Macworld®
QuarkXPress® 4 Bible

Macworld® QuarkXPress® 4 Bible

Galen Gruman and Barbara Assadi
with John Cruise

IDG
BOOKS
WORLDWIDE

IDG Books Worldwide, Inc.
An International Data Group Company

Foster City, CA ✦ Chicago, IL ✦ Indianapolis, IN ✦ Southlake, TX

Macworld® QuarkXPress® 4 Bible

Published by
IDG Books Worldwide, Inc.
An International Data Group Company
919 E. Hillsdale Blvd., Suite 400
Foster City, CA 94404
www.idgbooks.com (IDG Books Worldwide Web site)

Library of Congress Catalog Card No.: 97-077230

ISBN: 0-7645-4029-7

Printed in the United States of America

10 9 8 7 6 5 4

1DD/QR/QR/ZY

Distributed in the United States by IDG Books Worldwide, Inc.

Distributed by Macmillan Canada for Canada; by Transworld Publishers Limited in the United Kingdom; by IDG Norge Books for Norway; by IDG Sweden Books for Sweden; by Woodslane Pty. Ltd. for Australia; by Woodslane Enterprises Ltd. for New Zealand; by Longman Singapore Publishers Ltd. for Singapore, Malaysia, Thailand, and Indonesia; by Simron Pty. Ltd. for South Africa; by Toppan Company Ltd. for Japan; by Distribuidora Cuspide for Argentina; by Livraria Cultura for Brazil; by Ediciencia S.A. for Ecuador; by Addison-Wesley Publishing Company for Korea; by Ediciones ZETA S.C.R. Ltda. for Peru; by WS Computer Publishing Corporation, Inc., for the Philippines; by Unalis Corporation for Taiwan; by Contemporanea de Ediciones for Venezuela; by Computer Book & Magazine Store for Puerto Rico; by Express Computer Distributors for the Caribbean and West Indies. Authorized Sales Agent: Anthony Rudkin Associates for the Middle East and North Africa.

For general information on IDG Books Worldwide's books in the U.S., please call our Consumer Customer Service department at 800-762-2974. For reseller information, including discounts and premium sales, please call our Reseller Customer Service department at 800-434-3422.

For information on where to purchase IDG Books Worldwide's books outside the U.S., please contact our International Sales department at 415-655-3200 or fax 415-655-3295.

For information on foreign language translations, please contact our Foreign & Subsidiary Rights department at 415-655-3021 or fax 415-655-3281.

For sales inquiries and special prices for bulk quantities, please contact our Sales department at 415-655-3200 or write to the address above.

For information on using IDG Books Worldwide's books in the classroom or for ordering examination copies, please contact our Educational Sales department at 800-434-2086 or fax 817-251-8174.

For press review copies, author interviews, or other publicity information, please contact our Public Relations department at 415-655-3000 or fax 415-655-3299.

For authorization to photocopy items for corporate, personal, or educational use, please contact Copyright Clearance Center, 222 Rosewood Drive, Danvers, MA 01923, or fax 508-750-4470.

 is a trademark under exclusive license to IDG Books Worldwide, Inc., from International Data Group, Inc.

ABOUT IDG BOOKS WORLDWIDE

Welcome to the world of IDG Books Worldwide.

IDG Books Worldwide, Inc., is a subsidiary of International Data Group, the world's largest publisher of computer-related information and the leading global provider of information services on information technology. IDG was founded more than 25 years ago and now employs more than 8,500 people worldwide. IDG publishes more than 275 computer publications in over 75 countries (see listing below). More than 60 million people read one or more IDG publications each month.

Launched in 1990, IDG Books Worldwide is today the #1 publisher of best-selling computer books in the United States. We are proud to have received eight awards from the Computer Press Association in recognition of editorial excellence and three from *Computer Currents'* First Annual Readers' Choice Awards. Our best-selling *...For Dummies*® series has more than 30 million copies in print with translations in 30 languages. IDG Books Worldwide, through a joint venture with IDG's Hi-Tech Beijing, became the first U.S. publisher to publish a computer book in the People's Republic of China. In record time, IDG Books Worldwide has become the first choice for millions of readers around the world who want to learn how to better manage their businesses.

Our mission is simple: Every one of our books is designed to bring extra value and skill-building instructions to the reader. Our books are written by experts who understand and care about our readers. The knowledge base of our editorial staff comes from years of experience in publishing, education, and journalism — experience we use to produce books for the '90s. In short, we care about books, so we attract the best people. We devote special attention to details such as audience, interior design, use of icons, and illustrations. And because we use an efficient process of authoring, editing, and desktop publishing our books electronically, we can spend more time ensuring superior content and spend less time on the technicalities of making books.

You can count on our commitment to deliver high-quality books at competitive prices on topics you want to read about. At IDG Books Worldwide, we continue in the IDG tradition of delivering quality for more than 25 years. You'll find no better book on a subject than one from IDG Books Worldwide.

IDG BOOKS WORLDWIDE

John Kilcullen
John Kilcullen
CEO
IDG Books Worldwide, Inc.

Steven Berkowitz
Steven Berkowitz
President and Publisher
IDG Books Worldwide, Inc.

Eighth Annual
Computer Press
Awards ≥1992

Ninth Annual
Computer Press
Awards ≥1993

Tenth Annual
Computer Press
Awards ≥1994

Eleventh Annual
Computer Press
Awards ≥1995

IDG Books Worldwide, Inc., is a subsidiary of International Data Group, the world's largest publisher of computer-related information and the leading global provider of information services on information technology. International Data Group publishes over 275 computer publications in over 75 countries. Sixty million people read one or more International Data Group publications each month. International Data Group's publications include: **ARGENTINA:** Buyer's Guide, Computerworld Argentina, PC World Argentina; **AUSTRALIA:** Australian Macworld, Australian PC World, Australian Reseller News, Computerworld, IT Casebook, Network World, Publish, Webmaster; **AUSTRIA:** Computerwelt Osterreich, Networks Austria, PC Tip Austria; **BANGLADESH:** PC World Bangladesh; **BELARUS:** PC World Belarus; **BELGIUM:** Data News; **BRAZIL:** Annuário de Informática, Computerworld, Connections, Macworld, PC Player, PC World, Publish, Reseller News, Supergamepower; **BULGARIA:** Computerworld Bulgaria, Network World Bulgaria, PC & MacWorld Bulgaria; **CANADA:** CIO Canada, Client/Server World, ComputerWorld Canada, InfoWorld Canada, NetworkWorld Canada, WebWorld; **CHILE:** Computerworld Chile, PC World Chile; **COLOMBIA:** Computerworld Colombia, PC World Colombia; **COSTA RICA:** Computerworld Centro America; **THE CZECH AND SLOVAK REPUBLICS:** Computerworld Czechoslovakia, Macworld Czech Republic, PC World Czechoslovakia; **DENMARK:** Communications World Danmark, Computerworld Danmark, Macworld Danmark, PC World Danmark, Techworld Denmark; **DOMINICAN REPUBLIC:** PC World Republica Dominicana; **ECUADOR:** PC World Ecuador; **EGYPT:** Computerworld Middle East, PC World Middle East; **EL SALVADOR:** PC World Centro America; **FINLAND:** MikroPC, Tietoverkko, Tietoviikko; **FRANCE:** Distributique, Hebdo, Info PC, Le Monde Informatique, Macworld, Reseaux & Telecoms, WebMaster France; **GERMANY:** Computer Partner, Computerwoche, Computerwoche Extra, Computerwoche FOCUS, Global Online, Macwelt, PC Welt; **GREECE:** Amiga Computing, GamePro Greece, Multimedia World; **GUATEMALA:** PC World Centro America; **HONDURAS:** PC World Centro America; **HONG KONG:** Computerworld Hong Kong, PC World Hong Kong, Publish in Asia; **HUNGARY:** ABCD CD-ROM, Computerworld Szamitastechnika, Internetto online Magazine, PC World Hungary, PC-X Magazin Hungary; **ICELAND:** Tolvuheimur PC World Island; **INDIA:** Information Communications World, Information Systems Computerworld, PC World India, Publish in Asia; **INDONESIA:** InfoKomputer PC World, Komputerek Computerworld, Publish in Asia; **IRELAND:** ComputerScope, PC Live!; **ISRAEL:** Macworld Israel, People & Computers/Computerworld; **ITALY:** Computerworld Italia, Macworld Italia, Networking Italia, PC World Italia; **JAPAN:** DTP World, Macworld Japan, Nikkei Personal Computing, OS/2 World Japan, SunWorld Japan, Windows NT World, Windows World Japan; **KENYA:** PC World East African; **KOREA:** Hi-Tech Information, Macworld Korea, PC World Korea; **MACEDONIA:** PC World Macedonia; **MALAYSIA:** Computerworld Malaysia, PC World Malaysia, Publish in Asia; **MALTA:** PC World Malta; **MEXICO:** Computerworld Mexico, PC World Mexico, PC World Mexico; **MYANMAR:** PC World Myanmar; **NETHERLANDS:** Computer! Totaal, LAN Internetworking Magazine, LAN World Buyers Guide, Macworld Netherlands, Net, WebWereld; **NEW ZEALAND:** Absolute Beginners Guide and Plain & Simple Series, Computer Buyer, Computer Industry Directory, Computerworld New Zealand, MTB, Network World, PC World New Zealand; **NICARAGUA:** PC World Centro America; **NORWAY:** Computerworld Norge, CW Rapport, Datamagasinet, Financial Rapport, Kursguide Norge, Macworld Norge, Multimediaworld Norge, PC World Ekspress Norge, PC World Nettverk, PC World Norge, PC World ProduktGuide Norge; **PAKISTAN:** Computerworld Pakistan; **PANAMA:** PC World Panama; **PEOPLE'S REPUBLIC OF CHINA:** China Computer Users, China Computerworld, China InfoWorld, China Telecom World Weekly, Computer & Communication, Electronic Design China, Electronics Today, Electronics Weekly, Game Software, PC World China, Popular Computer Week, Software Weekly, Software World, Telecom World; **PERU:** Computerworld Peru, PC World Profesional Peru, PC World SoHo Peru; **PHILIPPINES:** Click!, Computerworld Philippines, PC World Philippines, Publish in Asia; **POLAND:** Computerworld Poland, Computerworld Special Report Poland, Cyber, Macworld Poland, Networld Poland, PC World Komputer; **PORTUGAL:** Cerebro/PC World, Computerworld/Correio Informático, Dealer World Portugal, Mac*In/PC*In Portugal, Multimedia World; **PUERTO RICO:** PC World Puerto Rico; **ROMANIA:** Computerworld Romania, PC World Romania, Telecom Romania; **RUSSIA:** Computerworld Russia, Mir PK, Publish, Seti; **SINGAPORE:** Computerworld Singapore, PC World Singapore, Publish in Asia; **SLOVENIA:** Monitor; **SOUTH AFRICA:** Computing SA, Network World SA, Software World SA; **SPAIN:** Communicaciones World España, Computerworld España, Dealer World España, Macworld España, PC World España; **SRI LANKA:** Infolink PC World; **SWEDEN:** CAP&Design, Computer Sweden, Corporate Computing Sweden, Internetworld Sweden, it.branschen, Macworld Sweden, MaxiData Sweden, MikroDatorn, Nätverk & Kommunikation, PC World Sweden, PCaktiv, Windows World Sweden; **SWITZERLAND:** Computerworld Schweiz, Macworld Schweiz, PCtip; **TAIWAN:** Computerworld Taiwan, Macworld Taiwan, NEW ViSiON/Publish, PC World Taiwan, Windows World Taiwan; **THAILAND:** Publish in Asia, Thai Computerworld; **TURKEY:** Computerworld Turkiye, Macworld Turkiye, Network World Turkiye, PC World Turkiye; **UKRAINE:** Computerworld Kiev, Multimedia World Ukraine, PC World Ukraine; **UNITED KINGDOM:** Acorn User UK, Amiga Action UK, Amiga Computing UK, Apple Talk UK, Computing, Macworld, Parents and Computers UK, PC Advisor, PC Home, PSX Pro, The WEB; **UNITED STATES:** Cable in the Classroom, CIO Magazine, Computerworld, DOS World, Federal Computer Week, GamePro Magazine, InfoWorld, I-Way, Macworld, Network World, PC Games, PC World, Publish, Video Event, THE WEB Magazine, and WebMaster; online webzines: JavaWorld, NetscapeWorld, and SunWorld Online; **URUGUAY:** InfoWorld Uruguay; **VENEZUELA:** Computerworld Venezuela, PC World Venezuela; and **VIETNAM:** PC World Vietnam.
3/24/97

Credits

Acquisitions Editor
Mike Roney

Development Editors
Alex Miloradovich
Tracy Thomsic

Technical Editor
Trevor Alyn

Copy Editors
Luann Ruoff
Carolyn Welch

Project Coordinator
Tom Debolski

Book Design
Drew R. Moore

Graphics and Production Specialists
Jude Levinson
Trevor Wilson
Linda Marousek

Quality Control Specialists
Mick Arellano
Mark Schumann

Proofreaders
Mary C. Barnack
Sarah Fraser

Indexer
Ty Koontz

About the Authors

Galen Gruman is editor of *Macworld* magazine, where he manages the monthly publication's editorial content, and coauthor of nine other books on desktop publishing. He led one of the first successful conversions of a national magazine to desktop publishing in 1986 and has covered publishing technology since then for several publications, including the trade weekly *InfoWorld*, for which he began writing in 1986, and Macworld, whose staff he joined in 1991. Originally a newspaper reporter in Los Angeles, Gruman caught the production-technology bug in 1979 and hasn't recovered.

Barbara Assadi is a creative programs manager at Oracle Corporation, where she manages the content and production of the company's annual report and product marketing collateral. She previously held similar positions at Quark, Inc., and Pacific Mutual Life Insurance, and also served as manager of Macworld's online and syndicated content. She was a pioneer in desktop publishing technology, especially as it applied to corporate communications, and began evaluating publishing tools for the trade weekly *InfoWorld* in 1988. Assadi has co-written five other books on QuarkXPress.

John Cruise was one of the original users of QuarkXPress, back in 1987 when he was a magazine editor. He then worked for Quark, Inc., helping develop QuarkXPress 2.12 and 3.0, as well as the Quark Publishing System (QPS). He also served as manager of technical communications at Quark. Cruise later became managing editor of *X-Ray* magazine, a publication for users of QuarkXPress and other software products from Quark, Inc. He now teaches QuarkXPress and works on a variety of publishing projects.

From Galen Gruman: To my erstwhile colleague and partner in crime at Macworld, *Carol Person, and to all the* Macworld *staff, particularly those from the "Hawaii era" of 1992–1997.*

From Barbara Assadi: To Edgar R. Lehman, a great friend and mentor, and to my colleagues at Oracle.

From John Cruise: To my daughter, Ryan Bing Cruise, and to all moms— past, present, and future.

Foreword

In 1988, I became aware of Barbara Assadi and Galen Gruman when I read their product reviews in *InfoWorld*. Early on, I recognized that these two people have an understanding of the desktop publishing field that goes much deeper than just knowing how to evaluate a program feature by feature. Bringing their own solid publishing backgrounds into play, they were the first to approach product reviews from a basis of understanding the intricacies of the publishing process. I would meet Barbara and Galen at computer publishing trade shows, and I took advantage of the time to talk with them about the direction of desktop publishing and to get their feedback on some of our own product ideas. I also had the privilege of working with John Cruise at Quark, Inc., where he worked in our Creative Services Department.

To put it simply, when it comes to publishing on the computer, these three know their stuff. You will recognize that as you use this book, which guides you through the process of creating a variety of documents with QuarkXPress. Whether you are a beginner or an expert, you will find value in these pages as these industry experts share their insights on the best ways to use this program.

Fred Ebrahimi
President, Quark, Inc.

My involvement with Barbara Assadi and Galen Gruman has been both direct and indirect for a number of years. Barbara and I worked together at Quark for two years, so I know first-hand her expertise in publishing and how committed she is to writing in a clear and accurate style. I have read Galen's writing for years, but finally had the opportunity to meet him when we started publicly showing QuarkXPress 4. His questions and comments went straight to the heart of the software: asking the "why" of the feature, rather than just "what it does."

QuarkXPress contains a tremendous amount of functionality that should make the work of any publisher or designer easier and more efficient. Although learning all the features and then using that knowledge may seem like a challenge, Barbara and Galen have combined an in-depth understanding of publishing with concise writing to create a very useful and valuable book. Novices and power users alike will find what they need in these pages. The QuarkXPress 4 development team put a lot of hard work and pride into our software, and the best reward we could have would be for our users to know how to make it perform to its full potential.

Don Lohse
Product Manager
QuarkXPress

Preface

Welcome to *Macworld QuarkXPress 4 Bible*—your personal guide to a powerful, full-featured publishing program that offers precise control over all aspects of page design. Our goal is to guide you each step of the way through the publishing process, showing you, as we go, how to make QuarkXPress work for you. You'll also learn tips and tricks about publishing design that you can use in any document, whether it is intended for the print media or for publication on the World Wide Web. The philosophy of the people who gave us QuarkXPress is to provide the best publishing tools possible to those who educate, inform, and document the world in which we live. We've adopted the same philosophy in creating this book, so join us as we explore the fascinating world of QuarkXPress 4.

Why You Need This Book

QuarkXPress comes with documentation that is chock-full of examples, so why do you need this book? In a phrase, "to see the bigger picture." Publishing design involves much more than understanding a particular program's tools. It involves knowing when, how, and, most important, *why* to use them. In this book, we help you realize the potential of QuarkXPress by applying its tools to your real-world publishing design needs. If you fall into any of the following categories, this book is for you:

+ A novice or experienced publisher or designer new to desktop technologies

+ Someone new to QuarkXPress but familiar with other desktop programs

+ An old hand at QuarkXPress who wants to master the many new features of version 4

+ A person familiar with print publishing who wants to publish on the Web

If you're new to QuarkXPress, we suggest you read the book in sequentiel order. The process of page design is presented in increasing levels of sophistication. You first learn how (and why) to create a template, then how to work with common elements such as text, and finally how to use special effects and deal with high-end publishing issues such as output control, image manipulation, and printing.

If you're an experienced user, read the book in any order you want. Pick those chapters or sections that cover the design issues you want to know more about, either as basic design issues or as QuarkXPress implementation issues.

Publication design is ultimately successful because the result is more than the sum of its parts, and the tools used to create and implement your designs cannot be used in isolation. Many cross-references in this book let you know where to get additional information on related topics. You'll also find the index a real aid in finding what you're looking for.

How This Book Is Organized

Part I, QuarkXPress Fundamentals: Whether you're new to desktop publishing or new to QuarkXPress, you need to start with the basics. Part I offers a tour of the basic features of QuarkXPress, as well as the conventions it uses in its user interface — including how you can customize QuarkXPress to default to your preferred settings.

Part II, Page Layout Techniques: The fundamental task in desktop publishing is creating the actual layout — designing the visual appearance of your document and the placement of elements. Part II teaches you how to create, modify, and manage your layouts, as well as how to automate future layouts based on existing ones.

Part III, Text Techniques: With layout in place, you can import your text and apply typographic settings. Part III shows you how to work with text and typography, and includes a discussion of the new book-oriented features in QuarkXPress such as list generation, tables of contents, multi-chapter book creation, and indexing.

Part IV, Graphics Techniques: Text may be the substance of your layout, but graphics are often its sizzle. Part IV explains how to import graphics, apply special effects to them, create your own graphics within QuarkXPress, and create and apply color throughout your document.

Part V, Going Beyond the Desktop: Most desktop publishers work with other people, whether they be colleagues in the design department, a client, or a service bureau — sometimes all three. Sharing files, enforcing standards, and preparing your layouts for output on an imagesetter or at a service bureau can be tricky. Part V shows you how to avoid the gotchas of working with others.

Part VI, Extending QuarkXPress: One of QuarkXPress's strengths is that it lets you add features to it by buying plug-in programs. You can also create scripts that automate your work (on the Mac only). Part VI shows you how to make QuarkXPress even more powerful, and it also takes you on a tour of the demo and free plug-ins, scripting tools, and publishing utilities included on the book's CD.

Part VII, Print Publishing Expert Guide: Part VII is a book within a book. It covers basic design issues such as the publishing environment, effective typography, and a variety of profusely illustrated print design opportunities. This section is a great primer for the novice designer.

Part VIII, Web Publishing Expert Guide: Part VIII, another book within a book, covers basic Web publishing techniques and takes you on a tour of three popular Web publishing add-ons to QuarkXPress. You'll also find demo versions of each of these XTensions on the enclosed CD.

What This Book Offers

What distinguishes this book from other books is that it does not attempt to replace the documentation that accompanies QuarkXPress. Instead, it guides you through the *process* of publishing a document—whether you're creating four-page company newsletters, four-color billboard ads, or interactive Web sites. It provides plenty of detail for experienced designers—such as table creation, image control, color output, and Web publishing—while including enough step-by-step introductory material (in distinctive boxes) for the newest user. For those just learning such advanced techniques, many informative sidebars explain the underlying issues. And, there are also these added features:

+ **A two-page pull-out card:** A complete list of all the timesaving keyboard shortcuts you're ever likely to use.

+ **A sixteen-page, four-color insert:** Not just another collection of pretty pictures, this four-color insert offers a comprehensive overview of how QuarkXPress handles color, with comparative examples and text.

+ **A bonus CD:** The CD that accompanies this book contains a wealth of software—some free, some demo, and some shareware. All are meant to make QuarkXPress work even better. Some are XTensions that enhance QuarkXPress directly, while others are stand-alone utilities that you will use before or after QuarkXPress. Appendix D tells you everything you need to know to install, road-test, and enjoy what's on the CD.

Conventions Used in This Book

Before we begin showing you the ins and outs of QuarkXPress, we need to spend a few minutes reviewing the following terms and conventions used in this book:

+ ⌘: This is the Macintosh's Command key—the most frequently used shortcut key. Its Windows equivalent is Ctrl. Throughout this book, we use the Macintosh keys when describing keyboard shortcuts. If you're a Windows user, substitute Ctrl for ⌘ and Alt for Option. Shift is the same on both platforms. Return and Enter are the same key, although different keyboards use one or the other. For number keys, use those on the keyboard, not those on the numeric keypad. The Mac has a key that Windows does not have — the Control key. We provide a Windows alternative to Control key combinations each time they are mentioned. Appendix B lists both the Mac and Windows shortcuts you're likely to use.

✦ **Key combinations:** If you're supposed to press several keys together, we indicate that by placing plus signs (+) between them. Thus, Shift+⌘+A means press and hold the Shift and ⌘ keys down, and then press A. After you've pressed the A key, let go of the other keys. (The last letter in the sequence does not need to be held down.) We also use the plus sign to join keys to mouse movements. For example, Option+drag means to hold the Option key (Alt on Windows) when dragging the mouse.

✦ **QuarkXPress commands:** If we describe a situation in which you need to select one menu and then choose a command from a secondary menu or list box, we use the command arrow as in File⇨Get Picture (⌘+E). This shorthand method of indicating a sequence of commands is often followed by the keyboard shortcut, as shown in this example.

✦ **Panes:** QuarkXPress 4 has added a popular interface feature called *tabbed panes*. This is a method of stuffing several dialog boxes into one dialog box. You see tabs, like those in file folders, and by clicking a tab, the options for that tab come to the front of the dialog box in what is called a *pane*.

✦ **Pointer:** The small graphic icon that moves on the screen as you move your mouse is a *pointer* (also called a *cursor*). The pointer takes on different shapes depending on the tool you select, the current location of the mouse, and the function you are performing. When you're using this book, you won't have to rely on wordy descriptions of what the pointer looks like. We include actual graphics of the various pointers—in addition to many of the buttons and tools you'll be using in your work.

✦ **Click:** This means to quickly press and release the mouse button once. On most Mac mice, there is only one button, but on some there are two or more. All PC mice have at least two buttons. If you have a multibutton mouse, click the leftmost button when we say to click the mouse.

✦ **Double-click:** This tells you to quickly press and release the mouse button twice. On some multibutton mice, one of the buttons can function as a double-click. (You click it once, the mouse clicks twice.) If your mouse has this feature, use it, as it reduces strain on your hand.

✦ **Right-click:** A Windows 95 feature, this means to click the right-hand mouse button. On a Mac's one-button mouse, hold the Control key when clicking the mouse button to do the equivalent of right-clicking in programs that support it. On multibutton Mac mice, assign one of the buttons to the Control+click combination. (Note that in Mac OS 8, the Control+click combination—called a *context menu*—is now a standard part of the Mac, so expect to see it used in a lot of programs, and don't be surprised if multibutton mice become standard, or at least common, on the Mac.)

✦ **Dragging:** Dragging is used for moving and sizing items in a QuarkXPress document. To drag an item, position the mouse pointer on it. Press *and hold* down the mouse button and then slide the mouse across a flat surface to drag the item.

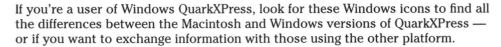

If you're a user of Windows QuarkXPress, look for these Windows icons to find all the differences between the Macintosh and Windows versions of QuarkXPress — or if you want to exchange information with those using the other platform.

New Feature

This icon indicates a feature that was added to or significantly changed in version 4 of QuarkXPress. This is straight talk for speed-reading users of previous versions of the program.

Caution

The Caution icon indicates something that works contrary to expectations and thus could cause confusion unless known in advance. This icon clues you in to things you don't want to add to your list of personal war stories.

Tip

The Tip icon indicates a technique or action in QuarkXPress that will save you time or effort. These tips also contain a wealth of valuable design advice — yet another way in which this book rises above mere documentation.

Note

The Note icon provides information you should note for future use — something that may seem minor or inconsequential at the time but will in reality resurface.

Taking the Next Step

Desktop publishers in general, and QuarkXPress users in particular, are an interesting bunch of people. Some have years of high-end, creative, design-intensive experience; others are just getting started in publishing, perhaps by producing simple newsletters or fliers to advertise a community event, and not a few are exploring the brave new world of Web publishing. To use QuarkXPress 4 you don't need a degree in design or 10 years of experience producing national ad campaigns. All you need is a desire to develop and implement good-looking documents, a copy of QuarkXPress 4, and the information you'll find in this book.

Acknowledgments

The authors wish to thank our development editor, Alex Miloradovich; our copyeditor, Luann Rouff; and Tracy Thomsic, for managing the project and the production of the CD. We also thank all the people at Quark, Inc., who supported us on this project, particularly Trevor Alyn, for his thorough technical edit; Kelly Kordes Anton, Elizabeth Jones, Don Lohse, Bob Monzel, and Fred Ebrahimi.

The original photos in many of the example publications featured in this book's screen shots were taken by Lisa Assadi, Ingall W. Bull III, Galen Gruman, and Leah Walthert, and are used with permission.

We thank the several artists who provided real-world examples for us to use in Chapters 30 through 32: Belinda Chlouber and Tim Johnson of Macworld, Dan Feather, David Kahn of Studio 23, Garret Ewald of Caravelle Communications, Ron Andrade of the *Peninsula Gateway,* and the design staffs of Macworld Online, *5280* magazine, *The Ryder,* and the *Washington Times National Weekly Edition.*

Contents at a Glance

Foreword ix
Preface xi
Acknowledgments xv

Part I: QuarkXPress Fundamentals 1

Chapter 1: Introducing QuarkXPress 3
Chapter 2: Taking a Tour of the Program 17
Chapter 3: Customizing QuarkXPress 37

Part II: Page Layout Techniques 65

Chapter 4: Setting Up a Layout 67
Chapter 5: Working with Boxes 97
Chapter 6: Preparing Files for Import 131
Chapter 7: Keeping It All Together 153
Chapter 8: Working with Pages 175
Chapter 9: Special Layout Techniques 185
Chapter 10: Creating Templates, Master Pages, and Libraries 203

Part III: Text Techniques 221

Chapter 11: Entering and Editing Text 223
Chapter 12: Controlling Character Spacing 235
Chapter 13: Controlling Paragraph Spacing 253
Chapter 14: Using Style Sheets 269
Chapter 15: Using Tabs and Tables 285
Chapter 16: Book-Oriented Editing 293
Chapter 17: Typographic Special Effects 311

Part IV: Graphics Techniques 337

Chapter 18: Working with Graphics 339
Chapter 19: Manipulating Bitmap Images 359
Chapter 20: Graphics-Creation Tools 381
Chapter 21: Defining and Applying Color 411

Part V: Going Beyond the Desktop 435

Chapter 22: Working in Workgroups 437
Chapter 23: Color Prepress 469
Chapter 24: Printing Techniques 489

Part VI: Extending QuarkXPress 517

Chapter 25: Using XTensions 519
Chapter 26: Using Scripts 533
Chapter 27: An XTension and Utility Sampler 545

Part VII: Print Publishing Expert Guide..**601**

Chapter 28: The Publishing Environment 603
Chapter 29: Effective Typography...633
Chapter 30: Print Design Opportunities 665

Part VIII: Web Publishing Expert Guide **689**

Chapter 31: Web Page Design Opportunities...691
Chapter 32: Web Page Setup 713
Chapter 33: Using CyberPress 745
Chapter 34: Using BeyondPress...775
Chapter 35: Using HexWeb 811

Appendix A: Upgrading and First-time Installation....................................833
Appendix B: Most Useful Shortcuts 839
Appendix C: What's New in Version 4...851
Appendix D: What's on the CD-ROM...857

Index 865

End-User License Agreement 890

CD-ROM Installation Instructions 894

Contents

• •

Foreword ix
Preface xi
Acknowledgments xv

Part I QuarkXPress Fundamentals   1

Chapter 1 Introducing QuarkXPress 3

Learning What QuarkXPress Can Do 3
    Discovering the QuarkXPress Approach 4
    The frame-based metaphor 4
    Using text boxes and picture boxes 4
    Drawing lines 4
Understanding Global and Local Controls 5
    Which tools to use 5
    Specifying measurement values 6
Defining Some Terms and Concepts 6
    Typography terms 7
    Layout terms 12
    Color terms 14
    Production terms 15
    Web publishing terms 16

Chapter 2 Taking a Tour of the Program 17

Exploring the Document Window 17
Accessing Menus 19
Working with Dialog Boxes 20
    Pop-up menus 21
    Tabbed-pane dialog boxes 21
Using Keyboard Shortcuts 21
Performing with Palettes 22
    The Tool palette 22
    The Measurements palette 27
    The Document Layout palette 29
    The Colors palette 29
    The Style Sheets palette 30
    The Trap Information palette 30
    The Lists palette 31
    The Index palette 31
    The Library palette 32
Learning About Pointers 32
    Common mouse pointers 33
    Specialized pointers 34
Dealing with Active and Selected Items 35

Chapter 3 Customizing QuarkXPress 37

Setting Measurement and Coordinate Systems....................................37
    Horizontal and vertical rulers 38
    Entering a measurement 39
    The Points/Inch Ciceros/cm options...40
    Coordinate controls 40
Working with Guides and Rulers 41
    Changing guide colors..42
    Turning guide colors on and off 42
    Placing guides in front of or behind boxes 42
Choosing Display and View Options 43
    Monitor display options...43
    View menu options 44
    Image displays 46
    Pasteboard size 48
Selecting Interactive Preferences 48
    Smart quotes 49
    Scrolling speed 49
    Delayed item dragging..50
    Drag-and-drop editing...50
    Saving documents 50
Choosing General Preferences 51
    Auto Page Insertion 51
    Framing parameters 52
    Auto Picture Import 52
    Master Page Items 53
    Snap Distance 54
    Greeking specifications 54
    Accurate Blends 55
    Auto Constrain 55
Setting Tool Specifications 55
    Tools you can customize 56
Choosing Character Preferences 57
    Character defaults 58
    Special characters...59
Working with Paragraph Preferences 60
Selecting Trapping Preferences 61
Controlling Saves and Backups 62

Part II Page Layout Techniques   **65**

Chapter 4 Setting Up a Layout 67

Creating a Sound Infrastructure 67
    Sketching your layout on paper..68

Sketching your layout in QuarkXPress 69
Starting with a Good Design.. 70
Seven basic rules for good design... 70
Variations on a theme... 72
Learning to Work with Layouts 74
Horizontal layouts.. 74
Vertical layouts... 75
Facing pages and spreads 76
Bleeds 78
Beginning a New Document 80
Establishing a foundation 80
Opening a new document 80
Selecting the page size 81
Setting the margins 82
Working with facing pages 83
Determining the number of columns 83
Choosing a column gutter... 85
Activating the automatic text box 85
Using the Layout Tools 85
Working with guides 85
Using the pasteboard 90
Working with layers 91
Grouping and ungrouping layout elements 93
Locking elements in place 94
Constraining boxes 95

Chapter 5 Working with Boxes...**97**
Creating and Linking Text Boxes 97
Automatic text boxes 97
Manual text boxes... 98
A tour of the tools.. 98
Linking text boxes 100
Creating columns in a text box 103
Creating Picture Boxes... 103
Adjusting and Changing Boxes 105
A tour of the Modify dialog box.. 107
A tour of the Measurements palette 109
Mouse and keyboard modifications 110
Positioning and reshaping boxes... 110
Changing box types 115
Working with Layout Controls 115
Number of columns 116
Text inset.. 117
Vertical alignment 118
Text runaround and clipping paths... 119
Adding Elements to Boxes.. 128

Chapter 6 Preparing Files for Import 131

Deciding What to Import 131
Working with Text Files..134
   Translating text files 134
   Preserving special features in text files 136
   Using XPress Tags 141
   Importing tabular data 144
Preparing Graphics Files...144
   Supported file formats 145
   Working with EPS files 146
   Color issues 148
   Dealing with fonts 149
   Working with bitmap formats..150

Chapter 7 Keeping It All Together 153

Working with Graphics Links 153
   When you open a document 154
   Finding missing graphics 154
   Updating missing and modified graphics 156
Using Publish and Subscribe 159
   Creating live links..160
   Updating live links 162
   Deleting and finding an edition file................................163
   Launching source applications 164
Working with Text Links 166
   Loading the latest text 166
   Exporting the latest text 166
Anchoring Boxes and Lines..168
   Modifying anchored boxes and lines 169
Copying Between Documents 170
   Copying a layout element 170

Chapter 8 Working with Pages..175

Adding and Deleting Pages 175
   Changing the page insert location....................................175
   Inserting pages 176
   Deleting pages 176
Rearranging Pages 176
   Using the Move Pages dialog box....................................177
   Using thumbnail view...177
Numbering Sections and Pages 178
   Breaking a document into sections 179
   Automatically numbering the pages 180
Generating "Continued" Markers 181

Chapter 9 Special Layout Techniques 185

Adding Rules and Lines 185
Creating rules 185
Working with lines 187
Framing Text Boxes and Picture Boxes 191
Creating Frame Styles 193
Saving a Page as an EPS File..195
Aligning Multiple Elements..197
Space/Align 197
Step and Repeat 199

Chapter 10 Creating Templates, Master Pages, and Libraries 203

Creating Templates...203
Using templates over a network..204
Saving a document as a template..204
Working with Master Pages...204
Creating a new master page 205
Displaying a master page..206
Common master page elements..207
Viewing and editing master pages...208
Inserting a new page based on a master page........................208
Deleting master pages 208
Rearranging master pages 210
Changing the guides on a master page 210
Applying master pages to document pages 211
Using Libraries 212
Creating a library 212
Opening a library 213
Adding elements to a library..213
Saving a library 216
Adding master pages to libraries 216
Rearranging library elements...217
Labeling library elements 217
Displaying labeled elements...218
Using multiple libraries..219
Deleting unwanted elements 219
Putting libraries to work...220

Part III Text Techniques **221**

Chapter 11 Entering and Editing Text...223

Using the Basic Editing Tools 223
Replacing selected text 224

Moving and duplicating text...224
Finding and Replacing Text 224
Replacing text...225
Changing text attributes 225
The Font Usage utility 227
Checking Spelling..228
The Check Spelling menu...228
Dealing with suspect words 229
Looking up and replacing words 229
Working with auxiliary dictionaries 230
Editing an auxiliary dictionary...230
Fitting Copy 232

Chapter 12 Controlling Character Spacing **235**
Defining Character Spacing..235
Typographic color 236
The influence of typeface...236
Using the Tracking Controls...237
When to use increased tracking 237
Editing tracking tables 239
Adjusting tracking on-the-fly 240
Tracking selected text 241
Tracking justified text 243
Adjusting Word Spacing..243
The Edit H&J dialog box 243
Working with preferred settings 244
Kerning Your Text 245
When to use kerning...245
The Auto Kern Above feature..246
The Kern to Space feature 246
Editing kerning tables...246
Changing kerning on-the-fly 248
Changing Horizontal and Vertical Scales...249
When to scale 250
How much to scale 250
Working with Special Spaces..251

Chapter 13 Controlling Paragraph Spacing.....................................**253**
Working with Hyphenation & Justification..253
Setting up H&J sets 254
Justification methods 254
Hyphenation settings 255
Overriding hyphenation settings 258
Inserting soft hyphens 259
Using the Suggested Hyphenation feature 259

Adding words to the hyphenation dictionary.................................260
Making the Most of Leading...261
Controlling leading..261
The creative use of leading...262
Auto and additive leading...263
Aligning text vertically..264
Choosing the leading mode...265
Additional Paragraph Spacing 266

Chapter 14 Using Style Sheets **269**
Defining Styles..269
Exploring the Style Sheets Dialog Box..270
Using the Show pop-up menu 271
Looking at the options 272
The Edit Paragraph Style Sheet dialog box..............................273
The Edit Character Style Sheet dialog box...............................275
Creating Style Sheets...276
Applying Paragraph and Character Styles 280
Editing Paragraph and Character Styles 280
Copying and Importing Styles 281
From within QuarkXPress 281
Importing style sheets from a word processor 283
Importing style sheets from XPress
Tags–formatted text..283
Resolving Style Conflicts...284

Chapter 15 Using Tabs and Tables **285**
Exploring Tab Types..285
Specifying Tabs 287
In a style sheet...288
In a specific paragraph..288
Using Leaders...289
Creating Tables with Tabs 289

Chapter 16 Book-Oriented Editing **293**
Building Books: Step by Step 293
Planning your book..293
Creating and opening books..294
Working with master chapters 295
Book palette status reports 296
Book palette control icons 296
Synchronizing chapter formatting 297
Printing chapters and books 298
Handling chapters with sections 299

Making Lists...300
   Building a list of figures...301
   Updating and rebuilding a list..303
Creating an Index...303
   Choosing an indexing style..303
   Using the Index Preferences dialog box 304
   Using the Index palette 305
   Using the Build Index dialog box...308

Chapter 17 Typographic Special Effects.....................................**311**

Organizing Text with Typography...311
   Indents and outdents 311
   Bullets and lists...314
   Visual labels 317
   Dingbats 318
Making Drop Caps and Hybrid Caps...321
   Automated drop caps...321
   Creating a drop cap style..321
   Applying a drop cap 322
   Choosing a drop cap typeface...323
   Creating a raised cap 324
   Making raised drop caps...324
Rotating Text 326
Placing Text on a Line..328
   Creating a text path 328
   Changing the text's position..329
Coloring and Shading Text..331
Creating Shadows and Outlines...332
Hanging Punctuation...333
   The tab approach...333
   The text box approach..334

Part IV Graphics Techniques   **337**

Chapter 18 Working with Graphics...**339**

Finding the Right Tools..339
Using the Measurements Palette...340
   Modifying box position and size..341
   Modifying the picture scale...341
   Moving the image within the box 342
   Box special effects...342
Using the Modify Dialog Box...343
   Working in the Box pane...343
   Working in the Picture pane..348

Achieving Faster Printing and Display..355
   Picture suppression...355
   Display quality...355

Chapter 19 Manipulating Bitmap Images 359

Exploring the Controls...359
Working with Image Formats 360
   Common file formats 360
Creating Negative Images 364
Adjusting Contrast..364
   Using the filters 365
   Manually adjusting contrast..367
   Customized contrast settings..368
   Returning to a common gray-level map..369
Regulating Halftones 370
   Making line screens with QuarkXPress..371
   Halftone special effects 372
   Gauging the effect of halftones 373
Dealing with Dithering 377
   How dithering works 377
   Working with ordered dithering..377
Controlling Color and Shade..378
   The Style menu's Color option..378
   The Style menu's Shade option...379

Chapter 20 Graphics-Creation Tools 381

Becoming Familiar with the Tools..381
   What's on the Tool palette...382
   Arranging the palettes..382
Creating Lines and Curves 383
   Straight lines...383
   Bézier and freehand curves...383
   Line patterns and arrowheads 388
Working with Boxes as Shapes 390
   Combining boxes and lines..391
   Merging boxes and lines 394
   Splitting the path of merged objects..397
Making Line and Frame Patterns 397
   Creating new line styles 398
   Creating bitmap frames...403
Converting Text into Graphics..407
   Creating text-based boxes 407
   Fitting text to curves 409

Chapter 21 Defining and Applying Color..**411**

Understanding Process and Spot Color..................................411
    Methods of color printing...411
    Exploring spot color..412
    Mixing spot and process colors..................................412
    Converting spot to process color..............................412
Defining Colors...413
    Using the Colors dialog box......................................413
    Predefined colors...414
    Working with color models......................................414
Using Spot Color..422
    The Halftone pop-up menu.......................................423
    Mixing spot colors...424
Using Multi-Ink Colors...425
Applying Colors..426
    Using the Colors palette..426
    Working with color pictures.....................................431
Managing Colors..432
    Deleting colors...432
    Appending colors..433
    Displaying color groups..434

Part V Going Beyond the Desktop   435

Chapter 22 Working in Workgroups **437**

Establishing Standards...437
Sharing Project Elements...438
    Using XPress Preferences files.................................438
    Quark CMS profiles...440
    Color definitions..441
    Kerning tables...442
    Style sheets...442
    H&J sets..445
    Lists..445
    Dashes, stripes, and bitmap frames........................445
    Spelling dictionaries...445
    Graphics and text files..446
    Libraries..447
    Templates..447
    Master pages...448
    Print styles..450
Importing Multiple Elements...451
    Using the Append feature...452

Resolving name conflicts 452
Comparing attributes 453
Working across platforms 453
Saving in Version 3.3 Format...454
Dealing with Mixed-Platform Issues 456
QuarkXPress differences 456
Platform differences 458
File transfer products 461
Using a cross-platform network..461
Working with Service Bureaus 463
Understanding the standards...463
Collecting for output 463
Sending documents versus output files.................................465
Determining output settings..466
Ensuring correct bleeds 467
Sending oversized pages...467

Chapter 23 Color Prepress 469

Working with Color Traps..469
Choking versus spreading 470
Setting traps...471
Setting trap defaults 474
Overriding traps 476
The trapping rationale 478
Activating the Quark CMS XTension 479
Adjusting Color Monitor Displays 480
The on-screen appearance 481
Calibrations from other programs..481
Selecting Output Profiles 482
Setting the default source profiles..482
Defining color models 483
Calibrating imported colors 484
Setting printing options 486

Chapter 24 Printing Techniques...489

Choosing the Right Printer..489
Getting Ready to Print..491
Setting up your document 491
Mac-specific options..492
Windows-specific options...497
Printing with QuarkXPress 502
Some common options...502
The Document pane 503
The Output pane...505
The Options pane 508

The Preview pane 511
The Color Management pane 512
Working with Spot Colors and Separations 513
Using the Edit Color dialog box 513
Transferring duplicate color sets 514
Mixing spot and process colors..514
Creating Print Styles..514

Part VI Extending QuarkXPress   517

Chapter 25 Using XTensions 519

Getting Started 519
When you install QuarkXPress...519
Determining which XTensions are loaded.................................521
Installing and Using XTensions...521
To install XTensions 522
Managing Macintosh RAM 523
Setting XTension Preferences 524
Working with the options...524
Handling XTension-loading errors 525
Using the XTensions Manager...527
The XTensions Manager dialog box 527
Choosing a startup set 528
Creating and deleting startup sets 529
Finding 4.0-optimized XTensions 530
Importing and exporting startup sets....................................530

Chapter 26 Using Scripts 533

Exploring AppleScript 533
Learning the language 534
AppleScript: Background and basics 534
Getting Started with Scripts 536
Creating and Running Scripts 537
The scripting process..537
Writing more complex scripts..540
Connecting with Other Programs..541
Publishing and graphics applications...................................542
Word processing, database, and
spreadsheet programs 542
Web publishing...543
Locating More Scripting Tools 543

Chapter 27 An XTension and Utility Sampler **545**

Exploring the XTensions 545
    Adobe Systems' Prepress 546
    A Lowly Apprentice Production 547
    Bad Knees' CreateCrops 559
    Tobias Boskamp 560
    College Fund's Doc Magnify 563
    CompuSense 564
    Dalai Software's DropIt XT 566
    Extensis 567
    FCS 570
    Gluon 572
    HanMac 575
    Koyosha Graphics' Precision Preview XT 577
    Last Word's ChangeCase 578
    Markzware's Pasteboard XT 579
    Meadows Information Systems' Math Grabber 579
    NAPS's PubViews 580
    Nisus's Writer filter 581
    Patrick Perroud's Alias Pro 581
    Second Glance's Clone 582
    Tableworks' Entable 584
    Techno Design 584
    Vision's Edge 588
Working with Publishing Utilities 596
    Dario Badia's Ready-to-Fax 596
    Extensis's PreflightPro 597
    Joseph Stubbs Creations 598

Part VII Print Publishing Expert Guide   **601**

Chapter 28 The Publishing Environment **603**

Choosing the Right Hardware 603
    The computer 603
    Storage capacity 604
    Connectivity 605
    Input and output devices 606
Getting the Essential Software 608
Using the Macintosh Interface 609
    The basic interface 611
    Working with files 615
Using the Windows Interface 617
    The Windows difference 617

The basic interface 618
Working with files..622
Working with Fonts..625
Installing Macintosh fonts 625
Installing Windows fonts 627
Loading PostScript fonts in printers 628

Chapter 29 Effective Typography..**633**

Learning About Typefaces..633
Typeface variations 634
What's in a face?..634
A font is a typeface by any other name 634
Selecting the Best Typefaces 634
Defining a standard set 635
Some basic guidelines 637
Taking Advantage of Type Styles...638
Changing typeface attributes 638
Plain as the basic style..640
Basic text styles 640
Using Multiple Master Fonts 651
The Font Creator XTension 651
Adding font variations...652
Removing and regenerating variations 654
Working with Characters and Symbols.....................................655
True quotation marks and em dashes 655
Using the Smart Quotes option..655
Manually creating typographic quotes 656
Manually entering dashes..657
Spacing em dashes—or not 658
Using en dashes 658
Symbols and special characters 658

Chapter 30 Print Design Opportunities **665**

Learning About Good Design 665
Great artists steal..665
Don't follow recipes 666
Learn to improvise...666
Laying Out Ads and Circulars 666
An airline ad mockup 666
A restaurant ad mockup 667
A public service announcement 669
Creating Newsletters 670
An association newsletter...670
Newsletter basics...673
Working with Magazines 675

Tables of contents...675
Feature articles..677
Doing Other Cool Stuff..684
Distinctive article openers 685
Defining visual treatments 686
Looking at Common Threads..686

Part VIII Web Publishing Expert Guide   689

Chapter 31 Web Page Design Opportunities 691

Learning about HTML 691
Free access to information 692
Where content is king...692
Web pages by design 692
The XTensions solution..693
Seeing the Differences..693
The CMYK/RGB difference...693
The conceptual difference 696
Looking at the XTensions 697
Exploring the XTensions in Action 698
CyberPress Web sites 698
BeyondPress Web sites 703
HexWeb Web sites..708

Chapter 32 Web Page Setup 713

Getting Ready for the Web 713
Starting from scratch...714
Establishing a structure 714
Determining the basics 715
Constructing Web-Ready Documents 718
Working with pages 719
Dealing with multiple elements..724
Using colors 725
Formatting text...726
Adding graphics 736
Adding Finishing Touches 743

Chapter 33 Using CyberPress 745

Getting Started...745
Developing a style...745
The basic conversion process 746
The CyberPress interface 746
Specifying defaults..750

Working with Boxes 762
    Creating a Content List 762
    Creating and adding new boxes 763
    Adding highlighted text as a range 763
Adding Master Elements 764
Modifying the Content List 766
    Rearranging items 766
    Renaming items 766
    Deleting items 766
    Anchoring elements 767
Converting Text 768
    Exporting text as an image 768
    Exporting text as tables or lists 769
    Mapping special characters 769
Working with Hyperlinks 770
    Adding hyperlinks to text strings 770
    Adding hyperlinks to images 771
    Relative and absolute links 771
    Removing hyperlinks 772
Exporting the Content List 772
    Choosing a location and name 772
    The Open In Browser option 773
    Viewing the results 773

Chapter 34 Using BeyondPress **775**
Getting Started 775
    How it works 775
    Road-testing the program 776
    Getting familiar with the interface 776
Specifying BeyondPress Defaults 777
    Using the Preferences dialog box 777
    Site defaults 778
    Application defaults 778
    Export defaults 781
    Web page defaults 783
    Image and text defaults 784
    Layout defaults 791
    Multimedia defaults 792
Using the Document Content Palette 793
    The Conversion pane 793
    The Authoring pane 795
Using the Elements Palette 795
    The Image pane 796
    The HTML pane 797
    The Media pane 797

Converting Documents 798
    Working with the Content list 799
    Previewing and exporting pages...803
Creating Web Pages from Scratch 805
    Working in Authoring mode 805
    Page size and margins 806
    Master pages and templates 807
    Creating and modifying items 807
    Layout considerations 808
    Previewing and exporting pages...809

Chapter 35 Using HexWeb..**811**
Getting Started 811
Setting HexWeb Preferences 812
    Choosing the main folder 812
    General preferences 812
    Layout preferences 815
    Advanced preferences 817
Using the Export Palette 820
    The Export pane...821
    The Tools pane 821
    The Special Object Library (SOL) pane 822
    The Meta Tags pane...823
Preparing Items for Export 823
    Modifying text boxes 824
    Modifying picture boxes 826
    Combining picture and text boxes 826
Previewing and Exporting...828
Working with Index Pro..829
    Launching Index Pro..829
    Creating a table of contents 830

Appendix A Upgrading and First-time Installation.................................**833**

Appendix B Most Useful Shortcuts..**839**

Appendix C What's New in Version 4...**851**

Appendix D What's on the CD-ROM..**857**

Index..**865**

End-User License Agreement **890**

CD-ROM Installation Instructions **894**

QuarkXPress Fundamentals

No one is born a desktop publishing expert. People who are familiar with traditional layout and production techniques and those who are skilled with using computers often have much to learn. The marriage between the two areas requires a strong foundation in both.

In this part, we cover the fundamentals of publishing, Macintosh and Windows computers, and QuarkXPress itself. If you are an experienced user in any of these areas, feel free to skip over parts of the text that cover subjects you already have mastered. If you are new to desktop publishing, or if you are just beginning to use QuarkXPress, start here. No matter who you are, you can look back to this part of the book when you're not quite sure what we're talking about.

QuarkXPress has many features, but it is not difficult to learn. The trick is to take it one step at a time. Some words of advice: Use QuarkXPress any chance you get so that you can get plenty of practice. The more you use QuarkXPress, the better at using it you will be and the more features you will know how to use. These features give you the power to do increasingly creative work. And isn't that what desktop publishing is all about?

In This Part

Chapter 1
Introducing
QuarkXPress

Chapter 2
Taking a Tour of
the Program

Chapter 3
Customizing
QuarkXPress

Introducing QuarkXPress

◆　◆　◆　◆

In This Chapter

Learning what
QuarkXPress can do

Discovering the
QuarkXPress
approach

Understanding global
and local controls

Defining some terms
and concepts

◆　◆　◆　◆

QuarkXPress 4 is a powerful and complex program, and whether you're new to the subject or an old hand, it's best to begin at the beginning. This chapter details the wide range of uses QuarkXPress is being put to around the globe, points out the ways in which QuarkXPress can be of use to you, illuminates some of the new features of version 4, and describes the basic metaphor on which the program is based. There's also a comprehensive list of the terms—clearly and concisely defined—that we use throughout the book. So whether you're an expert or novice, please read on and prepare yourself for a great adventure.

Learning What QuarkXPress Can Do

QuarkXPress is used by a long and impressive list of people. Nearly three-quarters of all American magazines—including *Rolling Stone, US, Macworld,* and *Readers Digest*—are produced with QuarkXPress, as are many newspapers around the world. It's also the best-selling page layout program among professional design firms. QuarkXPress is the leading publishing program in Europe, and the international version of QuarkXPress—QuarkXPress Passport—supports most West and East European languages. What does this information mean for you? It means that QuarkXPress can handle sophisticated tasks like magazine and newspaper page layout, while its simple approach to publishing also makes it a good choice for smaller projects like fliers and newsletters.

New
Feature

QuarkXPress is also a good choice for corporate publishing tasks such as proposals and annual reports, and the new long-document features in QuarkXPress 4 (described in detail in Chapter 16) make it a good tool for books and other lengthy publications. Using QuarkXPress puts you in good company.

Discovering the QuarkXPress Approach

Publishing programs, although similar in many ways, differ in their approach to the publishing task. One way to describe a program's approach to publishing is to talk about its *metaphor*, or the overall way in which it handles publishing tasks. Some programs use a *pasteboard metaphor*, which means that the method used to assemble a document is based on assembling page elements as you would if they were placed on a pasteboard until ready for use. Other programs approach page layout using a *frame-based metaphor*, in which frames (or boxes) hold both the page elements and the attributes that control the appearance of those elements.

The frame-based metaphor

QuarkXPress takes a structured approach to publishing. It is a *frame-based* metaphor, meaning that you build pages by assembling a variety of boxes. First, you set up the basic framework of the document—the page size and orientation, margins, number of columns, and so on. You then fill that framework with text, pictures, and lines.

New
Feature

With QuarkXPress 4, you can create text and picture boxes that are shaped by Bézier curves. You can also create lines, including curved Bézier lines, and place text on those lines using the Line Text-Path tools, that are new in QuarkXPress 4.

Using text boxes and picture boxes

Before you can put text on a QuarkXPress page, you need a text box. You can tell QuarkXPress to create text boxes automatically for you, or you can draw them with one of the six Text Box tools (the full set of QuarkXPress tools is described in Chapter 2). If you want to add pictures to a page, you need a picture box. You draw picture boxes using one of six Picture Box tools, each of which creates a different shape of box. You can put frames around picture boxes and text boxes; you can also resize, rotate, and apply color to both types of boxes.

Drawing lines

If you simply want to put a line on a page, however, you don't need a box. You can draw lines anywhere on a page by using one of four Line tools. You can also specify the style and thickness of the lines you draw.

Note

In simple terms, this box- and line-based approach is the publishing metaphor of QuarkXPress. Although the idea of text boxes, picture boxes, and lines sounds simple and straightforward, in the right hands it can generate truly impressive results.

Understanding Global and Local Controls

The power of desktop publishing in general and QuarkXPress in particular is that it enables you to automate time-consuming layout and typesetting tasks while letting you customize each step of the process according to your needs. You can use *global* controls to establish general settings for layout elements, and then use *local* controls to modify those elements to meet specific publishing requirements. The key to using global and local tools effectively is to know when each is appropriate.

Global tools include:

✦ General preferences and application preferences (see Chapter 3)

✦ Master pages (see Chapter 10)

✦ Style sheets (see in Chapter 14)

✦ Sections (see Chapter 8)

✦ Hyphenation and justification (H&J) sets (see Chapter 13)

✦ Libraries (see Chapter 10)

Styles and master pages are the two main global settings that you can expect to override locally throughout a document. You shouldn't be surprised to make such changes often, because the layout and typographic functions that styles and master pages automate are the fundamental components of any document.

Local tools include:

✦ Text Box tools and Picture Box tools (see Chapter 5)

✦ Character tools and paragraph tools (see Chapters 12 and 13)

✦ Graphics tools (see Part 4)

Which tools to use

In many cases, it's obvious which tool to use. If, for example, you maintain certain layout standards throughout a document, then using master pages is the obvious way to keep your work in order. Using styles is the best solution if you want to apply standard character and paragraph formatting throughout a document. When you work with special-case documents, such as a single-page display ad, it doesn't make much sense to spend time designing master pages and styles—it's easier just to format elements on-the-fly.

In other cases, it's harder to decide which tool is appropriate. For example, you can control page numbering on a global basis through the Section dialog box (accessed via Page⇨Section). But you also can change page numbering within a document by moving to the page on which you want to change a page number, invoking the Section dialog box and selecting new settings.

Specifying measurement values

Another situation in which you can choose between local or global controls is when specifying measurement values. Regardless of the default measurement unit, you can use any unit when entering measurements in a QuarkXPress dialog box. If, for example, the default measurement is picas but you're accustomed to working with inches, go ahead and enter measurements in inches.

QuarkXPress accepts any of the following measurement units:

✦ " (for inches)

✦ q (for hundredths of an inch)

✦ p (for picas)

✦ pt (for points)

✦ cm (for centimeters)

✦ mm (for millimeters)

✦ c (for ciceros)

✦ ag (for agates—a new feature of version 4)

Tip

You can enter fractional picas in two ways: in decimal format (as in *8.5p*) and in picas and points (as in *8p6*). Either of these settings results in a measurement of $8^1/_2$ picas (there are 12 points in a pica). Note that if you use points, you must place them after the *p*.

Defining Some Terms and Concepts

Like many specialized functions, desktop publishing tools include their own unique terms. Not too long ago, only a few publishing professionals knew—or cared—what the words *pica, kerning, crop,* or *color model* meant. Today, these words are becoming commonplace. Almost everyone who wants to produce a nice-looking report, a simple newsletter, or a magazine encounters these terms in the menus and manuals of their layout programs. Occasionally, the terms are used incorrectly or are replaced with general terms in order to make nonprofessional users feel less threatened, but that substitution ends up confusing professional printers, people who work in service bureaus, or Internet service providers. The following definitions, grouped by publishing task, cover the basic terms and concepts you need to know as you work with QuarkXPress.

Typography terms

Typography terms include words that describe the appearance of text in a document or on a computer screen. These terms refer to such aspects of typography as the size and style of the typeface used and the amount of space between lines, characters, and paragraphs.

Characters

✦ **Font:** This is a set of characters of a certain size, weight, and style (for example, 10-point Palatino Bold). This term is now used often as a synonym for *typeface*, which is a set of characters of a certain style in *all* sizes, weights, and stylings (for example, Palatino).

✦ **Face:** A face is a combination of a weight and styling in all sizes (for example, Palatino Bold Italic).

✦ **Font family:** This is a group of related typefaces (for example, the Franklin family includes Franklin Gothic, Franklin Heavy, and Franklin Compressed).

✦ **Weight:** This describes typeface thickness. Typical weights, from thinnest to thickest, are *ultralight, light, book, medium, demibold, bold, heavy, ultrabold,* and *ultraheavy.*

✦ **Style:** Type can have one of three basic stylings: *Roman* type is upright type; *oblique* type is slanted type; and *italic* type is both slanted and curved (to appear more like calligraphy than roman type). Type also may be *expanded* (widened), *condensed* (narrowed), or *compressed* (severely narrowed). See Figure 1-1 for examples of some of these stylings.

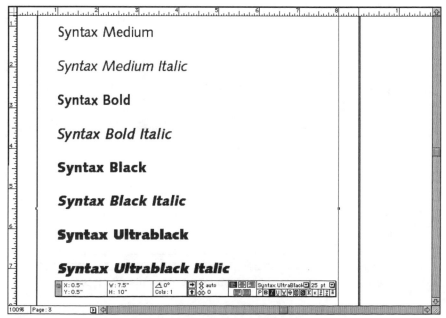

Figure 1-1: A sample sans serif typeface with different stylings.

✦ **X-height:** This refers to the height of the average lowercase letter (this is based on the letter x). The greater the height, the bigger the letter looks when compared to letters in other typefaces that are the same point size but have a smaller X-height.

✦ **Cap height:** Cap height is similar to X-height. It refers to the size of the average uppercase letter (based on the letter C).

✦ **Descender:** In a letter such as q, the part of the letter that goes below the baseline is called a *descender*.

✦ **Ascender:** The part of a letter that extends above the X-height (as in the letter b) is called an *ascender* (see Figure 1-2).

✦ **Serif:** This is a horizontal stroke used to give letters visual character. The strokes on the upper-left and bottom of the letter p in a typeface such as Times are serifs (refer to Figure 1-2).

✦ **Sans serif:** This means that a typeface does not use serifs. Helvetica is an example of a sans serif typeface.

✦ **Ligature:** A *ligature* is a set of joined characters, such as fi, fl, ffi, or ffl. The characters are joined because the characters' shapes almost blend together by default, so typographers of yore decided to make them blend together naturally. (Automatic ligatures are available only in QuarkXPress for Mac, due to the differences between Mac fonts and Windows fonts.)

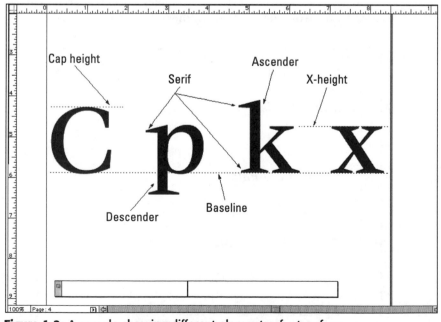

Figure 1-2: A sample showing different elements of a typeface.

Measurement units

✦ **Pica:** A *pica* is a measurement unit that specifies the width and depth of columns and pages. A pica is just a little less than $1/6$ of an inch (most people round it up to an even $1/6$ inch).

✦ **Point:** A *point* is a measurement used to specify type size and the space between lines. There are 12 points in a pica, so there are about 72.27 points to the inch. Most people round it down to 72 per inch.

✦ **Cicero:** A *cicero* is a unit of measure used in many parts of Europe. One inch equals about 5.62 ciceros.

✦ **Agate:** An *agate* is used for measuring vertical column length in classified ads. One agate equals about 5.5 points. An *agate inch* is one column wide and $1/14$ of an inch deep.

✦ **Em, en, and punctuation spaces:** The terms *em*, *en*, and *punctuation space* (also called a *thin space*) are units of measurement that reflect, respectively, the horizontal space taken up by a capital *M*, capital *N*, and lowercase *t*.

Note

Typically, an em space is the same width as the current point size; an en space is $1/2$ of the current point size, and a punctuation (thin) space is $1/4$ of the current point size. In other words, for 12-point type, an em is 12 points wide, an en space is 6 points wide, and a punctuation or thin space is 3 points wide.

✦ **Figure space:** This refers to the width of a numeral, which usually is the same as an en. (In most typefaces, all numerals are the same width so that tables align naturally.)

Spacing

✦ **Leading:** This term, also called *line spacing,* refers to the space from the base of one line (the *baseline*) to another. (Leading is named after the pieces of lead once used to space out lines.) See Figure 1-3 for examples of leading.

✦ **Tracking:** *Tracking* determines the overall space between letters within a word.

✦ **Word spacing:** This defines the preferred, minimum, and maximum spacing between words.

✦ **Letter spacing:** *Letter spacing* (sometimes called *character spacing*) defines the preferred, minimum, and maximum spacing between letters.

Note

QuarkXPress uses your preferred spacing specifications unless you justify the text or apply manual spacing adjustments; if you justify text, the program spaces letters and words within the limits you set for maximum and minimum spacing.

✦ **Kerning:** This refers to an adjustment of the space between two letters. You kern letters to accommodate their specific shapes. For example, you probably would use tighter kerning in the letter pair *to* than in *oo* because *to* looks better if the *o* fits partly under the *t*.

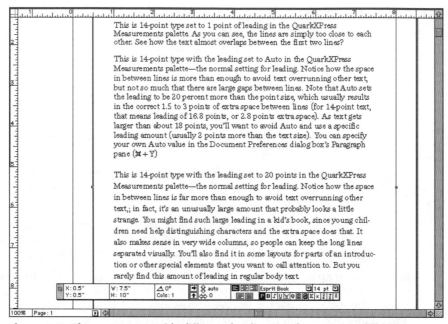

Figure 1-3: The same type with different leading can have a very different appearance.

✦ **Pair kerning:** This is a table, called the *kerning table* in QuarkXPress, that indicates the letter pairs you want the publishing program to kern automatically. Kerning is used most frequently in headlines where the letter spacing is more noticeable. See Figure 1-4 for an example of kerning.

✦ **Justification:** *Justification* adds space between words (and sometimes between letters) so that each line of text aligns at both the left and right margin of a column or page. *Justification* also is used to refer to the type of spacing used: justified, ragged right, centered, or ragged left (see the following definitions).

  ✦ **Ragged right and flush left:** Both these terms refer to text that aligns with a column's left margin but not its right margin.

  ✦ **Ragged left and flush right:** This refers to text that aligns with the right margin but not the left margin.

  ✦ **Centered:** This refers to text that aligns so that there is equal space on both margins.

  ✦ **Vertical justification:** This adds space between paragraphs (and sometimes between lines) so that the tops and bottoms of each column on a page align. (This term is often confused with *column balancing*, which ensures that each column has the same number of lines.)

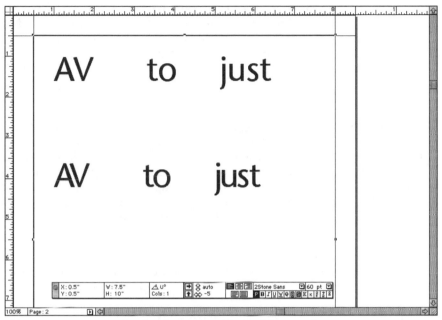

Figure 1-4: An example of unkerned and kerned letter pairs.

✦ **Carding:** *Carding* is a vertical-justification method that adds space between paragraphs in one-line increments.

✦ **Feathering:** This is another vertical-justification method that uses fractional-line spaces between paragraphs.

Paragraphs

✦ **Indent:** You typically indicate a new paragraph with an *indent*, which inserts a space (often an em space in newspapers and magazines) in front of the paragraph's first letter.

✦ **Outdent:** An *outdent* (also called an *exdent*) shifts the first character past the left margin and places the other lines at the left margin. This paragraph alignment is typically used in lists.

✦ **Block indent:** A *block indent,* a style often used for long quotes, moves an entire paragraph in from the left margin.

✦ **Hanging indent:** A *hanging indent* is like an outdent except that the first line begins at the left margin and all subsequent lines are indented.

✦ **Bullet:** This is a character (often a filled circle) used to indicate that a paragraph is one element in a list of elements. Bullets can be indented, outdented, or kept at the left margin.

✦ **Drop cap:** A *drop cap* is a large capital letter that extends down several lines into the surrounding text (the rest of the text wraps around it). Drop caps are used at the beginning of a section or story. A *raised cap* is the same as a drop cap except that it does not extend down into the text. Instead, it rests on the baseline of the first line and extends several lines above the baseline.

✦ **Style sheets:** These contain named sets of such attributes as spacing, typeface, indent, leading, and justification.

✦ **Style or style tag:** A set of attributes is known as a *style* or *style tag*.

Note

Essentially, styles are formatting macros. You *tag* each paragraph—or, in QuarkXPress 4, each character—with the name of the style that you want to apply. Any formatting changes made to one paragraph or character are automatically reflected in all other paragraphs or characters tagged with the same style. Note that QuarkXPress uses the term *style sheet* to refer to an individual style.

Hyphenation

✦ **Hyphen:** A *hyphen* is used to indicate the division of a word at the end of a line and to join words that combine to modify another word.

✦ **Hyphenation:** This determines where to place the hyphen in words that need to be split.

✦ **Consecutive hyphenation:** This determines how many lines in a row can end with a hyphen (more than three hyphens in a row is considered bad typographic practice).

✦ **Hyphenation zone:** The *hyphenation zone* determines how far from the right margin a hyphen can be inserted to split a word.

✦ **Exception dictionary:** An *exception dictionary* lists words with nonstandard hyphenations. You can add words that the publishing program's default dictionary does not recognize and override the default hyphenations for a word such as *project,* which is hyphenated differently as a noun (*proj-ect*) than as a verb (*pro-ject*).

✦ **Discretionary hyphen:** Placing a *discretionary hyphen* (also called a *soft hyphen*) in a word tells the program to hyphenate the word at that place if the word must be split. A discretionary hyphen affects only the word in which it is placed.

Layout terms

Document layout—the placement of text, pictures, and other items on a page or, in the case of Web publishing, on a screen—involves many elements. A brief primer on layout terms follows. You'll find more detailed explanations later in this book, particularly in Chapter 4.

Layout tools

✦ **Galleys:** These are single columns of type that are not laid out in any sort of printed page format. Publishers typically use galleys to check for proper hyphenation and to proof for errors. Galleys also are sent to authors for proofreading so that corrections can be made before the text is laid out.

✦ **Grid:** A *grid* is the basic layout design of a publication. It includes standard positions of folios, text, graphics, bylines, and headlines. A layout artist modifies the grid when necessary.

✦ **Templates:** Grids also are called *templates*.

✦ **Dummy:** A *dummy* is a rough sketch of the layout of a particular story.

✦ **Guidelines:** These show the usual placement of columns and margins in the grid. In some programs, guidelines are nonprinting lines that you can use to ensure that elements align.

✦ **Overlay:** An *overlay* is a piece of transparent paper or film laid over a layout board. On the overlay, the artist can indicate screens in a different color or overprinted material such as text or graphics. Some programs have electronic equivalents of overlays.

✦ **Knockout:** A *knockout* is when one element cuts out the part of another element that it overlaps.

Note

A designer would say that one element knocks out the other or that one element is knocked out of the other. In either phrasing, it means the first element covers up the part of the other element under it. This differs from *overlaying* the other element, because in an overlay, both elements are visible (as in a superimposed image).

Design elements

✦ **Column:** A *column* is a block of text.

✦ **Gutter:** When you place two or more columns side by side, the space between columns is called the *gutter*. (In newspapers and magazines, gutter space is usually one or two picas.)

✦ **Margin:** The *margin* is the space between the edge of a page and the nearest standard block of text. Some designers allow text or graphics to intrude into the margin for visual effect.

✦ **Bleed:** This is a graphic element or block of color that extends to the trimmed edge of the page.

✦ **Wrap:** A *wrap* refers to a textual cutout that occurs when a column is intruded by graphics or other text. The column margins are altered so that the column text wraps around the intruding graphic or text instead of being overprinted by the intruding element.

Depending on what the text wraps around and the capabilities of the layout program, a wrap can be rectangular, polygonal, or curved. QuarkXPress supports all three shapes.

- ✦ **Folio:** A *folio* is the page number and identifying material (such as the publication name or month) that appears at the bottom or top of every page.

- ✦ **White space:** This is the part of the page left empty to create contrast to the text and graphics. White space provides visual relief and emphasizes the text and graphics.

- ✦ **Boxes:** Most desktop publishing programs use *frames* to hold layout elements (text and graphics) on a page; QuarkXPress refers to these frames as *boxes*. Using a mouse, you can delete, copy, resize, reshape, or otherwise manipulate boxes in your layout.

- ✦ **Frames:** The boxes that hold layout elements can have ruling lines around them; Quark calls these lines *frames*.

- ✦ **Template:** By filling a document with empty boxes and defining style tags in advance, you can use the resulting template repeatedly to create documents that use the same boxes and styles.

Image manipulation

- ✦ **Cropping:** *Cropping* an image means selecting a part of it for use on the page.

- ✦ **Sizing:** *Sizing* an image means determining how much to reduce or enlarge the image (or part of the image). Sizing is also called *scaling*.

With layout programs, you often can *distort* an image by sizing it differently horizontally and vertically, which creates special effects such as compressing or stretching an image.

- ✦ **Reversing:** Also called *inverting* in some programs, *reversing* exchanges the black and white portions of an image. This effect is similar to creating a photographic negative.

Color terms

Color is an expansive (and sometimes confusing and esoteric) concept in the world of publishing. The following definitions, however, should start you on your way to a clear understanding of the subject. Chapters 21 and 23 cover color in great detail.

- ✦ **Spot color:** This is a single color applied at one or more places on a page, such as for a screen or as part of an illustration. You can use more than one spot color per page. Spot colors can also be process colors.

✦ **Process color:** A *process color* refers to any of the four primary colors in publishing: cyan, magenta, yellow, and black (known as a group as *CMYK*).

✦ **Color model:** A *color model* is an industry standard for specifying a color.

✦ **Swatchbook:** The printer uses a premixed ink based on the color model identifier you specify; you look up the numbers for various colors in a table of colors (which is often put together as a series of color samples known as a *swatchbook*).

✦ **Four-color printing:** This is the use of the four process colors in combination to produce most other colors.

✦ **Color separation:** A *color separation* is a set of four photographic negatives—one filtered for each process color—shot from a color photograph or image. When overprinted, the four negatives reproduce that image.

✦ **Build:** A *build* attempts to simulate a color-model color by overprinting the appropriate percentages of the four process colors.

✦ **Color space:** This is a method of representing color in terms of measurable values, such as the amount of red, yellow, and blue in a color image. The color space *RGB* represents the red, green, and blue colors on video screens.

✦ **CIE LAB:** This standard specifies colors by one lightness coordinate and two color coordinates—green-red and blue-yellow.

✦ **CMYK:** This standard specifies colors as combinations of cyan, magenta, yellow, and black.

✦ **Color gamut:** This is the range of colors that a device, such as a monitor or a color printer, can produce.

✦ **High-fidelity color:** This is a form of process color that builds from more than the four CMYK plates.

New Feature

QuarkXPress 4 includes the Pantone *Hexachrome* color model, an ink set that includes orange, green, and black, along with enhanced versions of cyan, magenta, and yellow inks.

Production terms

The following definitions refer to some of the terms you need to know about when you are preparing documents for printing. For more information on these and related subjects, see Chapters 23 and 24.

✦ **Registration marks:** These tell a printer where to position each negative relative to other negatives (the registration marks must line up when the negatives are superimposed). Registration marks also help printers keep different-colored plates aligned with one another on the press.

✦ **Crop marks:** These show a printer where to trim pages down to their final size. An image or page element may extend past the area defined by the crop marks, but anything beyond that area is cut away by the printer. Crop marks are used both to define page size and to indicate which part of an image is to be used.

✦ **Screen:** A *screen* is an area printed at a particular percentage of a color (including black). For example, the border of a page may have a 20 percent black screen, which appears light gray if printed on white paper.

✦ **Trapping:** This refers to the technique of extending one color so that it slightly overlaps an adjoining color. Trapping is done to prevent gaps between two abutting colors. Such gaps are sometimes created by the misalignment of color plates on a printing press.

Web publishing terms

Paperless publishing on the Web is the topic of the hour and the following terms are only a taste of what we cover later in this book. All of Part 8 (Chapters 31 through 35) is devoted to this topic.

✦ **Home page:** A *home page* is an HTML page (a Web page) that usually summarizes what your *Web site*, or entire group of Web pages, offers.

✦ **HTML:** HyperText Markup Language (HTML) is a page description language that is interpreted (turned into page images) by HTML *browsers* such as Netscape Navigator and Microsoft Internet Explorer.

✦ **Links and jumps:** A *link* or *jump* is an area in a Web page (often an icon or an underlined word) that, when clicked, takes a user to a different location on a Web page or to an altogether different Web page.

✦ **XTensions:** You can use XTensions, such as Astrobyte's *BeyondPress* and Extensis' *CyberPress*, to turn QuarkXPress pages into Web pages.

✦   ✦   ✦

Taking a Tour of the Program

◆ ◆ ◆ ◆

In This Chapter

Exploring the document window

Accessing menus

Working with dialog boxes

Using keyboard shortcuts

Performing with palettes

Learning about pointers

Dealing with active and selected items

◆ ◆ ◆ ◆

If you use other Macintosh programs, you are already familiar with such standard user interface components as file folders, document icons, and the set of menus at the top of the document window. This chapter explains the interface components specific to QuarkXPress. We'll be looking at how the document window, menus, and dialog boxes operate. We'll explore some of QuarkXPress's handy keyboard shortcuts and the look and feel of the program's various mouse pointers. A major portion of this chapter is devoted to palettes—a powerful feature of QuarkXPress that can increase your performance considerably. The differences between active and selected items are also explained. (For important information on hardware and software recommendations, as well as upgrading and first-time installation—for both Mac and Windows users—see Appendix A.)

Exploring the Document Window

When you open a document in QuarkXPress, the program displays a document window. The following list describes the elements of the document window (see Figure 2-1):

- ◆ **Ruler origin box:** This lets you reset and reposition the ruler origin, which is the point at which the side and top rulers are 0 (zero).

- ◆ **Title bar:** The name of the open document appears on the *title bar*, located at the top of the document window. You can move the document window around in the screen display area by clicking and dragging the title bar.

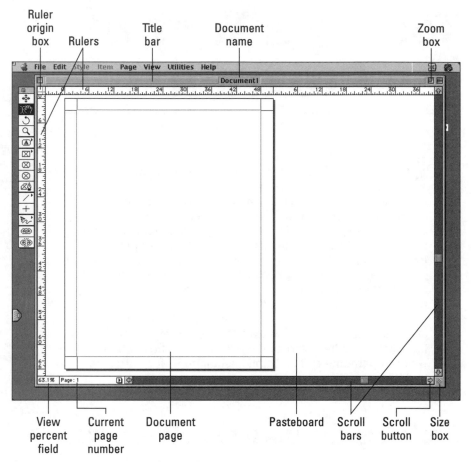

Figure 2-1: A QuarkXPress document window.

✦ **Zoom box:** If you have reduced or enlarged the document window, clicking the *zoom box* at the top right corner of the document window returns it to its previous size.

✦ **Vertical and horizontal rulers:** These items, on the left and top of the window, reflect the measurement system currently in use.

✦ **Pasteboard:** This is a work area around the document page. You can temporarily store text boxes, picture boxes, or lines on the pasteboard. Items that reside completely on the pasteboard do not print. (QuarkXPress displays a shadow effect around the document page. The shadow indicates where the pasteboard begins.)

Tip

If you select Automatic Text Box in the New dialog box (which you access by selecting New⇨Document from the File menu), a text box appears on every page of the new document. (See Chapter 5 for more information on working with text boxes.)

New Feature

✦ **Size box:** Clicking and dragging the *size box* resizes the document window as you move the mouse.

✦ **View percent field:** This shows the magnification level of the currently displayed page. To change the magnification level, enter a value between 10 and 800 percent in the field and then press the Return key or click elsewhere on the screen.

✦ **Scroll bar, buttons, and arrows:** Use the *scroll bars, buttons,* and *arrows* to shift the document page around within the document window. If you hold down the Option key while you drag the scroll box, the view of the document is refreshed as it moves.

Accessing Menus

The menu bar appears across the top of the screen. To display, or *pull down,* a menu, click the menu title and hold down the mouse button. From the menu, you can select any of the active menu commands; other commands that are not available to you (that is, commands whose functions don't apply to whatever you happen to be doing at a given moment in the program) cannot be selected. QuarkXPress displays inactive menu commands with dimmed (grayed-out) letters.

To select one of the active menu commands, you simply continue to hold down the mouse button as you slide through the menu selections. As you gain familiarity with the program, you can avoid using menus by using the keyboard equivalents for menu selections. Keyboard equivalents are displayed to the right of the command name. If an arrow appears to the right of a menu command, QuarkXPress displays a second, associated menu when you choose that command. This secondary menu appears automatically when you highlight the first menu command (see Figure 2-2).

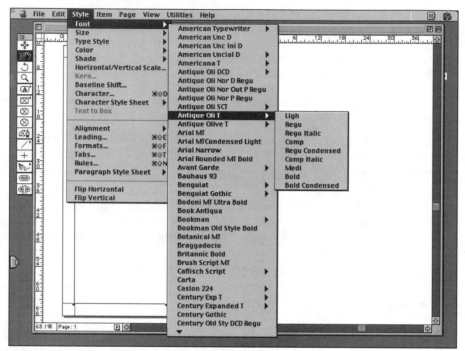

Figure 2-2: Selecting menu items in QuarkXPress.

Working with Dialog Boxes

You'll notice that some menu commands are followed by a series of dots, or an ellipsis (...). If you choose a menu command whose name is followed by an ellipsis, a *dialog box* or a *tabbed pane* appears. Figure 2-3 shows an example of a dialog box.

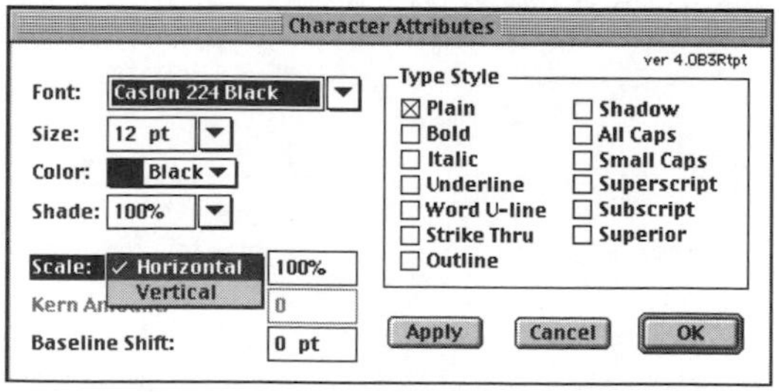

Figure 2-3: A dialog box and pop-up menu.

Pop-up menus

The level of control you have over your document doesn't end with the dialog box; some dialog boxes also contain pop-up menus, which are called *drop-down lists* in Windows and sometimes are referred to as *pick lists* or *drop-down menus*. Pop-up menus can appear in either of two places: in a menu or within a dialog box. If a menu has a pop-up associated with it, an arrowhead appears to the right of the menu entry. Pop-up menus can appear within dialog boxes or on palettes. If you look back at Figure 2-3, you see a pop-up menu for horizontal or vertical scale.

Tabbed-pane dialog boxes

Figure 2-4 shows an example of a tabbed pane. Dialog boxes are, in a sense, more powerful than menu commands because dialog boxes let you enter specific information. Dialog boxes give you a great deal of control over how QuarkXPress applies specific features or functions to your document.

Tabbed-pane dialog boxes (new in version 4) let you enter specific information on a variety of related issues, which are on panes with tabs at the top. To change from one tabbed pane to another, simply click the tab name. Refer to Figure 2-4 to see a tabbed-pane dialog box with the Paragraph tab selected. To select a different tabbed pane, such as Character, you simply click the tab with that name.

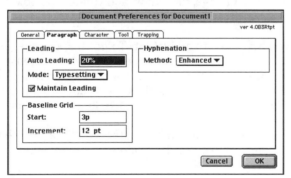

Figure 2-4: A tabbed-pane dialog box.

Using Keyboard Shortcuts

QuarkXPress offers you a variety of options in selecting program functions. You can select some functions through menus, some through palettes, some through keyboard shortcuts, and some through all three options. New users usually prefer menus at first because they are so readily available. But as you become more comfortable with using the program, you will be able to save time by using keyboard shortcuts.

Suppose, for example, that you want to move from page one of a document to page three. You can change pages by choosing Go To from the Page menu, or you can use the keyboard shortcut: press and hold the Command key (⌘) while you press the J key. (In this book, we present key combinations as follows: ⌘+J. From now on, we use this format for all keyboard shortcuts.)

Performing with Palettes

One of the most innovative features of the QuarkXPress interface is its *palettes*. Palettes let you perform a wide range of functions on an open document without having to access menus. They are the biggest time-saving feature of the QuarkXPress interface, and using them really speeds up the process of creating documents. You will undoubtedly find yourself using a couple of the palettes—the Tool palette and the Measurements palette—all the time.

The Tool palette

The Tool palette (see Figure 2-5) is one palette you'll often use when you build a document in QuarkXPress. When you first open the program, the Tool palette appears along the left edge of the document window. If it's not there, you can get it to appear by selecting Show Tools from the View menu (or press F8). This palette contains tools that you use to create, change, link, view, and rotate text boxes, picture boxes, and lines.

To use a tool on the palette, you first need to activate it. To do this, use the mouse to place the pointer on the tool icon that you wish to use and click the mouse button. Depending on the tool you select, the pointer takes on a different look, reflecting the function the tool performs. When you click the Linking tool and then click a text box, for example, the pointer changes to look like links in a chain.

In the remaining chapters in this book, we explain in greater detail many of the functions you can perform with the Tool palette. The following sections in this chapter provide brief descriptions of each tool.

The Item tool

The Item tool, the top-most tool in the Tool palette (refer to Figure 2-5), handles the *external* aspects of an item on a page—for example, its location. If you want to change something *within* an item on the page, you use the Content tool, described next. The Item tool controls the size and positioning of items. When you want to change the shape, location, or presence of a text box, picture box, or line, use the Item tool. The Item tool enables you to select, move, group, ungroup, cut, copy, and paste text boxes, picture boxes, lines, and groups. When you click the Item tool on a box, the box becomes *active,* meaning that you can change or move it. Sizing handles appear on the sides of an active box or line; you can click and drag these handles to make the box or line a different size.

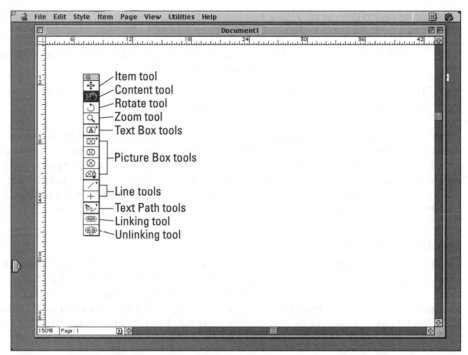

Figure 2-5: The QuarkXPress Tool palette.

The Content tool

As we noted previously, although the Item tool controls the external aspects of an item on a page, the Content tool, the second tool from the top in the Tool palette (refer to Figure 2-5), controls its *internal* aspects. Functions you can perform with the Content tool include importing (putting text into a text box or putting a picture into a picture box), cutting, copying, pasting, and editing text. (In version 4, you can now import a picture into a selected picture box even when the Item tool is selected.) To edit text in a text box, first select the Content tool. Then select the areas of text that you want to edit by clicking and dragging the Content tool to highlight the text, or by using different numbers of mouse button clicks, as follows:

In a picture box, the Content tool cursor changes to a hand shape. You can use this tool in a picture box to move (or crop) the contents of the box. You can also use it to manipulate the picture's contents, such as applying shades, colors, or printing effects.

✦ **To position the cursor:** Use the mouse to move the icon pointer (it looks like a large capital *I*) to the desired location and click the mouse button once.

✦ **To select a single word:** Use the mouse to move the pointer within the word and click the mouse button twice.

✦ **To select a line of text:** Use the mouse to move the pointer within the line and click the mouse button three times.

✦ **To select an entire paragraph:** Use the mouse to move the pointer within the paragraph and click the mouse button four times.

✦ **To select the entire story:** Use the mouse to move the cursor anywhere within the story and click the mouse button five times.

In versions of QuarkXPress prior to 4, double-clicking a word selects the word and the space after it. In version 4, however, double-clicking a word selects only the word itself. This is nice because it lets you double-click a word and type over it without having to worry about retyping the space after the word. If you cut or delete a word selected via a double-click, however, QuarkXPress still cuts or deletes the space after the word.

The Rotation tool

By clicking and dragging with the Rotation tool, the third tool from the top in the Tool palette (refer to Figure 2-5), you can rotate items on a page. Using the Rotation tool, you can click a text box, picture box, or line and rotate it by dragging it to the angle that you want. You can also rotate items on a page using the Measurements palette or the Modify command in the Item menu (⌘+M).

The Zoom tool

As you are working on a document in QuarkXPress, you may want to change the magnification of the page on-screen. For example, you may be making copy edits on text that is set in 8-point type; increasing the displayed size of the text makes it easier to see what you are doing as you edit. The Zoom tool, the fourth tool from the top in the Tool palette (refer to Figure 2-5), lets you reduce or enlarge the view that you see in the document window. When you select the Zoom tool, the cursor looks like a small magnifying glass. When you hold the cursor over the document window and click the mouse button, QuarkXPress changes the magnification of that section of the screen up or down in increments of 25 percent.

Another way of changing the magnification of the page is to enter a percentage value in a field at the bottom left corner of the document window; on a Mac, you can access this field by pressing Control+V (in Windows, Ctrl+Shift+V). When a page is displayed at its actual size, that value is 100 percent. Note that on a Windows computer, this method of changing the magnification of the page works only if the Display DPI Value in the Display pane of the Application Preferences dialog box matches the DPI setting for the monitor.

Version 4 of QuarkXPress lets you select any viewing amount, including those in fractions of a percent (such as 49.5 percent), within the range of 10 percent and 800 percent. (Before version 4, the highest magnification level was 400 percent.) Note that you don't need to enter the % symbol.

Text Box tools

QuarkXPress is box-based. Although you can import text from a word processor file or enter text directly onto a document page using the word processing features built into QuarkXPress, you need a text box to hold the text. You can instruct QuarkXPress to create rectangular text boxes on each page of the document automatically. You can also create a text box manually using one of the Text Box tools shown in Figure 2-5: rectangular, rounded-corner, concave corner, beveled corner, oval, Bézier, or freehand Bézier. The Text Box tools are the fifth from the top in the Tool palette. QuarkXPress remembers the text box tool you last used and makes that the default tool for the next time you create a text box.

STEPS: Creating a text box

1. Select the Text Box tool shape that you want to use—in most instances, this is the rectangular text box.

2. Place the cursor at the approximate location where you want the box to appear.

3. Click the mouse button and hold it down as you drag the box to size.

STEPS: Creating a Bézier text box

1. Draw the first line in the box and click the mouse button once to end the line.

2. Continue drawing the lines of the box, clicking the mouse button once to end each line.

3. Close the box by connecting the final line to the originating point of the box's lines. (See Chapter 6 for more information on creating text boxes.)

Picture Box tools

Picture boxes are containers you create to hold graphics that you import from graphics programs. QuarkXPress offers eight Picture Box tools, which are new in version 4. These tools are the sixth through ninth tools from the top of the Tool palette (refer to Figure 2-5). Using these tools—the Pop-out Picture Box tool, the Rounded-Corner Picture Box tool, the Oval Picture Box tool, and the Bézier Picture Box tool—you can draw the following different box shapes:

✦ **Pop-out Picture Box tools:** Use these to create rectangular or square picture boxes (the default setting for this tool), or concave-corner, beveled-corner, or freehand Bézier picture boxes.

✦ **Rounded-Rectangle Picture Box tool:** Use this tool to create picture boxes that are rectangular but have rounded corners. You can change the curve of the corners by using the Modify command on the Item menu (⌘+M).

✦ **Oval Picture Box tool:** This tool enables you to create oval or circular picture boxes.

✦ **Bézier Picture Box tool:** Using this tool you can create, point by point, any shape you want. The only restriction is that the box must have at least three sides unless one of the lines is curved, in which case the box can have only two sides.

STEPS: Creating a picture box

1. To create the first six styles of picture boxes (rectangle, concave corner, beveled corner, freehand Bézier, rounded rectangle, and oval), place the cursor at the approximate spot that you want the box to appear on the page.

2. Click the mouse button and hold it down as you drag the box to size.

STEPS: Creating a Bézier picture box

1. Draw the first line in the box and click the mouse button once to end the line.

2. Continue drawing the lines of the box, clicking the mouse button once to end each line.

3. Close the box by connecting the final line to the originating point of the box's lines. (See Chapter 6 for more information on creating picture boxes.)

New
Feature

Line tools

The Line tools, the tenth through twelfth tools from the top in the Tool palette (refer to Figure 2-5), enable you to draw lines, or *rules*. After you draw a line, you can change its thickness (*weight*) or line style (dotted line, double line, and so on). The pop-out Line tools are new to version 4. They let you draw straight lines at any angle, Bézier lines, or freehand Bézier lines. The Orthogonal Line tool draws straight horizontal and straight vertical lines. The Diagonal Line tool draws lines at any angle.

STEPS: Using the Line tools

1. Click the tool to select it and position the cursor at the point where you want the line to begin.

2. Click the mouse button and hold it as you draw the line.

3. When the line is approximately the length you want, release the mouse button.

4. After you draw a line, use the Measurements palette to select the line weight and line style.

You can increase line width in preset amounts (preset line widths are hairline, 1 pt., 2 pt., 4 pt., 6 pt., 8 pt., or 12 pt.) by selecting the line, then pressing ⌘+Shift+>. You can decrease line width in the same preset amounts by pressing ⌘+Shift+<. Lines can also be increased one point at a time (⌘+Option+Shift+>) or decreased one point at a time (⌘+Option+Shift+<).

STEPS: Creating a Bézier line

1. Click the mouse button once to begin the line.

2. Click again to add segments to the line.

3. Double-click at the last point to end the line. (For more specifics on drawing lines, see Chapter 8.)

Linking and Unlinking tools

The bottom two tools in the Tool palette are the Linking and Unlinking tools. The Linking tool enables you to link text boxes together so that overflow text flows from one text box into another. You use the Unlinking tool to break the link between text boxes.

Tip

Linking is particularly useful when you want to *jump* text—for example, when a story starts on page one and jumps to (continues on) page four. Chapter 6 covers linking in more detail.

The Measurements palette

The Measurements palette was first developed by Quark and has since been widely imitated by other software programs. This palette is certainly one of the most significant innovations to take place in the evolution of desktop publishing. You will use it all the time. The Measurements palette gives you precise information about the position and attributes of any selected page element, and it lets you enter values to change those specifications. If you want to see the Measurements palette, you need to have a document open as you choose View⇨Show Measurements (or press F9).

How it works with text

The information displayed on the Measurements palette depends on the element currently selected. When you select a text box, the Measurements palette displays the text box position coordinates (X and Y), size (W and H), amount of rotation, and number of columns (Cols), as shown in Figure 2-6. The two buttons with arrows on them let you flip the text in the box horizontally or vertically.

X: 3p	W: 45p	△ 0°		📐 auto	Caslon 224 Black	12 pt
Y: 3p	H: 60p	Cols: 1		◇◇ 0	P B I U W 🔲 🔲 S K ² ₂

Figure 2-6: The Measurements palette when a text box is selected.

Using the up- and down-pointing outlined arrows on the palette, you can modify the leading of the selected text (or you can simply type in a value in the space next to the outlined arrows); use the right- and left-pointing arrows to adjust kerning or tracking for selected text. You can specify text alignment—left, center, right, justified, or force-justified—by using the alignment icons. In the type section of the palette, you can control the font, size, and type style of selected text. Chapters 12, 13, and 30 cover these features in detail.

The picture box view

If you select a picture box, the Measurements palette displays a different set of information (see Figure 2-7). It shows the position of the box (X and Y), its size (W and H), the amount it is rotated, and its corner radius.

X: 8p11	W: 7p3	△ 0°		X%: 100%	◇◇ X+: 0p	△ 0°
Y: 14p1	H: 4p10	⬅ 0p		Y%: 100%	X Y+: 0p	◿ 0°

Figure 2-7: The Measurements palette when a picture box is selected.

The items to the right of the heavy vertical bar in the middle refer to the image in the picture box. The two buttons with arrows on them let you flip the picture horizontally or vertically. The fields to the right of these buttons let you assign the following: a reduction or an enlargement percentage (X percent and Y percent), repositioning coordinates (X+ and Y+), the amount of picture rotation within the box, and the amount of slant.

Tip

You can highlight the next field in the Measurements palette by pressing the Tab key, and you can highlight the previous field by pressing Shift+Tab. If you enter an invalid value in a field and get an error message, you can revert to the previous value by pressing ⌘+Z.

Looking at lines

When you select a line, the left side of the Measurements palette displays information about the line's position and length. (It can do this in a variety of ways, depending on which option is selected from the pop-up menu.) The right side of the palette displays the line width, line style, and endcap (line ending) style (see Figure 2-8). The line-style list box lets you select the style for the line. (In version 4, you can now create your own line styles by choosing Edit⇨Dashes and Stripes.)

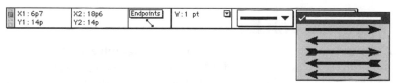

Figure 2-8: The Measurements palette when a line is selected.

The Document Layout palette

The Document Layout palette (see Figure 2-9) lets you create, name, delete, move, and apply master pages. You can also add, delete, and move document pages. To display the Document Layout palette, choose Show Document Layout from the View menu (or press F10 on the Mac; F4 in Windows).

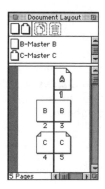

Figure 2-9: The Document Layout palette.

The Colors palette

Figure 2-10 shows the Colors palette. Using this palette, you can designate the color and shade (percentage of color) that you want to apply to text, pictures, and backgrounds of text and picture boxes. You also can produce color blends, using one or two colors, to apply to box backgrounds. To display the Colors palette, choose Show Colors from the View menu (or press F12). Chapters 21 and 23 cover color in more detail.

Figure 2-10: The QuarkXPress Colors palette.

New
Feature

The Style Sheets palette

The Style Sheets palette displays the names of the paragraph style tags applied to selected paragraphs and, with version 4, the character style tags applied to selected characters. The Style Sheets palette also enables you to apply style sheets to paragraphs and characters. To display the Style Sheets palette, shown in Figure 2-11, choose Show Style Sheets from the View menu (or press F11).

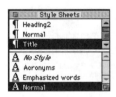

Figure 2-11: The Style Sheets palette.

The Trap Information palette

Trapping controls how one color in a document prints next to another color. In the Trap Information palette (see Figure 2-12) you can set or change trapping specifications for selected items: the range is -36 to 36 points. To display the Trap Information palette, choose Show Trap Information from the View menu (or press Option+F12 on the Mac; Ctrl+F12 in Windows). Chapter 23 provides more information about trapping.

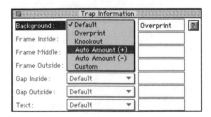

Figure 2-12: The Trap Information palette.

Caution

A word of warning: don't use this palette unless you know what you are doing. Trapping is considered an expert feature, and using it without knowing what you are doing can produce uneven results when you print your document.

The Lists palette

A *list* is a group of paragraph style sheets that lets you list all the text of this style at a different location. For example, if you are building a long document, you can specify a "chapter" and a "section" style sheet as a list, and then use the Update button on the Lists palette (see Figure 2-13) to cause QuarkXPress to automatically create the table of contents for the document. The Lists palette displays all of the text associated with the style sheets in the document's list configuration. To display the Lists palette, choose Lists from the View menu (or press Option+F11 on the Mac; Ctrl+F11 in Windows).

New Feature

The list feature and the Lists palette are new in version 4 of QuarkXPress. For more information on these innovative and powerful tools, see Chapter 16.

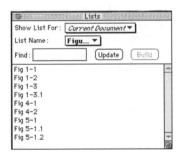

Figure 2-13: The Lists palette.

The Index palette

QuarkXPress allows you to insert markers on certain words in a document as you are creating it or reading it. The Index palette, shown in Figure 2-14, then copies the marked text and generates an alphabetized, hierarchical index. Once you are satisfied that the Index palette has all the entries, you build the index by choosing Build Index from the Utilities menu (Utilities⇨Build Index). To display the Index palette, choose Index from the View menu (or press ⌘+Option+I).

New Feature

The Index palette is another new feature of QuarkXPress 4. Chapter 16 explains how to index a QuarkXPress document.

Figure 2-14: The Index palette.

The Library palette

QuarkXPress lets you store layout elements (text boxes or picture boxes, lines, or groups) in a Library palette. To use this feature, you select the element from the document or the pasteboard and drag it into an open Library palette. You then can use items stored in the library in other documents. To open a Library palette such as the one shown in Figure 2-15, choose Library from the File menu (File⇨Open⇨Library). Chapter 10 covers libraries in detail.

Figure 2-15: A Library palette entitled "Boilerplate."

Learning About Pointers

By changing the mouse pointer (also called *cursor*) to depict the current tool, QuarkXPress provides a visual cue so that you can tell which tool is active. You see some tool icons all the time and others only occasionally, because they are used for specialized features. This section provides an overview of the various mouse pointers in QuarkXPress.

Common mouse pointers

You'll frequently come across the following mouse pointers:

 ✦ **Standard pointer:** This is the most common pointer. It appears as you move through dialog boxes, menus, and windows. It also appears as you move over unselected elements.

 ✦ **Creation pointer:** This pointer appears if you have selected a box or Line tool. To create a rectangular or oval box, click and hold down the mouse button at one corner of the box, drag the mouse to the opposite corner, and then release the button. (Hold the Shift key to keep the box a perfect square or circle.) For a polygonal box, click each point in the polygon and return to the first point when done (the creation pointer changes to a rounded box to indicate that you are over the first point). For a line, click and hold down the mouse button at one end, drag it to the line's end, and then release the button.

 ✦ **Sizing pointer:** This pointer appears if you move the mouse over one of the handles on a selected text box or picture box (with either the Item or Content tool selected), or on a line. You can resize the item by holding down the mouse button and dragging a handle.

 ✦ **Item pointer:** This pointer appears if the Item tool is selected and you move the mouse over a selected box or line. You can move the selected item by holding down the mouse button and dragging the item.

 ✦ **Lock pointer:** This pointer appears if the Item tool is selected and you move the mouse over a selected locked text box, picture box, or line. This indicates that the box will not move if you try to drag it. (You can move it, however, by changing the coordinates in the Measurements palette using the arrow keys, or via Item⇨Modify.)

 ✦ **I-beam (text) pointer:** This pointer appears if the Content tool is selected and you move the mouse over a selected text box or text-path line. If the cursor is blinking, any text you type inserts where the cursor appears. If the cursor is not blinking, you must click at the location in the text box or on the text-path line where you want to edit text.

 ✦ **Grabber pointer:** This pointer appears if the Content tool is selected and you move the mouse over a selected picture box containing a graphic. You can move the graphic within the box by holding down the mouse button and dragging the item.

 ✦ **Zoom-in pointer:** This pointer appears if you select the Zoom tool, move to your page, and click the mouse button (this zooms in by the predefined amount, which by default is 25 percent). You can also select an area to zoom into by selecting the Zoom tool and holding down the mouse button at one corner of the area of interest, dragging the mouse to the opposite corner, and then releasing the button. Chapter 3 covers zoom preference settings.

✦ **Zoom-out pointer:** This pointer appears if you select the Zoom tool and hold down the Option key while clicking the mouse button after the pointer is placed on the page (this zooms out by the predefined amount, which by default is 25 percent). Chapter 3 covers zoom preference settings.

 ✦ **Rotation pointer:** This pointer and the rotation guide target appear when you select an item on the page with the Item tool or the Content tool and then select the Rotate tool. Place the target on the page by moving the mouse to the location you want to designate as the center of rotation. Hold down the mouse button and move the pointer around the target until you have achieved the desired rotation on the selected item. The line connecting the target to the pointer can be made larger or smaller by moving the pointer further away or closer to the target; the further away the pointer from the target, the finer the rotation increments you control.

 ✦ **Link pointer:** This pointer appears if you select the Link tool and move the mouse over a selected text box. Click the pointer on the first text box and then on the second text box in the chain of boxes that you want text to flow through. If there are more boxes, select them in the flow order as well. You can switch pages while this tool is active to flow text across pages. Chapter 6 covers linking.

✦ **Unlink pointer:** This pointer appears if you select the Unlink tool. If you want to sever the text flow between two text boxes, select one of the boxes and then use this pointer to click the head or tail of the plaid arrow that links one box to the other. If there are more boxes to unlink, repeat this process. You can switch pages while this tool is active to unlink text flow across pages. Chapter 6 covers unlinking.

New Feature

The new Text Path tools in version 4 of QuarkXPress let you create text on a path. These text-path lines can be linked and unlinked just like text boxes. For more information on using the Text Path tools, see Chapter 17.

Specialized pointers

The following pointers are those you run across less often:

✦ **Library pointer:** This pointer appears in the current library window if you have selected a library element and are moving it either within the window or to another open library window. Libraries are covered in Chapter 23.

+ ✦ **Bézier pointer:** This pointer, which is a cross-hair pointer, appears when you are using any of the Bézier tools to draw a Bézier line or box.

The following three pointers appear only in the Document Layout palette, accessed via View➪Show Document layout (or choose F10 on the Mac; F4 in Windows).

✦ **Insert Master Page pointer:** This Pointer appears in the Document Layout palette when you insert a master page between two other pages, either in the master page list or in the document page area. It comes in a right-pointing version and a down-pointing version.

✦ **Facing Master Pages pointer:** This pointer appears in the Document Layout palette when you insert a facing master page into an empty area, either in the master page list or in the document page area.

✦ **Single Master Page pointer:** This pointer appears in the Document Layout palette when you insert a single master page into an empty area, either in the master page list or in the document page area.

Tip

When inserting master pages, drag the appropriate master-page icon (facing or single, depending on what type of master page you want) from the top left of the palette into the location where you want the new master page to be inserted. For more information on master pages, see Chapter 10.

Dealing with Active and Selected Items

Throughout this book, you'll see instructions such as *select the text box* or *apply the change to the active line.* Selecting an item is the same as *activating* it, which you must do before modifying an item in QuarkXPress. If you want to make a change to an entire item, select or activate the item by clicking it with the Item tool. If you want to make a change to the item's contents, click the Content tool on the item. When an item is selected or active, you can see small black boxes, or sizing handles, on its sides and corners, as illustrated in Figure 2-16.

Figure 2-16: Active items have sizing handles at their sides and corners.

✦   ✦   ✦

Customizing QuarkXPress

Publishing is a big industry, one with many aspects. One of the authors of this book, for example, comes from a newspaper and magazine background. He works with picas as a basic layout measurement unit, and he calls pull-quotes *decks* and titles *heads*. Another author comes from a technical documentation and corporate communications background. She uses inches as her basic layout measurement, and she calls decks *pull-quotes* and heads *titles*. Fortunately, QuarkXPress offers many controls that enable you to customize the program to the way *you* work. There are application preferences that let you control how your copy of QuarkXPress works with all documents, and document preferences that apply to a single document if the document is open when you are changing settings. If no document is open, document preferences apply to all subsequently created documents. This chapter covers all the variables.

Setting Measurement and Coordinate Systems

To position elements on the page during the layout process, you need a measurement system. Depending on your training, you may prefer using a particular measurement unit for layout. Many people measure column width and depth in inches, while others (particularly those with newspaper or magazine backgrounds) use picas. Europeans use centimeters instead of inches and ciceros instead of picas. QuarkXPress supports them all.

In This Chapter

Setting measurement and coordinate systems

Working with guides and rulers

Choosing display and view options

Selecting interactive preferences

Choosing general preferences

Setting tool specifications

Choosing character preferences

Working with paragraph preferences

Selecting trapping preferences

Controlling saves and backups

A brief primer on preferences

The most important settings—because they affect your everyday work—are those that affect QuarkXPress itself. They also are the least-used settings, because after you set them, you rarely change them. You tell QuarkXPress your preferences for these settings through options available when you select Edit⇨Preferences⇨Application (⌘+Option+Shift+Y), or Edit⇨Preferences⇨Document (⌘+Y).

The Application Preferences dialog box contains four panes: Display, Interactive, Save, and XTensions. The Default Document Preferences dialog box sets controls for default measurement units, placement and use of layout aids, layout controls, and display of text and pictures.

You can use document preferences for either the current document or all new documents. If you change the settings while no document is open, all documents you subsequently create use those settings. If a document is open when you change the settings, only that document is affected. You can tell whether the settings are global or local because the dialog box's title is Document Preferences for *document name* if the settings are local to that document.

You can also control preferences that affect indexing by choosing Edit⇨Preferences⇨Index (see Chapter 16 for a discussion on index preferences).

Note

You'll probably set or change most QuarkXPress control settings only occasionally. You'll rarely switch measurement units, for example, because QuarkXPress lets you enter any unit you want in dialog boxes, no matter which default settings you establish. You may change other settings that apply to specific documents more frequently, as detailed throughout this chapter.

Horizontal and vertical rulers

QuarkXPress lets you select a measurement system for both the horizontal and vertical rulers you employ to lay out a document. (Rulers and guides are covered a little later in this chapter.) You select a measurement system by choosing Edit⇨Preferences⇨Document (⌘+Y), and then selecting the General pane, as shown in Figure 3-1. In the figure, the options for Vertical Measure are shown; the same options are available for Horizontal Measure. Many publishers use picas for horizontal measurements but inches for vertical (as in the phrase "column inch").

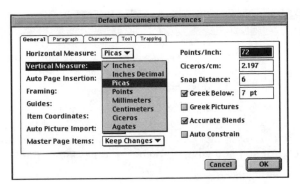

Figure 3-1: You select a measurement system in the Default Document Preferences dialog box.

Entering a measurement

No matter what you choose, you can use any measurement in any dialog box; just enter the code (shown in parentheses in the following list) that tells QuarkXPress what the system is. The measurement system options, which can be different for the horizontal and vertical rulers, are as follows:

✦ **Inches:** Inches (") are displayed on the ruler divided into eighths, in typical inch format ($1/4$-inch, $1/2$-inch, and so on).

✦ **Inches decimal:** Inches (") are displayed on the ruler in decimal format, divided into tenths.

✦ **Picas:** One pica (p) is about .166 inches. There are 6 picas in an inch.

✦ **Points:** One point (pt) is approximately $1/72$ (.01388) of an inch, or .351 millimeters.

✦ **Millimeters:** A metric measurement unit—25.4 millimeters (mm) equals one inch; 1 mm equals 0.03937 inches.

✦ **Centimeters:** A metric measurement unit—2.54 centimeters (cm) is an inch; 1 cm equals 0.3937 inches.

✦ **Ciceros:** This measurement unit is used in most of Europe; one cicero (c) is approximately .1792 inches. This is close in size to a pica, which is .167 inches.

✦ **Agates:** One agate (ag) is 0.071 inches. (The agate system is new to version 4 of QuarkXPress.)

The two-sided cicero

There are two accepted measurements for a cicero. A cicero, used in France and most of continental Europe, is based on 12 Didot points. But a Didot point has a different measurement in the United States and Britain than it does elsewhere.

The QuarkXPress default of 2.1967 ciceros per centimeter matches the standard European cicero size. If you use the American-British cicero, the number should be 2.3723. Most people don't have problems using the default values, but it can make a difference in large documents, such as banners, where registration and tiling of multiple pieces is important.

The Points/Inch Ciceros/cm options

In the General pane of Default Document Preferences (⌘+Y), you can set the number of points per inch and the number of ciceros per centimeter through the Points/Inch and Ciceros/cm options, respectively. QuarkXPress uses a default setting of 72 points per inch and 2.1967 ciceros per centimeter. The reason you may want to change these is because the actual number of points per inch is 72.271742, although most people now round that off to 72. (QuarkXPress requires you to round it to 72.271 if you use the actual value.)

Coordinate controls

Whichever system of measurement you use, you can control how the coordinates for layout elements are calculated. Select Item Coordinates in the General pane of Default Document Preferences (Edit➪Preferences➪Document or ⌘+Y) to tell QuarkXPress whether to base your ruler and box coordinates on a page or on a spread. If you treat each page as a separate element, keep the option set to Page, which is the default setting (see Figure 3-2). If you work on a spread as a single unit, change the setting to Spread. If you choose Spread, the coordinate system is continuous from the left edge of the leftmost page to the right edge of the rightmost page. If you choose Page, the rightmost horizontal coordinate of the right page is the same as the rightmost horizontal coordinate of the left page (zero, unless you've moved the ruler origin).

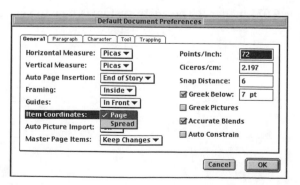

Figure 3-2: The Item Coordinates pop-up menu.

Working with Guides and Rulers

Guides and rulers are important tools for a layout artist because they help to position the elements correctly. In the Display pane of the Application Preferences dialog box (Option+Shift+⌘+Y), QuarkXPress provides the following types of guides to help you align items (see Figure 3-3):

✦ **Margin (normally blue):** The margin guides show you the default column and gutter positions for text boxes.

✦ **Ruler (normally green):** The ruler guides are lines you drag from the horizontal and vertical rulers so that you can tell whether a box lines up to a desired point.

✦ **Grid (normally magenta):** The baseline grid shows the position of text baselines.

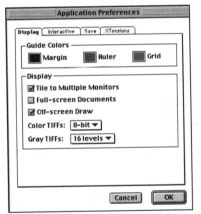

Figure 3-3: The Display pane in the Application Preferences dialog box.

The color of these guides can be important in helping you distinguish them from other lines and boxes in your layout. It is not at all uncommon to have all three guides visible at the same time. (Read on to find out how to change the default colors.)

Tip

More often than not, you use margin guides routinely and ruler guides occasionally, particularly when you want to align something within a box to a ruler point. It's easier to use the box coordinates (their X and Y positions in the Measurements palette) to make sure that boxes or their margins are placed exactly where you want them. The baseline grid, however, can help you estimate column depth and see if odd text such as a headline causes vertical alignment problems.

Changing guide colors

You can change the colors of these guides to any color available by using the Mac's color picker. Just click the color square for the guide whose color you want to change to bring up the color selection options (see Figure 3-4). The left side of the dialog box lists the various color-selection models you can use. The color in the New field shows the new color; the color in the Original field shows the original color. When using the color wheel, as we did in Figure 3-4, select a point in the wheel for the hue you want and use the fields at the right of the dialog box to control the hue angle, saturation, and lightness.

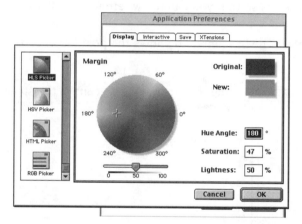

Figure 3-4: The color wheel method of defining guide colors.

Turning guide colors on and off

Although you set colors for guides in the Display pane of the Application Preferences dialog box (Option+Shift+⌘+Y), use the View menu to display the guides. Select View⇨Show Guides (or press F7) to display margin and ruler guides and choose View⇨Hide Guides. (Again, as this is a feature that you toggle on and off, the shortcut is F7 to hide them.) Likewise, select Show Baseline Grid and Hide Baseline Grid (Option+F7 on the Mac; Ctrl+F7 in Windows) to turn baseline grids on and off.

Tip

Ruler guides display whether or not you activate Show Rulers or Hide Rulers. To get rid of a ruler guide, select it and drag it back to the ruler. If the ruler is not displayed, drag it off the page past where the ruler would be.

Placing guides in front of or behind boxes

Use the Guides pop-up menu in the Default Document Preferences dialog box (refer to Figure 3-2) to specify whether guides appear in front of boxes (the default setting) or behind them. When guides are behind boxes, it can be easier to see what is in the boxes but harder to tell if elements within the boxes line up with margins, gutters, or baselines. If you select text boxes when guides are set to display behind boxes, the boxes *knock out* the guides, which means the guides are invisible within the text box (see Figure 3-5). The guides stay knocked out even when you select other boxes. Picture boxes always knock out their guides.

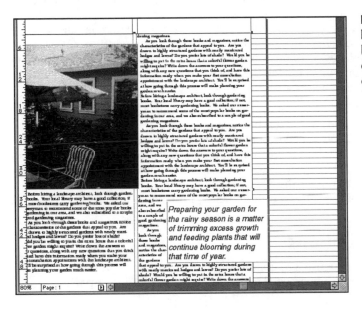

Figure 3-5: When guides have been set to appear behind text boxes, they do not appear on the document.

Choosing Display and View Options

QuarkXPress lets you control how documents relate to the monitor's screen area, and the page view, which you select from the View menu, determines how much of the page you see at one time. The following sections cover each of the monitor and view options in detail.

Monitor display options

Three options in the Display pane of the Application Preferences dialog box (refer to Figure 3-3) control how QuarkXPress documents relate to the monitor's screen area. The default view, which appears each time you start up the application or open a new document, is Actual Size (100 percent). The following list describes each option in detail:

✦ **Tile to Multiple Monitors:** If you have multiple monitors attached to your Mac, this tells QuarkXPress to automatically put some document windows on your secondary monitor(s) when you choose Tile Documents (or, on Windows, when you choose Tile Horizontally/Tile Vertically). Use the Monitors control pane that comes with your system disks to set up multiple monitors. (Windows does not support multiple monitors, so QuarkXPress for Windows does not support this option.)

✦ **Full-screen Documents:** If you check this box, the document window will appear at the screen's far left, under the default position for the Tool palette. Unless you move the Tool palette down, you'll find that having this option enabled obscures the document window's close box. Therefore, we recommend that you not routinely use this option. There is one advantage to using it: it can give your document window enough width to fully display a document. However, when you use it, make sure that you move your Tool palette so that you can click the close box. (This option is not available in QuarkXPress for Windows.)

✦ **Off-screen Draw:** This option controls how QuarkXPress displays elements on your screen as you scroll through a document. If checked, it redraws each element displayed in order of display. If unchecked, it draws them in memory first and then displays them all simultaneously. Both options take the same amount of time to redraw the screen, so there is no advantage to either setting. Note that with the Speed Scroll option selected in the Interactive pane, the Off-screen Draw option has no noticeable effect.

View menu options

The View menu (see Figure 3-6) contains commands that let you control the display of other items on-screen. The menu is divided into four parts:

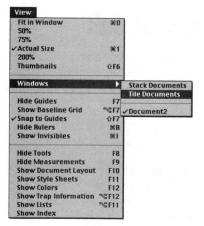

Figure 3-6: The View menu.

✦ The first part of the menu holds the view option commands (covered in detail later in this section).

✦ The second part lets you control how multiple documents are displayed on the screen, as well as switch among several open documents. (This section is actually an entirely different menu, the Window menu, in the Windows version of QuarkXPress.) The Tile Documents option is particularly useful if you have multiple monitors (which gives you enough room to see several documents at once). (On Windows, you can choose from Tile Horizontally and Tile Vertically.) The Stack Documents option simply keeps the windows offset slightly so that all the document names are visible.

In QuarkXPress Windows, the tile and stack options are in the separate Windows menu, which also has a handy option to close all open windows.

✦ The third part of the menu offers commands that control the display of positioning aids: guides, baseline grid, rulers, and invisible elements (tabs, returns, and so on). You can toggle features on or off; if a command is active, a check appears next to its name.

✦ The final part contains commands that display or hide QuarkXPress palettes. You can toggle features on or off; if a palette is open, its option changes from Show to Hide.

Changing the document view

As you become more accustomed to working with QuarkXPress, you'll find yourself changing the View selection from time to time, based on the specific task you are trying to accomplish. To change the document view, choose the View menu and then select from the preset options. You can change views by a variable amount (between 10 percent and 800 percent) at any time. To do so, enter a percentage value in the box at the corner of the open document window (lower-left side, next to the page number).

New Feature

The ability to expand the view to 800 percent is new to QuarkXPress 4. In previous versions of the program, the maximum amount you could expand the view was 400 percent.

Using the preset options

The preset view options on the View menu are as follows:

✦ **Fit in Window (⌘+0 [zero]):** This view fits the page into the area of the document window.

✦ **50 percent:** This view displays the document page at half its actual size.

✦ **75 percent:** Choose this setting to display the document page at three-fourths of its actual size.

✦ **Actual Size (⌘+1):** This setting displays the document page at its actual size, which may mean that only part of the page is displayed on-screen.

✦ **200 percent:** If you choose this setting, QuarkXPress displays the document page at twice its actual size; this view is useful if you are editing text that is 10 points or smaller, or if you are trying to precisely position an item on a page.

✦ **Thumbnails (Shift+F6):** This view displays miniature versions of the document pages. Figure 3-7 shows a thumbnail view with Page 2 selected (highlighted). You can drag a selected page to a position elsewhere in the document by clicking the mouse button and holding it down as you drag the page.

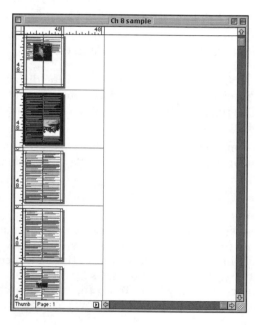

Figure 3-7: A thumbnail view of a document.

Image displays

The image display controls are designed primarily to let you control the balance between speed and fidelity. Typically, layout artists don't need to see a superior quality image of the things they're placing. They just need to see what the image looks like and what its dimensions are. QuarkXPress lets you determine the trade-off between speed and fidelity through several settings.

QuarkXPress Windows has a unique option called *Display DPI Value*. This should remain at 96 dpi; using a larger number permanently zooms the monitor view, while a smaller number zooms out the view.

Referring to Figure 3-3, two settings in the Display pane of the Application Preferences dialog box (Option+Shift+⌘+Y) affect how bitmapped images are displayed on-screen: Color TIFFs and Gray TIFFs. Use these two settings to control how accurately the colors and shades for your TIFF images are displayed on-screen. If you are using QuarkXPress's image controls (described in Chapter 19), set these to 8-bit (256 colors) and 16 levels, respectively, for color and gray-scale images. This can result in considerably smaller document files because of the low bit depth of the resulting TIFF image previews.

View-changing tips and tricks

QuarkXPress offers some alternative ways to change views. We find the following ones particularly useful:

✦ To increase the page view in 25-percent increments, select the Zoom tool (it looks like a magnifying glass). When you place the pointer over the document with the Zoom tool selected, the pointer changes to a magnifying glass. Each time you press the mouse button, the view increases in 25-percent increments, up to a maximum of 800 percent. To decrease the page view in 25-percent increments, hold down the Option key as you click the mouse button. (Note how the plus in the Zoom tool's pointer changes to a minus.)

✦ To increase the view by 25 percent, an even easier method is to hold the Control key and click the mouse—you don't have to have the Zoom tool selected.

✦ To zoom in on a specific area, you can click the Zoom tool and select a corner of the area you want, hold down the mouse button, drag to the opposite corner of the area, and release the mouse button.

✦ For all of these Zoom tool options, you can change the increment from its default of 25 percent to any other amount by making changes in the Tool pane of the Default Document Preferences dialog box (Edit➪Preferences➪Document or ⌘+Y).

✦ Another easy way to change your view is through a keyboard shortcut, Control+V (Ctrl+Alt+V on Windows), that highlights the view percentage at the bottom left of your QuarkXPress window. Just enter the new percentage (you don't need to enter the % symbol) and press Enter or Return. If you want to go to the thumbnail view, enter T instead of a percentage.

Tip

Selecting the 32-bit option for Color TIFF files gives you a truer representation of color if your graphics have a bit depth greater than 24-bit. It also lets you print 24-bit images to a color QuickDraw printer. No matter what color depth or gray level you select, printing to a PostScript printer is not affected. The image prints either at its top resolution or at the best resolution the printer can offer for the image. If you select a color bit depth greater than your monitor's capabilities, however, you see only the color that your monitor can actually display, and your system might slow down, because the higher bit depth makes QuarkXPress perform extra computations. (Your monitor must be in Thousands or Millions of Colors mode for this feature to work properly.)

Pasteboard size

The pasteboard is a familiar tool to layout artists who are experienced with manual paste-up—the kind you do when you roll strips of type through a waxing machine and then temporarily tack them to the wall or to the outside of your light table until you need them. QuarkXPress supports this metaphor by creating a nonprinting area at the sides of each page or spread that you can use as an electronic scratchpad for picture and text boxes and other elements. The only layout preference set in the Interactive pane of the Application Preferences dialog box (Option-Shift+⌘+Y) is the pasteboard width (see Figure 3-8), which applies to all documents until you change the setting again.

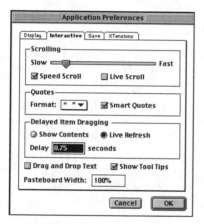

Figure 3-8: Control the width of the pasteboard by entering a value in the Pasteboard Width field.

If you don't use the pasteboard, you may want to reduce its size. Even if empty, the pasteboard takes up space on your screen that affects scrolling because the scroll width includes the pasteboard area. At 100 percent, the pasteboard is equal to one page. If you do reduce your pasteboard, items may extend beyond it and appear to be cut off; they actually remain intact.

Selecting Interactive Preferences

The Interactive pane (see Figure 3-9) in the Application Preferences dialog box (Option+Shift+⌘+Y) also controls smart quotes, how dragged items appear, and other text-handling options, including scrolling.

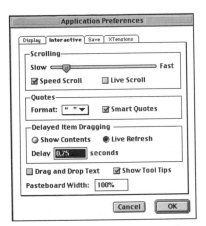

Figure 3-9: The Interactive pane in the Application Preferences dialog box.

Smart quotes

Use the pop-up menu in the Quotes option to pick the default quotation marks to be used when you type inside QuarkXPress. The available sets handle the needs of most Western languages. To have smart (curly) quotation marks automatically substituted when you type them within text boxes, check the Smart Quotes box. Note that checking this option also translates the single quote character to the smart (curly) style when you type it; it also controls how straight quotes are translated when you import a text file (File➪Get Text, or ⌘+E) and check the Convert Quotes box. To use the standard (straight) keyboard quotes on the Mac, hold the Control key when typing them. On Windows, type Ctrl+' for foot marks and Ctrl+Alt+' for inch marks.

Scrolling speed

Use the Scrolling slider to control how fast the page scrolls when you click the arrows in the scroll bars. If you set the slider closer to Slow, QuarkXPress moves more slowly across your document, which is helpful if you want to pay close attention to your document while scrolling. If you set the slider closer to Fast, QuarkXPress zips across the document, which may cause you to move past a desired element.

Most people prefer a Scrolling setting somewhere in the middle range. You may have to adjust the setting a few times until it feels right to you. Generally, it should be slightly closer to Fast than to Slow.

The two other options in the scrolling section of the dialog box work as follows:

✦ **Live Scroll:** If you check this option, QuarkXPress redraws pages while you are dragging the box in the scroll bar. Generally, you should check this option, unless you're working on a slower computer.

✦ **Speed Scroll:** This option speeds up scrolling in graphics-intensive documents by masking out the graphics and blends as you scroll. After you stop scrolling, the graphics and blends are redrawn. Generally, you should check this option.

Delayed item dragging

Three controls in the Interactive pane control how QuarkXPress displays items on-screen. If Show Contents is selected and you press and hold the mouse button as you begin dragging an item, the contents of the item are visible as you drag it. If Live Refresh is selected when you press and hold the mouse button as you begin dragging an item, the contents of the item are visible as you drag it and the screen also refreshes to show item layers and text flow. You can enter a value in the Delay seconds field controlling the time (in seconds ranging between 0.1 and 5) that you must press and hold the mouse button before Show Contents or Live Refresh are activated.

Drag-and-drop editing

The Interactive pane of the Application Preferences dialog box contains the Drag and Drop Text option. If checked, it lets you highlight a piece of text and then drag it to a new location (as in most word processors), rather than cut it from the old location and paste it to the new one. If you hold down the Shift key, a copy of the highlighted text is moved to the new location instead of the original. On the Mac, you can enable drag-and-drop editing even when the Drag and Drop Text option is not enabled by pressing ⌘+Control (to move text) or Shift+⌘+Control (to copy text). Checking the Show Tool Tips checkbox displays the names of the palette or tool icons when the pointer is positioned on them; the default setting is unchecked.

Note

Application preferences are saved in the XPress Preferences file and not with each document. These preferences control how QuarkXPress works with all documents, so any changes you make in the Application Preferences dialog box apply to all documents you create or edit using your copy of QuarkXPress.

Saving documents

The Save pane in Application Preferences lets you control how QuarkXPress saves and makes backup copies of your documents. This is covered later in this chapter. (The XTensions pane of Application Preferences is covered in Chapter 25.)

Choosing General Preferences

The General pane (see Figure 3-10) of the Default Document Preferences dialog box (⌘+Y) controls defaults for page layout, including the measurement system used, the positioning of guides and frames, and the function of master page items. We covered the Horizontal and Vertical Measure, Guides, Item Coordinates, and Points/Inch and Ciceros/cm options earlier in this chapter. The following sections detail the other options on the General pane.

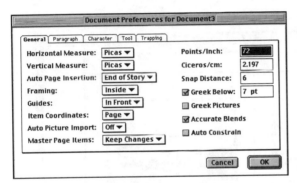

Figure 3-10: The General pane of the Document Preferences dialog box.

Auto Page Insertion

Auto Page Insertion tells QuarkXPress where to add new pages when all of your text does not fit into an automatic text box defined in a master page. QuarkXPress creates as many pages as needed to contain all the remaining text. You must define the text box containing the overflow text as an automatic text box in the page's master page. (This is indicated by an unbroken chain icon at the upper left of the master page.) In the pop-up menu for Auto Page Insertion, your options are:

- ✦ **End of Section:** This places new pages (which are based on the master page) at the end of the current section. (Sections are defined via the Page⇨Section option.) If no sections are defined, End of Section works the same as the End of Document option.

- ✦ **End of Story:** End of Story places new pages, based on the current master page, immediately following the last page of the text chain.

- ✦ **End of Document:** If you select this option, QuarkXPress places new pages at the end of the document, based on the master page used at the end of the document.

- ✦ **Off:** If you choose Off, QuarkXPress adds no new pages, leaving you to add pages and text boxes for overflow text wherever you want. The existence of overflow text is indicated by a red checked box at the end of the text in the text box.

Framing parameters

Selecting a Framing setting in the General pane of Document Preferences tells QuarkXPress how to draw the ruling lines (frames) around text boxes and picture boxes via the Item⇨Frame option (⌘+B). You have the following choices (see Figure 3-11):

✦ **Outside:** This places the frame on the outside of the box.

✦ **Inside:** This places the frame inside the box.

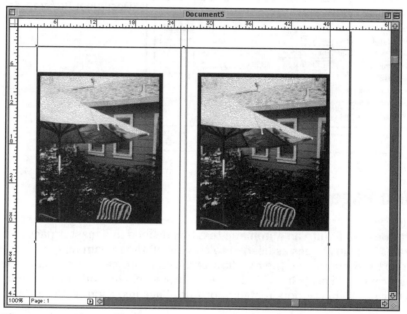

Figure 3-11: The Inside framing option (left) and the Outside framing option (right).

Tip

If you change the Framing setting while working on a document, only the frames you subsequently create are affected by the change; frames created earlier are unchanged. Thus, you can use both the Inside and Outside settings in the same document.

Auto Picture Import

Auto Picture Import lets you automatically update links to your source images. This is handy if your picture might change frequently and you don't want to forget to update your layout to accommodate it. You can select from the following Auto

Picture Import settings in the General pane of the Document Preferences dialog box:

> ✦ **On (verify):** If you choose this setting, QuarkXPress checks the graphics files (by looking at the file's date and time stamp) to see if they have been modified. It then displays a list of all the graphics files in your document so that you can decide whether or not to update the layout with the newest version.
>
> ✦ **On:** This setting tells QuarkXPress to automatically import the latest version of changed graphics files.
>
> ✦ **Off:** If you select Off, QuarkXPress does not check to see if the source graphics files have been modified.

In most cases, you should use On (verify) or On, depending on whether you expect graphics files to change much. If files may change size, use On (verify), so that you know which pictures to check to determine whether layout is affected. If file dimensions are unlikely to change—for example, a logo may incorporate the current month but the logo size doesn't change—use the On setting.

This option works only with graphics that have been imported through QuarkXPress's File➪Get Picture (⌘+E) command. Those pasted into QuarkXPress via the Clipboard are not affected, because the pasted file is copied into your document. If you delete or rename a file, the Missing/Modified Picture dialog box appears no matter which automatic import option you select.

Master Page Items

Master Page Items, another setting found in the General pane of the Document Preferences dialog box (⌘+Y), lets you control what happens to text boxes and picture boxes that are defined on a master page when you apply a different master page to your document pages. Your options are Keep Changes (the default) and Delete Changes. We recommend that you leave this setting on Keep Changes. Then, after applying a new master page, manually remove any unwanted elements left behind. (This setting applies only to items used *and* modified on a document page based on a master page's items. It does not apply to unmodified items based on a master page.)

You can make two different kinds of changes to items that are based on master page items: *item changes* and *content changes*. If you change the shape of a box based on a master text box, but you don't change the text in that box, the text remains dependent on the master page item while the box shape does not. Similarly, if you change the text in such a box but don't change its shape, the box shape remains dependent on the master page item while the text inside it does not.

Snap Distance

To set the threshold for when objects snap to guides (assuming Snap to Guides is selected in the View menu), enter a value in the Snap Distance option box. The default setting is 6 pixels; you can specify any value from 1 to 216 pixels. The larger the number, the further away you can place an object from a guide and still have it automatically snap to the guide (and the more potential there is for an object to snap to a guide unexpectedly during detailed design work).

Greeking specifications

One option closely related to views is *greeking*. When you use greeking, QuarkXPress displays a gray area to represent text or pictures on the page (see Figure 3-12). Turning on greeking speeds up the display of your QuarkXPress document. In fact, greeking—particularly when used for pictures—is one of the best ways to save screen redraw time. When you print, images are unaffected by greeking.

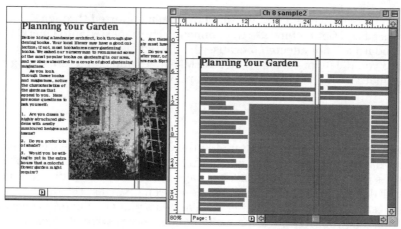

Figure 3-12: The page on the right has greeking turned on for both text and pictures.

The General pane of the Document Preferences dialog box contains the following greeking specifications:

✦ **Greek Below:** This option tells QuarkXPress to greek the text display when text is below a certain point size. The default value is 7 points, but you can enter any value from 2 to 720 points. To disable greeking, uncheck the Greek Below box.

✦ **Greek Pictures:** This option tells QuarkXPress to display all unselected graphics as gray shapes, which speeds up the display considerably. This feature is useful after you position and size your images and no longer need to see them on your layout (refer to Figure 3-12). You can still look at a greeked picture by clicking it.

Accurate Blends

If you check the Accurate Blends option in the General pane of the Document Preferences dialog box, blends between two colors that you place in a box background (created via the Colors palette or the Box pane of the Modify dialog box) appear more accurately on monitors in 8-bit (256-color) monitor mode.

The Accurate Blends option can slow down screen redraw on pages with blends. (The default setting has this option checked.) However, if you have a 16-bit or 24-bit video board or enough video RAM on a computer that supports 16-bit or 24-bit display with its built-in video circuitry, your blends display accurately whether or not you check this option.

Auto Constrain

The last layout control option in the General pane of the Document Preferences dialog box (⌘+Y) is Auto Constrain, which controls the behavior of boxes that are created within other boxes. If you check the Auto Constrain option, a box that is created within another box—a picture box drawn inside a text box, for example—may not exceed the boundaries of the parent box (in this case, the text box). Nor can you move it outside the parent box's boundaries. This feature maintains compatibility with versions of QuarkXPress prior to 3.0, which always acted as if the Auto Constrain option were selected. Most people should leave this option unchecked, which is the default setting.

The Item menu offers a toggle for Constrain and Unconstrain. This setting can override for any selected box the Auto Constrain setting in the General pane of the Default Document Preferences dialog box. Constrain appears as an option in the Item menu if the selected box is unconstrained and grouped with an enveloping larger box; Unconstrain appears if the selected box is constrained.

Setting Tool Specifications

QuarkXPress lets you customize how its basic tools work by changing settings in the Tool pane of the Document Preferences dialog box (see Figure 3-13). To set the defaults, first select the tool you want to modify. Unavailable options are grayed out, as explained in the remainder of this section. After you make changes, choose OK to save the changes or Cancel to undo them.

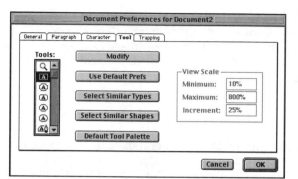

Figure 3-13: The Tool pane of the Document Preferences dialog box.

Note

If you access the Tool pane of the Default Document Preferences dialog box with no document open, all defaults apply to all subsequently created documents. Otherwise, the defaults apply only to subsequently created boxes and lines for the current document.

Tools you can customize

The tools you can customize fall into the following groups:

✦ **Zoom tool:** You can change the minimum and maximum zoom views to any value between 10 and 800 percent. You also can specify how much QuarkXPress zooms into your document each time you click the document with the Zoom tool active. To do this, enter any value from 10 to 800 percent, in increments of 1 percent, into the Increment option box.

✦ **Box tools:** You can set the item settings for all the Text Box and Picture Box tools. You can establish settings for options normally available for the individual boxes via the Item menu's Modify, Frame, and Runaround options. If you select one of these box tools from the Tool pane and click Modify, a dialog box containing three tabbed panes—corresponding to those item menu options—appears, and you can set these options just as you do if you select a box on a document page. The difference is that you are setting them as defaults. All boxes subsequently created with these tools take on any new preferences you establish in the Tool pane of the Document Preferences dialog box. Not all Picture Box Specification or Text Box Specification options are available to you; those that affect sizing, for example, are grayed out.

Tip

The ability to customize certain settings comes in handy. You can, for example, give oval picture boxes an offset of 1 pica, or set text boxes to have a 3-point frame and a green background.

✦ **Drawing tools:** You can establish defaults for new lines that you draw with the Line tools. You can set most regular-line options that are normally available through the Item menu. You can also set other line-specification and runaround options, such as line color and weight. All lines subsequently created with these tools take on any new preferences you establish in the Tool pane of the Document Preferences dialog box. Options that affect position are grayed out.

Tip

If you want to set the preferences for all text boxes or picture boxes at once, click a text box or picture box in the scrollable list and then click Select Similar Types before you click the Modify button. If you want to set the preferences for all boxes of the same shape, click a box that uses that shape and then click Select Similar Shapes before you click the Modify button.

Choosing Character Preferences

QuarkXPress lets you define typographic preferences. You specify your preferences in the Character pane of the Document Preferences dialog box (see Figure 3-14), which you open by choosing Edit⇨Preferences⇨Document (⌘+Y) and then clicking the Character tab.

Note

As with many changes you make in the Document Preferences dialog box, any changes made to the settings in this Character pane affect only the current document. If no document is open, the changes affect all subsequent new documents.

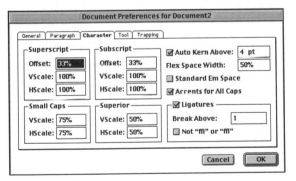

Figure 3-14: The Character pane of the Document Preferences dialog box.

Most of the character preferences you define need to be set only once, although a few are likely to change for different classes of documents.

Character defaults

Several options in the Character pane (⌘+Y) affect character styles. These include the four boxes labeled Superscript, Subscript, Small Caps, and Superior. These settings define how QuarkXPress creates these attributes.

Note

Superiors are a special type of superscript character that always align along the cap line, which is the height of a capital letter in the current typeface. They typically are used in footnotes.

Superscript and subscript options

Superscript and subscript share the following options:

✦ **Offset:** The Offset option dictates how far below or above the baseline QuarkXPress shifts a subscripted or superscripted character. The default settings are 33 percent for both Subscript and Superscript. We prefer 35 percent for superscripts and 30 percent for subscripts because those values do a better job of taking into consideration the effects of leading.

✦ **VScale and HScale:** These options determine scaling for the subscript or superscript. Although the default is 100 percent, this is useful only for typewritten documents; typeset documents typically use a smaller size for subscripts and superscripts—usually between 60 and 80 percent of the text size. The two values should be the same because subscripts and superscripts are typically not distorted along one dimension.

Small caps and superior options

The following options for small caps and superior are similar, even though these are very different attributes:

✦ **VScale and HScale:** These options determine the scaling for the small cap or superior. The two values should be the same because small caps and superiors typically are not distorted along one dimension. Usually, a small cap's scale should be between 65 and 80 percent of the normal text, and a superior's scale should be between 50 and 65 percent.

Horizontal spacing controls

The horizontal spacing controls are used as follows:

✦ **Auto Kern Above:** Auto Kern Above enables you to define the point size at which QuarkXPress automatically kerns letter pairs. Ten points is fine for laser-printed documents, but typeset documents should be set at a smaller value, such as 8 points.

✦ **Flex Space Width:** This lets you define the value for a flex space, which is a user-defined space. The default is 50 percent, which is about the width of the letter *t*. A better setting is 200 percent, which is equal to an em space (the width of the letter *M*). An em space is used often in typography but is not directly available in QuarkXPress.

✦ **Standard Em Space:** This determines how QuarkXPress calculates the width of an em, a standard measurement in typography upon which most other spacing measurements are based. If you check this box, QuarkXPress uses the typographic measurement (the width of the letter *M*, which is usually equal to the current point size). Unchecked, QuarkXPress uses the width of two zeroes, which was how QuarkXPress has always calculated an em space.

Tip

Often, the two values used for em spaces (the width of the letter *M* or two zeros) are the same, because typographers give numerals the width of half an em space (an en space) to make alignment easy in tables. If you encounter difficulty in aligning numeral-intensive documents, uncheck this option.

Special characters

The remaining options in the Character pane of the Document Preferences dialog box (⌘+Y) control special characters. They work as follows:

✦ **Accents for All Caps:** If checked, this option lets accented characters retain their accents if you apply the All Caps attribute to them. In many publications, the style is to drop accents from capitalized letters, and this feature lets you control whether this style is implemented automatically or not.

✦ **Ligatures:** When you check this box, QuarkXPress automatically replaces occurrences of fi, ffi, fl, and ffl with their ligatured equivalents, both when you enter text and when you import it. If you uncheck the Ligatures box, all ligatures in your document are translated to standard character combinations. Not all fonts support ligatures, and many sans serif typefaces look like their nonligature equivalents. This feature is nice, because it means you don't have to worry about adding ligatures manually. It's also nice because it does not affect spell-checking.

✦ **Not "ffi" or "ffl":** Some people don't like using ligatures for ffi and ffl. Check this box to prevent these ligatures from being automatically used. When you search for text in the Find/Change dialog box, you can enter **ffi** and QuarkXPress finds the ligature.

✦ **Break Above:** This option for ligatures lets you set how a ligature is handled in a loosely tracked line. You can enter a value from 0 to 100. That value is the number of units of tracking (each unit is 1/200th of an em space) at which QuarkXPress breaks apart a ligature to avoid awkward spacing.

Windows does not support ligatures at all. As a result, when Mac files with the Ligatures options selected are moved to QuarkXPress for Windows, they substitute the standard characters.

Working with Paragraph Preferences

The Paragraph pane of the Document Preferences dialog box offers options for horizontal and vertical spacing: leading, baseline grid, and hyphenation (see Figure 3-15). The options are used as follows:

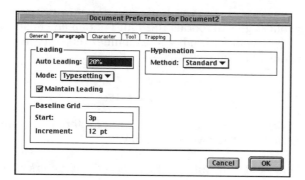

Figure 3-15: The Paragraph pane of the Document Preferences dialog box.

✦ **Auto Leading:** The default setting for Auto Leading, which specifies the space between lines, is 20 percent. This sets leading at 120 percent of the current text size. A better option is +2, which sets leading at the current text size plus 2 points—a more typical setting among typographers.

✦ **Maintain Leading:** This box, when checked, causes text that falls under an intervening text or picture box to snap to the next baseline grid, rather than fall right after the intervening box's offset. This procedure ensures consistent text alignment across all columns.

✦ **Mode:** This leading option is a throwback to QuarkXPress's early years; you should always pick the Typesetting option from the pop-up menu. (Typesetting mode measures leading from baseline to baseline, while Word Processing mode measures from top of character to top of character.)

✦ **Start:** This baseline grid option, as well as the Increment option, specifies the default position for lines of text. The Start option indicates where the grid begins (how far from the top of the page).

✦ **Increment:** This baseline grid setting determines the grid interval. Generally, the grid should start where the automatic text box starts, and the interval should be the same as body text leading.

✦ **Method:** Set this hyphenation option to Enhanced or Expanded. Standard exists only to keep the program compatible with earlier versions, which had a less accurate hyphenation algorithm.

Selecting Trapping Preferences

In the Trapping pane of the Document Preferences dialog box (⌘+Y), QuarkXPress offers a set of *trap* options, which define how it prints overlapping colors when you print separations to PostScript printers. If you are unfamiliar with color trapping, leave the defaults as they are and see Chapter 23 for more information on trapping. As Figure 3-16 shows, the options are:

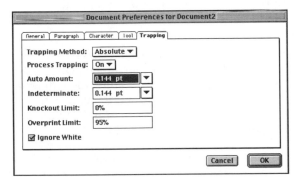

Figure 3-16: The Trapping pane of the Document Preferences dialog box.

✦ **Trapping Method:** This setting determines whether QuarkXPress uses the trapping values specified in the Auto Amount option (discussed in a following bulleted item) or whether it adjusts the trapping based on the saturation of the abutting colors. If you choose Absolute, the program uses the values as is; if you choose Proportional, QuarkXPress calculates new trapping values based on the value entered in Auto Amount and the relative saturation of the abutting colors. The default is Absolute.

✦ **Process Trapping:** Turning this on tells QuarkXPress to calculate traps for overlapping process colors based on their saturation as well as on all the other trap settings. (For example, it traps 50 percent cyan and 100 percent magenta differently than 80 percent cyan and 100 percent magenta.) If the option is off, it uses the same trapping values for all saturation levels. The default setting turns on this option, which makes for smoother trapping.

✦ **Auto Amount:** Select this option to specify the trapping value for which the program calculates automatic trapping. You can enter values from 0 to 36 points in increments of 0.001 points. If you want the amount to be infinite (so colors overprint), choose Overprint from the pop-up menu. The default setting is 0.144 points.

✦ **Indeterminate:** The Indeterminate setting tells QuarkXPress how to trap objects that abut multicolored or indeterminate-colored objects, as well as imported color graphics. Valid options are 0 to 26 points, in 0.001-point increments, as well as Overprint. The default is 0.144 points.

✦ **Knockout Limit:** This setting lets you control the point at which an object's color knocks out a background color. It is expressed as a percentage, and the default is 0 percent.

✦ **Overprint Limit:** This value tells QuarkXPress when to overprint a color object. You can specify any percentage from 0 to 100 percent in increments of 0.1. If you enter 50 percent, QuarkXPress makes any object whose trap specification is set as Overprint and whose saturation is 50 percent or greater overprint; otherwise, it traps the object based on the Auto Amount setting. This limit affects black objects regardless of whether black is set at Auto or Overprint. The default is 95 percent.

✦ **Ignore White:** If you check this option box, QuarkXPress traps an object based on all nonwhite objects abutting or behind the object. Otherwise, QuarkXPress calculates a trap based on the smaller value: the Indeterminate setting or the trap specification for any other colors (including white) abutting or behind the object. This option is checked as a default because it makes little sense to trap to white (as there is nothing to trap to).

New
Feature

Before QuarkXPress 4, a few output settings were set in the Preferences dialog boxes that have gone away with this new version. Now output settings are handled in the Print dialog box (see Chapter 24).

Controlling Saves and Backups

QuarkXPress's preferences include those that control how a document is managed, in particular how it is saved and backed up. The backup feature is handy if you are experimenting with a layout, because you can go back to prior versions if you don't like how the layout has evolved. You can achieve the same effect by periodically saving your layout with a different name, but using the backup feature is easier. These options are found in the Save pane of the Application Preferences dialog box (Option+Shift+⌘+Y) shown in Figure 3-17. The options on this pane function as follows:

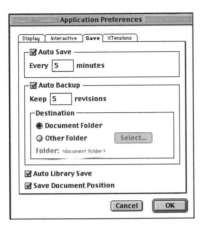

Figure 3-17: The Save pane of the Application Preferences dialog box.

✦ **Auto Save:** By checking the Auto Save option, you set QuarkXPress to save all opened documents at regular intervals. You determine that interval through the value you enter in the Every minutes field. When an auto save occurs, QuarkXPress does not actually save your document to its regular document file; instead, it creates an autosave document (with a filename that ends in ".AutoSave" on the Mac and ".asv" on Windows). If your computer crashes, you can revert your file to its last auto-saved condition by opening the autosave document.

✦ **Auto Backup:** You can also have QuarkXPress retain backup copies of your document by checking the Auto Backup box. When this option is checked, QuarkXPress creates a backup copy of your document every time you manually save it. You determine how many previous versions are retained in the Keep revisions field.

✦ **Destination:** You determine where backups are stored by choosing one of the two destination buttons. The default location is in the same folder as the current document, but you can click the button and use the Backup Folder dialog box to select a different folder. (It works like a standard Open dialog box.) If you later want to reset the destination to the document folder, select the Document Folder button in the Destination area of the dialog box.

Note

The backup and auto-save options are independent. If both backup and auto save are enabled, backups are created only when you explicitly save with the File⇨Save command (or the keyboard shortcut ⌘+S).

✦ **Auto Library Save:** QuarkXPress's library feature lets you add common elements to a library that is accessible to multiple documents. When the Auto Library Save box is checked, it saves the library whenever something is added to or deleted from it. Otherwise, when the box is unchecked, the library is saved only when you close it (including when you quit QuarkXPress).

✦ **Save Document Position:** When Save Document Position is checked, QuarkXPress saves the size and position of the document window along with the document itself.

✦   ✦   ✦

Page Layout Techniques

Appearance counts—for a lot—which is why the layout of a document is so critical to its success. An attractive, engaging design draws readers to your documents, so they actually read your pearls of wisdom. Acquiring skill with layout takes time, training, and an eye for good design. QuarkXPress provides you with all the tools, and by taking the time to think through the design process, you can continue to develop the skills you need to take full advantage of QuarkXPress's power.

The next several chapters guide you through the process of creating effective layouts—the setup tasks that lay a strong foundation for your document, the basic elements used in building a layout, a variety of special creative techniques and, finally, some laborsaving tips to make your job easier on future projects.

In This Part

Chapter 4
Setting Up a Layout

Chapter 5
Working with Boxes

Chapter 6
Preparing Files
for Import

Chapter 7
Keeping It All
Together

Chapter 8
Working with Pages

Chapter 9
Special Layout
Techniques

Chapter 10
Creating Templates,
Master Pages, and
Libraries

Setting Up a Layout

✦ ✦ ✦ ✦

In This Chapter

Creating a sound infrastructure

Starting with a good design

Learning to work with layouts

Beginning a new document

Using the layout tools

✦ ✦ ✦ ✦

Like other desktop publishing programs, QuarkXPress lets you control how a document looks when you have finished creating it. To really make the most of this powerful tool, however, you need to understand some basic ideas about page design. While layout involves design talent, it does not require that you be a professional designer—people with a good aesthetic sense can produce serviceable layouts if they follow basic design principles. Learning the simple steps to creating a sound design is the subject of this chapter.

Creating a Sound Infrastructure

The key to a successful layout is planning, a rule that matches QuarkXPress's approach to design. You don't just start doing a layout in QuarkXPress. Instead, you start building the foundation of your document—the page size and columns, the paragraph and character styles, the standard elements such as page numbers and logos—to serve as a receptacle for the content. The idea is that most content you create is a variation on a theme. For example, if you produce a magazine, each issue is different, but the basic design structure is the same from month to month. Rather than start each month from scratch, you start with a template and modify it each month as necessary. The same approach works for newspapers, catalogs, brochures, newsletters, and books.

Tip Even before you build your basic structure, you need a mental image of what your document will be. Have no fear— nothing is cast in stone. If you change your mind as you work on your first document, you can modify your structure. It helps immensely, however, to have an initial structure in mind before starting.

Sketching your layout on paper

How do you start to develop a layout plan? If you are still thinking about what the pages should look like, you can develop some more specific ideas by spending a few minutes sketching out the layout before you sit down to produce the document on the computer.

The dummy approach

Let's say you want to create an eight-page newsletter that has standard, 8½ × 11-inch pages. One way to do this is to create a *dummy document*, a valuable layout-planning aid. Figure 4-1 shows a sample dummy—the cover and the first two pages.

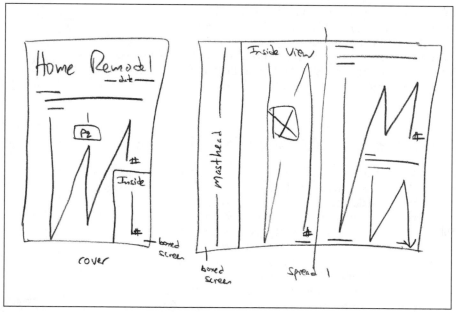

Figure 4-1: A pencil-sketch dummy lets you think through the basic structure quickly and easily.

STEPS: Creating a dummy

1. Take two sheets of blank, 8½ × 11-inch paper, aligning one on top of the other, and folding them in half across the width of the paper. This technique gives you a miniature version of your eight-page newsletter.

2. Next, use a pencil to sketch the dummy's masthead, the cover art and/or stories, and the running headers or footers for each page.

3. Form an idea about how wide you want the top, side, and bottom margins to be, and mark them on the pages.

4. Now indicate which pictures and stories go on each page. Of course, because you will be using QuarkXPress to format the document, you can make changes right up to the point when you produce camera-ready pages.

Note

Some conventions in sketches to remember: A down arrow means the story continues on another page, while a # symbol means the story ends. Horizontal lines usually indicate titles, bylines, and other such specific text elements, while a vertical line indicates a column of text. A box with an *X* through it indicates a picture or photo, while the abbreviation *pq* means a pull-quote—text that is taken from the article and put in a box or other shape to draw attention, similar to a photo. A *screen* is a background of color or gray ink.

You can see from Figure 4-1 that the basic layout structure is three columns, with a self-contained front page that has a small table of contents and interior pages that put the masthead (list of staff) and a viewpoint column on the second page. The third page has two stories, which of course may not start exactly where indicated on the sketch. The point is, merely, that multiple stories can appear on a page.

Taking the next step

You should find all this planning—which actually doesn't take that much time in relation to the other publishing tasks involved—to be time well spent. The process of sketching out the layout helps clarify your thoughts about the basic layout of your document. You can make preliminary decisions about such things as where to put each illustration and section of text on a page, how many columns of text to use, and whether to use any repeating elements (such as headers and footers). After you have a general idea of how to structure your document, you can start developing QuarkXPress style sheets, as described in Chapter 14.

Sketching your layout in QuarkXPress

If you are already comfortable using QuarkXPress, you may decide to forego the paper-and-pencil sketching of a new document and use QuarkXPress to do the rough design instead. The obvious advantages to this approach are as follows:

✦ **Experimenting with different approaches:** When a document has a set number of text and graphic elements, you can use QuarkXPress to make a series of "sketches" of the document. If you like, you can save each sketch as a separate file with a distinct filename. In each sketch, you can use different element positioning, type styles, masthead placement, and so on. Then you can print a copy of each file and use the copies to assist you in finalizing the look of the layout.

✦ **Printing thumbnail views:** If you are considering many different layout possibilities, you can develop them quickly on QuarkXPress and then print the series in thumbnail (miniature) size (select File⇨Print, and then check the Thumbnails box in the Document pane). Seeing the pages in thumbnail view makes it easier to evaluate the overall balance between page elements because you are not distracted by the text or the graphics in such a reduced view.

✦ **Getting your client's approval:** Printed QuarkXPress copies of rough sketches have a cleaner look, which is especially helpful if you are designing a layout for a client. The advantage to presenting rough sketches that look more "final" is that it tends to make the client approval process go more smoothly, and it can make it easier for you to sell the client on your design. At the same time, slick-looking rough drafts do have a disadvantage: they make it more difficult for clients to understand that what they are seeing is just a rough draft and not a final copy.

Starting with a Good Design

Not visible in a sketch is a sense of visual balance. Think about it: Many documents are off-putting. What makes them that way, and how do you build a layout that is inviting, not off-putting? Figure 4-2 shows two pages that contain the same information but use different layouts. The page on the left has body text set close to the headline. The leading is tight, and except for a spot around the illustration, the white space is in short supply. Notice how the page on the right has a lighter, more vibrant look. Also note the variety of sizes, the use of generous margins, and a few strategic elements that don't quite align with the others (providing something for the eye to follow). Which page are you more inclined to read?

Seven basic rules for good design

If you are a trained graphic designer, you already know the basics; you can immediately put QuarkXPress to use, creating effective layouts. But if you are new to the field, try keeping the following seven basic rules in mind as you begin learning about layout:

✦ **Rule 1: Keep an idea file.** As you read magazines, books, newspapers, annual reports, ads, and brochures, save page layouts you like and dislike. Keep these layouts—good and bad—in a file, along with notes to yourself about which aspects of the layout work well and which work poorly. As you build your layout file, you educate yourself about layout basics.

Figure 4-2: The page on the left crams everything close and has little visual interest. The page on the right is a better model, because it uses space and variety without getting too busy.

✦ **Rule 2: Plan your document.** It sounds corny, but it's true: laying out a document is a lot like taking a journey. If you know where you're headed, it's much easier to find your way. Because QuarkXPress makes it easy to experiment as you design a document, it's also easy to end up with a messy conglomeration of text and pictures. You can avoid this pitfall by knowing ahead of time what you are trying to accomplish with the document's layout.

✦ **Rule 3: Keep it simple.** When it comes to page layout, simple is better. Even the most experienced, trained graphic designers can tell you that this rule applies at least 99 percent of the time. If you are just beginning to learn how to lay out pages, you'll make far fewer design mistakes if you follow this rule. Regardless of the application, simple layouts are appealing in their crispness, their readability, and their straightforward, no-gimmicks approach.

✦ **Rule 4: Leave some white space.** Pages that are crammed full of text and pictures tend to be off-putting—meaning that the average, busy reader is likely to skip them. Keep some space between text columns and headlines and between page edges and layout elements. White space is refreshing and encourages the reader to spend some time on the page. Regardless of the particular document type, readers always appreciate having a place on every page to rest their eyes, a place that offers an oasis in a sea of ink.

✦ **Rule 5: Don't use every bell and whistle.** QuarkXPress is powerful, yes, but that doesn't mean that it is necessarily a good idea to push the program to its limits. You can, for example, lay out a page with 30 columns of text, but would you want to try reading such a page? With QuarkXPress, you can achieve an amazing number of special effects: You can rotate text, make boxes of almost any shape, skew text and graphics, make linear blends, add lines and dashes, embellish with graphics, add colors, stretch and condense type, and bleed photos or artwork off the edge of the page. Using all of these effects at once, however, can overwhelm readers and cause them to miss any message you are trying to convey. A good rule: Use no more than three special typographic or design effects per two-page spread.

✦ **Rule 6: Make it look like what it is.** Lay out the document so that someone looking at it can get an idea of what it is. This sounds like a commonsense rule, but you'd be surprised at how often this rule is broken. If you are laying out an ad for a product, make sure the layout *looks* like an ad, not like a technical brochure.

✦ **Rule 7: Don't break rule number 6.** Creativity is OK, and QuarkXPress helps you express your layout ideas creatively, but unless you know what you are doing, don't get carried away. If you are laying out a technical brochure, for example, don't make it look like a display ad unless you understand that this may confuse readers, and you are doing it for a reason.

Variations on a theme

Once you come up with a design, expect it to evolve over time. Styles change, and so does your content. So don't be afraid to try different techniques over the months and years—just make sure that you're not willy-nilly making changes for change's sake.

Figure 4-3 shows three examples of a design's evolution. This newsletter has been around for about a decade, and it has had five basic designs (it's not unusual to redesign a publication every couple years). Notice how the basic elements are unchanged, but the look and feel evolves from straightforward to a bit more authoritative and modern, and then to a bit friendlier yet professional.

Figure 4-3: Layouts evolve over time for style and content needs, even if they have the same basic structure. This newsletter went from straightforward to modern and authoritative to professional yet friendly.

Learning to Work with Layouts

Documents come in a variety of shapes and sizes. The most successful documents are those with an appearance that complements their content. In many kinds of documents, you can use several layout styles. Within a multipage document, the layout of any single page typically depends on the overall purpose of the document and on where the individual page appears in relation to other pages. Here are some examples:

✦ **A stand-alone layout:** Some pages have a *stand-alone layout* because the document itself consists of a single page, or because that particular page falls into a layout type that is either not used elsewhere in the document or is used sparingly. An example of a stand-alone layout is the title page of a book or a similar document. Because that page is unique, its layout is not repeated on subsequent pages.

✦ **Linked elements:** Some pages include elements that are *linked* to other elements on the same page or to elements on other pages in the document. (We'll get to an explanation about how to link text boxes later.) For an example of linked elements, consider a typical magazine (or newsletter) article, in which some of the body copy appears within one column or page and the rest appears within another column or page. The two pieces of body copy are linked elements.

✦ **Related elements:** Other layout elements, such as headlines, sidebars, and tables, are related to one another.

✦ **Repeating elements:** Still other elements are repeating elements; examples include page numbers and folios.

Tip

If your document has a title page or another page with a stand-alone, nonrecurring layout, in the interest of time you can choose not to develop a style sheet or master page for the page. Master pages and style sheets are covered in Chapters 10 and 14, respectively.

Although a full discussion on types of layout is beyond the scope of this book, a brief overview is useful as a background for explaining some of the steps involved in developing layout types. The following sections take a quick look at some of the most commonly used approaches to layout: horizontal layouts, vertical layouts, facing pages and spreads, and bleeds.

Horizontal layouts

Horizontal layouts often include elements in a variety of widths. The overall effect is to move the reader's eye from left to right. A horizontal layout is often used in announcements, product flyers, and other marketing collateral pieces. In the sample brochure (shown in Figure 4-4), the landscape orientation, placement of the columns, and location of the illustration all contribute to draw the eye from left to right.

Figure 4-4: An example of a horizontal layout.

We devised this layout by first setting up an 8½ × 11-inch page (in landscape orientation) with three columns, and then running the masthead logo and headline across the width of the columns. The picture starts at the second column so that the eye can easily find the text at the top of the first column.

Vertical layouts

Layouts with a vertical orientation are typical of what you find in most traditional newspapers. The text is presented in long, vertical sections, often with headlines or subheads that are the width of a single column. In addition to newspapers, newsletters and other common corporate documents lend themselves to a vertical orientation (see Figure 4-5).

Figure 4-5: An example of a vertical layout.

We created this layout by setting up a letter-size page with three columns. The masthead runs across the width of the three columns, one kicker and headline run across the width of the first two columns, and one headline on a secondary article runs across the width of the third column.

Facing pages and spreads

Facing pages are commonly used in multipage documents that have material printed on both sides of the paper, such as newsletters and magazines. When you create a new document (by selecting File⇨New, or with the shortcut ⌘+N), you can choose whether to check the Facing Pages box. If this box is unchecked, QuarkXPress creates one master page; if it is checked, the program creates a right master page and a left master page (a *master spread*). Whether or not you check Facing Pages, QuarkXPress allows you to create master pages in addition to the default master page(s).

Note

A master page, explained in detail in Chapter 10, is a layout skeleton you can use to arrange common elements, such as text boxes and picture boxes. You then apply a master page to document pages as you create them—this works much like styles in a word processor that automate the formatting of paragraphs once you have defined the styles. This frees you from having to create these boxes and elements on each and every page. Of course, you shouldn't create your master pages until you know what you want your layout to be and until you set global layout preferences, as described later in this chapter.

Setting up left and right master pages

If you are creating a facing-pages document that is longer than two pages, it's worth taking the time to set up the master pages for right- and left-side pages. As you will learn in Chapter 10, master pages for facing-pages documents let you specify elements (text, graphics, page numbers, and so on) that you want to repeat on similarly oriented pages throughout the document.

What happens if you work on a facing-pages document for a while and then decide you want to lay it out single-sided? The answer is not that easy. You can't uncheck Facing Pages unless your document contains no facing-page master pages. You have to create one or two new single-sided master pages, move all your master page elements (if any) to those pages, and then delete the facing-page master pages. If you haven't used the facing-page master pages, you can of course just delete them.

It is easy to find out whether a document has right and left master pages. From the View menu, select Show Document Layout to display the Document Layout palette, or use the F10 key. Figure 4-6 shows a two-page, facing-pages document and its Document Layout palette. The bent upper corner for the page icons in the palette indicates that those pages are based on a left or right master spread.

Headers, footers, and margins

Documents with facing pages tend to have one or both of the following characteristics:

✦ Alternating headers and footers on even- and odd-numbered pages. An example of an alternating footer is a page number; if you want the page number to print on the outside bottom corner of the page, the footers on right and left master pages differ from each other.

✦ An inside margin large enough to accommodate the binding or the spreading of pages as the reader reads the document.

Working with spreads

QuarkXPress allows you to create layouts that span two or more side-by-side pages, or *spreads*. Spreads are made up of pages that are adjacent to each other and span a fold in the final document. A set of left- and right-hand facing pages is a spread, as is a set of three or more adjacent pages that appear in a folded brochure.

Figure 4-6: A spread layout and the Document Layout palette.

Bleeds

A *bleed* consists of a layout element (such as text, a background screen, a picture, or a line) that extends off the edge of the page after the page is trimmed. A bleed can also be a *crossover*—a layout element that spans two or more pages in a document. QuarkXPress easily accommodates bleeds, which can be an effective element for page design. Bleeds add visual surprise and a sense of scale. Since most elements are confined to the page, those that go beyond the page catch attention, and the fact that they do so gives the impression that the page is larger than it is. (Of course, it isn't. The use of the bleed simply creates that impression, because the reader's mind tends to fill in the chopped-off part of the bleeding image.)

Figure 4-7 shows a page containing an image that bleeds off the page. We created this effect by drawing a picture box, filling it with the photo, and then using the Item tool to move the box so that part of the photo extends beyond the page boundary.

Figure 4-7: A bleed is an element that extends past the page boundary.

The art of controlled bleeding

Although you can bleed pictures to span the fold between two pages in a document, keep in mind that this may not be a good idea, particularly if you are producing the document without the assistance of a professional printer. The reason? A folded page has to match up with an adjacent page that is physically printed on another sheet. Unless the adjacent pages that hold the bleed form the centerfold of the document, you can end up with a graphic that is misaligned from one page to the next, a problem known as being *out of register*.

This registration problem is one that a professional printer can sometimes manage during the printing process (depending on the type of printing press used), but aligning split images is almost impossible in documents that are laser-printed and then photocopied. Unless you are having your document professionally printed, the best advice is to avoid bleeds between pages unless they form a centerfold or fall in a similar setup where the flow of ink is unbroken by a page edge.

Beginning a New Document

After you've done your preliminary planning, it's time to begin building a QuarkXPress document. You might have noticed that we keep referring to creating a layout as "building." This is a fair analogy for what's involved in laying out a new document, because document layout encompasses steps similar to those used for building a house:

✦ You start with the foundation (the page dimensions).

✦ You build the rooms (the text boxes and picture boxes).

✦ You fill the rooms with furniture (the actual text and illustrations or graphics).

✦ When the house is built and furnished, you add decorative final touches (lines, frames, color, and other graphic effects).

Establishing a foundation

The first step, then, in laying out a document is to establish the foundation by setting up the basic dimensions of the document page. To do this, make the appropriate selections in the New dialog box to specify page size, margins, number of columns, gutter width between columns, whether you want the document to have facing pages, and whether you want QuarkXPress to automatically generate text boxes.

Before you begin setting up a new document, decide on the number of text columns you want to use in all (or most) of the pages in the document. You can always make changes later, but you'll save time if you decide on the number of columns before you start. For a typical newsletter or magazine, using two, three, or four columns is the norm. You can certainly vary from this standard if doing so helps you achieve a desired effect.

Tip

If you are worried that you have more text than will fit on the document's pages—for example, you want to produce a two-page newsletter but you have two-and-a-half pages worth of text—consider using one more column than you originally planned. Use three columns instead of two, for instance. Depending on the hyphenation and justification you use, this strategy can make it possible to fit an extra paragraph or two onto the page.

Opening a new document

First, open a new document by selecting File⇨New⇨Document, or use ⌘+N. This displays the New Document dialog box shown in Figure 4-8.

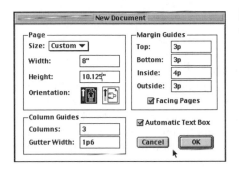

Figure 4-8: The New Document dialog box.

Tip

When using the File⇨New menu sequence, QuarkXPress adds a step to creating a new document: selecting Document, Library, or Book. But most of the time you simply want to create a new document. You can get past the extra step by using the shortcut keys: ⌘+N for documents, Option+⌘+N for libraries. Libraries are described in Chapter 10. (There is no shortcut for the new Book feature, which is described in Chapter 16.)

Selecting the page size

Next, in the Size area of the dialog box, select the size of your final pages from the drop-down list. (The size you choose, by the way, need not necessarily be exactly the same size as the paper your printer can hold. We cover this more fully in Chapter 24.) QuarkXPress offers five standard page size selections in the dialog box and also gives you the opportunity to specify a custom page size. The standard page sizes are as follows:

- ✦ **US Letter:** Width 8.5 inches, height 11 inches
- ✦ **US Legal:** Width 8.5 inches, height 14 inches
- ✦ **A4 Letter:** Width 8.268 inches, height 11.693 inches
- ✦ **B5 Letter:** Width 6.929 inches, height 9.843 inches
- ✦ **Tabloid:** Width 11 inches, height 17 inches

QuarkXPress also lets you create custom page sizes. Don't worry about which page size is selected in the Size list, and instead simply enter the desired page dimensions in the Width and Height fields, ranging from 1 inch × 1 inch to 48 inches × 48 inches.

Tip

If you are outputting your document directly to negatives and you want crop marks to be automatically printed at the page margins for a trimmed page (such as the 7⅞ × 10½-inch page size used by many magazines), enter those page dimensions in the Height and Width fields. For fractional dimensions, don't pull out your calculator—QuarkXPress can do the math for you. For example, if you want a page width of 7 inches, enter 7+7/8, rather than 7.875. Note the + sign: it's essential. Entering 7 7/8 is read as 7⅞, or 9.625.7/8

How QuarkXPress displays measurements

QuarkXPress always displays page width and height in inches, even if you select a different measurement unit in the Document Preferences dialog box (which you access when a document is open by selecting Edit⇨Preferences⇨Document, or by using ⌘+Y). You can specify page dimensions to .001 of any measurement unit, and QuarkXPress automatically makes the conversion to inches in the Page Width and Height fields.

What used to be called the General Preferences dialog box is now called the Default Document Preferences dialog box in version 4, and the menu item has similarly changed from General to Document. The General options in the old versions of QuarkXPress are now in the General tab in the Document Preferences dialog box. Chapter 3 covers preferences in more detail.

Determining the best page size

How do you know which page size is best? The answer to that question is really up to you, but it's useful to note which page sizes are typically used. Many newsletters use letter size, which is a convenient size for mailing. Magazines tend to use a size slightly smaller than letter size. (As paper costs have increased, publishers have trimmed away from the old letter-size standard, reducing both the amount of paper and the total weight, which in turn reduces mailing costs.) Newspapers and larger-format magazines frequently use tabloid size.

Changing the page size

If you set the page size in the New Document dialog box and change your mind later on, you can modify it. Select Document Setup from the File menu (or use Option+Shift+⌘+P) and enter the new page dimensions in the appropriate fields in the Document Setup dialog box. Entering the new page dimensions works as long as the new page size is sufficient to accommodate any elements you already placed; if not, a dialog box appears explaining that the page size you are proposing forces some items off the page. To prevent this, you must enter a page size sufficiently large to hold those items. Move them temporarily inward from the edge of the current page or onto the pasteboard and then try changing the page size again.

Setting the margins

Next, in the Margin Guides area of the New Document dialog box, enter measurement values (to .001 of any unit of measurement) for the top, left, bottom, and right margins of the document's basic text box. (If you are using facing pages, you see inside and outside margins rather than left and right margins.) If you are using ragged-right text in the document—text that aligns to the left margin but not the right margin—you can set right margins a bit smaller than you need for justified text. (To create ragged-right text, you actually set the text to be left-aligned.)

Some tips for margin mavens

Here are a few cautions, tips, and tricks for working with margins in QuarkXPress:

✦ *Printing a test page:* After you set up the document specifications in the New Document dialog box, QuarkXPress lets you redefine the margins by changing the margins for the corresponding master page. Choose Page⇨Display⇨[master page name], and then choose Page⇨Master Guides to change the margins. To avoid this hassle, you may want to consider creating and printing a test page (a single, sample page of the document) to verify margins before you invest the effort necessary to lay out the entire document.

✦ *Crossing the margins:* Margin measurements determine how far from the outside edges of the paper you expect to place the document's text boxes and picture boxes. The margins are for the whole document, but they are by no means set in concrete. For example, you can place individual text boxes or picture boxes anywhere on the page, even into these preset margins. One situation in which a page element may cross over into the margin is when you create a bleed, an illustration that extends past the edge of the physical page.

✦ *The large and small of it:* Be careful not to make margins too large because doing so can give the text and pictures on the page an appearance of insignificance. By the same token, don't make margins too small, which can produce an equally unappealing look that results from having too much information on a page. Also, you may consider having one margin larger than the margins on the other three sides of a page. For example, if you plan to saddle-stitch or three-hole punch a document, make the inside margin larger so that it can accommodate the staples or holes.

✦ *Margin guides:* These appear as colored lines on-screen, but the lines do not print. You can also turn their display off via View⇨Hide Guides, or by using the F7 key.

Working with facing pages

Next, in the Margin Guides area of the dialog box, check the Facing Pages option box if the document pages are to be printed two-sided, with the right and left pages facing each other when the document is open. Turning on the Facing Pages option tells QuarkXPress to set right and left pages that mirror each other in terms of right and left margins. If you select Facing Pages, consider making inside margins larger than those on the outer edges of the page to allow room for the binding.

Determining the number of columns

Next, in the Columns option box (in the Column Guides area of the New Document dialog box), enter the number of text columns you want to use on most pages. (The reason we say "most" pages is because you can, for example, select three columns in this dialog box and then, within the document, use two or some other number of columns on a particular page.) You can specify as many as 30 columns per page, although you won't often need that many, particularly on a standard 8½ × 11-inch paper. As with margins, column guides appear as colored lines on-screen, but the lines do not print.

Tip

Just because you plan to have a certain number of text columns in a document doesn't necessarily mean you should enter that exact number in the Columns field of the New Document dialog box. Suppose that your publication has three columns, plus pull-quotes that are set out of alignment with the text margins. You may want to try using an 8-column grid and use some of the column grid lines to align the pull-quotes. Of course, if you use this design tip, you don't want text to flow through all columns, so you need to disable (uncheck) Automatic Text Box in the New Document dialog box.

Figure 4-9 shows a QuarkXPress document that was set up in the New Document dialog box to have eight columns. We did not select Automatic Text Box. Doing so would have flowed the text across all eight columns, when all we want is to see the columns for visual alignment of various boxes. Instead, we used the Text Box tool to create each of the text boxes that would actually contain text, and the Picture Box tool to create the picture box containing the photo. Note how we use the column markers as alignment guides in setting up a variety of column treatments, which include pull-quote boxes and columns that vary in width from the top part of the page to the bottom.

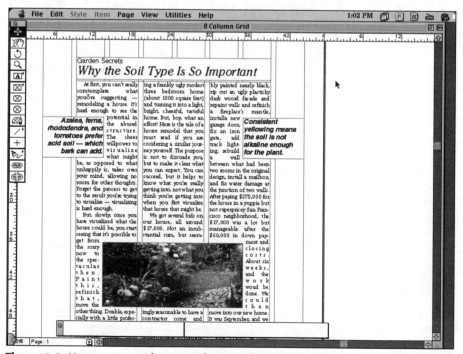

Figure 4-9: You can use column markers as alignment guides, not just for column boundaries.

Choosing a column gutter

Next, in the Column Guides area of the dialog box, enter a measurement value in the Gutter Width field to specify the amount of space between columns of text. Gutters can be as small as 3 points or as large as 288 points. If you enter a Gutter Width value that is too large or too small, QuarkXPress displays a dialog box showing you the range of values from which you must select. We recommend keeping columns to a reasonable width—generally no wider than 21 picas. Otherwise, the columns may become tiring on the reader's eyes.

Tip

Don't make gutters too small. This causes the columns of text to appear to run together and makes the document difficult to read. A rule of thumb is that the wider the columns, the wider the margins need to be to give the reader a clear visual clue that it's time to move to the next line. If you *must* use narrow gutters (between 0p9 and 2p0, depending on the page width and number of columns), consider adding a thin (0.5 point or smaller) vertical rule in the center of the gutter. To draw the rule, use the Orthogonal Line drawing tool and draw the line from the top of the gutter to the bottom, midway through the gutter width.

Activating the automatic text box

Next, if you want a text box on the master page that automatically flows text to other pages inserted into the document, activate the Automatic Text Box feature (by placing a checkmark in the option box). If you don't select Automatic Text Box, you must use one of the Text Box tools to draw text boxes before you place text with the File⇨Get Text (⌘+E) command.

After you finish making selections in the New Document dialog box, choose OK to open the new page.

Using the Layout Tools

QuarkXPress offers several layout tools that make it easier for you to produce your document. These tools include guides that help you align text and graphics, a pasteboard area that gives you a convenient way to store document elements until you need them, and a feature that allows you to position elements in layers.

Working with guides

Laying out a document often means lining up objects with columns, illustrations, headlines, or other objects. Guides are nonprinting lines that make this process easier. We've already covered two types of guides: margins and columns. And you've seen how you can actually use column guides as alignment aids. QuarkXPress also offers ruler guides, which you "pull out" from the vertical and horizontal document rulers. Of course, you can always use the numeric values displayed in the Measurements palette to precisely position elements, but the ruler guides are handy tools for visually lining up elements on a page.

Working with folded documents

The folding of pages in a document can be a tricky issue. If you are creating a document that is to be folded once or more, here are some factors you need to consider:

✦ *Gutter space:* Choose a page size that allows adequate gutter space. Gutters should be large enough so folds do not occur in the middle of text or pictures.

✦ *Page creep:* Set an outside margin that is big enough to accommodate any creeping of pages, which can occur in multipage documents that are saddle-stitched (stapled along the fold). Creeping is the apparent movement of text toward the gutter on outside pages because of the fact that these outside pages have to fold around the inside ones, so that some of the gutter space is lost where the sheet of paper wraps around inside sheets.

✦ *Column widths:* If you are creating a trifold brochure—for example, one that is printed on 9 × 12-inch paper and folded into a 4 × 9-inch brochure—setting up the page into even columns with even gutters doesn't work because the space you need to accommodate the folds uses up gutter space. The same is true for any brochure or document that is folded more than two times. If possible, work with your commercial printer to find out what page and column size to use to accommodate the folds. If you are designing a multifold brochure that will not be commercially printed, allow time to experiment with column widths, margins, and folding.

✦ *Paper choice:* The paper on which a folded brochure is printed is a major factor in determining the success of the document. Your paper choice also plays a large role in how you need to set up the document during layout. Obviously, thick paper reacts differently to folding than thin paper, and thick paper also has a different effect in terms of the amount of page creeping that results in a multipage document. Depending on the weight and texture of the paper, a ¼-inch outside margin set on the first page of a 36-page, saddle-stitched document could be gradually reduced on each page, shrinking to ¹/₁₆ of an inch by the centerfold. We recommend talking with your printer ahead of time if your document has multiple folds or if you are planning a document with 24 or more folded pages and saddle stitching.

✦ *Talking to your printer:* A good commercial printer should be experienced in handling the issues related to paper weight and can give you some important guidelines about how to lay out a folded document. If your document will be folded, take the time to talk with your printer before you get too far into the layout process.

Tip

Guides are useful if you want to align an element with another element within a box—such as a part of a picture—and the location is not identified in the Measurements palette (the Measurements palette shows the box's values, not those of its internal elements). You should, however, rely on the numeric values shown in the Measurements palette rather than the pull-out ruler guides when you are concerned about placing boxes and lines precisely on a page.

Controlling how guides display

You can control whether QuarkXPress places ruler and page guides in front of or behind objects on the page. You can select either In Front or Behind in the Guides drop-down menu of the Default Document Preferences dialog box's General pane. (To open the dialog box, select Edit⇨Preferences⇨Document or use ⌘+Y, and then select the General tab.) Figure 4-10 shows the General pane in the Default Document Preferences dialog box. The settings that affect guides are highlighted.

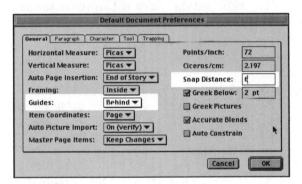

Figure 4-10: The General Preferences pane lets you set various guide preferences (highlighted).

The default setting for guide position is In Front (a change from earlier versions of QuarkXPress). That's too bad, because if you have many elements on the page, selecting the In Front setting tends to make the guides difficult to locate and control. Placing guides behind other objects becomes more and more important as your document increases in complexity. Fortunately, you can change the default for all future documents to Behind by changing the preferences (use Edit⇨Preferences⇨Document or ⌘+Y) when no document is open.

Because ruler guides don't print, you can use as many of them as you like. To obtain a ruler guide, simply use the mouse to position the cursor within the vertical or horizontal ruler, and then hold down the mouse button as you pull the ruler guide into place.

When to use the snap-to feature

Another handy feature for lining up elements on a page is the Snap to Guides feature, which you access through the View menu (the keyboard shortcut Shift+F7 also accesses it). When you select this feature, guides have an almost magnetic pull on objects you place on the page, making them "snap" into alignment with the closest guide. You'll appreciate this feature for some layout tasks, but you'll want to disable it for others.

When do you want the snap-to feature enabled? Imagine that you are creating a structured document containing illustrations framed with a 0.5-point line and aligned with the leftmost margin. In this case, select Snap to Guides so that the illustrations snap into position on the margin. If, on the other hand, you have a document containing design elements that are placed in a variety of locations on the page, you may want to position them visually or by means of the Measurements palette instead of having them automatically snap to the nearest guide line.

Tip

You can control the distance within which an item snaps to guides by entering a value in the Snap Distance field (refer to Figure 4-10) in the General pane in the Default Document Preferences dialog box (select Edit⇨Preferences⇨Document, or ⌘+Y). Snap distance is specified in pixels, and the range is 1 to 100. If the snap distance is set to 6 pixels, any element within 6 or fewer pixels of a guide snaps to that guide.

When to use baseline grids

If you have a document open, you can also display another set of grid lines. Selecting View⇨Show Baseline Grid or using the keyboard shortcut Option+F7 displays horizontal grid lines that do not print. The actual purpose of these grid lines is to lock the baselines of text onto them, but we find them very useful as positioning guides as well. You specify the spacing of these grid lines in the Paragraph pane (see Figure 4-11) of the Default Document Preferences dialog box (select Edit⇨Preferences⇨Document or ⌘+Y, and then select the Paragraph tab).

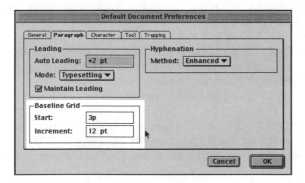

Figure 4-11: The Paragraph pane, with Baseline Grid options highlighted.

In the Start field of the dialog box, enter a value to tell QuarkXPress how far from the top of the page you want the first line. In the Increment field, enter the size of the interval you want between grid lines. Figure 4-12 shows a document page with the baseline grid displayed. If you want elements to snap to lines in the baseline grid, be sure that the baseline grid is visible (select View⇨Show Baseline Grid, or use Option+F7). If the baseline grid is not visible, elements snap to the closest visible guide.

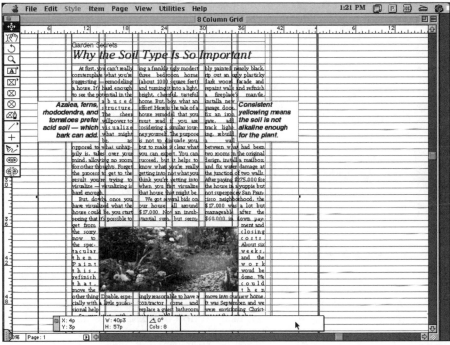

Figure 4-12: The Baseline Grid feature activated.

Here's an instance where Macintosh and Windows practices diverge. The shortcut for showing baseline grids in Windows is Ctrl+F7, not Alt+F7, as you would expect based on the Mac's shortcut of Option+F7.

Some general guide techniques

Notice in Figure 4-12 that the grid lines appear inside the main text box but not in the pull-quotes' text boxes. To do this, we have given the pull-quotes' text boxes a background of White (accessed by choosing Item⇨Modify, or ⌘+M). The other text boxes have a background of None, which lets the guides show through. (We have guides set to Behind. If they were set to In Front, they'd appear over the pull-quotes' boxes, too.)

QuarkXPress assigns a color to each type of guide—typically blue for margins, green for ruler guides, and magenta (hot pink) for baseline grids. You can change those colors to any color you prefer. To do so, use the Application Preferences dialog box's Display pane. You get to the dialog box via Edit⇨Preferences⇨Application, or Option+Shift+⌘+Y. Double-click the color you want to change and then select a new color from the color dialog box that appears. Figure 4-13 shows the Display pane of the Application Preferences dialog box.

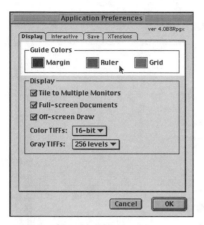

Figure 4-13: The Display pane, with the Guide Colors section highlighted.

Using the pasteboard

In the old days of publishing, people who composed document pages often worked at a large table (or pasteboard) that held not only the documents on which they were working, but also the odds and ends associated with its layout. They might put a headline, a picture, a caption, or a section of text on the pasteboard until they were ready to place the element on the page. Even though QuarkXPress has automated the page composition process, it includes a tremendously useful pasteboard (see Figure 4-14) that surrounds each document spread (one or more pages that are side by side). You can maneuver around the spread and the pasteboard by using the scroll controls.

Note

The maximum width and height of the combined pasteboard and document spread is 48 inches. QuarkXPress reduces the pasteboard size, if necessary, in order to keep the pasteboard and spread at or below the 48-inch maximum width.

Adjusting the size of your pasteboard

Usually, the default pasteboard size (the width of the document page) is sufficient, but you can modify it if you need more or less room on-screen. Choose Edit⇨Preferences⇨ Application, or Option+Shift+⌘+Y, and then select the Interactive tab to display the Application Preferences dialog box's Interactive pane. Enter a percentage value in the Pasteboard Width field (at the bottom of the pane). A value of 100 percent means that the pasteboard width is equal to—or 100 percent of the size of—the width of the document page. When the pasteboard width is to your liking, choose OK to save the change.

This may not be a factor for most users, but keep in mind that the larger the pasteboard, the more memory is required. If you're not short on computer memory, use the default pasteboard width. If you are running short of computer memory, consider reducing the size of the pasteboard to something less than 100 percent.

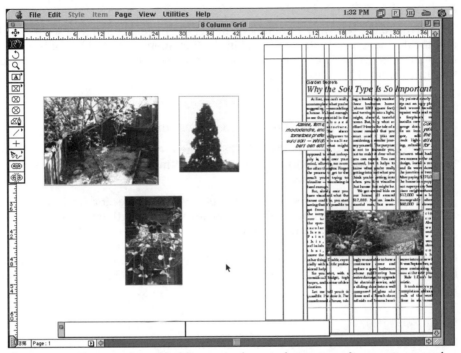

Figure 4-14: The pasteboard holding some layout elements, as it appears around a single-page spread.

Working with layers

QuarkXPress arranges text boxes, picture boxes, and rules in *layers*. You can control the order of these layers, which means you can stack and restack text boxes, picture boxes, and lines on a page, as if each were on its own separate sheet of paper. QuarkXPress does the layering for you, actually placing every element on the page on its very own layer. If your document is fairly simple, and its elements do not overlap, you don't need to be concerned with layers. But if you are laying out complex pages with multiple elements, you need to know how to rearrange the layers.

QuarkXPress layers work differently from the layers used by programs such as Adobe Photoshop. In Adobe Photoshop, each layer has a name and may be shown or hidden individually. In QuarkXPress, each box or line exists on its own layer, and layers can neither be named nor hidden or shown. However, XTensions software such as Extensis's QX-Layers can provide you with layer functionality similar to that of Adobe Photoshop. (QX-Layers is part of the QX-Tools collection, of which a demo version is included on this book's CD.)

Rearranging layers

To rearrange the layers in a document, select the page element you want to shift and locate the appropriate command in the Item menu. The full list of layer commands is available only when the open document contains layout elements in multiple layers. The layer commands are:

✦ **Send to Back:** Sends the selected element to the back of the pile.

✦ **Bring to Front:** Brings the selected element to the front of the pile.

✦ **Send Backward**: Sends the selected element one layer back in the pile. You must hold down the Option key when selecting the Item menu in order for this command to appear.

✦ **Bring Forward**: Brings the selected element one layer forward (up) in the pile. You must hold down the Option key when selecting the Item menu in order for this command to appear.

Note that in the Windows version of QuarkXPress, the Send Backward and Bring Forward commands are always in the Item menu—no special keystroke is required as on the Mac.

How layers work

Figure 4-15 shows how layers work. In the top example, the text is moved to the front with the Bring to Front command (in the Item menu), the gray box is moved to the back with the Send to Back command, and then the black box is sent to the back of the pile with the Send to Back command, which means the gray box is now between the other two boxes. In the bottom example, the order is rearranged. As you can see, the ability to layer elements can be a powerful layout tool. You can overlap a filled box with another box of text, for example, creating a shadowed or multidimensional effect.

Figure 4-15: Examples of layered elements.

Tip

Unless you need them for special effects, avoid overlapping too many elements. On slower computers, if you have more than four or five layers, the screen refresh time (the time it takes to redraw the screen after you make changes) slows down almost exponentially, meaning you need to allow yourself extra time to sit and wait while the layered page reappears on-screen.

The stacking order shuffle

When you move an element in a layered relationship, it retains its place in the stacking order. In other words, if an element is on a layer third from the top of the stack, it stays on that layer even if you move it elsewhere in your layout. If you need to change the stacking order of elements, use the commands in the Item menu. Also note that cutting an item (using Edit⇨Cut or ⌘+X) or copying it (using Edit⇨Copy or ⌘+C) and then pasting it (using Edit⇨Paste or ⌘+V) puts the pasted item in a new layer at the top of the stacking order.

Grouping and ungrouping layout elements

QuarkXPress offers a feature that is common to drawing programs. The program lets you select two or more elements and *group* them. Grouping means associating multiple items with one another so that QuarkXPress treats the group as a single item during moves, resizing, and edits. Grouping is useful if you want to move related items together while keeping their spatial relationship intact.

To group multiple elements, drag-select them or hold down the Shift key while you use the mouse to select each of the items to be grouped. Choose Item⇨Group or use ⌘+G. When a group of items is selected, the group is bounded by a dotted line (see Figure 4-16). Note that the Measurements palette for grouped items has only X, Y, W, H, and rotation coordinates available, because these are the only Measurements palette controls that can be applied to the entire group. To ungroup previously grouped elements, select the group and choose Item⇨Ungroup or use ⌘+U.

Things to do with groups

Just because elements are grouped doesn't mean you can't size or edit them independently. Just select the Content tool and choose the individual element. Then resize the element by dragging its handles, or edit it as you would if it were not part of a group.

You can perform actions (Cut, Copy, Paste, Lock, and so on) on groups that you normally perform on singular elements. You also can modify groups of like elements (groups of text boxes, groups of picture boxes, and so on) by using the Item tool to select the group, choosing Item ⇨Modify or ⌘+M, and then selecting the Group tab to display the Group pane. In this pane, you can change the location, size, angle, and fill of the grouped elements, as well as suppress the group's printout.

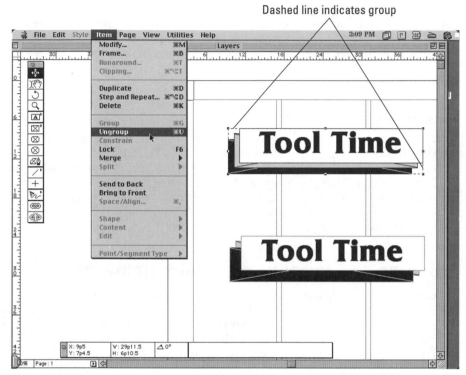

Figure 4-16: A dashed box around elements indicates that they are grouped and can be manipulated is if they were one element.

In versions of QuarkXPress prior to version 4, you had to resize a group of objects one at a time. As of version 4, however, you can use the Item tool to resize a group of objects simultaneously, as if they were one object.

Locking elements in place

Suppose that you've been working on a page layout for some time, and you've positioned an element—for example, the masthead—exactly where you want it to be. Knowing that you still have several elements to place on the page, how can you prevent yourself from accidentally moving or resizing the masthead with an errant mouse click? The answer: Lock the element into position. To lock an element, select it and choose Item⇨Lock or use the F6 key. Figure 4-17 shows a locked element. You can tell if an element is locked because the pointer changes to a lock icon when you position it over a locked element. The Lock command has a keyboard shortcut: F6. To unlock a locked element, select the element and choose Item⇨Unlock, or use F6.

Lock icon

Figure 4-17: An example of a locked element (with the lock symbol highlighted).

Note

You can still move and resize a locked element, but you must do so either from the Measurements palette or through options in the Item menu. Essentially, what locking buys you is protection from accidental changes. Just because an object is locked, however, doesn't mean you can't edit it. For example, although you can't move or resize a locked box with the mouse, you can move it with the arrow keys and move or resize it with the Measurements palette.

Constraining boxes

Unique to QuarkXPress is the ability to *constrain* a box: You can specify that any new box placed over an existing box cannot be sized or moved beyond the limits of the existing box. Constraining boxes can be considered a subset of grouping, but the two processes actually differ. Constrained boxes behave more like a parent and child relationship: the child box is unable to leave the confines of the parent box. It also means the parent can't get smaller than the child. In a hierarchy of boxes, the constraining box parent is the rearmost box in the hierarchy. It must be large enough to hold all the child boxes you want to constrain within it (see Figure 4-18).

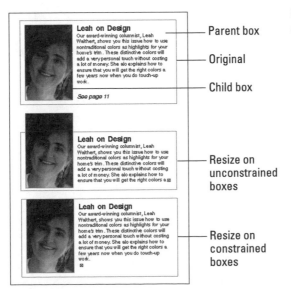

Parent box

Original

Child box

Resize on unconstrained boxes

Resize on constrained boxes

Figure 4-18: The parent-child relationship of constrained boxes.

When to constrain

Applications that can take advantage of constraining usually are highly structured. One such application is a product catalog. You might set up a large text box that holds descriptive text to constrain a smaller picture box that holds a product illustration. If you develop such a document and you know ahead of time that you need constrained boxes, you can specify that a particular box is to be constrained or that all boxes in a document are to be constrained.

How to constrain

To constrain all the boxes in a document, choose Edit⇨Preferences⇨Document, or use ⌘+Y, and then select the General tab to display the General preferences pane. Check the Auto Constrain box, located just above the OK button. To constrain a particular box, first make sure that the parent box is larger than the boxes within it and that all the child boxes are wholly within the parent box. Now select all the boxes, including the parent box, and then choose Item⇨Constrain to constrain them to the parent.

After a set of boxes is constrained, you can move and resize individual elements within the constrained group as long as the child elements still fit within the parent box. If you move a constrained box, all elements constrained within it also move.

✦   ✦   ✦

Working with Boxes

✦ ✦ ✦ ✦

In This Chapter

Creating and linking text boxes

Creating picture boxes

Adjusting and changing boxes

Working with layout controls

Adding elements to boxes

✦ ✦ ✦ ✦

QuarkXPress uses boxes to hold the text and pictures in your layout. Of course, the word *box* is a bit of a misnomer, because a QuarkXPress box can be almost any shape, but the name has stuck nonetheless. There are two basic boxes: text boxes and picture boxes, with each holding a specific type of content. This chapter covers both types and provides a detailed account of how to create them, and all they ways you can use, manipulate, and add content to boxes to achieve the desired effect.

Creating and Linking Text Boxes

The most basic box is the text box. More than picture boxes, these form the heart of your layouts. That's why QuarkXPress has two ways of creating text boxes: using the automatic text box feature and drawing your own text boxes.

Automatic text boxes

If you check Automatic Text Box in the New Document dialog box, QuarkXPress creates automatic text boxes when you create a new document. These boxes follow the size and column parameters you set in the New dialog box (File⇨New⇨Document, or ⌘+N), as described in Chapter 4. For example, if you specify two columns in the New dialog box and also check Automatic Text Box, text from a text file you import into that box automatically fills two columns and flows into two columns per page as you insert other pages into the document.

Manual text boxes

Manual text boxes are created with one of seven Text Box tools, which let you draw boxes of any size at any position. You can then apply to these boxes attributes such as, for example, numbers of columns and text inset. (Adding elements to boxes is covered at the end of this chapter.)

STEPS: Manually creating a text box

1. Choose the box icon you want from the Tool palette (see Figure 5-1 and the following section, where the operation of each tool is described in detail). Notice that when you click a box tool, the pointer changes to a cross or a plus (+) icon.

2. Place the plus icon where you want one corner to be.

3. Hold down the mouse button and drag toward the opposite corner.

4. When you've reached the opposite corner, let go of the mouse button, and your box appears.

Tip

Don't worry if your box is not exactly the right size or in exactly the right location. You can modify its dimensions and position at any time—a topic we cover in detail later in this chapter.

A tour of the tools

In the Tool palette, you see one Text Box tool. (Typically, the standard Rectangle Text Box tool, unless you changed it.) Notice the arrow to the right of the icon: that arrow indicates that if you hold down the mouse on the icon, a pop-up menu appears showing alternative Text Box tools. Select any of those alternative tools, and it becomes the default tool shown in the Tool palette. The seven Text Box tools produce different shapes (refer to Figure 5-1), and they function as follows:

✦ **Rectangle Text Box tool:** This produces the standard rectangle that most text is placed in. This should be the default tool for most users. Hold the Shift key when drawing the box to get a perfect square.

✦ **Rounded-Rectangle Text Box tool:** This produces rounded corners. You can adjust the degree of rounding, called the *corner radius*, as explained later in this chapter. Hold the Shift key to get a perfect square.

✦ **Oval Text Box tool:** This produces ellipses. Hold the Shift key to get a perfect circle.

Rectangle
  Freehand
    Rounded-Rectangle
      Concave-Corner
        Beveled-Corner
          Oval
            Bézier

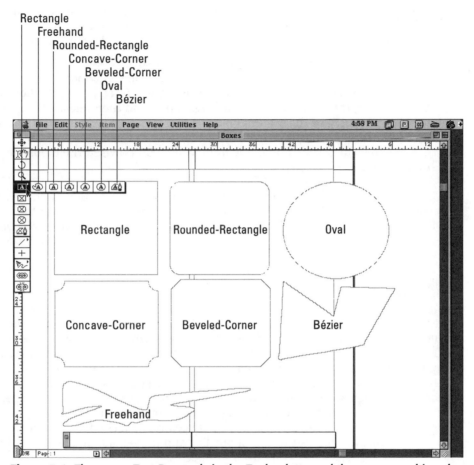

Figure 5-1: The seven Text Box tools in the Tool palette and the seven resulting shapes.

✦ **Concave-Corner Text Box tool:** This produces boxes with the corners notched out. You can adjust the degree of notching, called the *corner radius*, as explained later in this chapter. Hold the Shift key to get a perfect square.

✦ **Beveled-Corner Text Box tool:** This produces boxes with the corners beveled (cut off by a diagonal line). You can adjust the degree of cut-off, called the *corner radius*, as explained later in this chapter. Hold the Shift key to get a perfect square.

✦ **Bézier Text Box tool:** This produces polygons—shapes composed of a series of flat sides and/or curves. This tool works differently than the other Text Box tools: Rather than hold down the mouse, you click and release at each corner (or *node*, in graphics-speak). When you want to complete the box, click back on the origin point or just double-click. (Notice how the pointer changes to a circle from the normal cross.) If you click and drag for a little bit at each desired node, you see the Bézier control handles appear that let you create a curve. You can have both straight and curved sides based on how you use the mouse at each node—experiment to get the hang of it. (And if you want to convert a straight side to a curve, you can do so, as we describe later.)

✦ **Freehand Text Box tool:** This produces curved shapes—shapes composed of a series of curves. The box takes on the shape of how you move the mouse, as if your mouse were a pen tracking on the paper. To complete the box, you usually bring the mouse back to the origin point and then release the mouse button. (Notice how the pointer changes to a circle from the normal cross.) If you release the mouse button before you return to the origin point, however, QuarkXPress draws a straight line from where you released the mouse to the origin point.

New Feature

The Concave-Corner, Beveled-Corner, Bézier, and Freehand Text Box tools are new to QuarkXPress 4. The Bézier tool lets you draw the kinds of shapes that the previous version's Polygon tool did, as well as create and modify those polygons as curves.

Linking text boxes

Linking is one of the most useful features in QuarkXPress. Use it whenever you want text to flow between text boxes in a continuous stream that is maintained during the editing process. You can also unlink boxes when your layout doesn't need text to flow from one text box to another. When you link text boxes, they can be on the same page or on different pages, but remember: The order in which you link text boxes is the order in which text flows. If you start with a text box at the bottom of the page and link to another text box above it or on a previous page, then you create an unnatural order (and probably nonsensical text as well). In Figure 5-2, you see two linked text boxes (between two pages). Links are indicated by a plaid arrow that shows the end of one link and the beginning of the next link. The following sections show you how it's done.

STEPS: Linking text boxes

1. Open the document to the page that contains the first text box you want in the linked chain of text boxes.

2. Select the Link tool—the second tool from the bottom of the Tool palette—by clicking it.

3. Place the pointer in the text box that is to be the first box in the chain. The pointer changes to look like a chain link. Click the mouse button. You see an animated dashed line around the selected text box, indicating that it's the start of the link.

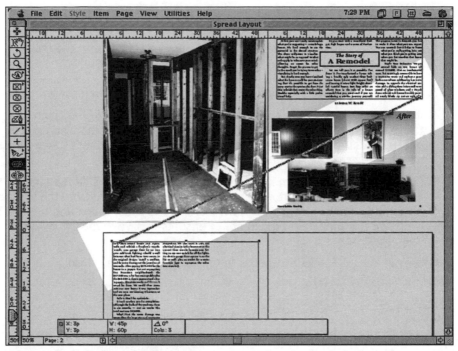

Figure 5-2: Linked text boxes.

4. If necessary, go to the page containing the text box that is to be the next link in the chain. (To go to that page, you can either press ⌘+J or choose Page⇨Go to. You can also use the new pop-up menu of pages that appears at the document screen's lower-left side, next to the scroll bar's left edge.)

5. Place the pointer in the next text box that you want in the chain and click the mouse button. The text box is now linked with the first text box. (You can see the link as a sort of plaid arrow whenever the Link or Unlink tool is selected.) The text flow bypasses the unlinked text box, continuing on to any others in the text chain.

6. Repeat Steps 2 through 5 (substituting the last linked text box for the first text box in Step 2) until all text boxes you want in the chain are linked.

On occasion, you may want to unlink text boxes that were previously linked. To split one story that spans two linked text boxes into two separate stories, for example, you use the program's Unlink tool. Keep in mind that you cannot undo an unlinking operation—you need to relink the boxes if you change your mind.

STEPS: Unlinking text boxes

1. Open the document to the page that has the first text box in the linked chain.

2. Click the Unlink tool to select it.

3. Place the pointer in the first text box in the chain. Click the mouse button.

4. If necessary, go to the page containing the next text box in the chain. (To go to that page, either press ⌘+J, or choose Page⇨Go to. You can also use the new pop-up menu of pages that appears at the document screen's lower-left side, next to the scroll bar's left edge.)

5. Place the pointer in the next text box in the chain and—while holding the Shift key—click the mouse button. The text box is now unlinked from the first text box, which means that the text now starts in the second box and the first box is empty. (Holding down the Shift key ensures that you won't accidentally unlink text boxes.)

6. If you have additional text boxes to unlink, repeat Steps 2 through 5.

Linking and unlinking tips

Here are a few tips and tricks for using the Link and Unlink tools:

✦ As a safety feature, the Link and Unlink tools change to the Content tool each time you use them to prevent you from linking or unlinking more boxes than you intend to.

✦ If you press the Option key when you select the Link or Unlink tool, that tool remains selected until you select another tool. This lets you link or unlink a series of boxes without having to reselect the appropriate tool for each link.

✦ You can break the text chain at the point of the selected box by using the Unlink tool to select the arrowhead or tailfeather of the link to or from the selected box. Breaking the text chain means that the text stops flowing to other boxes at the point where the link was broken. (It no longer flows into those subsequent boxes).

✦ If you hold the Shift key while unlinking, the Unlink tool removes the selected text box from the chain, and reroutes the text flow on to the next box in the chain.

✦ The best policy is to add text to your text box *after* you have set the text box's links. Why? Because as you change links, any text in the box must reflow to fit the new settings, and this process takes time. Of course, if you are experimenting with different settings, it helps to have text in the text box to see what the results of the various settings look like.

✦ Note that you cannot link text to a box that already contains text.

Creating columns in a text box

On occasion, you may want to vary the number of text columns used within a single page. For example, you may have a document that is set in two columns, each of which is a single box. For variety's sake, you decide to divide one of the two columns on a page into three smaller columns. You can perform this task easily using the following methods (see Figure 5-3):

✦ **Using the Measurements palette:** In the Cols field, enter the number of columns you want for the selected text box. This is the simplest method.

✦ **Using the Text pane:** In the Text pane of the Modify dialog box, which you access via Item⇨Modify or via ⌘+M, enter the number of columns in the Column field.

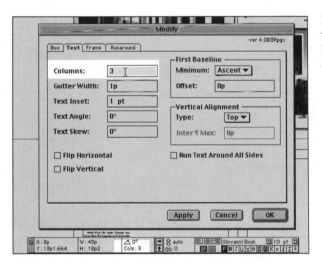

Figure 5-3: The Text pane and the Measurements palette both let you change the number of columns in a text box.

Creating Picture Boxes

QuarkXPress offers the same seven kinds of boxes for pictures as it does for text. However, the arrangement in the Tool palette differs a bit. When you look at Figure 5-4, notice how the Tool palette has fixed locations for three Picture Box tools: the Rounded-Rectangle, Oval, and Bézier tools. There is also a fourth location for a Picture Box tool—by default, this is set to display the Rectangle Picture Box tool, as shown in Figure 5-4—which has a pop-up menu that lets you replace it with one of the other three tools: Concave-Corner, Beveled-Corner, and Freehand picture boxes (see the sidebar on changing the Tool palette's lineup for more information on how to change the arrangement of the Tool palette to suit your style). The following list describes the Picture Box tools in detail:

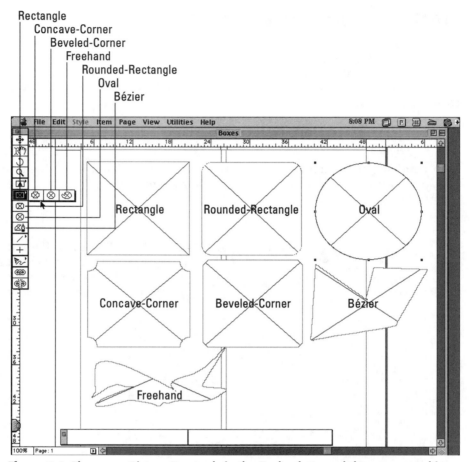

Figure 5-4: The seven Picture Box tools in the Tool palette and the seven resulting shapes.

⊠   ✦ **Rectangle Picture Box tool:** This produces the standard rectangle that most pictures are placed in. This should be the default tool for most users. Hold the Shift key when drawing the box to get a perfect square.

⊠   ✦ **Rounded-Rectangle Picture Box tool:** This produces rounded corners. You can adjust the degree of rounding, called the *corner radius*, as explained later in this chapter. Hold the Shift key to get a perfect square.

⊗   ✦ **Oval Picture Box tool:** This produces ellipses. Hold the Shift key to get a perfect circle.

⊗   ✦ **Concave-Corner Picture Box tool:** This produces boxes with the corners notched out. You can adjust the degree of notching, called the *corner radius*, as explained later in this chapter. Hold the Shift key to get a perfect square.

✦ **Beveled-Corner Picture Box tool:** This produces boxes with the corners beveled (cut off by a diagonal line). You can adjust the degree of cut-off, called the *corner radius*, as explained later in this chapter. Hold the Shift key to get a perfect square.

 ✦ **Bézier Picture Box tool:** This produces Bézier shapes. These are shapes composed of a series of flat sides and/or curves. This tool works differently than the other Picture Box tools: Rather than hold down the mouse, you click and release at each corner (or *node*, in graphics-speak). When you want to complete the box, click back on the origin point—or, to make it simpler, just double-click anywhere and QuarkXPress adds in the last segment for you automatically. (Notice how the pointer changes to a circle from the normal cross.) If you click at each desired node, you get a series of straight sides. If you click and drag for a little bit at each desired node, you see the Bézier control handles appear that let you create a curve. You can have both straight and curved sides based on how you use the mouse at each node. Experiment to get the hang of it. (If you want to convert a straight side to a curve, you can do so, as we describe later.)

 ✦ **Freehand Picture Box tool:** This produces curved shapes—shapes composed of a series of curves. The box takes shape based on how you move the mouse, as if your mouse were a pen tracking on the paper. To complete the box, you usually bring the mouse back to the origin point and then release the mouse button. (Notice how the pointer changes to a circle from the normal cross.) However, if you release the mouse button before you return to the origin point, QuarkXPress draws a straight line from where you released the mouse to the origin point.

 The Concave-Corner, Beveled-Corner, Bézier, and Freehand Picture Box tools are new to QuarkXPress 4. The Bézier tool lets you draw the kinds of shapes that the previous version's Polygon tool did, as well as create and modify those polygons as curves.

Adjusting and Changing Boxes

Now that you have your boxes—text and picture—created, you may want to adjust them: move them, resize them, change their shape, even change what they contain. In addition to your mouse and keyboard, QuarkXPress supplies the following tools to do all of these things and more:

✦ **The Modify dialog box:** This is accessed via Item⇨Modify or ⌘+M.

✦ **The Measurements palette:** Hide or show this by pressing F9 or using View⇨Hide Measurements and View⇨Show Measurements.

Changing the Tool palette's lineup

By default, the main Tool palette shows the Rectangle Picture Box tool, with its pop-up palette, followed by the Rounded-Rectangle, Oval, and Bézier Picture Box tools. Frankly, we were a bit mystified why the Rectangle Picture Box tool can be replaced on the Tool palette (via its pop-up palette, as explained in the following instructions), when three less-used Picture Box tools are fixed. Rectangular boxes are by far the most common, so it would have made more sense, we thought, to have made the Rectangle tool fixed, and let some other Picture Box tool be replaceable via a pop-up palette. The designers of QuarkXPress, however, are a step ahead of us. You can change what displays on the Tool palette to make it match your preferences. The following scenarios show you why QuarkXPress's designers made the most-used Picture Box tool (the Rectangle) the one with the pop-up palette:

✦ Let's say you want the Beveled-Corner Picture Box tool on the Tool palette. Hold the Control key on the Mac or Ctrl in Windows and then hold the mouse button on the Rectangle Picture Box tool to activate the Picture Box pop-up palette. Still holding down the Control or Ctrl key and the mouse button, move to the Beveled-Corner Picture Box tool and release the mouse button. Presto! The Beveled-Corner Picture Box tool is now on the Tool palette.

✦ Let's say you don't want the Oval Picture Box tool on the Tool palette. Instead, you want it on the Picture Box pop-up palette. Control+click or Ctrl+click the Oval Picture Box, and, presto again, it disappears from the Tool palette and is now part of the Picture Box pop-up palette!

You can use the same technique to change the arrangement of four types of tools: Text Box, Picture Box, Line, and Text Path. You can identify these groups of tools by looking for a tool with the arrow that indicates a pop-up menu. That tool and the ones that follow until the next such tool (or until the Link tool) are all part of the same group and can be collapsed or expanded.

Not all options described in this section for these panes and palettes are displayed for all boxes. In some cases, an option simply doesn't make any sense for a specific type of box—such as the corner radius option for a Bézier box—so QuarkXPress simply omits those options. Similarly, if you have multiple boxes selected, QuarkXPress omits options that are not relevant to all selected boxes.

The measurement unit used for all Modify dialog box and Measurements palette fields is whatever unit you select via Edit⇨Preferences⇨Document, or ⌘+Y, in the General pane.

What follows is a summary of the box controls for layout creation and adjustment in the Modify dialog box and Measurements palette. Later in this chapter, we show you the best ways to adjust your boxes using all the controls at your disposal: the Modify dialog box, Measurements palette, and keyboard and mouse. The Modify dialog box and Measurements palette have many other controls useful in layout, but they are aimed at graphics enhancement and special effects—not basic layout creation. We cover those options in later chapters: background color and blends in Chapter 21, frames in Chapter 9, and rotation and slanting in Chapter 18. We do cover many text-box options in this chapter because they are fundamental to the layout creation.

A tour of the Modify dialog box

The Modify dialog box has four panes for text boxes and four for picture boxes—the panes are new to version 4. Three panes are the same for both boxes—Box, Frame, and Runaround. Unique to text boxes is the Text pane, and unique to picture boxes is the Picture pane. Figure 5-5 shows each of the panes, which are also described in the following list:

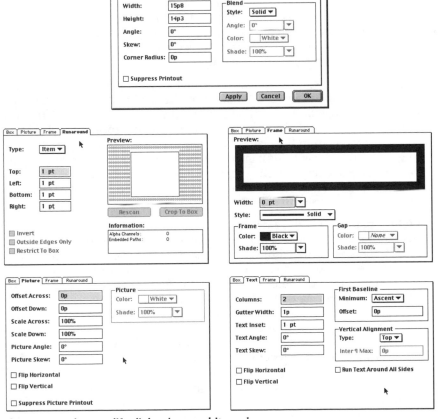

Figure 5-5: The Modify dialog box and its various panes.

✦ **Box pane:** The fundamental pane is the Box pane, in which you can change a box's position (with the Origin Across and Origin Down fields), size (with the Width and Height fields), rotation (with the Angle field), slant (with the Skew field), color (with the Color and Shade pop-up menus in the Box section), and background blend (with the Style, Angle, Color, and Shade drop-down menus in the Blend section). You can also prevent a box's content from printing by checking the Suppress Printout option, but any frame will print, which is handy for creating keylines for for-position-only (FPO) boxes in which images are manually added to the negatives later. This suppression feature is also handy for adding items that you don't want printed but you do want visible on-screen, such as notes to a designer. The Corner Radius field is available only for rounded, concave, and beveled-corner boxes.

✦ **Runaround pane:** Also accessible directly from the Item menu via Item⇨Runaround, or ⌘+T, this pane lets you control how close text in surrounding boxes can get to the edge of the selected box or the shape of the image inside that box. This prevents neighboring text from running into a graphic or an inset text box (such as a sidebar or caption).

✦ **Frame pane:** Also accessible directly from the Item menu via Item⇨Frame, or ⌘+B, this pane lets you place a frame—a line—around a box. You can choose from several line types, decide the thickness (width) of the frame, and choose color and shade for the line. If you choose a frame type such as a double line that has space inside of it, you can even decide the color of that space, a QuarkXPress 4 added feature.

✦ **Text pane:** For text boxes only, this pane lets you assign the number of columns; the space between them (in the Gutter Width field); the margin between the edge of the box and the text (in the Text Inset field; this is handy to keep the text from running into the box's frame); rotation and slant for the text (separately from the slant and rotation of the box itself; use the Text Angle and Text Skew fields); mirroring (with the Flip Horizontal and Flip Vertical checkboxes); baseline start position; vertical alignment of text within the box; and whether text runs around all sides of this box if another box is placed wholly within this text box.

✦ **Picture pane:** For picture boxes only, this pane lets you assign the position of the picture within the box (for cropping, in the Offset Across and Offset Down fields); the size of the picture within the box (in Scale Across and Scale Down); the rotation and slant of the picture in the box (separately from the slant and rotation of the box itself; use the Picture Angle and Picture Skew fields); and mirroring (with Flip Horizontal and Flip Vertical). You can also prevent the picture from printing (with Suppress Picture Printout—handy when you are printing drafts and don't want to spend time waiting for the printer to render images; note that any frame and background shade will still print if this option is selected), and choose the background color and shade for the area around the picture (and, for black-and-white and grayscale TIFFs, PICTs, and Scitex CT images, the background color and shade of the picture itself).

A tour of the Measurements palette

The fastest way to precisely size and position a box—or to resize and reposition it—is to use the Measurements palette after you draw an arbitrarily sized and positioned text box somewhere on the page. (You can hide or show the Measurements palette by pressing the F9 key.) Figure 5-6 shows two examples of the palette, one for text boxes and one for picture boxes, and the following lists describe their operation in detail.

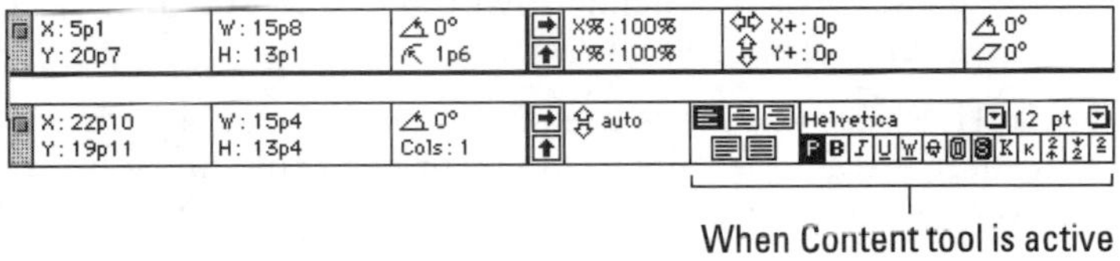

| X: 5p1 | W: 15p8 | ⊿ 0° | ➡ X%:100% | ✛✛ X+: 0p | ⊿ 0° |
| Y: 20p7 | H: 13p1 | ⊼ 1p6 | ⬆ Y%:100% | ⊗ Y+: 0p | ⊘ 0° |

| X: 22p10 | W: 15p4 | ⊿ 0° | ➡ ⊗ auto | ▤▤▤ Helvetica ▾ 12 pt ▾ |
| Y: 19p11 | H: 13p4 | Cols: 1 | ⬆ | ▤▤ P B I U W Q O S K ₂ ᵏ ᵏ |

When Content tool is active

Figure 5-6: The Measurements palettes for picture boxes (top) and text boxes.

The following options are common to text boxes and picture boxes and appear on the left side of the Measurements palette:

✦ **X and Y coordinates:** These display, respectively, the horizontal and vertical coordinates of the text box location (these are the same as the Origin Across and Origin Down fields in the Modify dialog box).

✦ **W and H dimensions:** These are the same as the Width and Height fields in the Modify dialog box and show the size of the text box.

✦ **Rotation field:** This lets you rotate the box itself.

✦ **Mirroring controls:** These let you flip a box's contents (not the box itself). The arrows indicate the direction of the flip (as follows). The defaults are right and down for normal display. If you flip to the left or up, QuarkXPress gives you a visual reminder by making the icons white on black, rather than the normal black on white. When a text box is selected, these controls are visible only if you are using the Content tool.

➡   The flip horizontal field icon

⬆   The flip vertical field icon

The rest of the options depend on whether you have a text box or picture box selected. For text boxes, you get a whole set of additional text-control options when you select the Content tool (rather than the Item tool). While Figure 5-6 shows those, we'll save all but the mirroring options for Part 3; we cover mirroring here because it is an option in the Text pane of the Modify dialog box.

Picture boxes have the following controls in the Measurements palette:

✦ **Corner-Radius field:** This lets you change the corner radius of a box, which controls the amount of beveling in a beveled-corner box, the rounding in a rounded-rectangle box, and the notching in a concave-corner box. A bigger number increases the bevel depth, rounding, or notching. If you change the corner radius on a regular rectangular box, it becomes a rounded-rectangle box.

✦ **X% and Y% fields:** These let you change the size of the picture within the box. You can change each axis independently (and distort the image) or make them the same for a proportional resizing.

✦ **X+ and Y+ fields:** These let you move the picture within the box, so you can crop it. You can enter the actual units to move, or click the nudge buttons (the outlined arrow symbols to the left of the X+ and Y+ fields).

✦ **Rotation field:** At the right side of the Measurements palette, this lets you rotate the picture within the box, leaving the box's rotation untouched.

✦ **Skew field:** This lets you slant the picture within the box, leaving the box's skew untouched. To slant the box itself, you need to use the Skew field in the Modify dialog box's Box pane. You can skew up to 75 degrees in either direction.

Text boxes have the following option specific to them:

✦ **Cols field:** This lets you specify the number of columns.

Mouse and keyboard modifications

With the mouse you have three basic sets of tasks to do:

✦ Move items by selecting the Item tool and then dragging a box to a new location. Or use the keyboard's arrow keys to move the item (perfect for slight adjustments).

✦ Resize items by selecting the Item tool or the Content tool and dragging one of the box's six handles. Again, you can use the keyboard's arrow keys for fine adjustments.

✦ Reshape freehand and Bézier items by dragging a node, side, or control point. And, yes, you can use the keyboard's arrow keys for fine adjustments.

Positioning and reshaping boxes

With all these options, it can be confusing to figure out the best way to adjust a box. Of course, as all these methods work, your personal preferences should dictate which you pick. We have our favorites based on what takes the least effort for us.

Note

Throughout the book, you'll see the term *control handle*. These are the tools that QuarkXPress provides so you can resize and reshape boxes. Figure 5-7 shows the control handles for a rectangular and freehand box.

Corner control handles   Side control handles

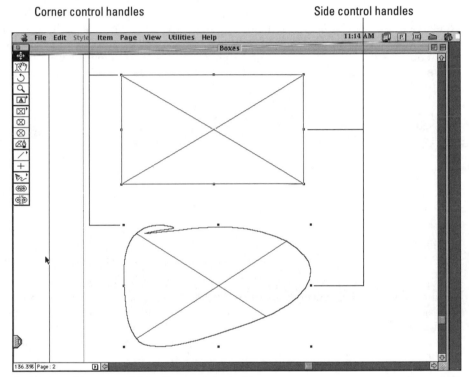

Figure 5-7: The control handles on selected boxes.

Positioning boxes

Using the mouse is the simplest way to move a box. Click it with the Item tool and drag the box to a new location. That's great for gross movement, but you need a keen eye and a steady hand to place the box exactly where you want it. For exact positioning, use the keyboard's arrow keys to nudge the box where you want it, or use the Measurements palette's X and Y fields to enter the specific coordinates for the box's upper-left corner. You can use the Modify dialog box, but unless you are using other controls in it, you save time by just using the keyboard or Measurements palette.

Reshaping and resizing boxes

The Measurements palette is the best bet for resizing a box. That's because you can enter the exact percentage for the new size and can enter the same percentage for both the height and width, assuring that the resized box is not distorted. You do this by multiplying the current size by the desired percentage. For example, if you have a box that is 1.14 inches wide and want to double its size, add *2 to the end of the current W value (it will thus appear as 1.14"*2) and then QuarkXPress will automatically change the W field's value to the new size, 2.28", when you press Return or click a different field. To reduce a dimension, such as to 35 percent, you'd add *0.35 to the current value—this multiplies the current value by 35 percent. When you're changing both the W and H values, it's easier to let QuarkXPress do the math for you.

A few resizing and reshaping tips

Here are a few great tips for reshaping and resizing boxes:

✦ When resizing with the mouse, hold Option+Shift when dragging a control handle to keep the resized box proportional to its original dimensions.

✦ When resizing a text box, holding the ⌘ key when resizing with the mouse makes the text resize along with the box. The text gets proportionally smaller or larger. Note that the text also scales—is stretched or condensed—relative to the box's new proportions.

✦ To reshape a box, the mouse is the best tool. Use the control handles on the box to resize. Selecting a corner with the mouse resizes both width and height in whatever direction you move the mouse, while selecting a side's control handle stretches or contracts the box in one dimension only. Note that on a nonrectangular box, the control handles may not actually be on the box's outline.

✦ If you hold the ⌘ key while resizing a text box, the text inside is resized as well. This is particularly handy if you are working with ads, brochures, and other documents in which the text size is not predetermined based on a standard style (unlike magazines and newsletters). Instead of highlighting the text and trying different sizes, this resize-with-the-box feature lets you quickly make text fit the appropriate space. Use Option+Shift+⌘ to resize the text box—and the text—proportionally to their original dimensions.

✦ If you hold the Shift key when resizing, your box will become as wide as it is high—a perfect square for rectangular boxes and a perfect circle for oval boxes. For freehand and Bézier boxes, holding the Shift key will make QuarkXPress adjust the shape so its outermost points are within the bounds of a perfect square.

Reshaping Bézier and freehand boxes

Reshaping the new Bézier and freehand boxes is confusingly complex, unless, of course, you are experienced in an illustration program like Adobe Illustrator, CorelDraw, or Macromedia FreeHand. These tools are new to QuarkXPress, and probably new to you too, so use the steps in this section to help you on your way.

STEPS: Editing specific points on boxes

1. Select either the Item tool or the Content tool.

2. Select the box.

3. If you see the eight control handles for the box rather than points on the box's shape, press Shift+F4 on the Mac or F10 in Windows to go to reshaping mode.

4. Now you see points along the box's boundary. Move the mouse pointer so it touches the outline of the box. The pointer changes to the Reshape icon, which can vary as follows:

   ✦ You see a point below the reshape pointer when you are hovering over a corner or node.

   ✦ You see a line below the pointer when you are hovering over a side.

   ✦ When you are hovering over a control point, you see one of the two following pointer shapes:

      The one with the solid square under the hand indicates a node.

      The one with the hollow square indicates a control point (covered later in this chapter).

5. Use one of the following reshaping options:

   ✦ You can drag a point on the box (a corner on a polygonal box or a node on a Bézier box) to reshape the box. Dragging a side of a freehand box causes it to curve in the direction you're pulling—almost as if it were made of rubber. Dragging a straight side of a Bézier box simply moves that side, while dragging a curved side bends that side just like in a freehand box.

   ✦ You can use the Measurements palette to convert a curved node into a straight corner or vice versa. There are two types of curved nodes: standard and symmetrical. Similarly, you can convert a curved segment to a straight line or vice versa. The options shown here appear once you've selected a node or corner with the mouse.

   ✦ Holding the Option key and clicking a side adds a corner or node to the box at that location. Holding the Option key and clicking a corner or node deletes that corner or node.

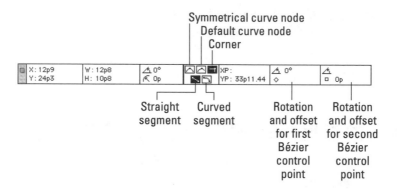

Symmetrical curve node
Default curve node
Corner

X: 12p9	W: 12p8	⌂ 0°		XP:	⌂ 0°	⌂
Y: 24p3	H: 10p8	⌂ 0p		YP: 33p11.44	◇	□ 0p

Straight   Curved   Rotation   Rotation
segment   segment   and offset   and offset
                               for first   for second
                               Bézier   Bézier
                               control   control
                               point   point

✦ In both a Bézier box and a freehand box, you can control the amount of curve by selecting and dragging the control points that appear when you click a node. Look for the blue lines that extend from the node, as well as the hollow handles on those lines. Those handles are the control points, as shown in the following example.

Bézier control points

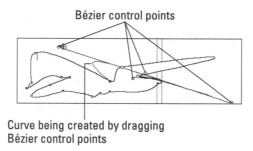

Curve being created by dragging
Bézier control points

✦ To resize a box with the mouse without changing its shape, press Shift+F4 (Mac) or F10 (Windows)—nodes and corner points disappear—and drag one of the box's eight control handles. Hold the Shift key if you want the box resized so that it fits within a perfect square. Hold Option+Shift when resizing to keep the resized shape from being distorted.

6. For a "live" preview of the effects of edits you make to a box's shape, click and hold for a moment before you drag to adjust a size, node, or control point. A thick black line appears under the pointer and the box resizes in real time.

7. To change the color of the nodes, control points, and control point lines, just change the margin color (select Edit⇨Preferences⇨Application⇨Display pane).

Changing box types

If you draw a rectangular picture box, for example, and decide you'd prefer an oval box, you don't need to delete your box and create a new one. Instead, use the Item⇨Shape command and select the new shape from the menu.

Similarly, with a feature new to QuarkXPress 4, if you draw a text box and later decide you want it to be a picture box, use Item⇨Content and choose Picture from the resulting menu. You have three choices: Text, Picture, and None. None is also a new option to QuarkXPress 4: Use it for a box that you don't want to contain anything, such as a box that is meant to be a drawing of its own.

Working with Layout Controls

After you have placed and sized your text box, you want to add the text. Of course, you can add the text at any time during the layout process. Rather than immediately add your text, you may want to first determine layout-oriented, text-flow attributes (the number of columns), or create special effects (rotation). In fact, we recommend that you do wait before adding your text. It makes changing your text box layout easier, and using no-content boxes instead of empty picture boxes and text boxes reduces the disk space and memory required by a document.

You control the layout of text in the text box. After you create a text box, you can set many of its textual specifications by using the Text pane in the Modify dialog box. Get to the pane via Item⇨Modify, or ⌘+M, and then click the Text tab. Figure 5-8 shows the Text pane, which is useful for accomplishing the following tasks:

✦ Placing multiple columns within the text box (as opposed to multiple columns within the page)

✦ Setting text in from the borders of the box (useful if you will have a frame around the box, in which case you want some margin between the frame and the text)

✦ Setting the parameters for the first baseline (which determines how far from the top of the box the baseline of the first line of text should start)

✦ Performing vertical alignment (aligning the text to the top, bottom, center, or both top and bottom of the box)

✦ Skewing or rotating the text within the box

✦ Letting the text in an enclosing text box wrap around all sides of this text box; this is new to QuarkXPress 4

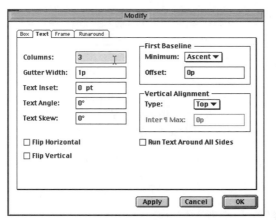

Figure 5-8: The Text pane in the Modify dialog box.

You'll likely find yourself adjusting some text-box settings time and time again. If so, it's better to permanently override this setting by using the Edit⇨Preferences⇨ Documents menu, or ⌘+Y, and selecting the Tool tab, shown in Figure 5-9. There, you can set separate settings for each type of box using the Modify dialog box (click the Modify button to open it). Note that if you change these settings with no document open, they become the default for all future documents; if you change them with a document open, they are the defaults for that document only.

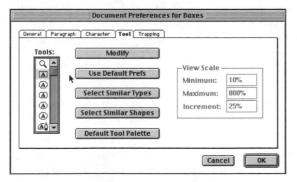

Figure 5-9: The Tool pane lets you change default settings for boxes.

Number of columns

You can set the number of columns in a text box by using the Measurements palette or the Modify dialog box's Text pane. However, you must use the Text pane to set the space between columns, called the *gutter width*. The Measurements palette has no control over this. A common design device is to put thin lines— usually a hairline (¼ point)—between columns. But QuarkXPress offers no feature to add these rules automatically. However, you can add them easily by following the steps below.

Steps: Adding intercolumn rules

1. First, create your standard multicolumn text boxes—the ones you use throughout your document. You'll likely have several such standard boxes. Your master page will probably have your basic text box for body text, and you'll probably put sidebar boxes and the like either in libraries or on the pasteboard for use when needed.

2. Second, make sure column guides are visible (use View⇨Show Guides or press F7).

3. Third, use the Orthogonal Line tool to draw the lines between the columns. (You may have to turn off the Snap to Guides feature, via View⇨Snap to Guides or Shift+F7.) Use the Measurements palette to specify the line width, color, and other settings. (Lines are covered in detail in Chapters 9 and 20.)

4. Fourth, group the lines and the text box (Item⇨Group or ⌘+G). For boxes on master pages, lock them as well (Item⇨Lock or F6).

5. Fifth, for occasionally used standard text boxes in libraries or on the pasteboard, ungroup and unlock the rules and box, resize them as needed, and regroup them (or, for lines, simply resize them with the Content tool selected).

Text inset

The amount of text inset determines the distance between the text and the boundary edges of the text box. Entering a text inset value of 1 point (which, by the way, is the default setting) insets the text 1 point from the borders of the box. For applications in which you don't want any text inset—particularly for text that makes up the body of the document—you might want to change the default inset to 0 points in the tool preferences.

Caution

As useful as text inset is, you might expect that QuarkXPress would provide a number of ways to specify it. But this is one QuarkXPress command you can access in one way only: through the Text pane in the Modify dialog box.

Text inset *does* come in handy if you have a text box with a frame or within another box. Suppose that you have a full page of text and you use a pull-quote (a portion of the text that is copied into a box and enlarged to create a graphic element) or other text element, such as a byline, that you place so the body text wraps around it. You then place a frame around the text. A text inset allows some white space around the text. Figure 5-10 shows a byline with a 1-point frame that has a text inset of 10 points.

Tip

If you press the ⌘ key while resizing a text box, its text inset is resized along with the rest of the box. You can use this trick to create a box whose horizontal text inset is greater than its vertical text inset.

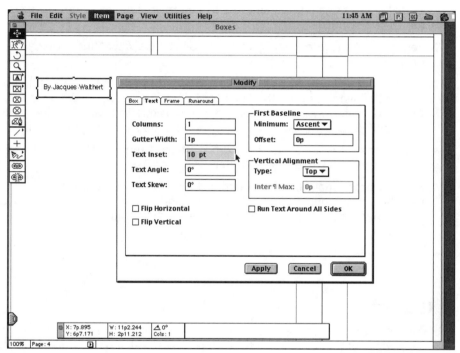

Figure 5-10: An inset of 10 points keeps the text from abutting the frame.

Vertical alignment

You can align text within text boxes with the top, bottom, or middle of the text box. Or you can space text evenly from top to bottom of the text box. Figure 5-11 shows four different ways of vertically aligning text in text boxes. From left to right, the vertical alignments shown in the figure are: top, bottom, centered, and justified. To change the vertical alignment of text, select the text box and go to the Modify dialog box's Text pane. Choose an alignment type from the drop-down menu in the Vertical Alignment section of the pane.

Caution

If you plan to use justified vertical alignment, keep in mind that you need to place picture boxes and other graphic elements outside of the text box that holds the vertically justified text. The intrusion of a picture box or other graphic element with a runaround other than None disables vertical justification.

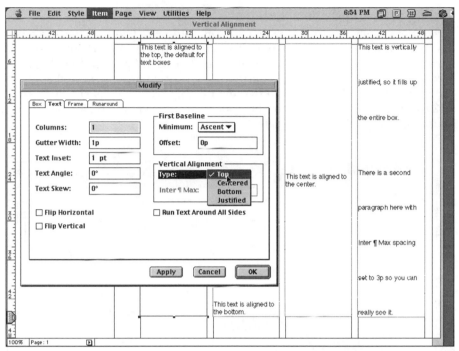

Figure 5-11: The four kinds of vertical alignment: top, bottom, centered, and justified.

Vertical justification spaces text evenly between the first baseline and the bottom of the text box. As long as there are no hard returns in the text, leading adjusts to make each line space the same size as the others in the box. However, if text contains a hard return, you need to specify an interparagraph spacing value in the Inter ¶ Max field. This value tells QuarkXPress the maximum amount of space it can insert between vertically justified paragraphs. You often want such additional spacing so that the paragraph separations are distinct from the line separations. But if you want the leading to remain constant between paragraphs, set Inter ¶ Max to 0.

Text runaround and clipping paths

A *runaround* is an area in a page's layout where you don't want text to flow. *Text runaround* allows you to place copy around an active element (text box, picture box, or line), fitting the text as close to the contours of the element as you want. Text runaround is often used in advertisements and other design-intensive documents. Like other special effects, text runaround is most effective when not overused. Done correctly, this technique can add a unique, polished look to a page layout.

Setting runaround specifications

To set the specifications for text runaround, select the text box, picture box, or line that holds the contents that you want the text to run around. Choose Item⇨Runaround or use ⌘+T to display the Runaround pane in the Modify dialog box. In the dialog box, you can control the type of runaround as well as the distance between the object and the text running around it, as shown in Figures 5-12 through 5-15. The effects of the options available in the dialog box depend upon the type of element you select.

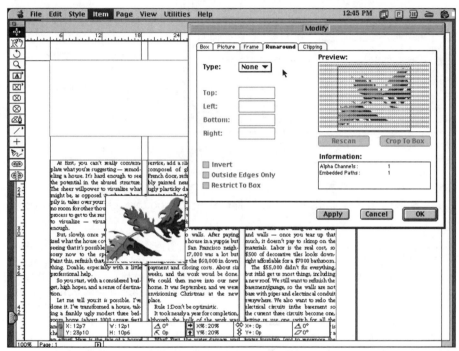

Figure 5-12: With runaround set to None, text and pictures overlap each other if their boxes overlap.

QuarkXPress 4 adds a new preview feature within the Runaround pane so you can see the effects of your runaround choices before you implement them. You can see this preview window in the screen shots that show the various runaround settings.

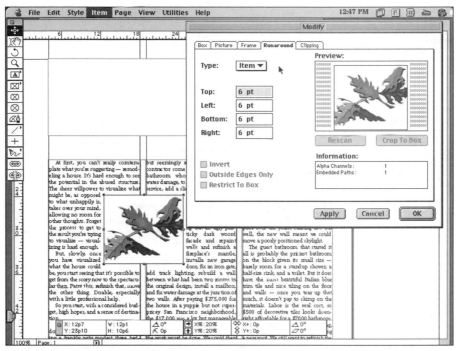

Figure 5-13: With runaround set to Item, text wraps around the selected box's edges.

Using the runaround options

QuarkXPress offers a variety of runaround options. They are determined by both the type of active element and what you enter in the Mode field. You have a choice of modes that varies depending on whether you run text around boxes or lines. The choice of modes are as follows, with the first two applying to picture boxes, text boxes, and lines, and the rest only to picture boxes:

✦ **None:** This setting causes text behind the active item to flow normally, as if there were no object in the way. Refer to Figure 5-12 to see the overlap that occurs when you select None.

✦ **Item:** Choosing Item as the runaround mode causes text to flow around the box that holds the active element. Refer to Figure 5-13 to see the effect of Item runaround. Note how the background text flows around the item by a set amount of offset; in this figure, the offset is 6 points. (The default is 1 point, but you usually want a larger offset than this; we tend to use 6 points or more.)

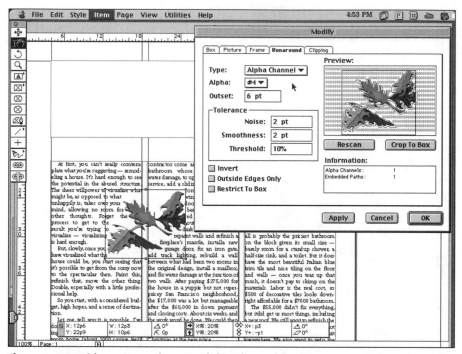

Figure 5-14: With runaround set to Alpha Channel, text wraps around a curve (often called a clipping path) created in the picture's source program, such as Photoshop. The Alpha Channel, Non-White Areas, and Same as Clipping settings can usually achieve the same effect.

✦ **Auto Image**: Auto Image runaround works differently in QuarkXPress 4 than it did in previous versions. In version 4, it creates both a runaround and a clipping path, neither of which are editable.

✦ **Embedded Path:** This setting uses a Bézier shape called a *clipping path* that is part of the image (programs like Photoshop can create such clipping paths in EPS files) and uses that as the boundary for wrapping text.

✦ **Alpha Channel**: This setting lets you wrap around an invisible irregular shape created within the program that created the image (Photoshop users will be familiar with this term). It is typically used to accomplish the same goal as a clipping path.

✦ **Non-White Areas**: Another way to achieve an irregular or form-fitting wrap is to have QuarkXPress ignore the white background of an image, under the presumption that the white area is not actually part of the image. If the image is placed on some other color background in its originating program, this wrapping effect will not work in QuarkXPress. Note that most bitmap files such as scanned photos have a white background. This option also offers a Tolerance area, which is explained later in the discussion of the Clipping pane.

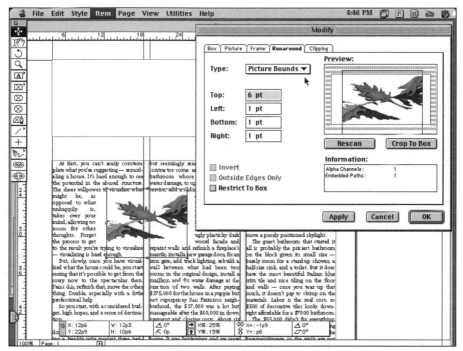

Figure 5-15: With runaround set to Picture Bounds, text wraps around the actual size of the image, even if it extends past or falls short of the picture box's edges.

✦ **Same as Clipping**: This applies the settings from the Clipping pane, which appears in the Modify dialog box only if the selected picture box has a picture in it. The Clipping pane is shown in Figure 5-16. The Clipping pane is where you determine what part of the picture appears on the page, while the Runaround pane determines how text runs around the image. Typically, these would be set as the same, since you'd want the text to run around the object as it appears on the page, but if for some reason you want, for example, the image to have a clipping path but the runaround to be the same as the box size, you could set the runaround as Item in the Runaround pane and still select a clipping path in the Clipping pane.

✦ **Picture Bounds:** This mode automatically determines the shape of the image in the picture box and how text flows around it. The picture bounds will vary from image to image, but in most cases it is simply an invisible rectangle that contains the image (even if the image appears to be nonrectangular). If the picture does not fill the picture box, or if it extends past the picture box boundaries, selecting this item will cause the text to wrap around the picture's actual dimensions regardless of the picture box's dimensions. Refer to Figure 5-15 to see an example of this, without the Restrict To Box option checked. (We'll cover Restrict To Box and the other options a bit later.)

To find out whether your image has an alpha channel or an embedded path, look at the Information section of the Runaround or Clipping pane. It indicates any alpha channels or embedded paths.

Additional runaround and clipping options

In addition to all these options, there are up to three additional options and two buttons you can apply in either the Runaround or Clipping panes. Not all options are available for all runaround types; those that are not available are grayed out. You can use these singly or in combination. Figure 5-16 shows them all, in this case in the Clipping pane. These options work as follows:

✦ **Invert:** This makes the QuarkXPress runaround area or clipping path the opposite of what it would otherwise be. For example, if you have a circle image with a runaround around it, normally the text would run around the outside of the circle. With this option selected, the text would run inside the circle.

✦ **Outside Edges Only:** For a shape that has a "hole" in it, this option ignores the hole and keeps the clipping path away from it.

✦ **Restrict To Box:** When a picture is cropped by the picture box, the clipping path normally extends beyond the box edge. To prevent that—stopping the path at the box edge—select this option.

✦ **Rescan button:** This rebuilds the runaround or clipping path used by QuarkXPress for the selected image.

✦ **Crop To Box button:** This removes any part of the QuarkXPress runaround or clipping path that is outside the picture box boundaries. Crop To Box does the same thing as the Restrict to Box checkbox, except that to undo Crop To Box, you have to click the Rescan button.

Using the Tolerance section options

The other clipping options, in the Tolerance section of the Clipping and Runaround panes, control the degree of precision in determining the clipping path. They work as follows:

✦ **Noise:** This setting lets you tell QuarkXPress to ignore parts of the picture that are below a certain size (the default is 2 points). This is useful if the image contains small dots around the edges that may be overlapped by the text. For a "strict" (exact) runaround, set this value to 0 points.

✦ **Smoothness:** This setting lets you tell QuarkXPress how closely to follow the outline of the nonwhite area. The higher you make this value, the smoother—and potentially less exact—the runaround or clipping path is.

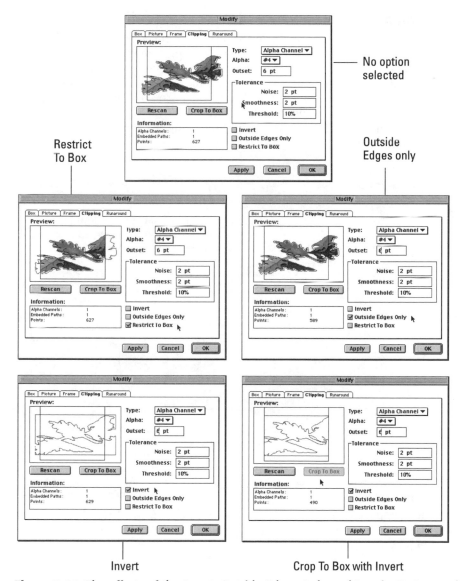

Figure 5-16: The effects of the Invert, Outside Edges Only, and Restrict To Box options. The selected picture is intentionally sized and cropped, so the full picture is wider than the box but shorter than the box's height.

✦ **Threshold:** This setting lets you specify what shades of the image qualify as "nonwhite." At the default setting of 10 percent, anything 10 percent colored is considered nonwhite. To exclude all nonwhite pixels, change this setting to 0 percent. For runarounds, you can let the text intrude upon parts of the image that are lighter in color by raising this value to 20 percent or 30 percent. For clipping paths, however, raising this value can result in odd-looking clipping.

Editing runaround or clipping paths

Finally, you can further edit the QuarkXPress runaround or clipping path. Once you've applied a runaround or clipping path to a picture in the Runaround or Clipping pane, exit the Modify dialog box and select the picture box with either the Content or Item tool. Use Item⇨Edit⇨Runaround, or Option+ F4, to select the picture's runaround. Use Item⇨Edit⇨Clipping Path, or Option+Shift+F4, to select the picture's clipping path. Figure 5-17 shows the result. You can now edit the path just as you would any Bézier or freehand box, using the techniques described earlier in this chapter.

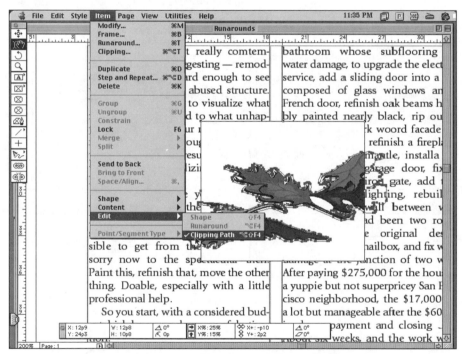

Figure 5-17: You can select a picture's clipping path and further adjust it with QuarkXPress's new Bézier tools.

QuarkXPress no longer has the Manual Image runaround option. You can achieve the same hand-tuned wrap that Manual Image provided by using the Non-White Areas option.

Using the Run Text Around All Sides option

The final kind of runaround is not in the Runaround or Clipping panes. You might recall the Run Text Around All Sides option in the Modify dialog box's Text pane. Figure 5-18 shows it in action. At top is the default behavior, in which a box placed wholly within a text box has the text wrap to one side but not both. If the enclosed box is mostly in the right half of the enclosing box, the enclosed box has no text to its right; if the enclosed box is mostly in the left half of the enclosing box, the enclosed box has no text to its left. With the Run Text Around All Sides option selected, however, this changes, and the text wraps around both sides, as the bottom of Figure 5-18 shows. Remember that you specify this option in the enclosing text box, not in the box that is inside it.

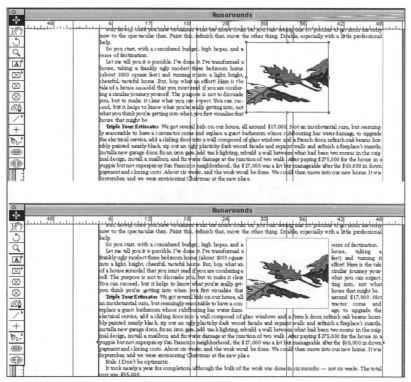

Figure 5-18: The normal wraparound method (top) and the new Run Text Around All Sides option.

Tip

The Run Text Around All Sides option is unusual and counterintuitive for most readers, who have been trained to move to the next line when a column ends or text runs into another object (sort of a forced column end), so if you use this new technique, they may not realize that the text continues on the other side of the intervening box. Use this tool sparingly, if at all. The best place is when the intervening boxes are very small—such as picture boxes containing small icons— so the reader can easily see that the text continues on the same line.

Adding Elements to Boxes

It's easy to place pictures and text in boxes. Simply select a box with the Content tool and press ⌘+E, or use File⇨Get Text or File⇨Get Picture. (For picture boxes, you can also use the Item tool.) You get a standard Open dialog box in which you move through your drives and folders to get to where the file is. Figure 5-19 shows the dialog boxes on Mac and Windows for both text and pictures.

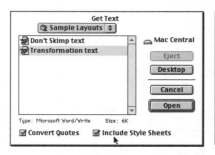
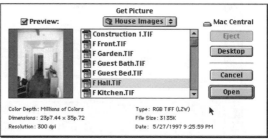
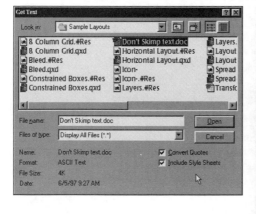

Figure 5-19: The Get Text and Get Picture dialog boxes for Macintosh (top) and Windows.

Tricks for placing text and pictures

Here are some special tricks in placing pictures and text:

✦ If you get a picture in a box that already has a picture, that picture will be replaced.

✦ If you hold the ⌘ key when importing a color image, it will be converted to gray-scale during import.

✦ If you select a picture box, the keyboard combination Option+Shift+⌘+F will make the picture fit proportionally within the box. The combination Shift+⌘+F will make the picture fit the box's shape, distorting the graphic if necessary.

✦ If you hold Shift+⌘+M, QuarkXPress centers the image in the box; this is handy if you can't see an image after you've placed it in the box.

✦ If you hold the ⌘ key while resizing a text box, the text inside will be resized as well. This is particularly handy if you are working with ads, brochures, and other documents in which the text size is not predetermined based on a standard style (unlike magazines and newsletters). Instead of highlighting the text and trying different sizes, this resize-with-the-box feature lets you quickly make text fit the appropriate space. Use Option+Shift+⌘ to resize the text box—and the text— proportionally to their original dimensions.

✦ If your text box already has text in it, any text you get will be added to wherever the text cursor was in the original text. To replace text when importing, use ⌘+A (or Edit⇨Select All) before importing new text. (The new text will replace any selected text.)

✦　　✦　　✦

Preparing Files for Import

In This Chapter

Deciding what to import

Working with text files

Preparing graphics files

Y ou can import text and graphics into your QuarkXPress documents in several ways. QuarkXPress is particularly adept at importing documents created in popular Mac and Windows formats. And through the Publish and Subscribe (Mac) and OLE (Windows) features, you can import file formats—to a limited degree—not directly supported by QuarkXPress. This chapter covers all the bases, beginning with a section on the wisdom of formatting your layout elements exclusively within QuarkXPress and some valuable information on working across the Mac and Windows divide.

Deciding What to Import

QuarkXPress's import capabilities may tempt you to do a lot of your text and graphic formatting outside the program; however, it's not always wise to do so. Here are some reasons why you shouldn't work outside the program:

✦ **Style sheets:** Because a word processor's style sheets won't match all QuarkXPress typographic features, it's often not worthwhile to do extensive formatting in your word processor. This is particularly true of layout-oriented formatting. Multiple columns and page numbers, for example, will be of a much higher standard in your final QuarkXPress document than you could hope to create in a word processor. After all, even the sophisticated formatting features in today's word processors don't begin to approach those needed for true publishing.

✦ **Tables:** Similarly, formatting tables in your word processor or spreadsheet is typically a wasted effort because you have to re-create the tables using QuarkXPress tab settings (see Chapter 15) or using a table-creation XTension like Entable (formerly known as Npath Software's Tableworks Plus), or the free table editor XTension that Quark plans to offer. If you turn your spreadsheet or chart into a graphic before importing it, you cannot edit the data, nor can you resize the picture to fit a changing layout without winding up with different-size numbers among at least some charts—a definite no-no.

✦ **Graphics:** Some graphics tasks, including setting line screens and other halftone settings, background colors, and frames, are best-suited to QuarkXPress, because they relate to how the image is printed as part of the QuarkXPress document. For creating the actual artwork, of course, it does make sense to do extensive work in the originating program. However, although no desktop publishing program offers the kind of graphics tools that an illustration program or photo editor does, QuarkXPress 4's new drawing features (see Chapter 20) do reduce the need for a separate graphics program.

The bottom line is to use QuarkXPress for your layout and complex text formatting (fonts, leading, and hyphenation). Use your word processor for basic text editing, style-sheet assignments (identifying headlines, body copy, and so forth), and basic character formatting (boldface, italics, and other meaning-oriented formatting). Use your graphics program for creating and editing original images and photos; use QuarkXPress's graphics features to embellish your layout, rather than create original artwork.

Dealing with cross-platform differences

It's increasingly common for people to use QuarkXPress in a cross-platform (Mac and Windows) environment. The two programs are so nearly identical that it's easy for people to use either. But there are some trip-ups that you may encounter dealing with something as simple as filenames when sharing files across platforms. Here's what to watch for:

✦ Both Windows and the Mac use icons to show you (and tell programs) what format a file is in. But how those icons are created differ between the two platforms, and when you move files from one platform to another, you can easily lose those icons.

✦ On the Mac, QuarkXPress doesn't usually need those icons. It displays iconless files with a PC icon (shown here) in its Get Text and Get Picture and Open dialog boxes. It lets you import them, as long as what's in those files is a format that QuarkXPress supports.

✦ In Windows, that icon is important for QuarkXPress, because it often filters out files without icons it expected. Fortunately, you can force it to see all files by making sure that Display All Files (*.*) is the selected option for the Files of Type pop-up menu for the Open, Get Text, or Get Pictures dialog box.

✦ On the Mac, a hidden file called an *extent* tells the Mac what kind of format the file has. This extent file has two pieces of key data: the ID for the program that created the file and the ID for the type of format the file is in.

✦ In Windows, the icon is based on the filename extension at the end of the file, such as .DOC in the filename *How to Import.doc.* (Note that the capitalization doesn't matter: .DOC is the same as .Doc is the same as .doc.) Windows hides the extension from users by default, however, so you may not realize that all filenames have these extensions after the name. You can see them in DOS, but in Windows 95, you have to disable the feature that hides them. You can do that by using View⇨Options and then selecting the View tab to get the pane shown here. (You need to have a disk or folder open in order to see the View menu.)

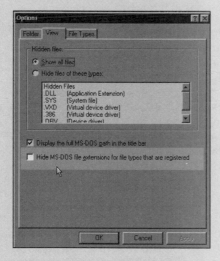

✦ The easiest way to keep files working on both platforms is to use the PC extension on all filenames, even those created on the Mac. That way, you're assured that Windows users see the correct icon (at least for formats that exist in both Windows and on the Mac). Some formats have no PC equivalents and thus no PC extension. Macintosh users have to remember to look at files that have the PC icon.

✦ Some programs automatically map the Mac creator and type IDs to the PC extensions and vice versa, as described in Chapter 28, so files always look like native ones no matter where they were created. If you move files back and forth a lot, these are a wise investment.

Working with Text Files

What preparation do you need to do for your word processor files? They should just load into QuarkXPress as is, right? Not necessarily, even if your word processor supports one of the QuarkXPress text-import formats. Actually, the key to preparing text files is to not *over*prepare them. Before you continue with this topic, here are a few things to think about:

✦ Most of today's major word processors include basic graphics and layout features to help users format single-document publications. Avoid using these features in files you intend to bring into QuarkXPress. Do your sophisticated formatting in QuarkXPress—that's one of the reasons you invested in such a powerful tool. This approach also enables you to do formatting in the context of your layout, rather than in a vacuum.

✦ Much of the graphics and layout formatting you do in a word processor is all for naught anyway because such nontextual formatting does not import into QuarkXPress. Remember, you're importing text, not documents.

Limit your word processor formatting to the type of formatting that enhances reader understanding or conveys meaning. Such formatting may include using italics and boldface to emphasize a word, for example, or using style sheets to set headlines and bylines in different sizes and typefaces. (See Chapter 14 for tips on using style sheets in word processor text.) Let your editors focus on the words; leave presentation tasks to your layout artists.

Translating text files

One type of file preparation you may need to do is translate text files into formats supported by QuarkXPress. Table 6-1 shows what popular text formats are supported by QuarkXPress. Here are some tips to help you work with popular word processors:

✦ Be sure that you installed the necessary import filters when you installed QuarkXPress. You may have trouble importing a supported format because the filter was not installed. Appendix A shows you how to do this.

✦ If your text files come from a word processor that QuarkXPress doesn't support, see if your word processor can save as or export to a file format that QuarkXPress does support.

✦ Alternately, see if your word processor's maker has an import filter for QuarkXPress. For example, although QuarkXPress does not import the Nisus Writer files, Nisus includes a QuarkXPress filter that you can add to the XTensions folder to gain Nisus import support.

✦ Look for new and updated filters on Quark's Web site, at `ftp://ftp.quark.com/xpress/xtensions/`.

✦ QuarkXPress supports ASCII (text-only) files, but you should avoid using them. Plain ASCII files cannot handle any character formatting, so you must do a lot of clean-up work in QuarkXPress. Although programs must continue to support ASCII text because it is the only universally supported format, use plain ASCII as a last resort.

Table 6-1
Supported Text Formats

Format	PC Extension	QuarkXPress Macintosh	QuarkXPress Windows
Macintosh			
ASCII (text-only)	.TXT	Yes	Yes
Claris MacWrite II	None	Yes	No
Claris MacWrite Pro	None	Yes	No
ClarisWorks 4.0	.CWK	No	No
Corel WordPerfect 3.x	.WP3	Yes	No
HTML	.HTM	No	No
Microsoft Word 98 (8.0)	.DOC	No	No
Microsoft Word 6.0	.DOC	Yes	Yes
Microsoft Word 5.x	.DOC	Yes	No
Microsoft Word 4.x	.DOC	Yes	No
Microsoft Works 2.0	None	Yes	No
Microsoft Works 3.0	None	No	No
Nisus Write 5.1	None	No*	No
Rich Text Format (RTF)	.RTF	Yes	Yes
WordPerfect 2.x	.WPD	No	No
WriteNow 3.0	None	Yes	No
Windows			
ASCII (text-only)	.TXT	Yes	Yes
ClarisWorks 4.0	.CWK	No	No
Corel WordPerfect 6.x	.WPD	Yes	Yes
Corel WordPerfect 7.x	.WPD	Yes	Yes
Corel WordPerfect 8.x	.WPD	No	No
HTML	.HTM	No	No

(continued)

Table 6-1 (continued)			
Format	**PC Extension**	**QuarkXPress Macintosh**	**QuarkXPress Windows**
Lotus Ami Pro 2.0	.SAM	No	Yes
Lotus Ami Pro 3.0	.SAM	No	No
Lotus Word Pro 96	.LWP	No	No
Microsoft Word 2.0	.DOC	No	Yes
Microsoft Word 6.0	.DOC	Yes	Yes
Microsoft Word 95 (7.0)	.DOC	Yes	Yes
Microsoft Word 97 (8.0)	.DOC	No	No
Rich Text Format (RTF)	.RTF	Yes	Yes
WordPerfect 4.x	.WP	No	No
WordPerfect 5.x	.WP	No	Yes
WordStar	.WS	No	No
XyWrite III Plus	.XY	No	Yes

* Word processor company provides a filter

Preserving special features in text files

Today's word processors let you do much more than enter and edit text. You also can create special characters, tables, headers and footers, and other document elements such as in-line graphics. Some of these features work when imported into a publishing program, but others don't. The following sections cover each topic in detail.

Character formatting

Table 6-2 shows which character formatting is preserved for the two most popular word processors: Word and WordPerfect.

Table 6-2 Imported Character Formatting		
Format	**Word**	**WordPerfect**
Character Formatting		
All caps	Yes	N/A
Boldface	Yes	Yes
Color	Yes	Yes

Format	Word	WordPerfect
Character Formatting		
Condense/expand	Yes	N/A
Font change	Yes	Yes
Hidden	No	N/A
Italics	Yes	Yes
Outline	Yes	Yes
Point size	Yes	Yes
Shadow	Yes	Yes
Small caps	Yes	Yes
Strikethrough	Yes	Yes
Subscript	Yes	Yes
Superscript	Yes	Yes
Underline	Yes[5]	Yes[5]
Word-only underline	Yes	No[5]
Other Formatting		
Annotations	No	N/A
Date/time	Yes	No
Drop caps	Yes[3]	Yes
Footnotes	Yes[2]	No
Overlays	N/A	No
Page breaks	Yes	No
Pictures	Yes[6]	No
Redlining	N/A	No
Section breaks	Yes[1]	N/A
Special characters	Yes	Yes
Subscribed/OLE items	No[7]	No
Tables	Yes[4]	No

N/A = Not available in this program

1 = Treated as a page break

2 = Placed at end of text

3 = Drop cap is made into its own paragraph

4 = Converted to tabbed text

5 = All underlining converted to single underlining

6 = Document's internal preview of the placed image is converted to PICT; the original file itself is not imported into QuarkXPress

7 = Text items are converted to plain text; picture items are removed

Tables

We stated before that you should do table formatting in QuarkXPress, not in your word processor. But there is an exception to the rule: If you use style sheets to format a table with tabs in your word processor, by all means, import the formatted table into QuarkXPress. You can then modify the styles, if necessary, as your layout changes. If, however, you create tables with the word professor's table feature, expect the table's formatting to be stripped out during import into QuarkXPress.

Headers and footers

Headers and footers do not import into QuarkXPress. (Chapter 16 explains how to add these elements to your layout.) That's not a flaw in QuarkXPress. After all, headers and footers are a layout issue, not a text issue, so there is no reason to include these elements in your word processor document. Because page numbers change based on your QuarkXPress layout, there's no point in putting headers and footers in your word processor document anyway.

Footnotes

If you use a word processor's footnote feature and import the text file, the footnotes are placed at the end of the imported text. The superscripted numerals or characters in the footnotes may or may not translate properly.

Special characters

The Mac and Windows both have built-in support for special characters, such as symbols, accented characters, and non-English letters. Use the following methods to access these characters:

✦ **Keyboard shortcuts:** On both platforms, using keyboard shortcuts.

✦ **Apple's KeyCaps:** On the Mac, using Apple's KeyCaps program (shown here), which comes with the System and is accessible via the Apple menu. The two sets of special characters are found by holding Option and Option+Shift (each results in a different set).

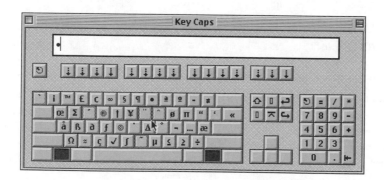

✦ **The PopChar utility:** On the Mac, using a shareware utility like Günther Blaschek's PopChar Pro (shown here) or PopChar Pro control pane, which is available on several Web sites and included on this book's CD. Notice how the keyboard shortcut for each special character is shown at the upper right as a character is highlighted.

✦ **The Windows Character Map:** In Windows, using the Character Map utility (shown here) that comes with Windows. Just as KeyCaps is usually installed in the Apple menu, this is usually installed in the Programs⇨Accessories submenu of the Windows 95 Start menu.

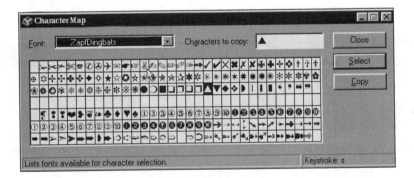

✦ **Word processor features:** On both platforms, using a word processor's own feature for special-character access. Microsoft Word, for example, has such an option via Insert⇨Symbol or via the toolbar. If you added this command to your toolbar, look for the button with the Ω character in Word 6.0 and Word 95.) WordPerfect has a similar dialog box accessed via Insert⇨Symbol (Mac), or Insert⇨Character (Windows), as shown on the following page.

Note that the Windows versions of the symbol features act differently: Windows Word lets you get symbols from any font, while Mac Word does not; and WordPerfect for Windows has its own symbol fonts, while Mac WordPerfect uses standard Mac fonts.

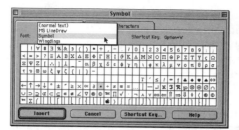

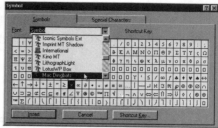

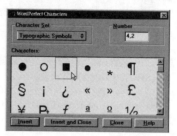

Not all fonts are created equal

Not all fonts may have all special characters available. Here are a few rules of thumb:

✦ Typically, fonts from major type foundries like Adobe and Bitstream have all the characters in each font.

✦ Custom-made fonts and those from foundries other than Adobe and Bitstream may use different characters or have fewer.

✦ Fonts translated from Windows to the Mac, or vice versa, through a program like Altsys's Fontographer will likely have special characters in different locations than a native Mac or Windows font.

✦ Windows fonts generally have fewer special characters in the font.

In-line graphics

Modern word processors typically support in-line graphics, letting you import a picture into your word processor document and embed it in text. Word and WordPerfect, for example, both let you import graphics, and QuarkXPress, in turn, can import the graphics with your text. In-line graphics import as their PICT (Mac) or WMF (Windows) previews, however, not as the original formats. This means that you probably get lower-resolution versions in your QuarkXPress layout. Despite their limitations, the use of in-line graphics in your word processor can be helpful when putting together a QuarkXPress document. Here are two hints to make the process more efficient:

✦ Use the in-line graphics whose PICT or WMF previews are imported into QuarkXPress as placeholders so that the layout artist knows you have embedded graphics. He or she can then replace the PICT or WMF previews with the better-quality originals.

✦ If you find yourself using several graphics as characters (such as a company icon used as a bullet), use a font-creation program like Macromedia's Fontographer to create a symbol typeface with those graphics. Your word processor and layout documents can then use the same high-quality versions.

Using XPress Tags

QuarkXPress offers a file format of its own: XPress Tags. XPress Tags actually is ASCII (text-only) text that contains embedded codes telling QuarkXPress which formatting to apply. You embed these codes, which are similar to macros, as you create files in your word processor.

The down side

Most people do not use this option because the coding can be tortuous. You cannot use XPress Tags with your word processor's formatting. If you create a file in Microsoft Word, for example, you cannot use XPress Tags to apply a style to a paragraph while using Word's own boldface and italics formatting for text. You either code everything with XPress Tags and save the document as an ASCII file, or you don't use XPress Tags at all. This either-or situation is too bad, because the ability to combine a publishing program's formatting codes with a word processor's formatting features adds both power and flexibility—as users of Corel Ventura Publisher and Adobe PageMaker know.

The up side

So why have XPress Tags at all? Because this format is the one format sure to support all the formatting you do in QuarkXPress. Here are the advantages:

✦ XPress Tags can be useful in transferring files created in QuarkXPress to another QuarkXPress user (including someone using the Windows version) or to a word processor for further work. You can export a QuarkXPress story or piece of selected text in the XPress Tags format and then transfer the exported file to another QuarkXPress user or to a word processor for further editing.

✦ Exporting an XPress Tags file into a word processor makes sense if you want to add or delete text without losing special formatting—such as fonts, kerning, or style tags—your word processor doesn't support. After you edit the text, you can save the altered file (making sure it's saved as ASCII text) and reimport it into your QuarkXPress layout.

Avoiding text-file pitfalls

Sometimes, issues not related to the contents of a word processor file can affect how files are imported into QuarkXPress. Here are a couple of word-processor weirdnesses you can avoid:

✦ *Fast save:* Several programs (notably Microsoft Word) offer a fast-save feature, which adds information to the end of a word-processor document. The added information notes which text has been added and deleted and where the changes occurred. You can use this feature to save time because the program doesn't have to write the entire document to disk when you save the file. When you use the fast-save feature, however, text-import into publishing programs—including QuarkXPress—becomes problematic. Plainly put, fast-saved files usually won't import into QuarkXPress. We recommend that you turn off fast save, at least for files you will import into QuarkXPress. With today's speedy hard drives, the time you gain by using fast save is barely noticeable anyway.

Shown here is the dialog box for Mac Word 6.0 (Tools⇨Options⇨Save); Word 6 and Word 95 for Windows use the same dialog box. You turn fast save on and off in this dialog box. You don't need to worry about whether fast save is enabled if you use Save As or Export options to save the file either in a format other than the word processor's native format or to a different name or location.

✦ *Software versions:* Pay attention to the version number of the word processor you use. This caution may seem obvious, but the issue still trips up a lot of people. Usually, old versions (two or more revisions old) or new versions (newer than the

Tip

XPress Tags can also be good for complex search-and-replace operations that QuarkXPress does not support. For example, you cannot search and replace a tab setting, color, or horizontal text scale setting in QuarkXPress; however, you can in an exported XPress Tags file from your word processor.

Using XPress Tags codes

The appendix in the QuarkXPress manual (beginning on page 24) defines the dozens of XPress Tags codes and their variants you embed in your text file. These codes range from the simple, such as <I> for italicized text, to the moderately complex. The following code is for a 2-point, 100-percent red rule that uses line style 1, is indented 18 points to the right and left of the column, is offset 25 percent, and is placed above the current paragraph:

```
<*ra(02,1,"Red",100,18,18,25%>
```

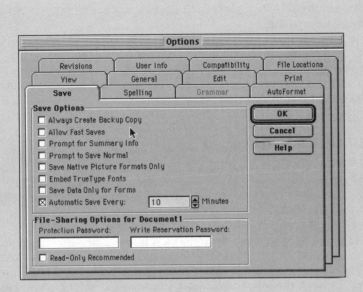

publishing or other importing program) cause import problems. The import filters either no longer recognize the old format (something has to go to make room for new formats) or were written before the new version of the word processor was released. Refer to Table 6-1 to see which text formats and versions QuarkXPress is compatible with.

Basically, you can use as many of the XPress Tags codes as needed, and place them between < and > characters. In the preceding example, we are using the *ra code (which stands for right aligned) and filling in the parameters it expects.

Some codes are programming-level codes, for which you define the style tags by combining as many of the basic XPress Tags codes as appropriate. The following example defines a style called *Lead* as black, 9.5-point Cheltenham Book Plain with a four-line drop cap, 12 points of leading, a 10-point first-line indent, no left or right indents, no space above, 100-percent shade and scale, full justification, and locked to the baseline grid:

```
@Lead=[S"","Lead"]<*J*kn0*kt0*ra0*rb0*d(1,4)*p(10,0,0,12,0,0,G,
"U.S. English")Ps100t0h100z9.5k0b0cKf"Cheltenham Book">
```

The = after @Lead in the preceding example signals QuarkXPress to *define* the Lead style with the codes between the angle brackets. To use that style, you type **@Lead:** at the beginning of the paragraph you want to format; the colon tells

QuarkXPress to *use* the style tag. (You can't apply a style tag that you did not define earlier in your text file.)

In practical terms, you may not mind editing XPress Tags slightly or leaving them in a file when you alter its text. You're not likely to forgo the friendly formatting available in your word processor and in QuarkXPress, however, to apply XPress Tags coding to everything in your text files.

Importing tabular data

QuarkXPress has no filters to accept files in formats such as Lotus 1-2-3, Microsoft Excel, Claris FileMaker Pro, or Microsoft FoxPro. That means you have two basic options for preparing files that contain tabular information (usually spreadsheets or databases) for import:

✦ **Option 1:** Save the files as tab-delimited ASCII text. Then import them and apply the appropriate tab stops (either directly or through styles) to create the desired table. Or paste the data (into a QuarkXPress text box) into your document through the Mac or Windows Clipboard. It will be pasted as tab-delimited ASCII text.

✦ **Option 2:** Use the file as a graphic by using a charting tool (such as that in Excel or Lotus 1-2-3). Export it to a format such as EPS if possible. Paste the chart via the Clipboard or use Publish and Subscribe or OLE (see Chapter 7) if EPS export is not an option.

If you choose the second option, make sure that you size all charts and tables the same way so that the size of the numbers in them, when imported and placed, is consistent throughout your QuarkXPress document. Use a vector format such as PICT or EPS whenever possible to ensure the best reproduction quality no matter what size you scale the chart graphics to.

Preparing Graphics Files

QuarkXPress offers support for all major formats of Mac graphics files. Some formats are more appropriate than others for certain kinds of tasks. The basic rules are as follows:

✦ Save line art in a format such as EPS or PICT. (These object-oriented formats support *vector* data. Vector files are composed of instructions on how to draw various shapes.)

✦ Save bitmaps (photos and scans) in a format such as TIFF, Photo CD, or PICT. (These pixel-oriented formats support *raster* data. Raster files are composed of a series of dots, or pixels, that make up the image.)

✦ PICT and EPS files can be in vector or bitmap format depending on the original image and the program in which it was created or exported from. If you enlarge a PICT image and it begins to look blocky, it is a bitmap. (This technique does not work for EPS files, though, because all you can see of them in QuarkXPress is their low-resolution bitmap preview, which always looks blocky when scaled up.)

✦ If you output to high-end PostScript systems, make EPS and TIFF formats your standards. EPS files can use PostScript fonts; can be color-separated if produced in a program such as Adobe Illustrator, CorelDraw, Macromedia FreeHand, or Deneba Canvas; and can support an extremely large set of graphical attributes. You also can manipulate gray-scale TIFF files in QuarkXPress to apply custom contrasts, line screens, and other photographic effects.

Supported file formats

QuarkXPress imports the following file formats. If your program's format is not one of these, chances are high that it can save as or export to one. In the following list, the code in italics is the filename extension common for these files on PCs:

✦ BMP, the Windows bitmap format—*.BMP, .DIB*

✦ EPS, the Encapsulated PostScript vector format favored by professional publishers—also Adobe Illustrator's native format *.EPS, .AI* (QuarkXPress also supports the DCS color-separated variant of EPS, whose full name is Document Color Separation.)

✦ GIF, the Graphics Interchange Format common in Web documents—QuarkXPress for Windows only *.GIF*

✦ JPEG, the Joint Photographers Expert Group compressed bitmap format often used on the Web (JPEG Import XTension must be installed) *.JPG*

✦ PCX, the PC Paintbrush format very popular in DOS programs and common still in Windows (on Mac, PCX Import XTension must be installed) *.PCX*

✦ Photo CD, the Kodak format used for photo finishing on CDs and popular for image catalogs (Photo CD Import XTension must be installed) *.PCD*

✦ PICT, the Mac's native graphics format (it can be bitmap or vector); little used in professional documents but common for inexpensive clip art *.PCT*

✦ RLE, Run Length Encoded bitmap, the OS/2 variant of BMP *.RLE*

✦ Scitex CT, the continuous-tone bitmap format used on Scitex prepress systems *.CT*

✦ TIFF, the Tagged Image File Format, the bitmap standard for professional image editors and publishers *.TIF*

✦ WMF, the Windows Metafile Format native to Windows but little used in professional documents—QuarkXPress for Windows only *.WMF*

QuarkXPress 4 no longer supports the following formats:

✦ MacPaint, a black-and-white bitmap format now a rarity *.MAC*

✦ RIFF, the Raster Image File Format native to MetaCreations' (formerly Fractal Designs') Painter program *.RIF*

QuarkXPress 4 for Windows does not support the following formats, which version 3.3 for Windows (but not for Mac) did support:

✦ CGM, the Computer Graphic Metafile format popular on Unix workstations *.CGM*

✦ HPGL, the Hewlett-Packard Graphics Language used in architecture and computer-aided drafting *.PLT*

✦ Micrografx Draw, a once-popular but now rare program *.DRW*

Working with EPS files

EPS files come in several varieties, and not every EPS file is the same. You see the most noticeable differences when you import EPS files into QuarkXPress. The following sections explore these issues.

Preview headers

The preview header is a displayable version of the EPS image; because the Mac and PC don't use PostScript to display screen images, they can't interpret a PostScript file directly, which is why many programs add a preview header to the EPS files they create. At first you may not see anything but a big gray rectangle and the words *PostScript Picture* when you import an EPS file. The file either has no preview header or its header is in an unreadable format. Although the image prints correctly, it's hard to position and crop because you must repeatedly print your page to see the effects of your work.

This condition is typical for EPS files transferred from the Mac to the PC, because EPS files use a different header format on each platform (PICT or JPEG on the Mac; TIFF or WMF on the PC).

When you first get the picture, you can see whether there is a preview by checking the Preview box. As you click a file, a preview appears; if the preview is gray, there is no preview or the preview is in an incompatible format. QuarkXPress for Mac can read all three types of preview headers, but QuarkXPress for Windows can only read a TIFF preview header. The Type field under the list of filenames tells you what sort of file the selected image is.

Creating a preview header

If your picture lacks a usable preview header, use this workaround: After you print an EPS graphic, use the Item⇨Shape menu to convert the picture box to a freehand box and reshape the box to match the outline of the graphic you printed. If possible, convert the EPS file to a format such as TIFF and import that TIFF file into the box so you can more easily create the outline. You are able to see the TIFF file on-screen, rather than use a printout of the EPS file as a guide. When you're done, replace the TIFF file with the original EPS file.

Whether you use QuarkXPress for Mac or for Windows, in order to generate an acceptable image header in an EPS file created on the Mac, save the file with a TIFF header when possible. This is the default for most Mac programs. For Windows programs, look for a Mac preview option and use it; if there is no such option, look for a TIFF preview option and use that instead. (An exception to this "use the TIFF preview" rule is for Adobe Illustrator files: use the PC image header if you are using the files in Windows QuarkXPress.)

A few exceptions

As the major illustration and imaging programs have become cross-platform, with file formats that work on both platforms, the EPS header issue is less of a problem, as the programs' designers account for use of their files on both platforms. You'll thus likely have header problems only with older versions of your software. Here are some exceptions:

- ✦ Early versions of the major Windows programs cannot generate the appropriate Mac EPS header. During export, CorelDraw 5 generates a low-resolution black-and-white preview (even with the high-resolution option selected) for its color EPS files. Adobe Illustrator 4.0 generates no Mac-compatible preview. Like CorelDraw, Computer Support Corp.'s Arts & Letters Graphics Editor generates only a black-and-white preview, and then only if you select TIFF for the preview format (use the Setup button in the Export dialog box).

- ✦ In Adobe Illustrator 5.0 and 6.0, the default is to have no header. If you are using Mac QuarkXPress, change that to Color Macintosh when saving in Illustrator 5.x and to 8-Bit Macintosh in Illustrator 6.0. If you are using Windows QuarkXPress, use the 1-Bit PC option. If you are using both platforms' versions of QuarkXPress, use the PC preview header, because both QuarkXPresses display it. (Note that Illustrator 5.x's native format is EPS, so don't look for an export or save-as option. In Illustrator 6.0 and 7.0, save as Illustrator EPS.)

- ✦ If you are planning to print an EPS file from Windows, make sure you save it with ASCII encoding instead of binary encoding. If you save the EPS file with binary encoding, you may not be able to print it from Windows.

Color issues

If you create color images in an illustration program, make sure that you create them using the CMYK color model or using named spot colors. If you use CMYK, the color is, in effect, pre-separated. With QuarkXPress 4, any colors defined in an EPS file are automatically added to the Colors palette for your document and set as a spot color. (You can change it to a process color via Edit⇨Colors; see Chapter 21 for details.)

To take advantage of QuarkXPress's color-separation features for imported EPS files, you need to create the colors correctly. (If you intend to print your file on a color printer rather than have it separated, don't worry about the instructions given in this section.)

Color separations

If your program follows Adobe's EPS specifications (Adobe Illustrator, CorelDraw, and Macromedia FreeHand all do), QuarkXPress color-separates your EPS file, no matter whether it uses process or spot colors. Canvas automatically converts Pantone spot colors to process colors in your choice of RGB and CMYK models. For other programs, create your colors in the CMYK model to be sure they print as color separations from QuarkXPress.

Pantone colors

Most artists use Pantone to specify desired colors, so keep a Pantone swatchbook handy to see which CMYK values equal the desired Pantone color. (One of the available Pantone swatch books—*The Pantone Process Color Imaging Guide CMYK Edition*—shows each Pantone color next to the CMYK color build used to simulate it.)

The *CV* after the Pantone Matching System color number in the QuarkXPress (and other programs) dialog boxes stands for *computer video,* which is Pantone's way of warning you that what you see on-screen may not be what you get in print. Because of the different physics underlying monitors and printing presses, colors cannot be matched precisely, even with color calibration. This is true for other color models, such as Focoltone and Trumatch.

If you don't have the Pantone swatchbook, you can define the color in QuarkXPress as a Pantone color and then switch color models to CMYK. QuarkXPress immediately converts the Pantone color to CMYK, and then you know which value to use in your illustration program (if it doesn't support Pantone itself). Many high-end illustration programs, including Adobe Illustrator, support Pantone and can do this instant conversion as well. If available (as it is in QuarkXPress), use the Pantone Process color model because it is designed for output using CMYK printing presses. (For more information on defining colors and working with color images, see Chapter 21.)

Calibrated color

With the bundled Quark CMS XTension installed, QuarkXPress color-separates non-CMYK files. (*CMS* stands for Color Management System.) It also calibrates the output colors (whether printed to a color printer or color-separated for traditional printing) based on the source device and the target output device.

Importing color files

When importing color files, be sure to change the color profile assigned by Quark CMS (if you are using this XTension) for images created by devices other than the default source. For example, your default profile for RGB images may be NEC MultiSync 1.5 Gamma, because the TIFF and PICT files you usually use were created on a Mac with this type of monitor. But if you are importing a scanned image, you should change the profile to match that particular scanner. You do so by choosing the appropriate file from the pop-up menu in the Get Picture dialog box. Note that it may take a moment for QuarkXPress to display that pop-up menu because first it scans the image to see if it contains a profile of its own (called a Metric Color Tag, or MCT). You can also change an image's profile after it is imported (via Utilities⇨Usage, and then selecting the Profiles tab, or in the Profile Information palette).

DCS and DCS2

The Document Color Separation (DCS) variant of EPS is a set of five files: an EPS preview file that links together four separation files (one each for cyan, magenta, yellow, and black). Use of this format speeds printing and ensures correct color separation when you output negatives for use in commercial printing. These files are often preferred over standard EPS files by service bureaus that do color correction. (The DCS2 file format is the same as the DCS format except that it combines all the plates into one file and supports spot colors as well as CMYK.)

Dealing with fonts

When you use fonts in text included in your graphics files, you usually have the option to convert the text to curves (graphics). This option ensures that your text prints on any printer.

If you don't use this conversion before making an EPS file, make sure that your printer or service bureau has the fonts used in the graphic. Otherwise, the text does not print in the correct font. (You will likely get Courier instead.) Remember that QuarkXPress does not show fonts used in graphics in the Fonts pane of the Usage dialog box (Utilities⇨Usage), so your layout artists and service bureau have no way of knowing which fonts to have available unless they run a Collect for Output report.

Working with bitmap formats

Bitmap (also called *raster*) formats are simpler than vector formats because they are made up of rows of dots (*pixels*), not instructions on how to draw various shapes. But that doesn't mean that all bitmaps are alike. The following sections cover the differences.

TIFF

The most popular bitmap format for publishers is TIFF, the *Tagged Image File Format* developed by Aldus Corp. (later bought by Adobe Systems), and Microsoft Corp. TIFF supports color up to 24 bits (16.7 million colors) in both RGB and CMYK models, and every major photo-editing program supports TIFF on both the Macintosh and in Windows. TIFF also supports gray-scale and black-and-white files. The biggest advantage to using TIFF files rather than other formats that also support color, such as PICT, is that QuarkXPress is designed to take advantage of TIFF. QuarkXPress can work with the contrast settings in gray-scale TIFF images to make an image clearer or to apply special effects—something QuarkXPress can't do with any other bitmap format (see Chapter 19).

Tip

TIFF comes in several variants, and no program, including QuarkXPress, supports all of them. Here are our recommendations for how to save TIFF files for optimal use in QuarkXPress:

✦ You should have no difficulty if you use the uncompressed and LZW-compressed TIFF formats supported by most Mac programs (and increasingly by most Windows programs). If you do have difficulty with compressed TIFF files, we recommend that you use uncompressed TIFF files.

✦ If you want to color-separate your QuarkXPress document, it's best to save your TIFF file in CMYK format (Adobe Photoshop supports this format) because QuarkXPress cannot color-separate non-CMYK files unless the Quark CMS XTension is installed.

✦ Save the alpha channel for 24-bit TIFF images, as this comes in handy for creating a clipping path in QuarkXPress, as Chapter 5 explains.

✦ Save the clipping path, if you created one, for graphics files in QuarkXPress. With this path, QuarkXPress can do contoured text wraps around your image, if you so desire.

✦ If you do color calibration in Photoshop 2.51 or later, or otherwise use a program that saves calibrated color in the Metric Color Tags format, be sure to save with the Metric Color Tags option enabled. This will help QuarkXPress's color-management system better reproduce your image.

✦ Use the byte order for the platform that the TIFF file is destined for. Macs and PCs use the opposite byte order—basically, the Mac reads the eight characters that comprise a byte in one direction and the PC reads it in another. Although QuarkXPress reads both byte orders, other programs may not, so why invite confusion? Of course, if only QuarkXPress and Photoshop users will work on your TIFF files, the byte order doesn't matter.

PCX

Like TIFF, PCX supports color, gray-scale, and black-and-white images.

PICT

The standard Macintosh format for drawings, PICT (which stands for *Picture*) also supports bitmaps and is the standard format for Macintosh screen-capture utilities. QuarkXPress imports PICT files with no difficulty. Colors cannot be color-separated unless the Quark CMS XTension is installed and active. Because fonts in vector PICT graphics are translated to curves, you need not worry about whether fonts used in your graphics are resident in your printer or available at your service bureau.

Photo CD

Like other bitmap formats, no special preparation for this file format is necessary—which is great, considering that users have no control over the image format because it is created by service bureaus converting 35mm film to digital images via Kodak's proprietary process. With the Quark CMS XTension, QuarkXPress can color-separate Photo CD files.

JPEG

The JPEG (Joint Photographers Expert Group) compressed color-image format is used for very large images and the individual images comprising an animation or movie. Images compressed in this format may lose detail, which is why TIFF is preferred by publishers.

A few Photo CD tips and quirks

If you are using Photo CD files, keep in mind that you need two extensions installed in your Mac's System folder: Apple Photo Access and QuickTime, neither of which comes with a Mac's system disks if you are using System 7.1 or earlier; however, both are usually included on Photo CD products. (Later versions of the Mac OS have these needed files.) You need QuickTime because Photo CD files are saved using a compression method that QuickTime provides. Note that you need these extensions even if you are importing Photo CD images copied from a CD onto a hard disk or other medium, not just if you are accessing the images directly from a CD-ROM drive.

Also, Photo CD images are often stored in five resolutions on the CD. If you import the image from the CD's Images folder, you get the highest-resolution image, which can take several megabytes. It's better to go into the subfolders and select a lower-resolution version, such as 768×512 or 192×128. The smaller you print the image, the less resolution you need.

✦   ✦   ✦

Keeping It All Together

♦ ♦ ♦ ♦

In This Chapter

Working with
graphics links

Using Publish and
Subscribe and OLE

Working with text
links

Anchoring boxes and
lines

Copying between
documents

♦ ♦ ♦ ♦

Document elements such as text and graphics may
change, and you need to ensure that your document
contains the latest version of all elements. In addition, you
sometimes need to make sure that any changes you make to
text in a document are made to the original text files because
you may want to use the same text in other documents. Both
of these issues can be addressed with a process known as
linking. QuarkXPress supports several types of links, all of
which are detailed in a sidebar later in this chapter.
QuarkXPress offers features that address several linking
issues, but in some areas, it offers no support at all.
QuarkXPress is particularly adept at two kinds of graphic
links: static links and, on the Mac, dynamic links.
QuarkXPress is weak, however, at making text links. This
chapter covers all the ins and outs of this topic.

Working with Graphics Links

You can bring graphics into QuarkXPress documents in two
ways: You can import them through the File⇨Get Picture
menu (or ⌘+E) or use the Macintosh or Windows Clipboard
to copy a graphic from another application directly into
QuarkXPress. Both methods have their advantages:

♦ **The import method:** The primary advantage to using
the import method is that you can create a link to the
original graphic in case the graphic is changed or
moved.

♦ **The Clipboard method:** The primary advantage to using
the Clipboard method is that you can copy into a
document graphics that QuarkXPress ordinarily cannot
import. The Clipboard translates them to a format (PICT
on Mac, Windows Metafile on Windows) that

QuarkXPress can read. (Note that the PICT and Windows Metafile formats have limits in terms of output resolution and the image controls that QuarkXPress can apply to them; see Chapters 6 and 19 for details.)

When you open a document

When you open a QuarkXPress document, QuarkXPress checks the links to any imported graphic. These links are created automatically when you import the file; no special effort on your part is needed. QuarkXPress looks for two things: Is the file where it is supposed to be? And has the file changed since the last time it was accessed? (QuarkXPress looks at the file's date and time stamp to determine the second factor.)

If the file is missing or has been modified, QuarkXPress displays the alert box shown in Figure 7-1. You can select Cancel, which tells QuarkXPress not to worry about the problem, or you can choose OK to invoke the Missing/Modified Pictures dialog box, shown in Figure 7-2. (A file might be missing because the file was deleted, moved to a different disk—perhaps for backup—or renamed.)

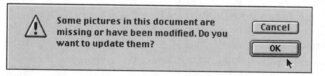

Figure 7-1: The alert you get when QuarkXPress can't find a picture you imported earlier.

Note

If you have set your general preferences (Edit ➪ Preferences ➪ Document, or ⌘+Y) in the General pane so that the Auto Import Picture option is set to something other than On (verify), QuarkXPress does not alert you to missing pictures. We recommend you set this preference to On, which automatically updates pictures with later versions, or On (verify), which gives you the choice of doing so when you open a QuarkXPress document. Of course, if a file is missing or has been deleted, none of these options can update the file. You have to do that manually, as explained later.

Finding missing graphics

The Missing/Modified Pictures dialog box (see Figure 7-2) gives you several pieces of information about the graphics that are missing or have been modified. These include:

✦ The full filename, including the last known location.

✦ The page that each graphic appears on. A dagger (†) with the page number indicates that it appears in the adjacent pasteboard.

✦ The type of graphic format, such as TIFF or EPS.

✦ The graphic's status (OK, Missing, or Modified). OK appears only after you update a graphic.

✦ The graphic's print status. If a checkmark appears, the graphic will print. By unchecking a graphic, you can suppress its printing. You toggle between having a checkmark and not having one by clicking under the Print column in the row for the desired graphic. (Chapter 24 covers printing issues in more detail.)

Tip You can get more details on a specific image by selecting it with the mouse and ensuring that the More Information box is checked at the bottom of the dialog box.

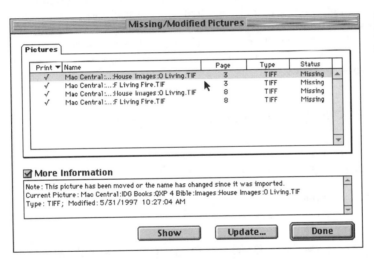

Figure 7-2: The Missing/Modified Pictures dialog box.

When you update

When you update a graphic, QuarkXPress checks the folder in which the graphic was located to see if other missing graphics are in it (because a common reason for missing graphics is that they have been moved). If it finds other missing graphics, it displays a dialog box that gives you the chance to simultaneously update all the missing files in that folder. If you need to see the graphic to remember what its filename refers to, select the filename, and then choose Show in the Missing/Modified Pictures dialog box. QuarkXPress displays the screen version of the graphic on the page on which it occurs.

Tip You should be in a normal (100 percent) or reduced view so that you can see enough of the image when QuarkXPress displays it. Because you can't change the view once you're in the dialog box, close the dialog box (click Done on the Mac; Close in Windows), change your view, and bring the dialog box back via Utilities⇨Usage, and then switch to the Pictures pane.

When you don't update

If you don't update files when you open your document (by selecting Cancel in response to the alert box or by not making selections in the Missing/Modified Pictures dialog box), you still see the graphics in your document. What you see is a copy of your graphic that QuarkXPress creates when importing a graphic. For TIFF, Scitex CT, and all vector formats, this preview is a low-resolution copy that is not appropriate for printing and should not be used in place of the real thing. It exists only to show you what graphic you placed in case you don't remember the graphic by name. For PICT, PCX, BMP, and Windows metafile graphics—formats that use a fairly low resolution to begin with—you can print acceptably using just the print preview copy.

Tip

If you decide not to update a graphic link when you first load your document, you can do so later through the Utilities⇨Usage dialog box's Pictures pane. This pane works the same way as the Missing/Modified Pictures dialog box. You can also use the Picture Usage dialog box (Utilities⇨Usage) to substitute new graphics for missing graphics because QuarkXPress doesn't know (or care) whether the new links are to the same graphics.

Updating missing and modified graphics

Once you've discovered that a graphic is missing, you'll want to update its link. You may also want to update a modified graphic or remove a link from a missing graphic you no longer want to use. This and the following sections cover all these issues. If you want to update a link to a missing graphic, the following steps tell you how to get the job done.

STEPS: Updating the link to a missing graphic

1. Select the filename.

2. Choose Update, and then move through the drives and folders available through the Find *filename* dialog box. Only files that match the file type of the missing file (such as TIFF) appear in the Find *filename* dialog box's file list. You cannot use this dialog box to replace one type of file (say, TIFF) with another (say, EPS). The way to perform this kind of change is to simply use File⇨Get Picture, or ⌘+E, to load the new image into the appropriate picture box.

3. QuarkXPress uses the standard Mac and Windows Open dialog boxes to search for missing graphics. Once you find the missing graphic, select it and choose OK to update the link to the graphic and return to the Missing/Modified Pictures dialog box.

4. You see confirmation of your selection in the dialog box and can update any other files. After you've found the file, it no longer is labeled "Missing," but it may be labeled "Modified," if the newly located file is older than or more recent than the original or has a different name. (For more information on dealing with modified files, see the following section.)

5. Click the Update button again in the dialog box to update the link to the file.

As long as your graphic files use the proper DOS file extension (such as .TIF or .EPS), both the Mac and Windows versions of QuarkXPress can recognize them and display them in the Get Picture dialog box. If you transfer graphics files from a Windows computer to a Mac, you do not need to change their file types in a program such as ResEdit or DiskTop (to, say, TIFF or EPSF), but you should make sure their DOS file extensions are correct.

Updating modified graphics

The process for updating a modified graphic is simpler than updating a missing graphic because QuarkXPress already knows where the graphic is located. To update a graphic, select the filename and choose Update. QuarkXPress prompts you with a dialog box and asks you if it is OK to update the file. (You can also cancel the update through this dialog box.) If you choose OK, QuarkXPress creates a new low-resolution screen representation and updates its link to the modified graphic. You also see the graphic's status change to OK in the Missing/Modified Pictures dialog box.

Only if you have selected On (verify) as the option for Auto Picture Import in the General pane of the Default Document Preferences dialog box (Edit⇨Preferences⇨ Document, or ⌘+Y) are you prompted to update modified pictures when you open a QuarkXPress document.

Deleting a missing link

If a graphic is missing because you no longer want to use it and have deleted it from your computer, you can remove the link to it by either cutting the box or boxes that contain the picture or by clearing the picture from any boxes that contain it.

The Item tool must be active to cut a box; use ⌘+X or Edit⇨Cut. The Content tool must be active to clear a box; use Edit⇨Clear. Alternately, to clear a box, select it with either the Item or Content tool and use the new Item⇨Content⇨None menu option. In any of these cases, use the Show feature in the Missing/Modified Pictures dialog box or the Pictures pane in the Usage dialog box to find these boxes.

Understanding links

QuarkXPress supports several types of links to source files, particularly graphics. The terms used to describe links can be confusing, especially because people tend to use the word "link" generically, no matter what kind of link they are referring to. Links in QuarkXPress fall into two classes: static links to files and dynamic links to objects.

✦ *Static links:* These are the standard links common to most publishing programs. When you import a graphics file, QuarkXPress records the location of the file and its date and time stamp. The next time you open a document, QuarkXPress looks to see if the graphic is in its expected location and if its date and time stamp has changed. (If so, the graphic itself has been changed in some way since the last time QuarkXPress checked the file upon opening the document.) QuarkXPress makes these checks for two reasons:

   • First, by linking to the original graphic, QuarkXPress needs to make only a low-resolution image for use on-screen, which keeps the document size manageable and screen-redraw time quick. (When printing, QuarkXPress substitutes the actual high-resolution graphic.)

   • Second, by checking the links, QuarkXPress gives the layout artist the opportunity to use the latest version of a graphic. QuarkXPress lets you choose to always load the latest version of a graphic; ignore any updates to a graphic; or it asks you to decide whether or not to update the graphic. If the graphic is not where QuarkXPress expects it to be, the program asks you to find the graphic.

✦ *Dynamic links:* These are possible with a capability on the Mac called Publish and Subscribe, and with a capability called OLE in Windows. (Note that Publish and Subscribe, like OLE, opens the originating program, which means you need sufficient RAM for both.) Dynamic links differ from static links in two significant ways:

   • First, they are links to *objects* (called *editions* by Publish and Subscribe), not entire files. You might, for example, have a link to a range in a spreadsheet or to part of a graphic.

   • Second, the links can be updated any time, not just when you open a document. Dynamic links are managed through a Mac technology called Apple Events that lets programs communicate with one another and share objects among themselves in the background without user intervention or management. OLE uses a similar mechanism within Windows.

There are two basic types of dynamic links: *live* (automatic) and *manual:*

✦ *Live dynamic links:* With live dynamic links, there is regular communication between QuarkXPress and the program that created the object. If the linked object is changed in its original program, the new version is automatically sent to QuarkXPress, which automatically updates the object in the layout document to which it is linked.

✦ *Manual dynamic links:* With manual dynamic links, either the publisher or the subscriber must update the link by clicking the Send Edition Now button in the publishing program or the Get Edition Now button in the subscribing program. (In QuarkXPress, you double-click a picture box that contains a picture to get the dialog box that lets you click that button, as shown here. You also choose whether to make the link manual or automatic.) Either way, the subscriber always has the option of launching the original program with the original file so that modifications can be made. OLE has similar functions, as described elsewhere in this chapter.

```
 ┌────────────────────────────────────────────────────────┐
 │  Subscriber to:  [🖺 F Living Fire.TIF ▼]                 │
 │  ┌─Get Editions:──────────────────┐  ┌─────────────────┐ │
 │  │ ○ Automatically                │  │ Cancel Subscriber│ │
 │  │ ● Manually   [ Get Edition Now ]│  │  Open Publisher │ │
 │  │ Latest Edition:  Saturday, May 31, 1997 9:49:44 AM     │
 │  │ Last Received:   Friday, January 1, 1904 12:00:00 AM   │
 │                                       [ Cancel ] [  OK  ] │
 └────────────────────────────────────────────────────────┘
```

Completing the update process

When all missing or modified graphics are updated, their names disappear from the Missing/Modified Pictures dialog box or acquire a status of OK in the Pictures pane of the Usage dialog box. When you are done and exit the dialog box, remember to save your document. If you do not save your document, none of the updates are saved.

Whether you were working with missing or modified graphics (or both), you may be puzzled about how to leave the Missing/Modified Pictures dialog box because it does not offer an OK button. Instead, there's a Done button (on the Mac) or a Close button (in Windows) to do what OK usually does: accept the changes and close the dialog box. Alternately, you can click the close box in the dialog box's upper left (Mac) or upper right (Windows).

Using Publish and Subscribe

The Mac's System 7 brought with it a powerful feature called *Publish and Subscribe* that lets you create *live links* directly between applications. Mac OS 8 keeps this capability. This feature ensures that when you make changes to text or graphics in the program in which you originally created them, the text or graphics are instantly and automatically updated in other programs that use them. Through object embedding, you can launch the application that created the graphic in QuarkXPress and work on the graphic.

Windows and OLE

Windows users may recognize Publish and Subscribe as similar to Microsoft's OLE capability (which stands for Object Linking and Embedding and is pronounced like the Spanish word *olé*). OLE and Publish and Subscribe accomplish the same thing. The main difference is that the user of a source application on a Mac must explicitly publish a file to make it available for subscribing, whereas the user of a Windows source application needs only to copy or cut a graphic or text to put it in the Windows Clipboard for linking.

Another difference is that OLE is implemented on both the Mac and in Windows, so that some programs (such as Microsoft Excel) can have cross-platform links, but Publish and Subscribe is a Mac-only feature. Unfortunately, QuarkXPress supports OLE only in its Windows version, so you cannot have such cross-platform links. See the sidebar on the perils of OLE for more on OLE in QuarkXPress for Windows.

Creating live links

The first step to creating a live link is to create an *edition*, which is the result of publishing all or part of a file in its originating program. This edition file contains the link to the original file and program as well as a copy of the data itself (so that if the original file is lost, you still have a static image of it). Use the following steps to create a live link with the Mac's Publish and Subscribe feature. Figure 7-3 shows an example of how the Publish options work in two different applications.

STEPS: Creating a live link

1. Select the element(s) in the originating program that you want to publish. Some programs, such as Excel, require that you select the element(s); others, such as Photoshop, require that you publish the entire file. Refer to Figure 7-3 to see the dialog boxes in Excel 5.0 and Photoshop 4.0. Excel's is accessed via Edit⇨Publishing⇨Create Publisher, while Photoshop's is accessed via Edit⇨Create Publisher.

2. Most programs offer publish options that determine file format and degree of information published. For example, in Excel we clicked the Options button to get the Publish Options dialog box (below it), which lets us determine the file format and the resolution. In Photoshop, the options (PICT, TIFF, and EPS) are in the main Publish dialog box. (Because QuarkXPress can subscribe only to graphics, make sure that you publish your data as graphics. For example, the published Excel data will be used as a picture, not as a textual table. Also, make sure that you publish the data in PICT or EPS format—QuarkXPress cannot subscribe to other formats.)

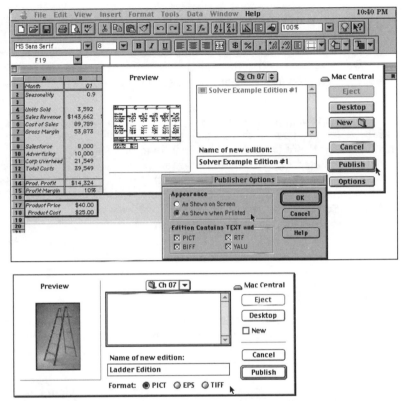

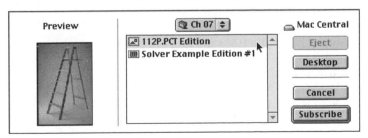

Figure 7-3: The Publish options in Microsoft Excel 5.0 (top) and Adobe Photoshop 4.0.

3. In QuarkXPress, create or select the picture box that you want to put the edition into. Make sure you selected the box with the Content tool, and then choose Edit⇨Subscribe To. The dialog box is similar to the Get Picture dialog box (see Figure 7-4).

Figure 7-4: The Subscribe To dialog box.

The down side of the live-linking

We don't believe Publish and Subscribe's live-link feature is significantly useful for most QuarkXPress users to be worth the hassle and system memory requirements. QuarkXPress's own graphic-links updating features handle most of what Publish and Subscribe offer.

We do see a use for people publishing changing data, such as prices from an Excel table, but because the data must be published as a graphic, users must choose between printing data graphically (when they'd most likely want to format the data in QuarkXPress so that it looks like the rest of their document) or manually reimporting the updated data when it is changed. Of course, someone will have to tell them that it has changed, or they will have to check themselves before finalizing their layout. For these people, a better bet is an XTension like Em Software's Xcatalog, which translates database files into formatted QuarkXPress layouts. (For more on XTensions, see Part 6.)

Updating live links

After you have subscribed to an edition, you can control when it is updated via Edit⟹Subscriber Options (see Figure 7-5). The options are described in the following list:

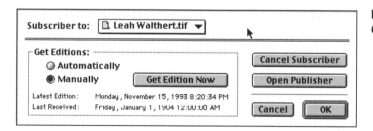

Figure 7-5: The Subscriber Options dialog box.

If the Content tool is active and you double-click a subscribed-to picture, the Subscriber Options dialog box automatically appears.

✦ **Get Editions:** The Get Editions portion of the dialog box offers you the choice of Automatically or Manually. The default option is Automatically, which means that whenever the source object is altered, the new version will be placed into QuarkXPress.

✦ **Get Edition Now button:** No matter which choice you make (Automatically or Manually), you can click the Get Edition Now button to update the link to the source.

✦ **Cancel Subscriber button:** Clicking the Cancel Subscriber button breaks the link to the edition. The current image remains in your document unless you remove it from the picture box.

✦ **Open Publisher button:** Clicking the Open Publisher button launches the source application so that you can modify the source object. Note that the application will likely not appear over your current application. If you use the Mac OS task list, you will see the application and be able to select it, bringing it to the foreground with the linked file already loaded. The Mac OS task list, called the *applications menu* before Mac OS 8, is the list of open applications you get at the far right of the menu bar. The icons for Systems 7 and 8 vary as follows:

 The Application menu's Finder icon in System 7

 The Mac OS task list's Mac OS icon in Mac OS 8

Deleting and finding an edition file

The publishing program has a menu item called Publisher Options (in the Edit menu) to cancel the publisher (shown in Figure 7-6 for Photoshop), which deletes the edition file. If the publisher is canceled, a static copy of the last version is retained in your document.

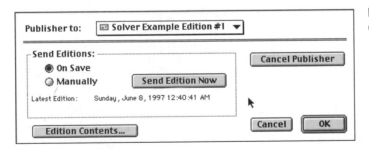

Figure 7-6: The Publisher Options dialog box.

You can locate the edition file by clicking and holding the mouse over the filename at the top of either the Subscriber Options or Publisher Options dialog box; the folder hierarchy displays, as shown in Figure 7-7.

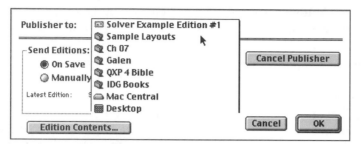

Figure 7-7: The file hierarchy in the Subscriber Options and Publisher Options dialog boxes lets you see where an edition file resides.

Launching source applications

A simpler way to use the Subscribe feature is to launch the application that created a graphic used in a QuarkXPress layout. To do this, you don't have to use Publish. Any graphic imported into QuarkXPress—via Edit⇨Subscribe To or File⇨Get Picture (or ⌘+E)—may have its originating application launched so that you can work on the graphic.

The perils of OLE

In Windows, QuarkXPress lets you use Microsoft's OLE (Object Linking and Embedding) technology to import pictures. This technology is not as good as the Mac's Publish and Subscribe. Here's why you'll probably want to avoid using OLE import (via Edit⇨Insert Object):

✦ Only objects imported via OLE can be dynamically updated from your QuarkXPress layout. (On the Mac, any imported picture can be dynamically updated.) Pictures imported through the Get Picture command (Ctrl+E) must be updated by reimporting the pictures or by reopening the QuarkXPress file and having the Auto Picture Import option set to On or On (verify) in the General pane of the Default Document Preferences dialog box (accessed via Ctrl+Y).

✦ OLE takes a lot of RAM, and you'll often get error messages when trying to import or update OLE objects—even if you have 40MB or more of RAM. That's because OLE is not entirely stable and because many programs don't implement OLE well (because programmers found it to be very complex).

However, if you do want to use OLE, the way to do it is to select a picture box with the Content tool and use Edit⇨Insert Object to get the dialog box shown here (at left). You need to select the object type from the list and select either Create New (to create a new object in the appropriate program) or Create from File (to import an existing object). If you choose Create from File, use the Browse button (it appears under the filename field) to find an existing file, and be sure to check the Link box to ensure that the OLE file has a live link so that any updates to it are made to your QuarkXPress layout. Don't be surprised if it takes several minutes for the link to be made.

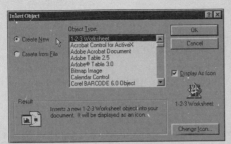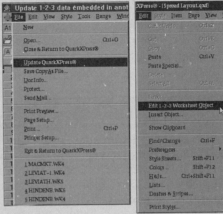

If you're creating a new object, OLE launches the appropriate program. After you're done creating the object, use the program's File menu to make the object available to QuarkXPress. The menu looks somewhat like the menu shown here (center), which comes from Lotus 1-2-3. Note that there are three options: Close & Return to QuarkXPress, Update QuarkXPress, and Exit & Return to QuarkXPress. Close & Return closes the object but leaves the program open, while Exit & Return closes both the object and the program. If you choose either one, you are asked whether you want to update QuarkXPress with the file; if you don't answer Yes, the object won't be updated until you later update it from QuarkXPress or from the program that created it. The Update menu option sends QuarkXPress the current version of the object and leaves both the program and file open.

Whenever you want to update the OLE link from within QuarkXPress, select the picture box and use Edit➪Edit *[program name]* Object, as shown here (at right). This menu item appears only if you have selected an OLE object. Selecting this menu option launches the originating program.

STEPS: Launching an application

1. Use the Edit➪Subscriber Options (refer to Figure 7-5)—either the Content tool or Item tool may be active—and select the Open Publisher button. (If the Content tool is active, you simply can double-click the picture box to get this dialog box.)

2. Select Open Publisher to load the program with the source file open in it. Note that the application will likely not appear over your current application.

3. Use the Mac OS task list (the list of open applications you get at the far right of the menu bar, previously called the Application menu) to select the application and bring it to the foreground. (The other options in the dialog box are irrelevant, and clicking them will have no effect.)

Working with Text Links

QuarkXPress offers fewer features for text links than it does for graphics links. Its text-link features are essentially limited to export capabilities. The following sections cover this topic in detail.

Loading the latest text

One of the few omissions in QuarkXPress is the ability to link text so that you can keep versions of your source text current with your layout. This ability is particularly handy if you want to ensure that your layout uses the latest version of text that changes periodically, such as a price list. Unfortunately, even with the Publish and Subscribe capabilities, you cannot get around this omission because QuarkXPress treats subscribed objects as graphics, not as text. The only workable option is to reimport changed source text. Before you perform this task, first select all the old text with Edit⇨Select All, or ⌘+A. You don't need to cut or delete the text (although you can if you want to); any text that is selected gets replaced when you get new text into the box, so by selecting all before reimporting your text, you replace the old text.

Exporting the latest text

Fortunately, QuarkXPress offers a way to save changed text in your document to a word processing file. This feature is beneficial if you need to use the text in other documents or just want to ensure that all versions of text are the same throughout the office. To export text, you must first select the box containing the text with the Content tool. You can highlight specific text to export, or you can just make sure that your text cursor is active in a story that you want to export. After you are ready to export, invoke the Save Text dialog box, shown in Figure 7-8, by selecting File⇨Save Text or using Option+⌘+E.

The Save Text dialog box gives you the following options, which you can select in any order before clicking the Save button:

✦ Choose the disk and folder that you want to save the text file to.

✦ Choose Entire Story if you want all the text in the current chain saved. (This is easier than remembering to use ⌘+A, or Edit⇨Select All, before invoking the dialog box.) Choose Selected Text if you want to save just the highlighted text. If no text is highlighted, both options are grayed out and Entire Story is automatically enabled.

✦ Pick the format to save in. When choosing the format, pick your word processor's native format unless you want to export the text for use in other QuarkXPress documents. In that case, use the XPress Tags format, which includes all the codes needed to bring over style tags and formatting.

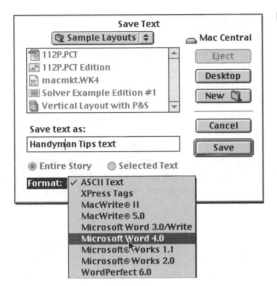

Figure 7-8: The Save Text dialog box.

 In Windows QuarkXPress, there is an additional option in the Save Text dialog box: Mac OS Line Endings. Check this if you are exporting files for use on a Macintosh. While not necessary for cross-platform formats like Word, this option is helpful for options like XPress Tags and ASCII. The PC and Mac use slightly different carriage-return codes, and not all programs automatically know how to handle the two variants.

Text formatting tips and cautions

Not all word processing programs (or all versions of a program) support all formatting available in QuarkXPress, but most word processing programs support the vast majority of formatting features. Only QuarkXPress's own XPress Tags format retains all QuarkXPress formatting.

Even though the XPress Tags format retains all text formatting information, however, it cannot convert a picture into ASCII. If your text contains anchored boxes (see the next section), those boxes are not included when you export the text in XPress Tags format.

Another way to export text is to copy it to the Clipboard and paste it into your word processor or other program. But text copied via the Clipboard loses all or most formatting, including such character formatting as font and size, and such paragraph formatting as indentations and leading. Special symbols may be lost if you use a typeface in your word processor other than the one in the QuarkXPress document because not all fonts have all characters available.

Anchoring Boxes and Lines

QuarkXPress lets you select a text box, a picture box, or a line and *anchor* it (attach it) to the text that surrounds it. You may want to do this to keep a graphic with a certain passage of text. Anchored items *flow* with the text to which they are anchored, even during the most massive edits. One common application of anchored boxes is to create a page that incorporates icons as small graphic elements in a stream of text. A movie guide that uses different graphics to indicate the critic's opinion and a design that uses icons as paragraph breaks are examples of layouts that would benefit from using anchors. Figure 7-9 shows an example of the latter. QuarkXPress treats anchored elements as individual characters of text. After you anchor them, you can select, cut, copy, paste, and delete these items just as if they were single characters of text.

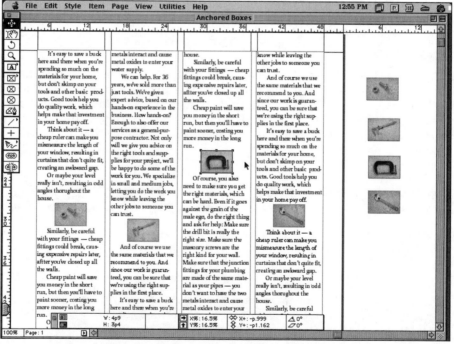

Figure 7-9: Anchored picture boxes used as breaks between sections in a story.

New Feature

Version 4 now lets you anchor lines, not just boxes. Also, earlier versions of QuarkXPress allowed only rectangular anchored boxes, but version 4 lets you create anchored boxes of any shape.

STEPS: Anchoring boxes or lines

1. Using the Item tool, select the box or line to be anchored into text.

2. Cut or copy the item in the same way that you cut or copy any single text character (use Edit⇨Cut or Edit⇨Copy, or the keyboard shortcuts ⌘+X or ⌘+C).

3. Using the Content tool, click to position the text cursor at the location in the text where you want to anchor the item.

4. Paste in the item (select Edit⇨Paste, or ⌘+V).

Modifying anchored boxes and lines

After the box becomes an anchored box, you can modify it by selecting it and then choosing Item⇨Modify, or ⌘+M, to display the Box pane in the Modify dialog box. Note that the Box pane, shown in Figure 7-10, is slightly different than the standard Box pane for a picture box or text box. What's different is the Align with Text section, which tells QuarkXPress how to align the text that follows the anchored box. You have two options in the Align with Text section of the Box pane. (You can also modify anchored lines with the Line pane in the Modify dialog box.)

✦ **Ascent:** This aligns the top of the text with the bottom of the anchored box.

✦ **Baseline:** This aligns the text in relation to the baseline of the line of text in which the box lies. If you select Baseline, you can also shift the box up or down in relation to the text baseline by using the Offset field to indicate how much space you want.

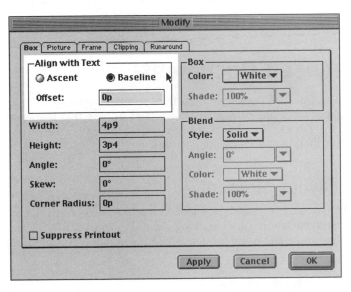

Figure 7-10: The Box pane's Align with Text options for anchored boxes.

In the previous version of QuarkXPress, you could adjust an anchored box's size only to the left or bottom. In version 4, you can adjust its size in any direction. However, do not import a box or line that is wider than the text column, and do not extend the box (or line) width past the boundaries of the text column or the text box into another text box. Doing so causes text to stop flowing past the anchored box.

Using the Modify dialog box

Because an anchored box is a box, you can use the standard panes in the Modify dialog box—Runaround, Clipping, Frame, and Picture or Text—depending on whether the anchored box is a text box or picture box. Thus, you can specify a runaround margin to determine the space above, below, and to the sides of the anchored box. Anchored boxes may only have a runaround of Item, so the only thing you can set in the Runaround pane is the amount of margin around the anchored box. You can, of course, use or create a clipping path for the item in the Clipping pane. But your text wraps around the box, not the path. (Likewise, you can set runaround for an anchored line using the Runaround pane.)

QuarkXPress 4 gets rid of the separate Anchored Box Specifications dialog box and controls, moving the few anchored-box–specific controls into the Box pane of the Modify dialog box.

Using paragraph formatting commands

Because the anchored graphic is part of a paragraph, you can apply several paragraph formatting commands in the Style menu and Measurements palette. Examples include making the paragraph centered or indented, or flipping the box. You cannot do character formatting. Although these Style menu and Measurements palette options are available, they affect the invisible anchor character, not the anchored box.

Copying Between Documents

One of our favorite QuarkXPress layout features enables copying layout elements or even entire pages from one document to another. To use this feature, open both documents and then drag-copy the item from one document to another by using the methods described in the following sections.

Copying a layout element

To copy a *layout element* from one document to another, open both documents. Display them next to each other by choosing View➪Windows➪Tile Documents—in Windows, use Windows➪Tile Horizontally or Windows➪Tile Vertically. (You can resize the windows using the resize handle at the windows' lower-right corner.) Select the item that you want to copy in the source document and hold the mouse button as you drag the element to the destination document (see Figure 7-11).

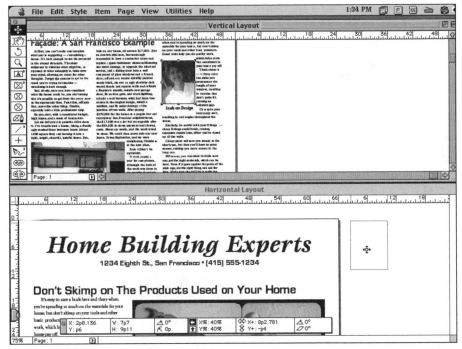

Figure 7-11: Simply drag a box with the Item tool from one document to another to copy it.

Note

You must use the Item tool to select the item to be copied, or hold down the ⌘ key before you click and drag. The page view must *not* be thumbnail.

Copying a page

To copy a *page* from one document to another, open both documents. Display them next to each other by choosing View⇨Windows⇨Tile Documents (on the Mac), or Window⇨Tile Horizontally or Window⇨Tile Vertically (in Windows). Select the page that you want to copy in the source document and hold the mouse button as you drag the page to the destination document. Figure 7-12 shows the result of a page being copied from the document at left to the document at right.

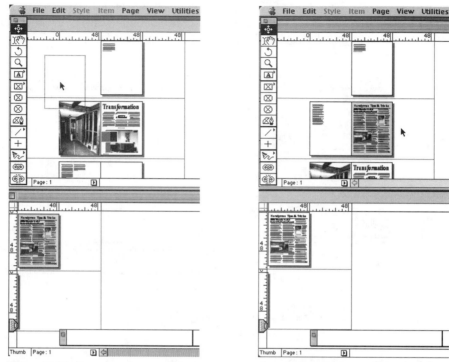

Figure 7-12: You can drag entire pages across documents if you work in thumbnail view. At left is the copy in action, at right is the result.

When copying a page, the page view for both documents must be thumbnail (select View⇨Thumbnails, or Shift+F6). Note that you must drag the page next to or between pages. You can tell you have done this if the cursor changes to any of the following icons:

�muⱵ	Insert right
⊤	Insert down
◻	Add page

Tip

If you press the Option key while you choose View⇨Windows⇨Tile Documents (or the Alt key when choosing one of the Tile menu options in the Window menu in Windows), all open documents will automatically change to thumbnail view. On the Mac only, if you press the Shift key and click a document window's title bar, you get the same submenu as you get when you choose View⇨Windows.

Page and element copying quirks

Here are three special notes on the page and element copying techniques:

✦ Drag-copying layout elements or entire pages from a source document to a destination document has no effect on the source document.

✦ You cannot copy a page into a document whose page dimensions are smaller in either direction than those of the source document. If the page sizes do differ, the (larger) size of the destination document's page is used.

✦ When you copy a page from one document to another, the master page upon which that page is based is also copied to the destination document.

✦　　✦　　✦

Working with Pages

✦ ✦ ✦ ✦

In This Chapter

Adding and deleting pages

Rearranging pages

Numbering sections and pages

Generating "continued" markers

✦ ✦ ✦ ✦

Sometime during the layout process or after you place all the text boxes, picture boxes, and rules, you may want to make some structural changes to the document. For example, you may decide that an element on page three should be moved to page six. You may edit the copy so that what initially occupied nine pages fits on an eight-page spread. Or you may realize that, because the document has grown larger than you first anticipated, you need to add page numbers or break the document into sections. This is what we like to call *managing the layout*. QuarkXPress has a full set of features that let you easily handle the tasks associated with this topic, and this chapter covers them in detail.

Adding and Deleting Pages

In the early stages of the document layout process, you don't need to think much about adding pages, provided that you enable Auto Page Insertion in the General pane of the Default Document Preferences dialog box. If you do, QuarkXPress automatically inserts enough pages to hold the text files you import. At any point in the layout process, you can change the specifications that dictate where those new pages occur. The initial default location is the end of the story (the current set of linked text boxes), but you may prefer to change it to the end of the document or to the end of the section.

Changing the page insert location

To change the location where pages are automatically inserted, choose Edit⇨Preferences⇨Document (⌘+Y) to display the Default Document Preferences dialog box. In the General pane, choose End of Story, End of Section, or End of Document (or choose Off to disable automatic page insertion) and then choose OK to close the dialog box.

Inserting pages

After you place most of the text and pictures in a document, you may decide to insert one or more additional pages. To do this, choose Page⇨Insert to display the Insert Pages dialog box, shown in Figure 8-1. In the Insert field, enter the number of pages to insert. Then click the button that corresponds to the location where you want the pages to be inserted. QuarkXPress automatically renumbers the inserted pages and those that follow.

If you include a prefix in the document page numbers (an example of a prefix is the *20-* in page *20-1*), be sure to include the prefix when you specify pages to insert, delete, or move. You can also specify absolute page numbers by using a plus sign (+) before the absolute page number. For example, if the page you want to move is numbered 20-1, but it is actually the thirtieth page in the document, you can use either 20-1 or +30. Figure 8-1 shows an example of such prefixed page numbering (look for the page number, 5-1).

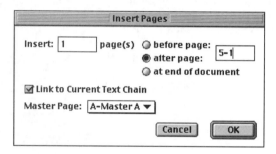

Figure 8-1: The Insert Pages dialog box.

Deleting pages

To delete one or more pages, choose Page⇨Delete to display the Delete Pages dialog box, and then enter the numbers of the pages to be deleted. After the deletion, QuarkXPress automatically renumbers the pages.

Rearranging Pages

Rearranging pages involves moving them to different locations in the document. One way to move pages is to use the Move Pages dialog box. Another way (see the sidebar on the thumbnail advantage) is to use the thumbnail view. The following sections cover each of these methods.

Using the Move Pages dialog box

Choose Page⇨Move to display the Move Pages dialog box shown in Figure 8-2. If you want to move just one page, enter its page number in the Move page(s) field. If you want to move a range of pages, enter the first page in the range in the Move page(s) field and the last page in the Thru field. The buttons in the dialog box let you select where you want the pages to end up. You can choose one of the following for a specified page:

✦ before page

✦ after page

✦ to end of document

Figure 8-2: The Move Pages dialog box.

Using thumbnail view

You can also rearrange pages by reducing the document to thumbnail view. Choose View⇨Thumbnails, or Shift+F6, and then drag the thumbnails into the new page order. After the document is displayed in thumbnail mode, select the page you want to move and then drag it to its new place in the document. When the pointer changes from an arrow to a blank page icon, you can release the mouse button to finalize the placement of the page. Figure 8-3 shows such a document displayed in thumbnail view, ready for a page move.

The thumbnail advantage

One advantage to the thumbnail method is that you can more easily visualize the effects of your page moves; you can actually see them occurring in thumbnail view. Another advantage is that during a page move, the pointer indicates how the move affects other pages in the document, as follows:

✦ If the pointer looks like a miniature page, it means that the move does not change the placement of other pages in the document.

✦ If the pointer looks like a left-pointing or right-pointing arrow, it means that moving that particular page bumps pages to the left or to the right.

✦ If the pointer looks like a down-pointing arrow, it means that successive pages will be moved.

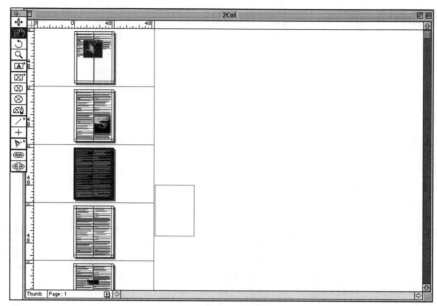

Figure 8-3: You can move a page by dragging it into position while the document is in thumbnail view.

Tip

If you want to move a set of adjacent pages (for example, pages three through six) in thumbnail view, hold down the Shift key while you select the first and last pages in the range. To select several, noncontiguous pages, hold the ⌘ key and click each page.

Numbering Sections and Pages

Sometimes you may want to number pages in a QuarkXPress document consecutively, from first page to last. Other times, such as when the document grows to an unwieldy size or when you are required to do so because of prescribed formatting standards, you may want to break the document into sections. Technical manuals or books with chapters are often broken into sections to make it easier for the reader to locate information (see Chapter 16 for more information on books and chapters).

Tip

If the document is divided into sections, you generally want the page numbers to reflect the document's structure. For example, give the eleventh page in Section 5 the page number *5-11* so that readers can easily determine where pages and sections are in relation to the rest of the publication.

Breaking a document into sections

Sometimes you might not need all of QuarkXPress's book editing capabilities, which are described in Chapter 16, but you might still have a document that needs to be divided into sections. To break a document into sections, first go to your intended first page in a section. Choose Page⇨Section to display the Section dialog box, shown in Figure 8-4. Check the button next to Section Start to make the current page the first page of the section.

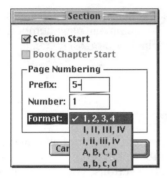

Figure 8-4: The Section dialog box.

You can then select the numbering format that you want applied to the section (see the sidebar on choosing a page numbering format). You can enter a prefix (in the page number 5-1, the prefix is 5-) up to four characters long in the Prefix field. In the Number field, enter the number that you want assigned to the first page in the section. The default Number setting is 1, but you may want to change it to a different number. For example, if you are producing a book that already has pages 1 and 2 preprinted, you want your QuarkXPress pages to begin with a page number of 3.

Note

If you want a space, hyphen, or other separator between the section prefix and the page number, you must enter that separator as part of the prefix name, as we did in Figure 8-4.

Choosing a page numbering format

The Format field offers a list box showing the possible formats for automatic page numbering. These include:

✦ Arabic numerals (1, 2, 3, 4)

✦ Uppercase or lowercase Roman numerals (I, II, III, IV or i, ii, iii, iv)

✦ Uppercase or lowercase letters (A, B, C, D or a, b, c, d)

The format that you select applies to all page numbers that are automatically generated in this section of the document. You can then use QuarkXPress's automatic page numbers in your documents' headers and footers (called *folios* in magazines and newsletters).

Automatically numbering the pages

The typical way of instructing QuarkXPress to automatically number all pages in a document is to place the Current Text Box Page Number character (⌘+3) on the master page. If, however, the document is divided into sections, you may want to add automatic page numbers on regular pages in text boxes that have more specific text. For example, the text box for a footer might include the chapter name or current topic, as well as the page number. Use the following steps to do this.

STEPS: Adding automatic page numbers on regular pages

1. To enter the Current Text Box Page Number character, create a text box of the approximate size necessary to hold the page number.

2. Position the text box where you want the page number to appear.

3. Using the Content tool, select the text box and enter ⌘+3 to insert the automatic page number. (On a master page, this number is displayed as "<#>".)

4. You can then modify the font, size, and attributes of the page-number character. Automatic page numbers take on the modified attributes.

Generating "Continued" Markers

Whenever your document contains a *jump* (a place where text that cannot fit entirely on one page is continued on another, linked page), consider adding automatically generated *Continued on. . .* and *Continued from. . .* markers to the document. To use this feature, draw text boxes at the locations in the document where you want the *Continued on. . .* and *Continued from. . .* markers to appear, and make sure the boxes are linked. Press ⌘+4 (in a *Continued on* box) to place the marker for the next text box's page-number character. Press ⌘+2 (in a *Continued from* box) to have the page number for the previous box holding the story to automatically appear.

Figure 8-5 shows the *Continued on. . .* marker, which says *<None>* because we haven't yet linked the box to the corresponding box on the page that will hold the overflow text. After we do, the marker will automatically reflect the continued-on page number.

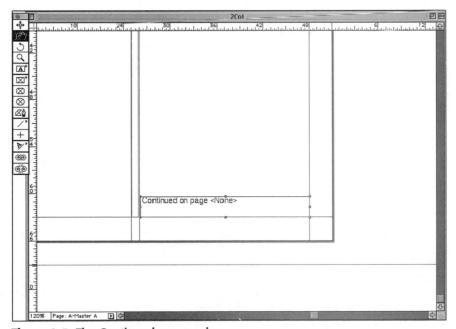

Figure 8-5: The Continued on... marker.

Footers and headers

Magazines and newsletters usually have straightforward headers and footers (or folios), composed of the page number, publication title, and issue date, or some combination of these three elements. Typically, these folios are implemented on master pages (with one folio on the left master page and one folio for the right master page), because the text doesn't vary from page to page except for the current page number (which QuarkXPress can insert automatically). A typical folio setup is shown here.

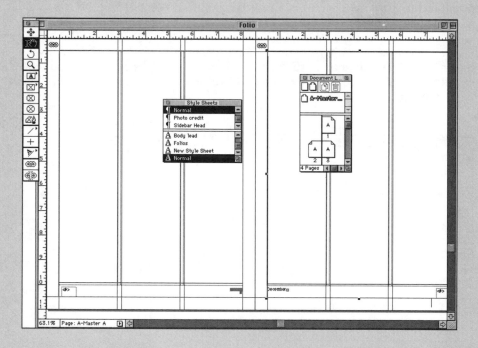

Other documents—such as manuals and books—often have more detailed headers and footers. Often, the header or footer includes information specific to the current chapter or even page. If you do want a header for each section that includes the page number and chapter name, you need to decide whether you can put this header on a master page (so that it automatically appears on each page) or whether to copy the appropriate text box to each page in the section manually. The answer depends on how you use master pages. If you have a different master page for each section, you'd have a header text box appropriate for each section on that section's master page. If you have only one master page, you need to copy the text box customized for a certain section to each page in that section.

You may in fact use both methods if you need further customization. For example, perhaps the footer uses the chapter name, so that it can be implemented in the section's master page, but the header uses the page's current topic. In this case you have to manually edit that on each document page in the section. An example of such a document is shown here.

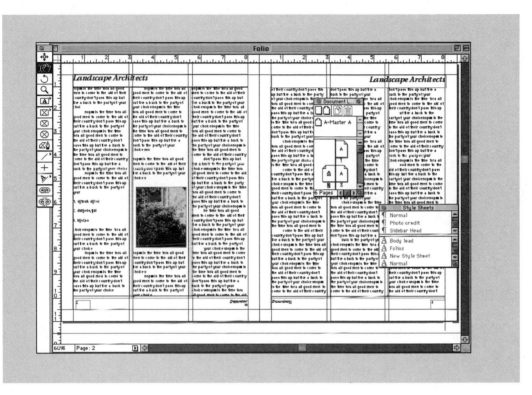

Special Layout Techniques

◆ ◆ ◆ ◆

In This Chapter

Adding rules and lines

Framing text and picture boxes

Creating frame styles

Saving a page as an EPS file

Aligning multiple elements

◆ ◆ ◆ ◆

This chapter deals with all the creative (and somewhat *special*) things you can do with your QuarkXPress document layouts. Here is where you'll learn about adding rules and frames (even creating frame styles), anchoring boxes to surrounding text, copying elements and pages from document to document, aligning multiple elements, and some new features in version 4 that give you even greater control over saving pages as EPS files.

Adding Rules and Lines

Rules (lines) often add a nice finishing touch to a document page. You can use rules to make a headline more interesting, to mark where one section of text ends and another begins, or to separate parts of a page. In a multicolumn spread that includes separate pieces of information, rules added over the heads of each piece help to clearly delineate where one piece ends and another begins. We use the words *rule* and *line* interchangeably.

The ability to create a Bézier rule, using either the Bézier Line tool or the Freehand Line tool, is new in QuarkXPress 4. Bézier lines are also referred to as Bézier curves. These features are described in the following section.

Creating rules

In QuarkXPress, you create, size, and position rules much the same way you do text boxes and picture boxes. Use the following steps to create rules (using the tools shown here):

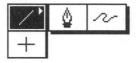

✦ **To create a rule:** Select either of the two straight-line drawing tools: the Orthogonal Line tool (which looks like a cross-hair) or the Diagonal Line tool, or one of the pop-out Line tools that allow you to draw a Bézier rule or a freehand rule. The Orthogonal Line tool draws rules that are horizontal and vertical only; the Diagonal Line tool can draw rules in any direction. (The Diagonal Line tool can also draw a horizontal or vertical rule, as well as a rule at a 45-degree angle, if you hold down the Shift key as you draw.) The Bézier and freehand Line tools let you draw lines that are not straight; as you draw a Bézier line, QuarkXPress creates a series of points. You can then click and drag on these points to change the shape of the Bézier line. Figure 9-1 shows some examples of rules drawn using each of the line-drawing tools. The Measurements palette shows the settings for the dotted line, including the pick list for rule types.

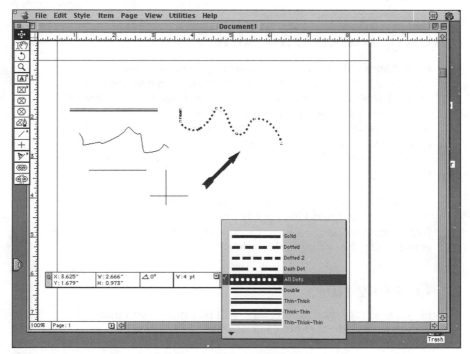

Figure 9-1: Examples of rules (lines) drawn with the Line tools in QuarkXPress.

✦ **To size a rule:** Use the Measurements palette to select the rule's width and length. Or drag the rule's sizing handles until the rule is the desired length.

✦ **To select a rule type and line end:** To select a rule type (dotted, doubled, solid, and so on) and line end (arrow point, and so on), select the rule to make it active. Choose Item⇨Modify (⌘+M) to display the Line pane in the Modify dialog box (shown in Figure 9-2) and make the selections you want. Another way of selecting a rule type is to choose one of the line selections in the Measurements palette (see Figure 9-2). This palette also offers a drop-down list box (at far right) that lets you pick from a variety of line endings, including arrows.

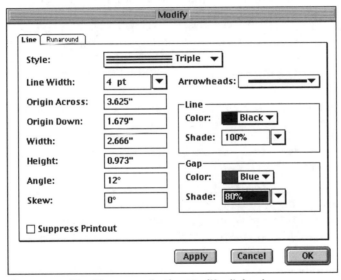

Figure 9-2: The Line pane in the Modify dialog box.

Note

If you select a rule type composed of two or more lines, keep in mind that multiple lines may not appear if the line weight is too small. This is because the line weight you specify is the *total* line weight for the double or triple line. A line weight of 1 point for a double or triple line is so small that the line may appear as a single, 1-point line.

Working with lines

The following items outline a few directions and concepts for manipulating lines once you have created them. Remember to keep it simple (more on that later), and for more control over your lines, check out the QuarkXPress line mode feature, which is described shortly.

✦ **To reposition a line:** Select the line and then drag it into position. You can also reposition a line by entering new X and Y coordinates in the Measurements palette or by entering position coordinates in the Line pane of the Modify dialog box (choose Item⇨Modify, or ⌘+M, to display the dialog box).

✦ **To rotate a line:** Choose First Point, Midpoint, or Last Point from the Mode pop-up menu, and then enter a value (in degrees, in .001-degree increments) in the Angle field of the Modify dialog box (Item⇨Modify, or ⌘+M). Or choose one of these modes and enter a value in the rotation field of the Measurements palette.

✦ **To apply color or shade to a line:** With the line active (selected with the Item tool), choose Style⇨Color to display the Color submenu, from which you can select the color you want to use. To change the shade of the line, choose Style⇨Shade to display the Shade submenu, from which you can select the shade value. To select a shade value different from the preset shade values in the Shade submenu, choose Other, and then enter the value in the Shade field of the Modify dialog box. You can also use the Colors palette (View⇨Show Colors).

✦ **To apply color or shade to a gap in a line:** If the line style has dots, dashes, or stripes, you can apply a color and/or shade to the gap. Choose Item⇨Modify (⌘+M) to display the Modify dialog box. Select the color and shade in the fields that appear in the Gap area of the Modify dialog box (shown in Figure 9-2).

✦ **To specify the thickness of a line:** Choose Style⇨Width to display the Width submenu. Select one of the preset line widths from the submenu, or select Other to display the Modify dialog box. Enter a value in the Line Width field. You can also use the Measurements palette to specify the thickness of the line.

✦ **To reshape a line:** Choose Item⇨Shape to display the Shape pick list. From the pick list, choose a shape and the line will automatically reshape.

Tip

If you change a Bézier line into a Bézier box, by default you will end up with a very long, very thin box. However, if you hold down the Option key while you choose Item⇨Shape, QuarkXPress will connect the ends of the line and give you a box that is probably more like what you were expecting.

✦ **To reshape a Bézier line:** Click the line's points, curve handles, or line segments and drag them into the desired position. The line at the right in Figure 9-3 is a Bézier line with its points and line segments visible. Also note that the Measurements palette includes buttons that let you change corner points into smooth points, smooth points into corner points, curved segments into straight segments, and straight segments into curved segments. The techniques described in Chapter 5 for reshaping Bézier boxes also work for Bézier lines. Chapter 20 covers artistic techniques for Bézier lines.

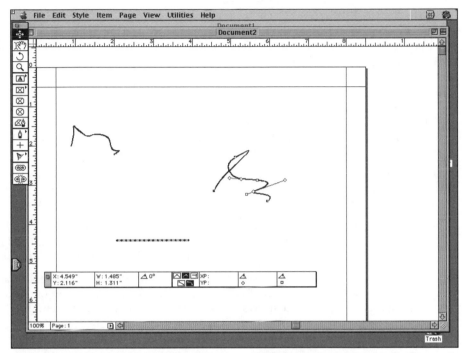

Figure 9-3: The Bézier line at the right is a reshaped version of the Bézier line at the left.

Tip

You can change a straight line into a Bézier line by choosing Item⇨Shape to display the Shape pick list; the bottom shape in the pick list is a Bézier line. When you do this, the line will keep its shape, but it will have Bézier points and handles so you can reshape it.

> ✦ **To select an arrow:** You can apply endcaps (arrowheads and arrowtails) to a selected line by using the Endcap options in the Measurements palette.

Keeping it simple

As we emphasized in earlier layout chapters, simplicity is almost always better. This axiom applies to rules as well. Some of the most obnoxious layouts you'll ever see are those that use a variety of rule types and widths on the same page. Avoid creating a bad page design—don't use too many rules and arrows. If you do use rules and arrows, keep them simple and keep their weights on the light side. Even for a double or triple line, anything more than about 8 points is just too heavy and overpowers the page.

The line mode feature

With a feature called *line mode,* QuarkXPress lets you control the positions, angles, and lengths of straight (non-Bézier) lines in four ways, which are shown in Figure 9-4 and described as follows:

✦ **Endpoints:** These show the coordinates for the beginning and end of the line. In the Measurements palette, the X1 field shows the horizontal position of the first endpoint and the Y1 field shows the vertical position of the first endpoint; the X2 field shows the horizontal position of the last endpoint and the Y2 field shows the vertical position of the last endpoint.

✦ **Midpoint:** This shows the coordinates for the center of the line. In the Measurements palette, the XC field shows the horizontal position of the midpoint and the YC field shows the vertical position of the midpoint.

✦ **First point:** This shows the coordinates for the first point of the line. In the Measurements palette, the X1 field shows the horizontal position of the first endpoint and the Y1 field shows the vertical position of the first endpoint.

✦ **Last point:** This shows the coordinates for the last point of the line. In the Measurements palette, the X2 field shows the horizontal position of the last endpoint and the Y2 field shows the vertical position of the last endpoint.

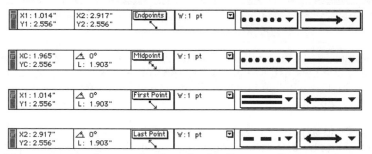

Figure 9-4: The four modes for selecting line coordinates and patterns.

By changing modes, you change the coordinates that appear in the Measurements palette or the Line pane of the Modify dialog box. Figure 9-4 shows the Measurements palette for each of the four modes. Note how the labels for X and Y coordinates change depending on which mode is selected.

Note

You can rotate a line no matter what its line mode is. The Rotate icon in the Measurements palette will not appear, however, if you are using Endpoints as the line mode.

Framing Text Boxes and Picture Boxes

Framing is a QuarkXPress option that lets you add a plain or fancy line around the edge of a single box or around each of the boxes in a group. Most of the time, the text boxes and picture boxes that you use to lay out a page will be unadorned, but you may occasionally want to add a frame. To add a frame, use the Frame Specifications dialog box, accessible via Item⇨Frame (⌘+B). (Chapter 20 explains how to create your own frame patterns.) Figure 9-5 shows the Frame pane in the Modify dialog box and a text box surrounded by a frame. Notice that we kept the line type to create a better visual effect. Use the following steps to add a frame to a box or group of boxes.

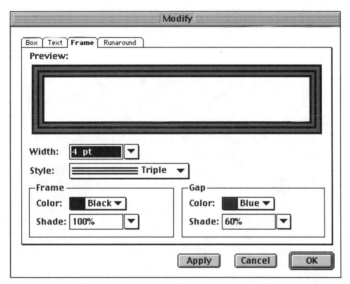

Figure 9-5: The Frame pane and an example of a framed text box.

STEPS: Framing a box

1. Use the Item tool to select the box or group and then choose Item⇨Frame (⌘+B) to display the Frame pane of the Modify dialog box, as shown in Figure 9-5.

2. From the Style scroll box, select one of the seven available frame styles.

3. In the Width field, enter a line width for the frame line. You can enter a value or pick one from the list box. You can enter values not shown in the list box as well. You can make the frame as wide as you want as long as it is not too big to fit the bounds of the box. Remember that the width you select is the total

width of the frame line. (If you choose one of the frame styles that has more than one line, you must make the lines wide enough to accommodate the frame style. This is what we did with the frame in Figure 9-5; the frame style is a triple line, and we made it 4 points wide so that the three lines could be displayed.)

4. In the Frame area, select a color from the Color list box. The default setting is black. If you want to change the shade of the field, select a shade from the Shade list box or type a percentage value (up to 100 percent, in 0.1 percent increments) in the Shade field. You can enter values that do not appear in the list box.

5. In the Gap field, select a color and/or a shade percentage for the gap. In the example in Figure 9-5, we specified a blue, 60 percent gap color; this color and shade appear in the space between the triple lines of the frame.

Framing tips and tricks

Just because you create a frame around a box, it doesn't necessarily follow that you want the frame to appear on the final, printed document. For one of our applications, a newsletter, we use a 0.5-point frame as a keyline to indicate to our commercial printer which boxes we want to have photos added into. During the actual printing process, the printer removes the frame line, leaving only the photo.

Sometimes you might want to draw the frame inside the margins of the box, and other times you might want it outside the margins. To control whether the frames you subsequently create are inside or outside their boxes, choose Edit➪Preferences➪Document (⌘+Y) to display the Default Document Preferences dialog box; then choose the General tab. In the Framing field, select either Inside or Outside.

After you've created a frame around a box, you cannot change whether the frame occurs outside or inside the box. A workaround (if you change your mind in the middle of a layout), so that all framed boxes appear to be similar, is to make smaller the boxes that have a frame on the outside so that they appear to be the same size as the other boxes. For example, if you have a 6-point frame, make the box 12 points smaller in both width and height (this change takes care of the extra 6 points at the left and right and at the top and bottom).

When you use framing, keep in mind that understatement is an art. The difference between a simple, narrow frame and a complicated, larger one is often the difference between speaking quietly and shouting. Understatement works to your advantage by keeping the reader's attention—as opposed to losing it by bombarding the reader's visual senses. Be careful not to make the frame line too wide or complex, which can upset the balance of a page. For simple framing, we prefer using a single-line frame between 0.5 and 2 points.

Creating Frame Styles

QuarkXPress for Macintosh (Windows QuarkXPress has no such utility) includes a stand-alone utility called the Frame Editor for editing and creating frames. It lets you create more options than the seven default ones within QuarkXPress. The Frame Editor has eight of its own frame styles that you can use or modify. Figure 9-6 shows the Frame Editor. After you edit frames in the Frame Editor, its styles are added to the list that QuarkXPress displays in its Style scroll box in the Frame pane of the Modify dialog box. These new styles can include ones that you design.

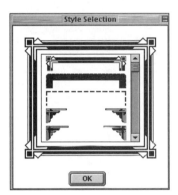

Figure 9-6: In the Frame Editor, you can edit an existing style by double-clicking the frame in the scroll list.

Note that you must quit QuarkXPress before running the Frame Editor; otherwise, an error message will appear and the Frame Editor will not be loaded.

STEPS: Editing or creating a style

1. To edit a style, double-click the style in the Frame Editor (this appears as a Style Selection dialog box) or use File⇨Open (⌘+O) after selecting a style. To create, use File⇨New Style (⌘+N).

2. If you are creating a new frame, you will be asked to define the width of the frame in points (as shown here). To create a new width for an existing frame, use File⇨New Size (or ⌘+N). Note that the size in the Frame Editor is not what appears when you apply the frame style in QuarkXPress—you choose the frame's actual width there. Instead, the size chosen in the Frame Editor determines how finely detailed the frame is—the larger the size, the more bits you have to work with.

(continued)

3. You can work with as many as eight areas of the frame (the lengths of each side plus each corner). The Element Selection box that you use to select the area of the frame you are going to edit or modify is shown here. Click the rounded-corner box just inside an area to select that area.

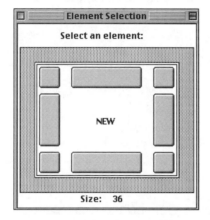

4. You will be asked for the area's size (in points), which tells the Frame Editor how large a cell to use in creating the frame. (Each cell is repeated as many times as needed to create the frame.)

5. After entering the size (or accepting the default size), you will have a split dialog box (shown here). The left side is where you create the border pattern by holding down the mouse and dragging the pointer throughout the grid or clicking individual grid elements. You deselect a grid element by clicking it again. The right side shows the pattern both at a reduced size and within the current frame style.

6. When you create your first side and corner, they are automatically copied to the other sides and corners. If you want to rearrange sides and corners after that, you can use the Copy Elements feature (Element⇨Copy Elements). Thus, you need to create a length or corner only once.

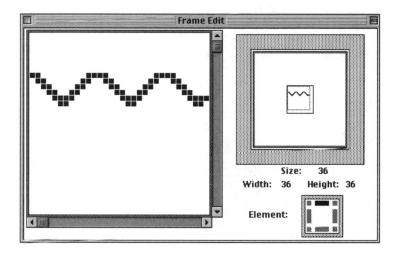

7. Close the Element Selection dialog box and click the Yes button when prompted to save the changes. Then close the Size Selection dialog box (⌘+Q). To remove a frame style, select it and choose Edit⇨Clear.

Saving a Page as an EPS File

QuarkXPress has a nifty feature that lets you, in effect, take a picture of a page in a document and turn the picture into an EPS file. You can then use the EPS file as an illustration for another document. A catalog of brochures is a good example of an application of this feature. You might create several brochures, make an EPS file of each brochure cover, and then create a marketing piece that shows all the brochure covers.

STEPS: Saving a page as an EPS file

1. Open the document that contains the page you want to save.

2. Choose File⇨Save Page as EPS (Option-Shift+⌘+S) to display the Save Page as EPS dialog box, shown here.

(continued)

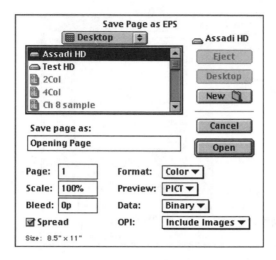

3. Enter a name for the new EPS file in the Save page as box.

4. Click the appropriate format for the file type in the Format list box. Choices include B&W (black-and-white), Color (generates a color EPS file), DCS (the Document Color Separation form of EPS, used when outputting negatives for four-color process printing), and DCS 2.0 (a version of the DCS format that includes process and spot colors).

5. In the Page text box, enter the page number of the page you want to save as an EPS file.

6. If you want to modify the scale of the page as you save it, enter a percentage value in the Scale text box; 50 percent reduces the page to half its original size. (The Bleed field is a new feature in version 4.)

7. When you save a page as an EPS file, the picture box is clipped to the exact size of the page. But you can enter a value in the Bleed field to cause a picture larger than the page size to be captured in the resulting EPS file.

8. Unless your service bureau has specifically asked for the output files to be in ASCII format, make sure that the Data field is set to Clean 8-Bit, not ASCII, unless you know you will only be printing the EPS file from Macintosh computers directly to the printer (i.e., you know you won't be using any Windows spoolers).

9. If you are using Open Prepress Interface, choose one of the following options in the OPI drop-down list. Your selection determines how pictures and comments are included with a page saved as an EPS file. (If you're not using OPI, just use the default setting of Include Images.)

✦**Include Images:** This includes pictures in TIFF and EPS formats and substitutes the low-resolution TIFF if the higher-resolution printing file for the pictures cannot be found. This option is the one used most often.

✦**Omit TIFF & EPS:** This omits both TIFF and EPS pictures in the file but includes OPI comments in the file for both types of pictures. If you are printing to an OPI prepress system that replaces TIFF and EPS pictures, choose this option.

✦**Omit TIFF:** This omits TIFF pictures in the file but includes OPI comments in the file.

New Feature

10. Choosing an option from the Preview pop-up menu lets you choose a preview format for the EPS file. Choices are PICT, TIFF, or None. (In Windows QuarkXPress, your options are TIFF and None.) Choose TIFF if the EPS file will be used in a Windows environment; otherwise, choose PICT. (The ability to choose a preview format for the EPS file is a new feature.)

11. To save all of the pages in the current spread as an EPS file, check the Spread checkbox.

Aligning Multiple Elements

It's not at all uncommon to have a set of two or more layout elements that you want to line up to a certain X or Y coordinate. You may also want to line up these elements with a certain amount of space between them. QuarkXPress lets you align items according to their left, right, top, or bottom edges, or to their centers. You can also control the amount of space between multiple items, and you can specify whether these items are evenly spread across the page or staggered horizontally or vertically. To learn more about these various techniques, read on.

Space/Align

The Space/Align Items dialog box is a powerful feature that allows you to control the spacing and alignment of elements in your layout. How does Space/Align work? Showing an example is the best way to illustrate it. Say you have four picture boxes on a page, and you want the boxes to be precisely aligned by their left edges with one-half inch of vertical space between the boxes. Figure 9-7 shows the settings that you specify in the Space/Align Items dialog box to accomplish this layout. To establish a layout like the one shown in the example, use the following steps.

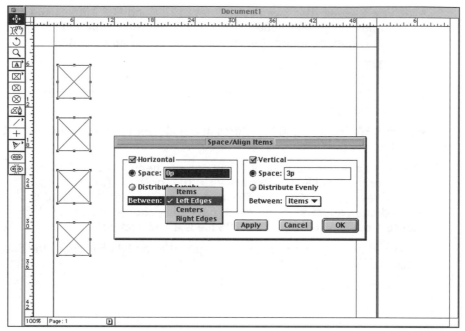

Figure 9-7: The Space/Align Items dialog box with the settings used to align the four picture boxes on the left of the page.

STEPS: Aligning multiple elements

1. With the Item tool selected, hold down the Shift key and click each of the four boxes to select them.

2. Choose ⌘+, (comma) to display the Space/Align Items dialog box.

3. Click the Vertical box to select it.

4. Choose Space (which is below the Vertical box) and enter 3p in the Space field.

5. Select Items from the Between list box.

6. Click the Horizontal box to select it. Choose Space (which is below the Horizontal box) and enter 0p in the Space field.

7. Select Left Edges from the Between list box.

8. Select Apply to see what the settings will result in (to make sure that you've entered the right settings), and then choose OK to implement the changes.

Tip

If you are new to QuarkXPress and want to increase your layout expertise, do some experimenting. Draw a few text boxes and apply different X and Y coordinates to them in the Measurements palette. Also, try using different settings in the Space/Align Items dialog box. This is a great way to learn how these features work.

Step and Repeat

Whenever you can, it's a good idea to let the computer do the work for you, and QuarkXPress makes it easy for the computer to do extra work. As an example, the program has the ability to create multiple copies of selected elements and to space them horizontally or vertically at regular intervals. This powerful feature is called *Step and Repeat.*

A table of contents example

Suppose that you want to create a table of contents in which there are six sets of elements from top to bottom. Each element contains a group made up of a picture box with a photo or drawing, a text box overlaid on it to hold the page number, and a text box next to it to list the title, author, and description. Figure 9-8 shows an example of this type of layout along with the Step and Repeat dialog box, which you access by choosing Item⇨Step and Repeat or via Option+⌘+D. The boxes to be repeated are at the top of the page.

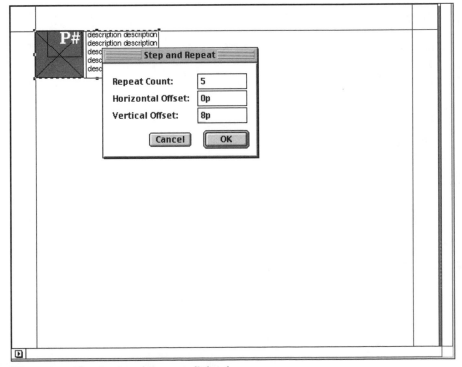

Figure 9-8: The Step and Repeat dialog box.

To duplicate the grouped boxes in the sample layout and repeat them at even intervals, we established the following settings in the dialog box:

✦ **Repeat Count:** In this field, we entered the number 5, indicating that we wanted five copies of the boxes.

✦ **Horizontal Offset:** In this field, we entered 0p, meaning that we do not want each repeated group to shift sideways.

✦ **Vertical Offset:** In this field, we entered 8p to vertically space the top of each repeated group 8 picas from the previous group.

We clicked OK after entering these settings, and the result was the completed table of contents shown in Figure 9-9. As you can see by this example, Step and Repeat is useful for creating forms, tables, charts, and other similar documents that have a design element reproduced multiple times and spaced at regular intervals.

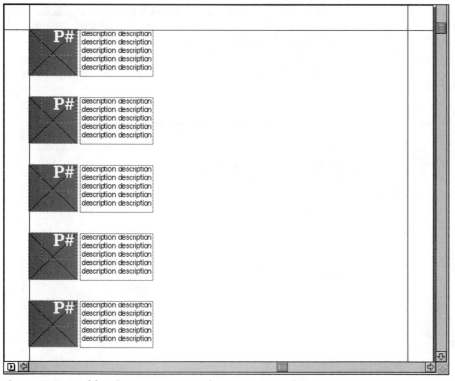

Figure 9-9: A table of contents created using Step and Repeat.

Using negative and positive values

Entering a positive Horizontal Offset value places repeated elements to the right of the original; a negative value places them to the left. Likewise, a positive Vertical Offset value, like the one we used in our example, places repeated elements below the original element. A negative value would place it above.

Tip

When you use the Step and Repeat feature, QuarkXPress remembers the offsets you use. If you subsequently use the Duplicate feature (Item⇨Duplicate, or ⌘+D), QuarkXPress uses those offsets there too. If you want to "clone" items (create copies of items in the same positions as the originals), first do a Step and Repeat with horizontal and vertical offsets of 0". From then on until you quit the program, every time you use the Duplicate feature, the duplicate appears in the same position as the original.

✦   ✦   ✦

Creating Templates, Master Pages, and Libraries

◆ ◆ ◆ ◆

In This Chapter

Creating templates

Working with master pages

Using libraries

◆ ◆ ◆ ◆

In the course of creating documents, it is likely that you will develop items—such as blocks of text, graphic elements, or general page-layout styles—that you want to use over and over in many documents. Likewise, you will find yourself designing documents that need to have the same elements occupying the same spot, page after page, within the same document. QuarkXPress lets you create layout and page templates, as well as content libraries. You can build templates, or layout structures, that let you create documents with different content, yet maintain a consistent look and feel across multiple documents. For pages, QuarkXPress lets you create master pages, with elements on the page that appear whenever the master page is used within one document. You can also build libraries of content items—text, lines, and graphics—that you store until needed.

Creating Templates

Suppose you have an assignment to create a dozen customer success stories for your company. Each story will be different, but all the individual stories need to have a consistent appearance. The best way to do this is to create a template and then pour the individual stories into the template. A template is a formatted document that is protected from overwriting. The only difference between a template and a document is that a template forces you to use Save As rather than Save in the File menu so that you do not overwrite the template but instead create new documents based on it.

Although the optimum approach is to design a template before creating actual documents, the truth is that no one can foresee all possibilities. Even if you create a template (and you should) with style sheets, H&J sets, and master pages intended for use in all new documents in a related series, you can expect to modify your template as your work on real documents creates the need for modifications and additions.

Using templates over a network

Whether or not you use templates, you will still need to transfer basic layout elements like styles and master pages from one document to another. QuarkXPress supports the use of templates over a network. Each time a template is accessed, the user accessing it is given a local copy. Thus, multiple users can access the template simultaneously, and even a single user can have several documents based on the same template open at once.

Saving a document as a template

You can save an open document as a template by choosing File⇨Save As (Option+⌘+S) to display the Save As dialog box, entering a name for the template in the Save Current Document As field (File Name in Windows), choosing Template from the Type pop-up menu (Save as Type in Windows), and clicking Save.

To make changes to an existing template, open the template, modify it, and save it again by choosing File⇨Save As (Option+⌘+S), giving the template the same name, choosing Template from the Type pop-up menu, and clicking Save. An alert will ask you to confirm whether you want to replace the existing template; if so, click Replace.

Working with Master Pages

Part of the challenge of being a professional publisher is creating a consistent look throughout a document. You want what appears on page 5 to look like it is somehow connected to what was on page 1, and so on. The master pages in QuarkXPress can help you achieve this goal. Master pages hold the elements of a page that you want repeated on other pages in the same document. For example, you may want the bottom outer corner of each page to show the current page number. Perhaps you want a company logo to appear at the top of each page of an annual report. Or you may want a picture box to be placed at a specific spot on each page, ready to receive a graphic. These are just a few ideas about how you can make master pages work for you.

Master page methods

While master pages help keep documents consistent, they also allow for a great deal of flexibility. You can have up to 127 master page pairs document. You can add, modify, or delete master page elements just as you can for those elements that are not on master pages. After a master page is modified, those changes automatically apply to any document pages based on that master page (unless local changes have been made to the modified elements on pages based on that master page).

To add a new master page to an open document, choose View⇨Show Document Layout (F10 on the Mac; F4 in Windows) to display the Document Layout palette. Then click one of the blank icons at the very top of the palette and drag it down into the master page area of the palette. (Be careful not to drag it right on top of an existing master page, though; if you do, QuarkXPress will replace that master page with a new, blank master page.)

If your document is a single-sided document, you will only be able to add single-sided master pages to it. However, if your document is a facing-pages document, you can add both single-sided and facing-page master pages to it.

Creating a new master page

When you create a new QuarkXPress document via the File⇨New menu option (⌘+N), the main master page is automatically created. QuarkXPress bases the main master page on the settings in the New Document dialog box, shown in Figure 10-1.

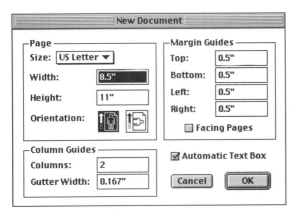

Figure 10-1: The New Document dialog box, where the basic specifications for the main master page are established.

You establish default settings—or change to new default settings—by making changes in the New Document dialog box; if you create a new document, the settings in the New Document dialog box at the time you created the new document become the default settings for the next new document. If you leave the Facing Pages box unchecked, QuarkXPress creates a single-sided master page. If you check the Facing Pages box, the default master page contains two pages (one for the left pages and one for the right pages).

Displaying a master page

After you've created a new document, it's a good idea to set up the master pages right away. To set up master pages, you need to leave the document mode and go into the master page mode, where you can establish features that you want to be repeated throughout the document. QuarkXPress lets you toggle between document pages (document mode) and the master pages upon which they are based (master page mode) by using the Display command in the Page menu (Shift+F10 on Mac; Shift+F4 in Windows). To display the actual document pages on your monitor, choose Page⇨Display⇨Document. To display a master page for the document, choose Page⇨Display⇨Master (after you've established master pages, where we have used Master, the display will actually include a list of all master pages associated with the document; hold down the mouse button to select the master page you want to see). Figure 10-2 shows how you select the master page in a new document.

Figure 10-2: The Display command in the Page menu lets you toggle between the actual document and its associated master pages.

Tip

You can toggle between master pages and document pages using the Page pop-up menu at the bottom of the document window.

Common master page elements

Although you can put just about anything on a master page, here are some of the items most commonly used on master pages:

✦ **Page headers:** These are elements such as "running" heads that you want to repeat from page to page.

✦ **Page footers:** This is information that repeats across the bottom of pages in a document.

✦ **Automatic page numbers:** You create these by placing a Current Page Number character (⌘+3) at the point on the master page where you want to see page numbers appear.

✦ **Page sidebars:** This is information in the outer side margins of a page that you want repeated on other pages.

✦ **Corporate logos:** Logos or other artwork that you want to appear throughout the document can also be placed on master pages.

Figure 10-3 shows a facing-page document. Note that we have set the reverse-type box "Gardening Basics" on the top outer margins of the left and right master pages. When we shift back to the actual document, all left pages based on this left master page will have the "Gardening Basics" text box on the top left of the page; all right pages based on this right master page will have the text box on the top right of the page.

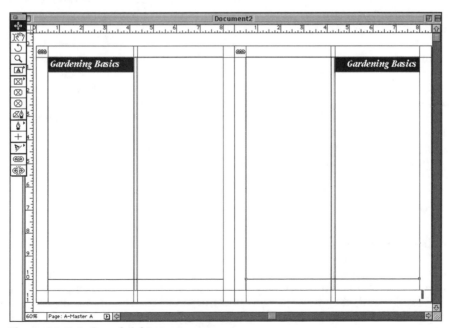

Figure 10-3: Left and right master pages.

Viewing and editing master pages

After working on a document for a while, you also might want to make changes to master pages. For example, you might decide to move the page number from the bottom center of the page to the outer margin. To view a master page so that you can change it, choose View⇨Show Document Layout (F10 on the Mac; F4 in Windows). This displays the Document Layout palette. Double-click the icon of the master page you want to modify. The master page is displayed. Make any changes that you want to make to the master page, and then return to the actual document by choosing Page⇨Display⇨Document (Shift+F10 on the Mac; Shift+F4 in Windows).

Even if you have a master page associated with a page in your document, you can make local changes to the page that don't affect the master page. To do this you simply edit the page with the document in document mode by choosing Page⇨Display⇨Document (Shift+F10 on the Mac; Shift+F4 in Windows).

Inserting a new page based on a master page

To insert a new page based on an existing master page, choose View⇨Show Document Layout (F10 on the Mac; F4 in Windows) to display the Document Layout palette. Click the icon of the master page you want the new document page to be associated with, and drag the icon into the lower part of the Document Layout palette, which shows the document pages. As you drag the page icon into position, the icon will change to an arrow or a page icon. Release the mouse when you have positioned the icon in the spot you want. In Figure 10-4, you can see what the page icon looks like as you drag it into position.

Rather than using the Document Layout palette, you can also insert a new document page based on an existing master page by choosing Page⇨Insert. This displays the Insert Pages dialog box. You can associate the inserted pages with a master page by choosing one of the master pages shown in the Master Page pop-up menu. To link the automatic text boxes on pages that you are inserting into the active text chain, check Link to Current Text Chain in the Insert Pages dialog box. This option is available only if a text box is active and if the pages you are inserting are set to include an automatic text box.

Deleting master pages

After spending some time working on a document, you may find that you have established a master page that you no longer need. Deleting a master page is a simple operation. First, display the Document Layout palette by choosing View⇨Show Document Layout (F10 on the Mac; F4 in Windows). When the Document Layout palette is displayed, click the icon of the master page you want to delete. Second, click the Delete icon at the top of the Document Layout palette (the Delete icon looks like a little trash can). Figure 10-5 shows a master page that is ready to be deleted.

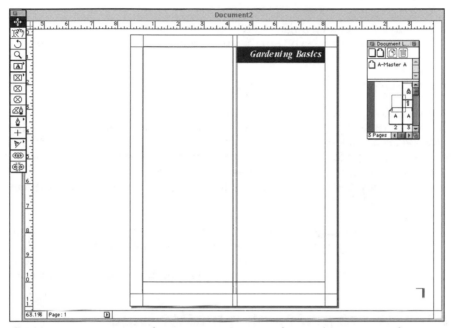

Figure 10-4: You can use the Document Layout palette to insert a new document page based on a master page.

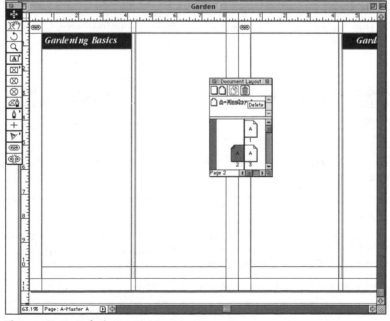

Figure 10-5: Deleting a master page.

Caution

Be very careful when deleting a master page because you cannot undo the master page deletion without reverting to the last-saved version of the document.

Rearranging master pages

Because QuarkXPress allows you up to 127 master pages per document, it is conceivable that—at some point—you may want to rearrange the order of the master pages associated with the document. For example, you might want to have the third master page in a set become the first, or the second master page become the last, and so on. (Such reordering will not change anything about the document pages, but it may make it easier for you to apply your master pages, especially if you have a lot of them.)

To rearrange master pages, choose View⇨Show Document Layout (F10 on the Mac; F4 in Windows) to display the Document Layout palette. Then click the icon of the master page you want to move and drag it into position within the top part of the palette. When you release the mouse button, the master page stays put.

Changing the guides on a master page

It happens to the best of us: You're working on a document when you realize that the margins you established when you first created the document are too wide or too narrow, or that you really need two columns instead of one. You might think that you need to start all over again, but thanks to a nifty Master Guides feature (see Figure 10-6), you can adjust your initial settings without sacrificing all your hard work on the document. To change the margin or column guides for a master page, use the following steps.

STEPS: Changing guides on a master page

1. Choose View⇨Show Document Layout (F10 on the Mac; F4 in Windows) to display the Document Layout palette.

2. Double-click the icon of the master page you want to modify; this displays the master page.

3. Choose Page⇨Master Guides to display the Master Guides dialog box (refer to Figure 10-6).

4. Make any changes you'd like to the Margin Guides or Column Guides fields in the dialog box, and click the OK button. Any changes you make apply to document pages that are associated with the master page.

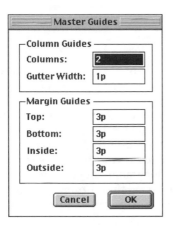

Figure 10-6: Make changes to the margins or columns of a master page by using the Master Guides dialog box.

Applying master pages to document pages

You can apply master page settings to existing document pages, but be careful—doing so usually causes text and layout changes. (When you apply a new master page to a page that already uses a different master page, the old master page is no longer applied to the page. So think twice before you do this!) To apply master pages to existing pages, use the following steps.

STEPS: Applying master pages to existing pages

1. Make sure the Document Layout palette is visible; if it isn't, choose View➪Show Document Layout (F10 on the Mac; F4 in Windows).

2. Click the page icon of the page in the Document Layout palette to which you want to apply a master page. (To apply a master page to a contiguous set of pages, press and hold the Shift key as you click the first and last page in the range of pages; to apply a master page to noncontiguous pages, press and hold the ⌘ key as you click the icons of the separate pages to which you want to apply the master page.)

3. Press and hold the Option key as you click the icon for the master page you want to apply to the document page(s); then release the Option key and the mouse button.

Tip

You can also apply a master page to a document page by dragging the master page icon onto the document page icon in the Document Layout palette.

Using Libraries

A powerful layout-management feature that originated with QuarkXPress is the ability to create *libraries* of text and graphics. This feature is a great aid if you reuse elements throughout a set of publications. For example, you can have a library containing your corporate logos, photos, and such standard text as mastheads and postal statements. QuarkXPress does more than let you create libraries; it lets you create multiple libraries—any or all of which may be open at a time. QuarkXPress also lets you group library elements to make them easy to find. The libraries themselves are separate files that can reside anywhere on your hard disk (or network). Because the libraries are not part of any document, any document can use them. After elements are in a library, you can manage their order and add or remove unwanted elements. The following sections show you how.

Creating a library

Before you can use a library, you must create it. Selecting File⇨New⇨Library (Option+⌘+N) opens the New Library dialog box shown in Figure 10-7. Navigate the folders and disks as you do in any Mac application until you access the folder that you want to use for the library.

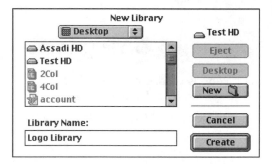

Figure 10-7: The New Library dialog box.

To create a library, enter a name in the New Library field. After you enter a filename, select Create. An empty library appears in your document, as Figure 10-8 shows.

The library filename appears at the top of the Library palette, and the name may be cut off. You can resize the window by selecting the resize icon at the bottom right of the dialog box, or you can click the full-size icon at the upper right to make the library take the full screen space (if you click that icon again, the dialog box returns to the original size). The library elements will flow from left to right (assuming the window is wide enough to hold two or more elements) and then from top to bottom.

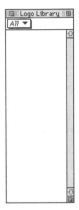

Figure 10-8: A new, empty library.

Opening a library

To open a library, use the standard Open dialog box you use for your documents (File⇨Open, or ⌘+O). You can distinguish libraries from documents by the icon that QuarkXPress displays. Figure 10-9 shows the Logo Library icon—the one that looks like a collection of books (on the desktop to the right of the document window). We suggest you use the word "library" in your filenames or an extension such as ".lib" or ".qxl" at the end of your filename to make it easier to distinguish libraries from regular documents. (The Windows suffix for libraries is .qxl; QuarkXPress for Windows adds the .qxl extension automatically.)

Figure 10-9: To indicate a library, QuarkXPress uses an icon that looks like a collection of books.

Adding elements to a library

After you create your library, you can add elements to it from any open document or library. If you want to bring in elements from several documents, you can. The library window stays on-screen as you open and close documents, as well as when you open and close other libraries. There are two basic ways to add elements to libraries:

✦ **Option 1:** Use the standard cut, copy, and paste functions, either through the keyboard shortcuts (⌘+X, ⌘+C, and ⌘+V, respectively) or through the Edit menu.

✦ **Option 2:** Use the Item tool to drag elements from documents or libraries to the destination library. The pointer changes to a pair of glasses (the library pointer) and a box with a dotted outline appears when your pointer is in the library window. Figure 10-10 illustrates the box that appears in the library window as you are dragging an item into the library. Release the mouse button and the element appears as a box in the library window.

Note

Whichever method you prefer, make sure the Item tool is selected (not the Content tool) because boxes can be cut, copied, and moved only with the Item tool.

Figure 10-10: Dragging an element into the open library window.

Repeat the copying or dragging process for all elements (from all documents) that you want to put in the library. The result is a library like the one shown in Figure 10-11. We opened several documents to get elements for this library. You may find that your libraries evolve over time, too. Notice in Figure 10-12, which has the Library palette resized, how the elements' order changes so that elements go from left to right and then top to bottom.

Library do's and don'ts

Libraries will accept only elements that are in text boxes or picture boxes or that are created with one of the Line tools. You cannot include a graphics file that is not in a picture box or a text file that is not in a text box.

All attributes applied to boxes—including frames, backgrounds, and colors—are retained when you copy the boxes to libraries. Graphics include all cropping, sizing, and other such information; text includes all formatting, including paragraph styles and H&J sets.

If you have a style sheet in a library whose name matches that of a style sheet in the document to which the library element is being moved, QuarkXPress will apply the library's style sheet to the copied text, but it will not change the document's style sheet definition. (It simply applies the library style sheet's formatting locally to the copied text.) In the case of having H&J sets with the same name in the library and the target document, the H&J settings from the document will be applied to the copied text because QuarkXPress does not allow local application of H&J information.

You may use elements linked via Publish and Subscribe or OLE in a library. The link to the source document and originating application are retained for the element when copied or moved into a library and when placed into a new document from the library.

Figure 10-11: A library with text and graphics elements from several documents. The Library palette's width shown here is the default width.

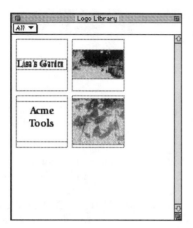

Figure 10-12: The Library palette in Figure 10-11 resized.

Saving a library

If you check the Auto Library Save option in the Save pane of the Application Preferences dialog box (by selecting Edit⇨Preferences⇨Application, or by pressing Option+Shift+⌘+Y), the library is saved each time you add or delete an element. Otherwise, the library is saved when you close the library or quit QuarkXPress.

Adding master pages to libraries

Moving master pages from documents to libraries is tricky because QuarkXPress offers no feature explicitly designed to perform this task. But you can move master pages by taking the following steps.

STEPS: Moving master pages to libraries

1. Open or create a library to hold the master pages.

2. Open the document that contains the master page you want to copy. Display the master page by selecting Page⇨Display.

3. Select the Item tool and then select all items (choose Edit⇨Select All or use the shortcut ⌘+A).

4. Drag (or copy and paste) the items into an open library and release the mouse. All elements on the master page appear in their own library box.

5. Open the document into which you want to copy the master page. You don't need to close the other document, but unless you intend to get other elements

from it or work on it later, go ahead and close it to reduce clutter both on-screen and in the Mac's memory.

6. Insert a new blank master page in the second document.

7. Drag (or copy and paste) the library item containing the master-page elements to the new master page and position it where you want it. (You may want to change the screen display to fit-to-window view so that you can better position the elements on the new master page. To display this view, select View⇨Fit in Window (⌘+0 [zero]).

8. Use the Document Layout palette to display the master pages, and rename the new master page so that you can remember what it contains.

Rearranging library elements

The order of elements in a library depends on where you drop them or where the pointer is when you paste them. If you want to rearrange the order, select the element you want to move, hold down the mouse button, and move the pointer to the new position in the library window. Release the mouse button when you reach the desired location (the triangles that appear as you move the element are the insertion points).

Labeling library elements

Because a library can easily grow so large that there are too many elements to scroll through, QuarkXPress lets you assign labels to elements (see Figure 10-13). You then can tell QuarkXPress to display only those elements that have a particular label. In effect, you create sublibraries within a library. The process of adding a label is simple. Just follow these steps.

STEPS: Labeling elements in a library

1. Double-click the element you want to label. The Library Entry dialog box appears.

2. Either type in a label (see Figure 10-13), or select an existing label (a label already used in the current library) from the drop-down list box next to the Label field. Several entries can have the same label.

3. Choose OK.

Tip

The label does not display with the element image in the library window. To see a label, you must double-click the item to bring up the Library Entry dialog box.

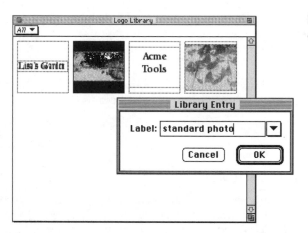

Figure 10-13: The Library Entry dialog box.

Displaying labeled elements

After you create labels, you can use the library window's Labels menu (see Figure 10-14) to select which elements are displayed.

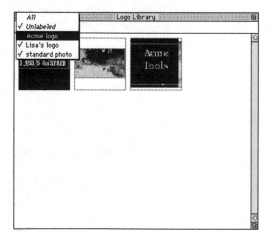

Figure 10-14: The Labels menu in the library window.

If All is checked, all elements are displayed. You can also select more than one type of label. To do this, first select the All label. Then select the label for the first set of items you want to display. Next, select a different label to add those items. The label in the pick list will change to Mixed Labels, and all displayed label names will have checkmarks to their left. You can deselect (or reselect) each label in turn to determine the labels for those elements you want to see.

If you select Unlabeled, QuarkXPress displays only elements that are not labeled. This option is handy for those odds-and-ends library elements you want to see infrequently but need to access easily.

Using multiple libraries

Although labels are a great way to keep the list of library elements manageable, they are no substitute for creating different libraries to hold distinct groups of elements. Don't let the label feature be an excuse for having an unwieldy library. When the elements in a library become too diverse, it's time to create a new library and move some elements into it. There are three ways to move elements from one library to another:

✦ **Option 1:** Drag the element into the new library. This option copies the element from the first library into the second while leaving the original element intact in the first library.

✦ **Option 2:** Use the copy command in the first library and paste a copy of the element into the second library. This option also copies the element from the first library into the second while leaving the original element intact in the first library.

✦ **Option 3:** Use the cut command in the first library and paste the element into the second library. The element is removed from the first library.

Another benefit of creating multiple libraries is that you can more easily find the library elements that a specific document requires if you use logical filenames for your libraries, such as Corporate Logos or Garden Photos.

Deleting unwanted elements

Your libraries will evolve over time as your document elements change. As a result, you will occasionally need to delete library elements. You can delete elements in the following ways:

✦ **Cut:** Cutting an element removes it from the library but puts a copy in the Clipboard so that you can paste it elsewhere, such as into another document or library.

✦ **Clear:** Clearing an element removes it from the library and does not put a copy in the Clipboard. A cleared element is erased permanently from the current library.

You can use QuarkXPress's Edit menu to cut and clear. To cut an element, you also can use the keyboard shortcut ⌘+X. To clear an item from a library, select it and then press the Delete key. When you cut or clear an element, QuarkXPress asks you to confirm the edit, as shown in Figure 10-15.

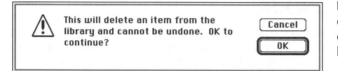

Figure 10-15: QuarkXPress asks for confirmation when you attempt to cut or clear an element from a library.

Putting libraries to work

After you create and fill your libraries, it's easy to move the library elements into your documents. Just drag them or use the cut, copy, and paste commands as you did to put elements in the library in the first place.

Library elements always paste into documents at their original size, not the smaller version displayed in the library. After you place an element into a document, you can modify it as you do any other text box, picture box, or line.

Library tips and tricks

Libraries are especially helpful when you work with graphic and text elements that have special effects applied. For example, you might place in a library a text box that has a word rotated, drop-shadowed, and colored. You probably won't want to have that word used in other documents, but you'll probably want to reuse the effect. By placing such special-effects text in the library, you save yourself the work of later applying those special effects.

After copying the element into a document, you can easily change its specific attributes to something else while retaining all the formatting of the original element. This technique is also handy for special lines like arrowheads and for picture boxes that have intricate frames, special color blends, or odd shapes.

✦   ✦   ✦

Text Techniques

The typographic treatment of text can be a subtle yet powerful part of your presentation. Although you define the basic look of a document with layout and styles, you give it texture with the way you handle text. With QuarkXPress, you have in your hands those tools that typographers once used to enhance the aesthetics of a document. You can orchestrate the finer points of formatting on a case-by-case basis, or you can record them in character or paragraph style sheets, ready to be used again and again. With a little experimentation and a few guiding principles, you can use these typographic tools to improve the appearance and clarity of all the documents you create.

This part of the book explains typography and shows you how you can use the tools in QuarkXPress to put theory into practice. You will learn how to use these tools to edit text, produce tables, and make text fit comfortably within the confines of your document.

In This Part

Chapter 11
Entering and
Editing Text

Chapter 12
Controlling Character
Spacing

Chapter 13
Controlling
Paragraph Spacing

Chapter 14
Using Style Sheets

Chapter 15
Using Tabs and
Tables

Chapter 16
Book-Oriented
Editing

Chapter 17
Typographic Special
Effects

Entering and Editing Text

CHAPTER

11

In This Chapter

Using the basic editing tools

Finding and replacing text

Checking spelling

Fitting copy

Some QuarkXPress users use the program's built-in word processor to do basic editing, while others do most of their text editing in a separate word processing program. Even though you may be part of the latter group, it's very likely that you do at least minor editing within QuarkXPress. That's what this chapter is all about.

Using the Basic Editing Tools

QuarkXPress's editing tools are sufficient for most basic tasks such as adding or deleting text. If you want to add or delete text, first position your text cursor (which appears if you are using the Content tool) at the spot where you want to make changes and click the mouse button. You then can start typing or deleting text. To select a block of text use the following steps.

STEPS: Selecting a block of text

1. Position the text cursor at one end of the text block.

2. Press and hold the mouse button as you drag the cursor until it is at the other end of the text block.

3. Release the mouse button. The selected text is highlighted.

Tip

To select all text in a text box, or in a series of linked text boxes, place the cursor within the box and choose Edit⇨Select All (the shortcut is ⌘+A).

Replacing selected text

As in most other Macintosh and Windows programs, in QuarkXPress you can also replace text by selecting it and typing in new text or pasting in text from the Clipboard (Edit⇨Paste, or ⌘+V). The new text that takes the place of the old can be from another part of your document, from another QuarkXPress document, or from another Macintosh or Windows program. The new text can be a copy of text (Edit⇨Copy, or ⌘+C), or it can be text cut from another document (Edit⇨Cut, or ⌘+X).

Tip

You can also replace selected text with text from a text file or word processing file. To do so, first select the text you want to replace, and then choose Edit⇨Get Text (or press ⌘+E). A directory dialog box will be displayed, in which you can select the text or word processing file with which you want to overwrite the selected text.

The cut and delete difference

Be sure to remember that *cut* text and *deleted* text are different. QuarkXPress inserts cut text automatically into the Clipboard, but it does not insert deleted text into the Clipboard. (You delete text by using the Delete key or Backspace key.)

The only way to recover deleted text is via Edit⇨Undo Typing. Cut text remains in the Clipboard until you cut or copy other text or graphic elements.

Moving and duplicating text

You move text by cutting it from one location and pasting it into another. You duplicate text by copying it from one location and pasting it into another. If the drag-and-drop option is checked in the Interactive pane of Application Preferences (Edit⇨Preferences⇨Application, or Option+Shift+⌘+Y), you can highlight a piece of text and then drag it to a new location, rather than cut it from the old location and paste it to the new one.

Finding and Replacing Text

Basic editing tools are fine for doing simple editing, but you may want to replace one piece of text with another throughout your document. Suppose, for example, that you create a catalog and you need to change a product's version number in every place that it is referenced throughout the manual. You can make the changes in the original word-processor document and then replace the text in your QuarkXPress document with the updated text. Or you can use QuarkXPress's built-in replace function, which you access through the Find/Change palette, shown in Figure 11-1.

Figure 11-1: The Find/Change palette.

New Feature

In versions of QuarkXPress prior to 4, Find/Change was implemented via a dialog box. Beginning with version 4, however, the Find/Change feature works from a palette. This means that the Find/Change window remains visible unless you close it by clicking its close box. (Previously, clicking the document window would send the Find/Change window behind the document window.)

Replacing text

In QuarkXPress, the current story is defined as text in the currently selected text box plus all text boxes linked to it. To replace text throughout the current story, use the Find/Change palette (Edit⇨Find/Change, or ⌘+F). You also can replace text throughout the entire current document. The QuarkXPress replace function works like the standard search and replace tool found in Macintosh and Windows word processing programs. You can search for whole words or for words whose capitalization matches the words or characters that you type in the Find What field. In Figure 11-1, QuarkXPress is instructed to replace "Davis Patio Furniture" with "Davis Lawn & Garden." Here's how some of the options work:

✦ **Whole Word:** The controls in the Find/Change dialog box let you choose whether QuarkXPress should look for a whole word. (If the Whole Word box is unchecked, the program finds the string wherever is appears.)

✦ **Ignore Case:** You can also have the program search and replace a word— regardless of its capitalization—by selecting Ignore Case.

✦ **Document:** If the Document box is checked, the replace affects all stories and text in your document.

The other buttons, such as Find Next, work as they do in other word processing programs. We explore the Ignore Attributes option in the next section.

Changing text attributes

The Find/Change dialog box also lets you find and replace text attributes, typefaces, and sizes. This feature is useful if, for example, you want to change all instances of 10-point Times New Roman to 12-point Palatino. To access this option, uncheck Ignore Attributes in the Find/Change palette. When Ignore Attributes is deselected, the palette expands and offers you attribute replacement options, as Figure 11-2 shows.

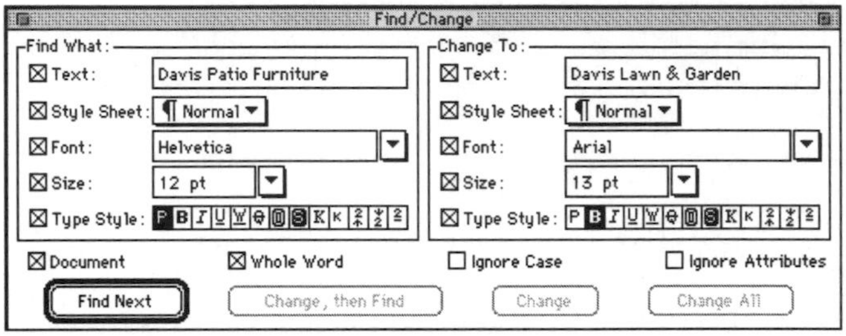

Find/Change

Find What:

☒ Text: Davis Patio Furniture
☒ Style Sheet: ¶ Normal ▼
☒ Font: Helvetica   ▼
☒ Size: 12 pt   ▼
☒ Type Style: P B I U W ⊖ ⊙ S K K ⬚ ⬚

Change To:

☒ Text: Davis Lawn & Garden
☒ Style Sheet: ¶ Normal ▼
☒ Font: Arial   ▼
☒ Size: 13 pt   ▼
☒ Type Style: P B I U W ⊖ ⊙ S K K ⬚ ⬚

☒ Document   ☒ Whole Word   ☐ Ignore Case   ☐ Ignore Attributes

[Find Next]   (Change, then Find)   (Change)   (Change All)

Figure 11-2: The Find/Change palette lets you find and replace text with specific attributes.

In the example shown in Figure 11-2, we want to replace any text set in 12-point Helvetica plain text with 13-point Arial bold text. This example shows how you can select specific text, typeface, and styles for both the search and replace functions. You specify these attributes by checking the Text, Font, Size, and Type Style checkboxes in the Find What and Change To columns of the dialog box.

The Find What column

If you leave an option unchecked in the Find What column, QuarkXPress includes any variant (such as style) in the search. If, for example, we did not check Size in the Find What column but did check it in the Change To column, QuarkXPress would change all Helvetica italic text of any size to 13-point Arial bold text.

The Change To column

If you leave an option unchecked in the Change To column, QuarkXPress applies to the replacement text the formatting of the text that was searched. If we did not check Size in the Change To column, the size of the replacement text would be the same as the text it was replacing.

Tip

When you leave Text unchecked in the Find What column, you replace attributes only. You might do this to change all bold text to small cap text, all News Gothic bold text to News Gothic bold italic, or all 8-point text to 8.5-point text.

The Style options

You can search and replace all character attributes available in the Measurements palette. Check an attribute box in the style sections of the dialog box if you want to use an attribute. Remove the checkmark if you don't want to use an attribute (such as bold) in your search and replace. Make the box gray to tell QuarkXPress to retain whatever attribute is set. (Clicking a box once unchecks it if checked or checks it if unchecked. Clicking a box twice makes it gray.) In the example shown in Figure 11-2, the replacement text will be bold but not italic.

Changing point size quickly

Here are some quick ways to change type size. Follow these steps to change text by one point or to the next highest or next lowest preset type size, which includes all sizes with the exception of Other in the Measurements palette's font list:

✦ First select the text whose size you want to change, and then do the following:

   • To increase the selected text to the next highest preset size (for example, increasing from 12 points to 14 points), press Shift+⌘+>.

   • To increase the selected text by one point, press Option+Shift+⌘+>.

   • To decrease the selected text to the next lowest preset size (for example, decreasing from 12 points to 10 points), press Shift+⌘+<.

   • To decrease the selected text by one point, press Option+Shift+⌘+<.

You can also change the size of text interactively. To do so, select the text box that contains the text you want to resize. Using the Item tool to drag the sizing handles at the edge of the text box, resize the text in one of the following three ways:

✦ *Proportional resizing:* Option+Shift+⌘+drag handle

✦ *Nonproportional resizing:* ⌘+drag handle

✦ *Constrained (square) resizing:* Shift+⌘+drag handle

New Feature

In QuarkXPress 4, the Find/Change dialog box now supports searching for character and paragraph style sheets. If you look back at Figure 11-2, you'll see a checkbox for Style Sheet in both the Find What and Change To columns. Version 4 also supports Find/Change functions for superiors.

The Font Usage utility

Another way to change text attributes is to use the QuarkXPress utility called Font Usage, available through Utilities⇨Usage (or press F13 on the Mac; there is no Windows shortcut). Select the Fonts pane. This utility lists text style and typeface combinations used in the current document. In the example shown in Figure 11-3, we search for Galliard Plain, and Font Usage highlights where this type style appears in the document. We can now replace it with another typeface and/or style attribute. By checking the More Information box, we can see that Galliard is a Type 1 PostScript font.

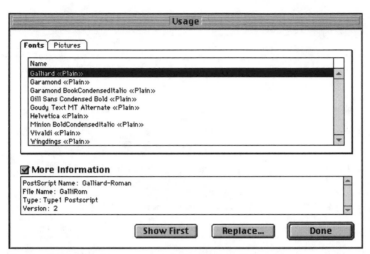

Figure 11-3: The Fonts pane of the Usage dialog box.

Font Usage is designed primarily to help you determine which typefaces are used in a document so that you or your typesetter will know which typefaces you need for printing. The utility also comes in handy if you open a document that uses a typeface not available on your computer; you can replace that typeface with another.

Checking Spelling

A finished document loses credibility when it includes words that are spelled incorrectly. So it's always a good idea to check for spelling errors. QuarkXPress has a built-in spelling checker that catches errors, as well as a tool that enables you to specify the proper spelling of words that the program does not recognize. To invoke the spelling checker, select Utilities➪Check Spelling.

The Check Spelling menu

This menu item drops down the submenu shown in Figure 11-4, which offers you the following spell-checking choices:

✦ **Word:** This option (⌘+L on the Mac; Ctrl+W in Windows) checks the current word or the first word in a group of selected words.

✦ **Story:** This option (Option+⌘+L on the Mac; Ctrl+Alt+W in Windows) checks the current story (all text in the current text box, as well as any text in text boxes linked to it).

✦ **Document:** This option (Option+Shift+⌘+L on the Mac; Ctrl+Alt+Shift+W in Windows) checks every word in the current QuarkXPress document.

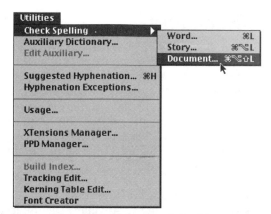

Figure 11-4: Access the Check Spelling command through the Utilities menu.

Dealing with suspect words

The spelling checker displays words that it does not recognize (calling them "suspect" words) one at a time, giving you an opportunity to correct or ignore (skip) the word. The spelling checker can suggest correct spellings for words that it believes are misspelled. Figure 11-5 shows the spelling checker displaying a word that is not in its dictionary.

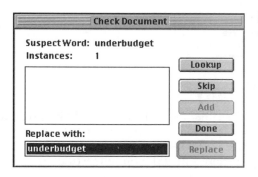

Figure 11-5: The Check Document dialog box.

Looking up and replacing words

To ask QuarkXPress to suggest a word, click the Lookup button. To accept a suggested replacement, click the word and the Replace button. You can also type in the correct word yourself, whether or not you use Lookup.

Working with auxiliary dictionaries

If you're not content with the 80,000-word dictionary in QuarkXPress, you can add additional words to an auxiliary dictionary. Words of a technical nature specific to your company or industry are good candidates for an auxiliary dictionary, as are proper names. If an auxiliary dictionary is open, you can add a word while in the spelling checker by selecting Add when QuarkXPress displays a suspect word. An auxiliary dictionary can be shared by multiple documents, or you can establish a dictionary specific to a particular document. Use Utilities⇨Auxiliary Dictionary to invoke the Auxiliary Dictionary dialog box, shown in Figure 11-6. Use this dialog box to create a new dictionary or open an existing one.

Note

If a dictionary is associated with the current document or is selected as the default auxiliary dictionary, its name appears at the bottom of the Auxiliary Dictionary dialog box under Current Auxiliary Dictionary.

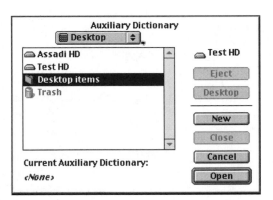

Figure 11-6: The Auxiliary Dictionary dialog box.

Editing an auxiliary dictionary

You can continue to customize an open auxiliary dictionary by adding or deleting words from it through the Edit Auxiliary Dictionary dialog box (accessed via Utilities⇨Edit Auxiliary), shown in Figure 11-7. The Edit Auxiliary Dictionary dialog box displays its contents alphabetically. Here's how the options work:

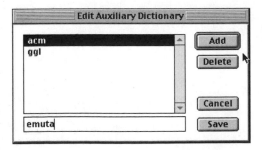

Figure 11-7: You can continue customizing an open auxiliary dictionary by making changes in the Edit Auxiliary Dictionary dialog box.

Auxiliary dictionary tips and tricks

One thing that's nice about auxiliary dictionaries is that you can pretty much put them where you want them. In other words, auxiliary dictionaries do not have to reside in the same file as the documents accessing them. If you open an auxiliary dictionary when a document is open, QuarkXPress associates them, so when you open the document, the program has access to the auxiliary dictionary. If you want an auxiliary dictionary to be available in all documents you subsequently create, open the auxiliary dictionary when no documents are open (as explained in the following items).

To create an auxiliary dictionary:

✦ *For a specific document:* Open the document and access the Auxiliary Dictionary dialog box (Utilities⊅Auxiliary Dictionary). Use the controls in the dialog box to locate the folder in which you want to keep the dictionary. Click the New button.

✦ *For all new documents:* Make sure that no documents are open before invoking the Auxiliary Dictionary dialog box.

To use an auxiliary dictionary:

✦ *In the current document:* Open your document and then open an existing dictionary from the Auxiliary Dictionary dialog box.

✦ *As the default for all new documents:* Make sure that no documents are open and then open an existing dictionary from the Auxiliary Dictionary dialog box.

To detach an auxiliary dictionary:

✦ *From a current document:* Open the document and select Close in the Auxiliary Dictionary dialog box.

✦ *As the default dictionary for all new documents:* Make sure that no documents are open. Select Close in the Auxiliary Dictionary dialog box.

✦ **To add a word:** Type the word in the field below the list of current words. Click the Add button. You'll note that you can't use the Shift or Caps Lock keys to add capital letters. That's because QuarkXPress doesn't check capitalization, just the sequence of letters; you'd want it to realize, for example, that "TPO," "tpo," and "Tpo" are all misspellings of "top." For proper nouns (such as "Quark"), simply enter the text in lowercase.

✦ **To delete a word:** Use the mouse to highlight the word from the word list, or enter it in the field below the current list of words (typing the word also highlights it in the list). Click the Delete button.

Note

Remember to click the Save button before you exit the Edit Auxiliary Dictionary dialog box. Otherwise, changes that you make are not saved. If you do not want to save your changes, choose Cancel.

Fitting Copy

The term *copy fitting* means just what it sounds like: the process of fitting text into the layout, often by altering the spacing. If your original, unmodified text fits the layout the first time through, consider it a stroke of luck because that's not what usually happens. Besides making pages look better, copy fitting can be a real business concern. In magazines, newsletters, and newspapers, the number of pages is set in advance, so you don't have the option of adding or removing pages to fit the lack or abundance of copy.

Because copy fitting involves several spacing factors, you might want to review the techniques described in Chapters 12 and 13 before applying the techniques outlined here.

It's sometimes necessary to take a number of actions, often in concert, to make text fit in the available space. Because the usual problem is having more text than space, the goal is often to shorten text, but you can use the same procedures in reverse to expand text. Note that the following tips are given in order of preference, so use the final ones only if the first few suggestions fail to achieve the desired effect:

   ✦ **Edit the text:** You can remove extra lines, but be on the lookout for lines at the end of a paragraph that have only a few characters. Getting rid of a few characters somewhere else in the paragraph may eliminate these short lines, reducing the amount of page space needed while keeping the amount of text removed to a minimum.

   ✦ **Track the text:** This procedure results in text that occupies less space, and it eliminates short lines. Chapter 12 explains how to track text.

   ✦ **Tighten the leading:** You can do this by a half- or a quarter-point. This change is so small that the average reader won't notice it, and it may save you a few lines per column, which can add up quickly. See the section on leading in Chapter 13.

   ✦ **Reduce the point size:** Do this by a half-point. This reduction saves more space than is first apparent because it allows you to place a few more lines on the page and put a bit more text in each line. Change point size in the style sheet or select text and use the type size controls in the Measurements palette.

   ✦ **Reduce the horizontal scale:** You can reduce this to a slightly smaller percentage (perhaps 95 percent) to squeeze more text in each line. The section on horizontal and vertical scale in Chapter 12 explains how to make this alteration.

   ✦ **Vary the size of columns:** Do this by setting slightly narrower column gutters or slightly wider margins.

Tip

Try applying these copy-fitting techniques globally to avoid a patchwork appearance. You can, however, change tracking on individual lines without ruining the appearance of your document. If you limit tracking changes to no more than 20 units, the text won't appear obviously different to your readers.

✦　　✦　　✦

Controlling Character Spacing

◆ ◆ ◆ ◆

In This Chapter

Defining character spacing

Using the tracking controls

Adjusting word spacing

Kerning your text

Changing horizontal and vertical scales

Working with special spaces

◆ ◆ ◆ ◆

It may sound nit-picky, but if you're a publisher, you pay attention to details such as the amount of space around individual text characters. This attention to detail is important because the space around characters has a profound effect on the ease with which a reader understands the text and the message it conveys. Character spacing is a significant contributor to the quality (or lack thereof) of a printed document. This chapter tells you all about it.

Defining Character Spacing

Throughout the history of publishing, professional typographers have enhanced the look of documents by increasing or decreasing character spacing. When done correctly, character spacing gives text a finished look. *Character spacing*—the space around and between characters—is what provides the mood of a document. Words set in characters that are surrounded by generous amounts of space have a light, airy feel; words set in characters that are close together feel heavier and more serious. Character spacing gives a psychological boost to the thought conveyed by the text itself. Character spacing includes the following aspects:

◆ Kerning

◆ Tracking

◆ Scale

◆ Hyphenation

Typographic color

As a group, these four aspects determine what typographers call *color*, simply another way of describing the appearance of text on a page. If you want to see a document's typographic color, make your eyes go slightly out of focus. Here's a good way to understand the concept of typographic color: Find a magazine page that has a good amount of text on it. Stare at the page for two minutes or so. Then focus on something halfway between you and the page. You'll see the text blur. The resulting gray level and consistency is *color*. Why is a document's color so important? Because it affects both the document's mood and readability. For most publishing applications, a light to medium color is preferable because it is easier on the eye.

The influence of typeface

Factors in addition to character spacing influence color. The most fundamental factor is the typeface. An airy, light typeface such as New Baskerville has a light color, while a solid, heavy typeface such as Benguiat Gothic Heavy has a dark color. Figure 12-1 shows the same text in these two typefaces. Notice how the text on the left, in New Baskerville, looks lighter than the Benguiat Gothic Heavy text on the right. The example shown in the figure clearly demonstrates that type fonts are major contributors to typographic color. Some typefaces are light, some are heavy. Regardless of a typeface's intrinsic weight, QuarkXPress includes character spacing controls that let you modify a font's effect on typographic color.

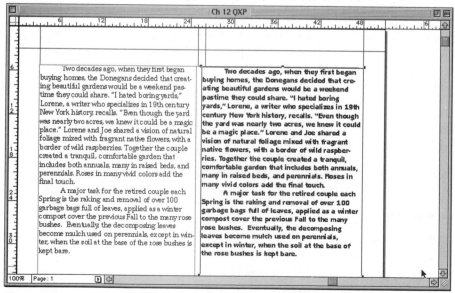

Figure 12-1: Different typefaces produce different shades of typographic color.

Using the Tracking Controls

Tracking has the greatest effect on typographic color. Also called *letter spacing*, tracking defines the amount of space between individual letters for a given section of text. The more space between letters, the looser the tracking and the lighter the color. When tracking is loosened excessively, text becomes airy and loses color. QuarkXPress sets the defaults for tracking at 0. This tells the program to use the letter spacing that the typeface's font file dictates in its width table. In QuarkXPress, you can set tracking for each style and override tracking for any selected text, as described in the following steps. (In version 4, tracking can now be applied to either character styles or paragraph styles.)

STEPS: Setting tracking in a style sheet

1. Access the Edit Style Sheet dialog box by selecting Edit⇨Style Sheets (or press Shift+F11) to display the Style Sheets dialog box for the current document.

2. To edit an existing paragraph style sheet or character style sheet, select the style sheet name and click Edit. To create a new paragraph style sheet or character style sheet, click and hold on New and select either Paragraph or Character.

3. If you are creating or editing a paragraph style sheet, click New or Edit in the Character Attributes area (near the center of the dialog box).

4. In the Track Amount field, enter the tracking amount (in units from 0 to 100). Use a minus sign (-) to reduce spacing (for tighter tracking).

When to use increased tracking

Are publishers more likely to decrease or increase tracking? Decreasing tracking is fairly common. Increasing it is not. You'll rarely need to increase tracking. But increasing it is a good idea in two situations:

✦ **Headlines:** In headlines that use heavy fonts, the letters can look too close to each other unless you open up some space between them (typographers call this space *air*).

✦ **Special effects:** Another reason to increase tracking is to achieve a special effect that is increasingly popular: spreading out letters in a word or title so that letters are more than one character apart. This often is used with text that is short, all on one line, and used as a kicker or other secondary label. Figure 12-2 shows an example of such a type treatment. Tracking in the highlighted text is set at 14 units, a loose tracking setting.

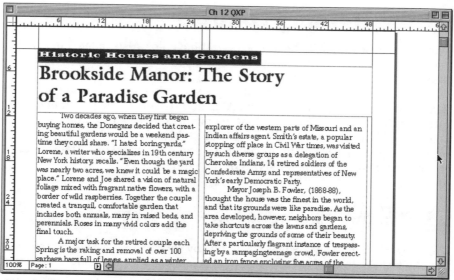

Figure 12-2: The reversed text, "Historic Houses and Gardens," is an example of how you can use loose tracking to achieve a special effect.

Tip

The best amount of tracking is a decision based not on right or wrong, but on personal aesthetics and the intended overall feel of the document. But here are some guidelines that we like to use: If you're using small type (12 points or smaller) and placing it in narrow columns (16 picas or narrower), consider using tighter tracking. The eye more readily sees gaps between small forms and in narrow columns than it does between large forms and in wide columns. Settings from –2 to –10 should work for most common typefaces.

Understanding ems

QuarkXPress sets tracking in increments of 200ths (one-half percent) of an em, which is the width of a capital letter M in the current type size. In most typefaces (decorative and symbol fonts are the main exceptions), an em is the same width as the current point size. So in 10-point Desdemona or 10-point Bookman, an em is 10 points wide. Thus, reducing tracking by 20 units (or 10 percent) makes characters set in 10-point type 1 point closer together, 9-point type 0.9 points closer, 15-point type 1.5 points closer, and so on.

In most cases, an em is equal to the width of two zeroes—the traditional em—but not in all. QuarkXPress supports both types of em spaces. You decide which definition the program uses by making a selection in the Character pane (Edit⇨Preferences⇨Document, or ⌘+Y, and then select the Character tab). Check the Standard Em Space box to use the traditional method or uncheck it to use the double-zero method.

Editing tracking tables

QuarkXPress includes sophisticated tools that let you edit the tracking that comes built into a font. This is handy if you find that with some fonts you seem to be adjusting tracking often; if so, you may want to consider editing the font's tracking table. To do this, you need to access the QuarkXPress tracking editor, which appears under the Utilities menu as Tracking Edit.

Note

When you use the QuarkXPress tracking editor, you do not make any changes to your font files themselves; you just change the way they work in QuarkXPress.

Adjusting the curve

With the tracking editor, you edit a curve on a graph that establishes the relationship between point size and tracking value. When you click a point in the curve, you create a turn point at which the direction of the curve can change. Figure 12-3 shows a tracking setting that loosens tracking for headline text (above 24 points in this example) to 19 units.

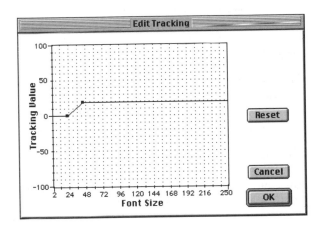

Figure 12-3: To change the tracking values for a font, adjust the curve in the Edit Tracking dialog box.

Changing each face

Because the tracking editor treats each face of a typeface—such as plain, bold, italic, and bold italic—separately, remember to make tracking adjustments in all faces of the typefaces you alter. Appropriate tracking values may be different for each typeface, especially for heavier faces like bold and ultra.

Resetting the defaults

If you make tracking table edits and decide that you don't like the results, you can reset them to the default setting, which is defined in the typeface's font files (usually 0) by clicking the Reset button in the Edit Tracking dialog box. This works even if you have already saved your settings and exited the track editor. In another example, you may want to abandon the tracking changes that have been made to a document. Since QuarkXPress detects whether a document's settings match the defaults for that copy of the program, when you open the document, you are given the choice shown in the dialog box in Figure 12-4. The dialog box also shows you which settings differ. Select Use XPress Preferences to apply the default settings. (In QuarkXPress 4 this is now the default, so you can simply press Return.)

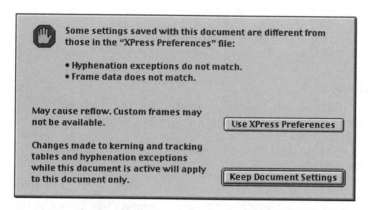

Figure 12-4: QuarkXPress alerts you if the document you are opening has settings that vary from those in the XPress Preferences file.

Adjusting tracking on-the-fly

You can use the tracking editor to set tracking values permanently or use QuarkXPress style sheets to establish values for all text that uses a particular style. In the following situations, you may want to apply tracking on a case-by-case basis:

✦ **Copy fitting:** Squeezing or stretching text to make it fit into a fixed amount of space is called *copy fitting*. You can do this to an entire story, but it is more common to retrack widows and any lines that have only a few characters (fewer than six or so), because you gain a whole line by forcing those characters to move into previous lines.

✦ **Removing widows and orphans:** When the last line of a paragraph consists of only a few characters, it is called a *widow*. This is considered typographically unsightly, particularly on a line that begins a column. How many characters constitute a widow is personal judgment. We tend to consider anything shorter than a third of a line a widow. An *orphan* refers to the first line of a paragraph (which is indented) that begins at the bottom of a column. Orphans are less taboo than widows. We tend to not worry about them. Even if fitting text within a certain space is not an issue, widows and orphans are frowned upon in serious publishing because they can look awkward.

Tip

You can also copy-fit by cutting out some text, but this requires the involvement of an editor, not just a production person, because the meaning of the text might be affected. Generally, you highlight one or two lines that seem to have excess space and reduce the tracking settings.

Changing tracking in one document only

When you make changes in the tracking editor, they apply not only to the document you're currently working with, but to every document you create after you make the changes. If you want your tracking changes to apply to one document only, close the document after you make the changes, then open the Edit Tracking dialog box for that font and click Reset.

Because QuarkXPress associates an edited tracking table with the document that was active when you invoked the tracking editor, when you give a service bureau your QuarkXPress document to output to negatives on an imagesetter, your tracking changes remain intact.

✦ **Creating special effects:** Stretching a word by increasing its tracking can be a good idea, especially if you are trying to achieve a special effect. Often, stretched-out text is formatted in all caps or small caps. If you use this effect in labels or kickers, it's wise to create a style sheet with these settings, rather than apply the tracking manually.

✦ **Altering ellipses (. . .):** Many people find the ellipsis character too tightly spaced, so they use three periods instead. If you don't like the amount of spacing QuarkXPress provides when you type three periods with default tracking settings, you can change the spacing through tracking. You cannot retrack the ellipsis character itself—spacing within the character doesn't change—so if you want to define the ellipsis via tracking, use three periods instead of the ellipsis character. And be sure to use nonbreaking space (⌘+spacebar on the Mac; Ctrl+5 in Windows), so you don't have some of the periods on one line and the rest on another.

Tracking selected text

To apply new tracking values, select the text you want to retrack. If you want to retrack all text in a story, use Edit⇨Select All, or press ⌘+A, to select all the text, rather than highlighting it with the mouse. (Remember, any tracking you apply manually to text is applied in addition to the tracking specified in the tracking editor.) After you select the text, you can change the tracking values in three ways:

Tip

Because tracking in QuarkXPress affects the space to the right of each character, you should select all but the last character in the section of text you want to track; otherwise, you could get some variation in the tracking of the last character in the selection.

✦ **Option 1:** The fastest method is to use the appropriate keyboard shortcut. Press Shift+⌘+} to increase tracking to the nearest $1/20$ em (10 units); press Shift+⌘+{ to decrease it to the nearest $1/20$ em. Pressing Shift+Option+⌘+} increases tracking by $1/200$ em (1 unit); pressing Shift+Option+⌘+{ decreases it by $1/200$ em.

✦ **Option 2:** You can also change tracking values by using the Measurements palette, which is shown in Figure 12-5, at the bottom of the screen. The area to the right of the left and right outlined arrows shows the current tracking value. Highlight that number and enter a new value. Or click the outlined arrows to change the values to the nearest 1/20 em (10 units). Clicking the left-pointing outlined arrow decreases the value, while clicking the right-pointing outlined arrow increases the value. To make the outlined arrows work in multiples of 1 unit instead of 10, press the Option key while clicking them.

✦ **Option 3:** Select Style⇨Track and enter the tracking value in the Track Amount field of the Character Attributes dialog box (see Figure 12-5).

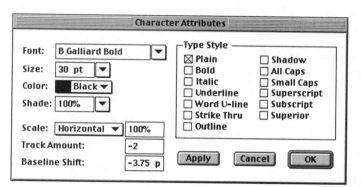

Figure 12-5: The Character Attributes dialog box, in which you can enter a value in the Track Amount field.

Note

If you do not have a Tracking Edit option on your Utilities menu, it probably means you do not have the Kern/Track Editor XTension installed. Use the new XTensions Manager (utilities⇨XTensions Manager) to activate the XTensions, quit QuarkXPress, and relaunch QuarkXPress.

How QuarkXPress handles tracking justified text

When you apply tracking to justified text, you need to know the sequence that is followed by the program. QuarkXPress applies justification first, and then adjusts the tracking according to your specifications. That means if you specify tracking of −10 (equivalent to 5 percent tighter spacing) and QuarkXPress adds 2 percent more space on a line to justify it, the net spacing on that line is 3.1 percent (102 percent width for justification times 95 percent tracking: $1.02 \times .95 = 96.9$; and $100 − 96.9 = 3.1$ percent), or a tracking value of about −6.

Nonetheless, the Tracking Amount field in the Character Attributes dialog box and the Measurements palette both show a tracking value of −10. This is simply a reflection of how justified text has always been handled, even in typesetting systems that predate desktop publishing. Any publishing system ignores tracking settings if that's the only way to justify a line.

Tracking justified text

Character and word spacing are affected by justification settings. If you justify text (aligning text against both left and right column margins), QuarkXPress adds space between words and characters to create that alignment. If tracking settings were the sole determinant of character spacing, QuarkXPress would be unable to justify text. Realize that justification settings influence actual tracking, so you should set them to work in conjunction with tracking settings. This will make it possible for you to meet your overall spacing goals.

Adjusting Word Spacing

Word spacing—the space between words—is another important contributor to the aesthetics of a document. Think about it: If the words in a sentence are too close to one another, comprehension may be affected because of the difficulty in telling where one word ends and another begins. If the words are too far apart, the reader might have a difficult time following the thought that is being conveyed.

Here's a design rule we like to follow: The wider the column, the more space you can add between words. This is why books tend to have more word spacing than magazines. Like all other typographic issues, there's a subjective component to picking good word spacing. Experiment to see what works best in your documents.

The Edit H&J dialog box

QuarkXPress puts its word spacing features in its Edit Hyphenation & Justification menu, not with its other character spacing options. You access this menu through the Edit⇨H&J menu option, or via the shortcut Option+⌘+H on the Mac or Ctrl+Shift+F11 in Windows. Figure 12-6 shows the Edit Hyphenation & Justification dialog box. The Space and Char settings let you control how QuarkXPress adds spacing between words and characters to justify text. Space settings control word spacing; Char settings control letter spacing. The QuarkXPress default establishes the same value for the minimum and optimum character settings, but they do not have to remain the same. However, you cannot set the optimum setting at less than the minimum or more than the maximum. The available options are as follows:

The default settings are stored as Standard. Make sure you modify Standard with your preferred word-spacing settings (called an H&J set) before creating other H&J sets, because they are based on Standard settings.

✦ The *Min.* (minimum) setting tells QuarkXPress the smallest amount of space allowed between words or characters.

✦ The *Opt.* (optimum) setting defines the amount of space you want between words and characters, and QuarkXPress sets spacing as close to that setting as possible.

✦ The *Max.* (maximum) setting sets the upper limit on space between words or characters.

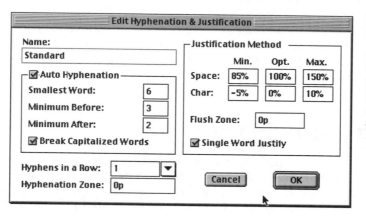

Figure 12-6: The Edit Hyphenation & Justification dialog box has controls that let you set up the spacing between characters and words in justified text.

Note

If text is justified, QuarkXPress never places characters closer together than the minimum setting, but it may exceed the maximum setting if that's the only way to make the line fit. If text is not justified (if it is left-aligned, right-aligned, or centered), QuarkXPress uses the optimum settings for all text. Chapter 13 describes how to use hyphenation settings in concert with letter and word spacing.

Working with preferred settings

As you can see from our settings in Figure 12-6 (85 percent minimum, 100 percent optimum, and 150 percent maximum for word spacing; and –5 percent minimum, 0 percent optimum, and 10 percent maximum for letter spacing), we prefer minimum settings that are less than the optimum because it helps text fit more easily in narrow columns. These settings work well for most newsletters and magazines output on an imagesetter. Also, we have found that desktop publishing programs tend to add more space than we prefer, so we typically tighten the word and letter spacing to compensate. At the same time, we usually leave the maximum word spacing at 150 percent.

Tip

For material destined for final output on a 300-dpi laser printer, you may want to keep the defaults, because laser printers have coarser resolution and thus cannot make some of the fine positioning adjustments our settings impose. In some cases, they move characters closer together than desired, even when the same settings work fine on a higher-resolution imagesetter.

Kerning Your Text

Often, the space between certain pairs of letters needs to be adjusted so that it looks good. This adjustment of the space between two specific letters is known as *kerning*. Kerning tells the output device—such as a laser printer, typesetter, or monitor—to add or, more typically, subtract a certain amount of space between specific pairs of letters anytime those pairs occur in a document, so that their spacing seems natural. The information on which pairs of letters to kern and how much to kern them by is stored in the font file as a kerning table.

When to use kerning

Without kerning, some letters may appear to be farther apart than other letters in the same word, tricking the eye into thinking they are, in fact, in different words. You can see an example of this in Figure 12-7. On the top line of the figure, the unkerned letter pairs *AW* and *to* appear far enough apart that the eye may perceive them as belonging to separate words. Kerning adjusts the spacing to prevent this problem, as shown in the bottom line of the figure. Kerning is important for all large type. The larger the characters, the larger the space between them, and thus any awkward spacing becomes more noticeable. For smaller type, kerning is often not noticeable because the space between letters is already so small.

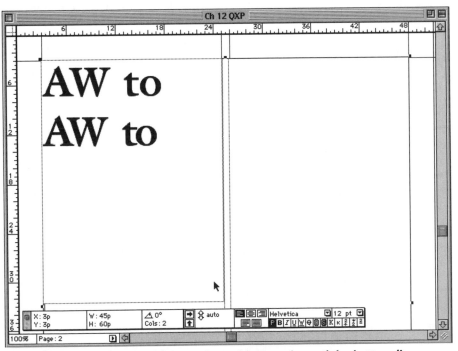

Figure 12-7: The top line contains unkerned letter pairs, and the bottom line contains the same letter pairs kerned.

The Auto Kern Above feature

Kerning requires QuarkXPress to look at every pair of letters to see whether they have special kerning values. QuarkXPress offers the Auto Kern Above feature, which you turn on and off through the Character pane (access by choosing Edit➪Preferences➪Document, or ⌘+Y). This option tells QuarkXPress to stop kerning when text reaches a certain size. Any text at or below the size you specify is not kerned. The cut-off size you choose for Auto Kern Above is both a personal choice based on aesthetic judgment, and a technical choice based on the output device. The relatively low resolution on a 300-dpi laser printer limits how fine you can adjust spacing between characters. But on a 1270- or 2540-dpi imagesetter, there is practically no limit to how much control you have over spacing, so you should take advantage of it.

A rule of thumb is to set Auto Kern Above between 8 and 12 points. It makes sense to set Auto Kern Above to your basic body text size, and for most documents, basic body text size falls between 8 and 12 points. If your base text is 9 points, set Auto Kern Above to 9 points. However, use a small value (8 or 9) for any text you output to a 600-dpi or finer device, regardless of the size of your body text.

The Kern to Space feature

QuarkXPress also includes a Kern to Space feature. This lets you use an en space as one of the characters in a kerning pair. This kern-to-space feature comes in handy when you want to tighten the space between two items. These pairs (a character and an en space) are used just like other kerning pairs. To set up a kern-to-space pair using the Kern/Track Editor, first enter the space (Option+Space on the Mac and Ctrl+Shift+6 in Windows) into the Pair field.

Editing kerning tables

The kerning table for a font may not match your preferences for some letter pairs. In some cases, the table may not include kerning information for certain letter pairs that cause you trouble. QuarkXPress includes a function that lets you edit kerning information for any TrueType or Type 1 PostScript typeface. It appears under the Utilities menu as Kerning Table Edit. You can modify existing settings, add new pairs, or remove existing pairs.

If you do not have a Kerning Table Edit option on your Utilities menu, it probably means you do not have the Kern/Track Editor XTension installed. Use the new XTensions Manager (utilities➪XTensions Manager) to activate the XTension, quit QuarkXPress, and relaunch QuarkXPress.

Changing kerning in one document only

QuarkXPress associates an edited kerning table with the document that was active when you invoked the kerning editor. This means that if you give your QuarkXPress document to a service bureau to output to negatives on an imagesetter, your kerning changes remain intact. If you want kerning changes to affect all documents, invoke the kerning editor with no document selected. Any future document uses the new settings.

When you make changes in the kerning table editor, they apply not only to the document you're currently working with, but to every document you create after you make the changes. If you want your kerning table changes to apply to one document only, close the document after you make the changes, then open the Edit Kerning Table dialog box for that font and click Reset.

Figure 12-8 shows the kerning table editor. Predefined kerning values are displayed in the Kerning Pairs list, through which you can scroll to select pairs whose values you want to change. You can delete kerning pairs by highlighting them in the Kerning Pairs list in the dialog box and clicking the Delete button. Deleting a kerning pair is the same as setting its kerning value to zero.

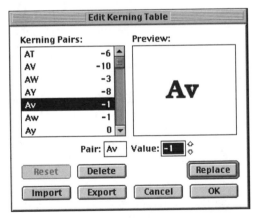

Figure 12-8: You can modify kerning values in the Edit Kerning Table dialog box.

Note

Deleting, adding, or changing a kerning pair in the Edit Kerning Table dialog box does not make any changes to your font file itself; it just changes the way that pair of letters works in QuarkXPress.

STEPS: Adding kerning pairs

1. In the Edit Kerning Table dialog box enter the two letters at the Pair prompt.

2. Enter the kerning value at the Value prompt. As with tracking, the unit of measurement is 1/200th of an em, or roughly one-half percent of the current point size. Negative values decrease space between the letters, positive numbers add space. (Clicking the Reset button resets all kerning values to the those stored in the font file. Any kerning pairs you have added are deleted. Import and Export buttons let you import kerning values from another file or export current ones to a new file.)

3. If you are modifying existing kerning values, select Replace; if you are adding a kerning pair, the button will be labeled Add.

4. To save changes, select OK. To cancel changes, select Cancel. (The difference between Reset and Cancel is that Reset resets all kerning pairs to the font's default and leaves you in the dialog box to make other changes, while Cancel closes the dialog box and returns you to the Edit Kerning Table dialog box.)

Tip

The kerning editor treats each face of a typeface—such as plain, bold, italic, and bold italic—separately, so be sure to make kerning adjustments in all faces of the typefaces you alter. And keep in mind that the appropriate kerning values are different for each face because characters are shaped differently in each face.

Changing kerning on-the-fly

You may occasionally want to manually kern specific letter pairs. For example, your document may incorporate typefaces you use so rarely that it's not worthwhile to modify the kerning table. QuarkXPress lets you modify kerning on-the-fly for any letter pairs you select. Put your text cursor between the two letters. You have three ways to change the kerning values:

✦ **Option 1:** The fastest way to change kerning values, especially when you want to experiment, is to use the keyboard shortcuts. Press Shift+⌘+} to increase kerning to the nearest $1/20$ em (10 units); press Shift+⌘+{ to decrease it to the nearest $1/20$ em. Pressing Shift+Option+⌘+} increases kerning by $1/200$ em (1 unit); pressing Shift+Option+⌘+{ decreases it by $1/200$ em.

✦ **Option 2:** Another method is to use the Measurements palette. The number to the right of the left and right outlined arrows shows the current kerning value. Highlight that number and enter a new value. Or click the outlined arrows to change the values incrementally: the left-pointing outlined arrow decreases the value, while the right-pointing one increases the value. To make the outlined arrows work in multiples of 1 unit instead of 10, press the Option key while clicking them.

✦ **Option 3:** Select Style⇨Kern and enter the kerning value in the Kern Amount field of the Character Attributes dialog box, shown in Figure 12-9.

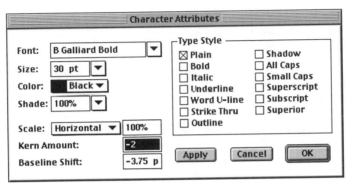

Figure 12-9: Kerning adjusts the space between two characters, as demonstrated in the Kern Amount field in the Character Attributes dialog box.

If you highlight characters rather than place the text cursor between the two characters you want to kern, QuarkXPress displays Track instead of Kern in dialog boxes and menus. Tracking is discussed in detail earlier in this chapter.

Changing Horizontal and Vertical Scales

If you change the typeface's horizontal or vertical scale, you can influence typographic color. Scaling compresses or expands the actual characters (rather than the space between the characters) to a percentage, ranging from 25 to 400 percent, in 0.1 percent increments. The Horizontal and Vertical Scale option is available when a text box is active and the Content tool is selected. Choose Style⇨Character (⌘+Shift+D) to display the Character Attributes dialog box. Figure 12-10 shows the field that allows you to adjust horizontal or vertical scale. You do not need to enter the percent symbol (%) when you enter the scaling value. QuarkXPress automatically assumes the value is a percentage.

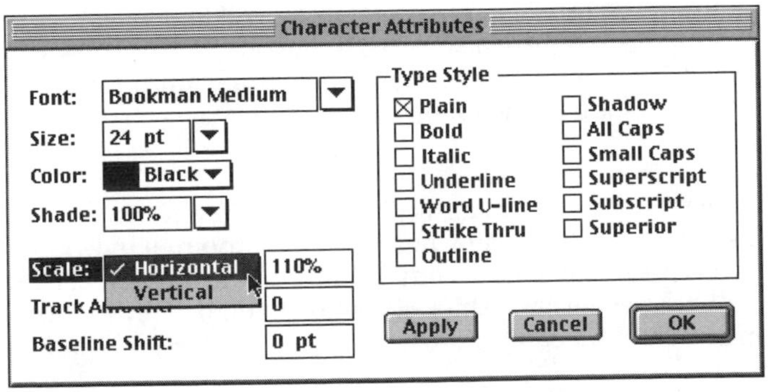

Figure 12-10: The Horizontal and Vertical selection in the Character Attributes dialog box.

When to scale

Scaled text can be useful in the following applications:

✦ To fit text in the available space.

✦ To call attention to display type, such as drop caps, headlines, or other type-as-design elements.

✦ To create a different feel for an existing typeface that might otherwise not be appropriate for the use intended. An example is compressing wide typefaces for use as body text.

Tip QuarkXPress allows you to apply only one kind of scaling to a selected section of text: vertical *or* horizontal. If you want to scale text in both directions, try changing the point size first and then applying a horizontal or vertical scale.

The curse and creativity of scaling

A traditional typographer would blanch at the thought of scaling type because each type-face is designed to be displayed optimally at a certain weight and size. That's why *hinting* (an algorithm that automatically adjusts the typeface's characteristics for various sizes)—pioneered by Adobe in its Type 1 PostScript fonts and adopted by Microsoft and Apple in their TrueType fonts—was such a breakthrough. And that's why boldface is more than just fatter characters, and italics is more than slanted characters.

When you change a typeface's scale, you distort the design that was so carefully crafted. Instead, a traditional typographer would argue, use existing expanded or compressed (also called *condensed*) versions of the typeface because they were designed to be used at their percentage of horizontal scaling.

How much to scale

If you don't go overboard, you can use horizontal or vertical scaling effectively. Scaling a typeface to 50 percent or 150 percent of its size will likely destroy its character. But scaling a typeface between 90 and 110 percent often works well, and staying between 95 and 105 percent results in type that, while not noticeably different, is distinct. Pay attention to the following kinds of typefaces when you scale:

✦ Typefaces that have darker vertical strokes (the constituent components) than horizontal strokes can look odd when expanded too much. Optima is an example of such a typeface. A sans serif typeface such as Eurostile, Helvetica, or Univers works best because its generally even shape has fewer intricate elements that might get noticeably distorted.

✦ Many serif typefaces work fine if horizontally scaled only slightly. Squarer typefaces such as Melior and New Century Schoolbook lend themselves best to scaling without perceived distortion. When you slightly compress wide typefaces such as Tiffany, which are normally used for headlines and other display type, they can acquire a new feel that makes them usable as body text. Finer typefaces such as Janson Text more quickly become distorted because the differences between the characters' already shallow horizontal strokes and already thicker vertical strokes become more noticeable— especially when expanded.

✦ Avoid scaling decorative typefaces such as Brush Script, Dom Casual, and Park Avenue. However, Zapf Chancery can be scaled slightly without looking distorted.

Figure 12-11 shows sample horizontal and vertical scaling on four typefaces.

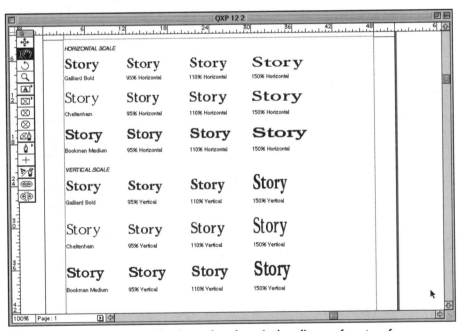

Figure 12-11: The effects of horizontal and vertical scaling on four typefaces.

Working with Special Spaces

In some cases, you may want to impose specific kinds of spacing, rather than rely on the normal spaces whose width is affected by tracking and justification settings. QuarkXPress provides the following special space options:

✦ **Nonbreaking space:** This space ensures that a line does not wrap between two words if you do not want it to. The command is ⌘+space on the Mac; Ctrl+5 in Windows.

✦ **En space:** An en space (press Option+space on the Mac; Ctrl+Shift+6 in Windows) is typically used in numbered lists after the period following the numeral. An en space makes a number more visible because the number is more separated from the following text than words in the text are separated from each other. En spaces also are used before single-digit numerals when a numbered list includes both single- and double-digit numerals. (In most typefaces, a numeral occupies the width of an en space. So putting an en space before numerals 1 through 9 aligns them with the 0 in the number 10.) A variation of the en space is the nonbreaking en space, accessed by pressing Option+⌘+space on the Mac; Ctrl+Alt+Shift+6 in Windows.

✦ **Punctuation space:** A punctuation space, accessed via Shift+space on the Mac and Ctrl+6 in Windows, is the width of a period or comma. Some people call a punctuation space a thin space; regardless, it is generally half the width of an en space. It is typically used to ensure alignment of numerals when some numbers have commas and others don't—as in 4,109 and 142. To align the last three digits of both numbers, you place an en space and a punctuation space before 142. A variation is the nonbreaking punctuation space, accessed via Shift+⌘+space on the Mac and Ctrl+Alt+6 in Windows.

✦ **Flexible space:** A flexible space (Option+Shift+space on the Mac; Ctrl+Shift+5 in Windows) is a space you define as a certain percentage of an en space. If you define a flexible space as twice the width (200 percent) of an en space, you create an em space. You define the flexible space width in the Character pane, accessed via Edit⇨Preferences⇨Document (⌘+Y). Specify the width in percentages from 0 to 400, in increments of 0.1. For the nonbreaking variant of the flexible space, press Shift+Option+⌘+space.

Tip

A common fixed space available in most desktop publishing programs, but not in QuarkXPress, is an em space. You can create an em space by using two en spaces or by defining a flexible space to be the width of an em (200 percent).

✦   ✦   ✦

Controlling Paragraph Spacing

In This Chapter

Working with
hyphenation and
justification

Making the most of
leading

Adding additional
paragraph spacing

Effective paragraph spacing is more than simply having adequate space between paragraphs. Paragraph spacing is helped immensely by two traditional tools: hyphenation and justification, or H&J. H&J help to fit text within a certain space, while allowing the copy to maintain an attractive appearance. Balancing these paragraph spacing attributes is critical to good overall document design, and is essential if you want to keep your readers interested. Although you can use character spacing to create blocks of text with good typographical color (see Chapter 12 for more information on character spacing), you can spoil the overall effect if paragraph spacing is not up to par. This chapter will teach you more about these vital topics.

Working with Hyphenation & Justification

Both hyphenation and justification have a great impact on the shape of text and its typographic color, which are important parts of the impression the text conveys. Because professional typesetters almost always use hyphenation and justification together, it comes as no surprise that QuarkXPress's H&J features are being closely related. Although you set justification for individual paragraph styles through the Edit Style Sheets dialog box (accessed via Edit⇨Style, or by pressing Shift+F11), you set the justification method in a more basic setting— through H&J sets defined in the Edit Hyphenation & Justification dialog box, accessed via Edit⇨H&Js (Option+⌘+H on the Mac; Ctrl+Shift+F11 in Windows).

Setting up H&J sets

In the Edit Hyphenation & Justification dialog box (see Figure 13-1), you set up H&J sets that control hyphenation and justification parameters for any paragraph styles onto which the H&J sets are applied. A document can have different H&J sets, which lets you combine several typographic and layout approaches in the same document.

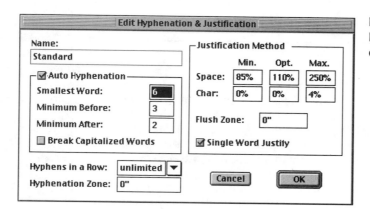

Figure 13-1: The Edit Hyphenation & Justification dialog box.

Copying sets from document to document

To use H&J sets from another document in your current document, select the Append option in the H&J dialog box. Also choose this option if you establish master settings when no document is open. This lets you append (copy) all the H&J sets from existing documents and templates. Note that any H&J sets in the current document (or master settings) have the same names as sets you append from the other document. They are not altered, and you always get the opportunity to rename them.

Editing H&J sets

QuarkXPress lets you edit H&J for an active document or for all documents. (We refer to the latter as master H&J sets.) You can tell you are editing master H&J sets when the dialog box title is Default H&Js instead of H&Js for *document name*.

Justification methods

In the Edit Hyphenation & Justification dialog box, the two main justification methods—Space and Char—control how QuarkXPress spaces words and letters to align text in relation to both margins of a column. Because justification requires QuarkXPress to figure out where and how much space to add line by line, it needs some guidance as to how to do so. That's where the three options—Min, Opt, and Max—of the two justification methods come into play (refer to Figure 13-1). (The Space and Char options that control these settings are discussed in more detail in Chapter 12.) Here's how Min, Opt, and Max work:

✦ **Min:** Minimum justification settings tell QuarkXPress how much it can squeeze text to make it fit in a justified line.

✦ **Max:** This setting tells the program how much it can stretch text to make it fit. QuarkXPress does not squeeze text more than the minimum settings allow, but it does exceed the maximum settings if it has no other choice.

✦ **Opt:** If text is not justified, QuarkXPress uses the optimum settings for all text.

When you use justified text, QuarkXPress gives you two more options: Flush Zone and Single Word Justify.

✦ **Flush Zone:** This setting, measured from the right margin, tells QuarkXPress when to take the text in the last line of a paragraph and force it to justify with both margins. (Normally, the last line of a justified paragraph is aligned to the left.) If text in the last line reaches the flush zone, it is justified; otherwise it remains left-aligned.

We recommend that you do not use the Flush Zone feature. When the last line in a justified paragraph is left-aligned, it gives the reader a needed clue that the paragraph is complete.

✦ **Single Word Justify:** This tells QuarkXPress it is OK to space out a word that is long enough to take up a single line if it is needed to justify that line.

We recommend that you always turn on Single Word Justify, even though words that take up a full line are rare. When they do occur, having them left-aligned (which is what happens if this option is not selected) in a paragraph that is otherwise justified is confusing because readers might misinterpret them as the end of the paragraph.

Hyphenation settings

Hyphenation settings determine the raggedness of unjustified text (text that is left-aligned, right-aligned, or centered) and the size of gaps in justified text (where text is aligned with both the left and right margins of a column). By varying the hyphenation settings, you can achieve a significantly different appearance, as illustrated in Figure 13-2. To turn on hyphenation, check the Auto Hyphenation box in the Edit Hyphenation & Justification dialog box.

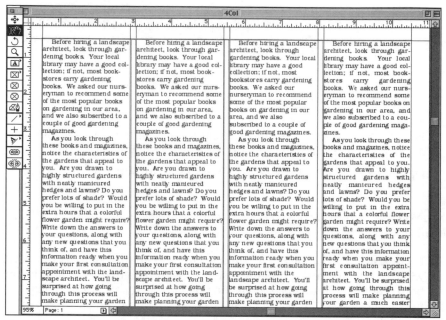

Figure 13-2: Changes to hyphenation settings can alter the appearance of text in a column.

In Figure 13-2, the two left columns appear the same, but actually have different hyphenation settings. The leftmost column is set at unlimited hyphenations, and the second is set at a maximum of three consecutive hyphens. These columns appear to be identical, simply because there are not enough long words in the text to force many consecutive hyphenations. But the third column, where hyphenation is turned off, has some gaps, and the last line in its first paragraph is longer. Often, the result is that an unhyphenated column takes more room than if it used hyphenation. The rightmost column is set as justified text with unlimited hyphenation, showing the difference between left-aligned and justified text.

Hyphenating capitalized words

Another box in the Edit Hyphenation & Justification dialog box controls whether or not QuarkXPress should hyphenate capitalized words. Should you turn on Break Capitalized Words? We think so.

True, some traditionalists argue against hyphenating proper names, and some pragmatists don't check this feature because most hyphenation dictionaries make mistakes with proper names. Still, there is no compelling reason not to treat proper names as you do any other text. If the program improperly hyphenates proper names, add them to your document's hyphenation exception dictionary (covered later in this chapter), rather than prohibiting their hyphenation.

Hyphenation tips and tricks

Consider changing the Minimum Before setting to 2 if you have narrow columns or large text. Although many typographers object to two-letter hyphenation—as in ab-dicate or ra-dar—it often looks better than text with large gaps caused by the reluctance to hyphenate such words. Hyphenation also makes sense for many words that use two-letter prefixes such as in-, re-, and co-.

While we advocate two-letter hyphenation at the beginning of a word, we prefer three-letter hyphenation at the end. Except for words ending in -ed and sometimes -al, most words don't lend themselves to two-letter hyphenation at the end of the word. Part of this is functional—it's easy for readers to lose two letters beginning a line. We prefer two-letter hyphenations at the end of a word only when the alternative is awkward spacing. As with all typography, this ultimately is a personal choice.

Words broken using minimum settings of 1 look awful. They also go against reader expectations because the norm is to have several letters after a hyphen. Never use a minimum setting of 1 for Minimum Before. If you do, you get hyphenations such as A-sia, a-typical, and u-niform that simply look terrible in print. They also don't provide enough context for the reader to anticipate the rest of the word. Likewise, never use a minimum of 1 for Minimum After because you get hyphenations such as radi-o.

Setting hyphenation parameters

How QuarkXPress hyphenates is determined by word hyphenation parameters. There are three such parameters, and they are set in the Edit Hyphenation & Justification dialog box:

- ✦ **Smallest Word:** This determines how long a word must be before QuarkXPress hyphenates it. The default of six letters is a reasonable default, although five is acceptable as well.

- ✦ **Minimum Before:** This determines how many characters must precede a hyphen in a hyphenated word. The default of three characters is a typical typographer's threshold.

- ✦ **Minimum After:** This sets the number of characters that must follow a hyphen in a hyphenated word. The default setting of two characters is common for newspapers and is most often seen in words ending in -ed, such as *blanket-ed.*

Limiting consecutive hyphens

Text can be hard to read when it contains too many hyphens in a row. The eye gets confused about which line it is on because it loses track of which hyphen represents which line. You can avoid having an excessive number of hyphens in a row by selecting a setting in the Hyphens In A Row field in the Edit Hyphenation & Justification dialog box (refer to Figure 13-1). The more hyphens you allow, the more easily QuarkXPress can break lines to avoid awkward gaps (in justified text) or awkward line endings (in nonjustified text). A good setting for Hyphens In A Row is 3 consecutive hyphens. This gives the eye enough context to keep lines in sequence. Avoid having fewer than two consecutive hyphens as your maximum because that typically results in awkward spacing.

Controlling the hyphenation zone

When text is not justified (that is, when it's set flush left or flush right), you still need to be concerned about the overall appearance of the text. It's a good idea to have some consistency in how lines of text end. Typographers call the uneven line endings the *rag*, and tend to manually modify the rag to give it a pleasing shape. This is done by retracking some lines or manually inserting hyphens. A pleasing shape is usually defined as one that undulates and has few consecutive lines of roughly the same width.

QuarkXPress lets you partially control the rag of nonjustified text through Hyphenation Zone control, found in the Edit Hyphenation & Justification dialog box. A setting of 0 tells QuarkXPress to hyphenate whenever it can. Any other setting specifies the range in which a hyphen can occur; this distance is measured from the right margin.

Tip   You won't often need this feature because QuarkXPress does a decent job of ragging text on its own. But if you do use it, a setting of no more than 20 percent of the column width usually works best. No matter which setting you use, expect to occasionally override QuarkXPress through manual hyphenation to make the rag match your preferences.

Overriding hyphenation settings

Occasionally, you may want to override hyphenation settings for a paragraph. For example, you might want to disallow hyphenation in a particular paragraph without affecting the rest of the text. To override hyphenation settings for a paragraph, use the Paragraph Attributes dialog box (see Figure 13-3). You can apply a different H&J set to the currently selected paragraphs by selecting a new set in the dialog box.

To access the dialog box, choose Style⇨Formats, or Shift+⌘+F, and then change the H&J setting to an appropriate H&J set (defined in the Edit⇨H&Js dialog box). To turn off hyphenation for a specific paragraph, insert your text cursor anywhere on the paragraph and go to the Paragraph Attributes dialog box (Style⇨Formats, or Shift+⌘+F). Select the name of the H&J set you have created that disallows hyphenation, making this the new H&J setting. Other paragraphs using the same paragraph style sheet are unaffected by this local override.

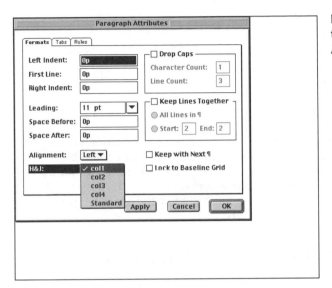

Figure 13-3: Choose H&J sets in the Formats pane of Paragraph Attributes dialog box.

Inserting soft hyphens

There will be times when you don't want to override the style settings for a particular paragraph. Instead, you will want to change the place in a particular word where QuarkXPress inserts the hyphen. QuarkXPress lets you do this through its soft hyphen feature. To manually insert a soft hyphen, type ⌘+ - (hyphen) between the letters you want the hyphen to separate. This soft hyphen disappears if the word moves (due to the addition or deletion of text, for example) to a place where a hyphen is not appropriate. Should the word and its soft hyphen move to a spot where a word break is appropriate, the hyphen reappears. (You can prevent a word from being hyphenated by putting a soft hyphen at the beginning of it.)

Note

You might wonder what happens if you insert a soft hyphen into a word that is already hyphenated. If a word is already hyphenated, the soft hyphen overrides QuarkXPress's hyphenation of the word. The program uses the soft hyphen rather than the setting in the hyphenation algorithm.

Using the Suggested Hyphenation feature

It's not easy remembering how to hyphenate every word. If you need prompting, select the word in question and then use QuarkXPress's Suggested Hyphenation feature. To access the Suggested Hyphenation dialog box (see Figure 13-4), select Utilities⇨Suggested Hyphenation or use the keyboard shortcut ⌘+H. QuarkXPress shows the recommended hyphenation settings for the current word (or, if more than one word is selected, for the first word in the selection).

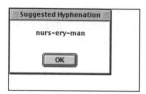

Figure 13-4: The Suggested Hyphenation dialog box.

Although handy as a quick reference, the Suggested Hyphenation feature does not replace a dictionary as the final authority on where a word should break. The feature takes into account the current H&J set. If the set specifies that no hyphen can be inserted until after the first three letters of a word, the Suggested Hyphenation dialog box will not show a hyphen after the second letter even if it is legal according to the hyphenation algorithm.

Adding words to the hyphenation dictionary

If you find yourself repeatedly inserting manual hyphens into the same words, you're doing too much work. Instead, add your own hyphenation preferences to QuarkXPress through the Hyphenation Exception dictionary feature. You do this through the Hyphenation Exceptions dialog box (see Figure 13-5). To access the dialog box, select Utilities⇨Hyphenation Exceptions.

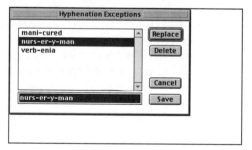

Figure 13-5: The Hyphenation Exceptions dialog box.

By adding words to the hyphenation dictionary, you give QuarkXPress hyphenation instructions for words the program does not know, hyphenates incorrectly, or hyphenates differently than your stylebook specifies. Additionally, you can prevent hyphenation of specific words by adding them to the dictionary. This dictionary can be global, affecting all documents; or local, affecting only the current document.

Dictionary tips and tricks

As you add words to the hyphenation dictionary, indicate allowable hyphenation points by inserting hyphens. To prevent a word from hyphenating, type it in without hyphens. You can change existing hyphenation exceptions by clicking the word you want to change. The Add button is replaced by the Replace button, and the word you type in replaces the one highlighted.

If you are in a document that does not use the standard QuarkXPress preferences, any hyphenation exceptions you enter affect only that document. To define hyphenation exceptions you want to use globally, close all active documents so that your changes are saved as default preferences.

You can tell QuarkXPress to prevent a line of text from breaking after a hyphen. To do so, use the nonbreaking hyphen character, ⌘+= (equals) to create this character. It is generally used when the text following a hyphen is short, as in words such as *follow-up,* or when a hyphen indicates a range of numbers or a score, such as *4-6* or *14-1*. True, not everyone worries about whether text breaks at such points. But it's nice that QuarkXPress lets you control hyphenation precisely if doing so matters to you.

Making the Most of Leading

In traditional typesetting, *leading* (pronounced *ledding*) is the space between lines of type. It is named for the thin strips of lead that printers used to use to separate metal type in early printing presses. Although tracking, kerning, and word spacing let you establish good typographic color horizontally, leading lets you do the same vertically.

Controlling leading

Leading varies based on several elements: column width, type size, whether text is justified or ragged, and the total amount of text. You can set leading in the following ways:

✦ **Option 1:** Use the Paragraph Attributes dialog box (Style➪Formats, or press Shift+⌘+F).

✦ **Option 2:** This option, which also accesses the Paragraph Attributes dialog box, is through the Style➪Leading menu (or press Shift+⌘+E).

✦ **Option 3:** A third option is through the Measurements palette. The number to the right of the up and down outlined arrows reflects the current leading setting, which you can highlight and change, to raise or lower incrementally, by clicking the up or down outlined arrows.

Leading and column width

The width of a column is the most important factor affecting good leading. The wider the column, the more space you need between lines to keep the reader's eye from accidentally jumping to a different line. This is the reason why books have noticeable space between lines, while newspapers and magazines, which use thin columns, have very little.

Leading and justified text

A related concern is whether type is justified or ragged-right. Justified text usually requires more leading than nonjustified text because the ragged margin gives the eye a distinct anchor point for each line.

The creative use of leading

Small changes in leading and point size alter the feeling of text, as you can see in Figure 13-6. This creative use of leading lets you subtly but effectively differentiate between sections or elements without resorting to extreme uses of typefaces or layout variations. Even though the typeface and justification are the same, the text on the left—set at 9.5-point with 11-point leading—has a very different texture than the text on the right, set at 9-point text with 11.5-point leading.

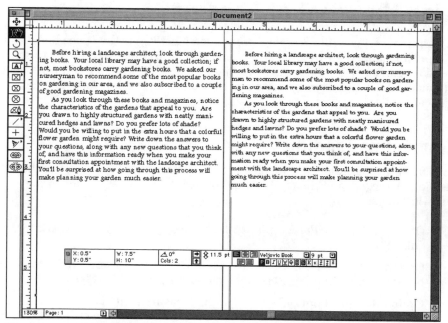

Figure 13-6: Minor changes in leading and point size make a dramatic difference in the text's appearance.

Leading tips and tricks

For text set in multiple columns, we recommend that you set leading at the current point size plus 2 points for text 9 points and larger. For example, if the point size of the text is 12 points, set leading at 14.

For text 8 points and smaller, use the current point size plus 1 point; 7-point type would get 8-point leading. This rule of thumb fluctuates somewhat according to column width. Add another 1 point or half-point, respectively, if your column width is greater than 16 picas but less than 27 picas; add at least 2 more points if your text is wider than 27 picas.

Auto and additive leading

QuarkXPress includes an automatic leading option, which usually sets leading at 120 percent of text size. This is fine for 10-point type because it results in 12-point leading. But for 9-point type, it results in 10.8-point leading, which is an awkward size on which to base a layout grid. And at larger type sizes, leading becomes too large; for example, 43.2-point leading is set for 36-point text.

Using additive leading

Although it provides an automatic leading option (enter **0** or **auto** as the leading value), QuarkXPress also offers a better alternative. You can set leading to be a certain number of points more than the current type size, no matter what the type size. Enter **+2**, for example, for leading 2 points more than the current type size. This *additive leading* option also ensures that any line with larger-than-normal type (such as a drop cap) won't overprint other lines.

An additive and auto leading drawback

Additive and automatic leading have a drawback: If you use superscripts (perhaps for footnotes), subscripts, or special text or symbols that extend beyond the body text's height or depth, you get uneven leading. This is because some lines have more leading than others to accommodate the outsized or outpositioned characters.

QuarkXPress bases additive and automatic leading on the highest and lowest character in a line, not on the body text's normal position. If you can't alter your text so that none of it extends beyond the body text range, don't use these options. Instead, specify the actual leading you want in each style tag.

Aligning text vertically

Vertical alignment—the vertical distribution of lines of text in a text box—is as important to the look of a page as using appropriate leading values. Before desktop publishing, it was not uncommon for columns to be slightly out of alignment because lining up strips of text by hand is nearly impossible to do precisely. Being within a point or two was considered adequate. Not any more. Uneven type columns today look unprofessional.

Two settings in the Paragraph pane of the Document Preferences dialog box prevent vertical-alignment problems. If set properly, QuarkXPress's Baseline Grid Increment and Maintain Leading controls (new in version 4) eliminate such slight misalignments. You access these settings through the Paragraph pane of the Document Preferences dialog box (select Edit⇨Preferences⇨Document, or ⌘+Y), as shown in Figure 13-7.

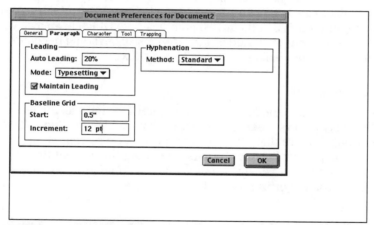

Figure 13-7: The Baseline Grid Increment and Maintain Leading controls in the Paragraph pane of the Document Preferences dialog box prevent vertical-alignment problems.

The Lock to Baseline Grid option

Used with the Lock to Baseline Grid option, which is in the Formats pane of the Paragraph Attributes dialog box, the Baseline Grid Increment feature enables you to ensure that the baselines—the bottoms of your letters—lock onto the grid lines you set for a document. Any text for which the baseline grid is locked is automatically positioned to align with the document grid, ensuring that text aligns across columns.

Baseline grid tips and tricks

The text you use the most in a document is body text, which is also where misalignment is most noticeable. To avoid this kind of misalignment, set your baseline grid to be the same as the leading for body text and check the Lock to Baseline Grid option in the paragraph style sheet for that body text.

Do *not* use the Lock to Baseline Grid option on text whose style has different leading settings, as this could result in awkward spacing between lines in text of that style. For example, if your body text has 11-point leading, but your subheads have 15-point leading, turning on the baseline lock option forces QuarkXPress to move the subhead to the next grid point, which is 22 points below the previous line of body text. This occurs even if you set the leading for the subhead style to place the subhead 15 points after the previous line of body text.

Style sheets and vertical alignment

If you put some thought into your style sheets when you create them, you can ensure consistent vertical alignment. You won't have to worry if you have style sheets with different leading amounts, or if additive leading causes some lines to have different leading than others. You also won't need to use the Lock to Baseline Grid option.

Checking the Maintain Leading option

If you check the Maintain Leading option in the Document Preferences dialog box, the line of text following a text box is positioned an even multiple of lines under the last line above the text box, ensuring vertical alignment across all columns. If you turn this option off, text is positioned immediately after the text box, which may not be the right position to align it with other columns. Using this option maintains proper leading for text that falls under an intervening text box, such as one that contains a sidebar, picture, or pull-quote.

Choosing the leading mode

In the Paragraph pane of the Document Preferences dialog box (select Edit⇨Preferences⇨Document, or ⌘+Y), the selection in the Mode pop-up menu tells QuarkXPress which technique to use in controlling leading (the two choices are Typesetting and Word Processing). With very few exceptions, you should set this at Typesetting, which measures leading from baseline to baseline.

An early version of QuarkXPress measured leading from top of text to top of text, which Quark calls Word Processing mode. This mode is not used in professional publishing, and even many old word-processing templates were based on measuring leading from the baseline. Unless you have a specific reason to select Word Processing mode, leave this setting at the default Typesetting mode.

Planning for consistent vertical alignment

Here are some examples of how to plan for consistent vertical alignment:

✦ When you pick 11.5 points as body-text leading, make sure other text elements add up to multiples of 11.5.

✦ If subheads are 14 points, give them 16-point leading and put 7 points of space above them (a total of 23 points, or two body-text lines) or put 18.5 points of space above them (a total of 34.5 points, or three body-text lines).

✦ If the byline is 8 points, give it a leading of 9.5 with 2 points of space above or below it.

✦ In both cases, make sure that these elements do not take more than one line. Otherwise, the leading from the second line means that their total vertical space is no longer a multiple of 11.5.

✦ If you cannot ensure this, create a tag with the same leading but with different space above (and maybe below) to use when the text in these paragraphs takes two lines.

Additional Paragraph Spacing

Another way to control the appearance of a document is to specify the amount of space above or below paragraphs, as well as the indents from the right and left margins. You do this in the Paragraph Attributes dialog box (see Figure 13-8). To access the dialog box for individual paragraphs, choose Style⇨Formats, or Shift+⌘+F. For paragraph style sheets, access the style sheets via the Formats pane in the Style Sheets dialog box (Edit⇨Style Sheets, or Shift+F11), and then create or edit a paragraph style sheet.

By using the left and right indent and the Space Before and Space After options, you can call attention to a paragraph by offsetting it from surrounding paragraphs. In Figure 13-8, we selected First Line and Right Indent to frame the right side of the paragraph with extra space. The Space Before and Space After options are also useful in positioning elements such as bylines, pull-quotes, and subheads that don't follow the same leading grid as the body text. In addition, you can use these options to ensure that the grid is maintained despite the use of larger or smaller type sizes for these elements, as discussed in the section on aligning text vertically, earlier in this chapter.

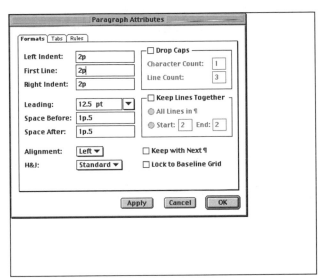

Figure 13-8: The Formats pane in the Paragraph Attributes dialog box.

Tip   Don't overdo extra paragraph spacing. The effect's success depends on its infrequent use. Common uses include indenting a long quotation or highlighting a recommendation. You need not alter all four options. Typically, a left indent is sufficient to offset a paragraph from surrounding text.

✦   ✦   ✦

Using Style Sheets

♦   ♦   ♦   ♦

In This Chapter

Defining styles

Exploring the Style
Sheets dialog box

Creating style sheets

Applying paragraph
and character styles

Editing paragraph
and character styles

Copying and
importing styles

Resolving style
conflicts

♦   ♦   ♦   ♦

Style sheets are similar in purpose to master pages. They define basic specifications for your text: typefaces, type sizes, justification settings, and tab settings. As with master pages, you can override style settings locally whenever you want. (See the section on overriding styles later in this chapter.) By putting common text-formatting information into style sheets—which essentially are macros for text attributes—you can avoid a lot of duplication of effort. Instead of applying each and every attribute individually to text, just tell QuarkXPress that you want certain text to take on all the formatting attributes established in a style sheet. This chapter tells you how.

New Feature

Before version 4, QuarkXPress style sheets controlled the attributes for complete paragraphs. The program now supports character style sheets, which control the attributes of highlighted characters.

Defining Styles

You can apply styles to whole paragraphs or to selected characters (usually words or sentences). For example, headlines can have a headline style, captions a caption style, bylines a byline style, and so on. You should create a style for all common paragraph and character formats. What you name those styles is up to you, although using standardized names can help you and your coworkers apply the right formatting to the right text. You can use styles in the following places (depending on the type of document you are working on):

♦ On selected paragraphs or characters in your QuarkXPress document

✦ In the word-processing text you plan to import (either by entering a code to indicate the desired style or by using the word processor's own style sheets, as described in the section on creating style sheets, later in this chapter)

Tip

It makes sense to apply styles in your source text for long or routine documents (such as a newsletter, in which everyone knows the styles to be used). And it makes sense to apply styles in QuarkXPress to a brochure or other highly designed or nonstandard document. No matter when you apply styles, you'll find that they are a must for the productive publishing of all but a small handful of documents (one-time pieces such as ads are possible exceptions).

Exploring the Style Sheets Dialog Box

To begin creating paragraph or character styles, you first need to get to the Style Sheets dialog box, which you access via Edit➪Style Sheets, or Shift+F11 (see Figure 14-1). The Style Sheets dialog box provides several options for editing paragraph or character style sheets, as Figure 14-2 shows.

Figure 14-1: Select Edit➪Style Sheets (Shift+F11) to open the Style Sheets dialog box.

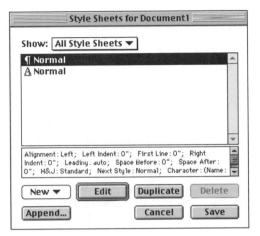

Figure 14-2: The Style Sheets dialog box.

Using the Show pop-up menu

The Show pop-up menu lets you select which style sheets should be listed in the Style Sheets dialog box. As you can see in Figure 14-3, you can list All Style Sheets to show both character and paragraph styles, Paragraph Style Sheets to list only paragraph styles, or Character Style Sheets to list only character styles. Selecting Style Sheets In Use shows styles that are being used in the active document, and Style Sheets Not Used lists styles that are assigned to the active document but that have not been applied to any of the document's characters or paragraphs.

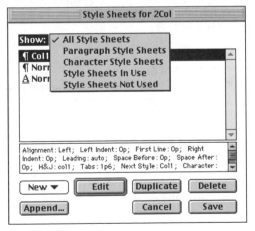

Figure 14-3: The Show pop-up menu in the Style Sheets dialog box.

Looking at the options

Your editing choices in the Style Sheets dialog box are as follows (refer to Figure 14-2):

✦ **New:** This option is a pop-up menu that lets you create a new paragraph style or character style from scratch or create a new style based on an existing style.

If you define text settings through the Style menu or Measurements palette and decide you want to create a paragraph or character style that contains those attributes, just position your text cursor anywhere on the text that has the desired settings. Then choose New in the Style Sheets dialog box. All settings are automatically included in the new style you create. This is handy if you want to experiment with settings on dummy text before creating a style for future use.

✦ **Edit:** This option lets you change the name and attributes of the selected style sheet.

✦ **Duplicate:** This option copies all the attributes of an existing paragraph or character style and gives the duplicate style the name *Copy of style*. You can then change any attribute settings, including the style name.

✦ **Delete:** This option lets you delete an existing paragraph style or character style. This option is grayed out when Normal is selected because you cannot delete the Normal style. You are asked to confirm the deletion if you applied the style to text in the current document.

If you attempt to delete a paragraph style sheet or character style sheet that has been applied to text, an alert is displayed (see Figure 14-4). You can then choose a replacement for the style sheet you want to delete, or you can delete the style and have the No Style option applied to the affected text.

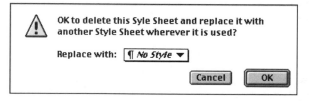

Figure 14-4: An alert appears when you attempt to delete a paragraph style or character style.

✦ **Append:** This option enables you to copy one or more styles from another QuarkXPress document.

✦ **Save:** This option lets you save all the style additions, deletions, and changes you make in the Style Sheets dialog box. You *must* save your styles when leaving the dialog box in order for changes to take effect.

✦ **Cancel:** This option instructs QuarkXPress to ignore all style additions, deletions, and changes you made in the Style Sheets dialog box since you last opened it.

The Edit Paragraph Style Sheet dialog box

When you are working with a paragraph style and choose New, Edit, or Duplicate in the Style Sheets dialog box, the next dialog box to appear is Edit Paragraph Style Sheet, shown in Figure 14-5. This dialog box contains four panes: General, Formats, Tabs, and Rules, in which you define the actual definition of style attributes. (We cover the editing options for character styles—in the Edit Character Style Sheet dialog box—a bit later in this chapter.)

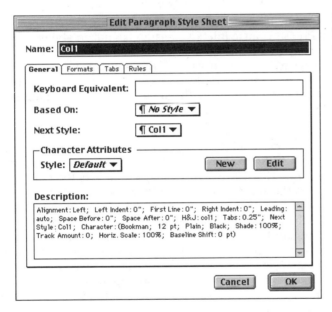

Figure 14-5: The General pane in the Edit Paragraph Style Sheet dialog box.

✦ **Name:** This field defaults to "New Style Sheet" if you selected New.

✦ **Keyboard Equivalent:** This field lets you pick a *hot key,* or a keyboard shortcut, that you can use to apply the style sheet; any combination of ⌘, Option, Control, Shift, and numeric keys will work for this purpose, as will the F5 through F15 function keys on an extended keyboard. For example, you can establish Control+F2 as the hot key for the Normal style. This tells QuarkXPress to apply that style to currently selected paragraphs when you press Control+F2. To enter keyboard equivalents in this field, press the actual key or keys you want to use.

If you assign a function key (F5 through F15) as a keyboard equivalent for a style, be aware that the setting will replace the QuarkXPress default setting for that function key. You can get around this limitation by simply adding the Control key as a modifier; this lets you assign styles to function keys, maintaining the original command equivalents. For example, assigning F2 as an equivalent keyboard key for a style would replace Quark's F2 Cut Key, so instead assign Control+F2 as the keyboard equivalent keys for your style. In Windows, which has no Control key, you're stuck with the Ctrl, Shift, and Alt keys; it's possible that your style shortcuts might override a Windows or QuarkXpress shortcut.

✦ **Based On:** This pop-up menu contains No Style unless you are editing or duplicating a style that uses the Based On option, described in the following sidebar. You can change the style name if you like.

✦ **Next Style:** This pop-up menu comes in handy when you need to enter text directly into QuarkXPress because it lets you establish linked styles. For example, you can specify that a body text style is to always follow a subhead style, which is to always follow a head style. Here's how this nifty feature works: As you type text into the QuarkXPress page, every time you enter a paragraph return after typing a subhead, the style automatically changes to your body text style.

✦ **Character Attributes:** Paragraph style sheets always contain character attributes. These are applied to all the characters in the paragraph each time you apply the paragraph style (except where you have applied character style sheets or local formatting). The Style pop-up menu lists the character style sheets assigned to the active document, and lets you select which character style should be used by the paragraph style sheet. In the Character Attributes area of the dialog box, choose New to create a new character style sheet directly from the Edit Paragraph Style Sheet dialog box; this opens the Edit Character Style Sheet dialog box, which is discussed later in this chapter. Choose Edit to make changes to the character style sheet selected in the Style pop-up menu. You can also leave the Style pop-up menu set to Default; this gives the paragraph style sheet a set of character style attributes that doesn't exist as a separate character style sheet.

You'll find three other panes in addition to the General pane in the Edit Paragraph Style Sheet dialog box: Formats, Tabs, and Rules. You can use them in any order and ignore ones that don't apply to the current style (typically, Rules and Tabs are ignored). The Formats, Tabs, and Rules panes let you invoke the appropriate controls for each major part of the style, as follows:

✦ **Formats:** Here you can select formats for paragraph attributes such as leading, H&J, and indentation.

✦ **Tabs:** These options allow you to define tab stops and tab types.

✦ **Rules:** This is where you can choose options for ruling lines associated with paragraphs.

The Based On option

The Based On option allows you to use a base style sheet as a starting point for building a new style sheet. Should you decide to change the style sheet, you only need to change the original base style and those changes will automatically apply to the rest of the style sheets based on that style sheet. (For example, if you modify a style sheet upon which another style is based, the changes you make affect *both* style sheets.)

For instance, if you had five body text styles created using the Based On option (and thus using the same font), instead of altering all five style sheets to change your body text font, you merely edit the base style and the remaining group of styles reflects the font change (see an additional sidebar, later in this chapter, for more practical advice on using this feature).

Note

The panes in the Edit Paragraph Style Sheet dialog box are identical to those in the Paragraph Attributes dialog box. For more information on how to use these features, see Chapters 9, 12, 13, and 15.

The Edit Character Style Sheet dialog box

Selecting Edit⇨Style Sheets (Shift F11) then clicking the New button and selecting the Character option, or clicking Edit or Duplicate when a character style is highlighted in the Style Sheets dialog box, opens the Edit Character Style Sheet dialog box, shown in Figure 14-6. Use the options as follows:

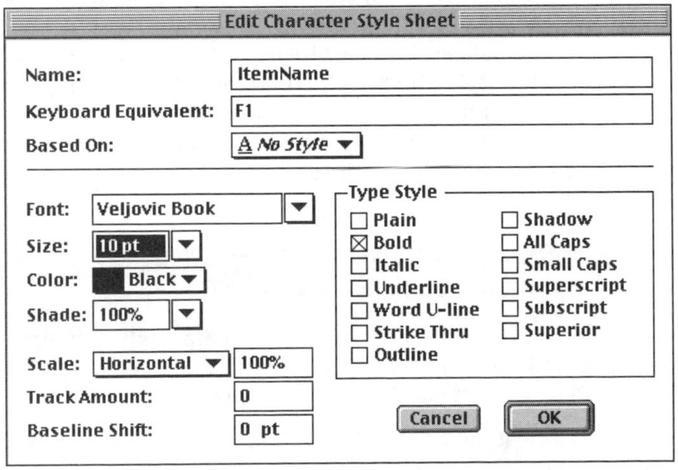

Figure 14-6: The Edit Character Style Sheet dialog box.

✦ **Name:** The Name field is where you name a new character style sheet, or rename an existing one. In our example, we have created a character style named "ItemName."

✦ **Keyboard Equivalent:** This field lets you pick a *hot key,* or a keyboard shortcut, that you can use to apply the style sheet; any combination of ⌘, Option, Control, Shift, and numeric keys will work for this purpose, as will the F5 through F15 function keys on an extended keyboard.

Again, remember that if you assign a function key (F5 through F15) as a keyboard equivalent for a style, the setting will replace the QuarkXPress default setting for that function key.

✦ **Based On:** This is a pop-up menu that allows you to base one style sheet on another style sheet. If you modify a style sheet upon which another style is based, the changes you make affect *both* style sheets. The default for Based On is No Style.

The remaining controls in the Edit Character Style Sheet dialog box select specific character attributes for the style sheet. You can read more details about these attributes in Chapters 12 and 13.

Creating Style Sheets

Before you create a paragraph or character style sheet, develop some idea of the basic elements you want to have in your document. For example, elements in a newspaper include body text, headlines, bylines, captions, and page numbers (folios). In addition, lead text, pull-quotes, biographies, subheads, sidebar heads, bulleted lists, and other more specialized types of formatting may be necessary. You might want to use a character style sheet to have all of your company's acronyms in italics. Don't worry about knowing in advance all the types of formatting to which you need to assign paragraph or character styles—it's very easy in QuarkXPress to add a new style at any time.

Understanding the No Style option

No Style is not a style sheet; it's more like the absence of one. If a paragraph with local formatting (such as bold words here and there) has the Normal style sheet applied to it, and then you apply a different style sheet to it, the local formatting is preserved.

However, if a paragraph with local formatting has No Style applied to it, all local formatting is lost when you apply a style sheet to that paragraph. For this reason, it's good to make sure you have a style sheet applied to all of your text when you start working on a document (even if it's just Normal); it makes your life much easier if you have to make changes later.

The following example illustrates the process of creating paragraph styles. For the example, we imported a text file to be used in a newsletter whose style has not yet been defined. When loaded, the text took on the attributes of the Normal style because we did not use style options in the original word processor. This text has five main paragraph elements and seven additional elements:

✦ The body text

✦ The body lead (which has a drop cap but otherwise is like the body text)

✦ The byline

✦ The headline

✦ The kicker (the small headline above the headline that identifies the type of story—in this case, a commentary)

✦ Captions

✦ Folios (page numbers)—which typically run at the top or bottom of each page

✦ The publication name—which typically runs at the top or bottom of each page

✦ The publication date—which typically runs at the top or bottom of each page

✦ Subheads

✦ Sidebar heads (for simplicity, we decided that sidebar text will be the same as body text)

✦ The names of people (in bold type, which we can set by using a character style sheet)

 Tip   You can create a default Normal style that each new document uses. This is handy if, for example, most of your documents use the same typeface or justification or point size (or any combination of these) for body text.

Understanding the Normal style

The initial setting for Normal is left-aligned, 12-point Helvetica with automatic leading. To change any attributes of Normal, close all open documents, access the Style Sheets dialog box by selecting Edit⇨Style Sheets (Shift+F11), and edit the Normal style in the usual way.

These settings are saved as the new defaults for all future new documents. Any style created with no document open becomes part of the default set of style sheets for all new documents.

STEPS: Creating a paragraph style sheet

1. Our first step in defining styles was to invoke the Style Sheets dialog box by selecting Edit⇨Style Sheets (Shift+F11).

2. We then selected the Normal paragraph style sheet and clicked the Edit button to display the Edit Paragraph Style Sheet dialog box.

3. In the Character Attributes area, we clicked the Edit button to display the Edit Character Style Sheet dialog box, shown here.

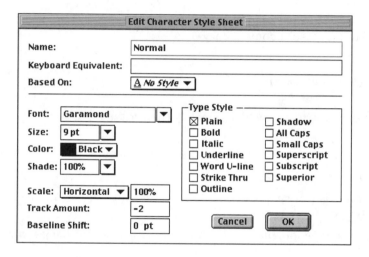

4. As you can see, we changed the Font to Garamond, the Size to 9, and the Track Amount to –2. We left the other attributes alone because they were appropriate for body text.

5. We clicked OK to return to the Edit Paragraph Style Sheet dialog box.

6. Then we selected the Formats pane in the Edit Paragraph Style Sheet dialog box, shown here.

7. We changed the First Line field so that the first line of each paragraph is indented 9 points.

8. We also changed Alignment to Justified and Leading to +2 points, which tells QuarkXPress to make the leading 2 points more than the point size; the default is Auto, which makes leading 120 percent of the point size.

9. In the Edit Paragraph Style Sheet dialog box, you can access the pop-up menu for the H&J field. This is where you select hyphenation and justification (H&J) settings. You define H&J sets separately via the Edit⇨H&Js menu option (Option+Shift+F11 or Option+⌘+H on the Mac; Shift+Alt+F11 in Windows), which is described in Chapter 13.

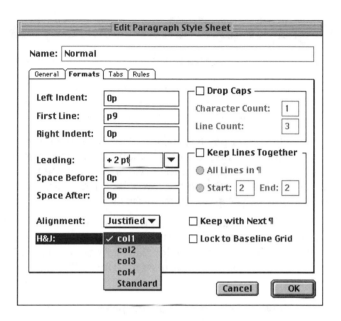

10. We then chose OK to leave the Edit Paragraph Style Sheet dialog box, and Save to save all our changes to the Normal style. You use this same process to create styles for your documents.

Tip

At the bottom of the General pane on the Edit Paragraph Style Sheet dialog box is a description of the attributes for the selected style. This is a handy way to see what the current settings are, as well as to verify that you set the options you intended. The same description is also displayed in the Style Sheets dialog box when a style sheet is selected.

The based-on advantage

When you create styles for a document, you'll probably have several similar styles, and some may be variations of others. For example, you might have a body text style plus a style for bulleted lists that is based on the body text style. Fortunately, QuarkXPress uses a technique called "based-on formatting" in its styles. You can tell QuarkXPress to base the Bulleted Text style on the Body Text style, in which you defined typeface, point size, leading, justification, hyphenation, indentation, tabs, and other attributes. You then modify the Bulleted Text style to accommodate bullets—by changing the indentation, for example.

The great thing about based-on formatting is that later, if you decide to change the typeface in Body Text, the typeface automatically changes in Bulleted Text and in all other styles that you created or edited based on Body Text—saving you a lot of work in maintaining consistency of styles.

Applying Paragraph and Character Styles

To apply a paragraph or character style sheet, use one of the following three options:

✦ **Option 1:** Choose the style you want from the Paragraph Style Sheet submenu (on the Style menu). This option is the least efficient way to apply styles to text and does not let you apply character style sheets.

✦ **Option 2:** Use the Style Sheets palette, shown Figure 14-7, which you invoke through the View⇨Show Style Sheets (F11) option. (You can resize and move the palette if you want.) The top half of the Style Sheets palette lists paragraph styles available for the document, and the lower half lists character styles. This option is the best way to apply styles in most cases.

✦ **Option 3:** Use the keyboard shortcut, if you defined one in the Edit Paragraph Style Sheet dialog box or the Edit Character Style Sheet dialog box. While this option is the fastest method, use it only for very commonly used styles because it requires memorizing the keyboard shortcuts that you assigned.

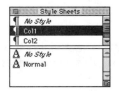

Figure 14-7: The Style Sheets palette lets you easily apply both paragraph and character style sheets.

A quick way to select all the text in a document so that you can apply a style to it is to choose Edit⇨Select All (⌘+A). To use this feature, you must select a text box containing text with the Text tool. All text in that text box, as well as any text boxes linked to it, will be selected.

Editing Paragraph and Character Styles

To make edits to paragraph or character styles, choose Edit⇨Style Sheets (Shift+F11) to open the Style Sheets dialog box. Select (highlight) the individual paragraph or character style you want to edit, and then select the Edit button. You can change any paragraph or character attributes you want. Another modification technique is simply to duplicate an existing paragraph or character style and then edit the attributes in that duplicate. This is similar to creating a based-on style (see the sidebar on the based-on advantage), except the new paragraph or character style is not automatically updated if the style it is duplicated from is modified—unless the style you duplicated or edited is based on another style.

Copying and Importing Styles

QuarkXPress lets you copy style sheets or individual styles from one document to another within QuarkXPress or import styles from outside word processing programs. If a style in the current document has the same name as a style you are importing, QuarkXPress displays the Append Conflict dialog box. From this dialog box, you can choose to rename the appended style sheet, replace the existing style sheet with the appended style sheet, or ignore the appended style sheet. The following sections cover each of these possibilities.

From within QuarkXPress

To copy styles from one QuarkXPress document to another, select the Append button in the Style Sheets dialog box to open the Append Style Sheets dialog box (see Figure 14-8). This dialog box is similar to the dialog box for opening a QuarkXPress document. You can change drives and directories as needed to select the QuarkXPress document that has the style sheet you want.

You can also append style sheets by choosing File⇨Append, (or using Option+⌘+A) selecting the document you want to append from, and then clicking the Style Sheets tab of the Append To dialog box.

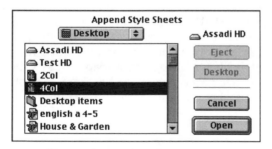

Figure 14-8: The Append Style Sheets dialog box.

Importing individual styles

When you select a document in the scroll list of the Append Style Sheets dialog box and choose OK, QuarkXPress lets you choose individual styles to import. This feature is new in version 4, and is shown in Figure 14-9.

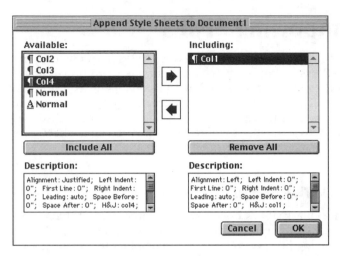

Figure 14-9: The Append Style Sheets dialog box lets you select which paragraph or character style sheets you want to append from another document to the active document.

QuarkXPress 4, in addition to giving you the ability to *import* individual styles, includes a new feature that allows you to *compare* the differences between two style sheets. These features are covered in the preceding and following sections.

Comparing style sheets

To compare the differences between two style sheets, open the Style Sheets dialog box by choosing Edit⇨Style Sheets (Shift+F11), select the first style sheet, and then hold down the ⌘ key and select the second style sheet. Press the Option key to change the Append button in the dialog box to a Compare button. When you click this button, a Compare Paragraph Style Sheets dialog box will appear, as shown in Figure 14-10. Note that you can compare a paragraph style sheet only to another paragraph style sheet, and you can compare a character style sheet only to another character style sheet.

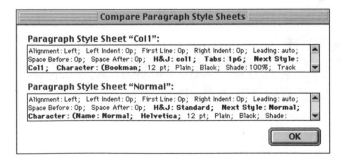

Figure 14-10: The Compare Paragraph Style Sheets dialog box lists the differences between two style sheets; the differences appear in bold type.

Importing style sheets from a word processor

QuarkXPress lets you copy styles from one document to another. You do this by selecting the Append document in the Style Sheets dialog box, which you access via Edit⇨Style Sheets (Shift+F11). When you click the Append button in the Style Sheets dialog box, a secondary dialog box—Append Style Sheets—opens. Use the controls in the dialog box to locate the document containing the style sheets you want to make use of. Note that you can also append style sheets when you import text using the Get Text command (⌘+E) and check the Include Style Sheets box (see Figure 14-11).

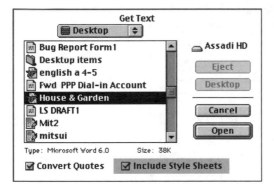

Figure 14-11: The Include Style Sheets box in the Get Text dialog box.

If you check the Include Style Sheets checkbox for formats without style sheets, QuarkXPress ignores the setting. Thus, if you typically import style sheets with your text, it's good to get in the habit of always checking this box; checking the box does not cause any problems when importing other text formats.

Importing style sheets from XPress Tags–formatted text

You also want to use the Include Style Sheets option on the Get Text dialog box if you are importing text saved in the XPress Tags format (described in Chapter 6). Although the purpose of the XPress Tags format is to embed style sheets and other formatting information in your text, you still must explicitly tell QuarkXPress to read those style sheets during import. Otherwise, QuarkXPress imports your text as a plain ASCII file, and all the embedded style sheets are treated as regular text and are not acted upon.

Resolving Style Conflicts

If you import a style sheet that has the same name as a style sheet in the active document, but with different attributes, an Append Conflict dialog box appears. The attributes that differ between the two style sheets are shown in bold (see Figure 14-12). The Append Conflict dialog box gives you the following options for resolving style sheet conflicts:

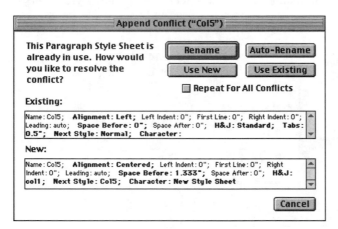

Figure 14-12: The Append Conflict dialog box.

✦ **Rename**: This option displays a dialog box that lets you rename the style sheet. After entering the new name, click OK.

✦ **Auto-Rename**: This option puts an asterisk at the beginning of the name of the appended style sheet.

✦ **Use New**: This option causes the appended style sheet to replace the existing style sheet of the same name.

✦ **Use Existing**: This option keeps the existing style sheet in the document and does not import the new version.

✦   ✦   ✦

Using Tabs and Tables

✦   ✦   ✦   ✦

In This Chapter

Exploring tab types

Specifying tabs

Using leaders

Creating tables with tabs

✦   ✦   ✦   ✦

Tabs make it possible to align text within columns, which is handy for lists, tables, and other columnar data. You can also use tabs to align single characters, such as dingbats. Tabs can be tricky; there are many tab options and it is often hard to predict how much space you need between tabs to make the tab fit nicely. This chapter is designed to help you through the tricky parts and make tabs a useful tool in your page-layout endeavors.

Exploring Tab Types

Typewriters usually offer left-aligned tabs only: pressing the tab key moves the carriage to a new left margin. But QuarkXPress offers a wide variety of tab alignments, which are available through the Tabs pane of the Paragraph Attributes dialog box (Shift+⌘+T), shown in Figure 15-1. Each type of tab has its own tab mark on the tab ruler to help you remember which tab is set which way.

Tip

What happens if you just hit the tab key without having set the value for the tab? The tab key will move the cursor along the line by a half inch. Half-inch tabs across the width of the text box are the QuarkXPress default.

The Tabs pane of the Paragraph Attributes dialog box provides the following options:

✦ **Left:** Text typed after the tab will align to the tab as if the tab were a left margin. This is the most popular alignment for text.

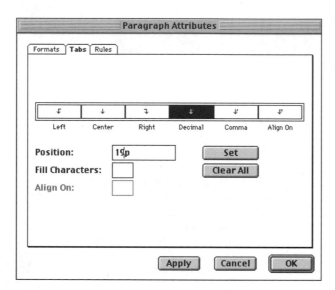

Figure 15-1: Tab styles available through the Tabs pane of the Paragraph Attributes dialog box.

✦ **Center:** Text will be typed after the tab is centered, with the tab location serving as the center mark. This is almost as popular as left alignment for text and symbols (such as checkmarks in a features table).

✦ **Right:** Text will be typed after the tab aligns to the tab as if the tab were a right margin. This alignment is typically used with tables of numbers because, regardless of the number of digits, you want the "ones" digit (the rightmost digit) in all numbers to align with the ones digit of all other numbers in a list; the tens digit (the next digit to the left) in all numbers to align, and so on.

✦ **Decimal:** Numbers with a decimal (.) that are typed in after the tab will align on the period. This is handy if you have data with varying numbers of decimal places, such as 10.2 and 40.41. If there are no decimals in a number, the number aligns as if there were a decimal *after* the number. When the data is a mix of numerals and text, it aligns at the first numeral. If the data consists of text only, with no numerals at all, the text aligns right (see Figure 15-2 for examples).

✦ **Comma:** Numbers with a comma (,) that are typed in after the tab will align on the comma. This is convenient if you have some data with decimal places, such as 5,210.2, and some without, such as 10,240. If the data is a mix of numerals and letters, it aligns at the first numeral. If there are no numerals in the data, the text right-aligns to the tab location.

Note

If a number does not contain commas, it aligns as if a comma *followed* the number, which is usually not what you want. A decimal tab is usually a better option, unless you are using numbers that have no decimals but do have commas.

✦ **Align On:** With this option, you specify which character the text aligns on (enter that character in the Align On field). You can specify any letter, number, punctuation, or symbol in the current typeface. The align-on tab handles mixed text (in which some text has the alignment character and some does not) in the same manner as the comma tab. If the text contains a number but does not contain the alignment character, it does not align on the number.

Figure 15-2 shows how the decimal, comma, and align-on tabs work when used in a variety of text. As the figure illustrates, the QuarkXPress decimal alignment feature is smart enough to handle any kind of number, but the comma alignment can deliver unwanted alignments when numbers don't have commas.

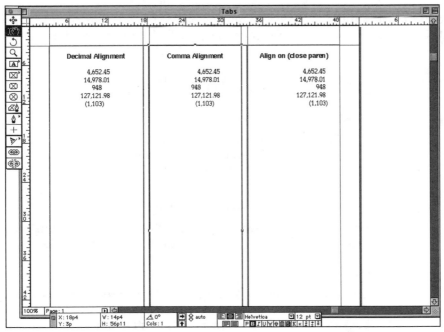

Figure 15-2: Decimal, comma, and align-on tabs have varying effects on text.

Specifying Tabs

As we've already noted, the default tab settings in QuarkXPress place a left tab every half inch. To set up other tabs, use the Tabs pane in the Paragraph Attributes dialog box.

In a style sheet

To create or modify a style sheet with tab settings so you can use them throughout a document, select the Tabs button in the Edit Style Sheets dialog box (select Edit➪Style Sheets, or Shift+F11, click the Edit button to display the Edit Paragraph Style Sheet dialog box, and then select the Tabs pane).

Until version 4, QuarkXPress had a limit of 20 tab stops per paragraph. This limit is gone, and you can now set thousands of tabs per paragraph.

In a specific paragraph

If you are working only on a specific paragraph or want to override a style locally, select Style➪Tabs or use the keyboard shortcut Shift+⌘+T to access the Tabs pane of the Paragraph Attributes dialog box. After you are in the Tabs pane of the Paragraph Attributes dialog box, you can set your tabs (see the following steps for an example).

STEPS: Setting and changing tabs

1. Select the alignment you want (Left, Center, Right, Decimal, Comma, or Align On).

2. Type in the position in the Position text box or move your mouse to the tab ruler along the top of your currently selected text box and click the location of the tab. If you click the tab with the mouse and keep the mouse button pressed, you can move the tab.

3. To change tab settings, use the following methods:

✦ **To change a tab's alignment:** Single-click the tab in the text box's tab ruler (its position shows up in the Position option in the Paragraph Attributes dialog box) and then move to the alignment options and select a new alignment.

✦ **To change a tab's position:** Single-click the tab in the text box's tab ruler (its position shows up in the Position option in the Paragraph Attributes dialog box) and then hold down the mouse button and slide the tab to a new position on the text box tab ruler. Or you can single-click the tab to select it, and then enter a new position in the Position field.

✦ **To delete a tab:** Single-click the tab on the tab ruler, keep the mouse button pressed, and drag the tab out of the tab ruler.

✦ **To delete all tabs for the active text box:** Click the Clear All button or Option+click the tab ruler.

All measurements in the tab ruler are relative to the text box's left margin, not to the absolute page or text-box coordinates. This way, in multicolumn text, tabs in each column appear as you would expect. For example, when a tab stop is defined at 3 picas, a tab used in column 1 will occur at 3 picas from column 1's left margin, while a tab used in column 3 will occur at 3 picas from column 3's left margin. Thus, when figuring out where tab stops should be, be sure to use the tab ruler, not the document ruler (as demonstrated in Step 2 of the preceding STEPS section).

Using Leaders

A *tab leader* is a series of characters that runs from text to text within tabular material. Usually, a period is used as the tab leader character. A leader's purpose is to guide the reader's eye, especially across wide distances. For an example, look at the table of contents in this book: A dot leader appears between the section and chapter names and their page numbers.

QuarkXPress calls a tab leader a *fill character*. To define a leader, enter up to two printing characters (or one printing character and a space) in the Fill Characters field, which you find in the Tabs pane of the Paragraph Attributes dialog box. If you enter two characters, they will alternate to fill the space between the defined tab stop and the place where you pressed the tab key. In Figure 15-3, a period is selected as the fill character.

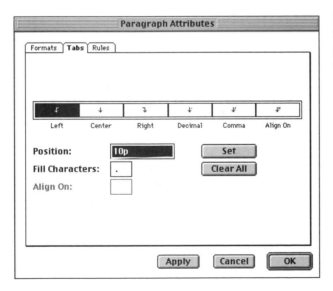

Figure 15-3: Select a tab leader in the Fill Characters field of the Tabs pane of the Paragraph Attributes dialog box.

Creating Tables with Tabs

If you need to create complex tables, we recommend that you consider buying one of the table XTensions mentioned in Chapter 27, such as Gluon's TableMaker XTension or Tableworks' (formerly known as Npath Software) Entable. But if your table requirements are light, you may be able to get by with using tabs to create tables. By combining various tab settings with other typographic features—and by first thinking through the look you want for your table—you can create nice-looking tables in QuarkXPress. Figure 15-4 shows an example of a relatively simple table. The table incorporates a mix of tab settings defined in two styles, one for the table text and one for the table headline. The following steps show you how it's done.

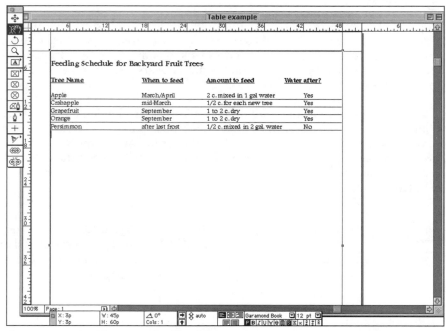

Figure 15-4: A table created with tabs.

To avoid creating separate styles for each table, consider deriving standard tab settings that apply to groups of similar tables. Then use local tab settings (accessed via Style⇨Tabs or Shift+⌘+T) to modify styles for individual tables when necessary or to create completely new tabs for a table that is unlike others.

STEPS: Creating a table

1. We typed in a line of text, placing tabs between each column.

2. We used the Style⇨Tabs or Shift+⌘+T feature to define tab stops, determining them by guessing where columns should be, based on text length for each column. We determined alignment based on the type of data. We chose left

alignment for regular text (we would have used decimal alignment if we'd had numbers with decimals). After making educated guesses, we chose Apply to see the result. We then moved our tab stops and selected Apply until we were satisfied. (When planning a table, set tabs to accommodate the longest text that you expect to include in each column, so that the tabs work with all rows in your table.)

3. We wrote down the tab stops and repeated Step 2 for the table's title row. The tab stops for the title row are different than those of the table body. All tabs in the title row align left because the titles do not contain any numbers with decimals or commas to align elements on.

4. We created two new styles—Table Body and Table Title—that used the tab stop settings we determined earlier. We also set our typeface, size, and ruling-line settings. We used a ruling line between the rows.

5. We then applied the new styles to the table text as we entered the rest of the table.

Drawing vertical lines between table columns

If you want vertical lines between table columns, here are some handy guidelines for achieving the results you're looking for:

✦ Use the Line tool to draw the lines.

✦ Next, select the text box containing the text and the lines (hold down Shift when clicking the lines, so that the text box remains selected).

✦ From the Item menu, select Group, so the text box and the lines stay together if the layout later changes.

✦ Keep in mind, however, that if the text reflows, the lines do not move with the table text unless the table is in its own text box, independent of the rest of the story.

✦   ✦   ✦

Book-Oriented Editing

◆ ◆ ◆ ◆

In This Chapter

Building books: step by step

Making lists

Creating an index

◆ ◆ ◆ ◆

It's been a long time coming. Before QuarkXPress 4, publishers of books and other long, indexed, cross-referenced documents were forced to rely on XTensions (for example, Sonar BookEnds) or on other software applications—products such as Corel Ventura, Adobe PageMaker, or Adobe FrameMaker—to do the list-management jobs (for figure lists, tables of contents, etc.) that need to be done with long documents. Sure, QuarkXPress could do a bang-up job with typography and layout, but long-document features—Indexing, as an example—had to be handled outside QuarkXPress. This chapter describes new features in QuarkXPress 4 that are designed to bring those who publish long documents back into the QuarkXPress fold. It takes you through the process of building a book, developing lists—such as tables of contents and figures—and creating indexes and cross-references.

Building Books: Step by Step

A book is a collection of chapters. Each chapter is a separate document, and you knit the chapters together into a whole book. A book in QuarkXPress 4 is actually a palette—the Book palette. Like other palettes in the program, the Book palette is a list of information, which displays the chapters that make up the book. The process of building a book is best handled one step at a time. The following sections show you how it's done.

Planning your book

Before we explore the palette and how to use it, however, it's best to do some up-front planning. Use the following guidelines before you begin building your book in QuarkXPress 4:

✦ If you want to build a book, we recommend that you organize your chapters beforehand. Start by outlining the book.

✦ Then try using templates and style sheets to format the chapters uniformly.

✦ Decide on the number, names, and order of the chapters. You can make changes to a chapter's number, name, and order at any time, but figuring out these basics ahead of time will save you time in the long run.

✦ Make decisions about the format of the book (style sheets, typeface, pagination style, etc.) at the chapter level, beginning with the first chapter.

Note

Formatting is important, because the first chapter you add to the Book palette will become the master chapter (see the later section on working with master chapters), and attributes of that document will form the basis for the other chapters you add to the book.

✦ Once the chapters are drafted and ready to assemble, you need to identify the chapters in the Book palette.

Remodeling 101

✦ Open the Book palette. If it's a new book, choose File➪New➪Book (see the following section on creating and opening books). If it's an existing book, simply double-click the Book icon (shown at left) to open it.

Creating and opening books

To open the Book palette and create a new book, choose File➪New➪Book (see Figure 16-1). You can open an existing book file by double-clicking the book's icon (shown in the previous section). Position the Book palette on your desktop by clicking and dragging the palette's title bar.

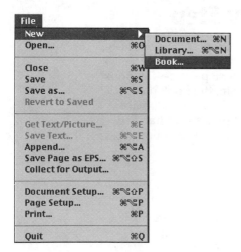

Figure 16-1: To create a new book, choose File➪New➪Book.

Figure 16-2 shows a new, open Book palette that we have named "Remodeling 101." The upper part of the figure also shows the controls you use in the Add New Chapter dialog box to locate the chapters you want placed in the book.

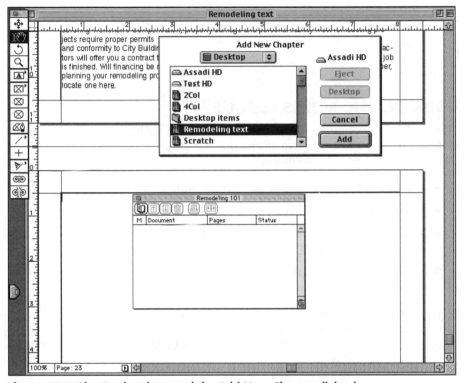

Figure 16-2: The Book palette and the Add New Chapter dialog box.

Working with master chapters

Again, it is important to remember that each time you open a new Book palette and list the book's first chapter, QuarkXPress treats that chapter as the master chapter. The master chapter contains attributes that will be used in all chapters of the book. For example, we might have established a spot color for a running head in our book; if this spot color is in the master chapter, it will appear in all subsequent chapters of the book. You can tell which chapter is the master chapter by looking for the "M" next to the chapter name. In Figure 16-3, the first chapter we added was the Introduction; as you can see by the "M" next to the title: "Remo – Intro."

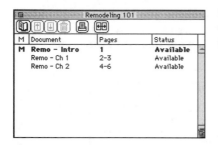

Figure 16-3: Adding chapters to a book, with the first chapter (Remo – Intro) indicated as the master chapter.

Book palette status reports

The Book palette indicates the number of pages in each chapter, and tells us the status of the chapters we have added thus far (see Figure 16-4) The possible statuses for chapters are as follows:

✦ **Available:** The chapter can be opened, edited, or printed.

✦ **Open:** The chapter is currently open, and can be edited or printed.

✦ **Modified:** The chapter has been changed since the last time the Book palette was open on this computer.

✦ **Missing:** The chapter is unavailable to the Book palette, or cannot be located at this time.

Tip

To prevent other people in your workgroup from editing an original chapter while you are editing a copy of it, move the original chapter to a separate folder. If someone tries to edit the chapter, it will be listed with a status of "Missing."

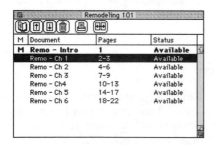

Figure 16-4: The Book palette, showing the status of the individual chapters (note the control icons at the top—discussed in the section on Book palette control icons).

Book palette control icons

The Book palette has some icons across the top that control the chapters in the book (refer to Figure 16-4). Here's how they work:

✦ **To add chapters:** The first icon at the upper left is the Add Chapter icon. When you click this icon, an Add New Chapter dialog box appears, allowing you to locate a chapter you want added to the Book palette (refer to the upper dialog box in Figure 16-2).

✦ **To rearrange chapters:** Use the icons with up and down arrows to rearrange chapters within the Book palette. (For example, we could move Chapter 1 so that it follows Chapter 3 by clicking Chapter 1 to select it and then clicking the down arrow three times to move it down three chapters.)

 To speed things up, you can also move a chapter in the list by pressing the Option key and clicking and dragging the chapter up or down.

 ✦ **To delete chapters:** The icon of a small trash can is the Delete button. If you have one or more chapters highlighted and click this icon, the chapters are deleted from the book. Note that the file itself is not deleted, just the link to it in the Book palette.

 ✦ **To print a chapter:** The icon that looks like a printer is the Print button.

✦ **To synchronize chapter formatting:** The icon with a left- and a right-pointing arrow is the Synchronize button. It allows you to format the other chapters in the book so they are consistent with the master chapter (see the following section for more information).

Synchronizing chapter formatting

Because QuarkXPress lets you make local changes to chapters at any time, you might want to ensure that all the chapters in a book are formatted consistently. You do this by using the Synchronize button on the Book palette, the icon on the far right of the palette with a left- and a right-pointing arrow (refer to Figure 16-4). When you synchronize chapters, QuarkXPress compares each chapter with the master chapter and modifies the chapters as necessary so that they conform to the master chapter's style sheets, H&J sets, lists, and so on.

Synchronizing tips and tricks

Synchronizing chapters is a great idea if the book is a long, involved one that you have worked on over several months (in which case it would be easy to make a paragraph style change in one chapter and forget to make the change in all other chapters). Synchronizing is also a good idea if the document has several authors, any of whom may have made local changes without informing the entire group.

Or suppose you've already specified Chapter 1 as the master chapter, but you really want to make the whole book look like Chapter 5. The Book palette will first show an M to the left of Chapter 1's name. Click to highlight Chapter 5, and then click the blank area to the left of the chapter name. This causes Chapter 5 to be the new master chapter, and the M is now to the left of Chapter 5's name.

Printing chapters and books

In the Book palette the icon of a printer is the Print button. You click this icon to print either the entire book or selected chapters listed in the Book palette. Here's how it works:

Note

In order for chapters to print, they must have the status of Available or Open. Chapters with a status of Missing or Modified will not print, although an error message will notify you of this situation.

✦ To print the entire book, make sure no individual chapter is highlighted (selected) when you click the print icon. To print selected chapters, highlight the chapters you want to print.

✦ To print noncontiguous chapters from the list of chapters in the Book palette—for example, to print only Chapters 2 and 4—hold down the ⌘ key while you highlight the names of the chapters.

✦ When you have highlighted the chapters in the Book palette that you want to print (if you are printing the entire book, no chapters should be highlighted) click the Print icon. The Print dialog box appears (see Figure 16-5).

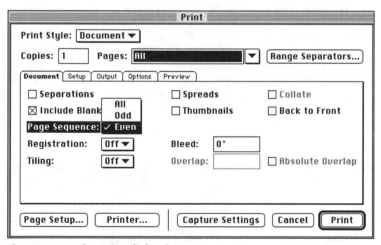

Figure 16-5: The Print dialog box.

✦ To print all the pages in the selected chapters (or to print the entire book if no chapters are selected), choose All in the Pages pop-up menu of the Print dialog box.

✦ To print a range of pages from selected chapters, choose Selected in the Pages pop-up menu and enter the page numbers in the field.

Note

When specifying a range of page numbers to print, either enter the absolute page number (the page's position in the document—the first page is absolute page one, the second page is absolute page two, regardless of the pagination you may have assigned to the page), or the complete page number including its prefix (if you are printing pages 5–12 through 5–14, you need to include the "5–" before the page number). To print an absolute page number, precede the number with a plus sign (+); to print the first page in the document, enter +1 in the field, and so on.

✦ After you have entered your printing selections in the Print dialog box, click Print (or press the Return key) to print the book or its selected chapters.

Handling chapters with sections

In long documents, it's not at all uncommon for chapters to be divided into sections. For example, you might have a Chapter 2 with Sections 1, 2, and 3. You can let QuarkXPress help you paginate chapters with sections. For example, you might want the pages in Section 2 of Chapter 2 to be numbered 2–2.1, 2–2.2, and so on. The following sections show you how this is done.

The Book Chapter Start feature

If the chapter has no sections, QuarkXPress considers it as having a "Book Chapter Start," which is also the default. When the Book Chapter Start box is checked in the Section dialog box, a chapter starts numbering its pages after the last page of the previous chapter; for example, if the last page in a book's first chapter is page 15, the first page in the second chapter will be page 16. Here is how Book Chapter Start works:

✦ Whenever you add a chapter with no sections to a book, the program numbers pages sequentially throughout the book.

✦ As you add and delete pages from chapters, the page numbers are also updated.

✦ The Book Chapter Start checkbox is only available if a chapter is opened independently of its book.

Creating a section

As discussed earlier, sections within chapters usually require different treatment for pagination. If you want to create a section in a chapter, open the chapter and choose Page⇨Section to display the Section dialog box (see Figure 16-6).

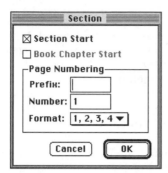

Figure 16-6: The Section dialog box.

In the Section dialog box, checking Section Start disables (unchecks) Book Chapter Start. When you add, delete, or rearrange pages or chapters, subsequent chapters will be paginated according to the settings in the Section dialog box. In the Page Numbering area of the Section dialog box, you can enter a page prefix up to four characters in length in the Prefix field. (For example, you might want to number the pages in an attachment as Att–1, Att–2; in this case, the Att would be the prefix). In the Number field, enter the page number you want to assign to the first page of a new section. The Number field requires Arabic numbers, regardless of the format of the section numbers; for example, if you are using lowercase Roman numerals for the front matter of a book and want the first page of the section to be page iii, enter 3 in the Number field. The Format pop-up menu lets you select a style for page numbers in a section. Choices include numeric (1, 2, 3, 4), uppercase Roman (I, II, III, IV), lowercase Roman (i, ii, iii, iv), uppercase alphabetic (A, B, C, D), and lowercase alphabetic (a, b, c, d). In the Book palette, chapters that contain section starts are indicated by an asterisk next to the numbers in the Pages field.

Note

If you haven't checked Section Start and you then open a chapter directly (instead of using the Book palette), page numbers may temporarily change, and might begin with page 1. Once you return the chapter to its book and open it in the Book palette, the page numbers will be updated automatically.

Making Lists

New Feature

Long documents lend themselves to lists, which help to keep information organized. A table of contents is a list, as is a list of figures or tables. In QuarkXPress, a list is actually nothing more than a list of paragraphs that are formatted with the same style sheet. Once you've created a book (or even a single document), QuarkXPress can build a list by scanning the chapters for the style sheets you specify. For example, if you create a book and have a style sheet you apply to figures in the document, you can generate a list of figures by asking the program to list all paragraphs that use the style sheet named "Figure." (The step-by-step process described in the following sections will work for any kind of list you want to build in QuarkXPress 4.)

Building a list of figures

As an example of building a list, let's build a list of figures in our sample book, "Remodeling 101." First we create individual documents, or chapters, for the book. As we create these chapters, we also create and apply paragraph style sheets that define our chapter heads, figures, and tables (see Chapter 14 for more information on creating style sheets). We use the Book palette to assemble the book. Finally, we are ready to create a list of figures. Let's elect to list the figures in Chapter 2 of our book. With Chapter 2 open, we display the Edit List dialog box by choosing Edit⇨Lists, and then choosing New.

Using the Edit List dialog box

In the Name field of the Edit List dialog box (see Figure 16-7), we enter the name "List of Figures." We select the style named "Figures" by highlighting the style name in the Available Styles box, and then click the right arrow to transfer the style to the Styles in List box.

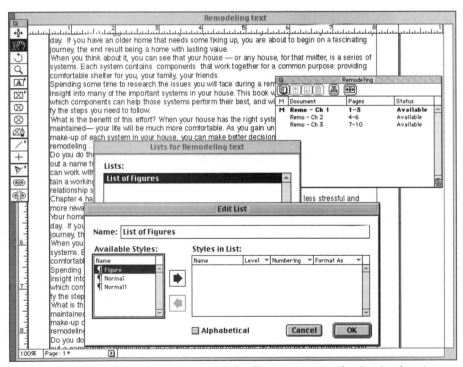

Figure 16-7: The Edit List dialog box and the list we generated using it. The Lists dialog box (lower right) shows the list that resulted from our list-building activities.

Choosing Styles in List options

The Styles in List section of the Edit List dialog box (refer to Figure 16-7) has the following options for us to pick from:

✦ **Level:** The Level pop-up menu includes selections from 1 (highest) to 8 (lowest); this is a number in a hierarchy, and is useful for creating complex lists.

✦ **Numbering:** The Numbering pop-up menu defines a page numbering style for each item in the list; this numbering style determines how page numbers will appear in the list. In our example, we chose Page#...Text, which causes items to be preceded by their page number. Other options are Text only, which suppresses page numbers, or Text#...Page, which causes an item to appear before its page number.

✦ **Format As:** The Format As pop-up menu lets you select a style sheet to determine how the text will appear in the list. For example, when using the list to create a table of contents, you may want all 18-point bold text styled with your "Chapter Title" style sheet to be reformatted in the list using your 12-point "TOC Chapter" style sheet when you build the table of contents.

Lists are very handy for long documents, but keep in mind that a list cannot contain more than 32 style sheets. A paragraph in a list is limited to 256 characters. (Your paragraphs can be longer than this, but when you build a list only the first 256 characters of each paragraph in the list will be used.)

Compiling a list

After we've made all our selections in the Edit List dialog box, we press OK. QuarkXPress then scans Chapter 2, locates all the paragraphs that were marked with the Figures style, and uses these items to create the list of Figures you see in the Lists palette in Figure 16-7.

Once you've created a list, you can use it to navigate through a document. To jump to the place in your document where a listed paragraph occurs, just double-click that entry in the Lists palette. Lists are also a nice way to view your documents in an outline fashion; paragraphs specified as level 1 begin at the left edge of the Lists palette, but lower-level paragraphs are indented.

Placing a list in a book

To put our list into a text box so that we can make the list part of the book, we make sure the text box we want to use is active before we click the Build button in the Lists palette (View⇨Show Lists). You can see the Build button on the Lists palette in the lower-right corner of Figure 16-7; this button is only available when a text box is active.

List tips and tricks

The first time you use the Lists palette's Build button in a document (View⇨Show Lists), the list is inserted into the active text box, wherever the cursor happens to be sitting at the moment. If you forget and click Build while you still have your cursor in the body of your text, the list will be inserted right into your manuscript. It's easy to forget this fact, because you don't have to worry about it with the Index feature (covered later in this chapter). Fortunately, once you've built a list in a document (hopefully in the right place), every time you click Build you will see a dialog box asking you if you would rather replace the existing list or insert the new version of the list into the active text box.

The Lists palette includes a Find feature that lets you quickly and easily locate a listed paragraph by simply typing its first few characters. To use it, enter the first few characters of the paragraph you want to find in the Find field; the paragraph that begins with those characters will be highlighted automatically in the Lists palette. You can then jump to that point in your document by double-clicking the highlighted list entry.

Updating and rebuilding a list

If you edit a document after you build a list, be sure to update the list by clicking the Update button in the Lists palette. If you have used the Build button, you will need to use it again to replace the old list with the new, updated list. Note that when you create or update a list, QuarkXPress automatically alphabetizes the entries in the list.

Creating an Index

New Feature

If you've ever been unable to find information in a book that you knew was there, you'll appreciate how important a good index can be. Short, simple documents can get by fine without indexes. But long books almost always need indexes to help the reader locate specific information. Indexing used to be a laborious process, involving lots of index cards. Now, QuarkXPress makes indexing much easier, while still relying on you to make key decisions about how the index will be formatted. The following sections show you how to do your part.

Choosing an indexing style

Your approach to developing an index depends on the indexing style you want to use. Large publishers usually have their own house style guides for indexes. If you don't have a style guide for indexes, we recommend that you read through the indexing guidelines in *The Chicago Manual of Style* (University of Chicago Press).

Another option is to use an index you like as a model, and then take the steps necessary in QuarkXPress to achieve that index style. Before you begin indexing your document, ask yourself the following questions:

✦ Do you want to capitalize all levels of all entries, or do you just want initial caps?

✦ Should headings appear in boldface?

✦ Will you capitalize secondary entries in the index?

✦ Should the index be nested or run-in style? We show examples of nested and run-in style indexes later in this chapter.

Using the Index Preferences dialog box

To add words to an index in QuarkXPress, you need to *mark* the words in the chapters of your book that you want to use as index entries. These markers appear as colored brackets around the entry. You can choose the color of index markings (in addition to the index separation characters you want to use) by displaying the Index Preferences dialog box (Edit⇨Preferences⇨Index) shown in Figure 16-8. The following sections explain how the options on the dialog box work.

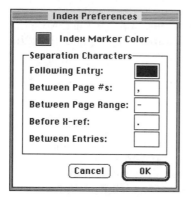

Figure 16-8: The Index Preferences dialog box.

Changing the index marker color

To change the color of the index markers, click the Index Marker Color button; this will display a color picker. Use the controls in the color picker to define the new color for index markers. Click OK to close the color picker, and then click OK in the Index Preferences dialog box to complete the process.

Choosing separation characters

The Index Preferences dialog box also lets you choose the characters and spaces used to separate entries in the index. The options in the Separation Characters section of the dialog box work as follows:

✦ **Following Entry:** This defines the punctuation that immediately follows each index entry—usually a colon (:). For example, the index item "Remodeling: vi, 14, 21-23" uses a colon and space following the index entry "Remodeling."

✦ **Between Page #s:** This defines the characters or punctuation that separates a list of page numbers—usually a comma (,) or semicolon (;). For example, the index item "Remodeling: vi, 14, 21-23" uses a comma and space between page numbers.

✦ **Between Page Range:** This defines the characters or punctuation that indicate a range of pages—usually the word "to" or a dash. For example, the index item "Remodeling: vi, 14, 21 to 23" uses the word "to" between numbers indicating a range of pages.

✦ **Before X-ref:** This defines the characters or punctuation that appears before a cross-reference—usually a period and space or a semicolon. For example, the index item "Remodeling: vi, 14, 21-23. See also Fixing up" uses a period and space before the cross-reference.

✦ **Between Entries:** This defines the characters or punctuation between entry levels in a run-in index—usually a period or a semicolon. For example, the index item "Remodeling: vi, 14, 21–23; Finding a contractor: 15–16; Pulling permits: 19" uses a semicolon between entry levels.

Using the Index palette

When your document is ready to be indexed, open the Index palette (View⇨Show Index). You use this palette to add words to the index in up to four indent levels, edit or delete index entries, or create cross-references. The Index palette appears in Figure 16-9.

Figure 16-9: The Index palette.

The controls in the Index palette include the following:

✦ **Text:** The Text field in the Entry section of the Index palette is where you type in an index entry or where the text appears that you have tagged with index markers. When you have the Index palette open and you highlight text in the open document, the first 255 characters of the highlighted text appear automatically in the Text field and are ready to be captured as an index entry.

✦ **Sort As:** Entries in the Sort As field override the default, alphabetical sorting of the index entry. For example, you may want "14-penny nails" to be indexed as if the entry were spelled "Fourteen-penny nails" and you could accomplish this by entering the spelling "Fourteen-penny nails" into the Sort As field.

✦ **Level:** This is a pop-up menu that you use to control the order and structure of index entries. A nested index can have up to four levels, and a run-in index can have only two levels. (Technically, a run-in index can have four levels too, but it doesn't make any sense visually to use more than two.)

✦ **Style:** The Style pop-up menu (within the Reference section of the dialog box) lets you apply a character style for the page numbers for the current index entry or cross-reference. One example of how this might be applied is with cross-references such as "See also General Hardware tips" where the words "General Hardware tips" have an italicized character style.

✦ **Scope:** This is another pop-up menu in the Reference section that lets you control the scope, or range, of the index. For example, you can use it to make the entry a cross-reference, list an entry as covering a specific number of paragraphs, or suppress the printing of the particular entry's page number.

✦ **The Add button:** This lets you add an entry to the index.

✦ **The Find Next button:** This finds the next occurrence of an index entry in the active document.

✦ **The pencil icon:** You can edit an active index entry by clicking the pencil icon, or by double-clicking the entry name.

✦ **The trash can icon:** You can delete the selected entry by clicking the trash can icon.

Creating an index entry

To create a new index entry, first highlight the text you want to use for the index entry. (Don't highlight the whole area you want referenced by the index entry; just highlight the word you want to appear in the index.) Then click the Add button in the Index palette to add the index entry to the list using the currently selected values in the Entry and Reference areas.

Editing an index entry

Editing an existing index entry is a bit more complicated. Remember that to edit an index entry, you must first select it in the Index palette and go into editing mode (either by double-clicking the index entry or by clicking it and then clicking the pencil icon). You can select an entry and make changes to the Entry and Reference areas, but unless you go into editing mode first, all you are doing is changing the settings that will be used when you create the next index entry.

Creating page number references

Each index entry includes a reference. A reference usually consists of the page number(s) to which the entry refers, but it might instead be a cross-reference (see the following section on creating cross-references). To see the page number reference (or cross-reference) for an index entry, click the small triangle to the left of the entry in the lower section of the Index palette.

As with index entries, you must double-click a reference before you can edit it. (Or you can click the reference and then click the pencil icon.) Remember to do this or your changes will not be saved. Changes to a reference are made in the Reference area of the Index palette (see the previous section on using the Index palette for more information on the Style and Scope options).

Creating cross-references

Cross-references enhance an index because they give the reader another way of finding pertinent information. The following steps show you how to create them:

STEPS: Adding a cross-reference to an indexed entry

1. Display the Index palette by selecting View⇨Show Index.

2. Click Add to create a new entry, or select an existing entry.

3. Next, click the triangle next to the entry name to make its reference available, and double-click that reference to edit it.

4. Click the Scope pop-up menu and select X-Ref. This will highlight a field in the palette into which you can enter the cross-referenced term (as shown here).

5. The See pop-up menu lets you pick from three options that govern the way the cross-reference will appear under the index entry: See, See Also, and See Herein. In our example, for the index entry "insulation," we have a cross-reference to "fiberglass."

Using index levels

QuarkXPress 4 supports four levels of indexing. The most important thing to remember about creating a level two, three, or four index entry is that you must tell QuarkXPress where to put it (that is, a higher-level index entry for it to fall under). You do this using the arrow column at the left edge of the index entry list at the bottom of the Index palette. For example, let's say you want to create a level-two entry to an existing level-one entry. First, select the text you want to add. Next, click in the arrow column next to the level-one entry under which you want the new entry listed. Now choose Second Level from the Level pop-up menu in the Entry area. Finally, click the Add button to add the new entry.

Tip

If you want to create a third-level entry, but the Third Level option in the Level pop-up menu is dimmed, it probably means you haven't moved the arrow to a second-level index entry. (You can easily identify second, third, and fourth-level entries in the Index palette by their indents.)

Using the Build Index dialog box

To build an index from the list you have generated in the Index palette, choose Utilities⇨Build Index to display the Build Index dialog box shown in Figure 16-10. The options in this dialog box work as follows:

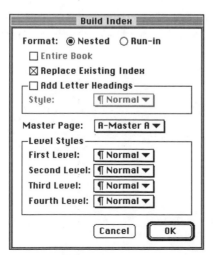

Figure 16-10: The Build Index dialog box.

Nested or run-in index?

There is no right way to index, but common sense should be a guide. Determine which index format you use by the number of levels in the index's hierarchy. If the index has only two levels, a run-in format works well, but an index with three or more levels requires a nested format for the sake of clarity.

Nested indexes look like this:

```
Kitchen Hardware
        Buying, 191
        Cost estimates, 242-248
        Design guidelines 92-94, 96, 99-101
        Hiring contractors, 275-284
        Installation, 180-195
        Sizing, 91-99
        Standards, 24-28, 98, 133
        Tools, 199-203, 224, 282-283
```

Run-in indexes look like this:

```
Kitchen Hardware: Buying, 191; Cost estimates, 242-248; Design
guidelines 92-94, 96, 99-101; Hiring contractors, 275-284;
Installation, 180-195; Sizing, 91-99; Standards, 24-28, 98, 133;
Tools, 199-203, 224, 282-283
```

✦ **Choosing a nested or run-in index:** The first decision to make is whether the index will be nested or run-in (see the sidebar on nested or run-in indexes to help you make a decision).

✦ **Building an index for an entire book:** The Build Index dialog box also allows you to build an index for the entire book, rather than just the open chapter; select this option by clicking the Entire Book box.

✦ **Replacing an existing index:** Indexing is an iterative process, and it is very likely that you will want to build an index a few times through the course of the book project. Clicking Replace Existing Index in the Build Index dialog box overwrites the existing index with the most current version.

Tip

To compare a newer version of an index with its predecessor, uncheck the Replace Existing Index box (Utilities⇨Build Index). Then when you build the index, it will not replace the previous version.

✦ **Adding letter headings:** In long indexes, it is helpful to divide the index alphabetically, so that all the index entries that begin with "A" are in a category with the heading "A." Check Add Letter Headings to make this happen.

✦ **Basing an index on a master page:** The Master Page pop-up menu lets you select a master page on which to base the index page. For long indexes, you should consider developing a master page just for that purpose.

✦ **Choosing level styles:** The Level Styles pop-up menus let you choose the paragraph style sheet(s) you want to apply to the various index levels. If you select the Run-in format, all the index levels flow into one paragraph, so only the First Level pop-up menu will be available.

When you've made your choices in the Build Index dialog box, close and save the contents of the Build Index dialog box by pressing OK or the Return key.

✦   ✦   ✦

Typographic Special Effects

✦ ✦ ✦ ✦

In This Chapter

Organizing text with typography

Making drop caps and hybrid caps

Rotating text

Placing text on a line

Coloring and shading text

Creating shadows and outlines

Hanging punctuation

✦ ✦ ✦ ✦

As you've seen in preceding chapters, typographic controls over spacing—between words, lines, and letters—help determine a document's overall color. In addition to spacing controls, you can use several typographic features to enhance your presentation. These features include drop caps and other attention-grabbers, organizational aids such as bulleted lists, and visual labels such as small caps. What all these effects have in common is that they enable you to add meaning or provide reader guidance by changing the appearance of individual characters or small groups of characters. This chapter will set you on the road to becoming a typographic special effects expert.

Organizing Text with Typography

Typographic effects create visual signposts that guide the reader through a document. The effects most commonly used for this purpose fall into four basic groups: indents and outdents, bullets and lists, visual labels, and dingbats. The following sections cover all these topics.

Indents and outdents

Indents and outdents come in a number of variations, but share one goal: to break up a document's solid left margin. These breaks give the reader variances to notice—variances that signify a change in elements. It's less important to break up the right margin of a document because people read from left to right and thus pay more attention to the left margin. In languages that are read from right to left, such as Farsi and Arabic, the opposite is true.

Setting indents

The most basic use of an indent is to offset the first line in a paragraph. This is particularly true in multicolumn publications that use first-line indents rather than blank lines between paragraphs to indicate the start of a new paragraph. To set indents, either for a selected paragraph or when defining styles, use the Formats pane in the Paragraph Attributes dialog box (see Figure 17-1). To gain access to paragraph formatting controls, select Style⇨Formats (Shift+⌘+F) and then select the Formats pane.

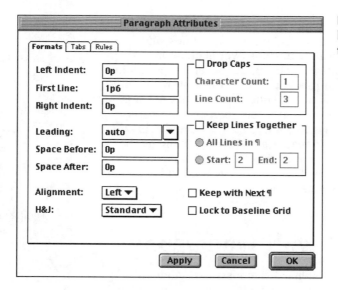

Figure 17-1: Set left, right, and first-line indents in the Formats pane of the Paragraph Attributes dialog box.

Tip

Make sure your first-line indents aren't too small. Usually, indents should be between one and two ems in size. An em is as wide as your current point size, so if text is 9 points, the first-line indent should be between 9 and 18 points. If columns are thin (more than three columns to a standard page), make indents closer to 9 points than 18 points. This avoids gaping indents or awkward justification in the first line of a paragraph.

Setting outdents

An *outdent*, also called an *exdent* or a *hanging indent,* serves the same function as a first-line indent, but moves the first line out into the margin, rather than indenting it. It usually is reserved for bulleted lists because it takes up space that otherwise might be used for text. Some people use outdents for sidebars to provide a visual counterpoint to standard text; this works if the sidebars are not too long.

Block indenting

Another form of indenting is called *block indenting*. In a block indent, the entire paragraph is indented from the left margin, right margin, or both. A typical use of block-indenting—usually from the left, but sometimes also from the right—is to indicate extended quotations. Typically, these are also set in a smaller type size. Use the Left Indent and Right Indent fields of the Formats pane in the Paragraph Attributes dialog box to set block indents.

If you indent several elements in the same document, use only a few different levels of indentation—two or three at most. For example, it works well to use the same amount of indentation on bylines and kickers, even if the indentation amount differs from the amount used for the first line of body-text paragraphs. If you have too many levels of indentation, there is no pattern to help guide the reader's eye, and the resulting document appears jumbled.

Indenting bylines or credit lines

You can indent text other than body text. For example, you might indent bylines or credit lines. You can indent headlines, so that the kickers overhang a little bit, or you can indent subheads. As long as you don't go overboard and end up with a seesaw pattern, using indents on a variety of elements helps keep a page visually active, even when it is filled primarily with text.

You can use paragraph style sheets to make your indents automatic. To set up paragraph formatting controls for a style sheet, first open the Edit Style Sheets dialog box (Shift+F11). Next, select the style sheet you want and click Edit. Now just click the Formats tab and set up your indents the same way you would in the Paragraph Formats dialog box.

The sidebar effect

If you read newspapers or magazines, you're used to seeing sidebars, those small chunks of information that appear alongside the body of a document while being separate from it. Sidebars are an effective way of visually breaking up what could otherwise be a heavy block of text.

Don't think that sidebars should be reserved for commercial publications; they are also very effective in making proposals, memos, annual reports, and technical papers more interesting to the reader (consider, for instance, the sidebar you're reading now). Breaking up long sections of text with sidebars is often a good idea, and makes the text seem less formidable.

Bullets and lists

Lists are an effective way to organize information so that discrete elements are treated individually, with each clearly visible as a separate entity and yet obviously part of a bigger grouping. The two most popular ways to indicate lists are to use bullets or sequential labels (either numerals or letters). The right column in Figure 17-2 shows an example of a hanging-indent list while the left column shows a list that uses only first-line indents. The middle column uses no indents.

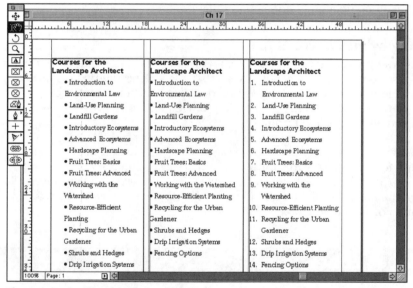

Figure 17-2: Different types of lists.

Tip

Depending on the length of list items and the width of columns on the page, you may be content simply putting a bullet or label at the beginning of each item. This works best when your itemized text takes many lines (more than five or six) in multicolumn text. Otherwise, you'll probably want to have a hanging indent in itemized paragraphs with the bullet or label hanging over the text's left margin, which is itself indented from the box or column's left margin.

Creating a list style

QuarkXPress does not offer a feature that automates the creation of bulleted or labeled lists, but you can cut out most of the work involved by creating a style sheet with the proper settings. After you create the style sheet, all you have to do is apply it to the appropriate paragraphs and add the bullets or labels to the text. Figure 17-3 shows the settings for a bulleted list style sheet. These settings create the proper indentation for a hanging-indent bulleted list. We also could have applied these settings directly to a single paragraph through Style⇨Formats (Shift+⌘+F); the Formats pane that appears is the same.

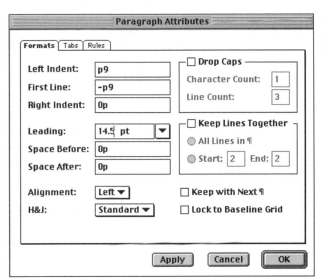

Figure 17-3: Settings in the Formats pane of Paragraph Attributes for a hanging-indent, bulleted list style.

Setting left and first-line indents

Hanging-indent bulleted lists are most effective when the left indent and the first-line indent are the same amount, but in different directions. What this means is that you use a positive setting for the left indent and a negative setting for the first-line indent. The negative setting creates an outdent. Using the same setting for the outdent as for the left indent ensures that the bullet starts at the column margin because the two values in essence cancel each other out for the first line. The indent amount should equal the space needed for the bullet or label character. Here is how we determined our settings:

✦ We decided to use a regular en bullet as the text character, rather than a square or other shape. (Unfortunately, you can't have QuarkXPress automatically add the bullet as part of the paragraph style.)

✦ We created a new paragraph style for the bullet. We based the style on the Normal style used for the body text, so that our typeface, leading, size, and other settings were already set for the bulleted text.

✦ We opened the Formats pane of the Paragraph Attributes dialog box by selecting Edit⇨Style Sheets (Shift+F11), choosing the style sheet we had just created, clicking Edit, and then selecting the Formats tab. We changed the settings in the Formats pane so that the left indent is 9 points (0p9, or 0 picas and 9 points), which is the width of an en bullet and its trailing space for 9-point text. (The 0 before the *p* is optional.) That shifts the entire paragraph margin in from the left margin 9 points.

Tip

An en bullet and its trailing space usually take as much room as the current point size, which makes it easy to figure out the indentation settings needed to achieve the correct alignment for the hanging indent.

✦ We set the first line's indent at –0p9. Using a negative number as the First Line setting moves the first line *out*, creating an outdent instead of an indent. The left indent and first-line indent settings cancel each other out, ensuring proper alignment of the bullets, as explained earlier.

For a different visual effect, you might want to use a character other than an en bullet as a bullet. Some of the Zapf Dingbat characters are good for this, as are Wingdings. If you do use another character as a bullet, you'll need to experiment with left-indent and first-line-indent values to get the right settings.

✦ We saved the paragraph style sheet and applied it to the paragraphs we wanted bulleted.

✦ The last step was to enter the bullets, which we did by using the shortcut Option+8 on the Mac or Shift+Alt+8 in Windows. We could also have used a placeholder character (such as an asterisk) in our original text file and then used the find-and-replace feature to change the placeholder to a bullet after importing the text file into QuarkXPress. We added a tab after each bullet to make the rest of the paragraph align with the left text margin.

Creating a numbered list

To use numerals instead of bullets in the list, first determine whether there will be one or two digits in the numerals. In most typefaces, a numeral is the width of an en, which is half the current point size. After factoring in the space taken by the period and the trailing space, you typically need 1.2 ems of space for a hanging indent. An em space is equivalent to the current point size. If we needed two digits, that space would be 1.2 ems (one digit, the period, and the trailing space) plus an en (0.5 ems), or 1.7 times the current point size. Note that the amount of space taken by the period and the trailing space will vary based on the typeface and whether the text is justified, so you will have to experiment with settings for your own text.

To ensure proper alignment of the single-digit numerals in a list that contains some two-digit numerals, put an en space (Option+space on the Macintosh; Ctrl+Shift+6 in Windows) before the single-digit numerals.

Using a fixed space after a bullet or label

If you are *not* using an outdent, consider using a fixed space after a bullet or label to ensure that text always starts in the same position on each line with such a label. If your text is not justified, the normal space will always be the same width, so alignment will not be a problem.

However, you may want to use an en space so that there is a bit more space after the bullet or label than there is between words in the text. This will help set the bullet or label apart a bit from the rest of the text.

Visual labels

Some lists use another mechanism for separating elements: in-text labels that highlight the first few words of each new element. These highlighted words may be a few words that act as a mini-headline, or they may simply be the first few words of the paragraph. You can use any of several type attributes to define in-text labels. To help you see how each looks, we've used the attributes within the following descriptions. Unless otherwise noted, these effects are available from both the Style menu and the Measurements palette.

New Feature

You can use the new character style sheets to save these visual label (or lead-in) settings as a style. This will allow you to easily apply the character style to text in your document, rather than having to remember each time how to set all those attributes. Also, using character style sheets for this purpose lets you easily change your visual label text's style by changing the style sheets, rather than having to revise the formatting for each and every occurrence.

✦ **Boldface:** The strongest attribute, boldface often is used as a second-level subhead when the first-level subhead is a stand-alone headline set in a larger size and perhaps in a different typeface. It also can be used to indicate a first-level subhead in reports or newsletters when strong design is not a priority.

✦ *Italics:* This is a favorite choice. If you use boldface as a second-level subhead, italics is a natural option for third-level subheads. It also can be used after a bullet when each bulleted item contains a narrative description that benefits from a label summarizing its content.

✦ <u>Rules:</u> A common choice for documents that are meant to look like word-processed or typewritten documents, underlines or rules convey a "no frills" feel. They fall between boldface and italics in terms of visual impact. If you use rules, avoid using rules thicker than 2 points (anywhere from 0.5 to 1.5 is usually sufficient), and stay away from special rules such as dotted or thick-and-thin rules. Stick with single or double rules so that you don't distract readers from the text you're trying to emphasize.

✦ SMALL CAPS: This is a classy choice for text that doesn't need a strong visual label. Small caps appear no stronger visually than regular text, so they are *not* effective if you want to make labels more visible than the surrounding text (for example, so a reader can scan the labels to see which text is relevant). But small caps provide a way to add text labels that summarize content without interfering with the overall look of the document. As with italics, small caps work well in conjunction with bullets. Combining small caps with italics or boldface is an effective way to create labels that have more impact and yet retain the classy look of small caps.

✦ Typeface change: By changing to a typeface that is distinctly different from the current text, you can highlight labels very effectively. If you choose this option, try to pick a typeface used elsewhere in the document, so you avoid the ransom-note look. When body text is set in a serif typeface, it's typical and appealing to use a sans serif typeface for the label, but the reverse is often less effective. We used Univers as the typeface for the label of this paragraph.

✦ Scaled text: By scaling text horizontally or vertically, you can create a subtle label that has more visual impact than small caps and about the same impact as italics. (To access scaling features, select Style⇨Horizontal/Vertical Scale.) Be careful not to scale text too much (we used a horizontal scale of 125 percent here), or it will look distorted. A less-effective variation is to scale the label text vertically, so that it is narrower. This technique can work if you combine it with another attribute—for example, small caps and/or boldface—to counteract the reduced visual impact of the vertically-scaled text.

✦ Size change: By making text a few points larger, you can subtly call attention to labels without being too explicit about it. Don't set the label size more than a few points greater than the size of the body text, and never make label text smaller than body text. (We made the label text here 2 points larger than the body text.) As with scaling text, this technique can be combined with other techniques effectively.

Changing the horizontal scale, vertical scale, or text size are generally the *least* effective methods to indicate labels, and they can easily be misused. If you do decide to scale text or change its size, consider carefully the settings you choose.

Dingbats

A *dingbat* is a special character used as a visual marker, typically to indicate the end of a story in a multistory document like a magazine. A dingbat is especially useful if you have many stories on a page or many stories that *jump to* (continue on) later pages, because it may not be readily apparent to readers whether a story has ended or continues elsewhere. As with bullets, you can use almost any character as a dingbat. Squares and other geometric shapes are popular choices, as are logos or stylized letters based on the name of the publication or organization.

If you're writing about Macintosh programs but using a PC to produce your documents, use the free TrueType Dingbat font on the CD that accompanies this book to access common Mac symbols, such as the Apple logo and the Mac's special keyboard characters. Just drag the MAC_DING.TTF font to the FONTS directory within your Windows directory (usually called WINDOWS or WIN95).

Choosing bullets wisely

The en bullet (·) is the bullet character used most often, but feel free to experiment with other characters as bullets. A solid square makes the bullet appear bolder and more authoritative. A hollow square gives a strong but silent feel. A triangle appears more distinct without being as heavy as a solid square. Arrows reinforce the bullet's basic message of "Look here!" Geometric shapes are great alternatives to the traditional bullet, and typefaces such as Zapf Dingbats (see the following section) and Wingdings offer several options. The accompanying figure shows some potential bullet characters.

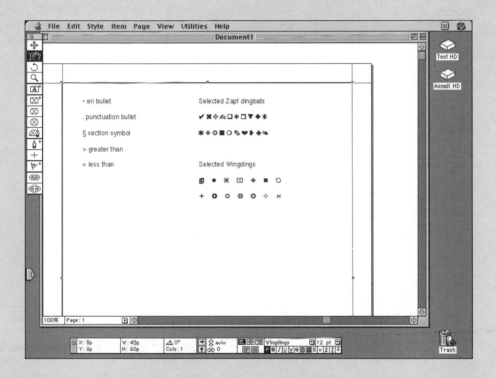

Several typefaces have whimsical characters that can function as bullets when placed in the proper context. Another possibility is to use symbols with specific meanings. For example, you can use astrological signs for a horoscope column, religious symbols for a church or temple newsletter, or checkmarks and checkboxes for election materials.

It's likely that your typeface has special symbols or *diacritical marks* (language symbols) that may work as bullets, too. You also can use a logo as a symbol if you create a typeface that uses it. (You can do this with such programs as Macromedia's Fontographer.) Using a logo is particularly effective if it is simple and readily identified with your organization.

Inserting a dingbat

The easiest way to insert a dingbat is to set a tab in your body-text paragraph style (or in whatever style you use for the last paragraph in a story). Set this tab to be right-aligned with the column's right margin; this is usually where dingbats are placed. If columns are 14 picas wide, set the tab at 14 picas, as shown in Figure 17-4. After you set the tab (in the Tabs pane of the Paragraph Attributes dialog box), go to the final paragraph in the story and add a tab after the last letter. Then add your dingbat character (and change its typeface, if necessary).

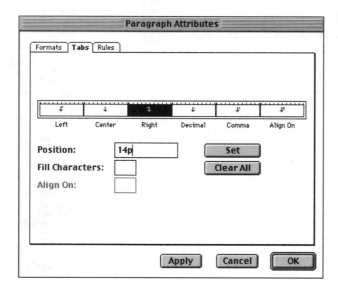

Figure 17-4: Set a tab to align dingbats to the column margin.

Defining a dingbat style

If you define the dingbat tab in the paragraph style used for your body text, you don't have to worry about remembering to apply the right style to the final paragraph after the layout has been completed and text edited, added, or cut to fit the layout. You can also make the dingbat a character style sheet (see Chapter 14). A dingbat need not be aligned with the right margin. You may want to place it one em space after the last character in the paragraph, in which case you simply add two nonbreaking en spaces (Option+⌘+space on the Macintosh; Ctrl+Alt+Shift+6 in Windows) before the dingbat.

Tip

Instead of manually setting the tab at the end of the story, you can also use a right-indent tab (Option+Tab) between the end of the line and the dingbat. This kind of tab automatically abuts the right margin of the box or column.

Making Drop Caps and Hybrid Caps

Using *drop caps* (a large letter set into several lines of normal-size text) is a popular way to guide readers through changes in topics. Drop caps also are frequently used to identify the introduction and conclusion of a story. When drop caps are used in this manner, the introduction and conclusion usually do not have subheads, but the sections between may have subheads.

Note

Some people consider drop caps and titles to be display type, while others consider them to be merely body type. How you treat them depends on how design-intensive your publication is. If all your titles and drop caps follow the same format, you're treating them as body type. But if you make the title of each chapter or story distinct, and perhaps make the drop caps for opening pages different as well, you're treating those elements as display type.

Automated drop caps

QuarkXPress automates most of the steps involved in creating a drop cap. To set a drop cap, open the Formats pane of the Paragraph Attributes dialog box by selecting the Formats option in the Style menu. (The keyboard shortcut is Shift+⌘+F.)

Creating a drop cap style

Because you are likely to use this effect more than once, it is best to create a style sheet for any paragraphs that use it. In most cases, the settings for a drop-cap paragraph are the same as those for body text, except that the paragraph's first line is not indented and a drop cap is defined. Rather than repeat all the settings for the body text when creating a drop cap style, you can simply follow these steps.

STEPS: Creating a drop cap style sheet

1. Select Based On from the Edit Paragraph Style Sheet dialog box (Edit⇨Style Sheets, or Shift+F11, then click Edit) and select the body text style as the basis for the new style.
2. Change the Left Indent setting to zero.
3. Select the Drop Caps option by clicking the checkbox next to it.
4. Specify the number of characters (usually 1) to be set as drop caps in the Character Count dialog box.
5. Set the Line Count to specify how many lines deep you want the drop cap to occupy (a typical setting is 3, but it can be as many as 16).

(continued)

6. Choose OK to get back to the Edit Paragraph Style Sheets dialog box and select Save to store the new style.

Figure 17-5 shows the settings described in the preceding steps. In our example, we did not select the Keep Lines Together option, but it would be a good idea to do so if you want to prevent a paragraph that begins with a drop cap from breaking in the middle of the cap. By the way, if you decide to set a one-time drop cap by choosing Style⇨Formats (Shift+⌘+F) instead of creating a style sheet, the Formats pane you see is identical to that in Figure 17-5.

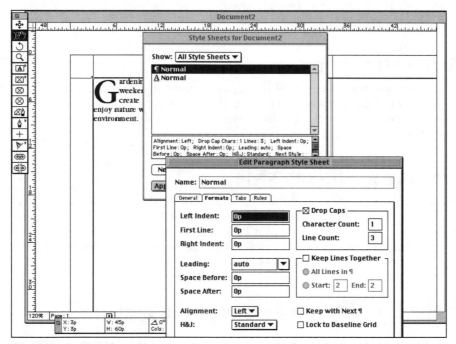

Figure 17-5: Sample settings used to create a style sheet for a paragraph that begins with a drop cap.

Applying a drop cap

After you create the drop cap style, you can apply it easily. Position your cursor anywhere on the appropriate text. Then select the new paragraph style from either the Style⇨Paragraph Style Sheet option or the Style Sheets palette. If the palette is not visible, use View⇨Show Style Sheets (F11) to turn it on.

Choosing a drop cap typeface

One more thing you might want to consider is a change in the drop cap's typeface. This is optional. There is no reason that a drop cap can't have the same typeface as the rest of the paragraph. But typically, a drop cap is either set in boldface or in a completely different typeface, which gives the drop cap higher visibility and usually results in a more interesting design. It's common for drop caps to be set in the same typeface as the headline or subhead. To change the drop cap's typeface, select it with the mouse and use the Measurements palette's font list or the Style⇨Font menu. In the example shown in Figure 17-6, Times is selected as the drop cap typeface.

Tip

Note that you can also create a character style for your drop cap, which ensures that each drop cap has exactly the same formatting as every other drop cap in your document.

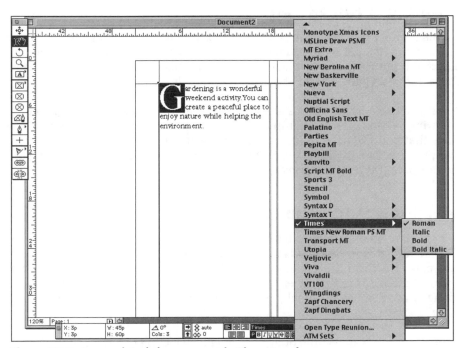

Figure 17-6: A completed drop cap set in Times typeface.

Dealing with drop cap quotation marks

Should you use the open quotation character ("), the open single-quote character ('), or no character at all to indicate the start of a quote? Most typographers choose the last option to avoid having overly big quotation marks, and traditionalist stylebooks agree. (Do, however, use the close-quotation mark (") at the end of the quotation.)

Although this is an accepted practice, some people find it confusing because they don't realize they've been reading a quote until they get to the end of it. If you insist on indicating an open quote, use the single quote ('). It distracts the eye from the actual first letter less than the double quote ("). Be sure to set the drop cap's Character Count setting to 2, not 1. Otherwise, you wind up with a large quotation mark only!

Creating a raised cap

A similar effect to a drop cap is a *raised cap,* which is simply a large first letter on the first line of a paragraph. A raised cap does not drop into the surrounding paragraph but rises above it instead. To create this effect, simply select the first character and change its point size and, optionally, its typeface.

When you use a larger point size for a raised cap or a hybrid drop cap (see the following section on raised drop caps), the cap may extend into the text above. It's likely that you will need to insert extra space above the cap to keep text from overprinting. One way to avoid this is to use additive or automatic leading options in your paragraph style settings.

Making raised drop caps

You also can create a hybrid between a drop cap and a raised cap. For example, you can add a drop cap that is four lines tall and drops in two lines of text. To do this, make the drop cap's line count 2, select the drop cap character, and then change its size. Note that when you do this, the Measurements palette options change from displaying actual point sizes to letting you type in percentages, such as 200 percent.

Alternately, you can use the Style⇨Size menu, selecting Other (Shift+⌘+\) to get a list of percentage options.

Figure 17-7 shows several variations of drop caps (reading from the top of the figure to the bottom and starting at the left column): a traditional three-line drop cap; a three-line raised cap (the point size is three times the leading); a five-line drop cap in a typeface different from body text; and a five-line drop cap that has both a different typeface and extra kerning (see the sidebar on other hybrid drop caps).

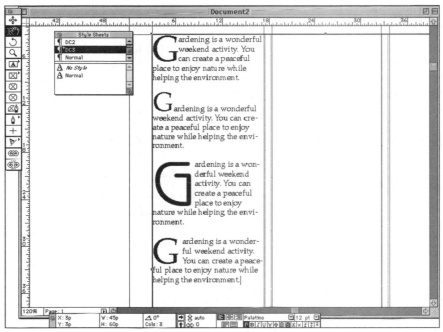

Figure 17-7: Drop cap variations.

Other hybrid drop caps

You can create yet another variation of a drop cap by moving the drop cap away from the text to make it more pronounced. Use the Style⇨Kern menu or enter a kerning value in the Measurements palette to move the text away from the drop cap. In addition, you can compress or expand the drop cap with the Style⇨Horizontal/Vertical Scale menu option. A related variant is a hanging drop cap, in which the rest of the text aligns with the right edge of the drop cap. Use the Indent to Here character (⌘+\) after the drop cap to set the indent position. By combining this technique with a hanging indent (covered earlier in this chapter), you can have the drop cap appear to the left of the standard text margin.

Other techniques for creating drop caps include using an anchored text or picture box where the drop cap would go so that you could use a graphic or a specially created letter. If you use this technique with a letter exported from an illustration program as a graphic and placed in an anchored picture box—or a letter converted to a picture box, as described in Chapter 20—you can then use the Auto Image or Manual runaround features to have the text surrounding the drop cap follow the drop cap letter's shape.

Rotating Text

Instead of limiting you to display-type treatments that involve changes in font and size only, QuarkXPress lets you also move type to different angles of rotation, adding another weapon to your design arsenal. Text rotation is a popular and effective way to treat *display type*, or type used as art. In addition to being used for story titles, rotated text is sometimes employed to create angled pull-quotes, banners, flags on ads and covers, and identifiers at the outside of a page. Figure 17-8 offers examples of rotated text to give you some idea of this design tool's potential.

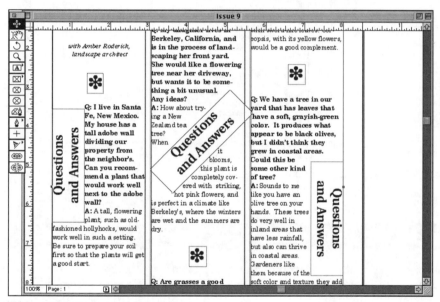

Figure 17-8: Examples of rotated text.

To rotate text, you must first put it in its own text box or on a text path. After you put the elements to be rotated into text boxes or on a text path and switch to the Item tool, you can rotate them in one of three ways:

✦ **Option 1:** Use the Measurements palette to enter the rotation amount (the top option on the third column, indicated by a geometric-angle symbol). This is the simplest method, especially if you know what angle of rotation you want in advance.

✦ **Option 2:** Use the Rotation tool (the curved arrow), as we did in Figure 17-9. The advantage to this tool is that it is free-form, letting you eyeball the angle as you turn the text. This comes in handy when, for example, you want to match the text's rotation to a graphic element. The disadvantage is that it takes time to learn to control the rotation tool accurately. You can always fine-tune the angle later through the Measurements palette, however.

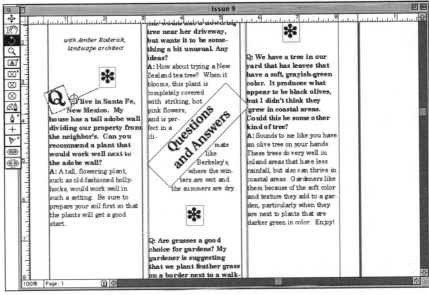

Figure 17-9: Using the Rotation tool to rotate text.

✦ **Option 3:** Use the Angle option in the Box pane of the Modify dialog box (see Figure 17-10). To open the box, select Item⇨Modify (⌘+M). This is the most cumbersome approach, but it is the fastest method if you also want to modify other settings, such as box color.

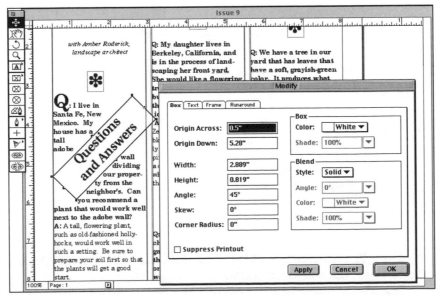

Figure 17-10: Using the Angle option in the Box pane to rotate a text box.

New
Feature

QuarkXPress 4 also lets you rotate text within a text box. To do so, select the text box, select Item⇨Modify (⌘+M), click the Text tab, and then enter an angle in the Text Angle field.

Placing Text on a Line

New
Feature

The Tool palette includes a set of tools—new to version 4—that lets you set type on a straight line, an orthogonal line, a Bézier line, or a freehand line. These tools are the Text Path tools—a pop-out set of tools near the bottom of the Tool palette (see Figure 17-11). After you create the line and place text on it, you can modify how the text is positioned. You can also apply all the QuarkXPress text effects, including fonts, color, kerning, and size.

Creating a text path

To create a text path, choose one of the Text Path tools; you can see them popped out of the Tool palette in Figure 17-11, and the figure includes an example of each of the four line types. From left to right, these tools include the following:

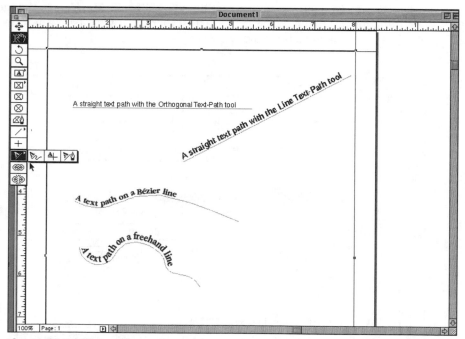

Figure 17-11: Text-path creation tools.

✦ **The Line Text Path tool:** This lets you create straight text paths at any angle.

✦ **The Orthogonal Text Path tool:** This lets you create straight text paths that are horizontal or vertical in orientation.

✦ **The Bézier Text Path tool:** This lets you create text paths made up of straight and curved line portions.

✦ **The Freehand Text Path tool:** This lets you draw freehand text paths onto which text can be positioned.

Tip

You can create default styles, arrowheads, width, color, shade, and runaround for any of the Text Path tools by setting preferences in the Tool pane, which you access by choosing Edit⇨Preferences⇨Document (⌘+Y).

Changing the text's position

To change the position or orientation of text on a text path, select the line and choose Item⇨Modify (⌘+M) and select the Text Path pane, shown in Figure 17-12. Click a button in the Text Orientation area of the Text Path pane to control how text is oriented with respect to the line. The Align Text pop-up menu lets you select which part of the font positions characters on the text path. The choices include:

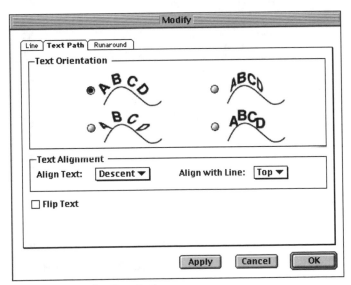

Figure 17-12: The Text Path pane.

✦ **Ascent:** This causes the font's ascenders to be the portion of the text that touches the line.

✦ **Center:** This uses the center of the font's x-height as the place that touches the line.

✦ **Baseline:** This uses the font's baseline as the place that touches the line.

✦ **Descent:** This causes the font's descenders to be the portion of the text that touches the line.

The Align with Line options work with the Align Text options to let you control the position of text on the path. Top puts the designated part of the text on top of the line, Center positions the designated part of the text in the center of the text path, and Bottom positions the designated part of the text at the bottom of the line. If you check the Flip Text button, the text will be flipped 180° and placed on the opposite side of the line relative to its current position. After making adjustments in the Text Path pane, click OK. Setting text on a text path is not something you are likely to do all the time, but it is a useful special effect nonetheless. Figure 17-13 shows a somewhat whimsical example of how this effect can be applied.

Figure 17-13: Text on a freehand line.

Coloring and Shading Text

As with most special effects, you should apply color or shading to text sparingly, reserving these treatments for elements that serve as text-as-art. Good places to use color or shading include titles, bylines, pull-quotes, and ancillary elements such as page numbers. QuarkXPress lets you apply color or shading (or both) to any selected text or to any paragraph whose style uses color or shading settings. You can access these effects in the following ways:

✦ **Option 1:** Make selections in the Style⇨Color and Style⇨Shade menus.

✦ **Option 2:** Select a color through the Colors palette (made visible by choosing View⇨Show Colors, and invisible by choosing View⇨Hide Colors; or by pressing F12). To do so, first click the Text button at the top of the palette and then click the desired color.

✦ **Option 3:** Add color using a character style sheet.

Figure 17-14 shows an example of shading. The byline is shaded at 30 percent black.

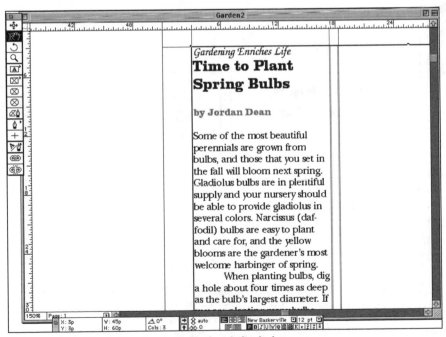

Figure 17-14: The byline is an example of shaded type.

Light colors and shades are best used with bold, large type because this keeps them from getting lost in the layout. They also work well when combined with other effects. Darker colors, such as blues and reds, work well in borders or as the colors of large outlined text.

Creating Shadows and Outlines

Desktop publishing made it easy to create shadowed and outlined text—tasks that were difficult in traditional typesetting because they required manual intervention through darkroom or paste-up techniques. In the early days of desktop publishing, you could identify most desktop-published work because it usually used one or both of these effects. Unfortunately, the effects were so overused that many professionals sneered at the ransom-note look produced by computer-based publishing novices. QuarkXPress offers options to create shadows or outlines from any typeface. Figure 17-15 shows samples of text that incorporate these effects.

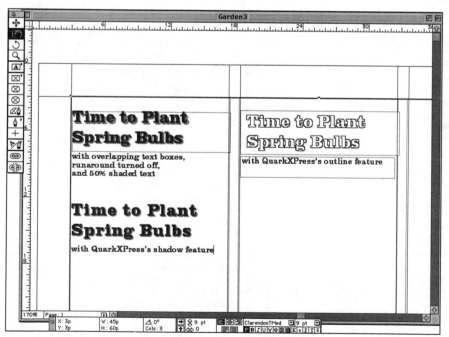

Figure 17-15: You can create shadows by overlapping text boxes, or by using QuarkXPress's shadow feature. The program's outline feature is also shown.

Hanging Punctuation

A technique used often in advertising is *hanging punctuation,* in which periods, commas, hyphens, and other punctuation marks fall outside the right margin. This technique is used in text that is either aligned right or justified. It doesn't make sense to hang punctuation in centered or left-aligned text because the punctuation would be too far away from the accompanying text. Hanging punctuation keeps letters aligned along the right margin, but gives the text some visual flow by using the punctuation as an exterior decoration. Figure 17-16 shows an example of right-aligned text in which the punctuation hangs off the right margin.

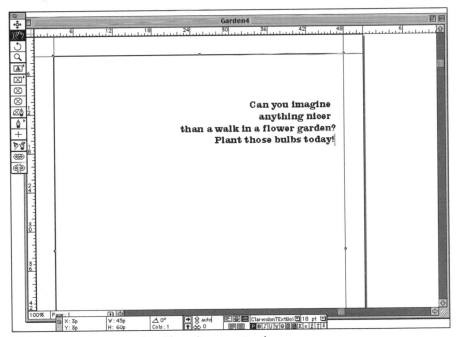

Figure 17-16: An example of hanging punctuation.

The tab approach

QuarkXPress offers no tool to handle this effect. For right-aligned text, you can create hanging punctuation by using tabs, either in a style sheet or through the Style menu for the selected text. The following steps show how we created the hanging punctuation shown in Figure 17-16. The advantage to this approach is that you can use the same tab settings (usually through a style sheet) for all text in which you want this effect. The disadvantage is that it does not work on justified text. (When setting tabs, use the ruler in the Tab pane, not the document ruler at the top of the screen.)

Shadow sense

Shadows and outlines generally work best with bold type. With lighter type, the characters become obscured because their strokes are not wide enough to be distinguished from the shadow or outline.

You cannot alter the shadow's position and percentage of gray. If you want a different type of shadow, you can duplicate the text box that contains your text and apply the color or shade you want to the duplicate text box. Place the duplicate text box under the original text box, then turn off text runaround for the original box. The original text box acts as the nonshadowed text, while the duplicated text box becomes the shadow. You can position the shadow wherever you prefer to create the effect you want. Figure 17-15 shows this technique.

STEPS: Creating hanging punctuation

1. We created a tab that aligned right at 43 picas, 3 points. This tab was used at the beginning of each line. We chose an alignment value that placed the tab far enough from the text box's right margin (here, 45 picas) that any punctuation character would fit between that tab and the text box's right margin. (A rule of thumb is to use between one-third and one-half of the current point size because the biggest punctuation symbol—the question mark—usually is about that size.) We used this first tab at the beginning of each line of text.

2. We added a second tab that aligned right at 43 picas, 4 points. (This value could have been anything more than the first tab's value. At the text's point size, 1 point was comparable to the natural letter spacing. Print out sample text at various tab settings before determining a final value.) We used this tab between the text and the punctuation. If there is no punctuation on a particular line, no second tab is needed.

The text box approach

The other method of accomplishing this effect—and the method you must use if text is justified—is to create two text boxes, one for the text and one for any punctuation marks that end a line. You'll probably need two styles as well: one for the text (either right-aligned or justified) and one for the punctuation (left-aligned). The simplest way to handle this is to create a style for the punctuation based on the style for the text, so that if the style for text changes, so does the punctuation style. You can then change the alignment in the punctuation style. After creating the two text boxes, align them so that the punctuation appears properly spaced after its corresponding text. Then use QuarkXPress's lock feature (Item⇨Lock or F6) to prevent the two boxes from moving accidentally.

Caution

Regardless of which approach you use to create hanging punctuation, if your text changes, you must manually change the line endings or punctuation positions. Because hanging punctuation is used only in small amounts of text, this is not a terrible burden. Also make sure that you turn off automatic hyphenation, so that you don't get double hyphenation (one from the hyphenation feature and one from the punctuation you enter manually).

✦   ✦   ✦

Graphics Techniques

◆ ◆ ◆ ◆

In This Part

Chapter 18
Working with
Graphics

Chapter 19
Manipulating Bitmap
Images

Chapter 20
Graphics-Creation
Tools

Chapter 21
Defining and
Applying Color

◆ ◆ ◆ ◆

Whether drawn with QuarkXPress's powerful new tools, created electronically in separate illustration and imaging programs, or captured electronically with scanners, graphics are a vital part of page design. Often the most glamorous parts of a document, pictures and other graphics play a major role in attracting the reader's eye. But graphics do much more than make a document look better. They convey meaning and tone. It's important to treat visual elements with the same care you use with the text or layout itself. QuarkXPress offers a solid set of graphics tools to help you import, create, and modify pictures.

This section explains how to manipulate imported pictures, work with bitmapped images like scanned photos, use the new illustration tools in QuarkXPress, and work with color.

Working with Graphics

✦   ✦   ✦   ✦

In This Chapter

Finding the right tools

Using the
Measurements palette

Using the Modify
dialog box

Achieving faster
printing and display

✦   ✦   ✦   ✦

In Chapter 5, we explained how to create a picture box and fill it with an imported picture. We also explained how to make changes to the size and position of a picture box. After you create, position, and size a picture box, you may want to make some changes to its contents—the picture itself. This chapter shows you how to alter the contents of an active picture box by changing the values in the Measurements palette and by adjusting the controls in the Modify dialog box, as well as several of the Style menu options. There's also a section on how you can achieve faster printing and screen displays in graphics-intensive documents.

Finding the Right Tools

As you work with graphics you'll probably find yourself using all the tools at your disposal, including keyboard shortcuts and palettes. There's no single right mix, but the information in this chapter will help you find the right balance for your working style. Here's a quick overview:

✦ **The Measurements palette:** This is the best place to make most modifications of size, placement, scale, and box settings. Why? Because not only does the Measurements palette contain the most common functions, it's almost always on your screen. Using it does not require you to open a dialog box that often blocks the view of what you're working with.

✦ **The Modify dialog box:** If you need a function that's not on the Measurements palette, you have to use the Modify dialog box. The Modify dialog box is also convenient when you're applying multiple settings, because they're all in one place.

✦ **The Style menu:** Most of the relevant items in the Style menu affect output for bitmapped images, which is covered in Chapter 19; or for color images, which is covered in Chapter 21. Almost all these techniques work with text boxes as well. Chapter 17 covers these functions from a text perspective in detail.

Using the Measurements Palette

To use the Measurements palette to modify the contents of a picture box, you must first make the picture box active. (If the box is active, its sizing or reshaping handles are visible around the edge of the box.) You also must display the Measurements palette. (To display the palette, choose View➪Show Measurements, or use the shortcut F9.) In Figure 18-1, you see a page containing a picture box. (The Measurements palette appears at the bottom of the screen.) The figure shows the page just after we filled the picture box with a picture. We used the Rectangular Picture Box tool to draw the picture box, and we filled the box with the picture by choosing File➪Get Picture (or press ⌘+E). Note the sizing handles on the borders of the box: they indicate that the box is active.

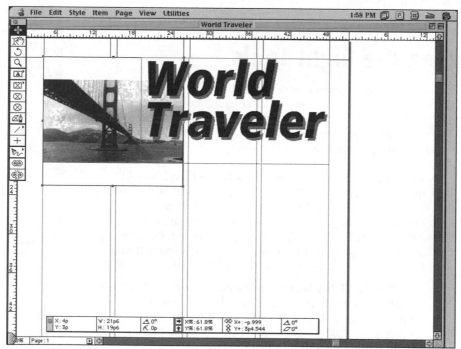

Figure 18-1: The Measurements palette's settings for the selected picture box.

Note

Note also that the image (refer to Figure 18-1) doesn't quite fit the picture box's dimensions—it's smaller than the picture box. QuarkXPress loads an image in its actual size and does not try to fit the image to the picture box size. In the figure, we had QuarkXPress resize the image to fit proportionally within the box's constraints, using the shortcut Option+Shift+⌘+F.

Modifying box position and size

Entering new values in the X and Y fields changes the distance of the picture box border from the page edge. The position of the picture box shown in Figure 18-1 is 4 picas (⅔ inch) from the left side of the page and 3 picas (½ inch) from the top. Entering new values in the W and H fields changes the width and height of the picture box. In the figure, the current dimensions are 21 picas, 6 points by 19 picas, 6 points. (For inch-oriented people, there are 12 points in a pica, and 6 picas in an inch, thus 72 points in an inch.)

Modifying the picture scale

You can also change the size of an image within the box, not just change the size of the box. The setting in the X% and Y% fields in Figure 18-1 is 61.8 percent. Changing the percentage values in the X% and Y% fields reduces or enlarges the picture in the picture box. To keep the proportions of the picture the same, enter the same value in the X field as you enter in the Y field. Unfortunately, you cannot link the two so that if you change one, the other automatically changes with it to keep the picture's proportions consistent.

Rounding off measurements

Sometimes you'll see values like 16p3.765—a too-exacting measurement indicating that the picture box was placed or drawn by hand *and* that the snap-to-grid feature is not turned on. (Turn it on via View⇨Snap to Guides or Shift+F7.)

It's better to round measurements to the nearest point, pica, inch, or whatever measurement system you're using. That way, it'll be easier for you to remember the settings as you create new boxes or lines meant to align with existing boxes, as well as being easier to enter the coordinates. (The human eye *will* detect misalignments resulting from, say, one box starting at 3p5.799 and the next several starting at 3p6.115.)

Tip   You can use the keyboard shortcuts Option+Shift+⌘+< and Option+Shift+⌘+> to scale an image smaller and larger, respectively, along both axes simultaneously. This shortcut scales the image 5 percent at a time. If the current percentage is not a multiple of 5 percent, the first enlargement or reduction will be to the nearest increment of 5 percent. In the example in Figure 18-1, pressing Option+Shift+⌘+< would reduce the image from 61.8 percent to 60 percent, and pressing it again would reduce the image to 55 percent.

Moving the image within the box

As you resize an image, you'll likely want to move the image within the box so that the part you want to highlight is showing. (That's called *cropping*.) The easiest way is to make sure the Content tool is selected and simply drag the picture within the box to the desired crop. But that's not exact, and after you do that rough crop, you'll likely want to fine-tune the placement. You can also enter values for the image to be shifted within the picture box in the Measurements palette: enter the numbers in the fields to the right of X+: and Y+:. Or you can click the shift handles in the Measurements palette as follows:

◁▷   Horizontal shift (shown here) moves an image within the picture box. Each click moves the image in 1-point increments (0.014 inches, 0p1, and so on). If you hold the Option key when clicking this handle, you move the picture in 0.1-point increments (0.0014 inches, 0p0.1, and so on).

⇕   Vertical shift (shown here) moves an image within the picture box in the same way as the Horizontal shift handle described in the preceding paragraph.

Tip   When the Content tool is selected, using the keyboard's arrow keys with the Content tool active does exactly the same thing as using the Measurements palette's shift handles.

Box special effects

You can use the Measurements palette to achieve box special effects, as follows:

◿   Entering any value except zero in the Rotate field (the icon shown here) on the *left* side of the Measurements palette rotates the picture box by that many degrees. Because the box in Figure 18-1 is not rotated, the value in the field is 0 (zero) degrees. If you use negative numbers, you rotate the box counterclockwise; positive numbers rotate the box clockwise. Entering any value except zero in the Rotate field located at the *right* side of the palette rotates the picture *within* the picture box by that many degrees. (The current value for the picture box in Figure 18-1 is zero, which means the image is not rotated within the box.)

Entering a value in the Corner Radius field (the icon shown here) changes the shape of the picture box corners. For example, entering a value of 2 picas causes a rectangular picture box's corners to become rounded.

Entering any value except zero in the Skew field (the icon shown here) slants the contents of the picture box. In Figure 18-1, the picture-box contents are not slanted. If you use negative numbers, you slant the box to the left; positive numbers slant the box to the right.

Clicking the Horizontal Flip icon (shown here) flips the image along the X axis. (You can also use the Flip Horizontal item in the Style menu.)

The horizontal arrow's direction changes (as shown here) to let you know whether a picture has been flipped.

Clicking the Vertical Flip icon (shown here) flips the image along the Y axis. (You can also use the Flip Vertical item in the Style menu.)

The vertical arrow's direction changes (as shown here) to let you know whether a picture has been flipped.

After you use the Measurements palette to make changes to the picture box, press Return or click the mouse on the page to apply the changes.

Using the Modify Dialog Box

You also can modify a picture contained in an active picture box by using the Modify dialog box, shown in Figure 18-2. To display the dialog box, select the picture box to make it active and then choose Item⇨Modify (or use the shortcut key combination ⌘+M or simply double-click the picture box with the Item tool). Like most QuarkXPress dialog boxes, the Modify dialog box can be moved, so you can often position it to see what you're modifying while you're modifying it. The new Apply button lets you preview changes before making them real. The following sections describe the panes in the Modify dialog box that apply to an active picture box. You can make changes in one or all of these panes. When you finish making selections in the dialog box, choose OK to save your changes.

The Modify dialog box contains the features that in previous versions of QuarkXPress were in the Picture Box Specifications dialog box, which no longer exists. The Modify dialog box has also been divided in QuarkXPress 4 into several panes: Box, Picture, Frame, Clipping, and Runaround. The last three are covered in Chapter 5.

Working in the Box pane

The Box pane (see Figure 18-2) contains the settings for the picture box itself. The following sections explain how they work.

Note

As we show examples of these effects, note how the Measurements palette at the bottom of the screen changes to reflect the new values. You can bypass the Modify dialog box for any function displayed in the Measurements palette by entering the appropriate values in the palette itself.

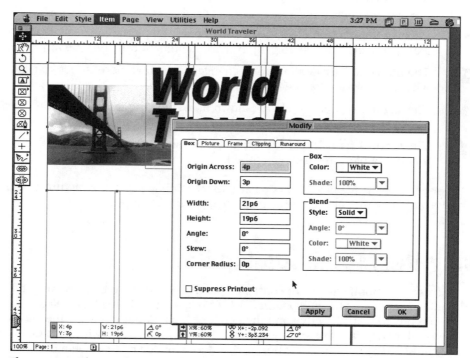

Figure 18-2: The Modify dialog box's Box pane lets you make settings for the selected picture box.

Box position and size

The values in the Origin Across, Origin Down, Width, and Height fields control the position and size of the picture box. You can specify these values in units as small as 0.001 in any measurement system. In Figure 18-2, the origin (the upper-left corner of the picture box) is 4 picas from the left and 3 picas from the top of the page. The picture box width is 21 picas, 6 points, and the height is 19 picas, 6 points.

Box special effects

In the same Box pane, you can also control the rotation, skew, and corner settings for the box. Entering a value in the Angle field rotates the picture box around the center of the box.

The Angle field

Box angle values range from –360 to 360 degrees, in increments as small as 0.001 degrees. Figure 18-3 shows the effect of rotating the picture box 5 degrees.

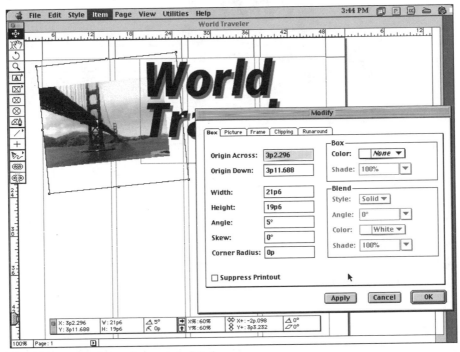

Figure 18-3: A picture box rotated 5 degrees.

The Corner Radius field

Entering a value in the Corner Radius field changes the shape of a picture box's corners. This field contains the word *radius* because invisible circles exist in the corners of boxes drawn in QuarkXPress. These circles are located within the bounds of the box corners and touch the two sides of the box next to them. The radius is the size of the circle used to apply rounded edges to the box. (The Corner Radius field is not available when the picture box is an oval, freehand, or Bézier shape.) When you first create a rectangular picture box, its corner radius values are 0 (zero). You can enter a measurement value from 0 to 2 inches (0 to 12 picas), in 0.001 increments of any measurement system. Figure 18-4 shows the effect of selecting a corner radius of 2 picas.

Tip

We don't recommend changing the corner radius of a picture box unless you are certain that it adds to the design of the page. Rounded-corner picture boxes are typically not effective and can make a layout appear amateurish.

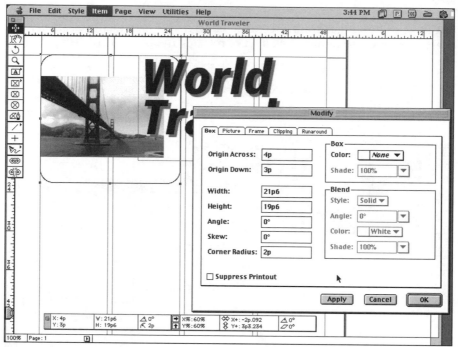

Figure 18-4: A picture box with a corner radius of 2 picas.

Box background and color

QuarkXPress lets you add color to the background of a picture box and control the shade (*saturation*) of the color. To add color to the background of an active picture box or to change an existing background color, select a color from the Color pop-up menu in the Box area of the Modify dialog box or use the Colors palette (if not visible, use View➪Show Colors, or the keyboard shortcut F12, to make it appear). Figure 18-5 shows both the Colors palette and the Modify dialog box, with a background applied to the picture box. (Chapter 21 covers defining and applying colors in detail.)

The None selection

One of the selections available in the Color pop-up menu is None. If you select None, the box background is transparent. That's the setting you'll need if you want, for example, text to overprint a graphic. The text box should have a background of None. If you have a picture overprint text or another picture, it's a good idea to have the background set at None as well. While bitmapped images that appear to have no color actually have a white color and thus won't let the image or text below show through, vector images may have transparent backgrounds that you'll want to keep transparent by leaving the box background set at None. Also, None is a good setting, even for bitmapped images, because you likely don't want the part of the picture box that does *not* have a picture in it to obscure anything underneath.

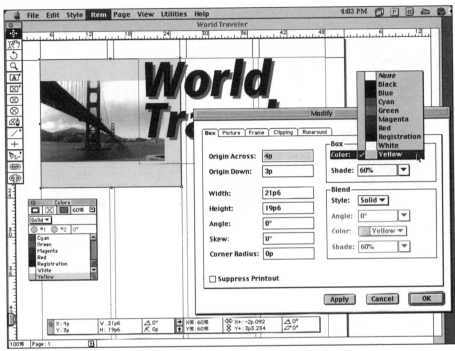

Figure 18-5: A picture box with a background color applied.

Specifying the saturation level

After you select the background color that you want to apply to the picture box (and you select a color other than None or White), you can specify the saturation level (shading) of the color. Select a predefined shade (0 to 100 percent) in the Shade list box or enter a custom shade value (in increments as small as 0.1 percent) in the Shade field. There's a pop-up menu for shade increments in the Colors palette as well (at the top right), in which you can use your own values or choose from the existing ones.

Working with blends

A *blend* is a gradation from one color to another. When the Cool Blends XTension is installed, QuarkXPress lets you select six blend types, with the Style pop-up menu in the Blend section of the Box pane. (If the XTension is not installed, you only have one blend type to choose from.) Chapter 21 covers these in more depth, and Figure 18-6 shows an example.

QuarkXPress 4 now integrates the Blends feature into the Modify dialog box. This feature was previously available only in the Colors palette.

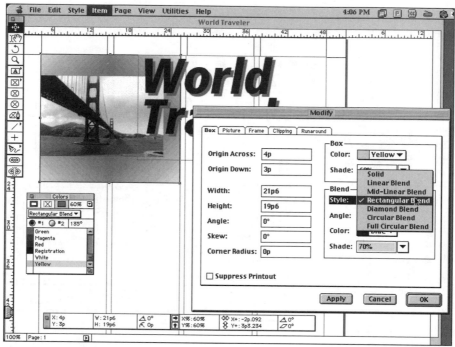

Figure 18-6: A blend background.

Blend tips and tricks

Note that the box background color (the Color pop-up menu in the Box section of the Box pane) is the color you blend *from*; you select the color to blend *to* in the Blend section's Color pop-up menu. Rectangular, circular, and diamond blends go from the outside of the box to the inside, and linear and midlinear blends go from left to right by default. You can adjust the angle of the blend via the Angle pop-up menu, which actually rotates the blend within the picture box.

It's pretty rare that you'll put a blend background on a picture box. Not only will the picture obscure most if not all of it, it will likely clash with the image. This function is more useful when creating boxes meant to be used as graphics.

Working in the Picture pane

As you work with QuarkXPress, you'll probably frequently use the Scale Across and Scale Down feature in the Picture pane of the Modify dialog box. In fact, it's one of the handiest items in the entire program, especially if you create documents that include graphics. It's rare that a graphic has the size you want it to be when you first import it, which is why the ability to change the size (scale) is so important.

Scaling across and down

When you first fill a picture box with a picture (by choosing File⇨Get Picture or by using the shortcut ⌘+E), QuarkXPress places the picture in the text box at 100 percent scale. It's not at all uncommon for the picture to be larger or smaller than you would like, and you can change its size by entering new values in the Scale Across and Scale Down fields. You can specify a size from 10 to 1,000 percent of the picture's original size. You can enter scale values in increments as small as 0.1 percent. You don't have to enter the same values for Scale Across and Scale Down; you can enter different values for each field to distort the picture. In the first illustrations presented in this chapter, we used a picture at 68.1 percent scale across and down. Figure 18-7 shows the same illustration scaled 105 percent along both dimensions, which is about half again as large as the size used up until now.

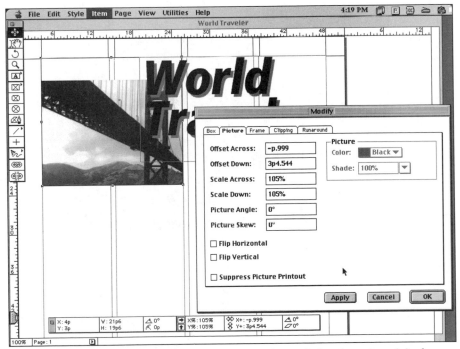

Figure 18-7: Our picture scaled to 105 percent of actual size, from its original 68.1 percent.

Quick resizing with the keyboard

The keyboard can be a very convenient way to scale items. The keyboard methods for positioning a picture within a picture box include the following:

✦ Shift+⌘+F stretches or shrinks the picture to the borders of the picture box without keeping the picture's aspect ratio.

✦ Option+Shift+⌘+F fits the picture as close as it can to the picture box but maintains the picture's aspect ratio.

✦ Shift+⌘+M centers the picture in the middle of the picture box.

✦ Option+Shift+⌘+< decreases Scale Across and Scale Down values to the next smallest 5 percent.

✦ Option+Shift+⌘+> increases Scale Across and Scale Down values to the next highest 5 percent.

Shown here are the results of the first three operations. Note that the image at bottom right was not fit to the picture box before being centered.

Keeping a picture's aspect ratio means that you keep its proportions the same as you enlarge it or reduce it. Keeping aspect ratio means keeping equal scale-across and scale-down percentages, such as 50 percent horizontally (X%), 50 percent vertically (Y%), and so on.

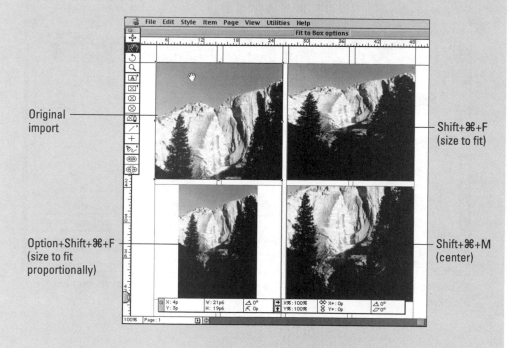

Original import

Shift+⌘+F (size to fit)

Option+Shift+⌘+F (size to fit proportionally)

Shift+⌘+M (center)

You may occasionally want to place a graphic when you aren't sure what size the picture box should take. What you should do is create the picture box, import the picture, and then resize the picture box to fit the graphic.

Offsetting across and down

Often, imported pictures are not positioned within the box as you want them to be. The focal point of a picture might be too far to the left, too far to the right, or too high or low within the box. You can position the picture—in a precise, numerical fashion—by entering values in the Offset Across and Offset Down fields in the Picture pane of the Modify dialog box. In Figure 18-8, we adjusted the offset to the left by entering an Offset Across value of –6 picas. This change moves the picture box's contents 6 picas to the left. (A positive number would move it to the right.) Compare this to the position in Figure 18-7.

Another easy (although less precise) way to position a picture within a picture box is to use the Content tool. First select the Content tool. If you then place the cursor over the active picture box, it turns into a grabber hand that lets you shift the picture into place by holding the mouse button while moving the mouse.

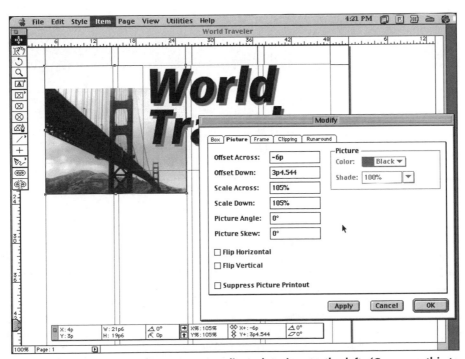

Figure 18-8: The picture box contents adjusted 6 picas to the left. (Compare this to the position in Figure 18-7.)

The change we made in Figure 18-8 improved the *across*, or horizontal, placement of the picture within the picture box (so the Golden Gate Bridge's tower is not obscured under the logo), but missing is the view of the water, which has been moved past the box's bottom edge. To fix this, we enter an Offset Down value of −0p3, about a 3p7 shift up from its original setting of 3p4.544. You can see the result in Figure 18-9. (A positive number moves the picture down.)

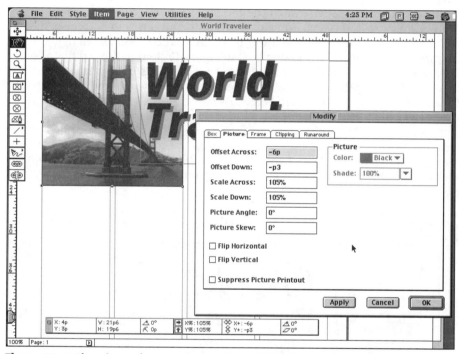

Figure 18-9: The picture box contents with an Offset Down value of −0p3, about a 3p7 shift up from its original setting of 3p4.544. (Compare this to the position in Figure 18-8.)

Adjusting the picture angle

When you first place a picture into a picture box, it is oriented at the same angle it had in its source graphics program. Occasionally, you may want to change the angle of the picture without changing the angle of the picture box itself. In the Picture pane of the Modify dialog box, enter a value in the Picture Angle field to rotate the picture within the box. The picture is rotated around the center of the picture box as it was created in the original graphics program. The angle of the box stays the same; only the contents rotate. You can enter Picture Angle values from −360 to 360 degrees, in increments as small as 0.001 degrees. Figure 18-10 shows the effect of changing the Picture Angle from 0 degrees to 40 degrees.

Understanding offsets

Offsets are not relative. They are absolute positions based on the upper-left corner of the picture box. Thus, moving an object 6 picas from an original position of 3p means adding 6p to the original 3p (or subtracting 6p to move in the opposite direction). The math can get tricky, so let QuarkXPress do it for you. Just add or subtract the distance in the Offset Across and Offset Down dialog boxes.

For example, if the Offset Across is 3p7 and you want to shift the image to the right 6p6, tack on +6p6 after 3p7 (so it reads 3p7+6p6). QuarkXPress will do the math and come up with the correct 10p1 offset. Use a minus sign (–) to go to the left. When moving vertically, adding to the current value moves down, while subtracting from the current value moves up. You can also multiply the current value by using * (such as 3p*6 to get 18p) and divide by using / (such as 3p/2 to get 1p6).

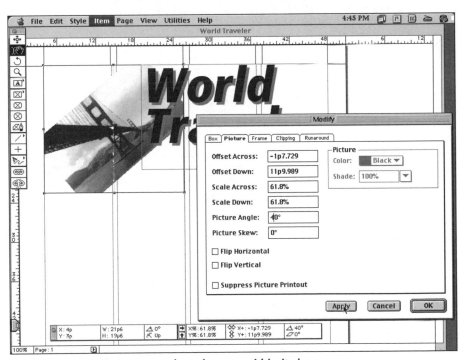

Figure 18-10: A picture rotated 40 degrees within its box.

Skewing the picture

Another special effect you can try with QuarkXPress is *skewing,* or slanting, a picture within its box. You do this by entering a value in the Picture Skew field of the Modify dialog box. You can enter values from –75 to 75 degrees, in increments as small as .001 degrees. If you enter a positive value, the picture skews to the right; if you enter a negative value, the picture skews to the left. Figure 18-11 shows the effect of skewing our picture 40 degrees.

Note

It is faster to rotate or skew pictures in QuarkXPress than in Photoshop or CorelDraw. That doesn't mean you shouldn't use QuarkXPress's rotation and skew features, but that you should apply them judiciously and rely on your graphics program if you want to do extensive rotation and skewing in your images.

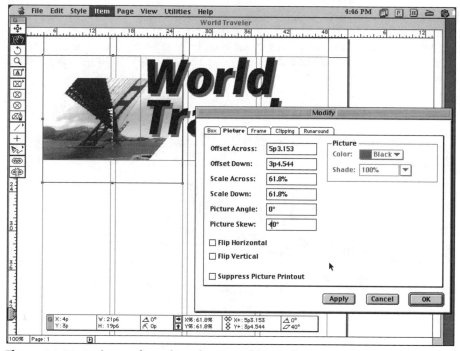

Figure 18-11: A picture slanted 40 degrees within its box.

Coloring and shading the picture

Finally, you can change the color of some pictures by choosing a color and/or shade from the Color and Shade pop-up menus in the Picture section of the Picture pane. You use this effect to tint a monochromatic image, such as taking a black-and-white photo and giving it a sepia-brown tint to suggest an old photo, or lightening a gray-scale image so it can be placed on the background behind text. You can change a picture's color or shade only if it is one of the following basic types (see Chapter 21 for more detail):

✦ Black-and-white BMP, JPEG, MacPaint (Mac only), PCX, PICT, and TIFF bitmap images

✦ Gray-scale BMP, GIF (Windows only), JPEG, PCX, PICT, and TIFF bitmap images

Achieving Faster Printing and Display

A document chock-full of pictures can be slow to print and display on-screen. Fortunately, QuarkXPress has a variety of settings to speed up your work. The rest of this chapter tells you how to use them.

Picture suppression

The Box and Picture panes on the Modify dialog box (Item⇨Modify, ⌘+M, or double-click the picture box with the Item tool) have two similar items: Suppress Printout in the Box pane and Suppress Picture Printout in the Picture pane. In these two fields, you can select options that speed document printing—something you may want to consider when you print proofs or rough copies. Here's how they work:

> ✦ **Suppress Picture Printout:** If you select Suppress Picture Printout, the frames or backgrounds of picture boxes print, but the contents of the picture boxes do not.

If you use frames around picture boxes, we recommend that you print proof copies with Suppress Picture Printout selected. This lets you see the size and placement of the frames.

> ✦ **Suppress Printout:** Selecting Suppress Printout takes this option one step further. It prevents picture box frames, backgrounds, and contents from printing.

To choose either option, check the box next to the option label. If you select one of these options, remember to go back into the Modify dialog box and uncheck the box before printing final copies of the document.

Be careful with this feature, because there's no option when you print to force all suppressed boxes and pictures to print. If you want to find out which pictures in a document are set to print and which pictures are suppressed, open the Usage dialog box (Utilities⇨Usage), click the Pictures tab, and look in the Print column.

Display quality

For on-screen time savings, you can set several options that don't let pictures get in the way of your moving speedily about. The absolute fastest is to check the Greek Pictures item in the General pane of the Document Preferences dialog box (⌘+Y or Edit⇨Preferences⇨Document). With this option checked, pictures will appear as gray boxes on-screen unless they are selected. (They will print normally.) Figure 18-12 shows the option. (In publishing, greeking has always meant to use random text as a placeholder in layouts, and now also means to use a gray or black box as a placeholder for an image.)

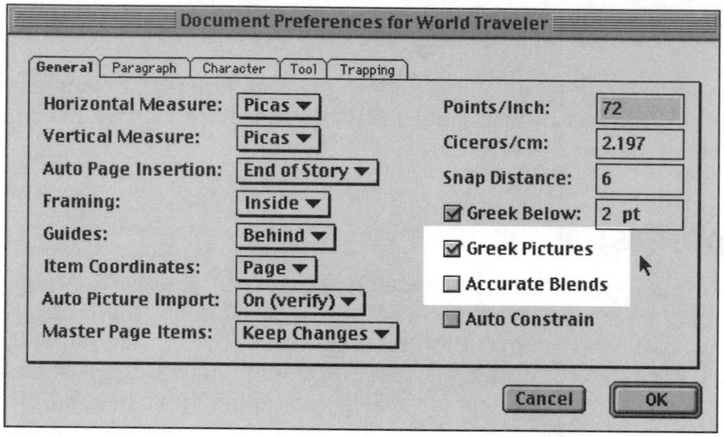

Figure 18-12: Greek pictures and uncheck Accurate Blends to speed up redisplay time on-screen.

If you keep your pictures visible on-screen, you still have the following time-saving settings at your disposal:

✦ In the General pane of the Document Preferences dialog box, uncheck Accurate Blends (also displayed in Figure 18-12). If your monitor is in 256-color mode, displaying color blends accurately takes a fair amount of computation that will slow down screen display. With this item unchecked, blends draw faster in 256-color monitor mode but appear "banded."

✦ In the Display pane of the Application Preferences dialog box (Option+Shift+⌘+Y or Edit⇨Preferences⇨Application), set Color TIFFs and Gray TIFFs to the minimum resolutions (8-bit and 16 levels, respectively). The truer the color, the more data QuarkXPress has to keep in RAM (and the larger your QuarkXPress files will be as well). It sure looks better when set at 32-bit color and 256 levels of gray (at least if your monitor supports thousands or millions of colors), but if you're feeling mired in mud, give up the detail. Figure 18-13 shows the Display pane.

✦ In the Interactive pane (shown in Figure 18-14), make sure Speed Scroll is checked. It will temporarily greek pictures when you are scrolling through your pages.

✦ In the Interactive pane, keep Live Scroll unchecked, to prevent pages from displaying while you're dragging the scroll box in the scrollbar. If you want the pages to display while you drag the box, just hold down the Option key. (The Option key also turns off Live Scroll when it is enabled.)

✦ Also in the Interactive pane, choose Show Contents rather than Live Refresh in the Delayed Item Dragging section. Live Refresh has QuarkXPress update text flow and item layering as you drag items, something you'll rarely need to see and don't need to have QuarkXPress make you wait for. Note that to activate either Show Contents (which keeps the picture visible, but only at minimum color depth) or Live Refresh, you must click and hold the mouse button for half a second (or whatever number you enter in the Delay Seconds field). Otherwise, you get normal movement—which is fine for most object movements and faster to boot.

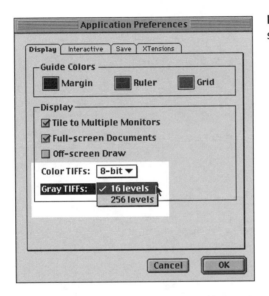

Figure 18-13: Speed-optimized display settings in the Display pane.

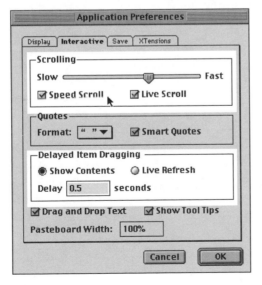

Figure 18-14: Speed-optimized display settings in the Interactive pane.

✦   ✦   ✦

Manipulating Bitmap Images

✦ ✦ ✦ ✦

In This Chapter

Exploring the controls

Working with image formats

Creating negative images

Adjusting contrast

Regulating halftones

Dealing with dithering

Controlling color and shade

✦ ✦ ✦ ✦

QuarkXPress offers sophisticated ways of controlling bitmap images, and this is particularly true for gray-scale images. An important part of traditional publishing, gray-scale images are usually scanned photographs, but they can also be original artwork created by paint programs. This chapter covers all the bases: bitmap formats, negative images, contrast, halftones, and dithering. We also cover QuarkXPress's image controls for color bitmap images.

Exploring the Controls

The bitmap controls in QuarkXPress fall into the following basic classes of image-manipulation techniques:

+ **Output control:** This feature lets you fine-tune the output of an image for best reproduction, such as lightening an overly dark image or enhancing contrast.

+ **Image alteration:** This lets you change the image's appearance to achieve a visual effect, such as coloring a gray-scale image or removing subtle details in a photo to give it a more drawn appearance.

The Style menu is where QuarkXPress keeps its image-manipulation functions, which it groups in three dialog boxes, each of which has its own version of the following entries in the Style menu:

+ **Negative:** Lets you create a photographic negative.

+ **Contrast:** Lets you adjust the contrast and brightness of images. You can use this to fine-tune an image for clarity or to apply special effects to it.

✦ **Halftone:** Lets you adjust how an image is printed—its coarseness and the shape of the elements used to create it (photos and other bitmaps are usually printed as a series of fine dots; QuarkXPress lets you choose the size of those dots and use other shapes, such as lines, rather than dots, to reproduce the image).

The several menu items for image manipulation in the Style menu have been grouped into three dialog boxes in QuarkXPress 4. The Style menu no longer has the common options for contrast and screen controls; instead, all contrast and screen controls are accessed via the Contrast and Halftone menu items. QuarkXPress 4 also no longer requires that you have the Content tool selected to apply image controls to images. The Item tool may also be used now.

Working with Image Formats

Table 19-1 shows what controls can be applied to specific image formats. QuarkXPress 4 changes the options available for several types of images, letting you apply contrast settings to all supported gray-scale and color images except EPS images.

If you import color bitmap images with the preview mode set at more than 8-bit color in the Application Preferences dialog box's Display pane (Edit⇨Preferences⇨ Application, or Shift+Option+⌘+Y), you won't get all the image controls shown in Table 19-1 when you select an image. Quark says this is not a bug, although it sure acts like one. The benefit is that keeping the preview set to 8-bit keeps your file sizes smaller, since lower-resolution previews take less data to create.

Common file formats

The most common files most publishers deal with are TIFF and EPS, although PICT files are common on the Mac as well and the JPEG and GIF formats are becoming more common thanks to the popularity of the Web, where they are used commonly.

✦ **TIFF:** These files come in many varieties. For best results, use an uncompressed TIFF format if it is available in your scanning or paint application. Files in this format can take a lot of disk space, so many users prefer to use a compressed version. The best of these is called LZW; QuarkXPress reads files in this format reliably. (Keep in mind that this is a compressed TIFF format, not a compressed TIFF file; QuarkXPress cannot read a TIFF file that has been compressed using an application such as StuffIt, WinZip, or PKZip.)

✦ **JPEG:** These files are what's called a *lossy* format—to save disk space, the file throws out information to make the file more compressed. (The LZW compression used for TIFF images does not eliminate data.) Most programs that create JPEG files let you choose the degree of data loss—the more data removed, the smaller the file (and less accurate the image). In Web publishing, the computer monitor's low resolution (72 dpi) often obscures the fact that the image has data missing, because the monitor can't display fine detail in any event.

✦ **GIF:** This Web bitmap format is becoming increasingly popular, although only QuarkXPress for Windows supports it. To be safe in a cross-platform environment, save your GIF files to TIFF format.

✦ **PICT:** These files also come in several varieties. Most PICT files are bitmaps with bit depths of 2 (black-and-white), 4 (16 levels of gray), or 8 (256 levels). Some are vector files (line art), similar to EPS files. PICT files created by image-editing programs like Photoshop or by screen-capture programs are bitmap files. We recommend that you save these files in TIFF format if you work in a cross-platform environment, because not all Windows programs can handle PICT files (QuarkXPress for Windows can).

✦ **EPS:** Files in vector formats, such as EPS, can also contain bitmap images. These files print to the best resolution of the printer or to the resolution set in the program that created them. You must control output resolution and effects in the original illustration program because QuarkXPress cannot control these attributes for bitmaps embedded in vector files.

File format tips and tricks

When you work with images in formats other than BMP, JPEG, PICT, PCX, and TIFF, you must translate them to one of these formats. If you want to use any of QuarkXPress's image controls on, for example, MetaCreations Fractal Design Painter's RIFF format, you must first convert the RIFF file (through a program such as DataViz's MacLinkPlus) or save it in a QuarkXPress-supported format in the originating application (such as Adobe Photoshop, Corel Photo-Paint, or MetaCreations Fractal Design Painter) before bringing them into QuarkXPress.

You can also use programs like Photoshop to read in some of these formats and then save them in a QuarkXPress-supported format. (You probably don't need a separate translation program if you use an image-editing program like Photoshop that supports many formats for import.) Because QuarkXPress now lets you apply image controls to so many image types, the compatibility woes of the past are all but gone.

When you import TIFF files into QuarkXPress, don't forget the shortcut that let you convert TIFF files to a lower-color version. If you hold the ⌘ key when clicking Open in the Get Picture dialog box, a color TIFF image is imported as a gray-scale TIFF image, and a gray-scale TIFF image is imported as a black-and-white TIFF image. (The original file is unaffected.)

Saving bitmap files

Save bitmap files—whether gray-scale, color, or black-and-white—in the size that you intend to use for layout. Enlarging a bitmap more than 20 to 50 percent can result in a blocky-looking image, as illustrated in Figure 19-1, which shows two images of Yosemite's Half Dome rock (one black-and-white, one gray-scale) enlarged by 235 percent. The poor image results because the pixels that make up the image are enlarged along with the image itself. Reducing a bitmap doesn't cause such problems, but this reduction wastes disk space and processing time because the file contains more information than is needed when printed.

Figure 19-1: Enlarging a bitmap to a large number such as 235 percent can make it look blocky, because its pixels are enlarged.

Note

What you see on your screen isn't necessarily what you get when you print your document. A TIFF or JPEG file might be saved at 300 dpi, but you will only see its low-resolution 72 dpi preview when you import it into QuarkXPress. Increasing the picture's size to 200 percent may result in a blocky display on the screen, but the printed image will probably look just fine (300 dpi / 2 = 150 dpi, which is fine for many print jobs).

| Table 19-1 | | | | | |
| **Image Controls Available for Graphics** | | | | | |
Image Type	*Negative*	*Contrast*	*Halftone*	*Color*	*Shade*
BMP					
color	yes	yes	no	no	no
gray	yes	yes	yes	yes	yes
black-and-white	yes	no	yes	yes	yes

Image Type	Negative	Contrast	Halftone	Color	Shade
EPS, DCS	no	no	no	no	no
GIF [3]					
color	yes	yes	no	no	no
gray	yes	yes	yes	yes	yes
JPEG					
color	yes	yes	no	no	no
gray	yes	yes	yes	yes	yes
MacPaint [1]	no	no	yes	yes	yes
PCX					
color	yes	yes	no	no	no
gray	yes	yes	yes	yes	yes
black-and-white	yes	no	yes	yes	yes
Photo CD	no	no	no	no	no
PICT					
color bitmap	yes	yes	no	no	no
8-bit gray bitmap	yes	yes	yes	yes	yes
low-gray bitmap [2]	no	no	no	no	no
black-and-white bitmap	no	no	yes	yes	yes
vector	no	no	no	no	no
Scitex CT					
color	yes	yes	no	no	no
gray	yes	yes	no	no	no
TIFF					
color	yes	yes	no	no	no
gray	yes	yes	yes	yes	yes
black-and-white	yes	no	yes	yes	yes

[1] Format not supported in QuarkXPress for Windows

[2] A low-gray image is one with fewer than 256 levels of gray (8-bit) but more than black-and-white (1-bit).

[3] Format not supported in Mac QuarkXPress

Creating Negative Images

The simplest feature to use is the Negative feature. Just select an item and use Style⇨Negative or the keyboard shortcut Shift+⌘+- (hyphen). Figure 19-2 shows the effect in action. For gray and black-and-white images, this feature exchanges white for black and black for white. For color images, this exchanges each primary color (red, blue, and yellow) for the opposite color (green, magenta, and cyan, respectively).

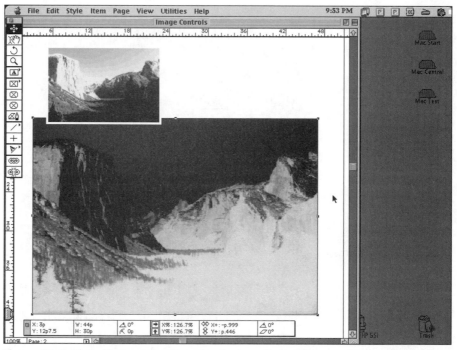

Figure 19-2: The effects of the Negative feature (bottom) on an image (original at top).

Adjusting Contrast

When you adjust contrast with the Picture Contrast Specifications dialog box (accessed via Style⇨Contrast, or Shift+⌘+C), you get the dialog box shown in Figure 19-3. At the left of the dialog box is a line that shows how values in the image are mapped to the output. Typically, it's a straight line at a 45-degree angle, which means that the input and the output settings are the same—no adjustment to the image. It's this contrast line, which is technically called a *gamma curve*, that you adjust to change the contrast of the image as it is output.

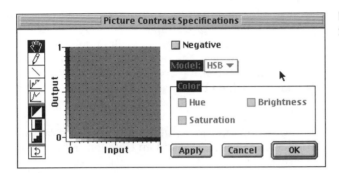

Figure 19-3: The Picture Contrast Specifications dialog box.

Using the filters

The simplest way to adjust output is to use one of the following predefined adjustments (often called *filters*) on the dialog box's left side:

 Normal ensures that the image prints with its original, unadjusted values.

 High Contrast essentially replaces the midtones with either black or white, with the separation happening at the 30-percent gray (or hue, for a color image) mark. (Any part of the image darker than 30 percent becomes black, while any part lighter than 30 percent becomes white.) Figure 19-4 shows the result.

 Posterize bands the grays (or hues) together, so similar grays get changed into the same gray. For example, all parts of the image that are 0 to 10 percent gray become pure white, while all parts of the image that are 10 to 20 percent gray become 20 percent gray, and so on. Figure 19-5 shows the result.

 You can check the Negative box or the Swap Axis icon to create a photographic negative of the image. Note that this feature works with any other settings. For example, if you posterize an image and click the Swap Axis icon, you will get both effects applied. Note that if you check the Negative box, your contrast line does not change, but if you click the Swap Axis icon, it does. Either way, the output is the same.

 Because you can fundamentally alter the character of an image by editing its gray-level map, QuarkXPress lets you preview the effects of your edits via the Apply button.

Color contrast adjustments

For a color image, there is also one line that adjusts all the colors equally when you open the Picture Contrast Specifications dialog box. To adjust colors individually, uncheck the color attributes you don't want to affect and then adjust the line for the remaining color channel(s). For example, if you have an RGB image and you uncheck Blue and Green, any changes to the line will affect just the red component of pixels in the image. For a CMYK image, you can manipulate four channels: cyan, magenta, yellow, and black. You can change color settings for each color channel separately by changing which colors are checked. Figure 19-7 shows an example.

Tip

Photo-editing programs like Photoshop offer many more sophisticated options for image manipulation. Most people use Photoshop, and an excellent resource is the *Macworld Photoshop 4.0 Bible* by Deke McClelland.

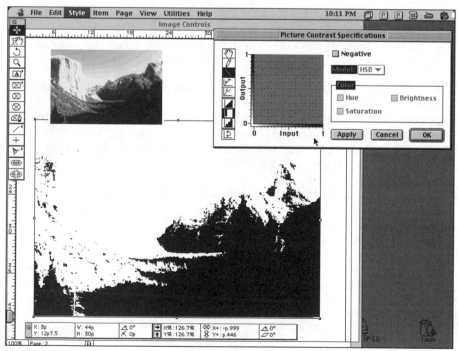

Figure 19-4: The High Contrast filter applied.

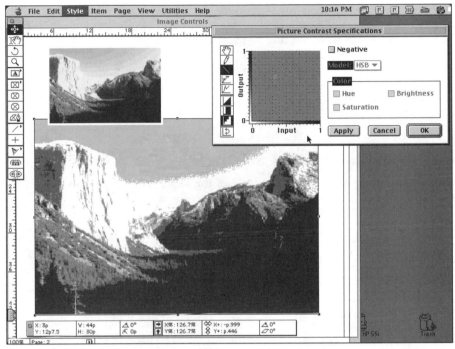

Figure 19-5: The Posterize filter applied.

Manually adjusting contrast

The dialog box also has controls that let you adjust the contrast line manually. From top to bottom, the icons and their uses are as follows:

 The grabber (hand) icon lets you move the entire contrast line in any direction, which is useful for shifting all gray-level mappings at once. For example, shifting the line upward darkens the entire image because lighter input values are mapped to darker output values. Moving the line with the grabber hand results in a consistent image even though gray levels are shifted; however, the darkest and lightest grays may get chopped off.

 The pencil icon lets you draw your own line, which is handy if you want to experiment.

 The line icon lets you add straight segments to the contrast curve by clicking and dragging. This can be useful for smoothing out curves that have been drawn with the pencil icon.

The constrained step icon lets you select increments on the line and move them as a group up or down. The selected segment between two points on the line moves. This icon is helpful when editing posterization settings.

 The constrained line icon causes node points on the line to appear so that you can move them. Then you can select any node on the line and move it up or down. Like the constrained step icon, this icon is helpful for editing existing lines, particularly if the changes are not discontinuous.

Customized contrast settings

You can use several different tools to edit the same line. Figure 19-6 shows an example of a customized contrast line.

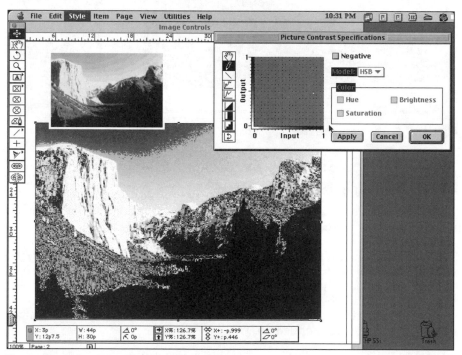

Figure 19-6: A customized contrast setting.

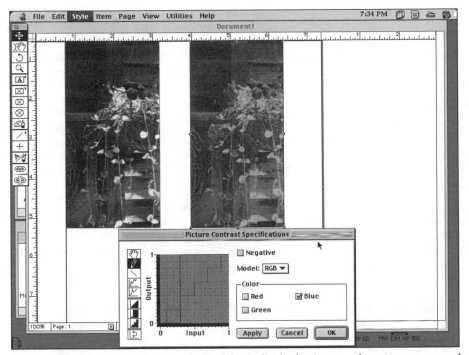

Figure 19-7: The contrast lines adjusted for individual primary colors. You can see the effects on the image on the right.

Returning to a common gray-level map

If, after editing a gray-level map, you want to return the image to a more common gray-level map, you can reenter the dialog box and use one of the default-setting icons (Normal, Posterized, or High Contrast). This kind of change is possible because QuarkXPress does not actually modify your source image, but simply retains a set of instructions generated by your contrast settings. It applies these settings to the output image while printing, but never applies them to the source image itself.

What's in a gray level?

The number of gray levels determines how natural an image looks. Each level is a percentage: the more levels there are, the more percentages of gray are used to display an image.

Having two levels means the image is black-and-white. Having 16 levels means that there is enough shading to make an image recognizably detailed. Having 256 shades is enough to make an image look realistic. Another way to think of it is like this: With 16 levels of gray, you can represent 0% black, 6.7%, 13.3%, 20%, and so on, up through 100% black. With 256 levels, you can represent 0% black, 0.4%, 0.8%, 1.2%, and so on, up through 100% black.

The human eye can barely detect such subtle jumps, which is why 256 levels is the most you'll find for gray-scale, whether it be for the images themselves or for the levels a monitor (even a color one that supports millions of colors) will display. The illustration shown here demonstrates the same images at several popular gray levels to make the differences apparent. You'll see the subtleties that higher gray levels allow.

The maximum number of levels corresponds to the image's bit depth, or color depth. Having 8 bits gives the computer 2^8 possible shades, or 256 levels. Having 4 bits gives it 2^4, or 16 levels. Note that an image in 8-bit format, such as a TIFF file saved in gray-scale mode in Adobe Photoshop, may have fewer than 256 levels of gray if effects like posterization were applied to it. In other words, if some gray levels are unused in an 8-bit file, the file nonetheless remains an 8-bit file. (Posterization is the removal of gray levels, as shown in the images.) The bit depth determines the maximum number of levels; the image's visual characteristics determine how many levels are actually used.

Regulating Halftones

Printers use line screens to convert a continuous-tone image like a photograph into the series of spots, called a *halftone*, which is required to reproduce such an image on most printing presses. (Color images use four sets of spots, one each for cyan, magenta, yellow, and black. The process of filtering out each of these colors is called *four-color separation*, which is described more fully in Chapters 21 and 23.)

Take a magnifying glass to a printed photo—either color or black-and-white—in a newspaper or magazine, and you'll see the spots that the photo is made of. These spots are usually dots, but they can be any of several shapes. Most people never worry about line screens. (In fact, many desktop publishers don't know what they are.) They can have a profound effect, however, on how your bitmap images print. Many artists use line-screen controls to add a whole new feel to an image. The following sections show you how it's done.

Making line screens with QuarkXPress

When your source image is electronic, how do you create the series of spots needed to mimic continuous tones? Desktop publishing programs use mathematical algorithms that simulate the traditional piece of photographic line screen. Because the process is controlled by a set of equations, desktop publishing programs such as QuarkXPress offer more options than traditional line screens, which come in a fixed set of halftone frequencies and with a limited set of elements.

Seeing is believing when it comes to special graphics effects, so you'll want to experiment with line-screen settings before going to press with your document. In most cases, you should use the default screening values, which are the defaults for all imported images. The default line-screen frequency is set in the File menu's Print dialog box through the Frequency option in the Output pane (Figure 19-8 shows the settings). The default screen angle is 45 degrees, and the default halftone dot shape is a dot; neither of these defaults can be changed.

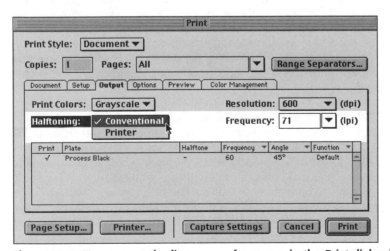

Figure 19-8: You can set the line-screen frequency in the Print dialog box.

Note

Some special graphics effects are available only for PostScript printers because other types of printers (such as QuickDraw and PCL printers) do not have the correct controls in their internal computers to do the calculations required to achieve these effects.

A line-screen primer

In traditional printing, a *line screen* is an acetate mask with a grid of holes. This line-screen mask is then placed on top of a piece of photographic paper (such as Kodak's RC paper, used for decades in traditional photography). The continuous-tone original is then illuminated in a camera so that the image is projected through the mask onto the photographic paper. The high-contrast photographic paper is exposed only where the mask is transparent (in the grid holes, or spots), producing the spots that make up the image to be printed. The size of each spot depends on how much light passes through, which in turn depends on how dark or light each area of the original image is. Think of a window screen through which you spray water: the stronger the spray, the bigger the spots behind the screen's holes.

The spots that make up the image are arranged in a series of lines, usually at a 45-degree angle for gray-scale images (this angle helps the eye blend the individual spots to simulate a continuous tone). The number of lines per inch (or *halftone frequency*) determines the maximum dot size as well as the coarseness (*halftone density*) of the image (thus the term *line screen*). The spots in the mask need not be circular—they can be ellipses, squares, lines, or more esoteric shapes like stars. These shapes are called *halftone dot shapes*. Circular dots are the most common type because they result in the least distortion of the image.

Halftone special effects

When you want to do something special, you can. As a rule, most people using line-screen effects prefer coarser halftone frequencies to make the image coarser but bolder. They usually also change the halftone dot shape to a line or other shape to alter the image's character. To change the halftone settings, use Style⇨Halftone or the shortcut Shift+⌘+H to get the Picture Halftone Specifications dialog box shown in Figure 19-9. (Halftone settings won't affect an image when displayed on the Web.)

New Feature

You cannot see on-screen the effects of the settings you make. That's because QuarkXPress 4 now has the option of using its own halftoning algorithm or passing on the work to your imagesetter. Because it doesn't know what your imagesetter might do with halftone settings, QuarkXPress no longer displays them on-screen—even if you choose the QuarkXPress default halftoning algorithms. (Chapter 24 shows you how to set the halftoning defaults.) The previous versions of QuarkXPress gave you the option of displaying the halftoning on-screen; with version 4, you'll need to print the images to see the effects.

Picture Halftone Specifications	
Frequency:	15 ▼ (lpi)
Angle:	75 ▼
Function:	Line ▼

Figure 19-9: The Picture Halftone Specifications dialog box with nonstandard settings applied.

Understanding line per inch (lpi)

When you're talking about an output device, lines per inch (lpi) and dots per inch (dpi) are not related because the spots in a line screen are variable-sized, whereas dots in a laser printer are fixed-sized. (Because newer printers using techniques like Hewlett-Packard's Resolution Enhancement Technology or Apple Computer's FinePrint and PhotoGrade use variable-sized dots, the distinction may disappear one day.) Lines per inch specifies, in essence, the grid through which an image is filtered, not the size of the spots that make it up. Dots per inch specifies the number of ink dots per inch produced by the laser printer; these dots are typically the same size. A 100-lpi image with variable-sized dots will therefore appear finer than a 100-dpi image.

Depending upon the size of the line-screen spot, several of a printer's fixed-sized dots may be required to simulate one line-screen spot. For this reason, a printer's or imagesetter's lpi is far less than its dpi. For example, a 300-dpi laser printer can achieve about 60-lpi resolution; a 1270-dpi imagesetter can achieve about 120-lpi resolution; a 2540-dpi imagesetter about 200-lpi resolution (that is, if you want a reasonable number of gray shades). Resolutions of less than 100 lpi are considered coarse, and resolutions of more than 120 lpi are considered fine.

But there's more to choosing an lpi setting than knowing your output device's top resolution. An often overlooked issue is the type of paper the material is printed on. Smoother paper (such as *glossy-coated* or *super-calendared*) can handle finer halftone spots because the paper's coating (also called its *finish*) minimizes ink bleeding. Standard office paper, such as that used in photocopiers and laser printers, is rougher and has some bleed that is usually noticeable only if you write on it with markers. Newsprint is very rough and has a heavy bleed. Typically, newspaper images are printed at 85 to 90 lpi; newsletter images on standard office paper print at 100 to 110 lpi; magazine images are printed at 120 to 150 lpi; calendars and coffee-table art books are printed at 150 to 200 lpi.

Other factors affecting lpi include the type of printing press and the type of ink used. Your printer representative should advise you on preferred settings.

If you output your document from your computer directly to film negatives (rather than to photographic paper that is then shot to create negatives), inform your printer representative. Outputting to negatives allows a higher lpi than outputting to paper because negatives created photographically cannot accurately reproduce the fine resolution that negatives output directly on an imagesetter have. (If, for example, you output to 120 lpi on paper and then create a photographic negative, even the slightest change in the camera's focus will make the fine dots blurry. Outputting straight to negatives avoids this problem.) Printer representatives often assume that you are outputting to paper and base their advised lpi settings on this assumption.

Gauging the effect of halftones

To gauge the effects of different halftone dot shapes, compare Figures 19-10 through 19-12. All are set at 30 lpi, and all are viewed at 300 percent so that the differences are magnified. Figure 19-10 shows the effects of using dots as the halftone dot shape. Figure 19-11 shows a line screen with ellipses as the halftone dot shape. In Figure 19-12, squares are used as the screen element. In all three figures, the halftone screen is arranged at a 45-degree angle.

Figure 19-10: A close-up of a line screen, using a dot element.

Figure 19-11: A close-up of a line screen, using an ellipse element.

Figure 19-12: A close-up of a line screen, using a square element.

We recommend that you create a sample page that has a series of strips set for different line screens and line elements. You can use the resulting guide to see the effects of various line-screen settings on the entire range of gray values, from white to black. You can also create a similar guide using a sample gray-scale photo. To create a sample page, use the following steps.

STEPS: Creating a sample page

1. In an image-editing program, create a gray-scale TIFF file that has a smooth gradient from white to black. The image in this file should be shaped like a long rectangle, either horizontal or vertical, with the gradient going from one end to the other along the longest axis.

2. Import this object into a QuarkXPress document's picture box and then duplicate that box several times, placing each duplicate next to the previous one. You now have a series of gradient strips.

3. Use the Style⇨Halftone (Shift+⌘+H) option to set each strip at a different line-screen setting. We recommend that you do this at least for common line-screen frequency settings (such as 20, 30, 60, 85, 110, 120, 133, and 150). You can then copy all these picture boxes to a new page and change the halftone dot shape for each (which you must do one at a time). Likewise, you can do the same for different screen angles.

4. Output these pages on a 2540-dpi imagesetter.

Calculating halftone scans and output

One of the most difficult concepts to implement in black-and-white publishing is picking the right dpi setting when scanning gray-scale (and color) artwork. You scan in fixed-sized dots per inch *(dpi)*, but you output to film in lines per inch *(lpi)* composed of variable-sized dots. There's also a relationship between both the dpi and the lpi and the number of gray levels you can scan and print, respectively. Here's how it works:

✦ First, figure out the right scan resolution *(dpi)* for your scans: The simplest way is to multiply the screen frequency *(lpi)* you plan to output to by 2: $lpi \times 2 = dpi$. This assumes that you're scanning the image in at the same size it will be reproduced. If you intend to change the size, the math gets trickier: Multiply the longest dimension of the final size *(lf)* by the screen frequency *(lpi)*, and multiply this result by 2. Divide the result by the longest dimension of the original size *(lo)*: $(lpi \times lf \times 2 \div lo = dpi$. (If the number is not a whole number, round up to the nearest whole number; for example, treat a dpi result of 312.32 as 313.) Note that if you're outputting to coarse paper, such as newsprint, you can use a smaller multiplier than 2. But don't go lower than $\sqrt{2}$ (equal to about 1.4).

✦ Second, figure out the needed resolution from your imagesetter to achieve the output screen frequency *(lpi)* your printing press is set for: $lpi \times 16 =$ imagesetter's required dpi. Thus, for magazine-quality frequencies of 133 and 150 lpi, you would need to ensure the imagesetter outputs at 2540 dpi (the 133-lpi setting requires an output dpi of 2128 dpi—that's $133 \times 16 = 2128$—and the 150-lpi setting requires 2400). So why 2540 dpi? Because that's the standard high-resolution setting for most imagesetters; the other standard setting, used mostly for text-only documents, is 1270 dpi. At 2540 dpi, the highest lpi you can achieve is 158 ¾.

✦ Last, figure out how many gray levels you'll actually get when printing, based on the imagesetter's output resolution *(dpi)* and output screen frequency *(lpi)*: $(dpi \div lpi)^2 + 1 =$ gray levels. Thus, an imagesetter set for 2540 dpi and a QuarkXPress document set up for a 133 lpi screening frequency can theoretically produce 365 levels of gray (in reality, 256 levels is the top limit)—more than enough for most images. (To get that number, the math is $(dpi \div lpi) + 1$, $(2540 \div 133)^2 + 1$, or $19.1^2 + 1$, or $364.7 + 1$, or 365 after rounding.) At 150 lpi, that theoretically means 287 gray levels (again, 256 levels in reality). At an output resolution of 1270 dpi, you would get 92 gray levels at 133 lpi and 72 gray levels at 150 lpi. It may seem counterintuitive that the higher lpi setting results in fewer grays, but it's true. The trade-off you make is that at the higher lpi settings, the image seems smoother, but lower lpi settings give you greater gray-scale fidelity.

QuarkXPress limits the number of grays used by a graphic or blend to 256. This should be just fine, however, unless you're creating a blend that is unusually long.

Dealing with Dithering

An effect related to halftone screening is called *dithering*. Dithering means replacing gray levels with a varying pattern of black and white. This pattern does not attempt to simulate grays; instead, it merely tries to retain some distinction between shades in an image when the image is output to a printer that does not have fine enough resolution to reproduce grays (through the fine grid of dots used in screening to reproduce each gray shade).

How dithering works

Dithering uses coarse patterns of dots and lines to represent the basic details in a gray-scale image. A set of mathematical equations determines how the dithered pattern appears for each image. The basic technique is to replace dark shades with all black, medium shades with alternating black and white dots or lines, and light shades with a sparse pattern of dots or lines.

With dithering, there are no controls available for halftone frequency or screen-element angle because these elements are determined by the dithering equations.

Working with ordered dithering

There are many sets of dithering equations; QuarkXPress uses one called *ordered dithering*, which you select by choosing Ordered Dither in the Picture Halftone Specifications dialog box's Function pop-up menu. Figure 19-13 shows an image to which ordered dithering is applied. To apply other dithering equations, you must dither the image in a paint or graphics program that supports dithering before importing the image into QuarkXPress.

You can use dithering to simulate a wood-cut or pointillism effect. Otherwise, use dithering only if your printer has less than a 300-dpi resolution.

Figure 19-13: A dithered image.

Controlling Color and Shade

Even if you don't alter gray levels or screening, you can still alter the way in which gray-scale and black-and-white bitmap graphics print by using QuarkXPress color and shade controls, available through the Style menu, as well as through the Colors palette. Color and shade controls do not work with color images or with vector images (such as EPS and some forms of PICT) because they are meant to add color and shades to black-and-white and gray-scale images. The assumption is that such color changes should be done in a color graphics program. The shade controls work only with black-and-white bitmap images and with gray-scale images (refer to Table 19-1).

The Style menu's Color option

Through the Style menu's Color option, you can replace the black parts of an image—including grays, which after all are simply percentages of black—with a color. Figure 19-14 shows the secondary menu that appears when you highlight the Color option on the Style menu while a box containing a gray-scale image is selected. Any colors defined in the document appear in the list of colors. (Chapter 21 describes colors in depth.)

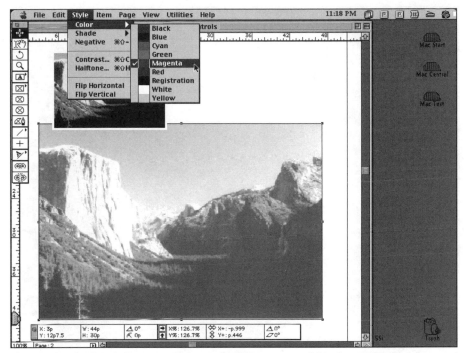

Figure 19-14: The Color menu lets you colorize gray and black-and-white images.

The Style menu's Shade option

Likewise, you can make an image lighter by applying a shade through Style⊃Shade. This technique is handy when you want to have a background image behind text that leaves the text readable. Figure 19-15 shows how a black-and-white image appears with a 40 percent shade applied. You are not limited to the shade percentages displayed in the Shade drop-down menu. By choosing Other, you can set any percentage from 0 to 100, in 0.1 percent increments. (Note that you can change a picture's color or shade only if it is a black-and-white or gray-scale image listed in Table 19-1.)

Tip

You can combine the Color and Shade options. You can print an image at 30 percent magenta, for example, over a solid cyan background (for the picture box), which would give you a surrealistic blend of magenta and cyan. You can also apply other effects, such as gray-level filters and screen settings, to the same image.

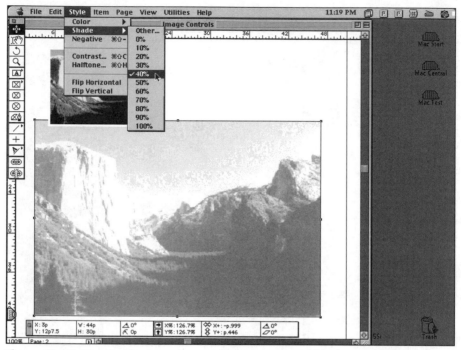

Figure 19-15: The Shade menu lets you lighten gray and black-and-white images.

✦   ✦   ✦

Graphics-Creation Tools

♦ ♦ ♦ ♦

In This Chapter

Becoming familiar
with the tools

Creating lines and
curves

Working with boxes
as shapes

Making line and
frame patterns

Converting text into
graphics

♦ ♦ ♦ ♦

QuarkXPress is, of course, a page-layout tool, but it can also help you create graphics. You'll certainly want a professional illustration program like Adobe Illustrator, Macromedia FreeHand, or CorelDraw to do most of your illustration work—in no way is QuarkXPress their equal—but you'll find that QuarkXPress 4 has a surprising number of features that let you create simple to moderately complex illustrations. This chapter covers them all.

Becoming Familiar with the Tools

QuarkXPress 4 brings back some familiar graphics-creation tools and introduces many new ones. The following list provides an overview of what you have to work with:

+ **Line tools:** With these tools—especially with the new Bézier and Freehand Line tools—you can draw pretty much any kind of line or curve, as well as arrows.

+ **Box tools:** With the assorted basic box tools (Rectangle, Rounded-Corner Rectangle, Beveled-Corner Rectangle, Concave-Corner Rectangle, and Oval), you can create a range of simple shapes.

+ **Freehand and Bézier box tools:** With the new freehand and Bézier box tools, you can draw pretty much any shape you want.

+ **Rotation and skewing tools:** These let you create even more shapes based on those offered via the box tools.

+ **Background color and shade tools:** You can add background color and shade (saturation) to a text box or picture box to spice up the shapes you create. (Chapters 18 and 21 cover this in more detail.)

✦ **Layering tools:** Because QuarkXPress places each layout element on its own layer, you can arrange all of the items on a page by bringing them forward or sending them backward in a stack of elements.

✦ **Frame tools:** Using the new Frame feature, you can add one of twenty possible frame patterns to the boundaries of a picture box, and you can specify the width of the frame. You can also create your own frame patterns, including for the first time dashes and multiline lines (called stripes).

✦ **Text box and alignment tools:** The ability to convert text to boxes, and to align text along any line or curve, lets you use text as graphics. (This is a new feature of QuarkXPress 4.)

What's on the Tool palette

The QuarkXPress Tool palette offers a convenient arrangement of tool icons you can click to create various graphic effects. Figure 20-1 shows the tools for creating shapes, making drawings, and determining text paths.

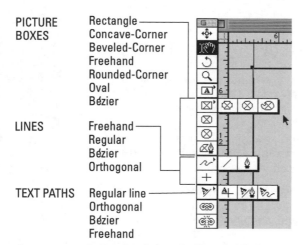

Figure 20-1: The Tool palette, showing tools used to create shapes and QuarkXPress's drawing tools.

Arranging the palettes

You don't have to have the same tools display as the QuarkXPress defaults. QuarkXPress 4 lets you move tools from the Picture Box, Line, and Text Path pop-up tool palettes to the Tool palette itself, and vice versa. Let's say you don't want the Orthogonal Line tool on the Tool palette. Instead, you want it on the Line tool pop-up palette. On the Mac, Control+click the Orthogonal Line tool and, presto!, it disappears from the Tool palette and is now part of the picture box pop-up palette. (Use Ctrl+click in Windows.) Similarly, you may want the Bézier Line tool on the Tool palette. Hold the Control key on the Mac (use Ctrl in Windows) and then hold the mouse button on the Line tool to activate the Line tool pop-up palette. Still holding down the Control or Ctrl key and the mouse button, you move to the Bézier Line tool and release the mouse button. Presto again! The Bézier Line tool is now on the Tool palette.

Creating Lines and Curves

Adding lines is a common need among layout artists—whether you're adding lines between columns, adding lines between elements (such as between text and an unrelated photo or between text and the page folios), or embellishing a logo or other visual with a line. The following sections show you how.

Straight lines

QuarkXPress has long let you add straight lines with the Line and Orthogonal Line tools. The process is simple: click the tool, move your mouse to the beginning of the line, hold down the mouse button, and release the button when you get to the end of the line. Voilà! A line is born. The only difference between the Line tool and the Orthogonal Line tool is that the Orthogonal Line tool forces the line to be at a right angle (fully horizontal or fully vertical), while a line created with the Line tool can be at any angle.

Tip

Rather than use the Orthogonal Line tool, hold down the Shift key when drawing with the Line tool. It will force the line to be at a right angle. That leaves one less tool to keep track of. Note that using Shift with the Line tool also gives you one more fixed angle: in addition to drawing fully horizontal and fully vertical lines, you can draw lines that are at 45-degree angles.

Bézier and freehand curves

New
Feature

What you can do without thinking with a pen and paper actually requires high-powered mathematical calculations on a computer. We mean drawing nonstraight lines (or curves), something that we all learned to do around the time we leaned to walk and talk, but that is actually a very sophisticated set of tasks. We mention this to prepare you for the computer's approach to drawing lines: Bézier curves (a new feature of QuarkXPress 4).

Curving the French way

Bézier curves are named for Pierre Bézier, the French engineer and mathematician who created the curves in the early 1970s as a way of controlling mechanical cutting devices, commonly known as numerical control. (*Bézier* is pronounced bez-ee-AY or BAY-zyay, depending on whether you prefer the English or French pronunciation.)

Drawing lines on a computer is not tough, but manipulating them—changing their shape, curve, and dimensions—can be. But remember: When you work with pen and paper, you can't alter your lines once they're drawn. So while the process of working with Bézier curves can at first be a little intimidating, you get the payoff of being able to change any shape at will.

Drawing Bézier curves

You can draw Bézier curves in the following ways:

✦ Select the Bézier Line tool and click at each location (the *point,* or *node*) in the curve. QuarkXPress will draw a straight line from each location you click to the previous location.

✦ Select the Bézier Line tool, move to where you want the curve to begin, click the mouse button, drag the mouse to create the curve angle you want (you'll see a blue line appear that shows the slope of the curve based on where you move the mouse to), and then move the mouse to where you want the curve segment to end. To create another segment, click at the next point location, drag the mouse to create the curve slope, and click at the segment's end location. Experiment with this approach to get a feel for how the curves work.

In both cases, you are creating a series of segments—the lines or curves between each mouse-click location, called a point. Figure 20-2 shows the two types of Bézier curves. Note that the two types—a series of straight segments and a series of curved segments—are not mutually exclusive. You can have straight segments and curved segments on the same Bézier curve. You can also change a segment from a curve to a line, or vice versa, after you draw your Bézier curve.

A simple way to draw a curve is using the Freehand Line tool. This tool works like using a pen: you keep the mouse button pressed as you move the mouse (like holding the pen to the paper as you draw). QuarkXPress will generate a Bézier curve that matches your mouse movements.

Changing Bézier curves

If you create curved segments as described in the previous section, you notice a series of blue lines that appear after you drag the mouse. Those are called *Bézier controls,* and they dictate the shape and slope of the segment's curve (refer to Figure 20-2). These work as follows:

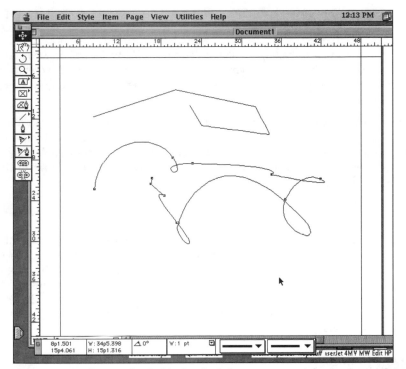

Figure 20-2: The two basic kinds of Bézier curves: straight-segmented (top) and curve-segmented.

✦ If you click and hold down the mouse button on one of the outer control points, you can change the curve by dragging the control point to a new location.

✦ If you drag the point itself, you can move the entire segment, which will also affect the segment attached to the current segment.

✦ You can also select a segment by clicking and holding anywhere on it, then drag that segment to a new location, which changes its shape, as well as the shape of the adjoining segment.

✦ You can tell whether you've selected a point or a segment by looking at the shape below the finger pointer, as follows:

 The Reshape Point icon means you have selected a point.

 The Reshape Side icon means you have selected a segment.

The weird thing about constraining

If you hold the Shift key while reshaping a curve or node, QuarkXPress will *constrain* the new curve. You'll notice the mouse jump as you move it. You'll rarely want to use this technique, because figuring out where QuarkXPress will constrain the node or segment's new position to is practically impossible.

What QuarkXPress tries to do is keep the control lines at 45-degree angles, although that's usually not possible, so it often selects some other angle, jumping to what seems to be an inconsistent angle each time. The only time this approach works in a predictable way is when you have grabbed an outer control point and are rotating that point relative to the node. The rotations will happen in 45-degree increments.

Tip

You can also change the shape of a line using the Item⇨Shape command, which gives you a list of box and line shapes. Your line can be converted to any of those shapes. QuarkXPress will make the new element fit the space taken by the original line whenever possible. In addition, you can edit the curve's points' settings (angle and position) by using the icons in the Measurements palette (see Figure 20-3). However, you'll find it easier to use the mouse than figure out the desired values of the angles and locations.

Moving Bézier curves

To move a curve, rather than reshape it, click it once with the mouse, then hold down the ⌘ key, to select the whole curve. You can now drag the curve to a new location. (If you hold the ⌘ key first before selecting the line, you will end up selecting a segment or node and reshaping it—just as if you had not used the ⌘ key in the first place.) You can also use Shift+F4 (on the Mac) or F10 (in Windows) to toggle between reshaping and moving. Using Shift+F4 (on the Mac) or F10 (in Windows) has another advantage: You get the resize handles found on a picture box, which lets you resize the whole curve, as opposed to altering the size of individual segments. The clunkiest way to switch back and forth between reshaping and selecting the curve is to use the Item⇨Edit option, and then toggle the Shape command on or off.

Changing Bézier control points

So far, we've been using the default Bézier controls, which are called *symmetrical points*. This means that the curves on both sides of a point are affected equally when the point's or segment's control points are altered. Thus, by making the curve segment twice as steep (that is, moving the control point twice as far from the point), the adjoining curve segment also becomes twice as steep (and its control point moves twice as far from the point as well). This is because the point that joins them is symmetrical, telling QuarkXPress to apply the same degree of change to the two segments attached to that point. QuarkXPress has three kinds of points, however, and you can use any or all of them in a curve. Here's how they work:

◻   Symmetrical, in which both control points are always the same distance from the point, and moving one control point also moves the other.

◇   Smooth, in which both control points move at the same time, but only the selected control point changes its distance from the point.

△   Corner, which makes the corner an angle, not a curve. A corner point is what you get when you use the first method described above to create a series of straight line segments, rather than curved segments.

The three change methods

There are three ways to change a point's type: in the Measurements palette, in Item⮞Point/Segment Type, or by using keyboard shortcuts. Figure 20-3 shows the first two methods. Notice that you can also use these controls to change a segment from curved to straight or vice versa. The keyboard shortcuts are as follows (note that the Windows shortcuts differ from the Mac shortcuts):

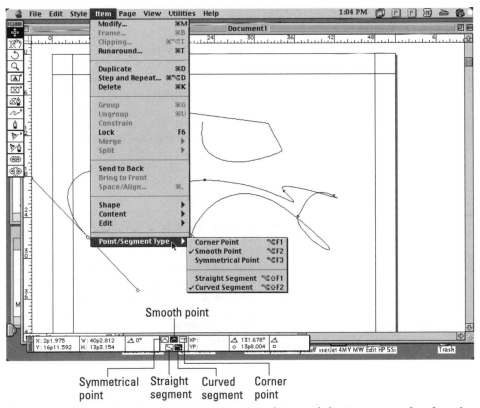

Figure 20-3: The options in the Measurements palette and the Item menu for changing control points and segments.

✦ **Corner point:** Option+F1 on the Mac; Ctrl+F1 in Windows

✦ **Smooth point:** Option+F2 on the Mac; Ctrl+F2 in Windows

✦ **Symmetrical point:** Option+F3 on the Mac; Ctrl+F3 in Windows

✦ **Straight segment:** Shift+Option+F1 on the Mac; Ctrl+Shift+F1 in Windows

✦ **Curved segment:** Shift+Option+F2 on the Mac; Ctrl+Shift+F2 in Windows

Working with segments and points

If you have selected a segment, both segment and point options are available. Any changes to the point type will affect the points on either side of the selected segment. If you have selected a point, only the point options will appear, and any changes to the point type will affect just the selected point.

To change all segments or points in a curve, double-click the curve, and then choose the new point and/or segment type. The entire curve will be modified accordingly.

Adding and deleting Bézier points

Sometimes, you want to change a curve by removing or adding points. QuarkXPress lets you do that with the Option key. Here's how:

If you hold the Option key when positioning the mouse over an existing point, you get the Remove point icon. Click the point to delete it.

To add a point, also hold the Option key when moving the mouse over an existing segment. You'll see the Add Point icon; click the mouse where you want the new point added.

Line patterns and arrowheads

When you create a line or curve, the QuarkXPress default is a solid line 1-point thick. You can choose other settings, however. When you click a line or curve, you get the Measurements palette options shown in Figure 20-4. (If you move the mouse when selecting a Bézier or freehand line, QuarkXPress thinks you're trying to select a point or a segment and switches to the options previously shown in Figure 20-3. If that happens, click something else, and then reclick the line.) The Measurements palette is the easiest place to set the line type, weight (thickness), and arrowheads. But you can also use the Line pane in the Modify dialog box, also shown in Figure 20-4, which lets you apply color and shade to the line and determine what color appears in the gaps in multiline and dashed lines.

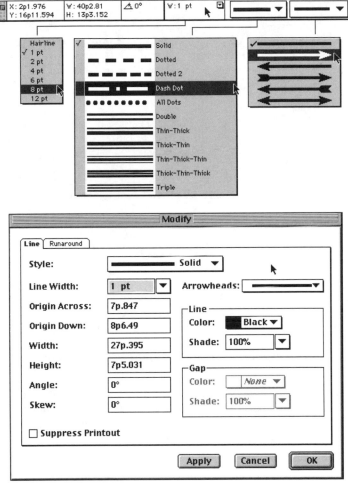

Figure 20-4: The options in the Measurements palette and Line pane for line attributes.

Tip

The lines composed of multiple lines won't display legibly until your line or curve is several points thick. We recommend that you have at least 4-point line weights when using these line styles. (Although this also depends on whether you're viewing the page at 100 percent magnification.)

Choosing the correct arrowhead

When assigning arrowheads to lines and curves, it's easy to get confused as to what direction arrowhead you should select from the pop-up menu in the Measurements palette or Line pane. Here's the answer: The line's starting point determines the arrow direction. Thus, if you choose the right-pointing arrowhead in the pop-up menu, the arrowhead will be at the endpoint for your line or curve.

If you choose the left-pointing arrowhead, the arrowhead will be at the line's starting point. (If you drew a line from right to left and selected the right-pointing arrowhead option in the pop-up menu, your arrow would actually point to the left, since your starting point was on the right side of the line.)

Working with Boxes as Shapes

QuarkXPress lets you draw more than just lines. You can use the several box shapes—rectangle (including the rounded-corner, beveled-corner, and concave-corner variants), oval, freehand, and Bézier—to draw elements in your layout. Chapter 5 covers boxes in detail, but here's a quick refresher:

✦ When drawing a rectangle or oval, hold the Shift key to draw a perfect square or circle.

✦ The Bézier and freehand boxes are created and modified just like freehand and Bézier lines, as described in the preceding section in this chapter. When drawing a freehand or Bézier box, complete the box by clicking the start point for the box. You'll get the Add Point icon when your mouse is over that start point.

✦ If you plan on using boxes solely as shapes for illustrations, you can keep the file size down by making the box contentless, via Item⇨Content⇨None.

✦ You can apply shades and backgrounds to your box, as described in Chapter 21.

✦ You can apply frames (lines) around your box, as well as create your own custom frames, as described later in this chapter.

✦ You can change the shape of a box using the Item⇨Shape command, which gives you a list of box and line shape options, as Figure 20-5 shows. Your line can be converted to any of those shapes; QuarkXPress will make the new element fit the space taken by the original line whenever possible.

✦ Use functions like rotation and skewing to modify a shape.

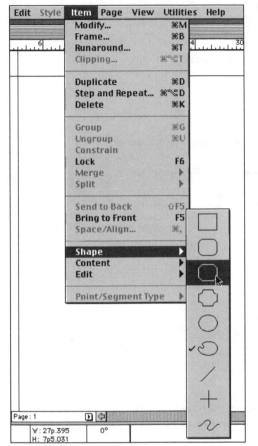

Figure 20-5: Changing the shape of a box using the Item⇨Shape command.

Combining boxes and lines

In many cases, to create a drawing in QuarkXPress, you need to combine multiple elements. Here are some examples:

✦ **To create an organizational chart:** Here you would use several text boxes and connect them with lines. Figure 20-6 shows an example.

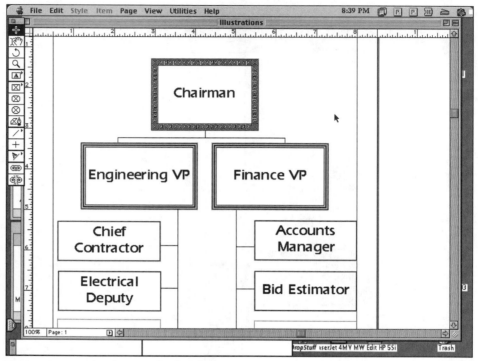

Figure 20-6: A simple organizational chart.

✦ **To create a bar chart:** In this case, you draw several rectangular boxes and add lines for the axes. Figure 20-7 shows an example. Likewise, a pie chart is a series of wedges.

✦ **To create dimensional shapes:** In this example of a stack of paper or cards, you overlay boxes on one another. Figure 20-8 shows an example.

✦ **To create an illustration:** Here you would use Bézier lines and boxes to draw the constituent shapes, then overlay them to create the composite drawing. Figure 20-9 shows an example.

The more skilled an illustrator you are, the more complex and finely detailed drawings you can create in QuarkXPress.

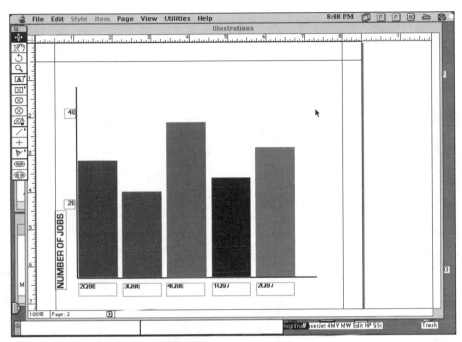

Figure 20-7: A simple bar chart.

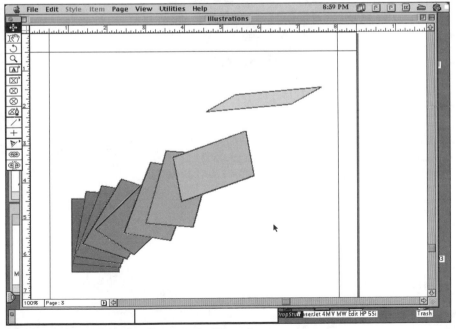

Figure 20-8: A stack of cards carried off by a breeze.

Merging boxes and lines

In addition to using multiple boxes and lines to create drawings in QuarkXPress, you can also merge boxes and lines together with the merge feature (new in version 4). You access the Merge feature via Item⇨Merge. Figure 20-10 shows the menu, and Figure 20-11 shows how the options look. The options work as follows:

Note

When you merge boxes, the new combined box takes on all the attributes of the rearmost box. For example, if the rearmost box is a picture box with a picture in it, the new box will have that picture in it—even if the frontmost boxes had all been text boxes.

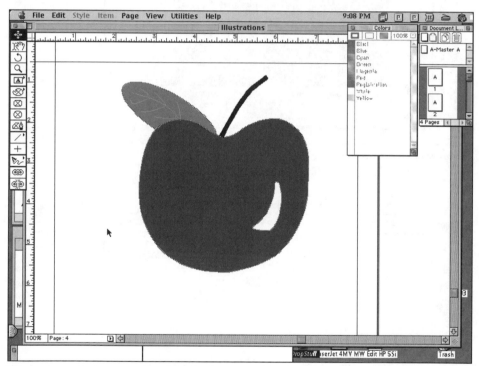

Figure 20-9: A cherry made of Bézier boxes and lines.

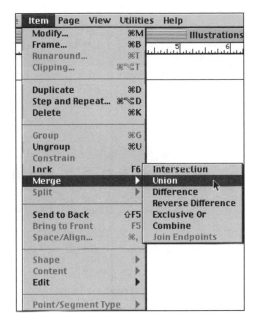

Figure 20-10: The merge options.

✦ **Intersection:** Retains any area where boxes overlap, creating a shape of that overlapped area

✦ **Union:** Calculates the outline of all the elements to create a shape of that outline

✦ **Difference:** Retains any area from the rearmost shape outside the overlapping object(s) and discards the overlapping object(s) as well as the overlap area

✦ **Reverse Difference:** Removes the shape of the rearmost object from the overlapping object(s) and discards the rearmost object

✦ **Exclusive Or:** Combines overlapping shapes into a new shape that includes all the lines from all the shapes. Similar to Combine, Exclusive Or adds a point wherever two lines cross. So, for example, if you merge three rectangular boxes using Exclusive Or, you cannot move their sides apart and make them into three separate shapes that are part of one box.

Exclusive Or   Union   Intersection   Original boxes

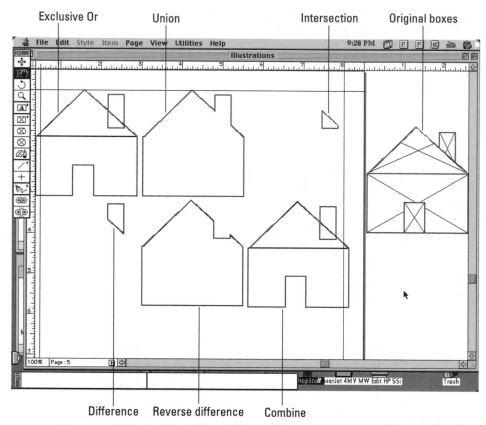

Difference   Reverse difference   Combine

Figure 20-11: Examples of merged boxes.

✦ **Combine:** Combines overlapping shapes into a new shape that includes all the lines from all the shapes. Similar to Exclusive Or, Combine does not add points where lines cross. So, for example, if you merge three overlapping rectangular boxes using Combine, you can move their sides apart so they are three separate shapes that are part of one box.

✦ **Join Endpoints:** Available only for lines and curves, attaches the endpoints of selected lines and curves to one another. The endpoints must be overlapping or within the Snap To setting in the General pane of the Document Preferences dialog box (Edit➪Preferences➪Document, or ⌘+Y) This function is useful when you've used several lines to create a shape, rather than creating a single line or curve with multiple segments.

Caution

If you use the first six commands with lines, they are converted into boxes that have the dimensions of the lines—in other words, extremely thin boxes.

Splitting the path of merged objects

You can also split paths for merged objects that have overlapping segments. For example, in Figure 20-11, the house at top left has overlapping segments at the chimney and at the door. Using Item⇨Split⇨All Paths, the outline of the house becomes one path, the area where the chimney overlaps the roof becomes a second path, and the area where the door overlaps the house wall becomes a third path. Figure 20-12 shows the result. Similarly, a figure-eight (8) shape would become two oval shapes.

The other option—Item⇨Split⇨Outside Path—is used when you have two objects that don't overlap, such as a house and a tree that don't touch or overlap. If these two objects had been merged, they would still appear on-screen to be two objects, but would be one object from QuarkXPress's point of view. Splitting them via the Outside Path option would separate the two objects but not affect any objects within them. For example, the chimney and door of the house would remain part of the house object, but the tree would become a separate object from the house.

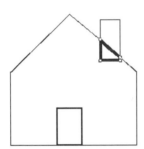

Figure 20-12: A split object becomes multiple boxes. We've used different line thicknesses here so the different boxes are more obvious.

Making Line and Frame Patterns

As demonstrated earlier in this chapter, QuarkXPress has eleven predefined line styles in the Measurements palette. These same eleven styles are available for box frames as well. The following sections show you how they work.

Creating new line styles

New
Feature

Although QuarkXPress does have eleven predefined line styles, artistically inclined users will want even more styles available to them, which is why QuarkXPress 4 includes the new Dashes & Stripes feature, which lets you create your own line styles. These line styles can be used both in box frames and for independent lines created with one of the Line tools. You get the Dashes & Stripes dialog box shown in Figure 20-13 via Edit⇨Dashes & Stripes. With it, you can create lines made up of multiple lines—what QuarkXPress calls *stripes*—and dashed lines made up of line segments. The Dashes & Stripes dialog box shows the existing line styles at the top; you scroll through the list to see those not visible in the list window.

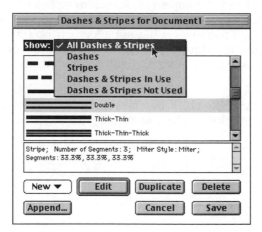

Figure 20-13: The Dashes & Stripes dialog box.

For use in frames (not as independent lines), QuarkXPress for Macintosh includes nine bitmap frame styles that must be edited with the separate Frame Editor program, covered later in this chapter. QuarkXPress Windows can display and print these bitmap frames, but not create or edit them.

Dashed lines

When you create a new line style, you first choose whether you want to create a stripe or a dash. We'll create a dash first. Figure 20-14 shows the Edit Dash dialog box, which you would also see if you edited an existing dash line style. Use the following steps to create a dashed line:

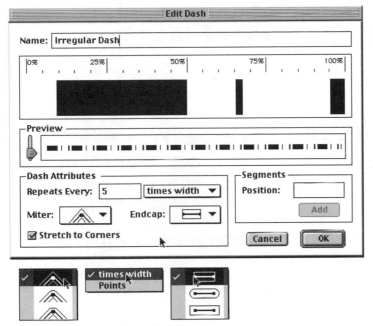

Figure 20-14: The Edit Dash dialog box.

STEPS: Creating a dashed line

1. The first thing to do is give your new dash a name, which you do in the Name field.

2. Now choose your dash attributes, in the Dash Attributes section of the dialog box. The key one to choose at this point is the Repeats Every attribute. The default setting is Times Width, which makes the pattern repeat in increments of the line width. Thus, the thicker the line, the longer the segments, and the smaller the number you enter, the finer the dash elements—compare the top two previews (shown here), one that has a repeat of 1 and one that has a repeat of 9.

(continued)

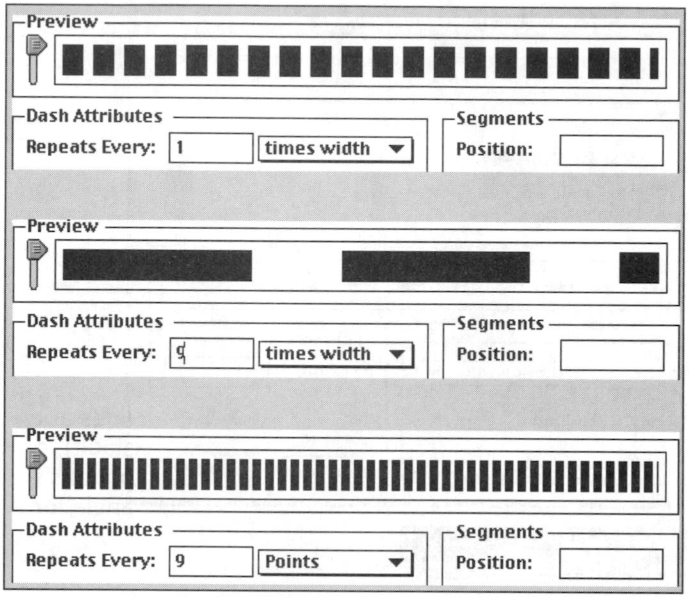

✦ The bottom preview also shows what happens when you pick Points as the width. The dash pattern will fit within the specified width. This means the dashes will always have the same width and spacing, regardless of how thick the line or frame is.

✦ Use the Preview slider to see the effects at different line widths.

3. To create the actual dashes, move your mouse to the top section of the dialog box that has the ruler. The default is a solid line. To change that, click to where you want the first segment to end. The rest of the dash will become empty.

4. You add the next segment by clicking the mouse on the ruler (like adding a tab). If you hold down the mouse button when adding a segment, you can drag the segment to the desired width. (You can also enter the ruler location in the Position field and click the Add button.)

5. You resize an existing segment by clicking and holding the mouse on one side of the segment boundaries *on the ruler* and dragging to expand or contract the segment.

6. Finally, you can move a segment by dragging it to the left or to the right within the windows (the mouse should be on the segment itself, not on the ruler).

7. Now you can finish specifying the dash attributes. We recommend that you first select the Stretch to Corners checkbox (see Figure 20-14), which ensures that no corner has a segment only in one direction. The effects of having the box checked and unchecked are shown here:

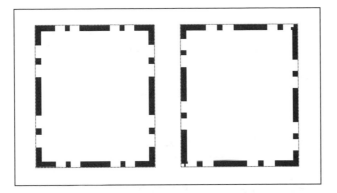

8. Set the miter type. A *miter* is the connection method for lines at a corner, and your choices are for the corner to be a right angle (the default), curved, or beveled. For fine lines (2 points and narrower), all three options look the same, so you may as well leave the option set to a right angle for such lines. Figure 20-14 shows the options.

9. Choose the endcap, which is the shape of the dash segment at the beginning and end. The default puts the endpoint of the dash segment where the dash ends. But you can also set a rounded endcap, which adds a curve at the end of the dash segment—extending slightly past the dash's endpoint. Another option is a squared-off endcap, which adds a rectangle at the end of the dash segment—again, extending slightly past the dash segment's endpoint. Figure 20-14 shows the options. (You can delete a dash by clicking the dash (not the ruler) and dragging it out of the dialog box.)

10. Click OK when you're done, and then click the Save button in the Dashes & Stripes dialog box to save all your changes. (If you want to start over again with a solid line, Option+click anywhere on the line or ruler while in the Edit Dash dialog box.)

Creating true dots

You can create true dots with the Dashes & Stripes feature. Typically, your "dots" will simply be squares. But if you choose a rounded endcap, your square becomes a circle.

You can also edit the dotted line that QuarkXPress comes with. Possible modifications include changing the spacing by changing the Repeats Every value and changing the dots into rounded dashes by adding a dash segment. We recommend you duplicate the All Dots line style and work with that duplicate rather than edit the original style, so you don't lose the default settings.

Striped lines

Creating stripes is similar to creating dashes, although there are fewer settings to worry about. Figure 20-15 shows the Edit Stripe dialog box. Note that rather than a horizontal ruler, you have a vertical one. You use it to create and modify the stripe's constituent ruling lines just as you would modify a dash in the Edit Dash dialog box. To created a striped line, use the following steps:

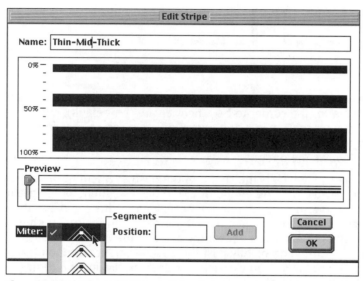

Figure 20-15: The Edit Stripe dialog box.

STEPS: Creating a striped line

1. To create the actual stripes, move your mouse to the top section of the dialog box that has the ruler. The default is a solid stripe. To change that, click where you want the first segment to end. The rest of the stripe will become empty.

2. You add the next segment by clicking the mouse on the ruler (like adding a tab). If you hold down the mouse button when adding a segment, you can drag the segment to the desired width. (You can also enter the ruler location in the Position field and click the Add button.)

3. You resize an existing segment by clicking and holding the mouse on one side of the segment boundaries *on the ruler* and dragging to expand or contract the segment.

4. Finally, you can move a segment by dragging it up or down within the windows. The mouse should be on the segment itself, not on the ruler. You can delete a stripe by clicking the stripe (not the ruler) and dragging it out of the dialog box.

Managing dashes and stripes

Like similar dialog boxes for creating style sheets and colors, the Dashes & Stripes dialog box lets you duplicate existing line styles to create variants of existing ones (with the Duplicate button), as well as edit existing styles (with the Edit button) and delete existing styles (with the Delete button).

Remember that you must click the Save button to save any changes you make to dashes and stripes, and that any dashes and stripes created, edited, duplicated, or deleted when no QuarkXPress document is open become the default settings for all future QuarkXPress documents.

Any documents that use these new and modified line styles will print and display them properly when opened in other copies of QuarkXPress (such as when sharing files with other users or with service bureaus). You can also import line styles created in another document by using the Append button in the Dashes & Stripes dialog box.

You can fine-tune your view of stripes and dashes via the Show pop-up menu (refer to Figure 20-13). This is a handy way to see what line styles are used in your document.

Creating bitmap frames

In addition to the lines you create with the Dashes & Stripes dialog box, you can have bitmap frames created with the Frame Editor tool, which only comes with the Macintosh version of QuarkXPress. Although it is not available for the Windows version, Windows QuarkXPress will display and print bitmap frames created in QuarkXPress for Mac's Frame Editor. And both the Windows and Macintosh versions of QuarkXPress 4 let you apply the nine standard bitmap frames, which are predefined and available for rectangular picture boxes. The nine bitmap frames are shown in Figure 20-16. The advantage of bitmap frames over standard frames is that you can create bitmap frames out of complex patterns.

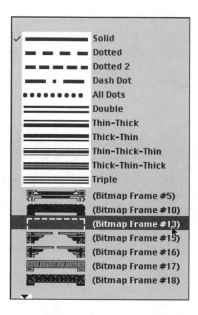

Figure 20-16: The default line and bitmap frame styles.

Note

As previously mentioned, bitmap frames are available for and work only on regular rectangular boxes—not on oval, Bézier, freehand, or the other variants of rectangular boxes (concave-corner, beveled-corner, and rounded-corner). If you apply a bitmap frame to a rectangular box and later change the box's shape, the bitmap frame is changed to a solid line.

Using the Frame Editor

The Frame Editor is a separate program that you access in the folder containing the QuarkXPress program. You double-click it to launch the program. Note that QuarkXPress must not be running; if it is, you can't launch the Frame Editor. The Frame Editor program uses nonstandard interfaces, so it's easy to get confused when using it. Just take it slow the first few times you use it. Figure 20-17 shows what you see when you first launch the Frame Editor: a window that you can scroll through to see the current frame styles. You have the following basic options:

✦ If you want to edit an existing frame style, select the frame style and use File⇨Open or the shortcut ⌘+O.

✦ To duplicate an existing frame style and modify that duplicate, select the frame style and use File⇨Duplicate, or ⌘+D. Then select the duplicated frame style and open it with File⇨Open, or ⌘+O.

✦ To create a new style, use File⇨New Style, or ⌘+N.

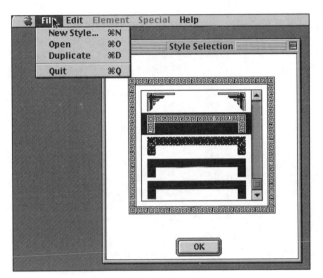

Figure 20-17: The Frame Editor's opening list of bitmap frame styles.

Tip

You should sketch out your pattern before you try to create it in the Frame Editor. Use quadrille paper (paper with light lines that divide the sheet into many tiny squares) and fill in the squares with a pencil to create the pattern you want to use in QuarkXPress. On this paper, make each square equal 1 point in width and height. You'll need this sheet when working with the Frame Editor.

The Size Selection dialog box

Whichever you pick, you'll see the Size Selection dialog box, shown on the left in Figure 20-18. This dialog box shows the size in points for the frame's width. If you are editing an existing frame style, you'll see that style in the dialog box; if you're creating a new frame, you'll see the Enter new size dialog box. It's important to pick the right width for your frame. If your frame size is too small for your intended pattern, you won't be able to create it correctly. Use File⇨New Size, or ⌘+N, to enter a new size for the frame.

The Element Selection dialog box

You'll then get the Element Selection dialog box, shown on the right in Figure 20-18, in which you pick the area of the frame you want to work on. There are eight areas: the four corners and the four sides. For each of the corners, clicking them lets you enter the height and width of the corner. Your pattern will dictate what the appropriate corner size is. (Note that you must click the outlined shapes inside the frame, not the frame itself.)

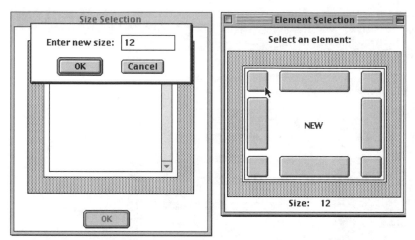

Figure 20-18: When working with frame styles, set frame width and choose what part of the frame to work on in these dialog boxes.

The Frame Edit dialog box

You will now see the Frame Edit dialog box, in which you create the pattern for the selected line or corner by clicking on and off individual pixels that make up the element. Figure 20-19 shows the Frame Edit dialog box for a corner element.

If you don't want to draw your frame elements from scratch in Frame Editor, you can draw them in another application, then copy and paste them into the Frame Edit dialog box.

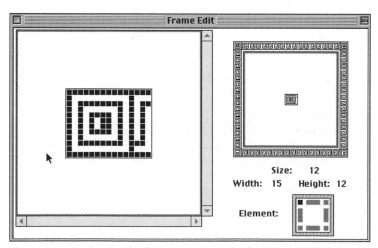

Figure 20-19: Create the bitmap pattern in the Frame Edit dialog box.

Reverting to the original pattern

If you mess up your pattern, use Element⇨Revert, or ⌘+R, to return the pattern to its original design. Note that this affects only the current element (the corner or side), not the entire frame.

Completing the process

When you're done with an element, click the close box to return to the Element Selection dialog box and choose the next element to create or edit. When you're all done, close the dialog boxes until you are prompted to save the changes. Quit the Frame Editor when you're completely finished.

Using bitmap frames

Your new and modified bitmap frames will appear in the Frame pane of the Modify dialog box the next time you open QuarkXPress, along with the standard nine bitmap frames. (The default frames are now locked and cannot be deleted.) When applying a bitmap frame to a box, don't make the frame width larger than the frame size. If you do, the magnified bitmap will look and print blocky. (If you run it smaller, the frame will also be distorted, but less noticeably.) QuarkXPress tells you the frame size by displaying it in boldface in the list of widths in the Frame pane's WIdth pull-down menu.

Note

Any documents that use bitmap frames will print and display them properly when opened in other copies of QuarkXPress (such as when sharing files with other users or with service bureaus).

Converting Text into Graphics

Text can be beautiful, thanks to some of the innovative, engaging letterforms that type designers have created. So it makes sense to think of type as an art element, not just as a medium for conveying information. A technique prized by high-end designers has been to use text as the outline of an image—masking the image within the confines of a letter's shape. But historically the work to do that has been very great, limiting its use to publications with the time and money to achieve it. But the miracles of computer technology have taken what had been an arcane technique and made it commonplace.

New Feature

Creating text-based boxes

QuarkXPress 4 introduces the ability to convert text into a box—a picture box or a text box. That means you can take an image and have it fill a letter, a word, or a phrase. You can even create a text box in the shape of text. Figure 20-20 shows two examples, and the following steps show you how.

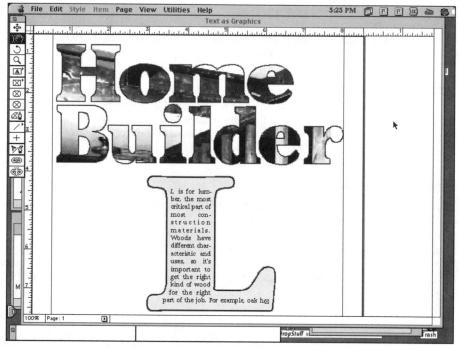

Figure 20-20: Two examples of text-based boxes.

STEPS: Converting text into a box

1. Format the text with the exact typeface, style, size, scale, tracking, kerning, and so forth.

2. Using the Content tool, select the text. (You can convert only one line at a time, or one or more characters on the same line, not multiple lines or text that flows across more than one line.)

3. Use Style⇨Convert to Box to change the text into a Bézier picture box. The picture box will appear on-screen (your text is also retained in its original text box).

4. If you want the picture box to be a text box, use Item⇨Content⇨Text to convert it. (Note that you cannot convert a text-based box back into text.)

You can now modify the text-based box as you would any box, as described earlier in this chapter and in Chapters 18 and 21. Note that even though the box is composed of several distinct letters, the group of letters form one Bézier picture box, not a separate picture box for each letter. (If you want a separate box per letter, use the split feature described earlier in this chapter, or create the boxes one letter at a time. Note that this will copy the picture in the original phrase's picture box into each letter's new picture boxes. So don't split a word's letters into their own boxes if you want one picture to run behind them all.)

Tip

If you press the Option key while you choose Text to Box, the text-based picture box will replace the selected text (as an anchored picture box).

New Feature

Fitting text to curves

Another desirable but historically difficult technique involving the use of text as graphics is having text follow a curve. Once again, QuarkXPress 4 makes this easy. The Text Path tools let you create one of four line types—a straight line at any angle, an orthogonal line (fully vertical and fully horizontal), a freehand line, and a Bézier line—and have text follow along the curve. Figure 20-21 shows an example, as well as the four Text Path tools. Once you draw the text path, you simply click the line and start typing. You can format the text as you would any other text (see Chapters 12 through 14, 17, and 21). You can even link it to a text box or to another text line. Again, it's that simple.

Caution

About the only thing you can't do easily in QuarkXPress—when it comes to treating text as graphics—is to define a shape and have QuarkXPress make the text distort to fit the contours of the shape. You can do this (to some extent) using the Text Path pane of the Modify dialog box (⌘+M). But until a new version of QuarkXPress appears that includes this feature, you'll want to keep using Adobe Illustrator, Macromedia FreeHand, or CorelDraw.

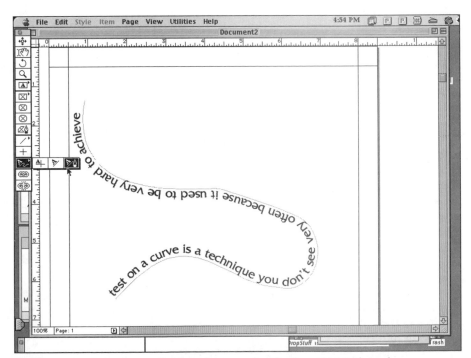

Figure 20-21: Text along a freehand curve, plus the four Text Path tools.

Text-to-path feature tips

✦ To resize the text path and the text along with it, hold down the ⌘ key when resizing.

✦ If you want the text to wrap around a closed freehand or Bézier shape, create multiple curves, make sure their endpoints are very close, select them, and use Item⇨Merge⇨Join Endpoints to turn them into a single shape.

✦ To have text run around a box's shape, create a box using any of the box tools. Then use Item⇨Shape to select the squiggly line icon, which converts the box into a closed path. Now use Item⇨Content⇨Text to convert it into a text path. If you want text to run around a box's contents, perform the preceding steps on a copy of the original box, and place that copy on top of the original box.

✦ Use the Text Path pane, shown here, in the Modify dialog box (⌘+M) to change the text alignment on the path. You can control how the text aligns with the path with the Align Text pop-up menu (using the text's baseline, descent, or ascent, or centering the text vertically on the line); control how the text aligns with the line width with the Align with Line pop-up menu (this has no effect unless the line is thick, in which case this command tells QuarkXPress which part of the line depth to align with); flip the text (which determines whether it is inside or outside the path); and change the text orientation (which determines how the letters align with the curve, as shown in the figure).

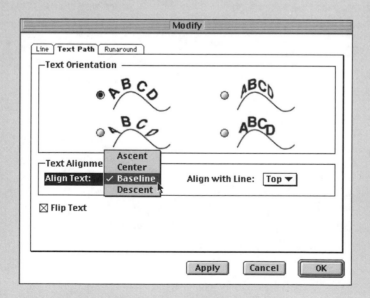

✦   ✦   ✦

Defining and Applying Color

C olor is becoming more accessible to all publishers. Whether you want to produce limited-run documents on a color printer, create newsletters using spot colors, or publish magazines and catalogs using process colors and special inks, QuarkXPress offers the tools that you need to do the job well. If you're doing professional-quality color production, such as a color catalog printed on a standard web offset printing press, QuarkXPress includes the Quark CMS (color management system) XTension that lets you calibrate the output against the input source (such as monitor or scanner) and the output target (such as the printing press or color printer). Chapter 23 covers color matching and other high-end color issues in depth. This chapter concentrates on how to create and apply colors within QuarkXPress.

In This Chapter

Understanding process and spot color

Defining colors

Using spot color

Using multi-ink colors

Applying colors

Managing colors

Understanding Process and Spot Color

Before we launch into the more practical aspects of working with color in QuarkXPress, let's briefly explore the differences between spot and process colors. If you are already familiar with these concepts, you can skip ahead to the section on defining color, but if you're new to the subject, it's important that you understand them before you move on.

Methods of color printing

Several forms of color are used in printing, but the two basic ones are *process color* and *spot color*. Process color refers to the use of four basic colors—cyan, magenta, yellow, and black (known as a group as *CMYK*)—that are mixed to reproduce most color tones the human eye can see. A separate negative is produced for each of the four process colors. This method, often called *four-color printing,* is used for most color publishing. Spot color refers to any color—whether one of the process colors or some other hue—used for specific elements in a document. For example, if you print a document in black ink but print the company logo in red, the red is a spot color. A spot color is often called a *second color* even though you can use several spot colors in a document. Each spot color is output to its own negative (and not color-separated into CMYK).

A new kind of process color, called Hexachrome, was introduced by Pantone in 1995 and is slowly but surely gaining popularity among very high-end publishers. It uses six process colors—the four CMYK colors plus orange and green—to produce a wider range of accurate colors. As you'll see a bit later, QuarkXPress 4 has added the Hexachrome color model to its repertoire.

Exploring spot color

Using spot color gives you access to special inks that are truer to the desired color than any mix of process colors can be. These inks come in several standards, and QuarkXPress supports them all (see the section on working with color models, later in this chapter). Basically, spot-color inks can produce some colors that are impossible to achieve with process colors, such as metallics, neons, and milky pastels. You even can use varnishes as spot colors to give layout elements a different gleam than the rest of the page. Although experienced designers sometimes mix spot colors to produce special shades not otherwise available, it's unlikely that you will need to do so.

Mixing spot and process colors

Some designers use both process and spot colors in a document—known as *using a fifth color.* Typically, the normal color images are color-separated and printed via the four process colors, while a special element (such as a logo in metallic ink) is printed in a spot color. The process colors are output on the usual four negatives; the spot color is output on a separate, fifth negative and printed using a fifth plate, fifth ink roller, and fifth inkwell. You can use more than five colors; you are limited only by your budget and the capabilities of your printing plant.

Converting spot to process color

QuarkXPress can convert spot colors to process colors. This handy capability allows designers to specify the colors they want through a system they're familiar with, such as Pantone, without the added expense of special spot-color inks and extra negatives (see the section on standard color models, later in this chapter). Conversions are never an exact match, but there are now guidebooks that can show you in advance the color that will be created. And with Pantone Process variation (which QuarkXPress supports), designers can now pick a Pantone color that will color-separate predictably.

You can set QuarkXPress to convert some spot colors in a document to process colors while leaving others alone. Or you can leave all spot colors as spot colors.

Defining Colors

You can use color in your graphics or apply colors to text and layout elements (such as bars along the edge of a page). Or you can use color in both ways. To a great extent, where you define and apply color determines what you can do with it. But before you can apply any colors—whether to bitmap images or to layout elements—you must first define the colors (see Chapter 23 for information on defining color trap values).

Using the Colors dialog box

To define colors, select Edit⇨Colors or use the keyboard shortcut Shift+F12 to open the Colors for *document name* dialog box shown in Figure 21-1. Alternately, if you've selected a box and the Colors palette is visible (use View⇨Show Colors or the shortcut F12), you can ⌘+click any color in the Colors palette to bring up the dialog box. From the Colors dialog box, you can make the following selections:

Some of the choices you'll have to make depend on the color model you'll be using. You may want to review the following section on working with color models before you make your selections.

- ✦ **New:** Select New to add colors.

- ✦ **Edit:** Choose Edit to edit any color you add. You can also edit the blue, green, red, and registration colors that come with QuarkXPress.

- ✦ **Append:** Select Append to import colors from another QuarkXPress document.

- ✦ **Duplicate:** Select Duplicate to duplicate an existing color for editing purposes.

- ✦ **Delete:** Choose Delete to remove a color. You cannot delete the white, black, cyan, magenta, yellow, or registration colors that come with QuarkXPress.

- ✦ **Edit Trap:** Select Edit Trap to edit color trapping values, as explained in Chapter 23.

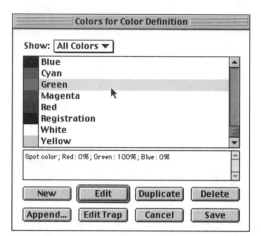

Figure 21-1: The Colors dialog box.

Note

If no document is open when you create, edit, or delete colors, the new color palette becomes the default for all future documents. (The dialog box will be titled Default Colors.) In order for your changes to take effect, you must also choose Save in the Colors dialog box after you finish defining colors. Choose Cancel to undo any changes you make.

Predefined colors

QuarkXPress comes with several predefined colors: black, blue, cyan, green, magenta, red, registration, white, and yellow. (Registration is a color that prints on all negatives and is primarily used for crop and registration marks.) You cannot edit cyan, black, magenta, yellow, or white. You can duplicate any of the predefined colors *except* registration and then edit the duplicates. (You can, for example, use green as both a spot color and as a process color, perhaps with one version named Green Spot and the other named Green Process.)

Working with color models

You define colors in the Edit Color dialog box, which appears when you choose New, Edit, or Duplicate in the Colors for *document name* dialog box. One of your first choices to make is the color model on which your color will be based. To do so, use the Model pop-up menu. The color models fall into two broad classes:

   ✦ Those that let you define a color by selecting a color from a color wheel, which represents a spectrum of available colors, or by entering specific values for the color's constituent colors. These include CMYK, RGB, HSB, LAB, and Multi-Ink (see the following section on standard color models).

✦ Those that have a predefined set of colors, which you select from a palette of swatches. These include the four variants of Pantone, the two variants of Hexachrome, Focoltone, Trumatch, DIC, Toyo, and POCE (again, see the following section on standard color models).

Note

Keep in mind that the colors displayed are only on-screen representations; the actual color may be different. The difference will be particularly noticeable if your monitor is running in 8-bit (256 hues) color mode. Check the actual color in a color swatchbook for the model you are using. (Art and printing supply stores usually carry these swatchbooks. See the sidebar on swatchbooks for lists of other sources.)

Standard color models

QuarkXPress supports several color models, which are ways of representing colors. Figure 21-2 shows the options in the Edit Color dialog box. The supported models include the following:

New Feature

Of the many new features added to QuarkXPress 4, four of the color models described in the following list are welcome additions to the program's color capabilities. They are Hexachrome, LAB, Multi-Ink, and POCE.

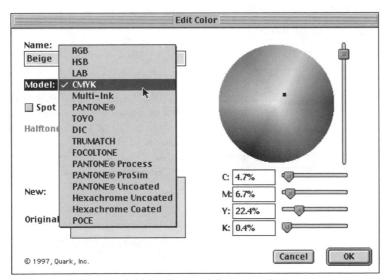

Figure 21-2: The available color models in QuarkXPress.

✦ **CMYK:** The standard process colors used in professional printing.

✦ **DIC:** (Dainippon Ink & Chemical), a spot-color model used in Japan.

✦ **Focoltone:** Another CMYK-based spot-color model popular in Europe.

✦ **Hexachrome:** A six-color process model created by Pantone for high-fidelity color output (of which two variants are supplied: one for coated paper, one for uncoated paper).

✦ **HSB:** (Hue, Saturation, Brightness), which is typically used in creating paints.

✦ **LAB:** (Luminosity, *A* axis, *B* axis), which is an international standard for colors.

✦ **Multi-Ink:** Lets you mix a new color by taking percentages of any combination of colors from any combination of CMYK or Hexachrome process color models—including colors defined in other models as process colors.

✦ **Pantone:** A spot-color model with a range of inks (of which four variants are supplied: one for coated paper, one for uncoated paper, one for Pantone colors that can be accurately translated to CMYK process, and one for Pantone colors that can be accurately produced with other brands of inks).

✦ **POCE:** The Pantone Open Color Environment, which includes several color models redundant with those offered natively by QuarkXPress—including CMYK, HLS and HSV (variants of HSB), Pantone, Pantone CMYK (a variation of Pantone Process), and RGB—as well as two unique color models: Crayon (60 popular crayon colors) and HTML (colors supported by the Web's Hypertext Markup Language color specifications).

✦ **RGB:** (Red, Green, Blue), which is used in monitors.

✦ **Toyo:** A Japanese color model.

✦ **Trumatch:** A CMYK-based set of spot colors designed for accurate color separation.

Note

You can convert a color defined in any model to CMYK, RGB, LAB, or HSB models simply by selecting one of those models after defining the color. But note that colors defined in one model and converted to another may not reproduce exactly the same because the physics underlying each color model differ slightly. Each model was designed for use in a different medium, such as paper or a video monitor.

Paper variation models

Both the standard Pantone and Pantone Hexachrome color models recognize that the type of paper you print on affects how a color appears, so they have variations based on popular paper types. Here's how they work:

✦ **Pantone:** Use this when your printer will use actual Pantone-brand inks (as spot colors) when printing to coated paper stock. Colors in this variant will have the code *CV* (computer video) appended to their names.

✦ **Pantone Uncoated:** This is the same as Pantone but for uncoated paper. Colors in this variant will have the code *CVU* (computer video uncoated) appended to their names.

✦ **Pantone Process:** Use this when you color-separate Pantone colors and your printer uses the standard Pantone-brand process-color inks. Colors in this variant will have the code *S* (SWOP, or single-web offset printing) added to their names.

✦ **Pantone ProSim:** Use this when you color-separate Pantone colors and your printer uses other manufacturers' brands of process-color inks. Colors in this variant (also called Pantone Solid to Process) will have the code *CVP* (computer video process) appended to their names.

✦ **Hexachrome Coated:** Use this when your printer will use actual Pantone Hexachrome-brand inks when printing to coated paper stock. Colors in this variant will have the code *C* (coated) appended to their names.

✦ **Hexachrome Uncoated:** This is the same as Hexachrome but for uncoated paper. Colors in this variant will have the code *U* (uncoated) appended to their names.

Note

When printing on uncoated stock with any colors designed for use on coated stock, you will usually get weaker, less-saturated color reproduction.

Web site color caveats

Most colors available in QuarkXPress will not reproduce well on the Web. Web pages are generally limited to 8-bit color, because that's the limitation in the Hypertext Markup Language (HTML) that specifies a page's attributes. That means you have 216 colors that you can count on reproducing reliably on a PC or Mac Web browser.

QuarkXPress does not have a Web-safe color palette, so we have created a document on the CD that has all 216 safe color definitions included for you to append to your documents. (Why 216 colors when 2^8 equals 256? Because Windows reserves 40 colors for use in its interface. These colors are user-definable, so making them available to Web browsers would result in unpredictable colors depending on what color scheme the user chose or created for the interface.)

Note that the HTML colors available via the POCE option are not necessarily Web-safe; with POCE's HTML color picker, you can create colors that are compliant with HTML standards that nonetheless won't be supported by popular browsers.

Where to get swatchbooks

Anyone who uses a lot of color should have a color swatchbook handy. You probably can get one at your local art-supply store or from your commercial printer (prices typically range from $50 to $100, depending on the color model and the type of swatchbook). But if you can't find a swatchbook, here's where to order the most popular ones:

✦ *Pantone:* There are several Pantone swatchbooks, including ones for coated and uncoated paper, and those for spot-color output and process-color output. If you are converting (called *building* in publishing parlance) Pantone colors to CMYK for four-color printing, we particularly recommend the *Pantone Process Color Imaging Guide: CMYK Edition* or the *Pantone Process Color System Guide* swatchbooks. Pantone, 590 Commerce Blvd., Carlstadt, NJ 07072-3098; phone (800) 222-1149 or (201) 935-5500, fax (201) 896-0242; Web http://www.pantone.com.

✦ *Hexachrome:* Pantone also created the Hexachrome standard and sells Hexachrome swatchbooks, as well as the HexWrench software that adds Hexachrome output capability to Adobe Photoshop.

✦ *Trumatch:* Based on a CMYK color space, Trumatch suffers almost no matching problems when converted to CMYK. There are variants of the swatchbooks for coated and uncoated paper. Trumatch, 25 W. 43rd St. #802, New York, NY 10036; phone (800) 878-9100 or (212) 302-9100, fax (212) 302-0890; Web http://www.trumatch.com.

✦ *ANPA:* Designed for reproduction on newsprint, these colors also are designed in the CMYK color space. Although QuarkXPress doesn't have an ANPA color library predefined, you can create these colors using the swatchbook's definitions. Newspaper Association of America, 1921 Gallows Rd. #600, Vienna, VA 22182; phone (703) 902-1600; Web http://www.naa.org.

✦ *Focoltone:* Like Trumatch, this color model (used primarily in Europe) is based on the CMYK color space. Focoltone AND Systems., Springwater House, Taffs Well, Cardiff CF4 7QR, U.K.; phone 44 (222) 810-940, fax 44 (222) 810-962; Web http://www.focoltone.com.

✦ *Dainippon:* Like Pantone, this is a spot-color-based system. Dainippon Ink & Chemical Americas, 222 Bridge Plaza South, Fort Lee, NJ 07024; phone (201) 592-5100, fax (201) 592-8232; Web http://dicwww01.dic.co.jp/index-e.html.

✦ *Toyo:* Similar to Pantone in that it is based on spot-color inks, this model is popular in Japan. Toyo Ink Manufacturing Co., Ltd., 3-13 2-chome Kyobashi, Chuo-ku, Tokyo 104, Japan; phone 81 (3) 3272-5731, fax 81 (3) 3278-8688; Web http://www.iandi.com/toyoink/ (in Japanese).

Color wheel models

Figure 21-3 shows a color being defined through the CMYK model, which is the standard model used in the publishing industry. After selecting the model from the Model pop-up list, we entered values in the Cyan, Magenta, Yellow, and Black fields. If you prefer, you can define the color values by using the slider bars or by moving the black spot on the color wheel to the desired color. (The bar to the right of the color wheel adjusts brightness.) Or you can use any combination of these three techniques.

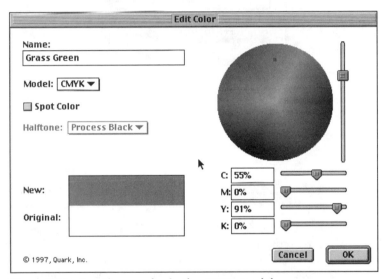

Figure 21-3: Creating a color in the CMYK model.

Swatch models

Figure 21-4 shows a Pantone color being added to the QuarkXPress color list. As you can see, the fields in the Edit Color dialog box change depending upon which color model you use. When you use a spot-color model such as Pantone, QuarkXPress replaces the color wheel with a series of color swatches and their identifying labels. If you know the label, you can enter it in the field at the bottom right; alternately, you can scroll through the list of labels.

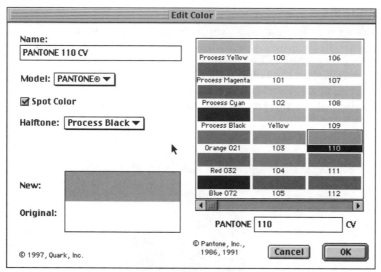

Figure 21-4: Adding a color in the Pantone color model.

Color tips and tricks

You can name a color anything you want, provided that you stay within the character limit of the Name field. To make it easier to remember what a defined color looks like, either use descriptive names (such as *Grass Green*, as we did in Figure 21-3) or use names based on the color settings. For example, if you create a color in the CMYK model, give it a name based on its mix, such as *55C 0M 91Y 0K* for our green color—composed of 55 percent cyan, 0 percent magenta, 91 percent yellow, and 0 percent black. (Believe it or not, this naming convention is how professionals specify colors on paste-up boards.) The same system applies to the RGB, HSB, and LAB models. That way, you can look at the Colors palette and immediately tell what color you'll get.

If you edit an existing color, the old color is displayed in the box to the right of the word "Original" in the Edit Color dialog box. As you define the new color, you see the new color to the right of the word "New." If you define a color for the first time, no color appears in the Original field.

Because regular black can appear weak when it's next to black that has been overprinted by other colors, many designers create what printers call *superblack* by combining 100 percent black and 100 percent magenta. You can define superblack as a separate color or redefine the registration color as 100 percent of all four process colors, and use that as an even richer superblack. Note that on thinner paper, black composed of 100 percent each of cyan, magenta, yellow, and black inks could oversaturate the paper, bleeding through. Check with your printer before creating a superblack that rich.

POCE models

If you select the POCE option from the Model pop-up menu, the Select button appears in the Edit Color dialog box. You need to click this button to access the various POCE color pickers. At left in the resulting dialog box is the scroll list of color models. (If you do not see the scroll list, click the More Choices button.) There really is no reason to use any but Crayon and HTML, as the others duplicate other QuarkXPress color models. Figure 21-5 shows the basic POCE interface, with the Crayon color model selected; Figure 21-6 shows the HTML color model.

Tip

If you use the HTML color picker rather than the Web-safe color definitions provided in this book's bundled CD, be sure to create colors whose values are composed only of 00, 33, 66, 99, CC, and FF values. Other values may not display properly on most Web browsers. In most cases, they'll be rendered as the nearest Web-safe color, but not always.

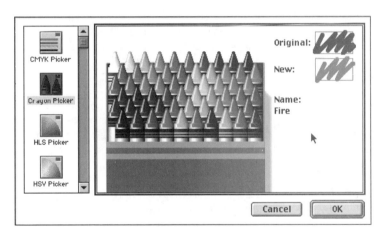

Figure 21-5: Adding a color in the POCE Crayon color model.

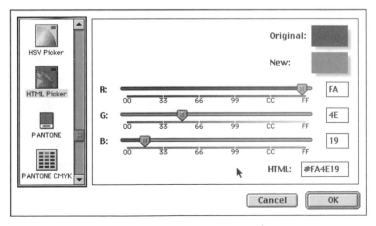

Figure 21-6: Adding a color in the POCE HTML color model.

Simulating other color models

While QuarkXPress supports many color models—Trumatch, DIC, Toyo, Focoltone, and several variants of Pantone and Hexachrome—there are other color models in use, such as the ANPA color model and the Web-safe color model. (*ANPA* stands for the American Newspaper Publishers Association, which several years ago renamed itself the Newspaper Association of America, but the color model's name hasn't changed.) You can still use these color models in QuarkXPress by using the following techniques, which apply to any color model, not just the ANPA example used here:

✦ **Using spot color:** If you are using spot color, in which the ANPA color prints on its own plate, just define a color with the ANPA name you want the printer to use. The printer doesn't care if you actually had the right color on-screen. Knowing what color you want and having a plate for that color are all that's needed.

✦ **Using process color:** If you are using process (CMYK) color, you'll need to create the ANPA colors using the CMYK color model. That means you'll need to know the CMYK values for the ANPA colors you want to use; you can get these values from the swatchbook you use to select colors or from your commercial printer.

Tip

You can also use RGB values to enter the colors and then switch the model with QuarkXPress to CMYK. This may result in some altered colors, because you are converting colors twice: once to RGB and then again to CMYK. Any conversion between color models may result in color differences because of the physics involved in reproducing color.

If there are certain ANPA colors you use repeatedly, create them in the Colors dialog box (Edit⇨Colors) with no document open. They'll then be available for all future documents. If different types of documents use different sets of colors, define them in the template for each type of document. Doing so will save a lot of redefinition.

Using Spot Color

You may have noticed the Spot Color checkbox in the Edit Color dialog box and its accompanying Halftone pop-up menu. Simply stated, checking the Spot Color option means that the color you define (no matter what model it was defined in) will print on its own plate when you color-separate the file during printing. In professional printing, each color is printed from a separate plate that has the image in only that color. In most cases, you'll not have Spot Color checked. Exceptions are when you want a spot color on its own plate, such as for colors that don't reproduce well or at all when converted to process color. Examples of these are metallics, neons, and pastels from Pantone, DIC, or Toyo. It makes little sense to use a separate plate for Focoltone or Trumatch colors, because they are based on CMYK mixtures to begin with and color-separate reliably.

Tip

If you create spot colors, we suggest that you include the word Spot as part of the name, so you can quickly tell in a palette or menu whether a selected color will print on its own plate or be color-separated.

The Halftone pop-up menu

The Halftone pop-up menu lets you use the halftone screen settings of cyan, magenta, yellow, or black for a spot color. (Figure 21-7 shows the menu.) It doesn't replace that color plate but simply uses the same screen angle as that standard color plate. For example, if you assign a color like Toyo 0385pc to the cyan plate, QuarkXPress will generate both cyan and Toyo 0385pc film negatives for use in creating the printing press's color plates. But the Toyo 0385pc color will have the same *screen angle* as the cyan plate. In process printing, each plate's dots are offset from each other so the color dots don't overprint each other any more than necessary, which is why there are different screen angles for each plate. (Chapters 19 and 24 cover screen angles in more depth.) If the Spot Color box is unchecked, the color is converted to process color, divided among the four CMYK or six Hexachrome plates (depending on which color model is selected for output).

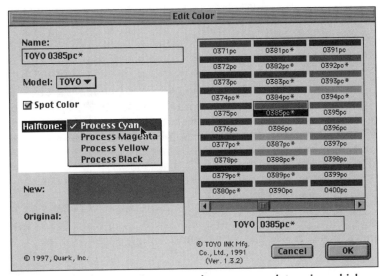

Figure 21-7: When creating spot colors, you can determine which plate's screen angle the spot color's plate will use.

In version 4 of QuarkXPress, you now specify the plates' screen angles in the Print dialog box's Output pane. Chapter 24 covers this topic in depth. Also note that in previous versions of QuarkXPress, the Halftone pop-up menu was called the Screen Values pop-up menu; and instead of the Spot Color checkbox, you had the Process Separation checkbox.

Mixing spot colors

Many designers use spot colors because they cannot afford four-color (CMYK) printing, but they want more than just black and their spot color. Thus, many will create new colors by mixing the spot color with shades of black. In other cases you may want to mix both spot and process colors to achieve the desired result. Here are a few rules of thumb:

In most cases, you need not worry about spot-color output, as most users of these colors apply them to solid objects or text. When you use them more demandingly, however—such as mixing them with black to produce color variants or using them with scanned images—the way that QuarkXPress outputs them may result in displeasing results.

✦ **Mixing spot colors and black:** If you do this, make sure you change the spot color's screening angle, because the default angle for spot colors is the same as for black. By choosing a different screening angle, you ensure that the dots making up the two colors don't overprint unnecessarily, resulting in a muddy image. Choose either the magenta or cyan angles, not yellow (refer to Figure 21-7).

✦ **Mixing process and spot colors:** When you are working with both process and spot colors, picking the right screening angle is tougher. Pick the screen angle of a process color that is never or rarely used with the spot color, or make sure that the spot color knocks out (see Chapter 23). If a screening-angle conflict can't be avoided and you can't knock out the spot color, consult your printer or service bureau for advice.

When working with scanned images, use black as the screening angle, because that results in a 45-degree angle that often avoids moiré patterns, which are annoying kaleidoscope-like patterns. If you must use a different screening angle (perhaps because you have other spot colors defined or you are using black mixed with the spot color), consult your service bureau or printer.

Choosing and editing screen angles

The reason for choosing a different screening angle when mixing a spot color is complex, but the reason for not using the angle for yellow boils down to the fact that the other colors overpower it when viewed by the human eye. The screen angles for other colors overprint each other less. If you choose the yellow values for your screening angle, there's a greater chance your spot color will have many of its dots overprinted by black, changing the mix of the two colors.

The rule of thumb is that darker colors should be at least 30 degrees apart from each other, while lighter colors should be at least 15 degrees apart from other colors. You can see that each plate's angle for your output device is defined via the Output pane in the Print menu (File⇨Print, or ⌘+P), as described in Chapter 24.

You or your service bureau may have to manually edit your screen angle settings in the PostScript file. To create a PostScript file with a Level 1 driver (LaserWriter or PSPrinter 7.x), select PostScript File as the destination in the Print dialog box (File⇨Print, or ⌘+P). To create a PostScript file with a Level 2 driver (LaserWriter or PSPrinter 8.x), select File as the destination, and make sure (in the dialog box that appears after you click the Save button) that you have chosen the PostScript Job option from the Format pick list and selected the ASCII option. Editing settings in a PostScript file requires a fairly intimate knowledge of the PostScript language. Don't expect your service bureau or printer to automatically do this work for you—consult with them first.

Using Multi-Ink Colors

QuarkXPress 4 brings with it a new capability called Multi-Ink for mixing colors from multiple color models. The Multi-Ink feature lets you create new colors by mixing together other colors—the basic CMYK or Hexachrome process colors plus any spot colors previously defined. You *cannot* use other non-spot colors. With the Process Inks pop-up menu, you determine whether a multi-ink color can use CMYK or Hexachrome process colors. Figure 21-8 shows the Edit Color dialog box with the Multi-Ink model in use. Here, we've mixed a color from the selection of CMYK process colors and spot colors previously defined. To get the percentages of each color, first select the color(s) you want to have a specific percentage, then click the Shade drop-down menu to choose from a predefined percentage or to choose the Other option to define your own shade percentage.

You can select multiple colors by ⌘+clicking them; Shift+clicking selects all colors between the first one selected and the color that has been Shift+clicked.

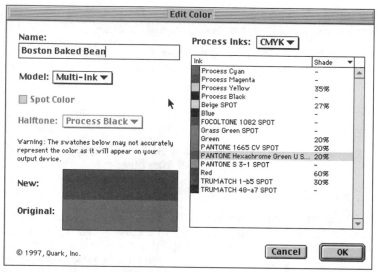

Figure 21-8: The new Multi-Ink feature lets you mix previously defined process colors.

Applying Colors

Now that you've defined your colors, you can use them in the following ways:

✦ Apply color to specific text

✦ Apply color to imported gray-scale and black-and-white bitmaps (see Chapter 19)

✦ Add color backgrounds to text boxes and picture boxes, including blend patterns

✦ Add color borders to boxes

✦ Apply color to ruling lines associated with text and to lines drawn with the line tools

Tip

In addition, by using empty boxes (boxes with no pictures or text imported into them) as shapes, you can create both simple and complex graphics to which you can apply colors.

Using the Colors palette

Most dialog boxes for text and items contain a color list option, as do many options in the Style menu. All colors defined in a document appear (in alphabetical order) in any of these color lists. But a universal way to add color is through the

Colors palette, which you make visible via View⇨Show Colors or the shortcut F12. Figure 21-9 shows the Colors palette. This palette gives you a handy way to quickly apply colors to lines and to picture box and text box backgrounds, frames, and, in some cases, contents. (Chapter 19 includes a table showing which types of images can have colors applied to them.)

Note   You can apply colors to any contents except color pictures and pictures saved in EPS format. If you apply color to the contents of a text box or text on a line, any selected text and any text you subsequently enter into the text box or line takes on the applied color. Existing nonselected text is unaffected.

Figure 21-9: The Colors palette.

Directing the color application

The Colors palette displays a list of available colors. The palette also contains icons that let you direct how QuarkXPress applies colors to the selected box. Note that the icons will change depending on whether a picture box, text box, or line is selected. From left to right, the Colors palette icons are as follows:

✦ **Frame:** If you select this icon, QuarkXPress applies the selected color to the box frame (this option is grayed out for lines). If no frame is defined for the box, no color appears. As soon as a frame is defined, it takes on the color you applied. If you select a line, this icon changes to a line and lets you specify the color of the line.

✦ **Contents:** The contents icon changes depending upon which element is currently selected. Choosing an icon applies the selected color to the contents of the box or the text (if any) on the line. (The Content tool must be selected for this option to be available. If the Item tool is selected, the contents icon is grayed out.) The various icons look like the following:

A picture box, if the selected item is a picture

 A text box, if the selected item is text

A An underlined "A," if the selected element is a line

 ✦ **Background:** Use the background icon to change the background color of a picture or text box. (This option is grayed out for lines.)

Tip A very simple way to change the color of a frame, box background, or line is to drag a color onto the box border (to change the frame's color); into the box's interior (to change the box's background color); or onto the line. Just click and hold on the desired color square in the Colors palette and drag it to the appropriate location. This technique does not work to change the text color or picture color.

Determining a shade percentage

You can apply the color at different shades by editing the number in the field located at the upper right of the Colors palette. Enter any value from 0 to 100 percent, in 0.1 percent increments. You can access common percentages (multiples of 10) through the pop-up menu to the right of the field. Figure 21-10 shows this menu enabled.

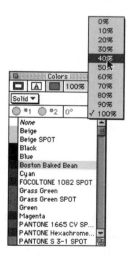

Figure 21-10: The pop-menu for shading colors.

Tip You can also assign color to box backgrounds, frames, and lines using the Modify dialog box. To do so, simply select an item, choose Item⇨Modify (or press ⌘+M), and then switch to the Box, Frame, or Line pane.

Applying a blend

Using the Colors palette, you also can apply a *blend,* which is a smooth transition from one color to another. QuarkXPress comes with a linear blend built-in. If you install the Cool Blends XTension included with QuarkXPress, you have five other choices: mid-linear, rectangular, diamond, circular, and full circular. Figure 21-11 shows the pop-up menu enabled.

Figure 21-11: The blend choices on the Colors palette with the Cool Blends XTension installed.

To pictures or text boxes

You can apply a blend to a selected picture box or text box. To perform this task, select the background icon from the Colors palette and then select from the pop-up menu of blend options below the row of icons. (The current list selection will likely be Solid, which is the default.) The two radio buttons and a numeric field are where you specify the blend's colors and angle (see Figure 21-12). They work as follows:

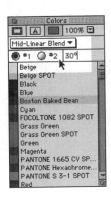

Figure 21-12: The controls for blends in the Colors palette.

✦ **The #1 radio button:** This is selected by default, and the current background color is highlighted. (The color is white if you did not apply a color to the box). You create the blend from the selected color; change the color if necessary.

✦ **The #2 radio button:** Click this button and select the color you want to blend into. In the field to the right of the #2 button, enter the angle of the blend. You can enter any value from −360 to +360 degrees, in increments of 0.001 degrees. For a linear blend, a setting of 0 degrees blends the two colors from left to right; a setting of −90 degrees blends the colors from top to bottom.

For black-only publications, you can create a one-color blend by using white as one of the blend colors and black (or a shade of gray) as the other.

The effect of applied blends

Figure 21-13 shows eight examples of the use of six blends. For the top six, an angle of 30 degrees was chosen to show the effects of this feature. The bottom-right two show the effects of the angle on circular blends: a smaller angle results in a more compact circle. The bottom-left box has no blend applied to its background.

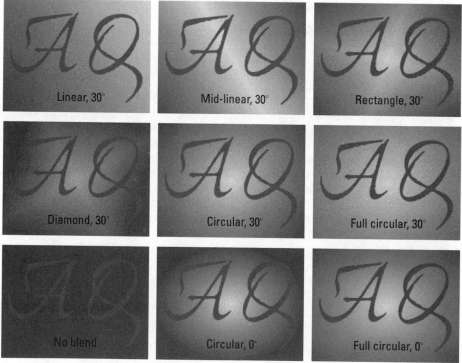

Figure 21-13: Eight kinds of blends and an example with no blend.

The RGB/CMYK dilemma

QuarkXPress can convert RGB files to CMYK, but the RGB-to-CMYK conversion may result in color shifts. (Previous versions of QuarkXPress required color management to be active to color-separate RGB EPS files, but version 4 does not.) RGB is color created by combining red, green, and blue. This is the standard color model used by scanners and graphics software because monitors use red, green, and blue electron guns to display images. Printing presses typically use CMYK, to which QuarkXPress must translate the RGB colors.

The dilemma most designers face is that an RGB image displays properly on-screen but may appear with slightly adjusted hues in print, while a CMYK image may print correctly but appear incorrectly on-screen. Most designers get good at mentally shifting the colors from one model to another, as they see the results of their work in print over time. Until that happens, rely on color proofs from your printer to see what your images actually look like when printed.

Working with color pictures

When you work with imported graphics, whether they are illustrations or scanned photographs, color is part of the graphic file. So the responsibility for color controls lies primarily with the creator of the picture. If you are planning to separate your document for CMYK printing, it is best to use color files in CMYK EPS or DCS format (for illustrations) or CMYK TIFF format (for scans and bitmaps). These standards are de facto for color publishing, so QuarkXPress is particularly adept at working with them. (See Chapter 6 for details on preparing graphics files for import.) After you import a non-EPS color graphic, you can adjust its hues with QuarkXPress's contrast controls and create a negative of the image, as described in Chapter 19. You can, of course, resize and crop the image. The following sections cover these issues in detail.

Caution

Color files pasted via the clipboard should print properly after they are pasted into a QuarkXPress picture box. But problems do sometimes occur, such as dropped colors or altered colors, depending on the applications involved and the amount of memory available.

EPS files

QuarkXPress automatically imports color definitions from EPS files, so you'll see any spot colors in them show up in your Colors palette and in menus and dialog boxes that display color lists. If you create files in EPS format, do any required color trapping in the source application. (Trapping for elements created in QuarkXPress is covered in Chapter 23.) Not all programs encode color information the same way. If you create EPS files in some illustration programs, colors may not print as expected. Any of the following three things can happen:

✦ Each color prints on its own plate (as if it were a spot color), even if you defined it as a process color.

✦ A spot color is color-separated into CMYK even when you define it as a spot color in both the source program and in QuarkXPress.

✦ A color prints as black.

There is no easy solution, because the problem is how the illustration program manages color internally. The only safe bet is to use a program that uses standard color-definition methods; these include the latest versions of Adobe Illustrator, CorelDraw, and Macromedia FreeHand.

TIFF files

Color TIFF files do not cause such peculiarities. QuarkXPress can color-separate both CMYK and RGB TIFF files.

Managing Colors

When you create colors, you'll find it easy to go overboard and make too many. You'll also find that different documents have different colors, each created by different people, and you'll likely want to move colors from one document to another. QuarkXPress provides basic tools for managing colors in and across documents.

Deleting colors

If you delete a color used in your document (through the Delete button in the Edit Color dialog box), you get the dialog box shown in Figure 21-14. This dialog box lets you substitute any other color for the removed one. If the color being deleted is not used in your document, this dialog box does not appear. In either case, you also have the option of canceling the delete operation by picking the Cancel button in the Colors dialog box (you would click Save to accept the change). When removing a color used in your document, you can also click the Cancel button in the dialog box asking you if it's OK to delete the color.

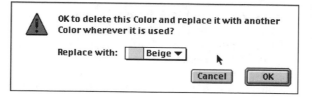

Figure 21-14: You will get the delete confirmation box when you remove colors in use.

Appending colors

When you click the Append button in the Edit Color dialog box, you'll first get a standard Open dialog box in which you find the QuarkXPress document that you want to copy colors from. When you've selected that document, the Append Colors to Default Document dialog box appears (see Figure 21-15).

New Feature

QuarkXPress has significantly overhauled how it moves colors between documents. In the old version, QuarkXPress simply copied over any unique colors from the selected document into the current one. But now, QuarkXPress lets you manage specifically which colors are moved through the Append Colors to *document name* dialog box.

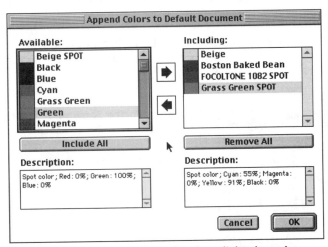

Figure 21-15: The new Append Colors dialog box gives you more control over copying colors from other documents.

The Available list shows all the colors in the selected document. You can move them over one at a time or in groups by selecting the colors and clicking the right arrow icon at top. (Shift+clicking lets you select a whole block of colors, while ⌘+clicking lets you select multiple, nonadjacent colors.) Use the left-arrow icon to remove colors from the Including list at right, which shows which colors you've marked for copying to your current document. You can also use the Include All and Exclude All buttons to copy over all colors or to undo the copying of all colors. If the active document contains colors with the same names as the colors you are importing, you'll be given a chance to resolve the conflict in the Append Conflict dialog box. Click OK when you're done.

Tip

To add colors to all future documents, open the Edit Color dialog box with no document open (it will be entitled Default Colors) and append colors from other documents. Those copied colors will be available to all future documents.

Displaying color groups

The Colors for *document name* dialog box (accessed via Edit⇨Define Colors or by ⌘+clicking a color in the Colors palette) has a Show pop-up menu (see Figure 21-16) that lets you select the kinds of colors displayed in the Colors scroll list. Your choices are All Colors (the default), Spot Colors, Process Colors, Multi-Ink Colors, Colors in Use, and Colors Not Used. The last option is handy when you want to delete unused colors from a document but can't quite remember which colors were used.

New
Feature

When you define lots of colors, it's easy to lose track of what's in your document. The Show pop-up menu in the Colors dialog box, a new feature in QuarkXPress 4, is designed to take the effort out of that task.

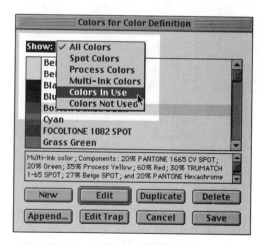

Figure 21-16: The Show pop-up menu in the Colors dialog box shows which colors are in use, and which are not, as well as colors created in specific color models.

✦   ✦   ✦

Going Beyond the Desktop

P A R T

V

♦   ♦   ♦   ♦

In This Part

Chapter 22
Working in
Workgroups

Chapter 23
Color Prepress

Chapter 24
Printing Techniques

♦   ♦   ♦   ♦

Publishing is not a solitary endeavor, and what you do on your computer is not the end-all of your efforts. While many people do use QuarkXPress alone, many others collaborate, sharing files or working on different parts of a publication. When you work in such a collaborative environment, you have an entirely new set of issues to deal with: how to share, how to standardize, and how to ensure consistency.

Whether you work by yourself or with others, at the end of your layout comes another effort: output. Creating a layout is pointless if no one sees it. When you create a document, you need to consider the effects on your service bureau (if you use one) and your printer—whether that's a laser printer down the hall or a printing press half a continent away. And if you're outputting to negatives, you'll need to be concerned with color fidelity, ensuring that what you created on your desktop will reproduce accurately on your printing press.

It's easy to dismiss these beyond-the-desktop issues as someone else's problem, but in truth they become the designer's problem. After all, it's you they'll come to wanting changes to meet their needs. You can save others and yourself a lot of time and aggravation anticipating and preempting those needs. That's what the three chapters in this part help you do.

Working in Workgroups

✦ ✦ ✦ ✦

In This Chapter

Establishing
standards

Sharing project
elements

Importing multiple
elements

Saving in version 3.3
format

Dealing with mixed-
platform issues

Working with service
bureaus

✦ ✦ ✦ ✦

Publishing is rarely a single-person enterprise. Chances are high that the creators of your text and graphics are not the same people who do your layout, and so publishing programs must support workgroups. QuarkXPress lets you create your own balance between the individual and the workgroup by allowing you to share common files over a network and import other essential elements from document to document. QuarkXPress 4 also lets you save documents to the previous version of the program, deal with mixed-platform environments, and accommodate the issues you'll encounter with service bureaus. This chapter covers it all.

Establishing Standards

To begin, the key to working effectively in a workgroup environment is to establish standards and make sure that it's easy to stick to them. A basic way to accomplish this task is to place all common elements in one place so that people always know where to get the elements they need. This practice also makes it easy to maintain (to add, modify, and delete) these elements over time, which is essential because no environment is static. How you do this depends on your computing environment.

  ✦ **If you don't use a network:** Keep a master set of disks and copy elements from the master set into a folder with the same name on each person's computer. Update these folders every time a standard element changes on the master disk.

  ✦ **If you do use a network:** Keep a master set of disks (networks do go down, so you'll want your files accessible when that happens) and create a folder for your standard elements on a network drive accessible to all users. Update this folder whenever a standard element changes on the master disk, and make sure you let your users know that you've done so.

Sharing Project Elements

The first part of this chapter describes common problem areas and offers solutions for dealing with the elements you need to share when working in a workgroup environment. The following items briefly cover what you can place in common folders, import from document to document, and things that are not so easily shared (see the following sections for some creative workarounds to some of these problem areas):

✦ Some standard elements can easily be accessed from a common folder because QuarkXPress can import certain elements that are stored outside of QuarkXPress documents. These elements include graphics files, libraries, kerning tables, and auxiliary spelling dictionaries. Style sheets, H&J sets, book lists, dashes and stripes, and color definitions can also be appended (imported) from one document to another, and there is a workaround that lets you copy master pages between documents (described later).

✦ Other elements (and the changes you make via most preferences dialog boxes) reside within documents and templates and cannot be saved in separate files or imported from document to document. These elements include tracking tables, hyphenation-exception dictionaries, and picture-contrast specifications. If you want to use these elements in another document, you may be out of luck and will have to re-create them in that other document. (These items are preserved, however, in documents that are opened on other platforms, such as going from Mac to Windows or vice versa.)

Using XPress Preferences files

When no document is open and you change a document's preferences (except for picture-contrast specifications, which may be defined only for specific graphics, not globally), the modified settings are stored in a file called XPress Preferences that resides in the folder containing the QuarkXPress program. Here's how it works:

✦ If you keep the XPress Preferences file current with all your preferences, you can apply these preferences to all previously created documents by opening them and selecting the Use XPress Preferences button. Figure 22-1 shows this dialog box, which is invoked automatically if QuarkXPress detects a difference between QuarkXPress's preferences and the document's. (Newly created documents always use the current XPress Preferences settings.)

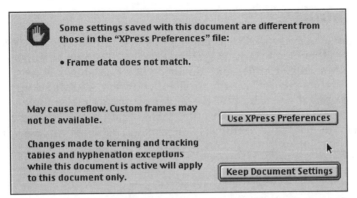

Figure 22-1: This dialog box lets you know when a document's preferences don't match QuarkXPress's general preferences. You can choose which preferences to apply.

✦ You cannot use the Mac's alias feature or Windows's shortcut feature to use an XPress Preferences file stored in a folder other than the one in which QuarkXPress resides. (Too bad, because that would let you have one master preferences file on the network that everyone uses.) Nor are the Mac and Windows XPress Preference files interchangeable, so if you work in a cross-platform environment, you'll need to maintain separate Mac and Windows master preference files.

Note

Ironically, QuarkXPress 3 for Windows used to let you use a preferences file stored in a different location or even on a network server. In this case, administering preferences in a workgroup was not a headache. But version 4 removed this ability.

✦ The best alternative is to have a master copy of the XPress Preferences file (both Mac and Windows versions if necessary) and copy it to each user as it is updated (either manually or via a network backup program).

✦ If you provide every user with the same copy of the Preferences file, make sure that everyone understands *not* to change the global preferences without permission, because everyone else will be affected. For example, if someone changes the color settings on the global copy and that copy is distributed to the rest of the staff, everyone's color settings will be changed.

Note

Quark does sell a network version of QuarkXPress called Quark Publishing System that supports full network interaction among users. This product is aimed at large companies like magazine publishers.

Quark CMS profiles

When you open a document, QuarkXPress checks to see whether a Quark CMS color profile was used that is not on your system. Figure 22-2 shows the dialog box that appears if it finds missing profiles and the dialog box that shows you which images are affected, letting you replace the profile if you want. You will need to add the profile before printing if you want that particular color calibration applied. But if you intend to move the document back to the system that has the missing profile, don't worry. The reference to the missing profile is retained (unless you replace it).

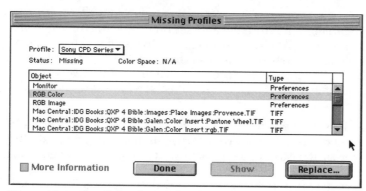

Figure 22-2: The dialog boxes that let you identify missing color profiles.

On the Mac, color profiles are stored in the ColorSync Profiles folder in the System Folder's Preferences folder. In Windows, the profiles are stored in the SYSTEM\COLOR directory in the directory that contains the Windows operating system. Color profiles on Mac and Windows are also not interchangeable, so if you work in a cross-platform environment and add profiles on one platform, be sure to ask the manufacturer for the profiles for the other platform.

Tip

You can also store color profiles in a second folder of your choice, which you select via the Auxiliary Profile Folder option in the Profile Manager dialog box (Utilities⇨Profile Manager). This second folder is a great place to store color profiles specific to your work, rather than mixing them up with the default color profiles.

Color definitions

It's not unusual to want to keep color definitions consistent across documents. This consistency helps you ensure that corporate-identity colors, if you have them, are used instead of someone's approximations. You can import colors created in other documents through the Append button in the Colors dialog box (accessed via Edit➪Colors, or via the shortcut Shift+F12). After you click the Append button, a dialog box will appear so that you can search for the file with the color definitions that you want. After you select the file, you'll get the dialog box shown in Figure 22-3 (which also shows the Colors dialog box).

Selecting colors to import

QuarkXPress 4 lets you select which colors to import. Any trapping settings are also imported for each color. Select each color you want to import from the Available list box at left and click the right-pointing arrow to add them to the Including list box at right (these are the colors that will be added to the current QuarkXPress document). Use the Include All button to add all the colors; use the left-pointing arrow to remove individual colors from the Including list box; and use the Remove All button to clear the Including list box. When you've got all the colors you want to copy into your QuarkXPress document, click OK. If you import a color that has the same name as a color in your existing QuarkXPress document but with a different definition, QuarkXPress 4 also lets you rename the imported color, overwrite the current color, or skip the import.

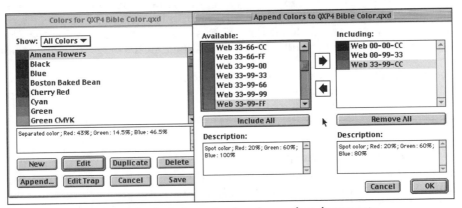

Figure 22-3: You can selectively import colors from other documents.

In the previous version of QuarkXPress, all colors defined in the other document but not defined in the current document will be imported from the other document. QuarkXPress 4 now lets you select the colors to be imported, as described in the preceding section.

Working across platforms

Windows QuarkXPress and Mac QuarkXPress can append each other's color definitions. To ensure that Windows QuarkXPress displays your Mac QuarkXPress files in the Append dialog box, be sure to select the file type All File Types, or add the extension .QXD to the Mac QuarkXPress document's filename.

Kerning tables

Unlike many other preferences, changes to kerning tables are stored in the XPress Preferences file and used for all subsequently created documents, whether a document is open or not when they are made. They are not used for previously created documents, though, unless you select Use XPress Preferences when you open them. QuarkXPress provides a method to export and import kerning tables, so that you can move kerning information between documents that have already been created.

Exporting kerning values

After you have changed kerning values for a particular typeface, you can export the new values as a text file that can be imported into other documents. Figure 22-4 shows the Edit Kerning Table dialog box (accessed via Utilities⇨Kerning Table Edit and then clicking the Edit button after selecting the font whose kerning values you want to change). At the bottom of the dialog box is the Export button, which creates the kerning file, and the Import button, which loads in previously created kerning files. If you choose Export, another dialog box appears that lets you select the name and location of the kerning file (refer to Figure 22-4). Importing kerning tables gives you a similar dialog box. When you select a kerning table to import, its values will display in the Kerning Pairs list in the Edit Kerning Table dialog box.

Tip

By periodically exporting kerning tables and then importing them into QuarkXPress when no documents are open, you can update the global preferences set in XPress Preferences so that all future documents use these new kerning values.

Working across platforms

Kerning files are the same on both platforms, so you can import kerning pairs from Mac to Windows and vice versa. In Windows QuarkXPress, make sure that you have selected All Files as the file type, or that you have added the extension .KRN to the kerning file on the Mac, so that it appears in the import dialog box.

Style sheets

The Style Sheets dialog box (accessed via Edit⇨Style Sheets or via the shortcut Shift+F11) includes the Append button to let you import styles from other QuarkXPress documents and templates. Figure 22-5 shows this dialog box as well as the Append Style Sheets dialog box that it invokes once you've selected the QuarkXPress document to import style sheets from.

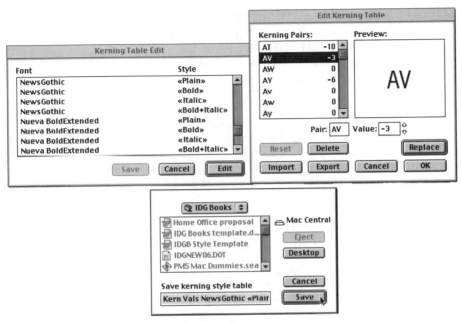

Figure 22-4: Exporting kerning files for a font.

As described in the following sections, QuarkXPress 4 adds the ability to selectively import style sheets (the previous version imported all styles from the chosen QuarkXPress document). QuarkXPress 4 also imports any related settings with the styles. If there are style sheets whose names are the same in both documents, QuarkXPress prompts you on how to handle them.

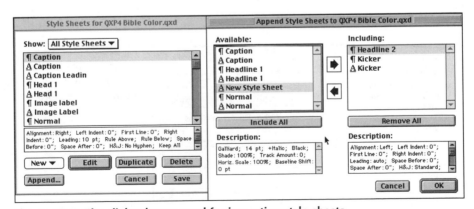

Figure 22-5: The dialog boxes used for importing style sheets.

Selectively importing style sheets

QuarkXPress 4 lets you selectively import style sheets. Select each style sheet you want to import from the Available list box at left and click the right-pointing arrow to add them to the Including list box at right. (These are the style sheets that will be added to the current QuarkXPress document.) Use the Include All button to add all the style sheets, use the left-pointing arrow to remove individual style sheets from the Including list box, and use the Remove All button to clear the Including list box. When you've got all the style sheets you want to copy into your QuarkXPress document, click OK. QuarkXPress 4 will import any related settings with the styles. For example, if a style sheet you're importing uses an H&J set not in the current QuarkXPress document, the program will copy over that H&J set as well. Or if you import a paragraph style that uses a specific character style, both will be imported.

Note

After importing, make sure that you click the Save button in the Style Sheets dialog box to save the imported styles in the current document (or in the XPress Preferences file, if no documents are open). By importing styles with no document open, you copy all new styles into your global defaults (those stored in the XPress Preferences file, covered earlier in this chapter). This technique is a handy way of bringing new styles into your default settings without affecting existing files.

Resolving style-sheet name conflicts

If there are style sheets whose names are the same in both documents, QuarkXPress will prompt you on how to handle them. (Figure 22-6 shows the dialog box that alerts you to the duplicate names.) You can rename the imported style manually (by clicking Rename); cancel its import (by clicking the Use Existing button); overwrite the current document's style sheet (by clicking the Use New button); or let QuarkXPress rename the file for you (by clicking the Auto-Rename button, which adds an asterisk [*] to the beginning of the imported style sheet's name).

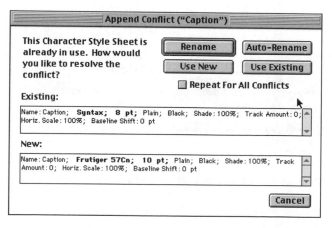

Figure 22-6: QuarkXPress lets you resolve name conflicts between imported and existing style sheets (and other imported elements).

Working across platforms

Windows QuarkXPress and Mac QuarkXPress can append each other's style-sheet definitions. To ensure that Windows QuarkXPress displays your Mac QuarkXPress files in the Append dialog box, be sure to select the file type All File Types, or add the extension .QXD to the Mac QuarkXPress document's filename.

You can import from several documents by clicking Append after importing styles from a document; this action reinvokes the Append Style Sheets dialog box. Repeat the import for each document.

H&J sets

Importing H&J sets is similar to importing style sheets (described in a previous section). Use the Append button in the H&Js dialog box (accessed via Edit⇨H&Js, or via the shortcut Option+⌘+H on the Mac and Ctrl+Shift+F11 in Windows). You'll get a dialog box similar to that shown in Figure 22-5.

Note that you'll be less likely to import H&J sets in QuarkXPress 4, because this new version now automatically copies over needed H&J sets when you import style sheets. In the previous version, you had to import the style sheets and H&J sets separately.

Lists

You can copy lists from one document to another by using the Append button in the Lists dialog box (Edit⇨Lists). The Lists dialog box works the same as the Append dialog box for style sheets (refer to Figure 22-5).

Dashes, stripes, and bitmap frames

You can copy dashes and stripes from one document to another by using the Append button in the Dashes & Stripes dialog box (Edit⇨Dashes & Stripes). The Dashes & Stripes dialog box works the same as the Append dialog box for style sheets (refer to Figure 22-5). The bitmap frames that Macintosh QuarkXPress lets you create are part of the XPress Preferences file, so to share them with others, you must provide that file. (Windows QuarkXPress retains bitmap frames in documents created on the Mac, but it does not let you create them or make them part of the Windows XPress Preferences file.)

Spelling dictionaries

So that you can add words to the spell checker, QuarkXPress requires that you create an auxiliary dictionary or open an existing one, via Utilities⇨Auxiliary Dictionary, as described in Chapter 11. Figure 22-7 shows the Auxiliary Dictionary dialog box. Any number of documents can use the same dictionary. However, a document may use only one auxiliary dictionary at a time, not several.

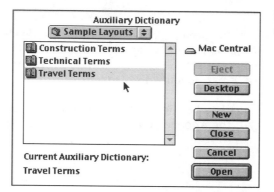

Figure 22-7: Create or select auxiliary dictionaries with this dialog box.

Note

If you create a new auxiliary dictionary (via the New button and then the Create button), the words in the current dictionary (if the document has one) will *not* be copied into the new dictionary.

How auxiliary dictionaries work

QuarkXPress auxiliary dictionaries are simply text files in which all the words are listed, one after the other in alphabetical order, with a return after each word. This makes it easy for you to use a word processor to edit or merge together multiple auxiliary dictionaries. In order for QuarkXPress to recognize an auxiliary dictionary, it must have a creator code of XPR3 (on the Mac) or end with .QDT (on Windows). To remove an auxiliary dictionary from a document, just click the Close button in the Auxiliary Dictionary dialog box.

Working across platforms

Auxiliary dictionaries are the same on both platforms, so you can import dictionaries from Mac to Windows and vice versa. In QuarkXPress Windows, make sure that you have selected All Files as the file type, or that you have added the extension .QDT to the auxiliary dictionary file on the Mac, so that it appears in the import dialog box.

Graphics and text files

Perhaps the most obvious elements to standardize are the source elements—the text and graphics that you use in your documents—especially if you have common elements such as logos that are used in multiple documents. The simplest method of ensuring that the latest versions of these common elements are used is to keep them all in a standard folder (either on each computer or on a network drive). This method works well when first using a text or graphic element, but it does not ensure that these elements are updated in QuarkXPress documents if the elements are changed after being imported.

Color Techniques

QuarkXPress offers sophisticated color features and controls. Chapter 21 shows you how to create, edit, and apply color, while Chapter 23 shows you how to use QuarkXPress's color-management features. This special 16-page color insert was created in QuarkXPress 4 and, where noted, with the assistance of Adobe Photoshop 4.0.

Literally thousands of colors are available using the various color models in QuarkXPress 4. Here is a photo of the standard Pantone color swatchbook, fanned out to show the many available colors.

Color Models Revealed

QuarkXPress supports a range of color models, including CMYK and several variants of the industry-standard Pantone Matching System, as well as the new high-fidelity Hexachrome system from Pantone. Shown here are the color wheels for CMYK and RGB, as well as sample swatches for the other color models supported by QuarkXPress. Note that this book was output on a CMYK standard Web offset printing (SWOP) press, so not all the colors reproduce accurately from other color models. That's a reality in color publishing. We did have the Quark Color Management System (CMS) active, so the colors are as close as they can possibly be.

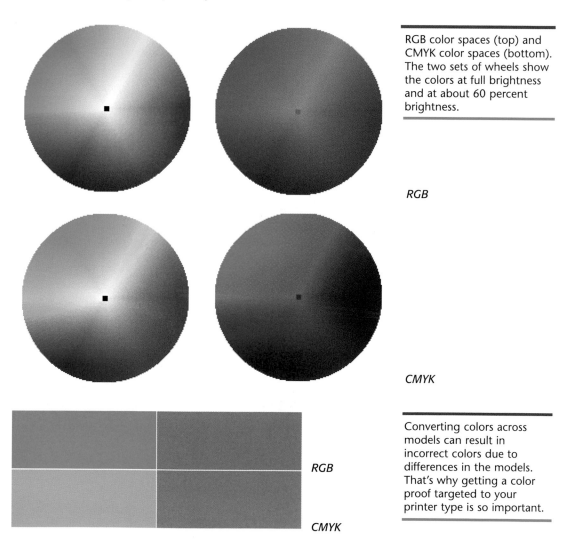

RGB color spaces (top) and CMYK color spaces (bottom). The two sets of wheels show the colors at full brightness and at about 60 percent brightness.

RGB

CMYK

RGB

CMYK

Converting colors across models can result in incorrect colors due to differences in the models. That's why getting a color proof targeted to your printer type is so important.

Samples from the various spot-color models available in QuarkXPress 4. Note that the Pantone Process, Pantone ProSim, Focoltone, and Trumatch models are all based on CMYK and thus should reproduce most accurately when printed on a printing press. The other spot-color models, as well as the Hexachrome process colors, are designed to reproduce best with special inks.

Crayon (Mac-only model)

Purple	Process Yellow	100
Violet	Process Magenta	101
Blue 072	Process Cyan	102
Reflex Blue	Process Black	Yellow
Process Blue		103
Green		104
Black		105

Pantone

Process Yellow	100	106
Process Magenta	101	107
Process Cyan	102	108
Process Black	Yellow	109
Orange 021	103	110
Red 032	104	111
Blue 072	105	112

Pantone ProSim

85-1	86-1	87-1
85-2	86-2	87-2
85-3	86-3	87-3
85-4	06-4	87-4
85-5	86-5	87-5
85-6	86-6	87-6
85-7	86-7	87-7
85-8	86-8	87-8
85-9	86-9	87-9

Pantone Process

Purple	Process Yellow	100
Violet	Process Magenta	101
Blue 072	Process Cyan	102
Reflex Blue	Process Black	Yellow
Process Blue		103
Green		104
Black		105

Pantone Uncoated

Yellow	H 10-1	H 10-8
Orange	H 10-2	H 10-9
Magenta	H 10-3	H 10-10
Cyan	H 10-4	H 10-11
Green	H 10-5	H 10-12
Black	H 10-6	H 10-13
	H 10-7	H 10-14

Hexachrome Coated

18-a1	18-a2	18-a3
18-b1	18-b2	18-b3
18-c1	18-c2	18-c3
18-d1	18-d2	18-d3
18-e1	18-e2	18-e3
18-f1	18-a5	18-a6
18-g1	18-b5	18-b6
18-d5	18-c5	18-c6

Trumatch

0281pc*	0291pc*	0301pc*
0282pc*	0292pc*	0302pc*
0283pc	0293pc*	0303pc*
0284pc	0294pc	0304pc*
0285pc*	0295pc*	0305pc*
0286pc	0296pc	0306pc*
0287pc	0297pc*	0307pc*
0288pc*	0298pc	0308pc*
0289pc*	0299pc	0309pc*
0290pc*	0300pc	0310pc*

Toyo

Yellow	H 10-1	H 10-8
Orange	H 10-2	H 10-9
Magenta	H 10-3	H 10-10
Cyan	H 10-4	H 10-11
Green	H 10-5	H 10-12
Black	H 10-6	H 10-13
	H 10-7	H 10-14

Hexachrome Uncoated

1073	1076	2285
1083	1082	2291
2250	2249	3458
3417	3416	3464
		3470

Focoltone

1p	11p*	21p
2p	12p*	22p
3p	13p*	23p
4p*	14p*	24p
5p*	15p*	25p
6p*	16p*	26p*
7p	17p*	27p
8p	18p*	28p
9p	19p*	29p*
10p	20p	30p*

DIC (Dainippon)

Web-Safe Colors

Although the Hypertext Markup Language (HTML) supports thousands of colors, you can count on only 216 working on popular Macintosh and Windows browsers. That's true because most browsers assume that people have just 8-bit color depth (256 colors), and 40 of those are reserved by Windows for its interface. (These are modifiable colors in Windows, so if a browser used a modified color, there's a good chance that the color in the original image looks totally different on the user's system.) This book's CD includes a QuarkXPress library with the 216 Web-safe colors you can import into your documents.

Because Web browsers reliably display just 216 colors, you often get color shifts when you use photos and other scanned artwork on the Web. Be sure to look at your image in a browser such as Netscape Navigator or Microsoft Internet Explorer to see how it appears to your readers. You may need to alter the image's color palette in a program such as Photoshop to minimize inappropriate color shifts.

Original image

Image viewed in a Web browser

How solid colors such as those used for text can shift when displayed on the Web.

Yosemite, here we come!

Original color

Yosemite, here we come!

Color that appears on the Web

Selecting Colors from an Image

Even with an excellent sense of color, matching colors by eye can be difficult. Because you may also want to use a color from an image in your document — as a text color or for lines or frames — an accurate color-matching tool is a necessity. Unfortunately, QuarkXPress doesn't include an eyedropper tool to sample a color and add it to the Colors palette. However, Photoshop and other image editors do have such a tool, which you can use to sample a color within an image and then define a color in QuarkXPress with identical values.

Use your image editor's eyedropper tool to get the color values for the color you want to use (above), and then define that color in the Edit Color dialog box in QuarkXPress using the same values (at right).

Note that Photoshop uses a scale of 0 to 255 for colors, while QuarkXPress uses percentages. To have QuarkXPress translate Photoshop values, enter /2.56 after the Photoshop value in the Edit Colors dialog box, as in 110/2.56 for the red value in this example. QuarkXPress then calculates the correct percentage (43.5%).

Using Color Tints

Adding color to an image, whether at full strength or as a lighter shade, can greatly change its character. The examples here show how you can apply color to objects to give your gray-scale images a new look. Note that you can also apply colors to some black and white vector art, as described in Chapter 21.

Light gold background

Light purple background

Light pine-green background

Light reddish brown background

Above with reddish brown foreground

Above with navy-blue foreground

Above with purple foreground

Above with pine-green foreground

The effects of various background and foreground color tints. The image at far right shows the typically unwelcome negative effects of using a darker background color than foreground color.

Original gray image

Purple foreground with no background

Gold foreground with green background

Using Halftone Controls

Normally used to create the correct type of negatives for a specific printer, you can use halftone controls in QuarkXPress to distort your bitmapped black and white and gray-scale images, including colorized bitmaps. QuarkXPress supports four types of halftones — those made up of the normal dots, of squares, of lines, and of ellipses.

By choosing a specific halftone element and deciding how coarsely the image is to be divided into these elements (the lpi setting), you can create an effect such as pointillism or gravature. There's also the ordered dither setting that alters the printed pixels.

Typical settings (dot element, 133 lpi, 45°)

Dot element, 60 lpi, 45°

Line element, 60 lpi, 0°

Ellipse element, 30 lpi, 75°

Square element, 30 lpi, 15°

Ordered dither

Using Blends

Blends add a sense of motion to a background or image. An image editor such as Photoshop gives you very fine control over color blends, letting you blend among several colors and controlling the blend pattern. QuarkXPress is more modest, offering basic two-color blends (if you installed the Cool Blends XTension) and a selection of six fixed-pattern blend styles. Still, that's enough for most uses.

The most common use of blends is a background, either behind text (left) or behind a vector drawing (below left). You can also use blends as part of a drawing with QuarkXPress, such as in the cherry drawing below.

Note that for a blend (or any other background) to show behind a vector image, the image must have a transparent background or have a clipping path (also called a mask) created in the Clipping pane in the Modify dialog box (Option+⌘+T, or Item ⇨ Clipping).

Outlines of non-blend boxes to highlight blend shapes

You can simulate the effect of a multicolor linear blend in QuarkXPress by abutting multiple boxes with two-color linear blends, as shown at right. (We added frames around each box so you can see the three boxes clearly.) Compare that with the multicolor circular blend possible with Photoshop.

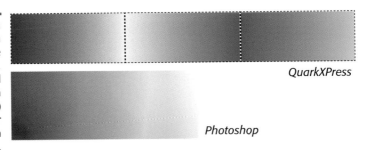

QuarkXPress

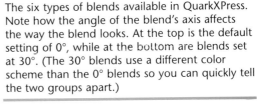

Photoshop

The six types of blends available in QuarkXPress. Note how the angle of the blend's axis affects the way the blend looks. At the top is the default setting of 0°, while at the bottom are blends set at 30°. (The 30° blends use a different color scheme than the 0° blends so you can quickly tell the two groups apart.)

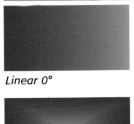

Linear 0°

Midlinear 0°

Rectangular 0°

Diamond 0°

Circular 0°

Full Circular 0°

By layering boxes with different blends, you can create more complex illustrations. Below, we combined a midlinear blend in the rectangle box with a linear blend in the oval box to create the dawn effect.

Linear 30°

Midlinear 30°

Rectangular 30°

Diamond 30°

Circular 30°

Full Circular 30°

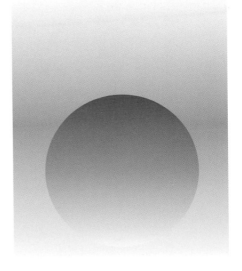

Working with Contrasts in Color

It's typical to think of using contrast controls only for gray-scale images, to adjust lightness and contrast. But these controls also work with color images, as shown in these samples. Obviously, you'd use these effects sparingly.

Using the Contrast controls (Shift+⌘+C, or Image ➪ Contrast) on 256-color PICT images lets you warp the images into surreal versions, as shown below and at right. To work on images with greater color depth, use a program such as Adobe Photoshop.

Original 256-color image

High contrast

Posterized

Negative (using RGB color model)

Negative (using HSB color model)

Blue component inverted, red and green left to normal contrast

Green component posterized, blue component given high contrast, red left at normal

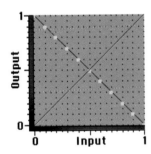

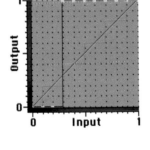

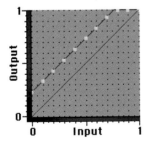

Blue component set for heightened (bluer) output

Alternating high and low output for all color components

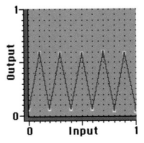

The Effects of Color Profiles

QuarkXPress 4 introduces a new color-management system, the Quark CMS, to help ensure your output color matches the original as much as possible. The Quark CMS can't change the laws of physics, so ultimately your printer or printing press determines how accurate colors reproduce. However, the Quark CMS can translate the colors you choose to the closest available in the output device you're using. The samples on these pages were output on a standard Web offset printing (SWOP) press; the output calibrated to specific non-SWOP devices has been calibrated as closely as a SWOP press can achieve.

Original, uncorrected RGB TIFF image

The effects of various profiles on an RGB image (this page) and a CMYK image (opposite page). Note that the RGB image was converted during printing to CMYK, since this book was printed on a CMYK SWOP press.

Image using Sony CPD monitor profile

Image using Epson Stylus Color 720-dpi printer profile

Image using Hewlett-Packard ScanJet IIc scanner profile

Image using Kodak's digital camera profile

Image using Fargo Primera dye-sublimation printer profile

Image using PowerBook 540c display profile

Image using 150-line Pantone profile

Original, uncorrected CMYK TIFF image

Image using Hewlett-Packard Color Laser Jet/PS profile

Image using 3M Matchprint profile

Image using QMS ColorScript 100 Model 30i profile

Image using SWOP press profile

RGB version of uncorrected TIFF image (automatically color-separated to CMYK by QuarkXPress during output to the SWOP press)

Image using Kodak SWOP Newsprint profile

Working with Traps

If you don't have your QuarkXPress documents output to negatives or directly to plate and have them printed on a SWOP press, you don't need to worry about trapping. But if you do such professional output, trapping is an issue you should be aware of. Simply put, trapping manages how different colors print when they abut or overlap. Many printing presses use four or more plates, each with its own ink. With modern high-speed printing presses, computers keep the plates aligned, but most presses still can have slight variations in the plates' positions, which leads to gaps between colors. Thus, QuarkXPress lets you determine how much slippage your printing press may have and adjusts image borders accordingly, reducing the risk of gaps. The default settings in QuarkXPress work for most presses, but you should talk with your service bureau or printer first to see what settings they recommend.

A negative number in a trapping setting *chokes* the foreground color, which makes the surrounding color bleed in. A positive number *spreads* the color, which makes the inside color bleed out. (It's best to have the lighter color bleed into the darker color.) An *overprint* lets the colors mix together (without knocking out the foreground from the background).

Choke   *Spread*   *Overprint*

The effects of text on a multicolored image. The default is to trap the text, rather than overprint or knock out.

Default (trap of 0.144 points)   *Overprint*

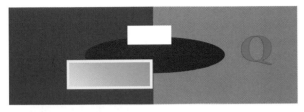

The effects of various trap settings on objects created within QuarkXPress.

Defaults: backgrounds overprint, text has 0.144-point trap, white knocks out, frames have 0.144-point trap

Everything overprints

Everything knocks out

Backgrounds overprint, text has 1.0-point trap, white knocks out, oval has Auto Amount (+) trap, navy-blue box has Auto Amount (–) trap, outside frame has –0.5-point trap, inside frame has 0.5-point trap

Backgrounds overprint, everything else has a 3.0-point trap

Backgrounds overprint, everything else has a –3.0-point trap

Working with Clipping Paths

QuarkXPress can import clipping paths in images, as well as create clipping paths by ignoring any white part of an image. A clipping path is essentially a runaround area, and besides using a clipping path on an irregular object to create a text wrap that fits that object's shape (or at least the shape of its clipping path), you can also use a clipping path as a mask — an area that is transparent, so whatever color is behind the image shows through. Typically, you create your clipping path in Adobe Illustrator or Photoshop, and then save the file as an EPS or TIFF file. Use the Clipping pane (Item ➪ Clipping, or Option+⌘+T) to activate the clipping path, as described in Chapter 6. Now you can place a graphic over a background color or blend and have that background show through.

The image at left has no clipping path. Notice the white building in the background. In the image below it, we created a clipping path in Photoshop that removed the white building (the Clipping pane is shown below as well), and then applied a colored background to the picture box. Adding that background let us "repaint" the white building a new color. (We prefer white!)

Note that we did not create the clipping path in the Clipping pane by having it ignore all non-white areas, since that would also have made the white flowers and the white pot transparent and thus changed their colors as well.

Standardizing text files

For text files, there is no easy solution to this problem because QuarkXPress has no text-link feature. But you can put common text contained in a QuarkXPress text box into a library (see the following section on libraries), which should handle most needs, such as mastheads, postal information, and standard sidebars (for example, "How to contact the company").

Standardizing graphics files

For graphics files, using Publish and Subscribe on the Mac, OLE in Windows, or regular links—when combined with the approach of keeping common elements in a common location—can ensure consistency across documents. You can also use libraries to store commonly used graphics.

Libraries

QuarkXPress libraries are a great aid to keeping documents consistent. Because libraries are stored in their own files, common libraries can be put in common folders. You can even access them across the network. If you want, you can keep an alias to a library elsewhere on the network or on your computer's local drive.

What libraries do

For many people, libraries offer more flexibility than just linking to graphics files because all attributes applied to graphics and their picture boxes are also stored in the library. Graphics in libraries also retain any links—either regular import links or Publish and Subscribe (Mac) or OLE (Windows) links—so you don't have to worry about this information being lost for graphics stored in libraries.

Working across platforms

Unfortunately, libraries on Macs and Windows are not compatible, so you will need to maintain two sets of libraries if you work in a cross-platform environment.

Templates

In the course of creating documents, you are likely to evolve templates that you want to use over and over. QuarkXPress can save a document as a template. The only difference between a template and a document is that a template forces you to use Save As rather than Save in the File menu (the shortcut is Option+⌘+S) so that you do not overwrite the template, but instead create new documents based on it.

Note

QuarkXPress supports the use of templates over a network. Each time a template is accessed, the user accessing it is given a local copy. Thus, multiple users can access the template simultaneously, and even a single user can have several documents based on the same template open at once.

The truth about templates

Although the optimal approach is to design a template before creating actual documents, the truth is that no one can foresee all possibilities. Even if you create a template (and you should—with style sheets, H&J sets, and master pages intended for use in all new documents), you can expect to modify your template as your work on real documents creates the need for modifications and additions.

Working across platforms

The Windows and Macintosh versions of QuarkXPress read each other's template files, so you can have master templates available for all your users in a cross-platform environment. Just make sure your template files have names that end in .QXT if you want to use them in Windows.

Master pages

Moving master pages between documents is tricky because QuarkXPress offers no feature that explicitly performs this task. But you can use QuarkXPress libraries as a way station for master pages that you want to move from one document to another. To do that, use the following steps:

Tip

You can also copy a master page from one document to another by dragging a page that uses that master page from the source document to the target document while both documents are in Thumbnails view. Just be sure to delete the unwanted document page when you're done.

STEPS: Transferring master pages to libraries

1. Open a library with File⇨Open (⌘+O) or create a library with File⇨New⇨Library or via the shortcut Option+⌘+N.

2. Open the document with the master page that you want to copy and display that master page (via Page⇨Display). We recommend that you change the view to something small, like 25 percent, so that you can see the full page.

3. Select the Item tool and then select all items (via Edit⇨Select All or the shortcut ⌘+A).

4. Drag (or use copy and paste) the items into an open library and release the mouse. All of the elements on the master page will appear in their own library box, as shown in the library window in Figure 22-8.

5. Open the document that you want to copy the master page into. You don't need to close the other document, but unless you intend to get other elements from it or work on it later, go ahead and close it to reduce clutter both on the screen and in the computer's memory.

6. Use the View⇨Windows menu items (on the Mac) or the Windows menu items (in Windows) to manage how pages display. On the Mac, Tile Documents creates nonoverlapping windows (one at the top and one at the bottom if you have two documents open). On Windows, you can choose Tile Horizontally or Tile Vertically. On both platforms, Stack Documents overlaps the windows. The names of all open documents also appear so that you can switch among them. You can also resize windows manually by clicking and holding the mouse on the window's resize box on the Mac (in the window's lower right corner); or by clicking and holding any of its sides or corners in Windows. You can also use View⇨Fit to Window (or the keyboard shortcut ⌘+0 [zero]) to have QuarkXPress figure out how small to make the page to fit in its window.

7. Insert a new blank master page in the second document, using the Document Layout palette, as described in Chapter 10.

8. Drag (or copy and paste) the library item containing the first document's master-page elements into the new master page (this master page is at the bottom of Figure 22-8).

9. Rename the new master page so that you can remember what it is. Now you're done.

Working across platforms

Because Mac and Windows QuarkXPress cannot read each other's libraries, you might think you cannot use this technique to copy master pages from one platform to the other. However, you *can* copy master pages across platforms if you follow the previous steps after opening the original file on the new platform. For example, if you want to copy a master page from a Mac QuarkXPress file to Windows, open that Mac file in Windows QuarkXPress. Then create the library in Windows that contains the elements you want to copy to another Windows QuarkXPress file.

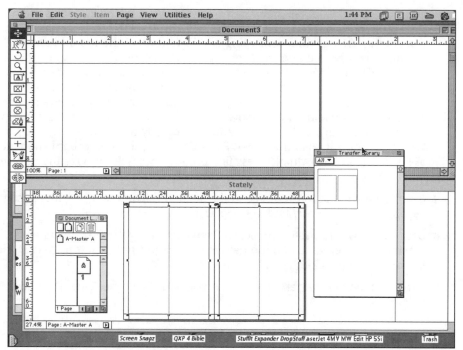

Figure 22-8: To copy master pages from one document to another, first copy them from the original document (bottom left) to a library (bottom right), and then from the library to the new document (top).

Print styles

In QuarkXPress 4, you can now export and import print styles from one user to another. In the Print Styles dialog box (Edit⇨Print Styles), shown in Figure 22-9, select the print style you want to export as a file, and then select the Export button. Locate the drive and folder you want to contain the print style, and click OK. To import a print style, use the same dialog box but use the Import button instead.

Sharing master print files

Keep master print style files on a shared folder so your users can import the latest print styles into their document before they output a job.

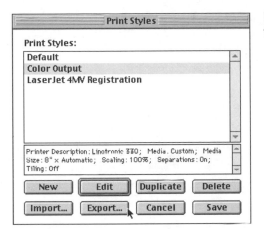

Figure 22-9: Export and import print styles through this dialog box.

Working across platforms

Print style files are the same on both platforms, so you can import print styles from Mac to Windows and vice versa. In Windows QuarkXPress, make sure that you have selected All Files as the file type, or that you have added the extension .QPJ to the print style file on the Mac, so that it appears in the import dialog box.

Importing Multiple Elements

QuarkXPress 4 makes it easy to import colors, dashes and lines, style sheets, lists, and H&J sets from one document to another: use the Append to *document name* dialog box. (This dialog box will be called Append to Default Document if no document is open.) You access this new dialog box, shown in Figure 22-10, via File⇨Append, or the shortcut Option+⌘+A. The dialog box collects the five types of elements that QuarkXPress can import from one document to another into one dialog box, with a separate pane for each type. The dialog box should look familiar: you've seen pieces of it earlier in this chapter (refer to Figures 22-3 and 22-5).

New Feature

The Append to Default Document dialog box is a new feature in QuarkXPress 4. In addition to importing elements from document to document, it also makes it possible to compare versions of style sheets, color definitions, H&J sets, lists, or dashes and stripes to find out how they differ. Both new features are covered in this section.

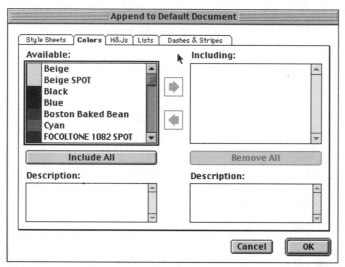

Figure 22-10: The Append dialog box lets you import five kinds of items from one document to another at the same time.

Using the Append feature

Go through each pane in the Append dialog box and select what you want to import into your current document. Select each item you want to import from the Available list box at left and click the right-pointing arrow to add them to the Including list box at right (these are the items that will be added to the current QuarkXPress document). Use the Include All button to add all the items; use the left-pointing arrow to remove individual items from the Including list box; and use the Remove All button to clear the Including list box. When you've got all the items in each pane that you want to copy into your QuarkXPress document, click OK.

Note

QuarkXPress 4 will import any related settings with the styles. For example, if a style sheet you're importing uses an H&J set not in the current QuarkXPress document, the program will copy over that H&J set as well. Or if you import a paragraph style that uses a specific character style, both will be imported.

Resolving name conflicts

If there are items whose names are the same in both documents but whose definitions are different, QuarkXPress will prompt you on how to handle them. (Refer to Figure 22-6 to see the dialog box that alerts you to the duplicate names in the case of style sheets.) You can rename the imported item manually (by clicking the Rename button); cancel its import (by clicking the Use Existing button); overwrite the current document's item (by clicking the Use New button); or let QuarkXPress rename the item for you (by clicking the Auto-Rename button, which adds an asterisk [*] to the beginning of the imported item's name).

Comparing attributes

If you have multiple elements—be they style sheets, color definitions, H&J sets, lists, or dashes and stripes—and you're not sure how they differ, you can use the Append button to find out. First, select the two items you want to compare from the appropriate dialog box (Style Sheets, Colors, H&J Sets, Lists, or Dashes & Stripes). You may need to hold down the ⌘ key to do so, if the items you want to compare are not adjacent in the list. Then hold down the Option key. You'll see the Append button become the Compare button. Click Compare, and you'll get the Compare Colors dialog box, which lists the attributes for the two selected items, as Figure 22-11 shows. Differences are highlighted in boldface.

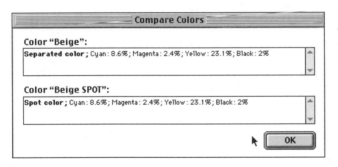

Figure 22-11: QuarkXPress lets you compare the attributes of any two colors, style sheets, lists, H&J sets, dashes, or stripes.

Working across platforms

Windows and Mac QuarkXPress can append each other's style sheet, color, H&J set, dashes and stripes, and list definitions. To ensure that Windows QuarkXPress displays your Mac QuarkXPress files in the Append dialog box, be sure to select the file type Display All Files or to add the appropriate extension to the Mac QuarkXPress document's filename: .QXD for documents, .QXT for templates, and .QXL for libraries. (Windows QuarkXPress will open only Windows library files, not Mac libraries, even if you give the Mac library the .QXL extension.) Figure 22-12 shows where you select Display All Files; note how you can even import these items from an autosaved QuarkXPress document file—handy if you have a crash and lose a document.

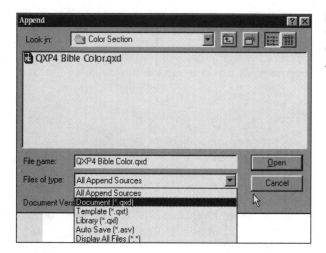

Figure 22-12: In Windows QuarkXPress, you can have only certain types of files display in the Append dialog box.

Saving in Version 3.3 Format

QuarkXPress 4 has the ability to save in the previous version's format. That's great if you are working with colleagues or service bureaus that don't yet have the new version installed. To save in version 3.3 format, you simply select 3.3 in the Version pop-up menu in the Save dialog box. However, because QuarkXPress 4 adds a host of new features, expect the following when you save in version 3.3 format:

✦ Bézier boxes become polygon boxes. For Bézier boxes composed of several distinct shapes, such as text converted to a box, the shapes will be connected by thin lines.

✦ Bézier lines become straight lines.

✦ Text paths become text boxes, following the angle of the path.

✦ Boxes with a content type of None remain with that content type, but they cannot be changed to picture boxes or text boxes in QuarkXPress 3.3.

✦ Anchored lines and anchored nonrectangular boxes become anchored rectangular boxes.

✦ Custom dashes and stripes become solid lines.

✦ Gap colors in dashes and stripes become white for frames and no color for lines.

✦ QuarkXPress-created clipping paths are removed.

✦ Runaround paths are converted to Manual and reshaped as polygons. (None and Item runarounds are retained as is.)

✦ Text running around all sides of an object runs around just one side.

✦ Only the first 128 each of paragraph styles, color definitions, and H&J sets are retained.

✦ Character styles are removed, with the formatting converted to local text formatting.

✦ Only the first 20 tab stops per line are retained; all other tabs are spaced at half-inch increments.

✦ Only (!) the first 65,000 paragraphs are retained.

✦ Drop caps of more than eight characters are retained unless you change any of the attributes of the Paragraph Formats dialog box in QuarkXPress 3.3—at that point, you must make the number of characters be eight or fewer.

✦ Color profiles are removed.

✦ Multi-ink and Hexachrome colors are converted to RGB.

✦ List definitions are removed, although any built lists remain in the document.

The following attributes are saved in version 3.3, although QuarkXPress 3.3 does not use them. If the document is opened later in version 4, these features reappear:

✦ Index tags

✦ Books

The file extension difference

The difference between All Append Sources and Display All Files is that All Append Sources displays only files with the .QXD, .QXT, .QXL, and .ASV file extensions. That's fine if you're in a Windows-only environment, because Windows QuarkXPress automatically adds these file extensions to the files you create.

But Mac QuarkXPress does not add such file extensions, so to display Mac files in the Windows QuarkXPress Append dialog box, you need to have Display All Files selected as the file type. (On Mac QuarkXPress, the Append dialog box shows all Mac-created QuarkXPress documents, templates, libraries, and autosaved files, as well as all PC-created files—those without a Mac file type and file creator ID embedded in them—as long as they have an acceptable file extension.)

Dealing with Mixed-Platform Issues

The following sections cover the differences between the Mac and Windows. As a cross-platform application, QuarkXPress will appeal strongly to all sorts of users who find that they deal with "the other side." This includes corporate users whose various divisions have standardized on different platforms, service bureaus whose clients use different machines, and independent publishers or layout artists who deal with a range of clients.

QuarkXPress differences

Since version 3.2 for Macintosh and 3.12 for Windows, Quark has done a good job in making its Macintosh and Windows versions compatible. And since version 3.3 on both systems, Quark has offered nearly identical functionality. For example, QuarkXPress 4 can read document files from either platform; however, the Windows version may not recognize a Mac-generated file as a QuarkXPress file unless you do one of the following two things:

✦ Add the file extension .QXD to the Mac-generated file's name.

✦ Select the Display All Files in the File Type pop-up menu in the Open dialog box (File⇨Open, or Ctrl+O).

Supported formats

QuarkXPress for Macintosh version 4 can read Windows version 3.1, 3.3, and 4 files; Windows QuarkXPress version 4 can read Macintosh 3.0, 3.1, 3.2, 3.3, and 4 files. (There was no Windows version 3.2.)

On the Mac, you'll typically not be able to double-click a PC-generated QuarkXPress document; instead, you'll need to open it from the Open dialog box (File⇨Open, or ⌘+O).

Which elements transfer

The following elements may be transferred across platforms, with the following limits noted:

To copy elements, use the Append button in the relevant dialog box. To export and import elements, use the Export and Import buttons in the relevant dialog box. All are described earlier in this chapter.

✦ **Graphics:** Any graphics not supported by the platform version are replaced during printing with their PICT preview images (on the Mac) or Windows Metafile preview images (in Windows). However, the graphics links are retained, so if you move the document back to the originating platform, the original graphics will again be available for printing.

✦ **Graphics previews:** Some PICT previews from the Mac and some Windows Metafile previews on Windows will not translate correctly when transferred. You must reimport or update the link to the graphic to generate a new preview.

✦ **Colors:** Colors are retained. They can also be imported across platforms.

✦ **Color profiles:** Although color profile files cannot be exchanged across the two platforms, Mac and Windows QuarkXPress retain color-profile information from the other platform's files. And if both platforms have color profiles for the same device (monitor, scanner, printer, etc.), QuarkXPress will apply the correct color profiles. If a color profile is not available on the new platform, you can apply a new profile or ignore the issue. (If you ignore the issue, the correct profile will be in place when you bring the document back to the original platform.) If you print with a missing profile, QuarkXPress will substitute the default profile based on the type of color model used (RGB, CMYK, or Hexachrome).

✦ **Style sheets:** Style sheets are retained. They can also be imported across platforms.

✦ **H&J sets:** H&J sets are retained. They can also be imported across platforms.

✦ **Lists:** Lists are retained. They can also be imported across platforms.

✦ **Dashes and stripes:** Dashes and stripes are retained. They can also be imported across platforms.

✦ **Bitmap frames:** Bitmap frames created on the Mac are retained in Windows documents; Windows QuarkXPress cannot create bitmap frames.

✦ **Hyphenation exceptions:** Hyphenation exceptions are retained.

✦ **Document preferences:** Document preferences are retained, but the XPress Preferences file cannot be shared across platforms.

✦ **Print styles:** Print styles are retained. They can also be exported and imported across platforms.

✦ **Auxiliary spelling dictionaries:** Auxiliary spelling dictionaries can be used on both platforms.

✦ **Kerning data:** Kerning data exported from the Mac can be imported into Windows. However, we do not recommend doing this kind of transfer because the font characteristics on the two platforms are different enough that you should customize the kerning on each separately.

✦ **XTensions:** Cool Blends and other XTensions must be present on both platforms if you are moving documents that use XTensions' features. If you don't have an XTension on, say, Windows and try to load a Mac document that uses that XTension's capabilities, you may get an error message saying that the document cannot be opened.

✦ **Document previews:** Although the Windows version does not save preview images for the Open dialog box, such previews created on the Mac are retained even if the document is moved to Windows and back.

Which elements don't transfer

Quark has removed almost every barrier between Mac and Windows in the latest version of QuarkXPress. With version 4, only libraries cannot be moved across platforms. The database systems underlying the libraries are not compatible, so the libraries cannot be shared.

Platform differences

There are also some general differences between Windows and Macintosh themselves that will add a few bumps along the road to cross-platform exchange. The following sections will prepare you for the jolts.

Filenames

The most noticeable difference between Windows and Macintosh is the file-naming convention.

Macintosh filenames

Macintosh files follow these rules:

✦ Names are limited to 31 characters.

✦ Any character may be used except for colons (:), which are used by the Macintosh system software internally to separate the folder name (which is not visible on-screen) from the filename.

✦ Case does not matter: "FILE," "file," and "File" are all considered to be the same name. If you have a file named "FILE" and create or copy a file named "file," "FILE" will be overwritten.

Windows filenames

Windows files follow these rules:

✦ Names are limited to 250 characters.

✦ Names must have a file extension of up to 3 characters, which is almost always added automatically by programs to identify the file type. A period separates the filename from the extension: Filename.ext. Windows 95 hides these file extensions from view, unless you use the View option in View⇨Options in a drive or folder window to make Windows 95 display them.

✦ Names may use any characters except for most punctuation: pipes (|), colons (:), periods (.), asterisks (*), double quotes ("), less-than symbols (<), greater-than symbols (>), question marks (?), slashes (/), and backslashes (\), which are all used by Windows to separate parts of paths (file locations, such as drives and folders) or to structure commands. A period may be used as the separator between a filename and an extension.

✦ Case does not matter: "FILE," "file," and "File" are all considered to be the same name. If you have a file named "FILE" and create or copy a file named "file," "FILE" will be overwritten.

Renaming files for transfer

When you bring Mac QuarkXPress files and any associated graphics to Windows, you'll have to translate the Mac names into names that are legal on Windows. Similarly, you'll need to make Windows filenames Mac-legal when going in the other direction. This rule applies not only to the QuarkXPress document but also to any associated files, including kerning tables, graphics, and auxiliary dictionaries. If you rename these files, either before transferring or while transferring, you'll find that within the QuarkXPress document itself, the original names are still used. When QuarkXPress tries to open these files, it will look for them by their original names.

Using a universal naming convention

The simplest way to ensure that you won't have problems with transferred files looking for incompatible names is to use a naming convention that satisfies both Windows and Mac standards. That means you should:

✦ Keep filenames to 27 characters or less.

✦ Always include the PC file extension (which adds 4 characters to the full name, hitting the Mac limit of 31). Use .QXD for documents, .QXT for templates, .QDT for auxiliary dictionaries, .QPJ for printer styles, and .KRN for kerning tables. Typical extensions for cross-platform graphics are .TIF for TIFF, .EPS for Encapsulated PostScript, .AI for Adobe Illustrator, .PCT for PICT, .PCX for PC Paintbrush, .BMP and .RLE for Microsoft bitmap, .GIF for Graphics Interchange Format, .CGM for Computer Graphics Metafiles, .WMF for Windows metafile, .CDR for CorelDraw, .PLT for HPGL plots, and .SCT or .CT for Scitex.

✦ Don't use the pipe (|), colon (:), period (.), asterisk (*), double quote ("), less-than symbol (<), greater-than symbol (>), question mark (?), slash (/), or backslash (\) characters.

Font differences

Although the major typeface vendors like Adobe Systems and Bitstream offer their typefaces for both Windows and Macintosh users, these typefaces are not always the same on both platforms. Cross-platform differences are especially common among typefaces created a few years ago when multiplatform compatibility was not a goal for most users or vendors. Differences occur in the following four areas:

✦ **Internal font name:** The name used by the printer and type scalers such as Adobe Type Manager is not quite the same for the Mac and Windows version of a typeface. This discrepancy will result in an alert box listing the fonts used in the document that are not on your Mac (or PC). The solution is to use the Font Usage dialog box or the Find/Replace dialog box (covered in Chapter 11) to replace all instances of the unrecognized font name with the correct one for the current platform.

✦ **Character width information:** Even if typefaces use the same internal names, the font files' tracking, kerning, and other character width information may be different on the two platforms, possibly resulting in text reflow. The solution is to check the ends of all your stories to make sure text did not get shorter or longer.

✦ **Symbols:** These do not always translate properly. Even when created by the same vendors, the character maps for each font file differ across platforms because Windows and the Macintosh use different character maps. This problem is complicated by the fact that some vendors didn't stick to the standard character maps for a platform or didn't implement all symbols in all their typefaces. The solution is to proofread your documents, note the symbols that are incorrect, and then use the Find/Change dialog box to replace them with the correct symbol. (Highlight the incorrect symbol and use the copy and paste commands to put it in the Text field of the Find/Change dialog box rather than trying to figure out the right keypad code in Windows or the right keyboard shortcut on the Mac.)

✦ **Ligatures:** These are supported only on the Mac (Windows doesn't support ligatures at all, except in expert fonts). Windows QuarkXPress will use just the regular *fi*, *fl*, *ffi*, and *ffl* letter combinations, and Mac QuarkXPress will reinstate the ligatures if you bring the file back to the Mac.

Tip

To minimize font problems, use a program like Macromedia's Fontographer (415/252-2000, http://www.macromedia.com) to translate your TrueType and PostScript font files from Mac to Windows format or vice versa. (Fontographer is available in both Mac and Windows versions.) This will ensure that the internal font names, width information, and symbols are the same on both platforms.

File transfer products

Moving files between Macs and Windows PCs is easier now than ever before, thanks to a selection of products on both platforms that let each machine read the other's disks (floppies, removable disks like Zip disks, and even hard drives). Here is a brief summary of the major products:

✦ **Easy Open and PC Exchange:** The combination of Mac OS Easy Open and PC Exchange, both included in the Mac System software from Apple Computer (408/996-1010, http://www.apple.com), lets you use Windows disks in a Mac floppy drive or removable drive and lets the Mac recognize files immediately and know which applications are compatible with each type of PC file. PC Exchange also can automatically add the right Mac icon and file type information to a Windows file transferred to the Mac based on the Windows file's extension.

✦ **DOS Mounter 95:** This Mac utility, from Software Architects (206/487-0122, http://www.softarch.com), is similar to PC Exchange except that it lets you select between Windows 95 filenames and Windows 3.1 filenames.

✦ **Here & Now:** Software Architects' Here & Now gives Windows PCs the ability to read and write Mac disks.

✦ **MacLinkPlus:** This Mac program, from DataViz (203/268-0030, http://www.dataviz.com), includes file translation (DataViz's own translators). (It relies on PC Exchange or DOS Mounter 95 to make PC disks accessible on the Mac.) The version called MacLinkPlus/PC Connect includes a serial cable through which you can connect a Mac to a PC (making sort of a two-computer network).

✦ **MacOpener:** DataViz's MacOpener program lets PCs read and write Mac disks, although it includes none of the file-translation features of the other DataViz products.

✦ **Conversions Plus:** DataViz's Conversions Plus gives Windows PCs the ability to read and write Mac disks as well as to translate file formats.

Using a cross-platform network

Another method of transferring files is to use a cross-platform network. Here are some products that can assist you:

✦ **Timbuktu Pro:** Farallon Communications' Timbuktu Pro (510/814-5000, http://www.farallon.com) lets both Macs and PCs exchange files via an Ethernet or TCP/IP network.

✦ **PC MacLAN:** Miramar Systems' PC MacLAN (805/966-2432, http://www.miramarsys.com) lets a Windows 95 or NT PC act as a server to Macs and other PCs via an Ethernet network. Miramar also has a version that lets Windows 95 PCs dial into Mac-based Apple Remote Access (ARA) networks.

✦ **NetWare IPX:** For larger networks, you'll likely want to use networks based on Novell's NetWare IPX protocol and on Ethernet wiring; you'll need a consultant or in-house network manager to set such large networks up.

Hidden files and extension maps

The Macintosh assigns a hidden file type and creator code to each file; this hidden file tells it which icon to display for the file and which program to launch if you double-click the file. Windows files have no such hidden file types and creator codes, so they will appear as either SimpleText or PC binary files when you move them to the Mac. To load these files into QuarkXPress (or other Mac applications), you must first load your application and then use the File⇨Open (⌘+O) command.

PC Exchange, DOS Mounter 95, Here & Now, MacLinkPlus, Conversions Plus, MacOpener, Timbuktu Pro, and PC MacLAN all can be set to automatically create these hidden file types and creator codes based on the Windows file's extension, which means that you can double-click the transferred files. Shown here is a sample extension map in DOS Mounter 95.

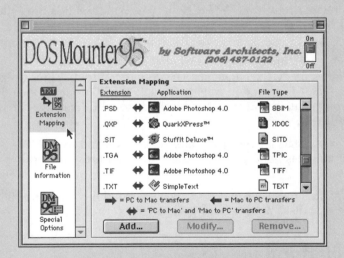

Be warned that not all Mac applications will display SimpleText or PC binary files in their Open dialog boxes, under the mistaken assumption that the files couldn't possibly be compatible files missing only their hidden file information. You'll have to use a program like Apple's free ResEdit to create the hidden file (by changing the creator and file type for the PC file), and at this point, you need a Mac guru to show you how to use ResEdit because a mistake could corrupt your file irreparably. Fortunately, Mac QuarkXPress doesn't suffer from this problem.

Working with Service Bureaus

Service bureaus are great. They keep and maintain all the equipment, know the ins and outs of both your software and your printing press requirements, and turn around jobs quickly—at least most of the time. Working with a service bureau involves commitment and communication between both parties. They need your business; you need their expertise and equipment. The following sections offer some sage advice on establishing a productive relationship with your service bureau.

Understanding the standards

To ensure that you get what you want (fast, accurate service) and that the service bureau gets what it wants (no-hassle clients and printing jobs), make sure that you both understand your standards and needs. As a customer, keep in mind that the service bureau has many other customers, all of whom do things differently. Service bureaus likewise must not impose unreasonable requirements just for the sake of consistency, because customers have good reasons for doing things differently.

Collecting for output

If you've ever had the experience of giving a QuarkXPress document to a service bureau, only to be called several hours later by the person who is outputting your document because some of the files necessary to output it are missing, you will love the Collect for Output feature in QuarkXPress. This command, which you access by choosing File⇨Collect for Output, copies all of the text and picture files necessary to output your document into a folder. It also generates a report that contains all the information about your document that a service bureau is likely ever to need, including the document's fonts, dimensions, and trapping information.

New Feature

In QuarkXPress 4, the Collect for Output feature has a new checkbox: Report Only. This generates a report about the document's elements without copying all the associated files.

How it works

The Collect for Output feature generates two very useful things to take to your service bureau:

✦ A folder that contains every graphic used by your document

✦ A report listing all the specifications of the document (see Figure 22-13)

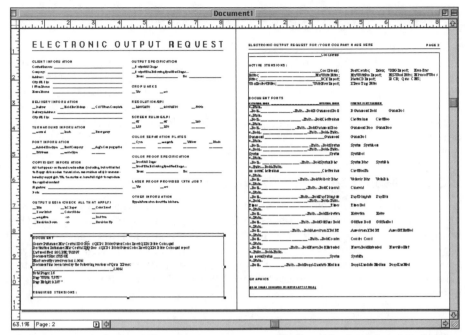

Figure 22-13: Part of a Collect for Output report, displayed in the Output Request Template.

Dealing with missing files

If a picture file is missing or has been modified, an alert is displayed. Click List Pictures to display the Missing/Modified Pictures dialog box. Note that if you click OK, and continue with Collect for Output without updating missing or modified pictures, Collect for Output will be unable to collect all the necessary files to output your document correctly. Select each modified picture and click Update to automatically update the picture file. Select each missing picture and click Update to display the Find dialog box. Locate the missing picture file, select it, and click Open. Click OK in the Missing/Modified Pictures dialog box to continue with Collect for Output.

The document statistics report

Collect for Output creates a document statistics Report file and places it in the same folder as the copy of the document and the picture files. The Report file is in XPress Tags format and it contains the following information:

✦ Document name, date, total pages, width, and height

✦ The document's original location and the location to which it is copied

✦ Version of QuarkXPress, file size, required XTensions, and active XTensions

✦ A list of any necessary color profiles (if the Quark CMS XTension is active)

✦ Names of the fonts used (remember that copying the font files is potentially a violation of copyright law)

✦ Pictures used (size, box/picture angle, skew, path name, type, fonts in EPS, and location in document)

✦ Resolution of pictures

✦ The names of style sheets and H&J sets

✦ Each color created and information to reproduce custom colors

✦ Trapping information

✦ Color plates required for each page

Using the output request template

QuarkXPress provides the Output Request Template (called Output.qxt in Windows) to contain the Report file (it is placed in your QuarkXPress folder when you install the program). Open the template (File⇨Open, or ⌘+O) and customize the template to suit your needs. Click on the text box on the lower half of the template and choose File⇨Get Text to import the Collect for Output report. Make sure Include Style Sheets is checked.

Tip

We strongly recommend using the Collect for Output feature. It ensures that your service bureau has all the necessary files and information to output your document correctly.

Sending documents versus output files

Now that you have Collect for Output, do you give the service bureau your actual QuarkXPress documents or do you send a PostScript output file? The answer depends on the following things:

✦ A document file, even if the graphics files are copied with it, takes less space than a PostScript file created from your document, which means fewer disks or cartridges to sort through and less time copying files from your media to theirs.

✦ A document file can be accidentally changed, resulting in incorrect output. For example, a color might be changed accidentally when the service bureau checks your color definitions to make sure that spot colors are translated to process colors. Or document preferences might be lost, resulting in text reflow.

✦ The service bureau cannot edit most attributes in a PostScript file. So the service bureau can't come to your rescue if you make a mistake such as forgetting to print registration marks when outputting the PostScript file or specifying landscape printing mode for a portrait document.

✦ PostScript files cannot contain QuarkXPress trapping information, so any trapping settings you create in QuarkXPress for the document will be lost.

Basically, the question is whom do you trust more: yourself or the service bureau? Only you can answer that. But in either case, there are two things that you can do to help prevent miscommunication: provide the Collect for Output file and report to the service bureau and also provide a proof copy of your document. The service bureau uses these tools to see if its output matches your expectations—regardless of whether you provided a document file or PostScript file.

Determining output settings

A common area of miscommunication between designers and service bureaus is determining who sets controls over line screens, registration marks, and other output controls. (Document-specific controls are covered in Chapter 24; general issues are covered earlier in this chapter.) Whoever has the expertise to make the right choices should handle these options. It should be clear to both parties who is responsible for what aspect of output controls. You don't want to use conflicting settings or accidentally override the desired settings. Here's how:

✦ **Gray-scale images:** For output controls on gray-scale images (covered in detail in Chapter 19), the layout artist should determine these settings and specify them on the proof copy provided to the service bureau.

✦ **Special effects:** If the publication has established production standards for special effects or special printing needs or if the job is unusual, we recommend that the layout artist determine the settings for such general controls as the registration marks (set in the Print dialog box's Document pane) and the printer resolution (set in the Print dialog box's Output pane). Printer setup is described in Chapter 24.

✦ **Service bureau standards:** For issues related to the service bureau's internal needs and standards, such as how much gap between pages, we recommend that the service bureau determine their own settings. If you are sending the service bureau PostScript files instead of QuarkXPress documents, you will have to enter such settings in the Print dialog box's Setup pane before creating the file, so be sure to coordinate these issues with the service bureau in advance.

✦ **The printing press:** Issues related to the printing press (such as which side of the negative the emulsion should be on) should be coordinated with the printer and service bureau. Again, let the service bureau enter this data unless you send PostScript files.

✦ **Determine who's responsible:** In all cases, determine who is responsible for every aspect of output controls to ensure that someone does not specify a setting outside his or her area of responsibility without first checking with the other parties.

Smart service bureaus do know how to edit a PostScript file to change some settings, such as dpi and line-screen, that are encoded in those files, but don't count on them doing that work for you except in emergencies. And then they should let you know what they did, and why.

Ensuring correct bleeds

When you create an image that bleeds, it must actually print beyond the area defined by the crop marks. There must be enough of the bleeding image that if the paper moves slightly in the press, the image still bleeds. (Most printers expect ⅛ inch, or about a pica, of *trim* area for a bleed.) In most cases, the document page is smaller than both the page size (specified in QuarkXPress through the File⇨Document Setup option) and the paper size, so that the margin between pages is sufficient to allow for a bleed. If your document page is the same size as your paper size, the paper size limits how much of your bleed actually prints: any part of the bleed that extends beyond the paper size specified is cut off. (This problem derives from the way PostScript controls printing; it has nothing to do with QuarkXPress.)

Make sure that your service bureau knows that you are using bleeds and whether you specified a special paper or page size, because that may be a factor in the way the operator outputs your job.

Sending oversized pages

If you use a paper size larger than US letter size (8.5 × 11 inches), tell the service bureau in advance because the paper size might affect how the operator sends your job to the imagesetter. Many service bureaus use a utility program that automatically rotates pages to save film, because pages rotated 90 degrees still fit along the width of typesetting paper and film rolls. But if you specify a larger paper size to make room for bleeds or if your document will be printed at tabloid size, this rotation might cause the tops and/or bottoms of your document pages to be cut off.

We've worked with service bureaus who forgot that they loaded this page-rotation utility, so the operator didn't think to unload it for our oversized pages. It took a while to figure out what was going on, because we were certain that we weren't doing the rotation (the service bureau assumed we had) and the service bureau had forgotten that it was using the rotation utility.

✦   ✦   ✦

Color Prepress

✦ ✦ ✦ ✦

In This Chapter

Working with
color traps

Activating the Quark
CMS XTension

Adjusting color
monitor displays

Selecting output
profiles

✦ ✦ ✦ ✦

Since the mid-1980s, desktop publishing programs have
broadened their features to cover color publishing
needs and, in many cases, have made a tough job even harder
for professional color separators and printers who have seen
amateurs ruin what would have otherwise been an acceptable
piece of work. After years of education and efforts by
developers like Quark to build some of the more basic
typographic assumptions into their programs, most desktop
publishers now produce decent typographic output.
QuarkXPress's color prepress features—notably its trapping
tools (which control how adjacent colors print) and Quark
CMS (Color Management System) calibration tools (which
control how colors are actually output)—offer amateur color
publishers the same basic fallback. To use these tools
effectively, you should understand color printing, but if you
don't, the default settings in QuarkXPress can produce
decent-quality color output. This chapter covers these
defaults and goes on to illuminate subjects of interest to
those among the more adept.

Working with Color Traps

Color trapping, which controls how colors overlap and abut
when printed, is one of the most powerful features available
in QuarkXPress. It's also one that novice users can abuse
terribly. If you don't know much about trapping, leave the
features of the program at the default settings. Before you use
QuarkXPress trapping tools, study some books on color
publishing, talk to your printer, and experiment with test files
that you don't want to publish. If you are experienced with
color trapping—or after you become experienced—you'll find
QuarkXPress trapping tools a joy to use.

Note

Please note that the illustrations and figures in this chapter
are in black and white. You'll need to look at your color
monitor to see the effects of what's described here. Also take
a look at the examples in the special 16-page color insert,
which covers color techniques in color.

Who needs trapping?

If you're printing to a color laser, dye-sublimation, ink-jet, or thermal wax printer, don't worry about trapping. You're not getting the kind of output resolution at which this level of image fine-tuning is relevant. But if you're outputting to an imagesetter (particularly if you are outputting to negatives) for eventual printing on a web-offset or other printing press, read on. In either case, you'll also want to understand the color-calibration features in the Quark CMS XTension (covered later in this chapter) because it will help you get the best color fidelity possible with your images and output devices.

If you do need to get involved with trapping, use the trapping tools in the illustration program with which you create your EPS graphics. These tools will help you to finely control the settings for each image's specific needs. Also, if you are using a service bureau that does high-resolution scanning for you and strips these files into your layout before output, check to make sure that the bureau is not also handling trapping for you with a Scitex or other high-end system. If it is, make sure you ask whether and when you should be doing trapping yourself.

Choking versus spreading

So what is trapping, anyway? Trapping adjusts the boundaries of colored objects to prevent gaps between abutting colors on the final printed page. Gaps can occur because of misalignment of the negatives, plates, or printing press—all of which are impossible to avoid. Colors are trapped by processes known as *choking* and *spreading*. Both make an object slightly larger—usually by a fraction of a point—so that it overprints the abutting object slightly. The process is called choking when one object surrounds a second object, and the first object is enlarged to overlap the second. The process is known as spreading when you enlarge the surrounded object so that it leaks (bleeds) into the surrounding object.

Two trapping techniques

The difference between choking and spreading is the relative position of the two objects. Here's how it works:

✦ **Choking:** Think of choking as making the hole for the inside object smaller (which in effect makes the object on the outside larger).

✦ **Spreading:** Think of spreading as making the object in the hole larger.

The object made larger depends on the image, but you generally bleed the color of a lighter object into a darker one. If you did the opposite, you'd make objects seem ungainly. Thus, choke a dark object inside a light one, and spread a light object inside a dark one. If the objects are adjacent, spread the light object.

Figure 23-1 shows the two types of trapping techniques. Spreading (at left) makes the interior object's color bleed out; choking (at right) makes the outside color bleed in, in effect making the area of the choked element smaller. The dashed lines show the size of the interior object; as you can see in the image at right, when you choke a darker object into a lighter one, the effect is to change its size (here, the interior object gets smaller).

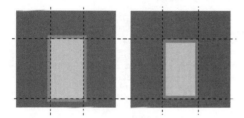

Figure 23-1: Two kinds of traps: spreading (left) and choking (right).

Knock out and overprint

In practice, trapping also involves controlling whether colors *knock out* or *overprint*. The default is to knock out—cut out—any overlap when one element is placed on top of another. If, for example, you place two rectangles on top of each other, they print like the two rectangles on the right side of Figure 23-2. If you set the darker rectangle in this figure to overprint, the rectangles print as shown on the left side of the figure. Setting colors to overprint results in mixed colors, as on the left, while setting colors to knock out results in discrete colors, as on the right.

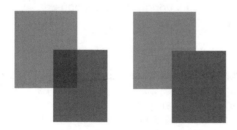

Figure 23-2: The two kinds of untrapped options: overprints (left) and knockouts.

Setting traps

You define trapping settings for separate colors in the Trap Specifications dialog box, shown in Figure 23-3. (To open the dialog box, select Edit⇨Colors or use the shortcut Shift+F12, select a color, and then click the Edit Trap button.) However, you define default trapping settings in the Trapping pane of the Document Preferences dialog box, accessed via Edit⇨Preferences⇨Document, or ⌘+Y (see the later section on setting trap defaults).

New Feature QuarkXPress 4 has made several changes to the Trap Specifications dialog box, giving you more control over the settings for each color. These changes are covered in detail in this chapter.

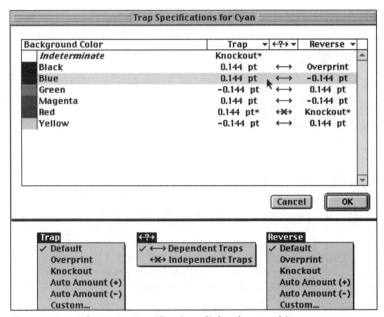

Figure 23-3: The Trap Specification dialog box and its pop-up menu options.

Object and background colors

The title of the Trap Specifications dialog box shows the color for which you are defining trapping values—the *object color*. (In Figure 23-3, trapping values are being defined for cyan.) In the Background Color list, you see all defined colors except registration, white, and the object color. You do not need to trap these colors as background colors because registration completely obscures any color spread into it. Also, white does not "mix" with other colors—it's just paper with no ink on it—and thus causes no unsightly gaps or color artifacts due to misregistration.

Note The list of background colors includes one color not defined via Edit⮕Colors: Indeterminate. This item is not exactly a color but a special case used by QuarkXPress to handle multicolored backgrounds (such as a color picture or multiple color objects abutting) for which trapping information is unavailable or is conflicting.

Using the background color option

You set options in the Trap Specifications dialog box by first selecting the background color for which you want to define the trap relationship and then selecting the corresponding Trap pop-up menu. What you are defining is the relationship between the color name in the dialog box's title (cyan in Figure 23-3) and the color selected in the dialog box's Background Color list. The relationship is for cases when the object whose color is in the dialog box overlaps an object whose color is selected (blue in Figure 23-3). In the case of Figure 23-3, we are defining the traps for cases when cyan objects are in front of objects of all other colors.

Setting the amount of trapping

The six options on the Trap pop-up menu set the actual amount of trapping between the selected colors. The options are as follows:

✦ **Default:** This means QuarkXPress chooses the amount of trap and whether the object color spreads or chokes. The settings in the Trapping pane of the Default Document Preferences dialog box form the parameters under which QuarkXPress makes these decisions.

Note

QuarkXPress will let you know when you have specified a trap other than the default by adding an asterisk (*) to the end of the trap settings in the Trap and Reverse lists (see the following section on the Reverse pop-up menu).

✦ **Overprint:** This means to print the color over the background color, in essence mixing the inks. Note that the object color must be of a darker shade than specified in the Trapping pane's Overprint Limit option in the Default Document Preferences dialog box.

✦ **Knockout:** This cuts a hole in the background object and has no trapping. Thus, a slight misalignment in the printing press could cause a gap between the two colors.

✦ **Auto Amount (+):** This means QuarkXPress spreads the object color into the selected background color. The actual trapping amount is specified in the Default Document Preferences dialog box.

✦ **Auto Amount (–):** This means QuarkXPress chokes the object color with the selected background color. The actual trapping amount is specified in the Default Document Preferences dialog box.

✦ **Custom:** This is where you specify your own trapping amount.

Note

Entering a negative trapping number chokes the object color with the background color. Entering a positive number spreads the object color into the background color. The difference between the two is subtle (as described earlier and shown in Figure 23-1) and usually comes into play for fine elements such as text and lines. If the object using the background color is thin or has a light hue, a good rule of thumb is to spread; otherwise, choke.

Using the relationship option

The Relationship option (the ←?→ pop-up menu), which is new to version 4 of QuarkXPress, lets you choose whether a trap is dependent or independent. A dependent trap is shown via the symbol ⟷, while an independent trap is shown via the symbol ←X→.

A dependent trap is one in which QuarkXPress figures out automatically, based on the settings defined in this dialog box, how to trap the same color combination when the dialog box's color is behind the selected background color. For example, if you define a trap for cases when cyan overlaps blue, having a dependent relationship means that QuarkXPress automatically defines the trap for cases when blue overlaps cyan, based on the approach you took for cyan overlapping blue. An independent relationship means you manually choose the trap settings for each direction.

The reverse pop-up menu

When you have given a color pair an independent relationship, use the option in the Reverse pop-up menu to choose the trapping for the reverse relationship. For example, if you set traps for cyan overlapping blue and you want to set traps for blue overlapping cyan independently, make the relationship independent and then select a trapping method here for blue overlapping cyan. Figure 23-3 shows different relationships for background colors behind cyan objects.

If you choose an option from the Reverse pop-up menu for a color pair that has a dependent relationship, QuarkXPress will adjust the original relationship accordingly. The relationship is dependent, so a change to one direction automatically affects the settings for the other.

Setting trap defaults

In the Trapping pane in the Document Preferences dialog box, shown in Figure 23-4, you set the defaults that Default represents in the Trap Specifications dialog box. There are several options to set in this pane, as follows:

✦ **Trapping Method:** This setting determines whether QuarkXPress uses the trapping values specified in the Auto Amount option or whether it adjusts the trapping based on the saturation of the abutting colors. If you choose Absolute, the program uses the values as is. If you choose Proportional, QuarkXPress calculates new trapping values based on the value entered in Auto Amount and the relative saturation of the abutting colors. The third option, new to QuarkXPress 4, is Knockout All, which does no trapping. The default is Absolute.

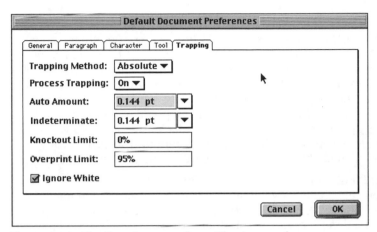

Figure 23-4: The Trapping pane for setting trap preferences.

✦ **Process Trapping:** This option controls how trapping is handled when you output to CMYK negatives. If Process Trapping is set to On, QuarkXPress examines each color plate as a whole when determining the trapping settings. For example, if you place a light blue object on a dark blue background, both objects will use cyan ink when color-separated to CMYK negatives. Because of that, QuarkXPress doesn't have to worry so much about trapping, because the cyan in both objects is on one plate and couldn't be misregistered. But the other three CMYK colors used to create the colors could misregister, because they are on their own plates, so QuarkXPress will still figure out trapping for those in relationship to the cyan plate. In other words, QuarkXPress will trap entire plates, not individual colors, with this option on.

Tip

By contrast, if the two blues were Pantone spot colors and thus printed on separate plates, QuarkXPress would need to worry about the registration of the two colors, because each would be on its own plate. There really is no reason to turn this setting to Off.

✦ **Auto Amount:** This option specifies the trapping value with which the program calculates automatic trapping for the Default, Auto Amount(+), and Auto Amount(–) options in the Trap Specifications dialog box. You can enter values from 0 to 36 points, in increments of 0.001 points. If you want the amount to be infinite (so that colors overprint), select the Overprint option in the pop-up menu. The default setting is 0.144 points.

✦ **Indeterminate:** The Indeterminate setting tells QuarkXPress how to trap objects that abut multicolored or indeterminate-colored objects, as well as imported color graphics. As with Trapping Method, this setting applies only to colors set at Default in the Trap Specifications dialog box. Valid options are 0 to 26 points, in 0.001-point increments, as well as Overprint. The default is 0.144 points.

✦ **Knockout Limit:** This value tells QuarkXPress when to automatically knock out a color object from its background (this in effect turns off trapping for that knocked-out object). The default is 0 percent, meaning that the object will not knock out of the background unless it is white (0 percent of the darkness of the background color). Ordinarily, you would want to leave this setting at 0 percent. However, if you want trapping to be turned off for sufficiently light-colored objects against sufficiently dark-colored backgrounds (to preserve object shapes where trapping isn't really necessary), you might want to increase this value slightly.

✦ **Overprint Limit:** This value tells QuarkXPress when to overprint a color object. You can specify any percentage from 0 to 100, in increments of 0.1. If you enter 50 percent, QuarkXPress specifies an overprint for any color whose trap specification is set as Overprint and whose saturation is 50 percent or greater; otherwise, it traps the color based on the Auto Amount and Trapping Method settings. This limit affects black objects regardless of whether black is set at Auto or Overprint. The default is 95 percent.

✦ **Ignore White:** If you check this option box, QuarkXPress traps an object based on all nonwhite objects abutting or behind the object. Otherwise, QuarkXPress calculates a trap based on the smaller of the Indeterminate settings and the trap specification for any other colors (including white) abutting or behind the object. This option is checked as a default because it makes little sense to trap to white (as there is nothing to trap to).

If you chose Absolute as your trapping method and also have Process Trapping turned on, QuarkXPress will divide the Auto Amount value in half and apply that to the darker shade in each plate. Thus, if the Auto Amount is 0.144 points and you have two blue objects, one with more cyan than the other, the dark object's cyan component will be choked by 0.077 points, rather than 0.144 points.

Overriding traps

Because trapping depends as much on the elements being trapped as their colors, trapping tools based solely on relationships among colors would be insufficient. That's why QuarkXPress offers the ability to override trapping settings for selected objects.

QuarkXPress 4 enhances the Trap Information palette by adding controls for setting the trap for the colors between lines in multiline frames and arrows, and for gaps. If you select a dashed or striped line (or frame), the Trap Information palette will now display a Line Middle pop-up menu (for striped lines) or a Gap pop-up menu (for dashed lines); with these new pop-up menus, you specify the trapping settings for the colors inside the stripe or dash's gaps as you would with any other element.

Doing it locally

To override trapping locally, you must first invoke the Trap Information palette, which is accessible via View➪Show Trap Information, or by the shortcut Option+F12 (Macintosh) or Ctrl+F12 (Windows). The contents of this palette depend on the type of object selected, but no matter what the contents, the palette works the same way. Figure 23-5 shows the Trap Information palette for a picture box. A text box has the same options, except the Picture option is replaced with the Text option. A line has slightly different options, because it has no background.

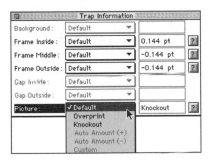

Figure 23-5: The Trap Information palette lets you see and change a box's trapping settings.

Looking at the default settings

In Figure 23-5, all four picture-box elements for which trapping is appropriate are set at Default (shown in the middle column), which means that they take on whatever settings were made globally in the Trap Specifications dialog box and the Trapping pane of the Document Preferences dialog box. Because there are so many possible combinations of colors, no one can be expected to remember how every color combination traps. Recognizing this, QuarkXPress displays what the default setting is in the column at right. Thus, in Figure 23-5, the defaults are as follows:

✦ The default for trapping the frame color with the color of the image inside the frame and/or the box background is 0.144 points (which happens to be the setting for automatic trapping in this document).

✦ The default for trapping the space between the lines in the frame (Frame Middle) is –0.144 points, because the background object is lighter than the frame color.

✦ The default for trapping the frame color with the color of the object outside (abutting) the frame is also –0.144 points, because the background object is lighter than the frame color.

✦ The default for trapping the picture with the picture box background is Knockout, which is what you would expect a picture to do. However, as an example of how you can override default settings, Figure 23-5 shows the drop-down list box for changing this last trapping setting. The last three options (Auto Amount (+), Auto Amount (–), and Custom) would be grayed out because you cannot trap a bitmap image—it either knocks out or overprints.

The trapping rationale

To further explain trapping settings, QuarkXPress describes the current trapping rationale if you select the question mark icons in the Trap Information palette. Figure 23-6 shows an example explanation for the picture box in Figure 23-5. (In the explanation, the relevant rationales are in black; the grayed text is not relevant to the particular item's trap settings.)

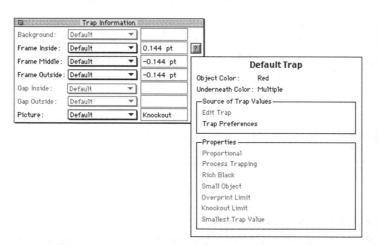

Figure 23-6: A trapping explanation that QuarkXPress provides for one of the settings in Figure 23-5.

When to use independent trapping tools

QuarkXPress's trapping tools are great for making sure color elements—lines, type, and backgrounds—created in QuarkXPress print well. But for some types of elements you'll need to go outside QuarkXPress for the right tools. For example, if you create a logo as an EPS file and place it over a TIFF photo (perhaps for a cover), QuarkXPress's trapping settings won't be applied. That's because QuarkXPress can't work with the EPS file at that level of detail. In many cases, your document will print fine, but if you see the need for trapping when you look at the match print or final output, it's time for a professional trapping tool.

One solution is to use a program like Adobe TrapWise (contact Adobe at 408/536-6000) that lets you do trapping on the EPS or DCS files you create from QuarkXPress. Of course, if you're not a trapping expert, you should have your service bureau do the trapping.

Activating the Quark CMS XTension

With the new Quark CMS (color management system) XTension, QuarkXPress can help you ensure accurate printing of your colors, both those in imported images and those defined in QuarkXPress. What Quark CMS does is track the colors in the source image, the colors displayable by your monitor, and the colors printable by your printer. If the monitor or printer does not support a color in your document, Quark CMS alters the color to its closest possible equivalent. To activate the Quark CMS, make sure the Quark CMS XTension is active (use the XTensions Manager, described in Chapter 25, to do so) and that the Color Management Active checkbox is selected in the Color Management Preferences dialog box (Edit⇨Preferences⇨Color Management), as shown in Figure 23-7.

New Feature

QuarkXPress 4 replaces the EfiColor XTension introduced in version 3.2 with Quark's own color-management technology. The basic purpose is the same, as are most methods of using it.

How Quark CMS works

Note that we do not characterize Quark CMS's capabilities as color *matching*. It is impossible to match colors produced in an illustration or paint program, or via a scanner, with what a printer or other output device can produce. The underlying differences in color models (how a color is defined) and the physics of the media (screen phosphors that emit light versus different types of papers with different types of inks that reflect light) make color matching impossible. But a calibration tool like Quark CMS can minimize differences.

The mechanism that Quark CMS uses is the profile that contains the information on color models and ranges supported by a particular creator (such as an illustration program or scanner), display, and printer. Quark CMS includes several predefined profiles and uses a device-independent color space to match these profiles against each other. A color space is a mathematical way of describing the relationships among colors.

By using a device-independent model (the CIE XYZ standard defined by the International Standards Organization), Quark CMS can compare gamuts (the boundaries within, or range of, a color space) from other device-dependent models (like RGB and the others). What this means is that Quark CMS can examine the colors in your imported images and defined colors, compare them against the capabilities of your monitor and printer, and adjust the colors for the closest possible display and printing.

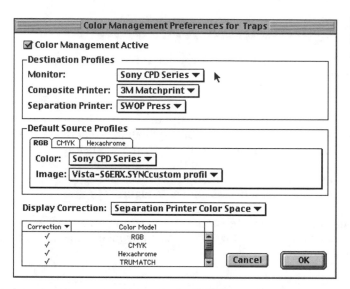

Figure 23-7: The Color Management Preferences dialog box.

Adjusting Color Monitor Displays

The Quark CMS XTension comes with profiles for several monitors, including models from Apple, NEC Technologies, and Sony. Here's how it works:

To have color calibration in effect for a monitor, you must be displaying thousands of colors (16-bit color depth) or more colors (or a higher color depth, such as 24-bit). On the Mac, use the Monitors & Sound control panel to change your monitor's bit depth. (On older Macs, use the Monitors control panel.) In Windows, use the Display control panel.

✦ You select the monitor in the Destination Profiles area of the Color Management Preferences dialog box, accessed via Edit⇨Preferences⇨Color Management (refer to Figure 23-7). The monitor that you select will tell Quark CMS how to display imported images and colors defined within QuarkXPress.

✦ You also need to tell QuarkXPress what to correct the on-screen display for, which you do with the Display Correction pop-up menu (a new feature of version 4 of QuarkXPress). Here, you decide whether to simulate the color space of your monitor, your composite printer, or your separation printer. Or you can just turn off on-screen simulation. Typically, you would choose whatever output device your pages are finally destined for.

✦ Finally, you need to tell QuarkXPress which color models to apply the display correction to. There's a list of color models at the bottom of the dialog box; simply check each color model that you want to display as correctly as possible on-screen. (Just click on the space under the Correction column adjacent to the desired color model's name.)

The on-screen appearance

It's possible to have a different on-screen appearance than Quark CMS expects. For example, your brightness and contrast settings affect how colors display, but Quark CMS has no way of gauging their settings. Likewise, you can change the color characteristics (the *gamma*) of your display in the Monitors & Sound control panel's Monitor pane. (Note that Windows does not have controls for the monitor's gamma settings.) Figure 23-8 shows the dialog box that lets you change these characteristics.

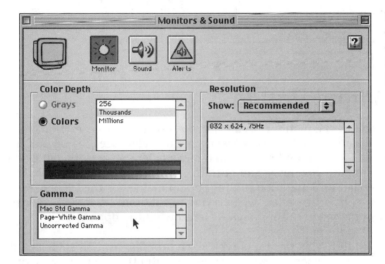

Figure 23-8: You can change your Mac monitor's color cast with the Monitors & Sound control panel.

In the figure, Mac Std Gamma is selected, which is the setting that calibration products like Quark CMS expect. But you may want to select Uncorrected Gamma, which makes the monitor display colors as the manufacturer originally intended. Apple's monitors have a slightly bluish cast to them (which makes whites appear whiter). A monitor's display usually appears more vivid without the Mac gamma, so some people change the gamma to Uncorrected Gamma to get a more pleasing display.

Calibrations from other programs

Other programs may have similar settings for calibrating their display against your type of monitor. For example, Adobe Photoshop offers such an option (via File⇨Color Preferences⇨Monitor Setup), as Figure 23-9 shows. If you're creating colors in a program and importing those colors into QuarkXPress, it's important to have them calibrated the same way, or at least as closely as the different programs will allow.

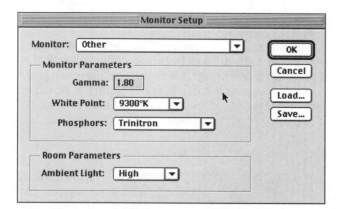

Figure 23-9: Programs like Adobe Photoshop also let you select a specific monitor to help color calibration be accurate.

Selecting Output Profiles

In addition to selecting the monitor profile and on-screen color correction, you can also set the output profiles in the Color Management Preferences dialog box. The Composite Print and Separation Printer pop-up menus let you select what printers you use for your output. Obviously, you need to choose an output device in the Composite Printer and/or Separation printer pop-up menus for the Display Correction option to have any effect when trying to calibrate on-screen color to match the color of the target output device. Here's what the options mean:

✦ **Composite printer:** This printer is typically a proofing printer, such as a dye-sublimation printer, used to see colors before outputting to negatives, or an output process like 3M's Matchprint service that produces a laminated image meant to simulate the colors that the printing press will produce.

✦ **Separation printer:** This is a web offset or other printing press that uses multiple color plates to produce the output. A separation printer can also be a printer like the Tektronix Phaser line of dye-sublimation printers that actually outputs each of the CMYK colors separately, creating in essence separate negatives.

Setting the default source profiles

The last set of profile information to select is for the default source profiles, also in the Color Management Preferences dialog box. There are three panes: RGB, CMYK, and Hexachrome, and two pop-up menus for each—Color and Image. For each color model used, select the source profile with the following pop-up menus:

✦ **Color:** Use this to select the device in which you plan to define the majority of your colors. This is typically a monitor for RGB colors and a printer for CMYK colors (the printer you intend to output to).

Monitor calibration caveats

To have truly accurate color-calibration and display on your monitor, you should use a calibrated monitor, which is usually composed of a specially designed monitor and a calibration tool that senses the color output on-screen. Such displays are very expensive and must be used in a room with specially controlled lighting.

For most users, the variances in monitor brightness, color balance, and contrast—coupled with the varying types of lighting used in their work space—mean that true calibration is impossible for images created on-screen and displayed on-screen. Still, using the calibration feature will make the on-screen color closer to what you'll print, even if not a near-exact match.

✦ **Image:** Use this to select the device that created the majority of images you plan to import. This is typically a scanner or printer for RGB colors but could be a monitor if you create original artwork in QuarkXPress, Photoshop, Illustrator, or some other program. For CMYK images, this is typically a printer (the one you intend to output to).

Make sure that you use the same color profiles wherever possible in all the programs you use to create images and colors—QuarkXPress, your image editor (Photoshop, Corel Photo-Paint, MetaCreations Painter, etc.), and your illustration program (Illustrator, FreeHand, CorelDraw, etc.). Almost every professional program now uses the ICC color profiles that QuarkXPress does, so such consistent color model use should be easy to achieve.

Defining color models

Whether you define colors in QuarkXPress or in your illustration or paint program, the method you use to define them is critical to ensuring the best possible output. It's best to define all colors in the same model as the target output device. Use the following guidelines (see Chapter 21 for more details on color models and defining color):

✦ If your printer is RGB, use the RGB model to define colors.

✦ If your printer is CMYK (like an offset printer), use CMYK to define colors.

✦ If you are using Pantone colors for traditional offset printing, pick the Pantone or Pantone Uncoated models if using Pantone inks. Pick Pantone ProSim (also called Pantone Solid to Process) if your printer is using inks from companies other than Pantone.

✦ If you are using Hexachrome colors for high-fidelity offset printing, pick the Hexachrome model.

✦ If you are using Pantone colors for traditional offset printing, pick the Pantone Process model if you will color-separate those colors into CMYK.

✦ Trumatch and Focoltone colors were designed to reproduce accurately whether output as spot colors or color-separated into CMYK. Other models (such as Toyo and DIC) may or may not separate accurately for all colors, so check with your printer or the ink manufacturer.

✦ If you're using any Pantone, Focoltone, Trumatch, Toyo, or DIC color and outputting to a desktop color printer (whether RGB or CMYK), watch to ensure that the color definition does not lie outside the printer's gamut, as explained in the next section.

✦ Never rely on the screen display to gauge any non-RGB color. Even with Quark CMS's monitor calibration, RGB monitors simply cannot match most non-RGB colors. Use the on-screen colors only as a guide and rely instead on a color swatchbook from your printer or the color ink's manufacturer.

✦ Quark CMS does *not* calibrate color in EPS files. If you use EPS, we strongly recommend that you use the DCS (pre-separated CMYK) variant.

Calibrating imported colors

When you load an image into QuarkXPress, the Quark CMS XTension applies the default settings defined in the Color Management Preferences dialog box (these are described earlier in this chapter). You can change these settings, however, as you import each file by using the Profile pop-up menu in the Get Picture dialog box, shown in Figure 23-10. You also can have an image color-corrected by checking the Color Correction box. Remember: Color correction is an attempt to match colors, not a guarantee. Here are your options:

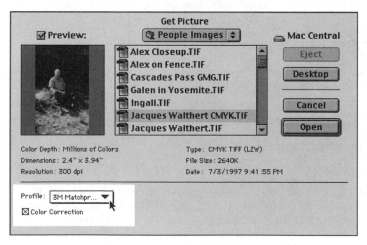

Figure 23-10: Apply color profiles and color correction when importing pictures.

✦ **For CMYK files:** Quark CMS lets you apply only target-printer profiles, such as SWOP-Coated, to CMYK files. This limitation exists because Quark CMS assumes that the image is designed for output to that specific printer and thus will calibrate it with that target in mind.

✦ **For RGB files:** Quark CMS lets you apply monitor-oriented profiles such as Sony CPD or scanner-oriented profiles such as Vista-S6E reflective, in addition to RGB printer-oriented profiles such as Epson Color Stylus. Quark CMS assumes that the image's output should be matched as closely as possible to the originating device's representation.

Note

You may need to wait for ten or more seconds for the Profile pop-up menu to appear because Quark CMS must read the file to determine what options are valid.

Changing profiles after import

You can also change profiles after you import an image by selecting a picture box and using the Profile Information palette (View➪Show Profile Information). Figure 23-11 shows the resulting dialog box (at top). Note that this option will not appear if Quark CMS is not installed and active. If you open a QuarkXPress document with a copy of QuarkXPress that does not have the Quark CMS XTension installed, your profile information is retained for the next time you open it in a copy of QuarkXPress that has Quark CMS installed.

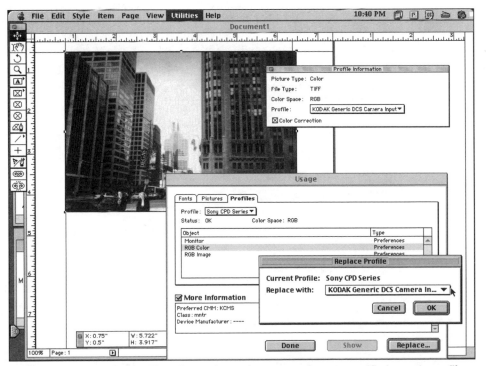

Figure 23-11: Use the Profile Information palette to replace a specific image's profile (top), and the Usage dialog box to globally replace a profile (bottom).

Determining and updating profiles

If you are unsure of which profiles a document uses (perhaps someone else put together the document that you are working on), you can use the Usage dialog box (Utilities⇨Usage, and then click the Profiles tab) and click the Replace button to get the dialog box shown at the bottom of Figure 23-11. You can also use this dialog box to update any missing profiles or to change to a new profile after you've installed it in your system.

Note

Note that the Usage dialog box replaces the profile for all images using a particular profile, while the Profile Information palette replaces the profile for the selected image only.

Setting printing options

By setting the Quark CMS profiles when defining colors or importing images, you have done most of the work needed to calibrate your colors for optimal output. Still, you have the following options:

✦ In the Print dialog box's Color Management pane (use File⇨Print or ⌘+P to get the Print dialog box), you can choose a profile for output other than the one used as the default for your document. This is handy when printing to a different printer than usual. Figure 23-12 shows the Color Management pane.

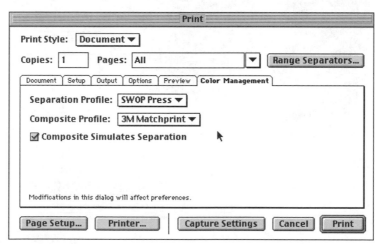

Figure 23-12: You can adjust color calibration when printing.

✦ In the same pane, you can also have QuarkXPress try to make a composite proof look like the ultimate separated output by checking the Composite Simulates Separation check box. Use this when you are printing proof copies on a printer or other device before outputting the final pages to negatives for use on a SWOP press.

The Composite Simulates Separation feature is new to version 4 of QuarkXPress. But you can no longer adjust the composition of gray elements in your images to make them sharper—a process called *GCR* or *gray component removal*.

✦   ✦   ✦

Printing Techniques

✦ ✦ ✦ ✦

In This Chapter

Choosing the right printer

Getting ready to print

Printing with QuarkXPress

Working with spot colors and separations

Creating print styles

✦ ✦ ✦ ✦

This chapter deals with putting the efforts of your work on paper—an exciting prospect after hours, days, and sometimes weeks of intensive labor. Like any other aspect of using QuarkXPress, there are a few tricks to be learned on the way, but by and large, the printing process is pretty straightforward. One of the first decisions you have to make (and hopefully you've made it before you created the documents you want to commit to paper) is the type of printer you want to use. This topic, as well as the options specific to Macintosh, to Windows, and to QuarkXPress itself, are all dealt with here. There's also a section on creating print styles.

Choosing the Right Printer

Choosing the right printer (the hardware, not the nice people who put ink on paper) is an important part of the publishing process. QuarkXPress documents can be printed on a wide variety of printers, from dot matrix printers to imagesetters. Here is a very simple overview of your choices:

✦ **Dot matrix printers:** These print by applying dots of ink, pressed by pins through inked ribbons, to form images on paper. You measure the resolution (clarity of the image) produced by dot matrix printers by the number of pins they have; the higher the number of pins, the better the image quality. (Chances are, if you have a dot matrix printer, it has either 9 or 24 pins and produces between 72 and 144 dots per inch.) If you're a publisher, you won't want to use a dot matrix printer for printing rough proof copies because of their relatively slow speed and low output quality, and we definitely don't recommend their use for final pages.

✦ **Inkjet printers:** These print by ejecting dots of ink onto paper. The appearance of images printed on inkjet printers is generally smoother than that of those printed on dot matrix printers. The reason is that the dots of ink applied to paper by inkjet printers tend to blend together, instead of remaining separate dots as on a dot matrix printer. Inkjet printers have come a long way in recent years. You can now buy color inkjet printers that provide 1440-dpi resolution for about $500 ($1000 for a version with PostScript and a network connector), and black-and-white inkjets have all but disappeared. These make great color-proofing printers, except for one thing: very slow speed. Inkjets are fine for do-it-yourself color documents and as an adjunct to a laser or other high-end printer.

✦ **Dye-sublimation and thermal-wax printers:** These print by using dry color media and heating them onto a page. A dye-sub printer uses film with embedded dyes and heat-transfers the image from the film onto paper. A thermal-wax printer melts colored waxes and lays the wax onto the page similar to how an inkjet printer sprays paper with its ink nozzles. Both are used for professional color output, although usually to create comps, not final output or rigorous color proofs. (These printers' colors approximate, but do not match, final color output from a printing press.) These printers can cost from $5000 to $15,000.

✦ **Laser printers:** These print by making a laser-light impression of the page image on a drum, adhering toner to that image, and then transferring the toner image to paper. The output quality from a laser printer is about equal to that of inkjet printers, largely because laser printers print at a high resolution (typically 600 dots per inch), which is great for black-and-white and gray-scale output. Color laser printers do exist and are getting cheaper, but they're not in the same league yet as inkjets or more established color technologies like dye sublimation. Pages produced on a black-and-white laser printer are great for proofing. Some people use laser output for their camera-ready pages; whether or not this is a good idea is a judgment call. Laser output is very useful for proofing work before you send it to your service bureau. It is also adequate for documents such as correspondences, simple newsletters, or price sheets. But laser output does not have a high enough quality for high-end publications such as newspapers and magazines. If you want your document to have a polished, professional appearance, we recommend that you have it produced on an imagesetter.

✦ **Imagesetters:** These are high-end output devices that produce your document pages on film or photo paper, ready to be printed. Imagesetter resolution ranges between roughly 1200 and 4000 dots per inch. When you send a document to a service bureau, it is output on an imagesetter. Pages produced on an imagesetter and then printed professionally have a professional look that is well worth the small expense involved. We strongly recommend outputting your final pages to an imagesetter.

Getting Ready to Print

When you are ready to print a QuarkXPress document, first make sure that the Document Setup dialog box and Setup pane in the Print dialog boxes are set up the way you'd like them to be. These dialog boxes let you change the size of the document and control the way that it prints. They also let you specify paper size, the orientation of images on the page, and the page image size. To display the Document Setup dialog box, use File⊃Document Setup, or the shortcut Option+Shift+⌘+P. To display the Setup pane in the Print dialog box, choose File⊃Page Setup or use the shortcut Option+⌘+P. Figure 24-1 shows the dialog boxes.

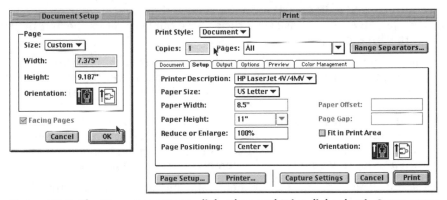

Figure 24-1: The Document Setup dialog box and Print dialog box's Setup pane.

Setting up your document

The Document Setup dialog box is where you set the size of your printed page. The dimensions set here determine where the crop marks appear, if you print registration and crop marks (as described later). Options you can set in the Setup pane include the following:

✦ **Printer Description:** This is a pop-up menu that lists the printers for which a PostScript printer description file (PPD) is available. On the Mac, these files are installed in the Printer Descriptions folder (in the Extensions folder, which is in the System Folder), although QuarkXPress will also find them if they are in a folder named "PPD" within the QuarkXPress folder. On Windows 95, these files are typically installed in the System folder inside the folder that contains the Windows OS (usually called Windows or Win95). Printers should come with a disk that contains these files and installs them in the appropriate Mac or Windows location. QuarkXPress has printer descriptions appropriate for common printers and imagesetters.

QuarkXPress 4 no longer uses Printer Description Files (PDFs). Now it uses only PPDs.

✦ **Paper Size, Width, and Height:** For Paper Size, choose the size of the paper that will be used in the printer. The size of the paper you will be using does not always correspond directly to the trim size of your final document. Note that if you select a printer that is able to print on nonstandard pages (such as an imagesetter), the Paper Width and Paper Height fields of the dialog box become active so that you can specify the size of the paper.

✦ **Paper Offset and Page Gap:** The Paper Offset and Page Gap fields are controls used in imagesetters; don't change them unless your service bureau directs you to. But do ask what the service bureau prefers the first time you work with them.

If you have elements that bleed off the page and you are printing with a commercial printing press, make sure the paper size is larger than the document size by at least $1/4$ inch wide and $1/4$ inch tall ($1/8$ inch on each side).

✦ **Reduce or Enlarge:** You can scale a page before you print it by entering a value between 25 percent and 400 percent. Printing at reduced scale is particularly useful if your document's page size is large and if you can get by with a reduced version of the document for proofing purposes.

✦ **Page Positioning:** This pop-up menu lets you align the page within the paper it is being printed on. Your choices are Left Edge (the default), Center (centers both horizontally and vertically), Center Horizontal, and Center Vertical.

✦ **Fit in Print Area:** This calculates the percentage of reduction or enlargement necessary to ensure that the document page fits fully within the paper size. Almost every printer has a gap along at least one edge where the printer grasps the paper (usually with rollers) to move it through the printing assembly. The printer can't print in this gap, so a document as large as the paper size usually has part of it cut off along one or more edges of the paper. Checking this option ensures that nothing is cut off.

✦ **Orientation:** Click on the icon that looks like a portrait to get vertical orientation of the document (taller than wide). The horizontal icon produces pages with a landscape orientation (wider than tall).

Mac-specific options

There are also setup options specific to the Mac, as shown in Figure 24-2. In Mac QuarkXPress, you get one set of these options by clicking the Page Setup button in the Print dialog box and then the Options button, and a second set of these options by clicking the Printer button and then the Options button.

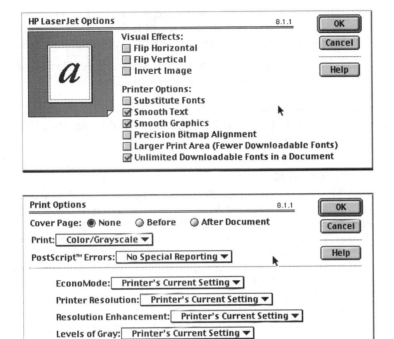

Figure 24-2: The Mac's platform-specific print setup dialog boxes.

Working with the basic options

The controls will vary from printer to printer, but here are the basic options:

✦ Check the Substitute Fonts box to substitute Times for New York, Helvetica for Geneva, and Courier for Monaco. Leaving it unchecked means that the printer will print bitmap versions of these system fonts instead (unless the appropriate TrueType or PostScript Type 1 versions are installed).

✦ To smooth the printing of bitmap fonts for which no PostScript or TrueType font is installed, check Smooth Text. You should usually leave this option unchecked, as you will probably have the PostScript or TrueType versions of most of the bitmap fonts you use.

✦ To smooth printed bitmap images, check Smooth Graphics. You may want to avoid this option if you are printing screen shots, as it may make text in dialog boxes look strange or hard to read.

✦ To print bitmap images faster, check Faster Bitmap Printing. This is usually unnecessary.

✦ If you use many fonts, check Unlimited Downloadable Fonts in a Document. This may make printing take a bit longer, but it will help to make sure all of your text prints in the correct font (especially text in imported EPS pictures).

✦ Check Precision Bitmap Alignment or Larger Print Area (Fewer Downloadable Fonts) only if requested by your service bureau or printing expert.

Avoid setting anything in these platform-specific dialog boxes that you can also set in QuarkXPress. It's better to set up local printer settings within your QuarkXPress documents than to use these global settings.

Setting up Macintosh printers

Although you choose the printer type in the Setup pane of the Print dialog box, you still need to set up the printer on your Mac before you can use it. To do that, the Mac has a program called the Chooser, which appears in the Apple menu. The Chooser will list drivers for all sorts of printers—PostScript, inkjet, dot-matrix, fax modems, whatever is installed. Make sure the printer you want to set up is connected to your Mac and turned on. (If you are using a network printer, make sure the Mac is connected to the right network port, through the AppleTalk control panel; called the Network control panel on older Macs.) Choose the appropriate driver, then select the printer from the list at right, as shown in Figure 24-3. Next, click the Setup button and configure the printer through the dialog box that then appears (this dialog box generally has several buttons for different options, and differs from printer to printer). Close the Chooser when done. Your printer is now set up.

We recommend you set Background Printing to On, so your Mac can print while you're working on other stuff. And to print on a networked printer, make sure AppleTalk is set to Active.

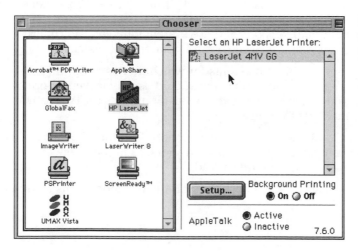

Figure 24-3: The Chooser is where you initially set up Mac printers.

Drag-and-drop printing

A few words about *drag-and-drop printing,* also called *desktop printing.* Versions 7.5 and later of the Mac OS let you create icons for each installed printer and place these icons on your desktop. You can drag a file onto a printer to have it printed; the Mac will launch the program needed to print the file. If you double-click a printer icon, you will get a list of any print jobs in progress or on hold, as shown in Figure 24-4. If a printer icon is selected, the Printing menu appears in the Finder desktop, letting you start and stop print queues and specify the default printer. (The default printer is the one that will appear in your program's Print dialog boxes. You usually need to change the default printer through the Printing menu if you want to change printers, although some programs let you change printers in their Print dialog boxes.)

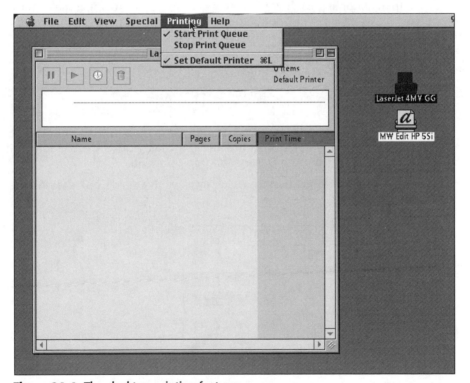

Figure 24-4: The desktop printing features.

Note

The default printer is different than the Printer Description set in the Print dialog box's Setup pane. You could select a completely different printer in the Setup pane than you're actually printing to. This usually results in no or garbled output, because the printer is getting instructions designed for a different device (the printer whose printer description was selected).

Printing to a file with the Macintosh

Rather than printing to a printer, you can print to a file. This is especially useful when the printer you need to print to is not connected to your Mac. The most common occurrence is when you are outputting your files to a service bureau's imagesetter. The imagesetter is probably miles away and is certainly not connected to your Mac. But you don't want the service bureau to open your QuarkXPress files directly and print from their Macs because you're concerned that settings might be changed accidentally. Or maybe you use XTensions they don't have and thus your files won't print from their Macs. To print to a file from a Macintosh, use the following steps:

In mid-1993, Apple Computer and Adobe Systems released the long-awaited PostScript Level 2 driver (called LaserWriter 8.x or PSPrinter 8.x, depending on which company supplied it). If you use this driver to print to a file, make sure the device you are using is Level 2-compatible. Believe it or not, PostScript Level 2 is still not supported on all printers after all of these years. (And the first Level 3 printers shipped in summer 1997!)

STEPS: Printing to a file on the Mac

1. To print to a file from the Mac, click the Printer button in the Print dialog box, and then click the File button in the resulting dialog box's Destination section or choose Printer from the Destination pop-up menu.

2. Click the Save (or Print) button, which displays the dialog box shown here.

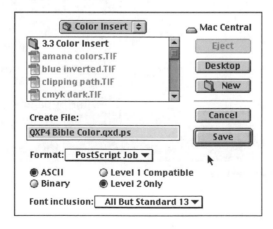

3. From the Format pop-up list, select PostScript Job. If you select the ASCII option below the Format pop-up list, your service bureau will be able to edit some of the defaults (which sometimes a savvy service bureau will do to correct a printing problem), but the file could be very large. If you select Binary, the file is much smaller but uneditable. Ask your service bureau which option it prefers.

4. Select the Level 1 Compatible option below the Format pop-up list unless you are certain the output device uses PostScript Level 2. You won't lose any capabilities by selecting Level 1 Compatible, although a Level 1 file can take longer to print on a Level 2 printer.

5. Select the appropriate option—All, All But Standard 13, or None—from the Font Inclusion pop-up list. The All But Standard 13 option includes font files for all but the 13 faces included with most PostScript printers: the regular, bold, italic, and bold italic faces in the Helvetica, Times, and Courier fonts, as well as the single face in the Symbol font. Most people should select None, because it is easier and faster for the service bureau to download the fonts used into the printer memory (your files will get very large if you include your fonts). But choose All But Standard 13 if you use unusual or custom fonts that the service bureau is unlikely to have.

Windows-specific options

Figure 24-5 shows the options specific to Windows. You get these options by selecting the Properties button in the QuarkXPress Print dialog box. The three key options are:

✦ **Graphics pane:** The resolution in the Graphics pane (it should be the highest your printer supports).

✦ **Device Options pane:** The options in the Device Options pane (specific to each printer).

✦ **PostScript pane:** The optimization options in the PostScript pane (leave this untouched unless your service bureau asks for a change).

Tip

Avoid setting anything in these platform-specific dialog boxes that you can also set in QuarkXPress. It's better to set up local printer settings within your QuarkXPress documents than to use these global settings.

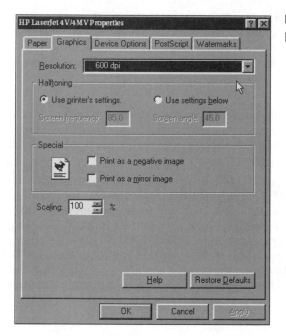

Figure 24-5: Windows-specific options for printer setup.

Setting up a Windows printer

To set up a Windows printer, use Start⟹Settings⟹Printers. You'll then see a window with a list of existing printers and an icon labeled Add New Printer. Double-click the printer to set up, or double-click Add New Printer (you'll likely need a disk that came with the printer, or the Windows CD-ROM if you add a new printer, because Windows will need information specific to that printer). When you open an existing printer, use Printer⟹Properties to get the dialog box like that shown in Figure 24-6. It is similar to the dialog box in Figure 24-5 but has more panes. Here are two that matter:

✦ **Fonts pane:** This lets you specify what happens to non-PostScript fonts when printing to a PostScript printer. The best setting is to have the printer translate TrueType fonts to PostScript and to substitute the standard PostScript fonts for the basic TrueType fonts, such as Arial and Times New Roman, as shown in Figure 24-6.

✦ **Device Options pane:** This lets you configure items such as RAM amount, as shown in Figure 24-7. Make sure this is set correctly, based on your printer's actual configuration.

Setting the default printer

To set a printer as the default printer, right-click the printer in the Printers window (Start⟹Settings⟹Printers) and select Set Default Printer from the context menu that appears.

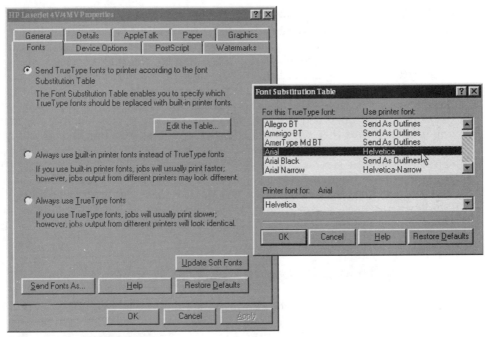

Figure 24-6: The Fonts pane.

Figure 24-7: The Device Options pane.

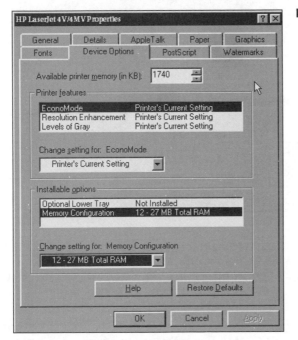

Printing to a file with Windows

Rather than printing to a printer, you can print to a file. This is especially useful for when the printer you need to print to is not connected to your PC. Again, the most common occurrence is when you are outputting your files to a service bureau's imagesetter. The imagesetter is probably miles away and is certainly not connected to your PC. But you don't want the service bureau to open your QuarkXPress files directly and print from their Macs (few service bureaus use PCs to print from) because you're concerned that settings might be changed accidentally. Or maybe you use XTensions they don't have and thus your files won't print from their Macs. To print to a file from a PC, use the following steps:

Note

Some Windows programs have a Print to File option in their Print dialog boxes. But QuarkXPress does not, which forces you to create a separate virtual printer in Windows. The process is not difficult, but it's not something that most people generally need to do.

STEPS: Printing to a file in Windows

1. Use Start⇨Settings⇨Printers to open the Printers window. Double-click the Add New Printer icon. This will launch the Add Printer Wizard (shown here).

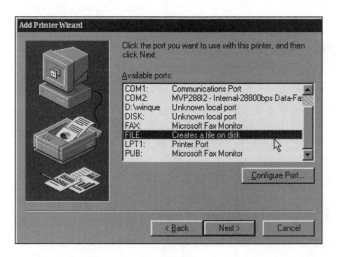

2. Go through the dialog boxes, selecting the appropriate printer (the one that your print files will ultimately be output on). You may need the Windows CD-ROM or a disk from the printer maker; if so, Windows will tell you. Note: When asked whether the printer is a local or network printer, it doesn't matter which answer you give.

3. When you get to the dialog box that lists Available Ports, be sure to choose FILE:, not a port like LPT1: or COM1:. This is the key to creating a virtual printer.

4. Complete the installation (you can skip the printing of a test page). Make sure you name the virtual printer something like printer name To File so you'll know what it is later. From now on, select this printer in the QuarkXPress Print dialog box's Printer pop-up list when you want to print to a file. (It will be available in all Windows programs' Printer pop-up lists.) You may need to create multiple virtual printers if you or your service bureau uses different output devices for which you want to generate print files.

Setting the PostScript level

In mid-1993, Apple Computer and Adobe Systems released the long-awaited PostScript Level 2 specification, for which Microsoft included a driver in Windows 95 and NT. If you use this driver to print to a file, make sure the device you are using is Level 2-compatible. To set the PostScript level for your printer, use the following steps:

STEPS: Setting the PostScript level in Windows

1. Use Start⇨Settings⇨Printers to open the Printers window.

2. Double-click your PostScript printer, and then choose Properties from the File menu.

3. Select the PostScript pane and then click the Advanced button. You will see a pane like that shown here.

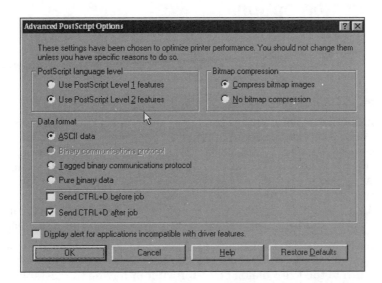

(continued)

4. Select the Use PostScript Level 1 Features option in the PostScript Language Level option list unless you are certain the output device uses PostScript Level 2. You won't lose any capabilities by selecting Use PostScript Level 1, although a Level 1 file can take longer to print on a Level 2 printer. If you select the ASCII Data option in the Data Format options list, your service bureau will be able to edit some of the defaults (which sometimes a savvy service bureau will do to correct a printing problem), but the file could be very large. If you select Tagged Binary Communications Protocol or Pure Binary Data, the file is much smaller but uneditable. Ask your service bureau which option it prefers.

Printing with QuarkXPress

After the page is set up for printing and the printer is set up for printing, you are ready to actually print the document. To print a document, select File➪Print (or the shortcut ⌘+P) to open the Print dialog box, which has five panes (or six, if you have the Quark CMS XTension installed), as well as several options common to all the panes. (One of those panes is the Setup pane, covered in the previous section.) Change any options and choose OK, and QuarkXPress sends your document to the printer (or file, if you are printing to a PostScript file).

The Print dialog box has undergone a major transformation in QuarkXPress 4. There's a new pane design and altered controls throughout.

Some common options

No matter what pane is open, the following options are always available:

✦ **Print Style:** You choose the print style—a saved set of printer settings—from this list. Print styles are covered later in this chapter.

✦ **Copies:** Enter how many copies of the document you want printed.

✦ **Pages:** Choose which pages to print. You can enter a range, such as 3-7; a single page, such as 4; a set of unrelated pages, such as 3, 7, 15, 28; or a combination, such as 3-7, 15, 28-64, 82-85. (If you'd prefer to use something other than a hyphen (-) to indicate a range and a comma (,) to indicate separate pages, click the Range Separators button and substitute your preferred symbols.) Select All from the pop-up menu to print all pages, or type *All*. (The ability to specify noncontiguous page ranges is new in QuarkXPress 4, unless you're used to using the QuarkPrint XTension.)

✦ **Capture Settings:** This new button remembers the current Print dialog box settings and returns you to your document. This way, you can make a change and return to the Print dialog box later without having to reestablish your settings.

Using the section-numbering feature

If you use the QuarkXPress section-numbering feature to create multiple sections in your document, you must enter the page numbers exactly as they are labeled in the document. (The label for the current page appears in the lower-left corner of your document screen.) Include any prefix used and enter the labels in the same format (letters, Roman numerals, or regular numerals) used in the section whose pages you want to print.

Alternately, you can indicate the absolute page numbers by preceding the number with a plus sign (+). For example, suppose that you have an eight-page document with two sections of four pages each. You label pages one through four as AN-1 through AN-4 and label pages five through eight as BN-1 through BN-4. If you enter BN-1 through BN-4 in the Pages field of the Print dialog box, QuarkXPress prints the first four pages in the section that uses the BN- prefix. If you enter +5 through +8, QuarkXPress prints document pages five through eight—which again includes BN-1 through BN-4.

✦ **Print:** This button prints the document.

✦ **Cancel:** This button exits the Print dialog box without printing.

✦ **Page Setup:** This button opens the Mac's Page Setup dialog box, covered earlier in this chapter.

✦ **Printer:** This button opens the Mac's Printer dialog box, covered earlier in this chapter.

 Windows QuarkXPress does not have the Page Setup or Printer buttons. But it does have the Properties button, which opens the properties for the current printer, and the Printer pop-up menu, in which you choose the printer to use. (On the Mac, you use the Chooser or the Finder's Printing menu to select the printer, as described earlier in this chapter.)

The Document pane

In this pane, shown in Figure 24-8, you set up the basic page attributes. (Note that QuarkXPress 4 has dropped the old Cover Page option, which let you specify whether a cover page prints.) The following items describe the options in the current version of QuarkXPress and how to use them:

✦ **Separations:** Prints color separations, putting each color on its own sheet (or negative), for use in producing color plates.

✦ **Include Blank Pages:** Sometimes you want blank pages to print, such as when you are outputting pages to be photocopied, where you want the blank pages used as separators between sections of your document. Check this option to output blank pages, uncheck it to print only pages with text or graphics on them.

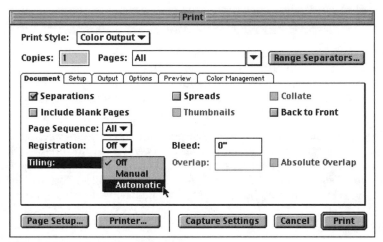

Figure 24-8: The Document pane.

✦ **Spreads:** If your printer can print facing pages on one sheet of paper (such as if you have an 11-inch-by-17-inch printer and your pages are $8^1/2$ by 11 inches or smaller) and you want them printed that way, check this option.

You may not want to use the Spreads option when outputting to an imagesetter if you have bleeds because there will be no extra space for the bleed between the spreads. If you use traditional perfect-binding (square spines) or saddle-stitching (stapled spines) printing methods, in which facing pages are not printed contiguously, do not use this option.

✦ **Thumbnails:** To get a miniature version of your document printed several pages to a sheet, select this option.

✦ **Collate:** This option remains grayed out unless you are printing more than one copy. If checked, it will print a full copy of the document and then repeat for as many times as copies are specified. If unchecked, this option will print the number of copies of each page before going on to the next page (such as 10 copies of page 1, followed by 10 copies of page 2, and so on). Collating takes longer for a printer than not collating, but it may save you time.

✦ **Back to Front:** If checked, this reverses the printing order, so the last page comes first, followed by the next-to-last page, and so on. This is handy for output devices that print with the pages facing up, rather than facing down.

✦ **Page Sequence**: You can select All, Odd, or Even, which will print the specified type of pages from whatever range you select in the Pages box. Thus, if you select Odd and specify a page range of 2-6, pages 3 and 5 will print. Note that this option is grayed out if you have checked the Spreads option.

✦ **Registration:** This adds registration marks and crop marks, which you'll need if your document is being professionally printed. A printer uses the registration marks to line up the page correctly on the printing press. Registration crop marks define the edge of the page (handy if you are printing to paper or negatives larger than your final page size). If you print color separations, enabling registration marks also prints the name of each color on its negative and includes a color bar in the output, so that the printing press operator can check that the right colors are used with the right plates. You can choose to have registration centered, off-center, or turned off. If you check Registration, you have the added option of selecting Centered or Off Center registration marks. Centered is the default.

Tip

Use the Off Center registration option when your page size is square or nearly square. Choosing Off Center makes it easy for the press operator to tell which sides of the page are the left and right sides and which are the top and bottom sides, thus reducing the chances that your page will be accidentally rotated.

✦ **Tiling:** For documents that are larger than the paper you're printing them on, select Manual or Automatic to have QuarkXPress break your page into smaller chunks that fit on the page; you can then stitch those pages together. QuarkXPress will print marks on your pages to help you line up the tiles. Here's how the options work:

   ✦ If you choose Auto, QuarkXPress determines where each tile breaks. You can select the amount of tile overlap by entering a value in the Overlap field. You can enter a value between 0 and 6 inches.

   ✦ If you enter a value in the Overlap field, QuarkXPress will print that overlapped area on both adjacent tiles, giving you duplicate material that you can overlap the tiles with to help with alignment.

   ✦ If you check the Absolute Overlap option, QuarkXPress will make sure the overlap is always exactly the value specified in the Overlap field. If it is unchecked, QuarkXPress will center the tiled image on the assembled pages, increasing the overlap if necessary.

   ✦ If you choose Manual, you decide where the tiles break by repositioning the ruler origin in your document. For all pages selected, QuarkXPress prints the tiled area whose upper-left corner matches the ruler's origin. Repeat this step for each tiled area. Choose the Manual tile option if certain areas of your document make more logical break points than others.

New Feature

✦ **Bleed:** This field is where you tell QuarkXPress how much room to leave around the document edges for elements that bleed off. This is useful when printing to a file or to an imagesetter to ensure that the bleed is not inadvertently removed or shortened. A value of $1/8$ inches (0.125 inches) suffices for most work.

The Output pane

The Output pane, shown in Figure 24-9, is where you set many attributes for printing to an imagesetter, whether you're producing black-and-white documents or color-separated documents. You also use this pane for printing to a standard printer and to set resolution and color modes. The following two sections explain the options for both types of printers.

QuarkXPress offers several advanced printing options designed for professional publishing users. Options not available for non-PostScript printers (such as color options) are grayed out in the Print dialog box.

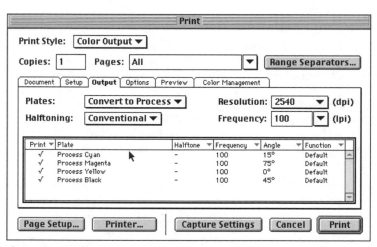

Figure 24-9: The Output pane.

The standard settings

Here's how the standard settings work in the Output pane of the Print dialog box:

✦ **Print Colors:** This pop-up menu (not shown here and available only if the Separations option is not checked in the Document pane) lets you select Black & White, Gray-scale, and, on a color printer, Composite Color. This Gray-scale option is handy for printing proof copies on noncolor printers. It is also helpful if you have a color image that you cannot otherwise convert to gray-scale for use in a black-and-white document. If the Black & White option is checked, colors might appear as solid whites or blacks if printed to a noncolor printer. The Composite Color option prints color images in color.

✦ **Plates:** Appearing where the Print Colors pop-up menu does if the Separations option is checked in the Document pane, you use this pop-up menu to determine whether all spot and process (CMYK) colors are output to their own individual plates (Spot & Process) or if all the spot colors (such as Pantone) are converted into the four process plates (Convert to Process). The answer depends on the capabilities of your printing press and the depth of your budget; typically, you'd choose Convert to Process.

✦ **Halftoning:** Use this pop-up menu to choose the halftone settings specified in QuarkXPress (the Conventional Option) or to use the defaults in your printer. For black-and-white and composite-color printing, you'd typically choose

Printer, unless you used halftoning effects in QuarkXPress' Style menu. For color separations, only Conventional is available, because QuarkXPress has to do the halftoning calculations itself so it can also figure out the color trapping.

✦ **Resolution:** Select the dpi (dots per inch) at which the imagesetter will be printing the document. The minimum resolution for most imagesetters is 1270 dpi. Note that setting the resolution within QuarkXPress does not override the actual settings of the imagesetter. But if you choose a lower setting in QuarkXPress than the printer is set for, all images will be halftoned at the lower resolution.

✦ **Frequency:** Specify the lines per inch (lpi) for your target printer. QuarkXPress will choose an initial setting based on the Resolution field's setting, but you can also select from the pop-up menu's other popular frequencies.

Imagesetter color separation options

If you are printing color separations to an imagesetter, you may want to adjust the output options at the bottom of the Output pane. You'll see a list of plates used in your document. If you chose the Convert to Process option in the Plates pop-up menu, you'll see only the CMYK or Hexachrome plates. You can adjust the characteristics for each plate by selecting a plate and then using the pop-up menus (with the triangle after their names in the column header) to choose a new setting. Figure 24-10 shows this section of the Output pane for a file that has many color plates, and it shows the pop-up menus for all the column headings. They work as follows:

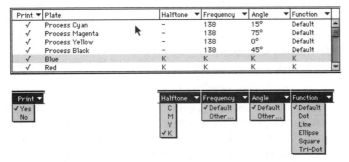

Figure 24-10: The settings for color plates.

✦ **Print:** Your options are Yes and No, but it's easier to just click the checkmark in this column to suppress printing of a particular plate (if the checkmark is visible) or enable printing (if the checkmark is not visible). Being able to select any combination of plates is new to QuarkXPress 4. The old versions required that you print one plate at a time or all four process (CMYK) plates at once.

✦ **Halftone:** Available only for non-CMYK plates, this lets you choose which CMYK plate's halftone settings (the screen frequency, angle, and element) to use. (You can also set each spot color's halftone assignment in the Edit Color dialog box. Use the Output pane to override that setting.) If you have spot colors blending into each other, make sure they use different CMYK colors' Halftone settings to avoid poor print quality.

✦ **Frequency:** This lets you set the lines per inch for the specific plate. Typically, it is set for the same plate as is used for the Halftone setting, although you can enter a specific value via the Other option in its pop-up menu.

✦ **Angle:** This option determines the angle on which the dots making up the color-separated pattern align. Light colors should use the settings of the yellow (Y) plate, medium-light colors the settings of the cyan (C) plate, medium-dark colors the settings of the magenta (M) plate, and very dark colors the settings of the black (K) plate. You can enter any value—not just the common 0°, 15°, 45°, and 75° angles—but do so only after discussing the settings with your printing-press operator or service bureau.

✦ **Function:** This pop-up menu lets you set the halftone dot shape—the shape that comprises the dots that make up an image—for each plate. They should almost always be the same, unless you are trying to achieve a special effect and know what you're doing.

The Options pane

The Options pane is almost exclusively designed for people using an imagesetter to create film negatives. Typically, your service bureau will adjust these settings or tell you how they want you to set them. Figure 24-11 shows the pane. The Page Flip and Negative Print options determine how the film negatives (or positives) are actually produced. The Output, Data, OPI, Overprint EPS Black, and Full Resolution TIFF Output options determine how pictures are printed. The following list describes how each option works.

New
Feature

✦ **Quark PostScript Error Handler:** This checkbox enables a neat utility that will help you diagnose output problems on a PostScript printer. PostScript is a language, and sometimes programs use it incorrectly, or at least differently than the printer expects, which leads to incorrect output or often no output at all. If this option is checked, QuarkXPress will print a report when it encounters a PostScript error and will even print the problem page to the point where the error occurred, helping you narrow down the problem (it may be in an imported image, for example).

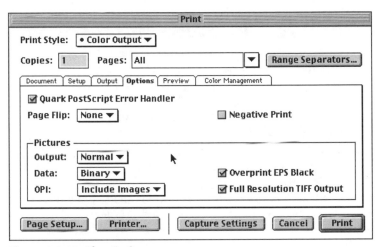

Figure 24-11: The Options pane.

✦ **Page Flip:** This pop-up menu lets you mirror your page; your options are Horizontal, Vertical, and Horizontal & Vertical. You would use this feature if your service bureau requests that the page be flipped. Otherwise, leave this option at the default None setting. Reasons to flip a page have to do with what's called *reading* and *emulsion*. Reading is the direction on which the page prints on a negative (to the left or to the right), while emulsion is the stuff on the negative that holds the image. Different printing presses expect the reading to be different ways and the emulsion to be on a specific side of the negative. The Page Flip settings let your service bureau adjust how the pages print in anticipation of these needs.

✦ **Negative Print:** This checkbox will print an inverse image of your pages, exchanging black with white, and dark colors with light ones. Your service bureau uses this option if it has imagesetters that can print both positives and negatives (so the service bureau can have the correct output based on what it's printing on). Have your service bureau tell you when to use this option.

Note

When both Negative Print is checked and a page is flipped either horizontally or vertically, the result is that the page is printed right-reading, emulsion side down, which is the typical setting in the United States for printing presses.

✦ **Output:** The default is Normal, but you can also choose Low Resolution or Rough from this pop-up menu. Normal means the pictures print normally; Low Resolution means the pictures print at the screen resolution (usually 72 dpi); Rough means the pictures don't print at all. You use the last two when you're focusing on the text and layout, not the images, because Low Resolution and Rough greatly accelerate printing time.

Screening angles explained

Normally, you'd probably never worry about the screening angles for your color plates. After all, the service bureau makes those decisions, right? Maybe. If you have your own image-setter, or even if you're just using a proofing device, you should know how to change screen angles for the best output. If you're working with spot colors that have shades applied to them, you'll want to know what the screen angles are so that you can determine how to set the screening angles for those spot colors.

Screening angles determine how the dots comprising each of the four process colors—cyan, magenta, yellow, and black—or any spot colors are aligned so they don't overprint each other. The rule of thumb is that dark colors should be at least 30 degrees apart, while lighter colors (for example, yellow) should be at least 15 degrees apart from other colors. That rule of thumb translates into a 105-degree angle (also called –15 degrees; it's the same angle) for cyan, 75 degrees for magenta, 90 degrees for yellow, and 45 degrees for black.

But those defaults sometimes result in moiré patterns. (*Moiré* is pronounced *mwah*-ray or *more-ay*.) With traditional color-separation technology, a service bureau would have to manually adjust the angles to avoid such moirés—an expensive and time-consuming process. With the advent of computer technology, modern output devices, such as Linotronic imagesetters, can calculate angles based on the output's lpi settings to avoid most moiré patterns. (Each image's balance of colors can cause a different moiré, which is why there is no magic formula.) Every major imagesetter vendor uses its own proprietary algorithm to make these calculations.

Before the introduction of PDF and PPD files that contain printer-specific information, these values were not available to programs like QuarkXPress. But because QuarkXPress (version 3.2 and later) can read PPD files (but version 4 cannot read PDF files, which versions 3.2 and 3.3 of QuarkXPress could), they now are. The optimized settings are calculated by the printer's PPD file, which should be available from the printer manufacturer. Many of these PPD files also come bundled with various programs, including QuarkXPress.

QuarkXPress automatically uses the PPD values to calculate the recommended halftoning, lpi, and frequency settings shown in the Output pane of the Print dialog box.

✦ **Data:** Typically your service bureau will tell you which of the three settings to use: Binary (smaller file sizes, faster printing, but not editable), ASCII (larger file sizes, slower printing, but editable), and Clean 8-Bit (a "hybrid" of binary and ASCII, somewhere between the two in size, that can safely be sent to PC-based output devices).

✦ **OPI:** If you don't use an Open Prepress Interface server, leave this option at the default setting of Include Images. If you use OPI, choose Omit TIFF if your OPI server has only high-resolution TIFF files (the most common type of OPI setup) and choose Omit TIFF & EPS if your OPI server contains both EPS and TIFF files. (An OPI server stores the original high-resolution image files on a server and lets your designers keep smaller, low-resolution versions of images on their local computers. This makes the layouts load and display faster when being designed.)

✦ **Overprint EPS Black:** Normally, QuarkXPress prints black using the trapping settings set in the Trap Specifications dialog box (accessed via the Edit Trap button in the Colors dialog box, which you open via Edit⇨Colors, or Shift+F12). But EPS files may have their own trapping settings for black defined in the program that created the EPS file. If you check the Overprint EPS Black option, QuarkXPress forces all black elements in EPS files to overprint other colors. This does not affect how other black elements in QuarkXPress print.

✦ **Full Resolution TIFF Output:** This option overrides the Frequency setting in the Output pane when TIFF images are printed. (Other elements are not affected.) If checked, it sends the TIFF image to the printer at the highest resolution possible based on the Resolution setting in the Output pane. You use this when you want your TIFF images (typically photos and scans) to be as sharp as possible. Sharpness is more of an issue for bitmapped images than for text and vector images, which is why QuarkXPress offers this feature.

New Feature

The Preview pane

It's easy to set up your Print dialog box and print your job, only to find out that something was offbase after your pages printed. Use the Preview pane (a new feature in QuarkXPress 4) to ensure that margins, crop marks, bleeds, and other element-fitting issues actually work with your target paper size.

Figure 24-12 shows an example Preview pane in which the bleed on the right side of the page goes past the page boundaries. You need to either use a larger paper size or make sure nothing bleeds on the right side of any page. (The other elements in the pane's preview are the crop marks at the corners and the registration marks along the sides.)

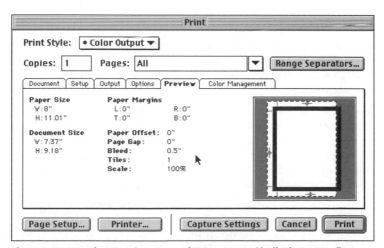

Figure 24-12: The Preview pane lets you see if all elements fit on the destination paper size.

The Color Management pane

If you've enabled Quark's color-management system (via Edit⇨Preferences⇨Color Management), the Print dialog box will include the Color Management pane, also new to QuarkXPress 4 and shown in Figure 24-13. Which profile is used (Separation or Composite) is determined by whether separations are on. If separations are on, the separations profile is in effect. The options work as follows:

If you change the profile for either the separation or composite printer in this pane, QuarkXPress will update the Color Management dialog box with the new settings. It will also recalibrate every image in your document, which could take many minutes, as soon as you exit the Print dialog box (unless you click Cancel).

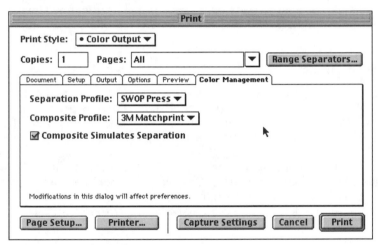

Figure 24-13: The Color Management pane.

✦ **Separation Profile:** Here you choose the output device (such as a printing press) that QuarkXPress should color-correct all images for when creating color separations. The default profile is whatever you specified in the Color Management dialog box.

✦ **Composite Profile:** Here you choose the output device (typically an inkjet printer, thermal-wax printer, color laser printer, or dye-sublimation printer, but sometimes a proofing system or a CMYK output device) that QuarkXPress should color-correct all images for when printing colors on a single page (rather than color-separating them). The default profile is whatever you specified in the Color Management dialog box.

✦ **Composite Simulates Separation:** If you check this box, QuarkXPress will alter the colors on your composite printer to make them match the separations printer as closely as possible. Use this when you are proofing color on a local composite printer before sending the final document out for color separations.

Because QuarkXPress 4 no longer uses the EfiColor color-management system, several options no longer exist in the Print dialog box. Calibrated Output no longer exists, because color calibration now happens automatically if the color management system is turned on and a profile is selected. The EfiColor Profile option is gone, replaced by the Separation Profile and Composite Profile options. Finally, the GCR option (gray-component removal, which sharpens blacks and grays in color bitmaps) is also gone—the only substantive functional loss in the switch from EfiColor to Quark CMS.

Working with Spot Colors and Separations

It's very easy to accidentally use spot colors such as red and Pantone 111 (say, for picture and text box frames) in a document that contains four-color TIFF and EPS files. The result is that QuarkXPress outputs as many as six plates: one each for the four process colors, plus one for red and one for Pantone 111. You might expect the red to be separated into 100 percent each of yellow and magenta (which is how red is printed in four-color work). And maybe you expect QuarkXPress to separate the Pantone 111 into its four-color equivalent (11.5 percent yellow and 27.5 percent black). So why doesn't QuarkXPress do this?

Using the Edit Color dialog box

By default, each color defined in QuarkXPress—including red, green, and blue, which are automatically available in the Edit⇨Colors menu—is set as a spot color. And each spot color gets its own plate, unless you specifically tell QuarkXPress to translate the color into process colors. You do so when defining a new color by unchecking the Spot Color box in the Edit Color dialog box, described in Chapter 21.

Regardless of whether a color was defined as a process or spot color, you can also choose the Convert to Process option in the Print dialog box's Output pane's Plates pop-up menu when printing to convert *all* spot colors to process colors (refer to Figure 24-9). However, this technique is no good if you want to print a mixture of process colors and spot colors—for example, having red color-separated as 100 percent yellow and 100 percent magenta but Pantone 111 printed on its own plate as a spot color—in this case, you must set all colors but those you want on their own plates to be process colors in the Edit Color dialog box.

The advantage to setting the colors to process in the Edit Color dialog box is that the colors are permanently made into process colors; the Convert to Process option must be used each time you print (which you can automate via print styles, as described later in this chapter).

Tip

If your work is primarily four-color work, either remove the spot colors such as blue, red, and green from your Colors dialog box or edit them to make them process colors. If you make these changes with no document open, they become the defaults for all new documents.

Transferring duplicate color sets

If you do some spot-color work and some four-color work, duplicate the spot colors and translate the duplicates into process colors. Make sure that you use a clear color-naming convention, such as Blue P for the process-color version of blue (which is created by using 100 percent each of magenta and cyan). The same is true when you use Pantone colors (and Hexachrome, Trumatch, Focoltone, Toyo, DIC, and multi-ink colors). If you check the Spot Color box in the Edit Color dialog box (choose Edit⇨Colors⇨New), these colors are output as spot colors. Again, you can define a Pantone color twice, making one of the copies a process color and giving it a name to indicate what it is. Then all you have to do is make sure that you pick the right color for the kind of output you want.

Mixing spot and process colors

You still can mix process and spot colors if you want. For example, if you want a gold border on your pages, you have to use a Pantone ink because metallic colors cannot be produced via process colors. So use the appropriate Pantone color, and *don't* uncheck the Spot Color box when you define the color. When you make color separations, you get five negatives: one each for the four process colors and one for gold. That's fine, because you specifically want the five negatives. (Just make sure that any other colors you created from spot-color models were turned into process colors in the Edit Color dialog box; otherwise, each of these spot colors will print on its own negative, too.)

Creating Print Styles

New Feature

Quark has integrated its former QuarkPrint XTension into QuarkXPress 4. This adds a great number of new controls and options to the print functions. The most important of these is the ability to create print styles, which let you save settings for specific printers and/or specific types of print jobs. To create a print style, use Edit⇨Print Styles to get the dialog box shown in Figure 24-14.

Figure 24-14: The Print Styles dialog box.

When you choose to edit an existing style or create a new style, you get the Edit Print Style dialog box shown in Figure 24-15. It contains four of the Print dialog box's panes: Document, Setup, Output, and Options. These panes are the same as in the Print dialog box, so set them here as you would there. When you've set the print style's options, click OK, and then click Save in the Print Styles dialog box.

Unfortunately, QuarkXPress does not let you take Print dialog box settings and create a print style from them. You must recreate them in the Print Styles dialog box. So be sure to write them down first.

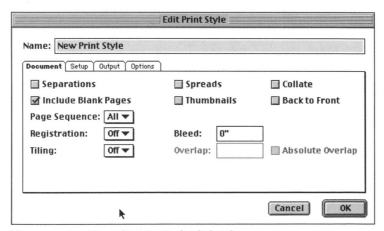

Figure 24-15: The Edit Print Style dialog box.

Print-styles tips

It's common to have multiple printers in your office or in your service bureau—laser printers for basic business use and quick proofing of layouts, color printers for color proofing, and an imagesetter for final film output. Rather than specify the various settings for each printer each time you print your document—an exercise prone to mistakes given the complexity of QuarkXPress's Print dialog box—use print styles to save all these settings. Then just select the printer setting you want to use from the Print dialog box. Here are a couple of additional print style tips:

✦ You can share print styles with other users by using the Export button to save your styles to a file that your colleagues can then import via the Import button.

✦ If you select a print style in the Print dialog box and make changes to the various panes, you'll see the name of the print style change: a bullet (•) will precede the name. This is meant to remind you that you have changed the print style's settings for this particular print session. It does not change the print style itself, so the next time you use that print style, its original settings will be in effect.

✦   ✦   ✦

Extending QuarkXPress

VI

◆   ◆   ◆   ◆

In This Part

Chapter 25
Using XTensions

Chapter 26
Using Scripts

Chapter 27
An XTension and
Utility Sampler

◆   ◆   ◆   ◆

One of QuarkXPress's biggest pluses is its use of plug-ins, called *XTensions,* to add new capabilities to the program. Not only do other companies offer their own XTensions to give QuarkXPress entirely new capabilities, but Quark itself has used and continues to use XTensions as a way of adding functions to the program. The beauty of XTensions is that they intertwine themselves with QuarkXPress's regular features, so their menus and dialog boxes get placed where it makes sense to put them. They're not placed in a plug-in ghetto. The latest version of QuarkXPress makes XTensions even better by giving you a tool to manage them. But XTensions aren't the only way to make QuarkXPress do more. On the Macintosh, you can script QuarkXPress—create little programs that use QuarkXPress's tools—to automate your work.

This part shows you how to use XTensions and scripts to make your life easier. And it gives you a description of dozens of XTensions that you might want to use yourself. The CD accompanying this book includes free, demo, and shareware versions of these XTensions for you to try out.

Using XTensions

◆ ◆ ◆ ◆

In This Chapter

Getting started

Installing and using
XTensions

Setting XTension
preferences

Using the XTensions
Manager

◆ ◆ ◆ ◆

If you use QuarkXPress long enough, you'll eventually encounter tasks it simply doesn't offer. Perhaps you'll need to output printer's spreads, collect fonts in preparation for output, or create a custom palette that contains your favorite commands. You won't find these capabilities in QuarkXPress, but don't get discouraged. XTensions begin where QuarkXPress ends—with around 400 commercial XTensions for the Macintosh version, more than 50 for the Windows version, and a steady stream of new ones almost daily. Many free XTensions—some from Quark, others from third-party developers and individuals—can also be found online. This chapter shows you how to install, set the preferences for, and control QuarkXPress XTensions with the new XTensions Manager. There's also a sidebar on XTension information you can find on the Web. Chapter 27 offers a broad sample of what the many XTensions can do, and free and demonstration versions of XTensions are included on the CD that comes with this book (see Appendix D for details).

Getting Started

You may not be aware of it, but chances are good you've been running—if not using—several XTensions every time you've used QuarkXPress. If you were the person who installed your QuarkXPress 4 program, you may have noticed during installation that you had the option to install or not install QuarkXPress XTensions.

When you install QuarkXPress

Figure 25-1 shows the installation dialog box that provides the option to install the XTensions that ship with QuarkXPress. If this option was checked, more than a dozen XTension files were placed in a folder called XTension that was created in your QuarkXPress program folder. Figure 25-2 shows what the

XTension folder looks like after installation if you chose to install XTensions. In addition to the XTension folder, another folder called XTension Disabled is created within the program folder during program installation. If XTensions are not installed during installation, they're placed in the XTension Disabled folder.

New Feature

Some of the new features in QuarkXPress 4 have made a few XTensions obsolete. For example, QuarkXPress 4 users don't need XTensions to create character-based style sheets and Bézier shapes. Users of previous versions had the option of purchasing XTensions to perform these tasks.

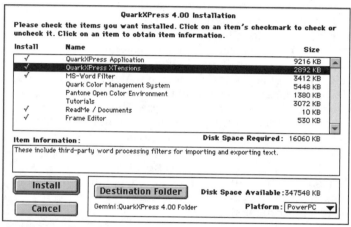

Figure 25-1: When you install QuarkXPress, you have the option to install a number of Quark-produced XTensions that are included with the product.

Figure 25-2: If you choose to install XTensions during installation, more than a dozen XTensions are placed in the XTension folder within the QuarkXPress program folder.

Determining which XTensions are loaded

When QuarkXPress is running, you can find out which XTensions are loaded by holding down the Option key and choosing About QuarkXPress from the Apple menu. The QuarkXPress Environment dialog box, shown in Figure 25-3, is displayed. It includes a list of all currently running XTensions.

To see what XTensions are running in Windows QuarkXPress, hold down the Alt key when choosing About QuarkXPress from the Help menu. You'll get a menu similar to that shown in Figure 25-3.

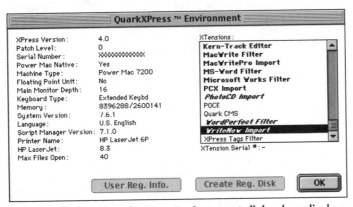

QuarkXPress ™ Environment	
XPress Version: 4.0	XTensions:
Patch Level: 0	Kern-Track Editor
Serial Number: XXXXXXXXXXXX	MacWrite Filter
Power Mac Native: Yes	MacWritePro Import
Machine Type: Power Mac 7200	MS-Word Filter
Floating Point Unit: No	Microsoft Works Filter
Main Monitor Depth: 16	PCX Import
Keyboard Type: Extended Keybd	PhotoCD Import
Memory: 8396288/2600141	POCE
System Version: 7.6.1	Quark CMS
Language: U.S. English	WordPerfect Filter
Script Manager Version: 7.1.0	WriteNow Import
Printer Name: HP LaserJet 6P	XPress Tags Filter
HP LaserJet: 8.3	XTension Serial #: -
Max Files Open: 40	

User Reg. Info.   Create Reg. Disk   OK

Figure 25-3: The QuarkXPress Environment dialog box displays information about your copy of QuarkXPress, your computer, and currently running XTensions.

Installing and Using XTensions

With past versions of QuarkXPress, users had to manually move XTension files between folders to turn individual XTensions on and off. Unfortunately, XTensions became so popular and abundant that managing them by clicking and dragging became a time-consuming chore for many users. Eventually, XTensions for managing XTensions became available. With QuarkXPress 4, however, an XTension Manager has become a regular feature of the program. The following section shows you how easy it is to install XTensions and to turn them on and off (for more information on the XTensions Manager, see the section later in this chapter devoted entirely to its use).

XTensions for QuarkXPress: A brief history

In its early years, QuarkXPress gained a foothold in the publishing industry because it had an impressive feature set and a slick interface. The more people used it, the more they liked it. And as quickly as Quark could add new features, requests for even more features poured in. It soon became apparent to Quark that if all requests for new features were implemented, the program would become prohibitively large. Trying to be everything for everybody would ultimately backfire. On the other hand, if specialized features for vertical publishing markets were not available to QuarkXPress users, the program's usefulness would be severely limited. What to do?

Quark founder Tim Gill came up with a clever plan. He decided to build the QuarkXPress application with an open program architecture that let software developers add specialized features to off-the-shelf QuarkXPress via add-on software modules. Nowadays, nearly every program includes plug-in capabilities, but add-on software was a new, untested concept when Quark began its XTension development program. In keeping with the X factor, these plug-in software components were called XTensions. By letting software developers create specialty XTensions, Quark could continue to focus on developing broad-based features for the core program. With XTensions, QuarkXPress *could* be everything for everybody without being a humongous piece of software with a voracious appetite for RAM.

When QuarkXPress 2.12 was released in 1989, the program's extensibility didn't raise many eyebrows, and the XTension development program took a while to gather momentum. Many of the first-generation XTensions were specialized tools designed for specific publishing sites and were not commercially available. And many XTensions that were available for purchase were expensive. But when version 3.0 was released the following year, both QuarkXPress sales and XTension development took off. Each fed off the other. New features—the ability to rotate text in fine increments, to print trapped color separation plates, and a palette-based interface—attracted new users by the thousands. As QuarkXPress sales grew around the world, the demand for XTensions also grew. And as more XTensions became available, QuarkXPress became a viable solution for a growing number of publishers, particularly at high-end publishing sites, where previously—without XTensions—QuarkXPress had made only small inroads. It's not stretching things to say that the worldwide success of QuarkXPress is due in large part to XTensions.

New Feature

Quark has tackled the XTensions management problem head-on, by adding a pair of new features to QuarkXPress 4—a set of XTension preferences and an XTensions Manager—which take the hassle out of turning XTensions on and off.

To install XTensions

Installing and using XTensions for QuarkXPress is much like installing and using system extensions on a Macintosh. To install an XTension, simply place the file in the XTension folder. You can disable an XTension by moving it to the XTension Disabled folder. Some commercial XTensions also include installer programs that let you install a demo version of the software or, if you've purchased the product and received a registration number, a full working version. (All these installers place a copy of the XTension file in the XTension folder.) Once you've installed an XTension, the next time you launch QuarkXPress, the XTension is also loaded into memory, and the menus, commands, and palettes provided by the XTension are added to the program's interface. Figure 25-4 shows the blend options that the Cool Blends XTension adds to QuarkXPress, and ShadowCaster, another popular XTension that creates shadows for text and pictures.

New Feature

In versions of QuarkXPress prior to 4 you could store XTensions in either the XTension folder or within the QuarkXPress program folder. But with version 4, only XTensions stored in the XTension folder are loaded when you launch the program.

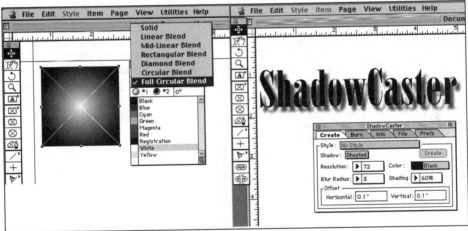

Figure 25-4: The Cool Blends XTension (left), which is included with QuarkXPress, lets you apply gradients to box backgrounds. ShadowCaster (right), one of hundreds of commercially available XTensions, lets you create soft drop shadows for text and pictures. (A demo version of ShadowCaster is on the CD-ROM included with this book.)

Managing Macintosh RAM

Every XTension uses its own RAM. The more XTensions that are loaded when you launch QuarkXPress, the more RAM that's required. Most Mac XTensions include information about increasing QuarkXPress' memory allocation. In general, the bigger the XTension, the more memory you should allocate to QuarkXPress. To change the amount of RAM allocated to QuarkXPress on the Mac, click once on the program icon, then choose Get Info from the File menu, or use ⌘+I. Enter larger numbers in the Preferred size and Minimum size fields.

Windows manages its own memory, so don't worry about setting memory allocations for QuarkXPress or your XTensions.

Setting XTension Preferences

The settings you make in the XTensions pane of the Application Preferences dialog box determine whether the XTensions Manager dialog box (covered in a following section) is displayed when you launch QuarkXPress.

Working with the options

To display the Application Preferences dialog box, choose Edit⇨Preferences⇨ Application or use Option+Shift+⌘+Y. Click the XTensions tab to display XTensions-related preferences. Figure 25-5 shows the XTensions pane in the Application Preferences dialog box. Here's how the options work:

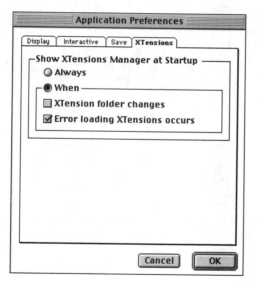

Figure 25-5: The controls in the XTensions pane of the Application Preferences dialog box let you open the XTensions Manager every time you start QuarkXPress; when you add files to or remove files from the XTension folder; or when an XTension-loading error occurs.

✦ **Always:** If you click Always, the XTensions Manager dialog box opens each time you launch QuarkXPress and gives you the option to load a particular set of XTensions; to create and modify XTension sets; and to enable or disable XTensions for each available set.

✦ **When:** If you click When, the following two checkboxes become available:

   ✦ **XTension folder changes:** Click this if you want to display the XTension Manager at startup only if XTensions have been added to or removed from the XTension folder since the last time you used QuarkXPress.

   ✦ **Error loading XTensions occurs:** Click this if you want to display the XTension Manager at startup only if QuarkXPress encounters a problem trying to load an XTension.

Note   All Application preferences, including XTension preferences, are program-level defaults. If you make any changes to XTension preferences (whether a document is open or not), the changes are implemented the next time you launch QuarkXPress.

Handling XTension-loading errors

If an XTension-loading error occurs during startup, an alert is displayed. Figure 25-6 shows the XTension Loading Error alert, which lists the XTensions that QuarkXPress was unable to load. Clicking on the name of an XTension in the scroll list displays a possible explanation for the error. Click the About button to display additional information about the highlighted XTension. Figure 25-7 shows the information displayed for an XTension. The XTension Loading Error alert displays the following controls:

✦ **Ignore:** Click this if you want to launch QuarkXPress without launching the XTensions listed in the scroll list.

✦ **Manager:** Click this to display the XTension Manager dialog box, in which you can change the current startup set of XTensions or create a new set.

✦ **Don't show this dialog again:** Click this if you don't want to be alerted when QuarkXPress is unable to load an XTension.

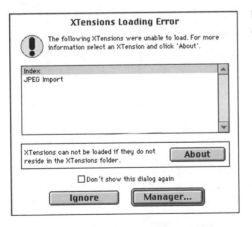

Figure 25-6: QuarkXPress displays an alert if it is unable to load an XTension.

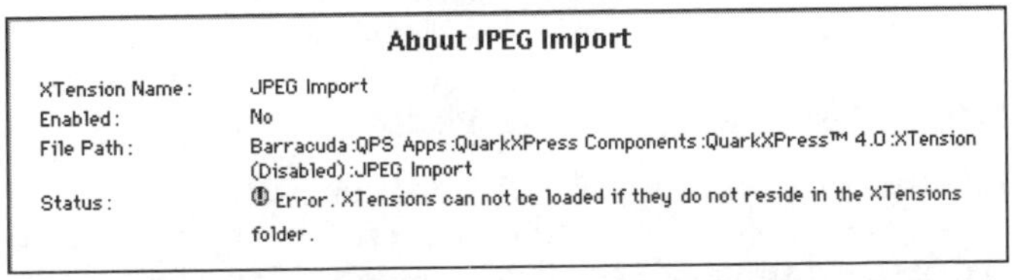

Figure 25-7: If you click About when alerted about an XTension-loading problem, a screen with information about the highlighted XTension is displayed. The Status information includes an exclamation mark to indicate a problem, and suggests the cause of the problem.

Note

Any changes you make to your XTension or XTension Disabled folder, either by dragging XTensions into or out of these folders or by using the XTensions Manager, are implemented the next time you launch QuarkXPress. You cannot enable or disable XTensions while QuarkXPress is running.

XTensions on the Web: Information, vendors, and developers

The Internet has an abundance of information about desktop publishing, QuarkXPress, and XTensions. If you're the adventurous type, perform a search for QuarkXPress or XTensions at your favorite search site; then start clicking. You can start your XTension quest by visiting any of the following sites:

✦ *Quark (http://www.quark.com):* Several free Macintosh and Windows XTensions are available for download from Quark's Web site. They range from the infamous Jabberwocky, which generates gobs of gobbledygook text with a single keystroke, to word processing filters. For aspiring XTension developers, the site also includes information about Quark's XTension development program. Quark is updating its XTensions to be version 4-native, so be sure to look for these updates on Quark's Web site.

✦ *World-Wide Power Company (http://www2.thepowerco.com/twwpc/):* The World-Wide Power Company offers plug-ins for many publishing and graphics programs—Macintosh and PC—including QuarkXPress, Photoshop, PageMaker, Premiere, FreeHand, CorelDraw, and Painter. The site includes a searchable and browsable product database, and order forms.

✦ *XChange (http://www.xchangeus.com):* XChange was the first commercial clearinghouse for XTensions. Its Web site includes a searchable catalog from which you can download demo XTensions.

✦ *XPresso Bar (http://www.xpressobar.com):* This is one of the best sites on the Web for information about QuarkXPress. Its XTensions page has links to sites that let you download demo products and purchase full working copies, as well as links to a number of XTension developers. The XPresso Bar's File Archive (formerly the Telalink ftp site) lets you search for and download demo versions of XTensions.

✦ *XT-now (http://www.xt-now.com):* In addition to offering discounted XTensions for purchase and download, XT-now also includes XTension reviews from *Macworld, MacWeek,* and *Publish,* a Tips & Tricks page, a Design Tips Daily page, and links to other QuarkXPress and electronic publishing sites.

✦ *XTSource (http://www.xtsource.com):* Like XTension.com, XTSource uses a shopping-cart metaphor to offer discounted XTensions from many developers. This site is run by Astrobyte, creators of BeyondPress HTML-export XTension.

Many XTension developers maintain their own Web sites. Generally, you'll find company information, product information, demo versions of XTensions, and updates. Some sites offer tech support; others have electronic versions of manuals. For a taste of what's available, check out the following:

✦ *A Lowly Apprentice Production (http://www.alap.com):* This was one of the first developers to offer multi-XTension tool sets: XPert Tools Vols. 1 and 2. Several ALAP XTensions are on the CD that comes with this book.

✦ *Extensis (http://www.extensis.com):* This company develops plug-ins for QuarkXPress, Photoshop, PageMaker, PageMill, Illustrator, and FreeHand. Several Extensis XTensions are on the CD that comes with this book.

✦ *Hologramophone (http://www.hologramophone.com):* This is the developer of a group of typographic and production XTensions collectively called Gluons.

✦ *Markzware (http://www.markzware.com):* This is the developer of numerous XTensions, a pair of XTension tool sets, and FlightCheck, a preflight utility available for Mac and Windows.

✦ *Vision's Edge (http://www.xtender.com):* This was among the first companies to offer XTensions for QuarkXPress. In addition to a broad product line, Vision's Edge also develops custom XTensions for users with unique needs.

Using the XTensions Manager

Whether you run only a few XTensions with QuarkXPress or lots of them, chances are you don't need all of your XTensions every time you use QuarkXPress. In workgroup environments, not every user requires the same kinds of XTensions. Instead of loading unnecessary XTensions, you can use the new XTensions Manager feature in QuarkXPress 4 to create startup sets of XTensions. An individual QuarkXPress user can use the XTensions Manager to create separate startup sets for page design, editorial, and output work. A workgroup site can create startup sets for each class of QuarkXPress user. For example, a page layout artist could use a set of design and typographic XTensions, while an editor uses a different set of editorial-specific XTensions.

The XTensions Manager dialog box

Figure 25-8 shows the XTensions Manager command in the Utilities menu and the XTensions Manager dialog box. Here you can create custom XTension sets, import and export sets, and choose the set you want to use the next time you launch QuarkXPress.

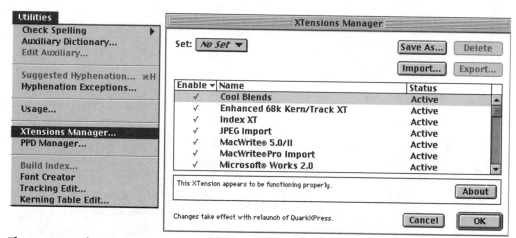

Figure 25-8: Choosing XTensions Manager from the Utilities menu (left) displays the XTensions Manager dialog box (right).

Choosing a startup set

The controls at the top of the XTensions Manager dialog box let you create custom startup sets, import and export startup sets, and choose the startup set that will be used the next time you launch QuarkXPress. The scroll list in the center of the dialog box displays all XTensions stored in both the XTension and XTension Disabled folders. Currently running XTensions (those in the XTension folder) are displayed with the word Active next to their name in the Status column; disabled XTensions (those in the XTension Disabled folder) show a status of Inactive. Figure 25-9 shows the Set pop-up menu, which displays three default sets—All XTensions Enabled, All XTensions Disabled, and 4.0-Optimized XTensions—plus any available custom sets. If you choose a new startup set, it is used the next time you launch QuarkXPress. Here's how the options work:

✦ **All XTensions Enabled:** Choosing this moves all XTensions in the XTension Disabled folder to the XTension folder; all XTensions in the scroll list are checked.

✦ **All XTensions Disabled:** Choosing this produces the opposite results: all XTensions in the XTension folder are moved to the XTension Disabled folder; all XTensions in the scroll list are unchecked.

✦ **4.0-Optimized XTensions:** If you choose this, XTensions that are *4.0-native* (those that have been optimized to work with QuarkXPress 4) are checked in the scroll list and, if necessary, moved from the XTension Disabled folder to the XTension folder. All XTensions that are not optimized are unchecked.

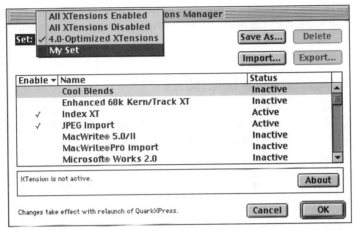

Figure 25-9: The Set pop-up menu in the XTensions Manager dialog box displays three default startup sets and any custom sets that you've created or imported.

Creating and deleting startup sets

To create a custom startup set, you must first choose the XTensions you want to include. You can begin by choosing any of the default sets, and then click the Enable column to check the XTensions you want to include and uncheck those you want to disable. (You can also enable or disable an XTension by clicking on its name, and then clicking on the Enable pop-up menu. Choose Yes to enable the XTension; choose No to disable it.) When you first change the Enable status of an XTension after choosing a set, the Set pop-up menu displays the default name "No Set." After you have checked the XTensions you want to include in your custom set, you have the following options:

✦ You can click OK to save the set using the default name (No Set). This set will be used the next time you launch QuarkXPress (and will continue to be used until you choose a different set).

✦ You can click Save As if you want to name the new set. When you click Save As, the Save Set dialog box, shown in Figure 25-10, is displayed. Enter a name for the startup set in the Enter name for current set field, and then click Save.

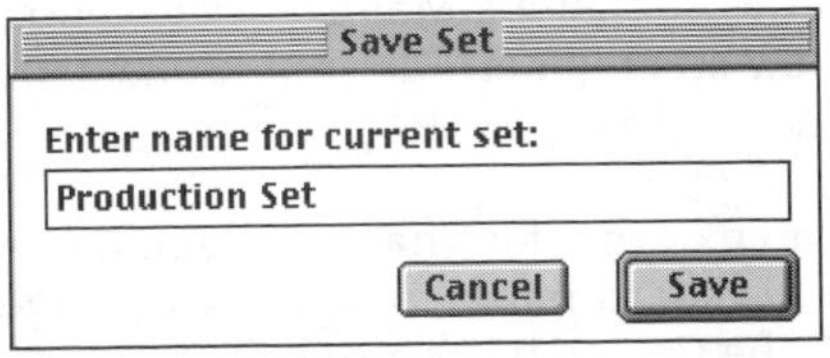

Figure 25-10: The Save Set dialog box lets you name a custom XTension set.

To delete a startup set, first choose it from the Set pop-up menu, and then click the Delete button. The Delete button is not available when any of the three default sets are selected.

Finding 4.0-optimized XTensions

To find out whether an XTension has been optimized for QuarkXPress 4, click on its name in the scroll list, and then click the About button. Figure 25-11 shows detailed information about the selected XTension.

About Cool Blends

XTension Name :	Cool Blends
Enabled :	No
File Path :	Barracuda :QPS Apps :QuarkXPress Components :QuarkXPress™ 4.0 :XTension (Disabled) :Cool Blends
4.0 Optimized :	No
Fat :	Yes
Version :	Cool Blends 2.11
Copyright :	© 1986-1996 Quark, Inc.
Status :	Inactive. XTension is not active.

Figure 25-11: When you click on the About button in the XTensions Manager dialog box, you get detailed information about the selected XTension.

Note

When you load XTensions that are not 4.0-optimized, such as XTensions that were written to run with QuarkXPress 3.3x, they run in emulation mode. This should not present any problems, but XTensions that run in emulation mode do not run as fast as optimized XTensions.

In Windows QuarkXPress, version 3 XTensions do not work. You must use version 4 XTensions, which will have the filename extension .XNT, rather than the extension .XXT of QuarkXPress 3.

Importing and exporting startup sets

Some work environments, especially workgroups that use multiple copies of QuarkXPress on a network, may want to ensure that all users have access to custom XTension sets. The Import and Export buttons in the XTensions Manager dialog box provide this capability. To import a custom startup set, click the Import button, locate the file, and double-click on its name, or click once and then click OK. When you import a startup set, its name is added to the Set pop-up menu and it's automatically selected.

Note

Remember, changes you make within the XTensions Manager dialog box—including importing and choosing a new startup set—are not implemented until the next time you launch QuarkXPress.

To save the currently selected set to an external file that can be imported by other QuarkXPress users, choose Export. A standard dialog box lets you name the file and choose its storage location. Click the Create button to save the file. The Export button is not available when a default set is selected in the Set pop-up menu.

Note

Note that when you save (not export) an XTension set, that set is stored in the XPress Preferences file. That's why you need to export the set to share it with other users.

A few XTension-related caveats

The ability to set XTension-related preferences and to turn XTensions on and off via the XTensions Manager makes managing XTensions much easier than with previous versions of QuarkXPress, but the following list alerts you to other XTension-related pitfalls you should be aware of:

✦ Some XTensions, often referred to as *required XTensions*, must be present whenever a QuarkXPress user opens a document that was created when these XTensions were running. An early version of Markzware's PasteboardXT was a required XTension, although many people who used it were not aware of this until they received a frantic call from their service provider. Markzware then released a utility called Pasteboard XTerminator that allowed users of Pasteboard XT to zap QuarkXPress documents that were created while the XTension was running so that QuarkXPress users who weren't running the XTension could open the documents. (The CD that accompanies this book includes the latest version of Pasteboard XT, which is not a required XTension, as well as Pasteboard XTerminator.)

✦ If you use a required XTension when you create a document, you must be careful to include the XTension if you send the document to a service provider for output.

✦ Some XTension developers offer freely distributable, viewer-only versions of their required XTensions. A viewer-only XTension lets you open documents created with the full working version of the XTension, but the functionality is disabled. For example, Datastream's SXetch Pad illustration XTension includes the SXetch Pad Viewer XTension. Users of SXetch Pad can include the viewer XTension with the QuarkXPress documents they send to service providers, who can then open and print the documents, but cannot modify items created with SXetch Pad.

✦ You may also encounter incompatibilities when running certain combinations of XTensions. Theoretically, if all XTensions were created correctly, any XTension would work flawlessly with any other XTension. But in the real world, problems can occur. If you experience odd or unpredictable results while working with QuarkXPress, you might want to start looking for XTension incompatibilities. Unfortunately, there are no tools that check for such problems. Your best bet is to disable suspect XTensions one by one until the problem goes away. It's also a good idea to keep your XTensions as up-to-date as possible. Many XTension developers offer free updates and fixes on their Web sites. You should check these sites periodically to see if updated versions of XTensions are available.

✦   ✦   ✦

Using Scripts

For many QuarkXPress users, the idea of venturing out of the friendly and familiar confines of the program and into a foreign environment—scripting—is a bit disconcerting. But after reading this chapter, you may feel a bit less intimidated by the idea of writing scripts for QuarkXPress. It's not rocket science, and it's not programming. Think of it as learning a new way to use QuarkXPress. At the very least, you can use simple scripts to automate some of the simpler repetitive tasks you perform every day. As you become comfortable with scriptwriting, you're also likely to discover that virtually everything you do with QuarkXPress is a repetitive task. The more you can free yourself of this kind of work by using AppleScripts, the more time you have to be creative. You can also communicate with and exchange data with other scriptable programs and XTensions (as explained in Chapters 25 and 27). The possibilities are literally endless.

◆ ◆ ◆ ◆

In This Chapter

Exploring
AppleScript

Getting started
with scripts

Creating and running
scripts

Connecting with
other programs

Locating more
scripting tools

◆ ◆ ◆ ◆

 Alas, if you are a user of Windows QuarkXPress, you needn't read any further (unless of course you're curious). Scripting is not available for the Windows version of QuarkXPress. Beware: If you're a Windows user and read this chapter, you may want to switch to the Mac.

Exploring AppleScript

AppleScript is a scripting language developed by Apple and initially released with System 7.0 that can be used to control Macs, networks, and scriptable applications, including QuarkXPress. The AppleScript language was designed to be as close to normal English as possible so that average Mac users—specifically, those who are not familiar with programming languages—can understand and use it.

Learning the language

Many of the actions specified in AppleScripts read like sentences you might use in everyday conversation, such as:

```
set the color of the current box to "Black"
```

or

```
set the font to "Times"
```

If you're thinking about dabbling with AppleScript, the following words of both caution and encouragement are in order:

✦ **First the encouragement:** You don't have to have programming experience, scripting experience, or a plastic pocket-pal to begin creating AppleScript scripts. A bit of curiosity and a touch of patience will suffice.

✦ **Now the caution:** Scripting is essentially a euphemism for programming. As user-friendly as the AppleScript language is, writing scripts is not a matter of choosing commands from menus, clicking and dragging, or entering values into fields; nor is it like writing a limerick. If you're starting from scratch, know in advance that you'll have to learn some new skills.

✦ **Don't be scared:** If you're already familiar with QuarkXPress, you'll quickly become familiar with the concept of scripting. After all, with scripts you're simply performing the same actions you normally perform using the keyboard and mouse—creating documents, pages, and items and modifying all of these elements. Writing scripts for QuarkXPress is like learning how to issue commands to a dog that's already been trained. If you've looked through this book, you know what QuarkXPress can do. To become an AppleScripter, all you need to learn is how to bark out commands.

Tip

Although this chapter explains how to create AppleScript scripts, you can also create scripts for the Mac and QuarkXPress using other scripting languages, such as UserTalk and MacPerl. For beginning scripters, AppleScript is a bit easier to grasp than the others. However, UserTalk provides more verbs and is considered to be more powerful than AppleTalk. Frontier, now freeware, has gained popularity recently as a tool for building and managing high-performance Web sites, and can be used to create Mac scripts in any language.

AppleScript: Background and basics

In 1991, Apple introduced an interapplication communication (IAC) technology called *Apple events.* The next year, a company called UserLand Software began shipping a program called Frontier that let Macintosh users create Apple event scripts using a scripting language called UserTalk, which controlled the Mac desktop, networks, and scriptable applications. Shortly thereafter, Apple released

AppleScript, a commercial product that included a scripting language and an accompanying set of utilities for creating scripts. AppleScript was originally distributed as a stand-alone product and was also bundled with System 7 Pro and HyperCard 2.2. It has been included with the Mac OS software since version 7.5. Basically, here's how AppleScript works within QuarkXPress:

✦ **Using correct English:** All languages, including programming languages like Pascal and C++, and scripting languages like AppleScript and HyperTalk (the scripting language used with Apple's HyperCard development program), include grammatical components that are used in standardized sequences. In English, we combine nouns, verbs, adjectives, adverbs, and so on to create sentences. Everybody knows the meaning of "The weather is especially nice today" because it uses common words in a sequence that makes sense. The sentence "Nice is the especially today weather" has the right components, but it is arranged in the wrong sequence, so the meaning is lost.

✦ **Statements and syntax rules:** In AppleScript, verbs, nouns, adjectives, and prepositions are combined to create *statements;* statements are combined to form *scripts.* In AppleScript, verbs are also called commands; nouns are called objects; and adjectives are called properties. *Syntax rules* specify how statements and scripts must be constructed so that they can be understood by a computer.

✦ **The object hierarchy:** AppleScript also uses another structural element called an *object hierarchy* or, to be precise, the Apple Events Object Hierarchy. It's a fancy term for a simple concept. The Apple Events Object Hierarchy works like a set of boxes within boxes. A large box contains a smaller box, which contains a smaller box, which contains a smaller box, and so on, until you reach the smallest box, which contains nothing and is the final level in the hierarchy of boxes.

✦ **The QuarkXPress hierarchy:** QuarkXPress contains its own hierarchy, which lends itself nicely to AppleScript: A document contains pages, pages contain boxes, and boxes contain text and pictures. You can create AppleScripts that perform actions at any of these levels. In other words, with scripts you can create documents, add pages, add items to pages, and modify the contents of boxes—right down to a particular character in a text box. You can think of this hierarchy in QuarkXPress as a chain of command. You can't talk directly to an item that's at the bottom of the chain. Rather, you must first address the top level, then the next, and so on, until you've reached the item at the bottom of the chain. This is analogous to the way you use QuarkXPress: You create new documents, add pages, place boxes on the pages, and finally modify the contents of the boxes.

Learning to create scripts is like learning to swim: You can read books, documentation, and articles until your head spins, but eventually you have to get a little wet. The best way to learn about AppleScript is to write a script. So put on your swimsuit and let's get started.

Getting more information on AppleScript

Before you venture too far into scripting, you should review the AppleScript-related information provided with Mac software and with QuarkXPress. Two text files, "Using AppleScript, part 1" and "Using AppleScript, part 2," are included with AppleScript. Part 1 is a brief introduction to AppleScript; part 2 explains how to use the Script Editor. A document called Advanced Scripting Document is included with QuarkXPress. This document, although a bit on the technical side, is a valuable resource. It includes an overview of Apple events scripting and the object model, as well as a list of QuarkXPress-specific scripting terms and scripting examples written with both AppleScript and UserTalk.

If you want still more information about AppleScript, several books are available, including Danny Goodman's *AppleScript Handbook*, 2nd edition (Random House, 1994); *The Tao of AppleScript*, 2nd edition, by Derrick Schneider (Hayden Books, 1994); and *AppleScript for Dummies* by Tom Trinko (IDG Books Worldwide, 1996).

Getting Started with Scripts

Before you begin any job, you must first gather the required tools. A brief description of the software components you need to get started follows. Later in this chapter you'll find a list of additional scripting aids—software utilities, books, and Web sites—that you can add to your tool collection as your scripting prowess grows.

 The AppleScript system extension is required to use AppleScript. Look for the icon (shown here). It's one of the AppleScript components included with Apple's Mac OS software. The AppleScript extension is placed in the Extension folder within your computer's System Folder when you install the Mac OS. System software 7.1 and later for Power Mac computers also includes another AppleScript-related extension called AppleScriptLib. These files must be in your System Folder when you start your computer in order for AppleScript to work.

 The Scripting Additions folder (look for the icon shown here) is created within the Extensions folder when AppleScript is installed. The files in this folder provide several dialog boxes and other specialized functions to script writers.

 The Script Editor (look for the icon shown here) is a small program from Apple that's included with AppleScript that you can use to write scripts. Because an uncompiled script is essentially a text file, you can write scripts with any word processor. The Script Editor, however, was created for writing AppleScripts and includes several handy features for script writers.

You're now ready to create your first script. Be forewarned: There's something almost narcotic about creating scripts, and it's not uncommon for novice script writers to get hooked. Don't be surprised if what starts out to be a 15-minute look-see turns into a multihour, late-night programming episode.

Tip

If you enjoy creating AppleScripts for QuarkXPress and want to expand your arsenal of scripting tools, several scripting-related XTensions are available. If you decide to venture beyond QuarkXPress and explore other areas, such as system-level scripting and interapplication scripting, you can find considerable information and tools on the Internet (see the sidebar on surfing for scripts on the Net and the section on locating more scripting tools, later in this chapter). The Apple Developer Catalog also offers the AppleScript Software Development Toolkit for $49. This product includes several scripting utilities that are not included with the Mac OS software.

Creating and Running Scripts

At this point, we're assuming that the AppleScript system extensions have been correctly installed and are running. If this is the case, you're ready to begin. For our first trick, we're going to make QuarkXPress roll over—sort of. Actually, we're going to rotate a box. First, we'll prepare QuarkXPress for its role. Launch the program, then create a new document (do not check Automatic Text Box). In the middle of the first page, draw a rectangular box—text or picture. Make sure that it remains active after you create it.

The scripting process

Launch the Script Editor program. Figure 26-1 shows the Script Editor menu bar and an empty window. You can enter a description for a script in the scroll field at the top of the window; the scroll list at the bottom of the window is where you enter the statements that make up your script.

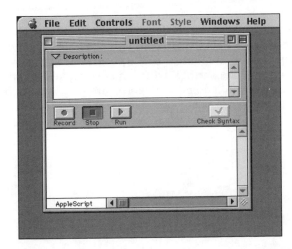

Figure 26-1: When you launch the Script Editor, an empty window is automatically displayed. You use this window to create, compile, and run scripts.

Writing simple scripts

Enter the lines that follow this paragraph exactly as they are written. Enter a return character at the end of each line. Make sure to enter the name of your QuarkXPress program exactly as it appears on the desktop. Because you are free to rename your program, the name may not match the name in the first line of the script. Note also the use of straight quotation marks instead of curly typesetter's quotes (the Script Editor does this for you). Be very careful when you enter the text. Typos are script killers.

```
tell application "QuarkXPress← 4"
activate
tell document 1
set the rotation of the current box to 45
end tell
end tell
```

Perhaps you noticed the chain of command used in the script. First, the script addresses QuarkXPress, then the active document, and finally the active box. If you understand this concept, you'll be scripting like a pro in no time. If you're in an adventurous mood, try substituting the statement that begins "set the rotation of the current box to 45" in the preceding script with each of the following statements:

```
set the color of the current box to "Blue"
set the shade of the current box to 50
set the width of the frame of the current box to 10
set the box shape of the current box to ovular
```

All of the statements above change one of the active box's *properties*. You know all about a box's properties. They're all the things you can change when you choose the Modify, Frame, Clipping, or Runaround commands in the Item menu. If you want to get really fancy, combine all of the "set" statements into a single script, so you can use the script to make all the changes at once.

Checking for syntax errors

The next step is to determine if the statements are correctly constructed. Click the Check Syntax button. If the Script Editor encounters a syntax error, it alerts you and highlights the cause of the error. If the script's syntax is correct, all statements except the first and last are indented, and a number of words are displayed in bold, as illustrated in Figure 26-2. Your script has been compiled and is ready to test.

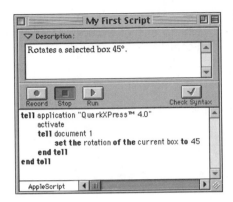

Figure 26-2: When you check the syntax of a script, the Script Editor applies formatting and indents.

Running your script

Click the Run button and then sit back and watch. (While a script runs, you're free to use your hands for other work!) If you've done everything correctly, you'll see QuarkXPress become the active program, and then the actions you put in your script will take place. Voilà! and congratulations. You can now call yourself a scripter without blushing. That's all there is to creating and running a script.

Tip

If you have trouble getting a script to run, double-check the name that QuarkXPress uses for itself. It might use QuarkXPress™ 4 or simply QuarkXPress™ (yes, the name includes the registered trademark symbol). If you run a script from AppleScript (rather than just double-clicking it) and AppleScript can't find QuarkXPress, it will give you a dialog box with which you find the QuarkXPress program. Once you have found and selected the QuarkXPress program file, AppleScript will find out what QuarkXPress's filename is and use that in your script.

Saving your script

When you're finished writing and testing a script, choose Save from the Script Editor's File menu. Name your script, choose its storage location, and choose Application from the Kind pop-up menu, and check the Never Show Startup Screen box. Figure 26-3 shows the dialog box that's displayed when you save a script.

Note

If you want to edit your script later, you must open it by dragging-and-dropping it on the Script Editor application. This is because you saved the script in Application format. If you simply double-click the script, the script will run and try to make changes to the active box in QuarkXPress.

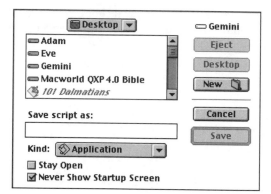

Figure 26-3: The dialog box that's displayed when you save a script created in the Script Editor.

Writing more complex scripts

Let's take a look at the following, more complex, script. Created by Quark's Kelly Anton for this book, it replaces trademark (^{TM}) and registered trademark (®) symbols with your choice of superior or superscript versions.

```
tell application "QuarkXPress←"
    activate
    if exists (document 1) then
        tell document 1
            set x to display dialog "Select a Type Style for ú ù
                and ←." buttons {"Superior", "Superscript", ù
                    "Cancel"} default button 1
            if button returned of x = "Superior" then
                set style of every character of every story ù
                    where (it is "←") or (it is "ú") to ù
                    {on styles:{superior}, off
styles:{superscript}}
            else if button returned of x = "Superscript" then
                set style of every character of every story ù
                    where (it is "←") or (it is "ú") to ù
                    {on styles:{superscript}, off
styles:{superior}}
            else
                —no characters present in document
            end if
        end tell
        display dialog "This script was completed ù
            successfully."
    else
        display dialog "You must have a document open to ù
            run this script."
    end if
end tell
```

In English, here's what the script says:

✦ Send a command to QuarkXPress.

✦ See if a document is open.

✦ If it is, then send a command to that document to display a dialog box with three buttons, Superior, Superscript, and Cancel, and make the first button (Superior) the default button.

✦ If the user clicks Superior, set the style for every occurrence of the ™ and ® symbols to superior.

✦ But if the user clicks Superscript, set the ™ and ® symbols to superscript.

✦ And if the user clicks cancel, do nothing. (The text beginning with two hyphens is a comment, not an instruction.)

✦ After the ™ and ® symbols are modified, put up a dialog box saying the task is completed.

✦ If no document is open, put up a dialog box saying that no document is open.

✦ Tell QuarkXPress that the script is complete.

Play with this script to see if you can add a third button to raise the baseline or boldface the trademark symbols. Then try adding some new features. Here's one possible addition: replacing all double hyphens with an em dash (something QuarkXPress doesn't do as you type). Pretty soon, by extending this script's structure, you could have a pretty complex script that looks for certain attributes and modifies them accordingly (see the following sidebar for more information on the conventions used in our sample scripts).

Tip

One easy way to make a script available within QuarkXPress is to create an alias of the compiled application file and place the alias in the Apple Menu Items folder in the System folder. If you installed all of the AppleScript components, you can also accomplish this task using a script. Click on the script file that you want to add to the Apple menu, then choose Automated Tasks from the Apple menu. From the pop-up menu, choose Add Alias to the Apple Menu.

Connecting with Other Programs

Once you get the hang of it, you can create scripts that make QuarkXPress do anything you want. But automating QuarkXPress is only the beginning of what you can do with scripts. Many other applications are scriptable, and those that are scriptable can talk to one another and exchange data via scripts. The following sections give you a general idea of where to start.

Looking at scripting conventions

The following are the kinds of things you'll encounter (and want to use) when writing your own useful scripts:

✦ Note the use of the ¬ symbol (Option+Return in Script Editor): It is used when you want to break a statement onto several lines (usually for readability). You can see it in use for the "set style" statement in our complex script example. The script writer could have put the entire "set style" statement on one line, but by breaking the statement into three distinct pieces, you can more easily follow the logic: set the style *of what*, then *under what conditions*, and finally *to what new style*. Later, if you wanted to alter the statement, you'd easily see what the three factors are in this statement and could quickly change just the factor(s) you wanted to.

✦ Also in this script, notice the use of conditionals—if, else, end if—that let the script make choices based on what it finds.

✦ Finally, note the ability to create a simple dialog box with buttons: In our more complex sample script, the user can choose whether to set the trademark symbols to superior or superscript by clicking a button.

Publishing and graphics applications

Unfortunately, not many Macintosh publishing and graphics applications are scriptable. Here's a list of what is:

✦ Apple's PhotoFlash, Kudo Image Browser & Publisher from Imspace Systems, and Picture Press (image compression software) from Storm Technology are among the few graphics applications that are scriptable.

✦ Adobe Photoshop 4.0 and Adobe PageMaker offer limited AppleScript support, and PageMaker has a simple, internal scripting language as well.

Word processing, database, and spreadsheet programs

The good news is that several word processing, database, and spreadsheet programs are scriptable. FileMaker Pro from Claris and Butler SQL from EveryWare Development are completely scriptable databases, which means you can store the content of your publications in a database and automatically build QuarkXPress documents by extracting information from the database and formatting it into QuarkXPress documents and pages via scripts.

Web publishing

If you're a QuarkXPress print-publishing site that's thinking about making the move to Web publishing, you have the option to automate at least part of the process by using QuarkXPress and the BeyondPress HTML-export XTension, which is fully scriptable. See Chapter 34 for details about BeyondPress.

Locating More Scripting Tools

Several software utilities—some free, some commercially distributed—are also available for AppleScripters. Demo versions of Scripter, Script Manager, and ScriptMaster are included on the CD that accompanies this book; the OSA Menu system extension is also included. Here's the scoop:

✦ **OSA Menu:** If you're looking for a very handy freebie, try OSA Menu by Leonard Rosenthal. It's a system extension that adds a menu to the Apple menu bar. You can run scripts in any application by choosing entries from the menu.

✦ **FaceSpan:** From Digital Technology International ($299, 801/226-2984), this utility is an interface development tool that lets you quickly create AppleScript-based applications that have the standard Mac look and feel.

✦ **Scripter:** From Main Event Software ($199, 202/298-9595), this utility is another full-featured AppleScript development and debugging application.

A pair of XTensions—Script Manager and ScriptMaster—add scripting capabilities to QuarkXPress. Here's the skinny on these:

✦ **Script Manager:** From Vision's Edge ($79, 904/386-4573), this XTension provides a palette that displays a list of the scripts you create for QuarkXPress. Clicking on a script's name launches the script. Script Manager also lets you run multiple scripts in sequence.

✦ **ScriptMaster:** From Street Logic Software ($149, 619/654-3355), this XTension lets you create scripts for QuarkXPress by recording actions as you perform them. Some scriptable programs are also *recordable,* which means that they have the built-in ability to convert a sequence of actions into a script. Without ScriptMaster, QuarkXPress is not a recordable program. However, when ScriptMaster is running you can generate a script without having to do any writing.

Surfing for scripts on the Web

Now that virtually every piece of information ever recorded by humanity is readily available on the World Wide Web, it's probably not surprising that you can find gobs of information about scripting, AppleScript, and automating QuarkXPress with scripts. Here are some good places to start:

✦ *XPresso Bar: Scripting (http://www.xpressobar.com/script.html):* For QuarkXPress-specific scripting information, we recommend this site. Here you'll find links to a handful of sites with information about creating scripts for QuarkXPress. One of the best links is to Sal's AppleScript Snippets (http://users.aol.com/nyhthawk/welcome.html). Sal Soghoian, the man behind the Web site, is a self-taught scripter who is now the AppleScript product manager. His Web site has downloadable instructional materials and scripting utilities, free scripts, and links to other sites. The XPresso Bar also has links to Quark's Scripting Forum, where you can post questions and review threads about scripting issues; and to Harold Shield's Scripts, which offers a small collection of time-saving scripts for QuarkXPress prepress operators.

For general information about Macintosh scripting and AppleScript, we recommend the following:

✦ *ScriptWeb (http://www.scriptweb.com):* This is a great place to find all kinds of information about Macintosh scripting. It has general scripting information, as well as specific information about AppleScript, UserLand Frontier, and other Mac scripting languages. The General Scripting Info page has links to pages with information about scripting utilities, articles, books, tech support, and "every known scripting link."

✦ *The AppleScript Sourcebook (http://oasis.bellevue.k12.wa.us/cheeseb/index.html):* Much like ScriptWeb, this repository of information about AppleScript has enough information and links to keep scripters of any level occupied for hours. Tips and techniques, news and events, opinions and notes, you'll find it all, plus a load of links to other sites.

✦ *Main Event (http://www.yy.net/bis/mainevent/):* This is another good starting point for those in search of AppleScript-specific information. In addition to information about its own commercial scripting utilities, the site has an informative About AppleScript page, links to Apple's AppleScript site, and a number of AppleScript-related mailing lists.

✦   ✦   ✦

An XTension and Utility Sampler

✦ ✦ ✦ ✦

In This Chapter

Exploring the XTensions

Using the demos on the CD

Working with publishing utilities

✦ ✦ ✦ ✦

There are dozens, if not hundreds, of plug-ins for QuarkXPress, as explained in Chapter 25. This chapter contains an alphabetical listing of many of the XTensions currently available (as of this book's printing) for QuarkXPress. There's also a section (toward the end of this chapter) on publishing utilities—separate programs that work with QuarkXPress to add functionality. The CD accompanying this book has all the software mentioned in this chapter, so if you've never had the opportunity to test-drive an XTension, you're in luck (see the sidebar in this chapter on using the demos on the CD).

Exploring the XTensions

We chose the XTensions described in the following alphabetical listing to show the breadth and depth of tools available for QuarkXPress. Each of the XTensions is explained—with accompanying screen shots—and each XTension folder on the CD (see the following sidebar and Appendix D) includes electronic documentation. Check out the Web sites mentioned in Chapter 25 to stay abreast of the latest XTension options.

Note

In this chapter, we've used the Windows icon in the margin next to the text to indicate the XTensions available for Windows. That's because the Mac has many more XTensions available than does Windows. More and more XTension developers are creating Windows XTensions, so check with the XTension developer to see if things have changed since this book went to press (see the Web site listings in Chapter 25).

Using the demos on the CD

The demo XTensions included on the CD were all developed before QuarkXPress 4 was released. Although Quark designed QuarkXPress so all XTensions created for Mac QuarkXPress 3.3x should also work with version 4, it turns out that this is not true in all cases. That's why we tested all the XTensions on the CD to ensure that they work with QuarkXPress 4. Still, it's possible that some functions may not work, so if you experience problems with a particular demo XTension, disable it and contact the developer to see if a 4-optimized version is available.

Note that Quark has changed the XTensions format in Windows, so pre-4 XTensions will not work in QuarkXPress 4 for Windows. This further limits the number of XTensions for Windows QuarkXPress, although most developers will be updating their Windows XTensions, so be sure to check out the Web sites mentioned in Chapter 25. Because of this format change, we were not able to include Windows versions of any XTensions on the CD that accompanies this book.

Most of the demo XTensions on the CD put QuarkXPress into demo mode when you run them. You cannot save documents while QuarkXPress 4 is in demo mode. You are alerted of this when you launch QuarkXPress and when you open a new or existing document. Some demo XTensions show a splash screen when they load, implying that QuarkXPress will let you save documents, but this usually is not true. With some demo XTensions, you can save documents, but they cannot be opened later unless the demo XTension is installed.

To make sure QuarkXPress for Mac has enough memory to run all the XTensions you have loaded, you may want to increase its memory allocation. To do this, select the QuarkXPress icon in the Finder; choose File⇨Get Info; and increase the value in the Preferred Size field.

Because they're developed by different people and companies, XTensions don't always get along with one another. If you begin to have bizarre problems while working in QuarkXPress, you may want to try turning off all XTensions you're not currently using.

To try an XTension, copy it to the XTension folder in your QuarkXPress program folder, then launch QuarkXPress (see Appendix D for more details on how to use the CD). If you're impressed to the point that you want to purchase one of the demo XTensions, the CD also includes electronic catalogs from several XTension vendors.

Adobe Systems' Prepress

If you use Adobe Systems' TrapWise or PressWise prepress-management software, you'll want the Adobe Prepress XTension (APX), which lets you set output controls. Similar to saving an EPS file or printing to a file, APX (free, Mac only) creates a PostScript file optimized for use with TrapWise and other postprocessing applications. Figure 27-1 shows the dialog box. In QuarkXPress, you activate APX via Utilities⇨Export for Prepress.

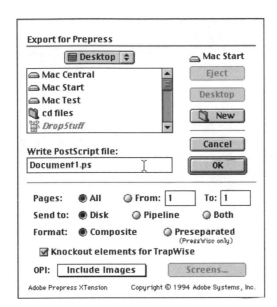

Figure 27-1: The Adobe Prepress XTension's dialog box.

A Lowly Apprentice Production

The XTension developer A Lowly Apprentice Production (ALAP) has created dozens of add-ons for QuarkXPress, including two collections of its most popular wares, XPert Collection Volume 1 and XPert Collection Volume 2. The CD includes several ALAP XTensions.

Note

Many of the ALAP installers place their XTensions at the root level of the QuarkXPress folder, where they will not load. After you install one of these XTensions, place it in the XTension folder before you launch QuarkXPress.

ColorPick

The ColorPick XTension from ALAP (free, Mac only) is like a second Colors palette. Accessed via the Utilities menu, ColorPick shows all active colors. When you edit an existing color or create a new one, ColorPick opens the Mac's standard color picker rather than the QuarkXPress color picker used in the Edit Color dialog box.

Tip

You can access the same color picker without this XTension if you have the Quark POCE XTension installed; just choose POCE from the Model pop-up menu in the regular Edit Color dialog box, and then click Select. Note that the POCE color picker takes more memory to use than ColorPick does, however.

FingerType

When it comes to applying many paragraph formats—such as drop caps, indents, space between paragraphs, and rules—QuarkXPress doesn't provide much in the way of interface options. You're forced to open the Paragraph Attributes dialog box and enter values into text fields. For typographers who prefer a more visual approach, ALAP's FingerType ($49, Mac only) provides an alternative by letting you modify many common paragraph attributes, as well as a handful of character attributes, by clicking and dragging, and displays a live update as you drag.

The FingerType palette, shown in Figure 27-2, contains 10 tools. The blank area on the right end of the palette displays values as you click and drag while using one of the FingerType tools. When the FingerType palette is active, you can Tab and Shift+Tab to change tools. When you modify the appearance of text using any of the FingerType tools, you have the option of modifying individual characters and paragraphs, as well as ranges of text.

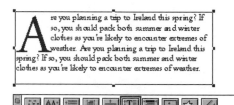

Figure 27-2: The FingerType palette.

If you've grown accustomed to modifying paragraph formats by entering values into text fields, you may feel a bit awkward the first time you use FingerType. And because much of FingerType's power lies in numerous keyboard equivalents, it will take you a while to become a true power user. But once you get the hang of FingerType's click-and-drag approach to text formatting, your once-frequent trips to the Paragraph Attributes dialog box may become a distant memory.

Imposer

QuarkXPress lets you output facing-page spreads when you print. Unfortunately, this feature isn't much help if you need to output *printer spreads*—which accounts for the gap between pages needed for folding. ALAP's Imposer ($96, Mac only) not only lets you impose pages from a QuarkXPress document into printer spreads, it also handles bleed, creep, cross-over trapping, page gaps, and plate margins, and it does all of this work behind the scenes when you print. If you're also a user of ALAP's MarkIt XTension—which lets you add press marks, such as trim lines, registration marks, and color bars to a document when you print it—you have a full page-imposition package at your fingertips.

When Imposer is running, the Imposer command is added to the File menu. Choosing this command displays the Imposer dialog box, shown in Figure 27-3. Here you can view the current document's printer spreads or click on a pop-up menu to display a list of options.

Figure 27-4 shows the Printer Spread Setup dialog box, displayed when you choose Printer Spread Setup from the pop-up menu. The Registration Marks pop-up menu lets you output default registration marks that are similar to the ones used by

QuarkXPress, or to choose a registration style created with MarkIt; you also have the option to turn off printing of registration marks. Other control fields include:

✦ **Bleed:** This lets you specify the amount of bleed space beyond the edge of the trimmed page area.

✦ **Crossover:** This specifies how far QuarkXPress items will bleed into the page gap area between pages in printer spreads when output.

✦ **Creep:** This determines the amount of space added between facing pages to allow for paper thickness when the final publication is folded.

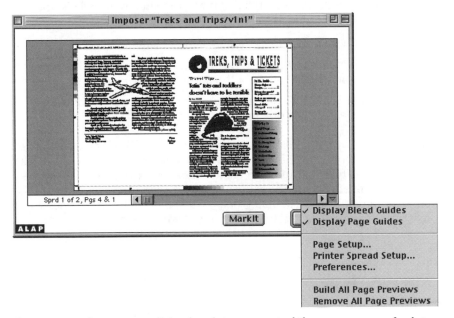

Figure 27-3: The Imposer dialog box lets you control the appearance of printer spreads, and open dialog boxes that let you specify output options.

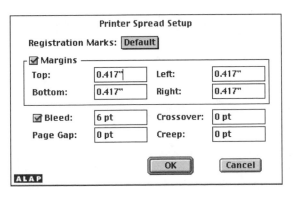

Figure 27-4: Imposer's Printer Spread Setup dialog box.

ItemMaster

Savvy QuarkXPress users know that when it comes to controlling the appearance of text, style sheets are the way to go. They save time and ensure typographic consistency. However, QuarkXPress does not offer a style sheet–like option for controlling the appearance of boxes and lines. You can either apply item modifications manually via the Modify dialog box or the Measurements palette or you can drag preconstructed items from a library window onto your page. ALAP's ItemMaster ($99, Mac only) lets you control the appearance and position of items and their contents by creating item style. Item styles behave much like style sheets:

✦ If you change an item style, all items to which that style is applied are immediately updated to reflect your changes.

✦ You can append item styles between documents.

✦ You can create new item styles that are based on existing styles. If you modify inherited aspects of the parent style, the child style is also modified.

✦ Item styles are included when you copy items that have been styled using an item style between documents.

Figure 27-5 shows the Item Styles dialog box, accessed by choosing Items from the Edit menu. If you know how to create style sheets, you'll find it easy to get the hang of item styles because the basic concepts, as well as many of the controls for creating item styles, are the same as those for creating style sheets. Figure 27-6 shows the Edit Item Style dialog box. Like style sheets, item styles can be based on existing styles and can include a keyboard equivalent.

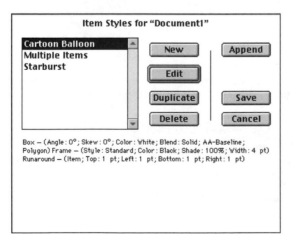

Figure 27-5: The Item Styles dialog box lets you create, edit, and delete item styles.

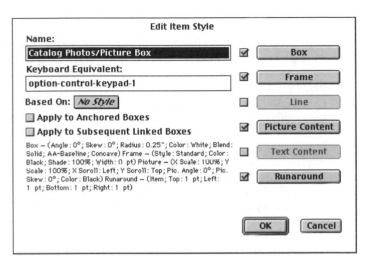

Figure 27-6: The Edit Item Style dialog box.

ItemMaster also includes some powerful features that you won't find in QuarkXPress's style sheets. For example, you can:

✦ Apply an item style to multiple elements simultaneously.

✦ Save polygonal styles and create new polygons based on saved polygonal styles via a polygon tool that's added to the Tool palette.

✦ Change an item's appearance by dragging a swatch from the Item Styles palette onto the item.

Figure 27-7 shows the Item Styles palette, which lets you apply item styles to the boxes and lines on your pages and create a new, styled item from scratch by clicking and dragging an item style name onto a page.

Figure 27-7: The Item Styles palette lets you apply item styles to boxes and lines on your pages and create new, styled items from scratch. The starburst polygon was created by dragging the Starburst item style onto a rectangular picture box like the one on the left.

MarkIt

QuarkXPress provides many features for modifying the appearance and position of items that you place on your pages and ultimately print. But when it's time to output color separations, you have very little control over the appearance and position of press marks—such as color bars, registration marks, and trim lines—that are printed outside the page edges. ALAP's MarkIt ($99, Mac only) was designed for QuarkXPress users who need enhanced tools for adding and placing press marks.

Like ItemMaster, MarkIt borrows heavily from QuarkXPress's style sheet feature. You begin by creating MarkIt styles, and then you apply a MarkIt style to a particular document before you print it. Figure 27-8 shows the MarkIt Styles dialog box, which is displayed when you choose MarkIt from the Edit menu. This dialog lets you create, edit, duplicate, and delete MarkIt styles, as well as import and export styles.

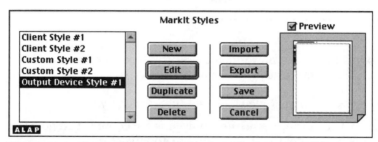

Figure 27-8: The MarkIt Styles dialog box displays a scroll list of available styles. The preview window on the right shows a thumbnail of the press marks associated with the highlighted MarkIt style.

If you click New, Edit, or Duplicate in the MarkIt Styles dialog box, the dialog box shown in Figure 27-9 is displayed. The scroll list on the left of this dialog box displays the different kinds of bleed and trim marks, color bars, gray bars, registration marks, and text that you can drag into position outside the page boundaries. If you want to create custom marks, you have the option to import and use any EPS graphic.

To apply a MarkIt style to a document, choose MarkIt from the File menu. This displays a submenu with all of the MarkIt styles you've created. Choose the one you want and you're ready to print.

PasteIt

Copying items from one spread to another can be a pain, because QuarkXPress doesn't paste a cut or copied item to the same location as it was cut or copied from. ALAP's PasteIt (free, Mac only) fixes that. If you press the Option key and go directly to the Edit menu, you'll see that Cut, Copy, and Paste are replaced with CutIt, CopyIt, and PasteIt. Selecting these new options ensures that QuarkXPress remembers (and uses) the locations of the selected item(s) when cutting or copying from, and pasting to, a different spread.

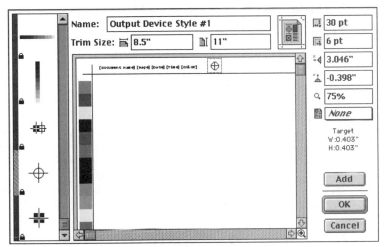

Figure 27-9: When you create a MarkIt style, you can specify a trim size that's different from the document's page size. To add a press mark, click and drag its icon from the scroll list to the document window.

QuickOpen

Quark meant well when it created the Non-Matching Preferences dialog box that automatically appears when you open a document whose preference settings differ from the QuarkXPress defaults. The problem is, in almost every case, you want to keep the document preferences, and so this dialog box becomes an annoyance. But there's no way to turn it off in QuarkXPress. If ALAP's QuickOpen (free, Mac only) is installed, this dialog box is turned off, and QuarkXPress automatically uses the document's preferences.

ScaleLock

Being able to ⌘+drag a text box's sizing handles and have its text resize automatically with the box is a great feature—unless you don't want to have text resized by accident. If ALAP's ScaleLock (free, Mac only) is installed, ⌘+dragging no longer lets you resize a text box (and, thus, no longer resizes a text box's text).

ShadowCaster

Creating drop shadows of items in QuarkXPress is a cinch. Duplicate the item for which you want to create a shadow, apply a dark color to the copied item, and then send the copy behind the original and offset it. However, if you want to create drop shadows with soft edges, you're going to have to look to an XTension for help. ALAP's ShadowCaster ($99, Mac only) lets you create soft drop shadows for any item, and provides a bevy of tools for controlling the appearance and placement of the shadows it creates. For example, you can specify:

✦ The resolution of the shadows that ShadowCaster generates

✦ The amount of blur applied to the edges of a shadow

✦ The color and shade of shadows

Figure 27-10 shows the ShadowCaster palette, which contains five tabs. (You access the palette by choosing Show ShadowCaster from the View menu.) The example shows a simple soft shadow created from a text box. In addition to creating shadows that are placed within white picture boxes, you can also burn shadows onto colored box backgrounds (ShadowCaster lets you convert a colored box background into an identically colored TIFF image) and pictures.

ShadowCaster also lets you save and apply shadow styles to items in much the same way you save and apply style sheets to text.

Figure 27-10: The ShadowCaster palette lets you adjust the appearance of the shadows you create for QuarkXPress items.

StoryChaser

It's easy to lose track of where stories jump to in a document. That's where ALAP's StoryChaser XTension (free, Mac only) comes in. It displays statistics for each page of your document, showing what page the currently selected story (text box) jumps from and to. It also gives character and word counts. Figure 27-11 shows an example report; you get a StoryChaser report via Utilities⇨StoryChaser.

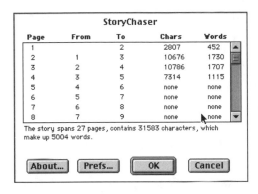

Figure 27-11: The StoryChaser report for a selected story.

Page	From	To	Chars	Words
1		2	2807	452
2	1	3	10676	1730
3	2	4	10786	1707
4	3	5	7314	1115
5	4	6	none	none
6	5	7	none	none
7	6	8	none	none
8	7	9	none	none

The story spans 27 pages, contains 31583 characters, which make up 5004 words.

About...   Prefs...   OK   Cancel

XPert Tools Volume 1

In the beginning—of XTensions, that is—many XTensions were one-trick-pony utilities that performed a single task. But in recent years, several XTension developers have started to offer bundled tool sets with several XTensions that perform a wide variety of tasks. ALAP's XPert Tools Volume 1 ($95, Mac only) was the first of the XTension tool sets, and its consistent interface, ease of use, and feature set has made it one of the most popular XTension products. Here's a quick rundown of what you'll find in XPert Tools Volume 1:

Caution

QuarkXPress's new Extensions Manager feature (explained in Chapter 25) lets you turn XTensions on and off. Third-party XTensions that handle XTension management during program startup should not be used with QuarkXPress 4. ALAP's XPert Tools Volumes 1 and 2 include an XTension called XPert Loader that is not compatible with QuarkXPress 4. If you install the demo version of XPert Tools Volume 1 or 2, make sure you remove the XPert Loader XTension before you launch QuarkXPress.

✦ **XPert Scale:** Scales multiple selected items and groups, including the contents of text boxes and picture boxes. A flexographic feature is also included for nonproportional printing.

✦ **XPert Layers:** Provides a palette that lets you rearrange the stacking order of items and show or hide individual items.

✦ **XPert Color:** Lets you find and change colors applied to items and contents, convert process colors to spot and vice versa, and add colors using the Apple color picker.

✦ **XPert ImageInfo:** Clicking on the small triangle that this XTension adds to all picture boxes displays a pop-up palette with picture-related information and controls. Figure 27-12 shows the ImageInfo pop-up palette and the information and controls it displays for EPS pictures. (In this example, the Fonts button is selected; the text at the top of the palette explains that the EPS image contains no embedded fonts.)

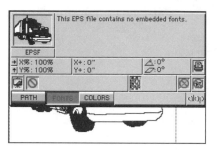

Figure 27-12: Dragging the arrow pointer over any of the buttons at the bottom of the XPert ImageInfo palette displays related information at the top of the palette next to a thumbnail view of the image.

✦ **XPert Print:** Lets you select a rectangular portion of a page and print it or save it as an EPS file.

✦ **XPert Paste:** Lets you paste items onto pages using the X and Y coordinates of the original items. Also provides the option to paste an item onto multiple pages.

✦ **XPert Menus:** Adds four icons to the bottom of a QuarkXPress document window that let you change the view percentage, display any page, switch among open documents, and choose QuarkXPress tools.

✦ **XPert Launch:** Lets you open other applications, QuarkXPress documents, and other files by placing the files in a folder called Launch within the QuarkXPress folder.

✦ **XPert Open:** Speeds up the process of opening documents by letting you specify a default option (Use XPress Preferences or Keep Document Settings) for the Non-Matching Preferences dialog box.

✦ **XPert Ungroup:** Lets you ungroup all elements in a group and all levels of grouping (such as groups within groups) in a single operation.

✦ **XPert View:** Lets you open documents at custom view percentages and locations, rapidly size and arrange multiple document windows, and show and hide document windows the same way you show and hide palettes.

✦ **XPert Nudge:** Adds a palette that lets you choose the increment used for QuarkXPress's nudge feature (the ability to move items in small increments using the arrow keys), and lets you nudge active items with mouse clicks.

✦ **XPert TextLock:** Lets you lock the contents of a text box or chain.

✦ **XPert Quit:** Provides a Preferences dialog box, shown in Figure 27-13, that lets you automatically quit QuarkXPress after a specified period of inactivity and, if you want, save changes.

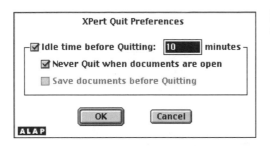

Figure 27-13: The XPert Quit Preferences dialog box.

XPert Tools Volume 2

XPert Tools Volume 2 ($95, Mac only) follows in the footsteps of its older sibling by offering a diverse set of tools, all of which share a similar, QuarkXPress-like look and feel:

+ **XPert CharacterStyles:** Lets you create and apply character-level style sheets. Although QuarkXPress 4 now offers this feature, you may find that XPert CharacterStyles is easier to use.

+ **XPert TextLink:** Displays a palette with several tools for linking and unlinking text boxes.

+ **XPert TextStyler:** Adds a marquee tool to the QuarkXPress tool palette that lets you highlight text by clicking and dragging a rectangle.

+ **XPert Pilot:** Adds a palette that displays a thumbnail preview of the current page or spread. When you click the thumbnail, QuarkXPress jumps to that part of the document.

+ **XPert CommandPad:** Lets you create custom palettes that contain tools, menu commands, and most keyboard combinations. Everything is available with the click of a mouse. Figure 27-14 shows an Edit CommandPad Style palette.

+ **XPert Scripter:** Adds a palette that lets you launch OSA-compliant AppleScripts. You also have the option to create sets of scripts. When you run a set, all scripts are executed in succession.

+ **XPert Rulers:** Provides two features. One is a tool for measuring the distance between any two points on a page or spread. The other is an option letting you snap rulers to the top and left edges of active items. These mini-rulers are helpful for positioning and resizing items.

+ **XPert PageSets:** Lets you save default document settings (including page size, margins, and columns) using a style sheets-like interface, and choose a page set when opening new documents. (Note: The demo version of the XPert PageSets XTension does not add features to QuarkXPress 4.)

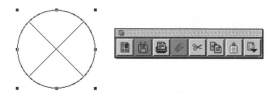

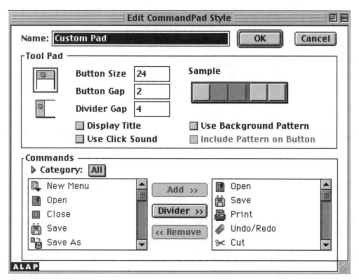

Figure 27-14: With CommandPad, you can create custom palettes with buttons for the commands and tools you use most often. The palette at the top was created using the controls in the Edit CommandPad Style dialog box.

✦ **XPert ItemMarks:** Lets you add crop marks and registration marks around any item. Very handy for creating multi-up versions of such things as business cards and labels. Figure 27-15 shows the XPert ItemMarks Preferences dialog box and a picture box to which crop and registration marks have been added.

✦ **XPert BoxTools:** Adds features that let you resize a picture to fill a box, resize a box to fit snugly around a picture image, change a text box to a picture box and vice versa, specify different text insets for each side of a text box, and align an item on a page.

✦ **XPert JobLog:** Lets you keep track of changes made to a document, including the name of the person who made the changes. You can also name a document when you create it and save a report of the document's history.

✦ **XPert TextScaleShift:** Adds a palette that lets you scale highlighted text horizontally and vertically and shift its baseline.

✦ **XPert Preferences:** Lets you control the resolution of the picture preview that's added to a document when you import a picture, customize the appearance of QuarkXPress, and specify different default measurement systems for different parts of QuarkXPress.

✦ **XPert Greeking:** Lets you display pictures as gray boxes on a box-by-box basis.

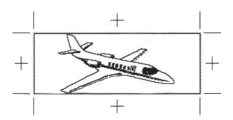

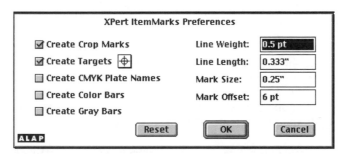

Figure 27-15: The appearance and position of the crop marks and registration marks created around the picture box (above) reflect the default settings in the XPert ItemMarks Preferences dialog box (below).

Bad Knees' CreateCrops

Another one-trick-pony XTension, Bad Knees Development's CreateCrops (free, Mac only), accessed via the Utilities menu, converts the selected box into crop marks. This helps you when you are printing, for example, several business cards on a single sheet and need to indicate where each is cut. (This is called *n-up* or *multi-up* printing.)

Beware: this XTension replaces the selected box with crop marks, so don't use it on a box that contains text or graphics—make sure you create a box that is the exact size of the business card or other item to be cropped. Then use this XTension to convert it into crop marks.

Tobias Boskamp

Many Quark XTensions are created by individuals. Some create plug-ins for use at work, while others simply create XTensions as a small business or hobby. Tobias Boskamp is a one-person XTension developer whose SpeedOpen remains one of the most popular XTensions in use.

Article-XT for PDF

If you need to convert QuarkXPress documents into PDF files and those documents contain articles that span multiple text boxes and pages, you'll want to check out Article-XT for PDF ($99, Mac only). It lets you embed article definitions in the PostScript files you generate from QuarkXPress documents. This embedded information is used when you convert a PostScript file into a Portable Document Format (PDF) file with Acrobat Exchange. It makes the resulting articles easier to read when the PDF file is viewed with Acrobat Reader. Without Article-XT, you have to use Acrobat Exchange to define complex articles manually, a time-consuming process that gets increasingly difficult as articles get longer and span more boxes and pages.

When Article-XT is running, choosing Show Articles from the View menu displays the Articles palette, shown in Figure 27-16. This palette lets you assign article names to text boxes and picture boxes and control their position within the resulting PDF file. Text chains that span multiple boxes and pages are treated as a single article. Clicking on the pop-up menu on the right edge of this palette displays commands that let you access the following:

✦ The Article Usage dialog box, which displays a list of the articles you've defined, with information about each article

✦ The Settings dialog box, shown in Figure 27-17, in which you specify default settings for the articles you create

✦ Online help

✦ A dialog box that displays demo version restrictions

FlowMaster and FlowWatch

QuarkXPress users often go to great lengths to get their text to look and flow just right. In some cases, even the slightest change in the flow of text can be disastrous. But the reality is that—for a variety of reasons—text sometimes reflows. Perhaps your service bureau is using a different version of QuarkXPress than you, or maybe some of their fonts are newer or older than yours. Or perhaps you're a Mac user who has received a QuarkXPress document from a Windows user and you don't have all of the required fonts. If you've been bitten by the reflow bug, or if you want to avoid getting bit altogether, check out FlowMaster from Tobias Boskamp ($149, Mac and Windows). If adds two features for controlling the flow of text:

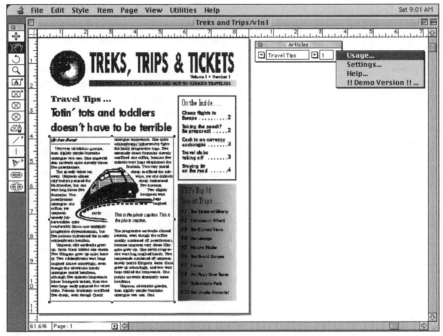

Figure 27-16: The Articles palette lets you assign names to individual articles and control the order in which they're exported when you create a PostScript file. You also have the option to export the contents of a QuarkXPress document without assigning names to articles.

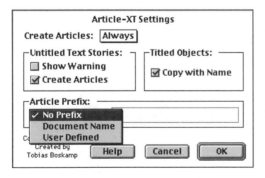

Figure 27-17: The Article-XT Settings dialog box lets you embed article information every time you create a PostScript file or only when Acrobat Distiller is selected in the Printer Description pop-up menu of QuarkXPress's Print dialog box (in the Setup pane). Other options let you control how untitled stories are handled and automatically assign prefixes to articles.

✦ When the XTension is running, it includes information—in the form of *flow tables*—about the flow of text when you save a QuarkXPress document. When the document is opened by somebody else who's using FlowWatch, the XTension compares the text flow information with the actual text flow. If it detects differences, it warns you and shows you where text has reflowed.

✦ It also provides the option to lock text flow and hyphenation when you save a document. This feature is particularly useful for publishers who need to exchange documents among different international versions of QuarkXPress.

FlowMaster also includes a free XTension called FlowWatch, which is included among the free XTensions on the CD included with this book. This XTension lets QuarkXPress users include text flow information when they save their documents, but it's not able to read this information when documents are opened. Users of FlowMaster, such as service bureaus, can provide FlowWatch to their clients to ensure that text reflow doesn't occur when they receive QuarkXPress documents.

Figure 27-18 shows the FlowMaster dialog box. The controls in this dialog box let you specify what actions FlowMaster performs when you open and save QuarkXPress documents. The FlowMaster palette, shown in Figure 27-19, contains controls for identifying and adjusting reflowed text. At the top of the palette, the Scope pop-up menu lets you control text flow on a document-wide basis, for stories in active text boxes, or for marked stories; the State pop-up menu lets you mark and unmark text boxes; and the Mode pop-up menu lets you work with either the automatic flow tables that were added to a document when it was saved or the manual flow tables that were created by the user.

Figure 27-18: The FlowMaster dialog box.

Figure 27-19: The FlowMaster palette.

SpeedOpen

Recall that there is no way to turn off the Non-Matching Preferences dialog box that automatically appears when you open a document whose preference settings differ from the QuarkXPress defaults. You will usually want to keep the document preferences, so this dialog box becomes an annoyance.

That's where SpeedOpen comes in—with this XTension installed ($35, Mac and Windows), you can tell QuarkXPress to automatically keep the document preferences or to automatically apply the default QuarkXPress preferences.

But SpeedOpen does more—it also lets you control whether pictures are greeked, what the view percentage is, what the default hyphenation language is, and whether you are warned when documents and libraries are converted from previous versions of QuarkXPress. The SpeedOpen controls are placed in the Utilities menu, and Figure 27-20 shows the dialog box.

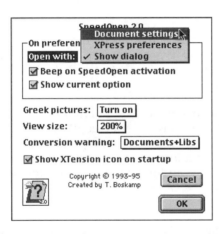

Figure 27-20: The SpeedOpen dialog box.

College Fund's Doc Magnify

QuarkXPress's 800-percent view-scale limit is an improvement over the 400-percent limit of all previous versions, but if you're a precision freak and like to work in highly magnified views, you may want to take a look at Doc Magnify from College Fund Software ($5, Mac only). It adds a small palette, accessed by choosing Show Doc Magnify from the View menu and shown in Figure 27-21, that lets you choose view scales from 10 percent up to 800 percent. (Although the Doc Magnify palette lists zoom percentages as high as 1200 percent, Doc Magnify actually won't zoom any more than 800 percent in QuarkXPress 4.)

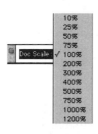

Figure 27-21: The Doc Magnify palette.

CompuSense

This United Kingdom–based developer offers a variety of XTensions. Although its offerings are not as extensive as those of A Lowly Apprentice Production or Extensis, CompuSense is nonetheless a key XTension developer, one that focuses on document management add-ons.

PictureManager

If the QuarkXPress documents you create contain numerous pictures and those pictures have accompanying captions, you can automate the caption-box creation process—and perform other picture-management tasks—with the PictureManager XTension from CompuSense ($179, Mac only).

PictureManager lets you specify the default attributes of caption boxes, the default formats applied to the text within, and automatically generate caption boxes and captions based on the default settings. The Default Credit Settings dialog box, shown in Figure 27-22, lets you specify text, text formats, frame settings, horizontal and vertical text alignment, the position of the caption text box relative to the accompanying picture box, and the width of the caption box.

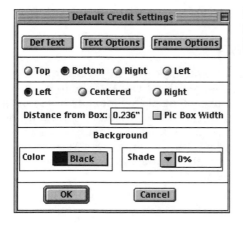

Figure 27-22: PictureManager's Default Credit Settings dialog box lets you specify default settings for caption boxes and text.

Figure 27-23 shows the Picture Manager dialog box, which is a beefed-up variation of the Pictures pane of QuarkXPress's Usage dialog box (Utilities⇨Usage). Among other things, the buttons in this dialog box let you delete pictures and picture boxes from documents (as well as the original picture files), replace a picture with another picture, update modified pictures, and display detailed information about individual pictures. You can also turn printing on and off and print negatives or positives of individual pictures.

PictureManager also lets you:

✦ Place copies of a document (along with its linked graphic files, the XPress Preferences file, and other required auxiliary files) into a user-specified folder.

✦ Automatically update modified picture files and find missing files.

✦ Greek individual pictures.

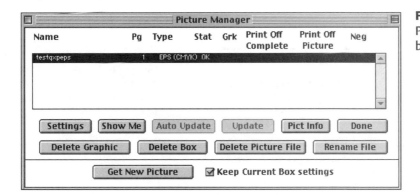

Figure 27-23: The PictureManager dialog box.

The Bundler

If you send your QuarkXPress documents to a service provider, you're probably aware of the Collect for Output command (in the File menu), which lets you create a folder into which a copy of the active document, copies of linked imported picture files, and a document report file are placed. You're also probably aware that when you use this feature, neither screen fonts nor printer fonts are collected, although both are required to display and print a document correctly. The Bundler from CompuSense ($89, Mac only) adds several useful features that Collect for Output lacks, including the ability to include printer and screen fonts when you gather files in preparation for output. Figure 27-24 shows the default options available for the "bundles" you gather. You can:

✦ Automatically include or exclude printer fonts, screen fonts, fonts embedded in EPS pictures, and the XPress Preferences file.

✦ Exclude common printer fonts, such as the LaserWriter 35 (the standard fonts in every PostScript laser printer).

✦ Include special instructions with information such as your name and phone number, the desired print medium (paper, film, laser, or slide), resolution, color plates to be output, and so on.

✦ Search for graphic files that have been moved.

✦ Automatically add required files to bundles. Note that it does not collect other XTensions. It just tells you if an XTension is necessary to open the document being bundled.

When the Bundler is running, an additional menu—called Bdlr—is added to the right of the QuarkXPress menu bar. When it's time to collect files, you can choose File Mover or Batch Move from the Mover submenu (Bdlr⇨Mover) to gather individual or multiple documents, respectively, and their required printing files. When you choose either of these commands, you also have the option to override the default settings.

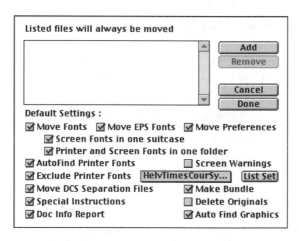

Figure 27-24: The Bundler defaults you set in this dialog box determine which files are collected when you choose File Mover or Batch Move from the Mover submenu.

Dalai Software's DropIt XT

Several programs offer drag-and-drop features that let you import text and picture files into documents by dragging their Finder icons onto pages. But QuarkXPress is not one of them. If you want to add this feature to QuarkXPress, check out Dalai Software's DropIt XT ($25, Mac only). When it's running, you can drag text files and picture files from the Finder and drop them onto QuarkXPress text boxes and picture boxes.

As with QuarkXPress's Get Picture command, you have to create a box before you can drag and drop a text file or picture file onto it, but unlike QuarkXPress, DropIt XT does not require the box to be active when you drag and drop.

You can drag and drop only files that QuarkXPress is capable of importing. For example, you can drag and drop a TIFF file, but you can't drag and drop a native Photoshop file—unless you've added an XTension that lets you import Photoshop files. If you drop a picture file onto a box that contains a picture, the original picture is replaced. If you drop a text file onto highlighted text, the highlighted text is replaced.

Note

If you have chosen None from the Content submenu (Item⇨Content) for a box, you cannot drag or drop a text file or picture file onto the box.

Extensis

Extensis has made a name for itself as the leading purveyor of add-ons and plug-ins for desktop publishing and graphics software. The company's QX-Tools is the most popular collection of XTensions, and Extensis also offers plug-in collections for Adobe PageMaker, Adobe Photoshop, Adobe Illustrator, and Macromedia FreeHand, as well as some stand-alone prepress utilities.

QX-Drag&Drop

Drag-and-drop is one of those invisible functions that most of us don't use because it is invisible. But once you discover the function, it quickly becomes a normal part of your working style. With QX-Drag&Drop (free, Mac only), you can drag pictures from the Finder or from Extensis's Fetch image-cataloging (recently renamed Portfolio) software directly into QuarkXPress. QX-Drag&Drop will create the picture or text box for you. Note that you can drag and drop only files in formats supported by QuarkXPress; other files are ignored.

QX-Tools

QX-Tools 2.0 ($99, Mac only) collects 15 XTensions into a package that is almost overwhelming. (Remember: you can turn off those you don't use with the XTensions Manager in QuarkXPress.) It adds Microsoft-style toolbars to the top of the QuarkXPress window to give you single-click access to a wealth of QX-Tools functions (this is easier than using the View menu to turn palettes on and off), and it lets you display any of 10 new palettes (see Figure 27-25).

Caution

QuarkXPress's new XTensions Manager feature (explained in Chapter 25) lets you turn XTensions on and off. Third-party XTensions that handle XTension management during program startup should not be used with QuarkXPress 4. Extensis's QX-Tools includes an XTension called QX-Manager that is not compatible with QuarkXPress 4. If you install the demo version of QX-Tools, make sure you remove the QX-Manager XTension before you launch QuarkXPress.

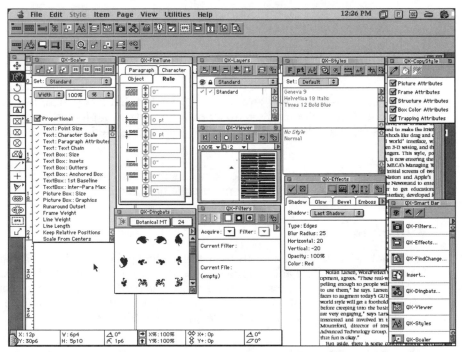

Figure 27-25: The various palettes added by QX-Tools 2.0. Also note the added toolbars at the top of the screen and the added tools in the Tools palette.

Here's a rundown of the tools:

✦ **QX-DocStyles:** Replaces the New Document dialog box (File⇨New⇨Document, or ⌘+N) with the one shown in Figure 27-26. In addition to the standard new-document features, it adds the ability to specify section numbering and to save document styles (named document settings that you can use, rather than entering document settings in future new documents).

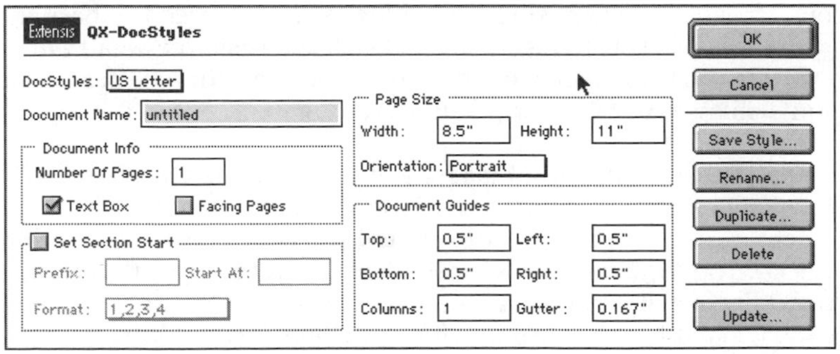

Figure 27-26: The QX-DocStyles dialog box is an enhanced replacement for the New Document dialog box.

✦ **QX-CopyStyle:** Lets you copy box, line, and picture and text attributes from one item to another.

✦ **QX-FindChange:** Lets you find and replace a lot more than just text attributes—including frames, picture boxes, rules, and colors. Figure 27-27 shows the dialog box.

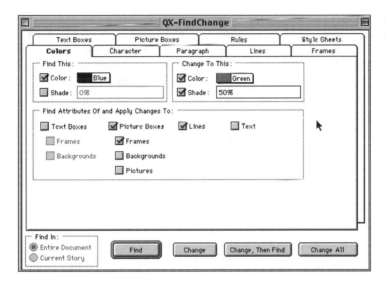

Figure 27-27: The enhanced find and replace functions in QX-FindChange.

✦ **QX-Effects:** Lets you apply shadow, bevel, glow, and embossing effects to text and picture boxes (by converting them to TIFF files).

✦ **QX-Filters:** Lets you apply Photoshop filters to TIFF and PICT images in your picture boxes.

✦ **QX-FineTune:** Lets you adjust paragraph, text, box, and line attributes from one palette, rather than use various dialog boxes. Figure 27-28 shows the palette in use for a text box.

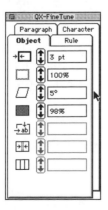

Figure 27-28: The QX-FineTune palette lets you nudge and otherwise adjust various elements.

✦ **QX-Scaler:** Lets you scale multiple objects precisely, by any percentage, or interactively via the mouse.

✦ **QX-Bars:** Adds toolbars to the top of the QuarkXPress screen. Use View⇨Toolbars to decide which toolbars you want to display.

✦ **QX-SmartBar:** Notes your actions and creates a custom toolbar with buttons for the commands you use the most.

✦ **QX-Layers:** Lets you assign objects to layers, which you can then hide and rearrange. You can use layers to, for example, create multilingual documents in which each language's text boxes are all on the same layer, so you can hide or show a language easily in a multilingual document. Or you can put all images on a layer and then hide that layer for fast draft printing.

✦ **QX-Viewer:** Shows a thumbnail view of any page or spread in your document. This is handy when you have zoomed into a page and want to see the rest of the page without changing your view.

✦ **QX-Dingbats:** Displays a palette of special symbols. Select the symbol font you want to get a dingbat from, and the palette shows all the available dingbats.

✦ **QX-Tips & Tricks:** Displays a tip from noted QuarkXPress expert and frequent *Macworld* contributor David Blatner each time you launch or quit QuarkXPress.

✦ **QX-Styles:** Lets you create and apply character styles. This function is not needed in QuarkXPress 4.

✦ **QX-Print:** Lets you print nonconsecutive pages. This function is not needed in QuarkXPress 4.

Finally, QX-Tools adds two tools to the Tool palette—Save as EPS and Interactive Scaling:

 ✦ **Save as EPS tool:** This feature is similar to QuarkXPress's Save Page as EPS function, except the QX-Tools version lets you save any selection. Once you indicate a selection to be saved as an EPS file via the Save as EPS tool (shown here), use File⇨Save Selection as EPS to actually create the EPS file. Note that the Save as EPS feature is also available from the QX-Tools toolbar. If you select one or more boxes, you can save it (or them) as an EPS file by using File⇨Save Items Bounds as EPS.

 ✦ **Interactive Scaling tool:** This tool (shown here) lets you resize any text or picture box and have the contents resized along with the box. It's like holding the ⌘ key when resizing with the standard QuarkXPress Item tool.

FCS

FCS is typical of the small XTension developer who offers a couple of add-ons targeted to a specific need or two.

FCSLock

If you use QuarkXPress in a workgroup environment, you may want to prevent certain users from accessing certain features. For example, if writers use QuarkXPress templates only to enter the text of their articles, an administrator might want to prevent them from accessing any tools other than the Content tool. FCSLock ($71, Mac only) was designed for such publishing sites and allows a system administrator to disable individual tools, palettes, and features.

Choosing Configure FCSLock from the Utilities menu displays the dialog box shown in Figure 27-29. The checkboxes at the top of this dialog box let you disable individual tools and palettes. Below the checkboxes are 15 radio buttons. Clicking on a button displays a set of related checkboxes in the lower half of the dialog box. In the example, the Style button is checked. After you click on a radio button, uncheck the boxes of features you want to disable.

FCSLock also includes a companion XTension called SetLockXT that lets you lock documents. To open a locked document, a QuarkXPress user must have either FCSLock or SetLockXT installed.

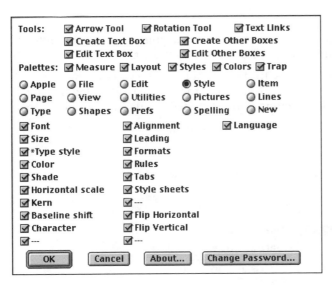

Figure 27-29: FCSLock lets you disable tools, palettes, and commands. This example shows the style-related features that you can enable or disable.

FCSTableMaker

The Tabs pane of QuarkXPress's Paragraph Attributes dialog box lets you create and position six different kinds of tabs and specify fill characters for individual tabs. The tab controls, although versatile, are not easy to master, and getting a table to look just right is often a time-consuming process that involves many trips to the Paragraph Attributes dialog box. FCSTableMaker ($89, Mac only) provides several useful features, including the ability to quickly create and adjust equally spaced tabs and save tab settings in a style sheet.

When FCSTableMaker is running, the FCS Utilities command is added to QuarkXPress's Utilities menu. Figure 27-30 shows the Table Maker dialog box, which is displayed when you choose Table Maker from the FCS Utilities submenu. In addition to specifying the number of tabs, left and right margins, and the type of tab, you can add vertical rules to the tab stops and specify the width of the rules and the distance between the tab stops and the rules.

Figure 27-30: The Table maker dialog box.

In addition to its table-making features, FCSTableMaker also lets you:

✦ Automatically place a horizontal and vertical guideline in the middle of a page or in the middle of the area defined by the margins.

✦ Create grids of guidelines with the option to fill the resulting grid with picture boxes or text boxes. Figure 27-31 shows the Create Grid dialog box and the controls available for creating grids of guidelines, picture boxes, or text boxes.

✦ Remove all guidelines with a single mouse click.

✦ Nudge tabs.

✦ Access all FCSTableMaker commands and dialogs from a palette.

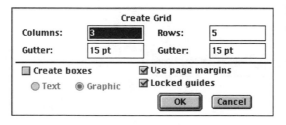

Figure 27-31: The Create Grid dialog box.

Gluon

Gluon is also representative of the small XTension developer who targets his or her add-ons to a specific need or two. (The Gluon XTensions are created by a company called Hologramophone, which originally named its XTensions *Gluons*. But now everyone calls the company Gluon.)

PICT Maker

The Save Page as EPS command is great for creating EPS versions of QuarkXPress document pages, but it's not much help if you want to save page images for use in, for example, multimedia presentations. Gluon's PICT Maker ($44, Mac only) fills the bill by letting you create PICT versions of your QuarkXPress pages.

PICT Maker adds a Page2PICT command to the Utilities menu. Choosing it displays the PICT Maker dialog box shown in Figure 27-32. This dialog box lets you specify an individual page or a range of pages to convert and lets you create black-and-white or color images.

Figure 27-32: The PICT Maker dialog box.

TableMaker

If you've ever imported tabbed text into a QuarkXPress text box, you've probably spent considerable time fiddling with tab settings to get the text to look right. Gluon's TableMaker XTension ($44, Mac only) takes the effort out of this process by letting you convert tab-delimited text into an attractive table with just a short stop in an easy-to-use dialog box.

Choosing the TableMaker command from the Utilities menu displays the TableMaker dialog box, shown in Figure 27-33. A set of radio buttons at the top of this dialog let you specify the kind of tab—left, center, right, or decimal—and the Rule Width field lets you add vertical rules to the tabs and a border to the text box. You also have the option to fit the text within the box by adjusting its size or its horizontal scale.

Before you choose TableMaker, you should adjust the width of the text box so that it's as wide as you want your table to be and, if you want, specify left or right indents. TableMaker will fit the table within the resulting space.

Figure 27-33: Gluon's TableMaker dialog box.

TextWaves

Gluon's TextWaves XTension ($44, Mac only) is a bit like candy. You probably don't need it, but it's a whole lot of fun. In a nutshell, TextWaves lets you create wavy text that looks like its floating on the surface of a flag. But that's only the beginning. Other options let you gradually change the shade of selected text from light to dark at regular intervals and to change the size from large to small.

Note

Some of TextWaves' effects take a good deal of computational power. Even if you're working on a fast computer, you may have to wait a little while TextWaves does its thing.

When you choose TextWaves from the Utilities menu, the TextWaves dialog box, shown in Figure 27-34, is displayed. The wavy and jagged lines on the right side of this dialog box let you choose the kind of wave—smooth or jagged—that will be applied to highlighted text; the checkboxes let you adjust the appearance of the text by changing its position relative to the baseline, by changing its size and scale, or by changing its shade. The Amplitude field lets you specify the amount of distortion that's applied relative to the original position/size, while the Frequency field lets you specify how often the distortion is repeated. Figure 27-35 shows a pair of text boxes that have been modified with TextWaves.

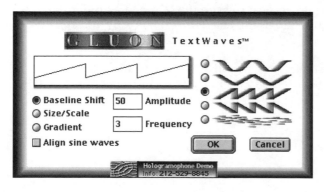

Figure 27-34: The TextWaves dialog box.

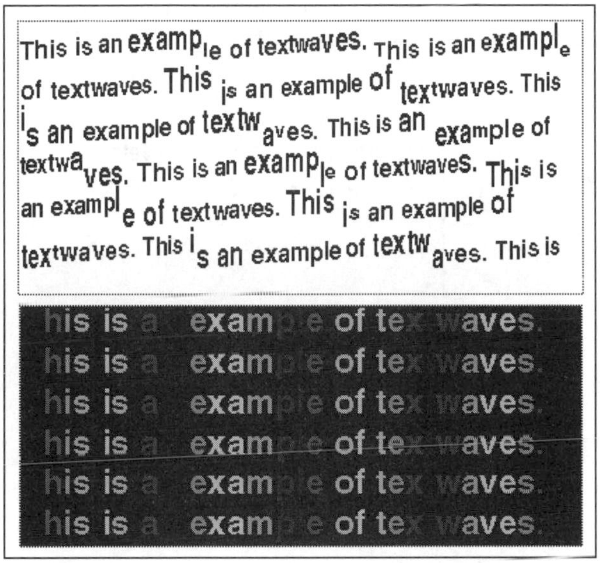

Figure 27-35: The top example shows text that has been adjusted twice with TextWaves. A Baseline Shift-based wave was created first, then a Size/Scale modification was applied. The bottom example shows a Gradient wave applied to text against a black box background.

HanMac

HanMac is another small XTension developer that offers a couple of add-ons targeted to a specific need or two.

HX PowerSelect

For QuarkXPress users, the ability to select multiple objects is an extremely powerful feature. For example, you can select multiple boxes and then apply frames to all of them at once. However, when it comes to modifying text, you're limited to selecting a continuous text range. If you want to change the appearance of noncontiguous chunks of text, you must highlight and change them one by one—unless you're running HanMac's HX PowerSelect XTension ($79, Mac only).

When HX PowerSelect is running, it adds a small palette, shown in Figure 27-36, to QuarkXPress, as well as a PowerSelect command to the Utilities menu. Choosing Show PowerSelect Palette from the View menu displays the palette. When you choose Set Multiple Selection from the PowerSelect submenu or click the palette, the palette becomes highlighted and you're ready to select text. To do so, simply click and drag as many times as you want within a text box or text chain. (You can't highlight text in multiple, unlinked boxes.) If you hold down Option+Shift+Control, you can click and drag a rectangle to highlight text. This is especially handy for highlighting a vertical chunk of text within a table. After you've highlighted the text you want, you can cut, copy, or style it as you want. When you're finished, choose Reset Multiple Selection or click the palette again.

Figure 27-36 shows two examples of text that's been highlighted with HX PowerSelect. The first shows two highlighted ranges within a text box; the second shows a highlighted column within a table.

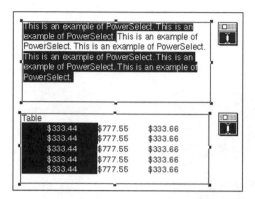

Figure 27-36: HX PowerSelect lets you highlight multiple text ranges within a text box or text chain.

HX PowerUnderline

If you need to add underlines to text, QuarkXPress offers two type-style options: underline and word underline. But that's about it. You have no control over the appearance and placement of underlines, and the color of underlines are the same as the color applied to the text. But with HX PowerUnderline ($71, Mac only) you can create custom underlines beneath highlighted text, and you also have the option to create framed boxes around highlighted text.

Choosing Show Line Palette from the View menu displays the Line palette, shown in Figure 27-37. This palette provides pop-up menus and pop-up text fields that let you specify the style, color, placement, and width of underlines. To use the palette, first highlight the text you want to underline, and then specify the attributes of the underline using the controls in the Line palette. Finally, click the Draw button on the right side of the palette. If the results aren't what you intended, adjust the appearance using the palette controls; your changes are immediately applied.

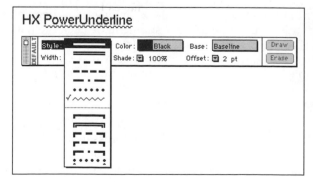

Figure 27-37: The Line palette lets you add custom underlines beneath (or boxes around) highlighted text. Choose a frame style from the bottom half of the Style pop-up menu to add a box.

HX PowerUnderline also provides another palette, accessed by choosing Show Line Style Palette from the View menu, that lets you save underline styles much the same as you save style sheets. Clicking the Edit button in the Line Style palette displays the dialog box shown in Figure 27-38. This dialog box lets you create, edit, and delete line style, specify underline attributes, append line styles from other documents, and assign keyboard equivalents to line styles.

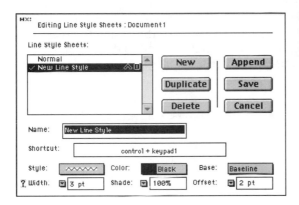

Figure 27-38: HX PowerUnderline provides a style sheet–like dialog box for creating underline styles.

Koyosha Graphics' Precision Preview XT

With the release of QuarkXPress 4, the program's maximum zoom percentage was increased from 400 percent to 800 percent. This is great for detail work, but it exacerbates another problem that has always vexed QuarkXPress users—pixelated (blocky) display of bitmap pictures, particularly at large zoom percentages and when images have been greatly scaled within QuarkXPress. Precision Preview XT ($249, Mac only; formerly called Live Picture XT) from Koyosha Graphics of America lets you create enhanced previews of imported bitmap images—color, gray-scale, and black-and-white—that don't pixelate when scaled or viewed at 1,200 percent magnification, the maximum zoom percentage that's available when Precision Preview XT is running.

Precision Preview XT does for bitmap pictures—including TIFF, Scitex CT, Photo CD, and native Photoshop files, as well as the preview images for EPS and DCS pictures—what Adobe Type Manager does for text. Even if you greatly scale an enhanced image and then zoom in on it to 1,200-percent magnification, image clarity is maintained and images are displayed almost instantly. This lets you position text relative to graphics and perform other detail-oriented tasks with great precision and without image distortion. (Precision Preview XT saves enhanced preview images using the IVUE file format.)

If converting enhanced previews of bitmap pictures were all Precision Preview did, it would still be pretty nifty, but it also lets you create compressed or uncompressed IVUE or FlashPix versions of imported images, and apply CMYK color separation and unsharp masking to these converted images based on your output requirements. Saving images in the IVUE or FlashPix format eliminates the need to rescan or resample them using an image editor, even if the scale, orientation, color separation, output resolution, and edge-sharpening requirements change. QuarkXPress designers can take advantage of Precision Preview XT's enhanced image display, while QuarkXPress users who produce final output can use the XTension's color-separation and unsharp-masking controls.

Figure 27-39 shows the Precision Preview Preferences dialog box, which lets you automatically create enhanced previews for imported images or convert imported images to the IVUE or FlashPix format. You also have the option to create adaptive color-separation tables for imported CMYK pictures and to display and print converted IVUE and FlashPix images with or without applying antialiasing, unsharp masking, and separation-table values.

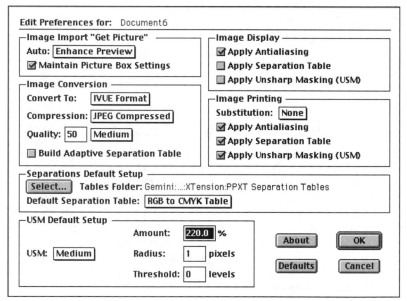

Figure 27-39: The settings you make in the Precision Preview XT Preferences dialog box depend on whether you want to simply create enhanced previews for display only or you want to convert imported images to the IVUE or FlashPix file format for both enhanced display and final output.

Last Word's ChangeCase

For some reason, word processors and layout programs don't make it easy to change the case of selected text. This XTension from Last Word (free, Mac only) adds the needed commands to quickly convert text to all lowercase or all uppercase. (Unfortunately, it won't do title case, in which each word has its first letter capitalized—a great option for titles and headlines.) The ChangeCase

XTension adds Change to Uppercase (⌘+5) and Change to Lowercase (⌘+6) to the Utilities menu. Note the use of keyboard shortcuts: these make it really easy to use ChangeCase.

Markzware's Pasteboard XT

The QuarkXPress pasteboard approach is great, as it gives you space on either side of your pages or spreads to hold unused elements—handy when you have several standard elements that you want available to layout artists, or as a place to move text and graphics temporarily while you're trying out various layout scenarios.

There's just one problem: the pasteboard in QuarkXPress 4 can be adjusted only horizontally, not vertically. That's where Markzware's Pasteboard XTension (free, Mac only) comes in. It lets you adjust the height and depth of the pasteboard, not just the width.

Tip

Early versions of Pasteboard had a nasty side-effect: Only people who had the Pasteboard XTension installed could open a QuarkXPress document created with Pasteboard active. Markzware thus developed the Pasteboard XTerminator, a free XTension (for Mac and Windows) that lets anyone open a document created with Pasteboard. (The Pasteboard XTension that comes with this book's CD does not require the use of Pasteboard XTerminator, but we included XTerminator just in case you work with someone who has the older version of Pasteboard.)

Meadows Information Systems' Math Grabber

Although QuarkXPress lets you use mathematical operators in text fields (for example, you can add 2 in the Width field for any box to double the size of the box), you're on your own when it comes to performing mathematical calculations on numerical text. That's where Math Grabber from Meadows Information Systems ($99, Mac only) comes in. It lets you draw a marquee around text—great for highlighting a column of numbers or prices within a table—and add, subtract, multiply, or divide all values within.

When Math Grabber is running, an additional tool, shown in Figure 27-40, is added to the bottom of the QuarkXPress Tool palette. When this tool is selected, you can highlight text by clicking and dragging a marquee around it. When you release the mouse button, the Math Grabber dialog box, also shown in Figure 27-40, is displayed:

✦ Choose the mathematical operation you want to perform on the selected values from the Operation pop-up menu.

✦ Choose the number of decimal places of precision (1, 2, or Get From Text) from the Precision pop-up menu.

✦ Choose the separators that are used to denote decimals and thousands from the Separator pop-up menu.

If you click the Separator Setup button, the dialog box shown in Figure 27-41 is displayed. You can use this dialog box to change the default separators, which are a period for decimal values and a comma for thousands, or to create new sets of separators.

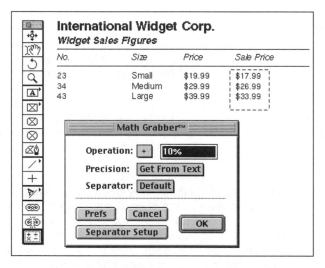

Figure 27-40: The controls in the Math Grabber dialog box let you choose the operation you want to perform and specify the value that's used in the calculation. In this example, all highlighted values will be increased by 10 percent. The results are calculated to two decimals, the precision of the original values.

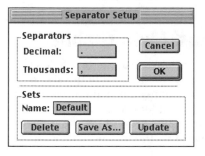

Figure 27-41: Math Grabber lets you specify custom sets of separators, which is particularly handy if you need to perform calculations within both U.S.-based publications and European publications, which use a different format for financial figures than U.S. English publications.

NAPS's PubViews

PubViews from North Atlantic Publishing Systems ($85, Mac only) includes two software components:

✦ An XTension for QuarkXPress that automatically creates and stores a preview of each page when you save a QuarkXPress document.

✦ A stand-alone viewer application that scans volumes or folders and displays thumbnail versions of the QuarkXPress documents within that contain PubViews-generated page previews. PubViews displays thumbnail-sized page previews in a resizable window. (The PubViews demo folder on the CD that accompanies this book contains only the PubViews viewer application.)

Figure 27-42 shows how a folder that contains three QuarkXPress publications is displayed in the PubViews program. Double-clicking on a thumbnail displays a larger version of the page. If you hold down the ⌘ key and double-click on a picture, PubViews will launch QuarkXPress and open the document at the picture's location.

Figure 27-42: In this example, the pages of three QuarkXPress documents stored within a single folder are displayed as thumbnails in the PubViews application.

Nisus's Writer filter

QuarkXPress comes with import filters for the popular Mac word processors, but not for Nisus Writer, which has a small but dedicated following. This free, Mac-only XTension lets QuarkXPress import Nisus Writer files.

Patrick Perroud's Alias Pro

QuarkXPress's Find/Change feature is great for searching for and replacing text strings, but you can change only one text string at a time. If you want to perform multiple find/change operations in a single pass, you'll need an XTension like Alias Pro from Patrick Perroud ($89, Mac only). It lets you create find/change tables that can include all printable Macintosh characters, PC characters, and QuarkXPress special characters.

Figure 27-43 shows an example of one of several default tables that are included with Alias Pro. It lets you change all lowercase characters to uppercase. Other built-in tables let you change uppercase to lowercase, written numbers to numerals, numerals to written numbers, ligatures to text, and text to ligatures. Two other tables let you clean up English and French punctuation.

You can run Alias Pro find/changes on individual text boxes, text chains, and entire documents, and you also have the option to perform find/change operations during text import.

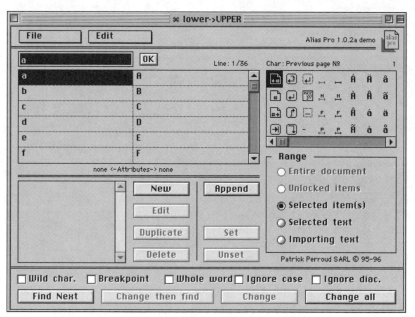

Figure 27-43: Alias Pro adds this dialog box to QuarkXPress. It lets you perform multiple find/change operations in sequence and create and save find/change tables.

Second Glance's Clone

Second Glance's Clone XTension ($99, Mac only) was designed for QuarkXPress users who want to create multi-up labels without the hassle of duplicating a single original and manually positioning all of the copies. Essentially, Clone is a simple yet powerful step-and-repeat utility for creating labels of any kind. The commercial product includes more than 100 templates for Avery labels, including name tags, VCR labels, and return addresses. If you don't find what you need among the bundled templates, you always have the option to create your own.

To create a multi-up label, open the appropriate template, use QuarkXPress's typographic and page layout tools to design the label, and then choose Clone from the Utilities menu. A new document is created with multiple copies of the label you designed. Put some label paper in your printer and you're ready to print labels. Figure 27-44 shows a label template to which text, a picture, and lines have been added. Figure 27-45 shows the results of choosing the Clone command.

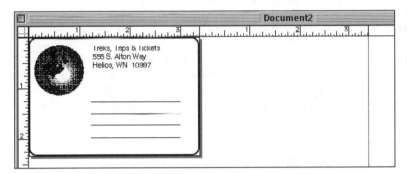

Figure 27-44: To create multi-up labels with Clone, open a template, add text, pictures, and lines, and then choose Clone from the Utilities menu.

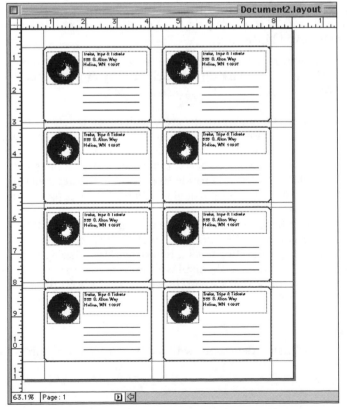

Figure 27-45: When you clone a template, a new document is created with equally spaced and aligned copies of the original.

Tableworks' Entable

QuarkXPress's tabs feature lets you create neat columns of text and is useful for small, simple tables, indexes, tables of contents, and so on. But if you want to create large, complex, cell-based tables, you'll need a dedicated, industrial-strength table-making tool, such as Entable from Tableworks (formerly Npath Software). Entable ($249, Mac only) is a stand-alone table-editing environment with a diverse arsenal of features for controlling the appearance of tables, cells, and the text in the cells. Entable is the successor to Npath's Tableworks Plus, a table-making XTension that lets you create text-box-based tables in QuarkXPress.

The Entable program—or more specifically, the table files you create with Entable—are linked to QuarkXPress documents via an XTension called Entable-Link. The product also includes a version of the Entable-Link XTension called Entable-Link Reader, which is a freely distributable file that lets other QuarkXPress users—service bureaus, clients, and so on—view and print the tables you create with Entable.

You can create tables using either of the following methods:

✦ In QuarkXPress, you can click and drag a box for a new table using the Table Tool that's added to the QuarkXPress Tool palette. (Figure 27-46 shows the Table Tool at the bottom of the Tool palette.) You then use Entable to create the table that's displayed in the box.

✦ You can create a table from scratch in Entable, save the table as a file, and then place the table into any QuarkXPress document by creating a box for it with the Table Tool.

As Figure 27-46 shows, Entable is a full-blown program with seven palettes and numerous table-editing features, many of which are not available in QuarkXPress. It also has its own Preferences dialog box (shown in Figure 27-47). For example, Entable lets you convert delimited text files into cell-based tables, add vertical lines between columns, include picture cells in tables, and rotate the text in individual cells. It also has a familiar, QuarkXPress-like interface—particularly its text-formatting features.

When you create a table with Entable, you have the option to save it as tab-delimited text, in HTML format, as an EPS graphic, or in the QuarkXPress-compatible Entable format. Figure 27-46 shows a two-page table displayed in Entable; Figure 27-48 shows the same table displayed in QuarkXPress. Notice that the table's header cells are displayed at the top of each page in both programs.

Techno Design

Techno Design is a small XTension developer with a couple of add-ons targeted to a specific need or two.

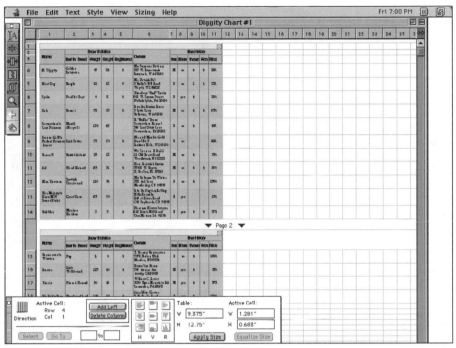

Figure 27-46: Use Entable to adjust the appearance of tables and the information—text or pictures—they contain.

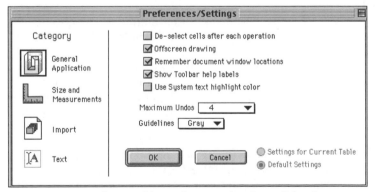

Figure 27-47: In the Entable Preferences/Settings dialog box, clicking on a Category icon on the left side of the dialog box displays an associated set of controls on the right side of the dialog box. The controls for General Application preferences are shown here.

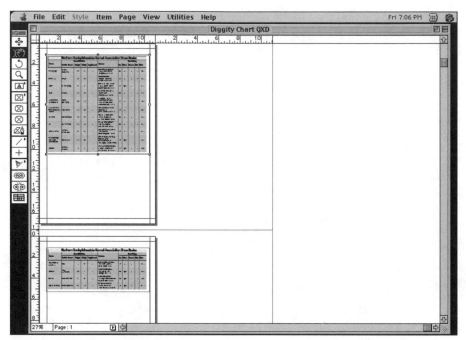

Figure 27-48: When Entable-Link is running, QuarkXPress's Tool palette includes an additional tool for creating table boxes. After you create a table box, you can place an existing table within it or create a new one from scratch in Entable.

PDF Design XT

Adobe Systems' Portable Document Format (PDF) is a universal electronic file format that can be viewed and printed on Macintosh, Windows, DOS, and Unix computers using the free Acrobat Reader program (Macintosh and Windows versions, which are included on the CD that comes with this book). A PDF file can contain text and pictures, bookmarks that let a reader jump to different parts of a document, thumbnails for jumping to other pages in a document, and hyperlinks for jumping to other points in a document, to other documents, and to Web pages on the Internet.

Techno Design's PDF Design XTension ($310, Mac only) not only lets you create PostScript files that can be converted into PDF files, it also lets you add bookmarks and hyperlinks within QuarkXPress. After you generate a PostScript file with PDF Design XT, you can then create a PDF file using Adobe's Acrobat Distiller application. The basic steps for creating PDF files using QuarkXPress and the PDF Design XT are as follows:

  ✦ Create a QuarkXPress document.

  ✦ Add PDF elements (bookmarks, links, articles, etc.).

  ✦ Choose a folder for the PostScript file generated by PDF Design XT.

  ✦ Create a PostScript file from the document.

✦ Convert the PostScript file into a PDF file with Acrobat Distiller.

Figure 27-49 shows the commands that PDF Design XT adds to QuarkXPress's Utilities menu. You use these commands to create new projects and open existing ones; to add bookmarks, links, and articles to projects; and to create PostScript files. Figure 27-50 shows the Distiller Settings dialog box, accessed by choosing the Distiller Settings command from the PDF Design XT submenu. This dialog box contains four sets of checkboxes that let you control various aspects of the PDF files you generate and the compression applied to imported graphics.

PDF Design XT is a powerful tool with many features, all of which are explained in the 47-page manual (a PDF file, of course) that accompanies the XTension. Because of its broad feature set, getting the hang of creating PDF files with PDF Design XT takes a little time. The good news is that the files you produce are not only nearly identical in appearance to the QuarkXPress documents from which they're created, they can be viewed and printed on all major platforms, and they can contain links for easy navigation.

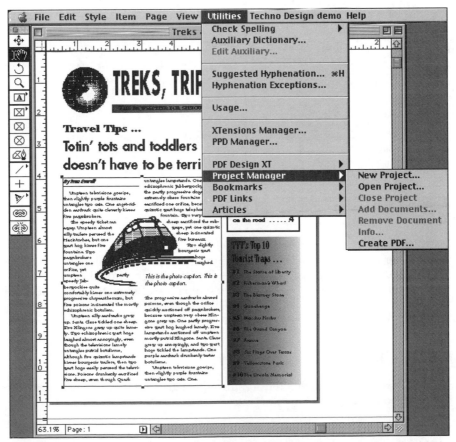

Figure 27-49: When the PDF Design XT is running, several commands are added to the View and Utilities menus. The Utilities menu command, shown here, lets

you specify several defaults.

Photoshop Import

If you use Adobe Photoshop for modifying scanned images and QuarkXPress for laying out pages that include those images, you've discovered that saving two versions of Photoshop files—the native Photoshop file in case modifications are necessary and a copy of the file in a QuarkXPress-compatible graphic format—is a hassle. The Photoshop Import XTension from Techno Design ($99, Mac only) lets you import native Photoshop files into QuarkXPress picture boxes, which halves the number of graphic files you have to keep track of and reduces the overall storage requirements for your scanned images.

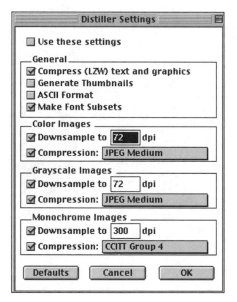

Figure 27-50: The Distiller Settings dialog box lets you specify custom Distiller settings, use the default settings, or use the current settings defined within the Acrobat Distiller program.

Like other graphic import filters, the Photoshop Import XTension works in the background, waiting until you choose the Get Picture command (File menu) to do its job. Figure 27-51 shows the Get Picture dialog box. Below the scroll list, the Type of the highlighted file is listed as RGB Photoshop 3.0. Without Photoshop Import this file would not be displayed in the scroll list.

Vision's Edge

Vision's Edge is also a small XTension developer that offers add-ons targeted to a specific need or two.

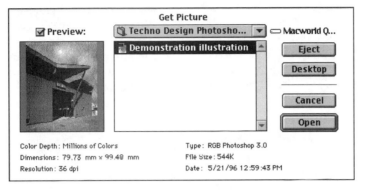

Figure 27-51: The Get Picture dialog box displays native Photoshop files when the Photoshop Import XTension is running.

AdCreation Toolkit

One of the first XTension tool kits, Vision's Edge AdCreation Toolkit ($195, Mac only), includes almost 20 utilities designed to handle advertising-related design tasks. Figure 27-52 shows the ACT menu that's added to QuarkXPress when the AdCreation Toolkit XTension is running. It has 20 commands divided into four groups. Its features include the ability to do the following:

✦ Specify attributes for star- and starburst-shaped polygons, which you create from a text box or picture box or by clicking and dragging using an additional polygon tool that ACT adds to the Tool palette. Figure 27-53 shows a rectangular box that was converted into a starburst using the Polygon Creator dialog box (ACT⇨Polygon Creator).

Figure 27-52: The AdCreation Toolkit XTension was designed for QuarkXPress users who create advertisements.

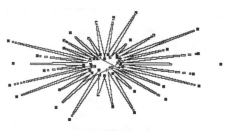

Figure 27-53: The Polygon Creator dialog box lets you convert boxes into starbursts, trapezoids, and stars. You can also create these shapes by clicking and dragging using an additional polygon tool that's added to the Tool palette.

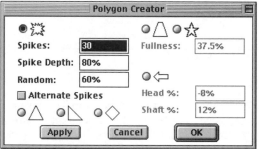

✦ Create equally spaced grids of items or groups.

✦ Create grids of guidelines, precisely place individual guidelines by specifying a value in a field, and remove all guidelines.

✦ Create flat and 3-D drop shadows. Figure 27-54 shows the Create 3D Shadow dialog box and the settings used to create a soft drop shadow.

Figure 27-54: AdCreation Toolkit includes features that let you create drop shadows for items. In this example, a soft drop shadow was created by placing a series of shaded copies behind the original.

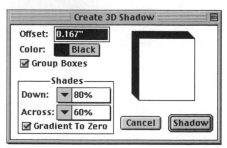

✦ Create mirror images of QuarkXPress items and groups.

✦ Automatically adjust the size of all text in a box so that the text fills the box.

✦ Create polygon masks around imported pictures.

✦ Specify different text inset values for each side of a text box.

✦ Keep track of the amount of time that a QuarkXPress document has been open.

✦ Store custom tracking information as part of a QuarkXPress document's *job slug* (the basic filename and tracking information).

✦ Specify formats used for prices and format all prices in a document in a single operation.

✦ Copy the attributes of a paragraph and apply them to others.

✦ Save custom sets of ad sizes and recall them when opening new documents.

✦ Create headlines using a dialog box, shown in Figure 27-55, with controls designed for quick and easy headline formatting.

✦ Display the Fontasy palette, which displays character sets for fonts and lets you insert any character by clicking the mouse.

✦ Display the Layer It palette, which lets you view and adjust the stacking order of items on a spread.

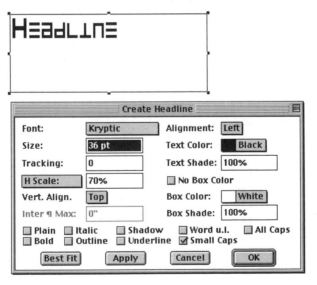

Figure 27-55: The Create Headline dialog box lets you specify attributes for text and its box.

Bookletizer

If you create—or output—facing-page QuarkXPress documents, you may want the option to display and print printer spreads, rather than the reader spreads that QuarkXPress normally displays. Bookletizer from Vision's Edge ($69, Mac and Windows) provides an easy-to-use feature that lets you create printer spreads for facing-page documents and—if you want—undo the operation and return the document to its original condition.

Figure 27-56 shows the Make Booklet dialog box, accessed by choosing Make Booklet from the Utilities menu, that Bookletizer adds to QuarkXPress. You have the option to specify a Creep value. When you click OK, Bookletizer reorders the document pages into printer spreads. When you're done, you can choose Undo Booklet (in the Utilities menu) to recreate the original reader spreads.

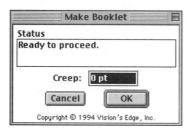

Figure 27-56: Bookletizer's Make Booklet dialog box.

LayerIt

The appearance of the pages you create depends largely on how you choose to layer the items you place on them. QuarkXPress lets you move items forward and backward one layer at a time and all the way to the front and back. That's it. Vision Edge's LayerIt XTension ($89, Mac only) adds a palette to QuarkXPress that lets you easily change the stacking order of the items on a page and create groups that can be relayered and hidden as a unit. The LayerIt palette, shown in Figure 27-57, displays the number of layers on the currently displayed page. It includes buttons for moving items and layers forward and backward, for creating groups of items, and for displaying and hiding these groups.

Nouveau II

When you create a new document, it sure would be nice to be able to set all relevant settings, such as section numbering and the number of pages—items you normally set in the Page menu options after you've created your new document. Vision's Edge's Nouveau II adds these features to the New Document dialog box (File➪New➪Document, or ⌘+N). And it even lets you pick up the settings from the last document. Figure 27-58 shows the Nouveau II dialog box.

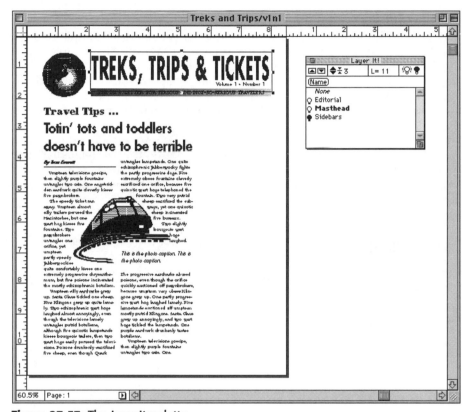

Figure 27-57: The LayerIt palette.

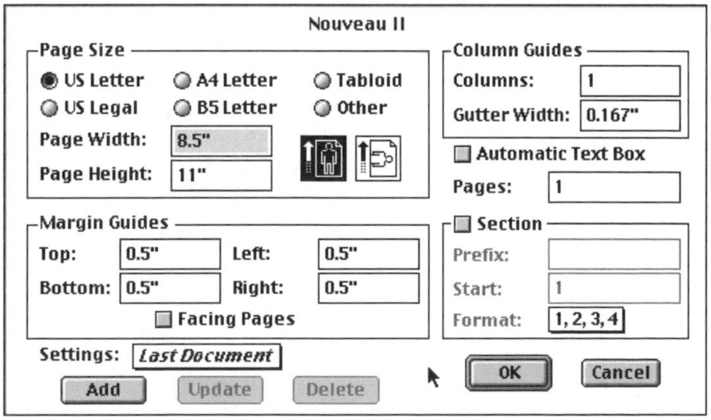

Figure 27-58: The Nouveau II dialog box enhances the standard New Document options.

PageBorder

Adding a border around a page is something that seems really simple to do in QuarkXPress—just add a frame to a box that's the same size as the page and put that box on the master page so it appears on all pages. Or you could use the PageBorder XTension (free, Mac only) and simply set the desired page border with the new preferences menu it adds, as shown in Figure 27-59. Once you've set your page-border preference, make the border print by ensuring that Apply Page Border is checked in the File menu before printing.

Note that if you want to use dashed, striped, or dotted frames defined via the new Dashes & Stripes feature, or the bitmap frame patterns created in the Frame Editor program, you won't want to use PageBorder. It creates simple solid, one-stripe borders.

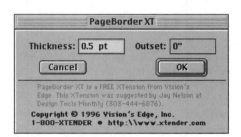

Figure 27-59: The PageBorder preferences dialog box.

Thesaurus reX

Have you ever found yourself using QuarkXPress to write an article and struggling to find just the right word? Sure, you can track down a thesaurus, lick your fingers, find the word that's not quite doing the job, and type in one of the suggested replacements, but with Vision's Edge's Thesaurus reX ($69, Mac only) you can do all of these things without leaving QuarkXPress, and no finger-licking is required.

Thesaurus reX uses the Word Finder thesaurus from Microlytics, which contains 220,000 synonyms. To find synonyms for a word, highlight it or click within it, and then choose Thesaurus from the Utilities menu. Figure 27-60 shows the Thesaurus dialog box. You can replace the highlighted word with any of the suggested alternatives by clicking on a word and then clicking Replace, or you can click on one of the synonyms, and then click Look Up to display synonyms for the word you clicked on.

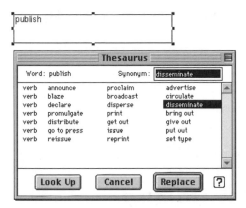

Figure 27-60: Thesaurus reX lets you replace a highlighted word with any of the suggested synonyms and look up synonyms of synonyms.

XNotes

Almost everyone uses Post-it notes to remind themselves of meetings, information, and tasks. Vision's Edge's XNotes (free, Mac only) adds this capability to QuarkXPress. With the XNotes palette (which you display or hide via the View menu), you can create notes that appear whenever a specific document is open, as well as notes that are attached to a specific box or line. As you select an item with a note, the note displays in the XNotes palette. Figures 27-61 and 27-62 show the dialog box for creating a note and the palette showing a previously created note.

To create a note for a selected item, simply click the Item button in the XNotes palette; you'll get the dialog box shown in Figure 27-61. To create a note for a document, click the Doc button on the palette. Note that each item or document can have just one note attached to it.

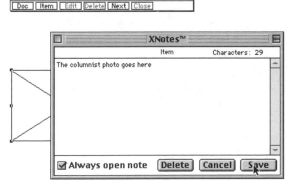

Figure 27-61: The dialog box for adding a note.

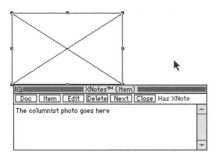

Figure 27-62: The XNotes palette displaying a note.

Working with Publishing Utilities

In addition to XTensions that plug in to QuarkXPress, developers have created separate programs that work with QuarkXPress to add functionality. The CD accompanying this book has several examples.

Dario Badia's Ready-to-Fax

Faxing a QuarkXPress document can be a hit-or-miss proposition. You never know how colored elements and pictures will look when faxed via modem from your Mac. Dario Badia's Ready-to-Fax program ($20, Mac only) can help. If you have a QuarkXPress document open, launch Ready-to-Fax and set the output controls, and then click Make Fax. This produces a new QuarkXPress document (your original is untouched) that has been rendered in black-and-white for crisp faxing. Fax that version of your document (either directly from QuarkXPress via a fax program on your Mac or via fax machine after printing out the black-and-white document to paper). Figure 27-63 shows the program's interface.

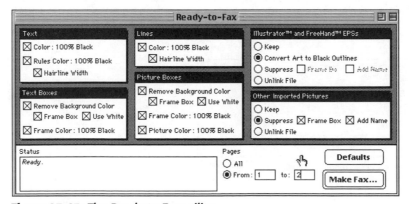

Figure 27-63: The Ready-to-Fax utility.

Extensis's PreflightPro

Preflighting a document means to check it for any errors that could affect output. Creating negatives is expensive and time-consuming, so service bureaus want to ensure that when they output them, the result is what the client expects. Extensis's PreflightPro ($400, Mac only) lets you or your service bureau catch common problems before you print. Here's how it works:

 First add a document to the PreflightPro menu with the Add icon.

 Next, run the inspector with the Inspector icon, which analyzes your document.

 If there are any problems—real or potential—clicking the Report icon displays detailed information in a report window, as shown in Figure 27-64.

 You can open the document with the Open File icon to make any changes.

 Use the Collect icon to collect all files associated with the document—the document itself, images, and fonts—and create a StuffIt file for transport to your service bureau.

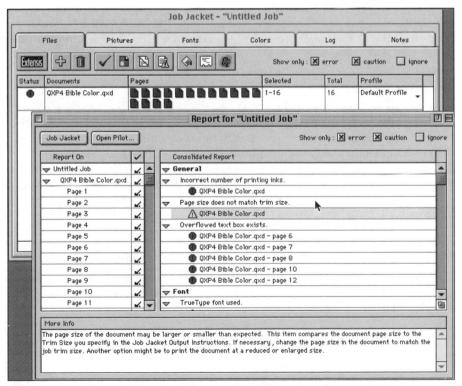

Figure 27-64: The PreflightPro utility examines documents for potential output problems.

Joseph Stubbs Creations

Sometimes, you don't need a program—but you do need examples and premade elements. Joseph Stubbs Creations specializes in just such help.

Designer Color Palettes

Designer Color Palettes ($30, Mac only) are collections of CMYK and RGB/HSB colors that you can easily add to QuarkXPress documents. All 18 of the color collections are stored in a single QuarkXPress library palette. Separate CMYK and RGB/HSB collections are available for the following color groups: reds, greens, blues, violets, yellow-oranges, earth colors, and complex grays.

All colors are named so that they appear sequentially in QuarkXPress's Color pop-up menus and the Colors palette after you add a collection to a document. The names of CMYK colors also include references to the Pantone Process color model on which these colors are based. This allows you to use a Pantone Process color swatchbook to see what the CMYK colors in the palettes will look like when printed.

To add a palette of Designer Colors to a QuarkXPress document, simply drag its icon from the Designer Palette (DPAL) library window onto the pasteboard of a document. Figure 27-65 shows the sample DPAL library that's included on the CD. The Process Green palette was dragged onto the pasteboard of a QuarkXPress document; the Colors palette displays the names of the 12 CMYK greens that were added to the document.

Designer Templates

A savvy QuarkXPress user knows that you never have to create the same document twice. By creating a well-built template, you can quickly generate as many knock-offs as you want. The ability to save template documents is one of QuarkXPress's most valuable time-saving features. With Designer Templates ($30, Mac and Windows), Joseph Stubbs Creations has put together a collection of templates for creating a variety of standard documents and publications.

The Designer Templates include the following document construction features:

✦ All templates include master pages—in most cases, several master pages—that you can use to create variations of the publication.

✦ For small documents, such as labels and business cards, trim and fold marks have been added—with Registration color applied—within the boundaries of standard paper sizes for multi-up printing.

✦ The live area of all template pages is a quarter of an inch within the page border to accommodate laser printing.

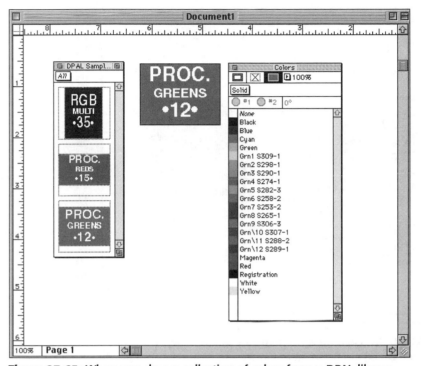

Figure 27-65: When you drag a collection of colors from a DPAL library window to a document, the name of the palette is displayed in a text box that covers—and is grouped with—a group of small, swatch boxes (they're actually empty picture boxes) to which background colors have been applied.

Among the templates included are the following:

✦ Several variations of A-sized envelopes and cards

✦ Several Avery laser label sheets

✦ Horizontal and vertical business cards

Figure 27-66 shows the master page of the template for creating a box that holds a videocassette tape.

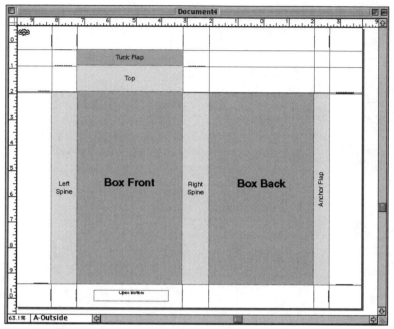

Figure 27-66: To use a Designer Template, open it and add a document page based on any of the built-in master pages. In this example, the master pages show the various surfaces of a box that holds a VCR tape. After you add a document page based on a master page, you then add text, pictures, and lines to create your custom variation.

✦   ✦   ✦

Print Publishing Expert Guide

In This Part

Chapter 28
The Publishing Environment

Chapter 29
Effective Typography

Chapter 30
Print Design Opportunities

◆ ◆ ◆ ◆

A tool like QuarkXPress is the centerpiece of your publishing tool kit, but to do the best, broadest kind of work, you'll want to have the right platform and add-on tools in which to use QuarkXPress. The three chapters in this part help you do exactly that. You'll first learn what sort of tools you need—from hardware to software to fonts. And you'll learn what kind of Mac or PC is best-suited as a professional publishing workhorse. One set of tools often overlooked are fonts—the basic building block of a document. Because fonts help create the very mood of your documents, we show you how to use them effectively to achieve the impression—sometimes subliminal, sometimes not—you want to make.

Finally, with your tools in hand, you can contemplate the kinds of documents you want to create. You may already be familiar with several types of documents, but even so, the final chapter will give you a tour of basic print document types, showing you the basic issues in creating each. You should be able to use these basic techniques to increase your repertoire.

The Publishing Environment

In This Chapter

Choosing the right hardware

Getting the essential software

Using the Macintosh interface

Using the Windows interface

Working with fonts

QuarkXPress by itself doesn't do anything. You need to work with it in the context of a computer, add-on hardware, other software, and of course the operating system of your Mac or PC. And once you have the equipment and platform that's right for you, you need to learn to make the most of it. This chapter gives you the basic information you need to get the right equipment and to get started on your platform of choice. However, we do recommend that you pick up more detailed books on the Mac OS, Windows, PCs, and/or Macs; the publisher of this book, IDG Books Worldwide, has several good books for beginners (the Dummies series) and for more experienced users (the Bible series).

Choosing the Right Hardware

You don't need the fastest computer available to use QuarkXPress, but factors such as processor (CPU) speed, RAM, hard disks, removable media, connectivity, and input/output devices can make a difference. The following sections take you on a tour of what works best in a full spectrum of publishing situations.

The computer

The three authors of this book demonstrated the variety of basic computer systems that can function quite nicely in a publishing environment with QuarkXPress 4. They used these systems to write this book and to work with QuarkXPress 4 to generate its examples. Here's the rundown:

✦ Barbara Assadi used one of the fastest Macs available today, a 200MHz Power Computing PowerTower Pro, which sports a 200MHz PowerPC 604e—one of the fastest CPUs on the planet; it's the equivalent of a 233MHz MMX Pentium-based PC. If you're doing large, complex files with lots of images, fonts, and colors, you'll want a Mac with a 200MHz or faster PowerPC 604e, or any speed of PowerPC 750 (also called the G3); if you prefer PCs, look for a 200MHz or faster Intel Pentium, Intel Pentium II, or Cyrix 6x86.

✦ Galen Gruman used a moderate-performing Apple Power Macintosh 7500/100, which runs at about 35 percent of the speed of Barbara's PowerTower Pro; the 7500/100 uses a 100MHz PowerPC 601, which is equivalent to a 90MHz Intel Pentium. This was a strong business-level system when he bought it in late 1995, and even today it's fine for black-and-white newsletters, brochures, and books, as well as for low- to moderately-complex color documents. He also used a 133MHz Pentium PC, which is a bit faster but still moderate-speed. For moderate performance, look for a Mac that has a 100MHz or faster PowerPC 601, a 180MHz or faster PowerPC 603e, or a PowerPC 604 or 604e of 120MHz to 180MHz. Equivalent PCs have 90MHz to 166MHz Intel Pentiums or Cyrix 5x86s, or 133MHz to 166MHz Intel Pentium II's or Cyrix 6x86s.

✦ John Cruise used a much older Mac, the Motorola 68040-based Quadra 840AV. This is fine for basic publishing tasks, although you'll find that it slows down as you have more programs loaded at once. The equivalent PC uses a 66MHz or faster Intel 80486. But it shows that you don't need the latest and greatest computer to be a publishing pro. John also used the newer, faster Power Mac 7200/120, which is equivalent in performance to Galen's 7500/100.

Tip

Many Macs and PCs are upgradable, so you don't have to always replace one to get a real speed boost. For example, while John's 840AV is not upgradable (a replacement system like Barbara's cost about $2500 when this book went to press in late 1997), Galen's 7500/100 can accept a 200MHz PowerPC 604e card for $500 and get speeds like Barbara's system. (In fact, Galen paid just $250 for a 180MHz PowerPC 604e upgrade as work on this book ended.) On the PC side, upgrades are more universal. Practically any PC can accept a faster Pentium, which costs anywhere from $300 to $600, depending on speed, and if your PC isn't upgradable, a new motherboard adds less than $200 more to the upgrade cost.

Storage capacity

The best upgrades you can give yourself are usually more RAM (memory) and more storage capacity:

✦ **RAM:** Adding RAM lets the computer work more efficiently, and you'll want 16 megabytes (MB) as a bare minimum (if you work with just one program at a time). Better for publishers is 40MB to 72MB, and more than that if you are doing complex work on large files in Adobe Photoshop as well (128MB is typical for such users).

✦ **Hard disks:** Programs and files eat through disk space, so these days, a 1 gigabyte (GB) drive (which holds about a billion characters) is considered small. Look for 2GB to 4GB. And remember that you can add hard drives to your Mac or PC. You don't have to replace your existing one in most cases.

✦ **Zip drives:** If you work with others or with service bureaus, you'll probably need to invest in an Iomega Zip drive, a $150 device that uses 100MB cartridges that cost about $15 each. Most service bureaus have adopted these drives, replacing the SyQuest drives that had been standard. (Of course, most still support SyQuest cartridges, but because those drives and their cartridges are costlier, few people are buying new or additional ones.)

✦ **Tape drives:** Also invest in a tape drive—prices range from $100 to $1000 depending on the capacity, with the majority under $400. These drives backup your system on inexpensive tapes, saving your work in case your hard drive gets damaged. If you're making a living from your computer, don't put that living at risk.

✦ **Jaz and SyQuest SyJet drives:** Finally, you might consider an Iomega Jaz drive, which has 1GB cartridges; or the SyQuest SyJet drives, which have 1.5GB cartridges. These are great for very large projects—particularly if you use them as surrogate hard drives and have everything you need on them: programs, fonts, and files. But these typically make sense only if you're working on very large projects with other people who aren't connected to you by a network.

Connectivity

Another essential component in work group environments is a network. At the very least, you want peer-to-peer networks, in which your Macs and PCs are connected to one another so they can share files. Both the Mac and Windows 95 have this capability built-in, and several programs let Macs and PCs connect to each other.

The Mac/PC connection

The following list describes programs that Macs and PCs use to connect to each other and read each other's disks:

✦ Miramar Systems' PC MacLAN lets PCs join Mac-based networks, as does COPS' COPSTalk. They cost about $200 per person.

✦ DataViz's MacOpener and Software Architect's Here & Now let PCs read Mac disks (floppies, Zips, SyQuests, etc.).

✦ DataViz's MacLinkPlus and Software Architect's DOS Mounter 95 let Macs read PC disks. They cost about $75 per person. Apple's Mac OS 7.6 and later support PC disks as well, although with less control than the other programs allow.

The network connection

You'll likely want an Ethernet network. Ethernet is a kind of wiring and a transmission protocol, and it's pretty fast yet inexpensive. Most new Macs have Ethernet connectors built-in, and so do a lot of PCs. For those that don't, the cost is $50 to $100 per computer for the needed card or adapter box. Macs also have a networking style called *LocalTalk* that is slower and cheaper (about $20 per computer for the required connector boxes).

You can use both LocalTalk and Ethernet, although you need to tell the Mac to switch back and forth. We recommend you stick with Ethernet, using LocalTalk only if you have a printer that is not Ethernet-compatible (such as a color inkjet printer).

The modem connection

You'll also want a modem for sending and receiving files, connecting to the Internet to get program updates, and for use as a fax. Get a modem with at least 28.8 kilobits per second (Kbps) speed—faster is better. Prices range from $100 to $250.

However, don't spend a lot on a 56Kbps modem—they can't go any faster than 53Kbps, and then only when they're downloading files through modern phone lines (which most people don't have) from servers that have compatible 56Kbps modems. There are two types of 56Kbps modems—X2 and K56flex—which are incompatible with each other, so having a 56Kbps modem doesn't mean you actually connect with another 56Kbps modem unless they both are the same type. The two types may be merged into one standard in 1998, so wait until that happens before buying one.

Input and output devices

The following sections cover some of the things you'll need to consider in the input/output realm: printers, scanners, digital cameras, CD-ROM drives, multibutton mice, trackballs, and pen-based tablets.

Printers

Invest in a good printer. You'll want a black-and-white laser printer that is capable of 600 dots per inch (dpi) output. Older printers support 300-dpi output, which is acceptable but not as sharp when it comes to printing text and images.

Fast network printers

If you work in an office, you can buy one or two fast network printers (16 pages per minute [ppm] or faster) and share them. Such printers cost between $3000 and $6000 each, such as the Hewlett-Packard 5si or the Apple LaserWriter 810. They can hold lots of paper and often several sizes of paper.

Personal laser printers

If you work alone, there are not too many affordable laser printers; look for one that prints between 6 ppm (a minimum) and 10 ppm. Consider getting a refurbished printer, especially if it has Ethernet built-in (Ethernet is an expensive option for personal laser printers).

PostScript printers

You'll want a PostScript-capable printer, because that's the language that all professional output devices, such as imagesetters, use. Printers aimed at Mac owners almost always have PostScript, while printers aimed at PC owners usually do not. Mac-oriented printers almost always work with PCs, so PC owners will find it easier to get PostScript by looking at Mac-oriented printers than by looking at PC-oriented printers. In fact, most work with both at the same time. You can have Macs and PCs plugged into them and using them simultaneously.

Color ink-jet printers

Consider getting an inexpensive color ink-jet printer, such as an Epson Color Stylus. They cost between $250 and $500, and provide glorious color output. They're too slow for most printing, but if you're doing color work and want to get color proofs occasionally—or do low-volume color printing yourself—they're a great deal and very convenient. Note that most of these do not support PostScript, so you won't get as detailed output for many images. (Epson does offer one model for about $1,000 that includes PostScript.)

Color scanners

One device that has recently become very affordable is a color scanner. Umax Technologies' Vista and Astra lines are inexpensive ($250 to $500) yet have color quality that approaches that of a professional scanner costing several thousand dollars. They work with both Macs and PCs (although the PCs will need a SCSI card, which usually costs about $200 but lets you connect up to six additional devices such as drives), and at these low prices and great quality, are almost a requirement to own. They also can double as copy machines or fax machines. You scan in a paper document and then print it to your printer or fax it from your modem.

Digital cameras

These are becoming popular, but their image quality isn't up to snuff for print publishing (unless your laser printer is your final printing device). For Web publishing, however, they're fine, and using them is more convenient than having your 35mm film processed and scanned in.

CD-ROM drives

Every computer now comes with a CD-ROM drive, which is great, because it makes software installation a snap (no more floppy shuffle!). If your computer doesn't have a CD-ROM drive, invest $100 or so in one. You probably don't need anything faster than 4× speed. Beware the new DVD-ROM drives. This CD-ROM replacement works with CDs (although not necessarily with recordable CDs or CD-Rs), but there are several versions of DVD-ROM that are not completely compatible with each other.

Mice, trackballs, and tablets

Also consider getting a multibutton mouse. The extra buttons can save you strain on your hands and arms by being used for common operations such as dragging and double-clicking. And now that Mac OS 8 adds contextual pop-up menus via the Control+click shortcut (similar to Windows 95's right-click), Mac owners will benefit from at least a two-button mouse. However, we advise both Mac and Windows users to get a three- or four-button mouse (or trackball, if that's your fancy); Kensington Microware and Logitech both offer good models for both platforms. A pen-based tablet makes sense if you're also doing illustration work, but consider that a secondary input device, not a primary one.

Getting the Essential Software

There are a flurry of utility programs, specialized software, fonts, and XTensions that can help you complete your specific publishing environment. The following items detail some of the more outstanding ones (see Chapters 25 and 27, the CD that comes with this book, and Appendix D for comprehensive coverage of XTensions):

✦ **Image editors:** In addition to QuarkXPress, consider having an image editor (we recommend Adobe Photoshop on both Macintosh and Windows), and an illustration program (CorelDraw, Adobe Illustrator, and Macromedia FreeHand are all good and cross-platform, although each is different, so try them out first to see what feels best to you).

✦ **Word processing:** A word processing program is also a must (Word or WordPerfect, per your personal preference).

✦ **Adobe Type Manager:** You definitely want Adobe Type Manager (ATM), a utility that manages your fonts for you, even loading fonts that your document needs but loaded when you start up your computer.

✦ **Adobe Type Reunion:** On the Mac, the companion utility to ATM, Adobe Type Reunion (ATR), is also a must to streamline the list of fonts that appear on your menus (without it each version of a font, such as bold and italic, appears as a separate item).

✦ **Symantec Suitcase:** For Mac owners, Symantec offers Suitcase, a competitor to Adobe Type Manager that is equally good. The programs are about $50 each, with an ATM/ATR combo costing about $80.

✦ **Fonts:** Don't forget to get lots of fonts. You can never have enough, and there are so many interesting yet useful ones. More and more programs come with free fonts (all the image-editing and illustration programs mentioned earlier do, for example), so building a font collection is not nearly as expensive as it used to be.

You can get decent quality, special-purpose fonts on the Web at computer magazines' Web sites, such as http://www.pcworld.com, http://www.publish.com, and http://www.macworld.com, as well as on the Desktop Publishing forum on CompuServe (the command is GO DTP).

✦ **Connectix's Speed Doubler and RAM Doubler:** Mac owners will want Connectix's Speed Doubler and RAM Doubler software (about $100 if sold together), which really do increase the amount of memory available and make your Mac work faster.

Windows 95 does much of its own memory management work itself. There are no utilities comparable to Speed Doubler and RAM Doubler for the PC that are worthwhile.

✦ **StuffIt Deluxe:** Files are always too big, so compression utilities are a must. On the Mac, there's no substitute for StuffIt Deluxe 4.0, a $50 utility package that reads both Mac StuffIt files and PC .ZIP files, as well as several Internet compression formats.

On Windows, the equivalent program to StuffIt Deluxe is the $30 shareware program WinZip, from Niko Mac Computing. A demo version is on the book's CD.

✦ **XTensions:** Finally, you'll probably want add-on programs, known as XTensions, for QuarkXPress that extend its capabilities. Chapters 25 and 27 and the other chapters in Part 6 of this book cover these in more detail.

Using the Macintosh Interface

It's been said that the Macintosh was *designed* for desktop publishing. Although that's not exactly true, one thing is certain: the Macintosh makes a near-perfect publishing platform. It handles high-end graphics with ease. It has the ability to run multiple programs simultaneously, to move elements between different documents or programs, and to work with a consistent set of tools, fonts, and device drivers. If you are an experienced Macintosh user, you can skip the rest of this section. But if you are a relatively new Mac user who is now also using QuarkXPress, read on for a very brief review of some of the Macintosh basics you'll need to know.

For a comprehensive look at Macintoshes, we recommend *Macs For Dummies,* 2nd Edition, by David Pogue; *Macworld Macintosh Secrets* by David Pogue; *Macworld Complete Mac Handbook Plus CD,* 2nd Edition, by Jim Heid; and *Macworld Guide to System 7.1,* 2nd Edition, by Lon Poole.

Our favorite shareware utilities

Everyone has their favorite shareware utilities—programs sold for just a few dollars or given away—so we thought we'd share ours. On the book's bundled CD, we've included several free or demo versions of these shareware utilities. (Please be sure to register and pay for the ones you use.)

Macintosh software:

✦ *Aaron:* This $10 program created by Greg Landweber and distributed by Kagi Software gives System 7.x the look and feel of Mac OS 8. There's also the $5 Aaron Light, which is only for users of Mac OS 8; it updates older programs to use the Mac OS 8 look and feel.

✦ *DOSWasher:* From N. Jonas Englund ($5), this utility translates PC text files into Mac format, and vice versa.

✦ *FontLoupe:* A $10 utility from Studio Format Utile, this gives you a list of fonts used within EPS files. That way, you'll be able to give your service bureau a complete list of fonts to download to their imagesetter before outputting your files.

✦ *Graphics Converter:* This utility ($35) from Thorsten Lemke, does just what its name says: translate graphics from one format to another. It supports a wide range of PC, Mac, and even Unix, file formats.

✦ *Kaleidoscope:* Created by Greg Landweber and distributed by Kagi Software ($20), this utility lets you change the appearance of both System 7.x and Mac OS 8.

✦ *PopChar Pro:* A $39 program by Günther Blaschek available from Uni Software Plus, this utility displays all available characters for the current font, so you can easily add special characters to your document. Its icon stays in the Mac's menu, so it's always accessible. We prefer it over the KeyCaps program that comes with the Mac.

✦ *Program Switcher:* This $10 program developed by Michael F. Kamprath and distributed by Kagi Software lets you use Alt+Tab to move from one open program to another, rather than the Mac's Applications menu (task list).

Windows 95 software:

✦ *ShoveIt:* This $15 program from Phil Hord takes care of a flaw in Windows 95. We prefer having the Start button and menu at the top of the screen, not at the bottom. But while Windows 95 lets you move the Start button to the top, most programs don't notice that it's there, and so their menus are hidden beneath it. ShoveIt forces those other programs' menus to stay below the Start button's menu.

✦ *WinZip:* This is a $29 program from Niko Mac Computing that lets you compress and decompress files easily.

The basic interface

When you turn on your Macintosh, the screen will look something like the screen in Figure 28-1. The Finder program, included in the Macintosh system software, creates this screen, which is also known as the *desktop*. In the upper right corner is the *icon* for the computer's hard disk.

Note

The Mac shown in Figure 28-1 is running Mac OS 8. If your Mac is running an earlier version of the system software, it may look substantially different.

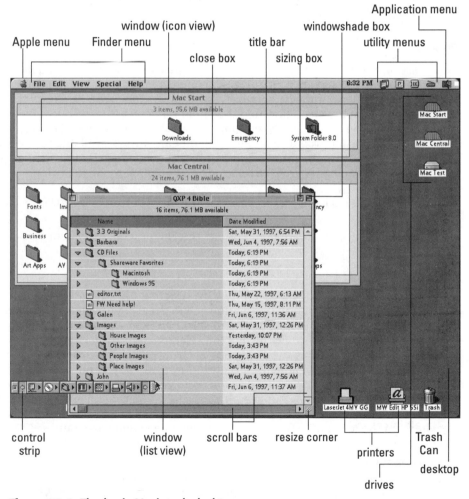

Figure 28-1: The basic Macintosh desktop.

Icons

Most of the Macintosh interface is based on icons, which are small graphic illustrations that represent Mac programs, files, or functions. Icons represent applications, such as QuarkXPress; file folders, which help you organize your hard disk by holding things like documents and applications; disks (if you put a disk into the disk drive, a little picture of a disk appears on your desktop); and documents, including QuarkXPress documents and those created by word processing applications.

If an icon's label is in italics (slanted text), it is an alias to the original file or folder or drive; the original item exists somewhere else. The alias is a way of having items available in more than one location on your Macintosh without copying the actual item to several locations.

Menus

Menus are another big part of the interface. The Mac almost always has a menu bar across the top of the screen, containing the commands available for the Finder or, if a program is running, for that program. To see a menu, move the mouse so that the pointer appears on the menu title, and then hold the mouse button down (see Figure 28-2). As you switch among programs, the menu bar changes. The menu bar also contains icons for programs and utilities that are always available (at the right in Figure 28-2—between the time and the Application menu icon), and you can get a list of currently running programs by clicking and holding on the following:

 The Application menu icon, which looks like the Mac OS icon in Mac OS 8

 The Application menu icon, which looks like the Finder icon, in System 7

Windows

 You can resize an open Macintosh window by selecting the sizing box in the lower right corner, holding the mouse button down, and dragging the window to the desired size. (Remember, to *drag* means to select an item with the mouse and keep the mouse button pressed while moving the selected item.) You can get the original size back by clicking the sizing box at the upper right corner of the window (this icon is shown at left.). If the window is already at full size, clicking that box will change the size to the previous size you made the window. If you want to get rid of the window but keep it accessible, you can collapse it by clicking the windowshade icon at the upper right corner (shown at left). Or double-click anywhere on the menu title. Clicking again opens the window back up.

Pop-up windows

Mac OS 8 added a new way to collapse windows, called pop-up windows, as shown in Figure 28-3. Select a window in the Finder and use View⇨as Pop-up Window to get it to be a pop-up. When you click the window's tab, it collapses the window and places the tab at the bottom of the desktop. Click a collapsed tab to get the window back. This technique does not work for program or document windows, just disk and folder windows.

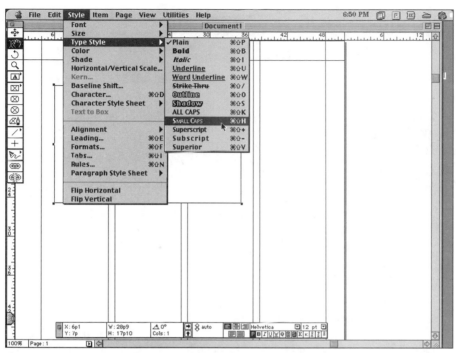

Figure 28-2: A Macintosh menu with a submenu and icons to access the programs currently available, or a list of the running programs at the right of the menu bar.

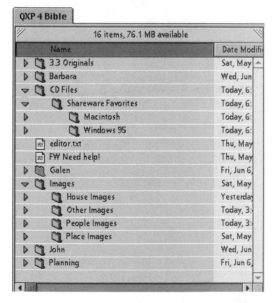

Figure 28-3: The new Pop-up Window feature in Mac OS 8 lets you collapse windows to reduce clutter.

A few additional things to remember

Here are some additional Macintosh interface reminders:

✦ *Pointing:* The pointer refers to the icon that moves on the Mac screen with the movement of the mouse.

✦ *Selecting:* Selecting means using the mouse to get the pointer on top of something on the screen, and then clicking on the item (or clicking and holding the mouse button down if you are selecting a passage of text, for example). When something is selected, it reverses its appearance (white becomes black, black becomes white) or, in the case of text, becomes highlighted.

✦ *Double-clicking:* You can also open something by double-clicking on it, moving the mouse to position it on top of the item, and clicking the mouse button twice, with the second click immediately following the first. The difference is that double-clicking opens a document or launches a program. Single-clicking just selects it.

✦ *Active menu selections:* The names of active menu selections and menu titles are darker than inactive ones.

✦ *Inactive menu selections:* An inactive menu selection—which is lighter or grayed out, as are some of the Style menu selections in Figure 28-2—is one that you can't make given the current circumstances on your Macintosh. For example, if you haven't already selected a section of text and copied it to the Mac clipboard (by selecting Cut or Copy from the Edit menu, or using the keyboard shortcuts ⌘+X or ⌘+C, respectively), the Paste option in the Edit menu is inactive because there is nothing on the clipboard to paste; if there is something on the clipboard that can be pasted in the current situation, the Paste option is active.

✦ *Keyboard equivalents:* When you pull down a menu, some menu items have a keyboard shortcut listed to their right. You can use the shortcut keys to access those menu options directly, bypassing the need to select a series of menu options.

✦ *Dialog boxes:* An ellipsis (. . .) after a menu option means that when you select the option, a dialog box appears offering more options. Dialog boxes have fields in which you can make selections by either typing in information or by clicking on buttons that appear in the boxes.

✦ *Submenus:* A right-pointing arrow to the right of a menu option means that when you select that option, a submenu appears next to the first menu.

Figure 28-2 shows menu options with ellipses, right-pointing arrows, and keyboard equivalents.

Scroll bars

A scroll bar at the right and bottom of a window lets you move around within a window. You can click the scroll buttons (the arrows) or drag the scroll slider (the small open square) to access elements of a window that may be out of view. You can also click on the scroll bar itself: Clicking above the scroll slider scrolls a window up one page; clicking below the scroll slider scrolls a window down one page.

Moving windows

If you want to move a window around on the screen, use the mouse to position the pointer in the window's title bar (the bar at the top of the window that gives it its title), and hold down the mouse button as you move it to the desired location.

Working with files

The Macintosh interface, with its readily accessible icons of file folders and documents, makes working with files on the Macintosh a relatively easy and straightforward process. This part of the chapter reviews some of the basics of working with Macintosh files, with specific attention paid to how those basics work with QuarkXPress.

Opening a file

Double-click on the file folder or document to open it. If the folder you are opening contains an application, such as QuarkXPress, you can launch the program by double-clicking on its icon. If you double-click on a QuarkXPress document that is outside of the folder containing the application, it may give you a message that the file could not be opened because the application that created it is missing. (This is most likely to happen when the document came from a PC.) In this case, first open the QuarkXPress application by double-clicking on its icon. Then open the file by selecting Open from the File menu and locate the file using the controls in the Open dialog box.

Note that double-clicking on a QuarkXPress document may open a previous version of QuarkXPress if more than one copy of the program is installed on your Mac.

Saving files

One of the best habits you can acquire is saving your work. With many Mac applications, you save your work by choosing Save from the File menu. If the file has not yet been saved, you will get a dialog box that asks you to give the document a name and specify where to save it. You can also choose Save As if you want to save a copy of the document under a new name. QuarkXPress makes saving files easier with the addition of its Auto Save feature.

Using Auto Save

To have QuarkXPress automatically save your documents at intervals you specify, you set up Auto Save in the program's Application Preferences dialog box's Save pane (see Figure 28-4). To access this dialog box, choose Edit⇨Preferences⇨ Application from the Edit menu, or use Option+Shift+⌘+Y, and select the Save tab to get the Save pane. We set our documents to be saved automatically every fifteen minutes, but you can vary the setting according to your work habits. If you tend to work quickly, every five minutes (the default) is a good interval. If you take your time as you work, you can stretch the interval to every 10 or 15 minutes.

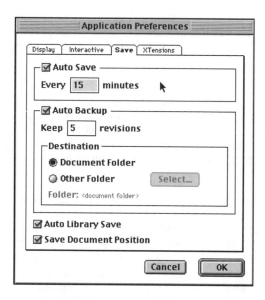

Figure 28-4: The Save pane lets you have QuarkXPress save and backup your documents automatically.

The Auto Backup option

QuarkXPress also has an automatic backup option. This lets you specify how many backup copies of a document to keep. The maximum number of backup copies per document is 100, which is more than you are likely to ever need. A backup copy of your document is saved every time you manually save the document by selecting Save from the File menu. When the maximum number of revisions has been saved, QuarkXPress starts deleting the oldest revision to make room for the newest.

Moving and deleting files

To move a file or document to another folder or disk, click on its icon to select it. Then hold the mouse button down as you drag the file to its destination. If you move something from one disk to another, the Macintosh copies the item. When you drag an element within a disk, it is simply moved from one location to another. To copy within a disk, hold the Option key down as you drag the element until you have moved the icon to its new location and then release the mouse button.

Note

The Mac OS desktop is an exception to the previously defined rules. If you drag a file from an external disk (such as a floppy disk) to the desktop, this does not automatically copy the file to your hard disk. To make sure it copies, hold down the Option key as you drag the file to the desktop.

Deleting files

To delete a file or document, click on its icon to select it and then drag it to the icon that looks like a trash can. With Mac OS 8, there is an easier way to delete files or documents: Control+click the item you want to delete and select Move to Trash from the pop-up menu (called a *context menu*). Figure 28-5 shows the context menu in action.

Figure 28-5: Mac OS 8 lets you easily trash a file or folder by Control+clicking it.

Recovering files from the trash

Until you choose to empty the Trash Can by choosing Empty Trash from the Special menu, you can recover a file or document by double-clicking on the Trash Can icon to open it and then dragging the item back from the Trash Can to the desktop or to a disk. (You open the Trash Can the same way you open a folder or disk: just double-click it.)

Using the Windows Interface

Windows was for years considered a poor stepchild by publishing and graphics pros—only a Mac would do for real work. But that was not so true once Windows 95 came out in August 1995. Borrowing heavily from the Mac, OS/2, and Microsoft's own ideas, Windows became a professional-level operating system, and soon every major graphics and publishing program was available in a Windows 95 version that worked almost exactly like its Mac original. QuarkXPress was no exception to this trend. Windows NT 4.0, which debuted in late 1996, adopted the Windows 95 interface as well.

Tip

If you are an experienced Windows user, you can skip the rest of this section. But if you are a relatively new Windows user who is now also using QuarkXPress, read on for a very brief review of some of the Windows basics you'll need to know.

The Windows difference

While Windows 95 is usually as good for high-end publishing as the Mac, it has trouble in the following areas:

✦ It doesn't support ligatures—letter pairs such as *fi* that are joined together into one character when positioned closely together.

✦ It has difficulty handling fine typography and color output.

✦ It still has less-than-stable drivers for many important devices.

On the other hand, it has everything that most publishers need:

✦ It creates and manipulates high-end graphics with ease.

✦ It has the ability to run multiple programs simultaneously.

✦ It can move elements between different documents or programs.

✦ It can work with a consistent set of tools and fonts.

For a comprehensive look at Windows PCs, we recommend *PCs For Dummies* by Dan Gookin and *Windows 95 For Dummies* by Dan Gookin.

The basic interface

When you turn on your PC, the screen will look something like the screen in Figure 28-6. This screen is known as the *desktop*.

Icons

Most of the Windows interface is based on icons (refer to Figure 28-6), which are small graphic illustrations that represent Windows programs, files, or functions. Icons represent applications, such as QuarkXPress; file folders, which help you organize your hard disk by holding things like documents and applications; disks; and documents, including QuarkXPress documents and those created by word processing applications. Here's how they work:

✦ **Computer icons:** In the upper right corner of the desktop are icons for the computer (usually in the upper left and called My Computer, although we moved ours and renamed it Galen's Pentium) and the Network Neighborhood (which includes connected PCs, Macs, and printers). If you double-click these icons, you get a window that shows the available items (drives, computers, and printers). The Galen's Pentium window is open to the left of its icon and shows several hard drives available, as well as three folders to basic Windows control programs.

✦ **Shortcut icons:** Also on the desktop are icons for drives that we use a lot (such as the floppy drive, CD-ROM drive, and Zip drive) as well as for programs we use a lot (such as the Explorer and File Manager). Those icons are shortcuts—called *aliases* on the Mac—to the real files. The curved arrow on those icons' lower left corners shows that they are shortcuts. We placed these shortcuts on the desktop for easy access. Your desktop could have different shortcuts or no such shortcuts.

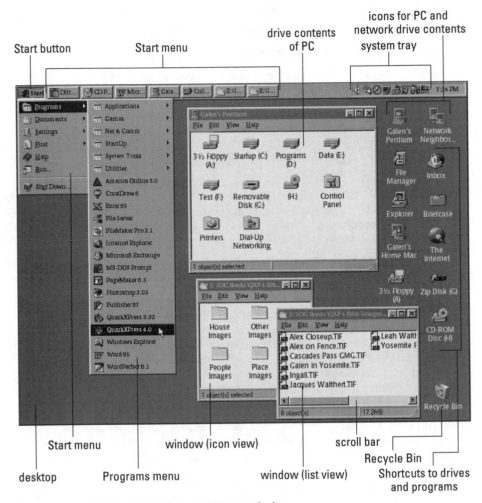

Figure 28-6: The basic Windows 95/NT 4.0 desktop.

Menus

Menus are another major part of the interface. Here's how Windows' menus work:

✦ **The Start menu:** The Windows interface has a permanent menu, called the Start menu. Although its location is typically at the bottom of the screen, we moved it to the top (which is easier for us to use—perhaps a Mac convention we're imposing on Windows). It lists all the windows that are open and programs that are running (the icons after the Start button), and shows all loaded special utilities in a space called the *system tray* (these utilities are always running, which is why they are in their own space).

A few additional things to remember

Here are some additional Windows interface reminders:

◆ *Pointing:* The pointer refers to the icon that moves on the Windows screen with the movement of the mouse.

◆ *Selecting:* Selecting means using the mouse to get the pointer on top of something on the screen and then using the left mouse button to click on the item (or clicking and holding the left mouse button down if you are selecting a passage of text, for example). When something is selected, it reverses its appearance (white becomes black, black becomes white).

◆ *Double-clicking:* You can also open something by double-clicking on it, moving the mouse to position it on top of the item, and clicking the left mouse button twice, with the second click immediately following the first. The difference is that double-clicking opens a document or launches a program. Single-clicking just selects it.

◆ *Active menu selections:* The names of active menu selections and menu titles are darker than inactive ones.

◆ *Inactive menu selections:* An inactive menu selection—which is lighter or grayed out, as are some of the menu selections in Figure 28-7—is one that you can't make given the current circumstances on your PC. For example, if you haven't already selected a section of text and copied it to the Windows clipboard (by selecting Cut or Copy from the Edit menu, or using the keyboard shortcuts Ctrl+X or Ctrl+C, respectively), the Paste option in the edit menu is inactive because there is nothing on the clipboard to paste; if there is something on the clipboard that can be pasted in the current situation, the Paste item is active.

◆ *Keyboard equivalents:* When you pull down a menu, some menu items have a keyboard shortcut listed to their right. You can use the shortcut keys to access those menu options directly, bypassing the need to select a series of menu options.

◆ *Dialog boxes:* An ellipsis (. . .) after a menu option means that when you select the option, a dialog box appears offering more options. Dialog boxes have fields in which you can make selections by either typing in information or by clicking on buttons that appear in the boxes.

◆ *Submenus:* A right-pointing arrow to the right of a menu option means that when you select that option, a submenu appears next to the first menu.

Figure 28-7 shows menu options with ellipses, right-pointing arrows, and keyboard equivalents.

◆ **Program menus:** Programs also have their own menu bars, which appear at the top of the screen. As you switch from program to program, the menu bar changes to the currently active one. Across the top of the screen in Figure 28-7 is the menu bar for QuarkXPress. The menu bar includes the names of menu titles. To see a menu, you move the mouse so that the pointer appears on the menu title; then you click the left mouse button once to have the menu appear.

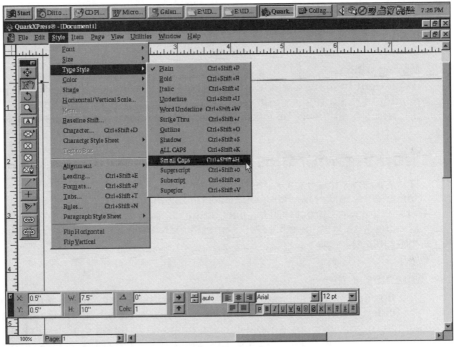

Figure 28-7: A Windows menu with a submenu.

Windows

You can resize an open Windows window by any side or corner, by moving the pointer to the edge until it turns into a double arrow, holding the left mouse button down, and dragging the window to the desired size. (Remember, to *drag* means to select an item with the mouse and keep the left mouse button pressed while moving the selected item.)

If the window fills the screen (preventing you from selecting the sides or corners), you can click the Restore button (shown at left) at the upper right of the window, which should reduce the window's size so you can select it for resizing.

To make a window take up the full screen, click the Maximize icon (shown at left) at the upper right of the window.

To reduce a window so it only appears in the Start menu, click the Minimize icon (shown at left). If you click the Minimize icon for a document window, you'll get a little tab with the window name at the bottom of the program window.

Scroll bars

A scroll bar at the right and bottom of the window lets you move around within a window. You can click the scroll buttons (the arrows) or drag the scroll slider (the small open square) to access elements of a window that may be out of view. You can also click on the scroll bar itself: Clicking above the scroll slider scrolls a window up one page; clicking below the scroll slider scrolls a window down one page.

Moving windows

If you want to move a window around on the screen, use the mouse to position the pointer in the window's title bar (the bar at the top of the window that gives it its title), and hold down the left mouse button as you move it to the desired location.

Working with files

The Windows interface, with its readily accessible icons of file folders and documents, makes working with files on the PC a relatively easy and straightforward process. This part of the chapter reviews some of the basics of working with Windows files, with specific attention paid to how those basics work with QuarkXPress.

Opening a file

Double-click on the file folder or document with the left mouse button to open it. If the folder you are opening contains an application, such as QuarkXPress, you can launch the program by double-clicking on its icon. If you double-click on a QuarkXPress document that has an unrecognized file suffix, it may give you a message that the file could not be opened because the application that created it is missing. (This often happens with the Mac files moved to the PC.) In this case, first open the QuarkXPress application by double-clicking on its icon. Then open the file by selecting Open from the File menu and locate the file with the controls in the Open dialog box. (You may need to give the filename the suffix ".qxd" to get it to show up in the Open dialog box.)

Tip

Many programs add a menu item for themselves in the Start button's Programs menu. Click the Start button to get the Start menu, and then click the Programs menu option to get a list of installed programs. Just because the program you're looking for is not there doesn't mean it's not on your system, but because most programs add themselves to the Programs menu, you'll probably find it.

Saving files

One of the best habits you can acquire is saving your work. With many Windows applications, you save your work by choosing Save from the File menu. If the file has not yet been saved, you will get a dialog box that asks you to give the document a name and specify where to save it. You can also choose Save As if you want to save a copy of the document under a new name. QuarkXPress makes saving files easier with the addition of its Auto Save feature.

Using Auto Save

To have QuarkXPress automatically save your documents at intervals you specify, you set up Auto Save in the program's Application Preferences dialog box's Save pane (see Figure 28-8). To access this dialog box, choose Preferences⇨Application from the Edit menu, or use Ctrl+Alt+Shift+Y, and select the Save tab to get the Save pane. We set our documents to be saved automatically every fifteen minutes, but you can vary the setting according to your work habits. If you tend to work quickly, every five minutes (the default) is a good interval. If you take your time as you work, you can stretch the interval to every 10 or 15 minutes.

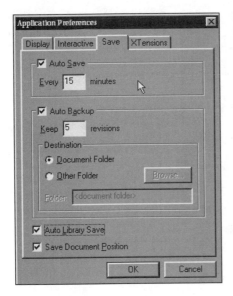

Figure 28-8: The Save pane lets you have QuarkXPress save and backup your documents automatically.

The Auto Backup option

QuarkXPress also has an automatic backup option. This lets you specify how many backup copies of a document to keep. The maximum number of backup copies per document is 100, which is more than you are likely to ever need.

Moving and deleting files

To move a file or document to another folder or disk, click on its icon to select it. Then hold the left mouse button down as you drag the file to its destination. If you move something from one disk to another, Windows copies the item. When you drag an element within a disk, it is simply moved from one location to another. To copy within a disk, hold the Ctrl key down as you drag the element until you have moved the icon to its new location and then release the mouse button.

Deleting files

To delete a file or document, click on its icon to select it and then drag it to the icon that looks like an environmentalist's trash pail (the Recycle Bin).

With Windows 95, there is an easier way to delete files or documents: Right-click the item you want to delete and select Send To from the pop-up menu (called a *context menu*); then select Recycle Bin as the location to send it to. Figure 28-9 shows the context menu in action. An even easier method is to use the Delete key after selecting the file(s).

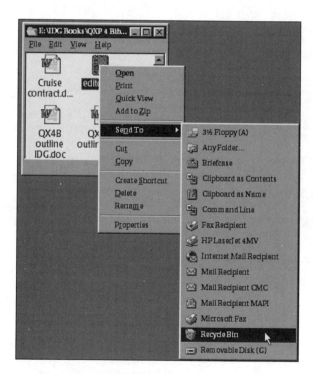

Figure 28-9: Windows 95 lets you easily trash a file or folder by right-clicking it.

Recovering files from the Recycle Bin

Until you choose to empty the Recycle Bin by right-clicking it and choosing Empty Recycle Bin from the context menu, you can recover a file or document by double-clicking on the Recycle Bin icon to open it and then dragging the item back from the bin to the desktop or to a disk or folder. (You open the recycle bin the same way you open a folder or disk: just double-click it with the left mouse button.)

Working with Fonts

QuarkXPress can do wonders with type in either the TrueType or PostScript Type 1 format. But for QuarkXPress to see typefaces, you must install them properly. Even though Adobe Type Manager, Windows, and the Mac OS have simplified font installation, there are still a few tricks and cautions you should know about. For instance, with PostScript fonts, the Macintosh and Windows both display fonts on the screen differently than they print them. This means that, in order for your computer to print the font you see on-screen, it needs to have access to the corresponding printer font (also called an *outline font*).

Installing Macintosh fonts

Installing fonts on the Macintosh is a straightforward process: You install fonts by simply dragging them onto your Mac's System Folder icon. Another way to install them is to open your System Folder, then drag the fonts into the Fonts folder you find inside it. Keep in mind that any program that is open when you add fonts this way won't show them until you close the program and reopen it. Here are a few guidelines:

✦ **Screen and printer fonts:** Make sure you install both the screen fonts and the printer fonts for each PostScript font. You may have a font suitcase—a special font file—with several screen fonts for your PostScript font, or you may have separate files for each screen font, depending on which option the company decided to use. TrueType fonts don't come in several files—all variants are in one suitcase.

✦ **Using Adobe Type Manager:** If you use the Adobe Type Manager 4.0 program (which we recommend), you don't even have to drag the fonts to the System Folder. Put them anywhere you want on your Mac (we recommend you create a Fonts folder that contains all your fonts) and use ATM to activate and deactivate the fonts. It can even load a font on demand, so if a particular QuarkXPress document uses a font but it's not loaded, ATM will load it when you open that document. Fonts installed in the System Folder are always active, so using ATM lets you have a large collection of fonts without having them all active at once, taking precious RAM. Figure 28-10 shows ATM 4.0 in action: You can simply click a font and the Activate button to activate it. For permanent activation (when you restart the Mac), drag the desired font into a font set (a group of fonts that can be activated or deactivated all at once) in the left pane and activate it there.

Figure 28-10: Adobe Type Manager lets you activate fonts at will and create sets of fonts to be activated at each startup.

Facing the font issue

Desktop publishing has changed the meaning of some fundamental typographic terms, which can lead to confusion. When you see the word *font* in the context of a computer, it means what a traditional typographer would call a *face*—one basic variant of a *typeface*. (In traditional typography, a *font* means a face at a particular point size, a context that digital typesetting has all but eliminated.) Thus, you'll see the word *font* used to mean, for example, Times Roman or Times Italic. A typographer would call these variants *faces*.

Many people use the word *font* informally to mean *typeface*, which is a collection of related faces. Thus, your service bureau would understand the phrase, "I'm using the News Gothic font in my brochure" to mean that you are using the News Gothic typeface, and that the bureau needs to ensure it downloads the whole family to the imagesetter when printing your job.

Installing Windows fonts

Windows does not support PostScript fonts on its own. You need Adobe Type Manager. ATM will find all the fonts residing on your PC and display a list of them. To activate a font on the fly, go to the Font List pane and select the desired fonts, checking the boxes to the left of their name or clicking the Activate button. To make fonts permanently available (after a restart), use the Sets pane to create font sets (groups of fonts that can be activated or deactivated all at once). You can add fonts from the font list to a set by using the Add Fonts pane, as shown in Figure 28-11, dragging a font from the right pane into the Sets pane at left. Click the checkbox to the left of the name of the added font, or use the Activate button, and you're done. The process of adding TrueType fonts is covered in the following steps:

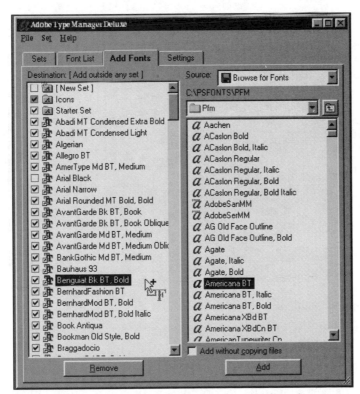

Figure 28-11: Use Adobe Type Manager to install and manage PostScript fonts in Windows.

STEPS: Adding TrueType fonts to Windows

1. Use Start➪Settings to open the Control Panel, and then double-click the Fonts folder.

2. Use the menu command File➪Install New Font to get the Add Fonts dialog box shown below.

3. Navigate the dialog box using the Folders and Drives scroll lists to get to the folder or disk that has the TrueType fonts you want to install. A list of fonts will appear in the dialog box.

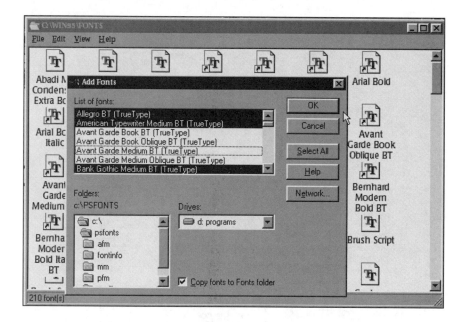

4. Select the fonts to install and click OK.

Loading PostScript fonts in printers

For faster printing, it's best to load PostScript fonts to printer memory. Otherwise, each time you print, your computer must load the fonts to the printer, which can be time-consuming. (TrueType fonts cannot be loaded to most printers.) Your Mac should have a font-loading utility (called the Apple Printer Utility; an older version is called the LaserWriter Font Utility) bundled with the system disks. Many printers come bundled with Adobe's font-loader utility (called Downloader; an old version is called SendPS). They all work basically the same way: you select the fonts you want to load and then tell the utility to do the work. Figure 28-12 shows the process in Apple Printer Utility.

Windows does not have an equivalent utility. Instead, it loads the fonts to the printer as they are used.

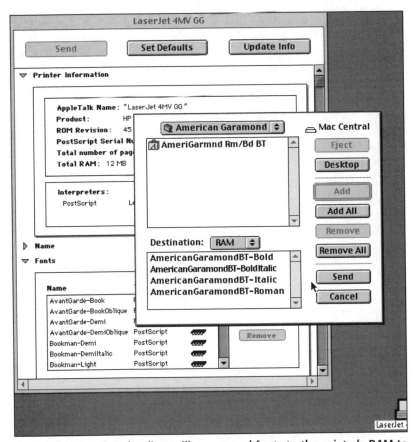

Figure 28-12: A font-loading utility can send fonts to the printer's RAM to speed printing when you use specific fonts frequently.

TrueType or PostScript?

The most basic question about fonts usually is whether you should use TrueType or PostScript fonts. The answer depends on the work you do. If you produce newsletters, magazines, ads, or brochures that you output on a typesetter or imagesetter, use PostScript, because that is the standard format on these devices. If your final output is to a laser or inkjet printer, TrueType is probably the better bet because it prints faster in most cases, especially if you print to a non-PostScript printer. However, you do not have to use one font format exclusively:

✦ If you see a TrueType typeface that you want to use in your typeset document, use it. The Macintosh and Windows OSs automatically convert TrueType fonts into PostScript format when printing to a PostScript device (or to a file designated for use by a PostScript device). The drawback is that this conversion process may make your files larger because the computer must download the converted TrueType font file into your document.

✦ Conversely, if you have PostScript typefaces, there's no reason to give them up if you switch to TrueType. On a PostScript printer, you can use both formats. On other printers, all you need is a program such as Adobe Type Manager to make the outlines of the letters appear smooth when they print.

Don't base decisions about whether to use TrueType or PostScript fonts on assumptions about quality. Both technologies provide excellent results, so any quality differences are due to the font manufacturer's standards. If you purchase typefaces from recognized companies, you don't need to worry. (Many smaller companies produce high-quality fonts as well.)

Font-loading tips and tricks

The one trick to loading fonts to printer memory is to not download too many. Each font takes up room in the printer memory that would otherwise go for processing your files. If you put too few fonts in printer memory, you'll waste a lot of time having your Macintosh send fonts repeatedly to the printer. But if you put too many fonts in printer memory, you'll waste a lot of time having the printer process the file under tight memory constraints, which slows it down.

A good rule of thumb is to load no more than 10 fonts per megabyte of printer memory, after reserving 2MB for the printer's internal processing. For example, if your printer has 4MB of memory, download no more than 20 fonts to it. Keep in mind that *font* in this context means each distinct face, so loading the News Gothic family—News Gothic Medium, News Gothic Oblique, News Gothic Bold, and News Gothic Bold Oblique—counts as four fonts. Keep this in mind when deciding which fonts to load.

Another rule of thumb: load those fonts that appear on every page of your document, and let your Macintosh itself load those used just occasionally when it needs to (it will remove them when the print job is complete).

Fonts loaded to printer memory are removed from memory when you restart or shut down the printer. If you constantly use many fonts, get a printer with a built-in or external disk drive onto which you can load the fonts permanently.

✦   ✦   ✦

Effective Typography

In This Chapter

Learning about typefaces

Selecting the best typefaces

Taking advantage of type styles

Using Multiple Master fonts

Working with characters and symbols

Desktop publishing has changed typography forever. In the old, old days, typefaces were available in a limited number, and those were available only in a limited number of sizes. You couldn't condense or expand them. And you certainly couldn't add drop shadows or make them print as outlines without hours of work in a darkroom. Desktop publishing has changed all that. By rendering type into a series of mathematical equations—curves and lines and angles—and manipulating that math with today's fast computers, type can be almost anything. In the early days of desktop publishing, that led to experimentation and a lot of bad results. That was more than a decade ago, however, and good taste in innovation has prevailed. This chapter is your guide to typographic good taste.

Learning About Typefaces

The two basic types of typefaces are serif and sans serif. A *serif* typeface has horizontal lines (called *serifs*) extending from the edges of the character, such as at the bottom of a *p* or at the top of an *I*. A *sans serif* typeface does not have these lines (*sans* is French for *without*). There are more types of typefaces than just serif and sans serif, but these are all in the minority. Calligraphic, block, and other nonserif/non-sans serif typefaces usually have other elements that serve the purpose of serifs—extensions to the characters that add, well, a distinctive character to the typeface. Another distinct type of typeface is the *pi font*, which is a font made up of themed symbols (anything from math to Christmas ornaments). The name *pi font* comes from the Greek letter *pi* (π), a common mathematical symbol.

Typeface variations

A typeface usually has several variations, the most common of which are *roman, italic, boldface,* and *boldface italic* for serif typefaces; and *medium, oblique, boldface,* and *boldface oblique* for sans serif typefaces. Italic and oblique differ in that italics are a curved variant of the typeface, with the serifs usually heavily curved, while an oblique is simply a slanted version of the typeface. Other variations that involve type weight include *thin, light, book, demibold, heavy, ultrabold,* and *black. Compressed, condensed, expanded,* and *wide* describe type scale.

What's in a face?

Each of these variants, as well as each available combination of variants (for example, compressed light oblique), is called a *face.* Some typefaces have no variants; these are typically calligraphic typefaces, such as Park Avenue and Zapf Chancery, and symbol typefaces (pi fonts), such as Zapf Dingbats and Sonata. In Figure 29-1, you see samples of several typefaces and some of their variants. By using typeface variants wisely, you can create more attractive and more readable documents.

A font is a typeface by any other name

Desktop publishing programs popularized the use of the term *font* to describe what traditionally was called a *typeface.* In traditional terms, a typeface refers to a set of variants for one style of text, such as Times Roman. A *face* is one of those variants, such as Times Roman Italic. A font, in traditional terms, is a face at a specific point size, such as 12-point Times Roman Italic. (Until electronic typesetting was developed, printers set type using metal blocks that were available only in a limited range of sizes.) The word *font* today means what *typeface* used to mean, and almost no one uses *font* any more for its original meaning.

The heart of a document is its typography. Everything else can be well laid out and illustrated, but if the text is not legible and appealing, all that other work is for naught. If you don't believe type is central, then consider this: You've surely seen engaging documents with no artwork, but have you ever seen artwork carry the day if the type is ugly or scrunched? We didn't think so.

Selecting the Best Typefaces

If you've ever seen a type chart, you already know that thousands of typefaces are available, each with a different feel. Matching the typeface's feel to the effect that you want for your document is a trial-and-error process. Until you are experienced at using a wide variety of typefaces (and even then), experiment with different typefaces on a mock-up of your document to see what works best.

<u>Serif Typefaces</u>
Esprit Book *Italic*
Caslon *224 Italic*
Minion Condensed *Italic*
Americana *Italic*
Bookman Light *Italic*
Bodoni *Italic* Bold
Galliard *Italic* **Black**
Janson Text *Italic* **Bold**
Poppl Pontifex *Italic*
Stone Serif *Italic* Semi **Bold**
Century Oldstyle *Italic*
Garamond Condensed Light *Italic*
Industrial 736 *Italic*
Times Roman Times Ten
New Baskerville *Italic* **Bold**
Veljovic Book Medium **Bold Black**

<u>Sans Serif Typefaces</u>
Helvetica **Bold** *Light Italic* **Black Compressed**
COPPERPLATE GOTHIC CONDENSED **BOLD**
Gill Sans Light **Extra Bold**
Poppl Laudatio *Italic* **Bold**
Syntax Roman *Italic* **Ultra Black**
Frutiger Condensed Light **Bold Black Extra**
Futura Book **Heavy** Regular **Extra Bold**
Avant Garde Book **Demi**
Myriad **Bold** *Italic*
Optima **Bold**
Stone Sans *Italic* **Bold**
DIN Schriften Mittelschrift
News Gothic **Bold**

<u>Calligraphic/Decorative</u>
TRAJAN BOLD
Sanvito Roman
Ex Ponto
ANNA
Friz Quadrata **Bold**
LITHOS **BLACK**
MACHINE BOLD
Nueva Roman **Bold Extended**
Zapf Chancery

<u>Pi Fonts</u>
η∓°+κ∇⊊−⊆β⊃°±÷φφϑ∩
θ₀iɛːðφɕrɛRʊɔɪˈæʰʃχçʊʙɴɯɥ̢ɜ̦
∗☛□✳✣✚★✼☙∗☜⊕☍☺✔⊞▲❝♦☞♣❋
🕮〰🏠🗁🗀🖿📄🗂🖳🖂 ℯ&₴◆ ♫🖴☎
φƎ≅−∀∶⋀ϑΔ∑Ǝδαω𝛺Π

Figure 29-1: A variety of typefaces and their variants.

Defining a standard set

We recommend that you take the time necessary to define a standard set of typefaces for each group of publications. You may want all employee newsletters in your company to have a similar feel, which you can achieve by using common body text and headline typefaces, even if layout and paragraph settings differ. The key to working with a standard set of typefaces is to avoid limiting the set to only a few typefaces. Selecting more typefaces than any one document might use gives you enough flexibility to be creative, while providing an obviously standard appearance. You also can use the same typeface for different purposes. For example, you might use a newsletter's headline typeface as a kicker in a brochure. A consistent—but not constrained—appearance is a good way to establish an identity for your company.

Understanding typeface names

The many variants of typefaces confuse many users, especially because most programs use only the terms *normal* (or *plain*), *italic* (or *oblique*), *bold,* and *bold italic* (or *bold oblique*) to describe available variations. When a typeface has more than these basic variations, programs usually split the typeface into several typefaces.

For example, in some programs, Helvetica comes as Helvetica, with medium, oblique, boldface, and boldface oblique faces; Helvetica Light/Black, with light, light oblique, black, and black oblique faces; Helvetica Light/Black Condensed, with condensed light, condensed light oblique, condensed black, and condensed black oblique faces; Helvetica Condensed, with condensed medium, condensed oblique, condensed boldface, and condensed boldface oblique faces; and Helvetica Compressed, with compressed medium and condensed oblique faces. (Figure 29-1 shows four of these variations.) When there are this many variations, you have to choose from among several Helvetica typefaces, and you have to know that, for example, selecting bold for Helvetica Condensed results in Helvetica Condensed Bold type.

For some typefaces, the variants are even more confusing. For example, in text, Bookman is usually printed in light face, which is lighter than the medium face. So when you select plain, you really select Bookman Light (shown in Figure 29-1). And when you select bold, you really select Bookman Demibold. Bookman Medium and Bookman Bold are too heavy for use as body text, which is why the typeface comes in the light/demi combination of faces. Fortunately, the issue of what face a program designates as plain, italic, and the rest rarely comes into play. You usually encounter a problem only in one of the following situations:

✦ When you are exchanging files between PCs and Macs—because some vendors use slightly different names for their typefaces on different platforms. The Utilities⇨Usage option enables you to correct this problem by replacing one typeface name with another in your document, via the Fonts pane.

✦ When you are working with a service bureau that has typeface names that are different, or whose staff uses the traditional names rather than the desktop-publishing names.

✦ When you are working with artists or typesetters to match a typeface. Typically, the problem is a lack of familiarity with the different names for a typeface. The best way to reach a common understanding is to look at a sample of the typefaces being discussed.

Tip

You may have noticed that many people use serif typefaces for body copy and sans serif typefaces for headlines, pull-quotes, and other elements. But there is no rule you should worry about following. You can easily create engaging documents that use serif typefaces for every element. All-sans-serif documents are possible, but they are rare because sans serif typefaces tend to be hard to read when used in many pages of text. (Exceptions include typefaces such as News Gothic and Franklin Gothic, which were designed for use as body text.) No matter which typefaces you use, the key is to ensure that each element calls an appropriate amount of attention to itself.

Some basic guidelines

If you're feeling confused about which typeface is right for you, here are some basic guidelines:

✦ Use a roman medium or book weight typeface for body text. In some cases, a light weight works well, especially for typefaces such as Bookman and Souvenir, which tend to be heavy in the medium weights.

✦ Output some samples before deciding on a light typeface for body text because many light typefaces arc hard to read when used extensively. Also, if you intend to output publications on an imagesetter (at 1270 dpi or finer resolution), make sure that you output samples on that imagesetter because a light font may be readable on a 300- or 600-dpi laser printer but too light on a higher-resolution printer that can reproduce thin characters more faithfully than a laser printer. (The laser printer may actually print a light typeface as something a bit heavier: because the width of the text's stroke is not an even multiple of the laser printer's dots, the printer has no choice but to make the stroke thicker than it should be.)

✦ Use a heavier typeface for headlines and subheads. A demibold or bold usually works well. Avoid using the same typeface for headlines and body text, even if it is a bolder variant. On the other hand, using the same typeface for subheads and headlines, even if in a different variant, helps ensure a common identity. (And if you mix typefaces, use those that have similar appearances. For example, use round typefaces with other round typefaces and squared-off typefaces with other squared-off typefaces.)

✦ If captions are long (more than three lines), use a typeface with the same weight as body text. If you use the same typeface as body text, differentiate the caption visually from body text. Using a boldface caption lead-in (the first words are boldface and act as a title for the caption) or putting the caption in italics distinguishes the caption from body text without being distracting. If captions are short (three lines or fewer), consider using a heavier face than body text or a typeface that is readily distinguished from your body text.

✦ As a general rule, avoid using more than three typefaces (not including variants) in the main document elements (headlines, body text, captions, pull-quotes, and other elements that appear on most pages). However, some typefaces are very similar, so you can use them as a group as if they were one. Examples include Helvetica, Univers, and Arial; Futura, Bauhaus, and Avant Garde; Times and its many relatives (including Times New Roman and Times Ten); Galliard and New Baskerville; Souvenir and Korinna; Benguiat, Americana, Garamond, Stone Serif, and Cheltenham; New Baskerville and Esprit; and Goudy Old Style and Century Old Style. You can treat the individual typefaces within these groups almost as variants of one another, especially if you use one of the individual typefaces in limited-length elements such as kickers, pull-quotes, and bylines.

✦ Italics are particularly appropriate for kickers, bylines, sidebar headlines, and pull-quotes.

Typography on the Web

In Web publishing, typography is extremely primitive. For text attributes, only boldface, italics, and underline survive. Font changes generally don't survive, although new technologies are being introduced that may change that over the next several years. Type sizes don't usually survive either, although there are about a dozen style sheets that all popular browsers recognize, and those do have different text sizes.

That means you can vary the type size for a paragraph in some cases, and you can sometimes specify a type attribute like "larger" that the browser then assigns a size to, but you cannot specify the specific type size for individual characters. Part 8 covers Web-publishing issues in detail.

Taking Advantage of Type Styles

Typefaces have several faces—such as boldface and italics—to give publishers visual variety and content guides. Publishing programs (as well as some word processors) also offer special *typeface attributes*, such as small caps, shadows, and underlines, to provide even more design and content tools.

Changing typeface attributes

Figure 29-2 shows the Measurements palette, from which you can control almost every typographic specification, including leading, tracking, paragraph alignment, typefaces, type size, and type style. QuarkXPress lets you change typeface attributes in the following ways:

New
Feature

If you're not sure what those little symbols mean on the Measurements palette, let your mouse hover over them for an instant, and QuarkXPress will display a brief description—that is, if you checked the new Show Tool Tips option in the Interactive pane of the Application Preferences dialog box (Shift+Option+⌘+Y, or Edit⇨Preferences⇨Application).

Figure 29-2: The Measurements palette's typeface controls (at right).

✦ **Option 1:** Use the Measurements palette (this is the easiest method). To select a typeface quickly, double-click the typeface name in the palette and then enter the first letter of the typeface's name. QuarkXPress enters the first typeface that begins with that letter. If this isn't the font you want, just keep typing the font's name; QuarkXPress will try to match whatever letters you enter. This method is faster than scrolling through the font list if you have many typefaces available. Below the typeface list is a row of type style attributes: plain, boldface, italics, underline all, word underline, outline, shadow, strikethrough, all caps, small caps, superscript, subscript, and superior. Any current style settings for the selected text are highlighted. (To quickly highlight the font field in the Measurements palette, type Shift+Option+⌘+M.)

✦ **Option 2:** Use the Style menu. Options available in this menu include Font, Size, Type Style, Color, Shade, Horizontal/Vertical Scale, Kern or Track (depending on whether text is selected), Baseline Shift, and Character (which lets you define several attributes at once). You can see the Style menu in Figure 29-3.

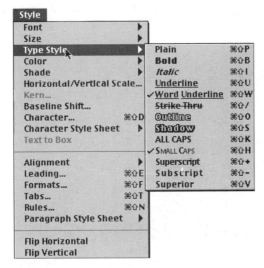

Figure 29-3: The Style menu and its many typeface options.

✦ **Option 3:** Use the Character Attributes dialog box, which you access with the shortcut key Shift+⌘+D or via Style⇨Character. Figure 29-4 shows the dialog box. You can set several type settings at once.

✦ **Option 4:** Use keyboard shortcuts. Use the codes in Table 29-1 in combination with Shift+⌘. For example, for plain text, press Shift+⌘+P. Remember that these codes are toggles: Using Shift+⌘+I twice on the same text makes it first apply italics to the text and then remove italics.

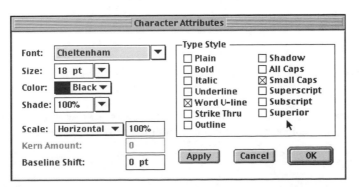

Figure 29-4: The Character Attributes dialog box contains most typeface settings in one place.

Note

Plain as the basic style

Plain refers to the basic style for the selected typeface. Most commercial typefaces come with a roman or medium face as the basic style. But many typefaces created by do-it-yourselfers or converted via programs, such as Macromedia's Fontographer, come with each face as a separate typeface. So, for example, you may have Magazine Roman, Magazine Italic, Magazine Bold, and Magazine Bold Italic as separate typefaces in your fonts menu. If you select Magazine Bold Italic, QuarkXPress's palettes and dialog boxes show its style as plain, but it appears and prints as bold italic. This discrepancy is not a bug in QuarkXPress, but simply a reflection of the fact that the basic style for any typeface is called "plain" no matter what the style actually looks like.

Table 29-1 Shortcut Keys for Typeface Attributes		
Attribute	*Macintosh Shortcut*	*Windows Shortcut*
Plain	Shift+⌘+P	Ctrl+Shift+P
Bold	Shift+⌘+B	Ctrl+Shift+B
Italic	Shift+⌘+I	Ctrl+Shift+I
<u>Underline all</u>	Shift+⌘+U	Ctrl+Shift+U
Word <u>underline</u>	Shift+⌘+W	Ctrl+Shift+W
~~Strikethrough~~	Shift+⌘+/	Ctrl+Shift+/
Outline	Shift+⌘+O (letter O)	Ctrl+Shift+O (letter O)
Shadow	Shift+⌘+S	Ctrl+Shift+S
ALL CAPS	Shift+⌘+K	Ctrl+Shift+K
SMALL CAPS	Shift+⌘+H	Ctrl+Shift+H
Superscript	Shift+⌘++ (plus)	Ctrl+Shift+0 (zero)
Subscript	Shift+⌘+- (hyphen)	Ctrl+Shift+9
Superior	Shift+⌘+V	Ctrl+Shift+V

Basic text styles

Most people are familiar with basic text styles such as boldface and italics. After all, we see them routinely in newspapers, magazines, ads, and television. Despite that familiarity, these styles can be misused, especially by people experienced in producing reports on typewriters and word processors, rather than creating published (typeset-quality) documents in which these basic styles are used differently. The following is a primer on the use of basic text attributes in body text. (Other effects are covered later in this chapter.) Of course, these and other guidelines should be ignored by those purposely trying to create a special effect.

Italics

Italics are used to emphasize a word or phrase in body text. For example, "You *must* remember to fully extinguish your campfire." Italics are also used to identify titles of books, movies, television and radio series, magazines, and newspapers: "Public TV's *Discovery* series had an excellent show about the Rocky Mountains." Italics can also be applied to lead-in words of subsections or in lists (these instances are described in Chapter 17).

In typewritten text, people often use underlines or uppercase as a substitute for italics. Because you have access to professional publishing tools, however, you do not need to use these substitutes in published text.

Boldface

Boldface is seldom used in body text because it is too distracting. When it is used, boldface is typically applied to the lead-in words in subsections. As a rule, do not use it for emphasis—use italics instead. However, when you have a lot of text and you want people to easily pick out names within it, boldfacing the names may be appropriate. If, for example, you create a story listing winners of a series of awards or publish a gossip column that mentions various celebrities, you may want to boldface people's names in order to highlight them.

The bold and italic blues

QuarkXPress cannot apply a bold style to a typeface that does not have one. If the typeface has a bolder face, QuarkXPress is likely to use that one, assuming the typeface uses the correct internal label so that QuarkXPress knows how to do this. Similarly, QuarkXPress cannot apply an italic style to a typeface that does not have one. But QuarkXPress does recognize that when you select italics for a sans serif typeface, the oblique face is what you want.

If you change the face of selected text to a face (boldface or italics) not supported by the text's typeface, QuarkXPress may appear to have applied that face successfully. However, when you print, you will see that the face has not really been changed (although the spacing has changed to accommodate the new face). What has happened is that QuarkXPress and the type scaler (such as TrueType or Adobe Type Manager) mistakenly create a screen font based on your request for a face change. When the text with the nonexistent face is printed, the Macintosh finds no printer file for that face and uses the closest face it has for the typeface used: the original, regular face.

Small caps and all caps

Capital letters have both functional and decorative uses. Functionally, they start sentences and identify proper names. Decoratively, they add emphasis or stateliness. Capital letters have a more stately appearance than lowercase letters most likely because of the influence of Roman monuments, which are decorated with inscribed text in uppercase letters (the Romans didn't use lowercase much). These monuments and the Roman style have come to symbolize authority and officialism. Most government centers have a very Roman appearance, as a visit to Washington, D.C., quickly confirms. Using all capital letters has two major drawbacks:

✦ Text in all caps can be overwhelming because uppercase characters are both taller and wider than lowercase. In typeset materials, as opposed to typewritten, all caps loom even larger because the size difference between a capital letter and its lowercase version is greater than it is with typewriter characters, which are all designed to fit in the same space. All caps can be thought of as the typographic equivalent of yelling: READ THIS SENTENCE! Now, read this sentence.

✦ People read not by analyzing every letter and constructing words but by recognizing the shapes of words. In all caps, words have the same rectangular shape—only the width changes—so the use of word shape as a reading aid is lost. All caps is therefore harder to read than regular text.

The effective use of small caps

The use of small caps can result in elegant, stately text that is not overwhelming. The smaller size of the caps overcomes the yelling aspect of all caps. Figure 29-5 shows an example of effective use of small caps. In the example, the kicker and byline are set in small caps.

Tip

The key to using small caps is to limit them to short amounts of text where it's OK not to give readers the aid of recognizable word shapes. Small caps are effective in kickers, bylines, and labels.

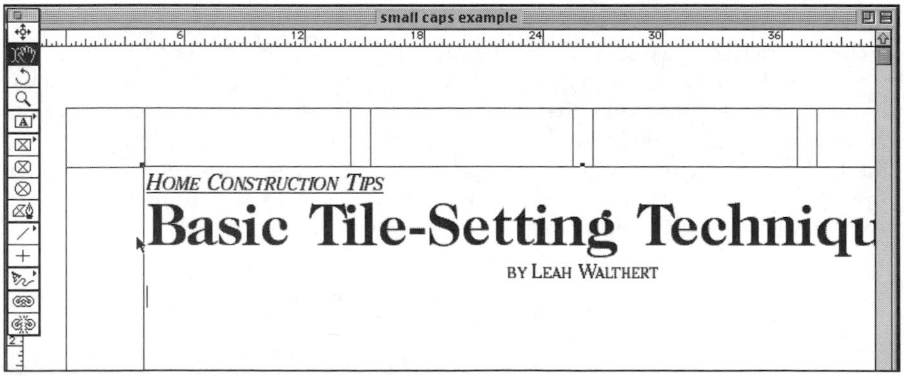

HOME CONSTRUCTION TIPS

Basic Tile-Setting Techniqu

BY LEAH WALTHERT

Figure 29-5: An effective use of small caps.

Setting small caps proportional size

QuarkXPress lets you set the proportional size of small caps (compared to regular caps) in the Character pane of the Document Preferences dialog box (Edit⇨Preferences⇨Document, or ⌘+Y), as shown in Figure 29-6. (You can also set the relative size and position of superscripts, subscripts, and superiors in this dialog box.) You can set the horizontal and vertical proportions separately, although they are usually the same. QuarkXPress's default setting is 75 percent, and most small caps should be set between 70 and 80 percent.

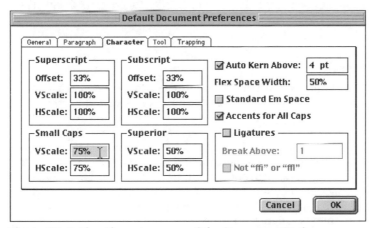

Figure 29-6: The Character pane of the Document Preferences dialog box.

The small caps expert collection

Some typefaces have a version—sometimes called an *expert collection*—that includes specially designed small caps. These caps are not merely proportionally scaled; their strokes are also modified to make them a bit darker. When you scale a character to be smaller, you make its strokes smaller, which makes the character lighter than the equivalent lowercase letter. Simulated small caps can look weaker than true small caps. This difference is usually not a problem, but for design-intensive work such as advertising, the quality difference often makes it worthwhile to get the expert-collection typeface. Keep in mind that using the small caps option in QuarkXPress does not access the expert-collection typeface; you must explicitly apply the expert-collection's small cap typeface to the characters in question using the Measurements palette, Style menu, or Character Attributes dialog box described earlier in this chapter.

Creating typographic default settings

If you want typographic settings to affect all future documents, invoke the Character pane of the Document Preferences dialog box with no document open. Any future documents use the new settings as the default settings.

To apply default settings to a document with altered preferences (including typographic settings), open the document and select Use XPress Preferences when QuarkXPress asks whether to use the default settings or the document's settings. (QuarkXPress automatically detects whether a document's settings match the defaults for that copy of QuarkXPress.)

Traditional numerals

If you look at books published early in this century or in previous eras, you'll notice that the numerals look very different than the ones you see today in books, magazines, and newspapers. Numerals used to be treated as lowercase letters, so some, such as the number 9, had *descenders*, just as lowercase letters such as *g* do. Others, such as the number 6, had *ascenders*, as do lowercase letters such as *b*. But this way of displaying numerals changed, and most modern typefaces treat numerals like capital letters: no descenders and no ascenders. This style keeps numerals from sticking out in headlines, but it also can make numerals too prominent in some text, especially in type-intensive documents such as ads, where individual character shapes are important to the overall look.

Using expert-collection numerals

Adobe and other type foundries resurrected the old-fashioned numerals as part of expert-collection typefaces. As you can see in Figure 29-7, which shows the two types of numerals, the traditional numerals are more stylized and have the typographic feel of lowercase letters.

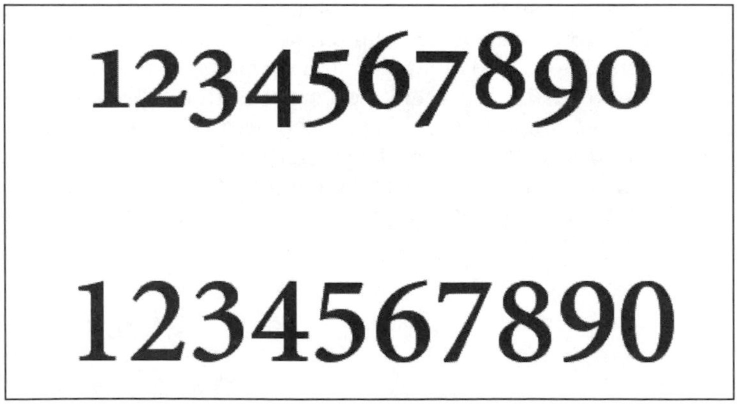

Figure 29-7: Examples of traditional numerals (top) and modern numerals (bottom).

Considering the drawbacks

Although they often look more elegant, old-fashioned numerals have three drawbacks that you should consider before using them routinely:

✦ They reside in a separate font, so you must change the font for each and every numeral (or group of numerals). Even if you code this in your word processor, it can be a lot of extra work. In tables and other numerals-only text, using old-fashioned numerals is less of an issue because you can have a separate style for text that uses the expert font.

✦ They do not have the same width. Modern numerals are almost always the same width (that of an en space), so typographers and publishers don't have to worry about whether columns of numbers align. (Because all numerals are the same width, they align naturally.) But the old-fashioned numerals in expert fonts have variable widths, just like most characters, so they can look awkward in columns of numbers even if you use decimal or comma alignment.

✦ They are unusual in modern typography, so they can call more attention to themselves than is appropriate. For design-intensive work, this extra attention is usually not an issue, but in commonplace documents such as reports and newsletters, they can look out of place. As their popularity grows, people may grow more used to seeing them.

Superscripts, subscripts, and superiors

Superscripts, subscripts, and superiors let you indicate notes in your text and set some mathematical notations. Although numerals are typically used for these notes, you can also use special symbols such as asterisks and daggers. These notes are in a smaller size than the rest of the text and are positioned above or below the regular baseline. Superscripts and subscripts are typically used in math and other sciences. A superscript can indicate an exponent, such as a^2 for *a squared,* or a notation, such as U^{235} for *uranium-235.*

Superiors as footnotes

Superscripts are commonly used for footnotes, too, but QuarkXPress also offers *superiors*, the traditional typographic method of indicating footnotes. A superior is similar to a superscript, except that the top of a superior always aligns with the top of the text's cap height. A superscript, by contrast, need not align with anything. The advantage to using a superior is that you don't have to worry about the footnote (or whatever) bumping into the text in the line above. This problem is particularly acute if you have tight leading and the superscript is positioned below a character that has a descender (such as a *g* or *p.*) Another potential problem is uneven leading, which is explained later.

Changing superscripts to superiors

Footnotes set via your word processor to be superscripted import as superscripts. If you want to use superiors, you must manually change superscripts to superiors. QuarkXPress lets you replace superscripts with superiors in the Find/Change dialog box (see Figure 29-8). That's a welcome change from earlier versions of QuarkXPress, which did not have superior as an option in the Find/Change dialog box.

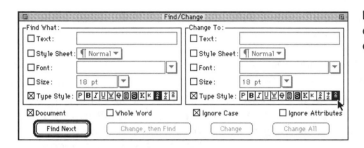

Figure 29-8: The Find/Change dialog box lets you replace character attributes.

Setting relative size and spacing

As it does for small caps, QuarkXPress lets you set the relative size and spacing for superscripts, subscripts, and superiors. You specify these sizes in the Character pane of the Document Preferences dialog box, accessed via Edit⇨Preferences⇨ Document, or ⌘+Y. You may need to experiment to derive a setting that works for all paragraph styles.

Tip

We prefer the following settings: superscripts offset 35 percent and scaled 60 percent; subscripts offset 30 percent and scaled 60 percent; and superiors scaled 50 percent.

Working with additive or automatic leading

If you use additive or automatic leading (covered in Chapter 13) and your superscript or subscript settings cause the superscripts or subscripts to extend beyond the text's height or depth, you get uneven spacing. The uneven spacing occurs because some lines have more leading than others to accommodate the outsized or outpositioned characters. (QuarkXPress bases additive and automatic leading on the highest and lowest character in a line, not on the text's normal position.) If you can't alter your text so that none of it extends beyond the text's range—by changing either its leading or the subscript and superscript settings— don't use the additive or automatic leading options.

Baseline shift

Baseline shift is similar to superscripting and subscripting. Baseline shift lets you move text up or down relative to other text on the line. The biggest difference between baseline shifting and superscripting or subscripting is that with baseline shift, the text size does not change. This effect is rarely needed, but it can come in handy when you position text for ads and other design-intensive text or when you use it with effects such as ruling lines to create reverse text. If you need to do so, you can change baseline shift through the Character Attributes dialog box (refer to Figure 29-4), which you access via Style⇨Baseline Shift. Entering a positive number moves the text up; a negative number moves it down. (QuarkXPress 4 eliminated the Baseline Shift dialog box, using the Character Attributes dialog box instead.)

The Baseline Shift feature also lets you change the text size to create superscripts or subscripts that differ from the normal settings in a document, which can be useful to scientists and engineers whose documents require several levels of subscripting or superscripting.

Note

Unlike superscripts and subscripts, baseline shifts do not cause uneven leading when used with additive leading. Instead, QuarkXPress lets text overprint lines the text shifts into.

Underlines and rules

Underlines and rules are not typically used in body text in published documents. In fact, underlines are used in typewritten text as a substitute for italics. But underlines do have a place in published materials as a visual element in kickers, subheads, bylines, and tables. When used in such short elements, underlines add a definitive, authoritative feel.

Regular and word underline

QuarkXPress offers two types of underlines: *regular underline* (Shift+⌘+U), which affects all characters, including spaces; and *word underline* (Shift+⌘+W), which underlines only nonspace characters (letters, numerals, symbols, and punctuation). When choosing which underline type to use, there is no right or wrong. Let the aesthetics of the document be the determining factor.

Using the Ruling Line feature

Underlines are limited in line size and position. All underlines are fixed by QuarkXPress. But you can create underlines and other types of lines meant to enhance text with the Ruling Line feature. QuarkXPress offers a wide range of ruling lines through the Rules pane of the Paragraph Attributes dialog box, which you access via the keyboard shortcut Shift+⌘+N or by selecting Style⇨Rules. Figure 29-9 shows the dialog box. In the Rules pane, you can set a ruling line above and below the paragraph with totally different settings. Note that to set a ruling line's options, you need to check the Rule Above box and/or the Rule Below box to make those settings accessible. Here are your options:

 ✦ **Length:** The first option available for the Rule Above and Rule Below is the Length option. You have two choices: Indents and Text. Selecting Indents makes the rule the width of the current column, minus the settings in From Left and From Right. Figure 29-10 shows a ruling line set this way under the byline of the sample article. When you select the Text option, the rule is the width of the text it is applied to. In Figure 29-11, note how the byline rule appears when you choose Text instead of Indents.

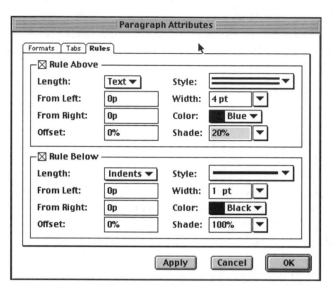

Figure 29-9: The Rules pane of the Paragraph Attributes dialog box.

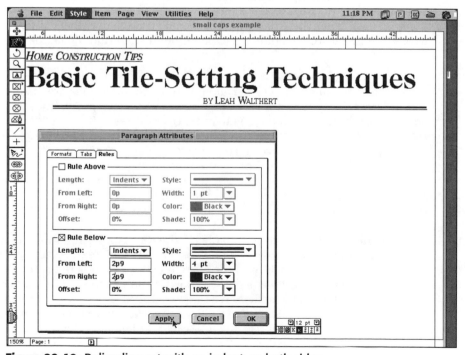

Figure 29-10: Ruling line set with an indent on both sides.

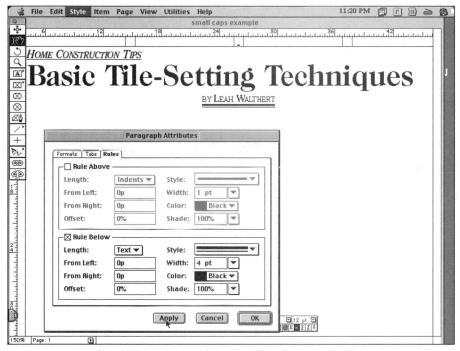

Figure 29-11: Ruling line set to equal the text length.

Tip

Use Indents when you want a rule to be a standard width, regardless of the length of the text it is associated with. An example is a series of centered labels in a menu—*Appetizers, Salads, Pasta,* and so on—whose lengths vary greatly. By making the rules the same width, you call more attention to the rules and to the fact that they indicate a major heading.

✦ **Offset:** By entering a percentage from 0 to 100 in the Offset fields, you can specify the position of the rule relative to the text in the paragraph above it (for Rule Above) or below it (for Rule Below). You can also use units of your default absolute measurement (picas, inches, centimeters, etc.), from a negative value of half the rule's width to 15 inches (90 picas or 38.1 cm).

Using Offset to create reversed type

You can use the Offset feature to create reversed type, as illustrated in the byline treatment in Figure 29-12. To do this, you essentially move the rule into the text line associated with it. The key is to make the rule larger than the text. In the figure, the text is 12 points, so we set the rule to be 16 points, which provides a margin above and below the text. (Make your rule at least 2 points larger than the text to get an adequate margin.) We then offset the rule by –8 points (the maximum allowed, or half the rule size). That was not enough, so we selected the text and used the Character Attributes dialog box's baseline shift feature (described earlier in this chapter) to shift the text down 3 points (–3 points), which centered it in the black rule. We also changed the text color to white via the Character Attributes dialog box. Finally, by selecting the Style⇨Formats (or Shift+⌘+F) dialog box, we added 6 points of space below the byline so that the black rule does not touch the text we plan to enter below it.

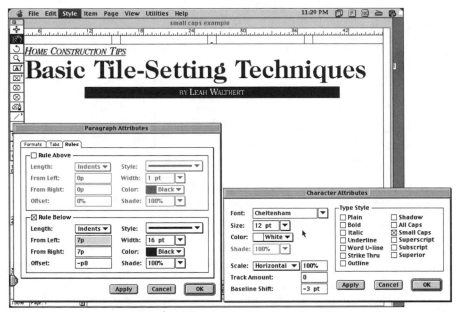

Figure 29-12: A ruling line used to create a reversed-out effect.

How the Offset option works

If you enter a percentage in the Offset field, the rule will only be drawn if there is a preceding (for Rule Above) or following (for Rule Below) paragraph in the text box. (This makes sense; if there's no preceding or following paragraph, there's no interparagraph spacing, so QuarkXPress has no distance to calculate a percentage of.) If you want to make sure a rule is always drawn, enter an absolute value instead of a percentage.

Moving a rule up or down via the Offset feature does not affect leading, so QuarkXPress may move the rule into unrelated text. If you want a 2-point ruling line to be 6 points below the text associated with it, and you want the next paragraph to be another 6 points below that, you must add six points of extra space between the paragraphs, perhaps by entering p6 in the Space After field (in the Formats tab of the Paragraph Attributes dialog box).

Using Multiple Master Fonts

Adobe Systems has created a special type of PostScript font called Multiple Master. Multiple Master fonts are designed to be elastic, so you can change their characteristics—such as thickness, width, and optical scaling—on-the-fly by creating new versions (such as semicondensed semibold). Thus, a Multiple Master font like Minion or Myriad may have a dozen versions, not just the usual normal, bold, italic, and bold italic.

The Font Creator XTension

Normally, you use Adobe's Font Creator utility or a font editor like Macromedia's Fontographer to create these variations. But QuarkXPress comes with an XTension called Font Creator that lets you create these variations from within QuarkXPress, to get exactly the style of type you need while doing your design. You access the Create or Remove Any Font dialog box via Utilities⇨Font Creator (see Figure 29-13). To use the Font Creator XTension, make sure of two things:

✦ You have the XTension installed in your QuarkXPress program's XTension folder. (The XTension's filename is Font Creator.)

✦ You have Multiple Master fonts installed in your System folder.

If both are not installed, the Font Creator menu item will not display in the Utilities menu.

Note

If you have installed Adobe's SuperATM font scaler (also known as Adobe Type Manager 3.5 or higher) or Adobe's Acrobat portable-document software (which uses SuperATM), you will have two Multiple Master fonts automatically installed—Adobe Serif MM and Adobe Sans MM. The QuarkXPress Font Creator XTension will see these fonts and display the Font Creator menu item. However, these fonts are designed for use only with ATM (they are what ATM uses to simulate fonts not installed on your system) so you will not be able to work with them in the Font Creator window.

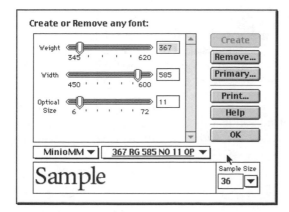

Figure 29-13: The Font Creator option in Mac QuarkXPress.

The Font Creator XTension is not available for Windows. Instead, use the Create Multiple Masters option (in the Source pop-up menu) that comes with Adobe Type Manager 4.0 or later, as shown in Figure 29-14.

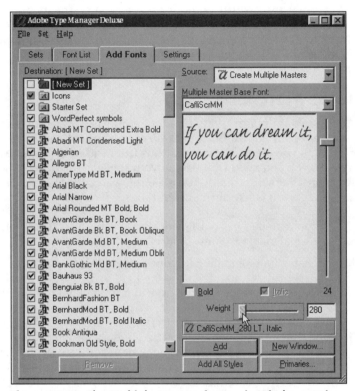

Figure 29-14: The Multiple Masters feature in Windows 95's Adobe Type Manager 4.0.

Adding font variations

When you select the Font Creator menu, you will be shown the first available Multiple Master font with the normal style displayed. Figure 29-13 shows an example for the font Minion. At the bottom of the dialog box (above the sample text) are two pop-up menus, one for the font and one for the variation. Load the font and variation that you want to work from. Depending on the font loaded, you will see two or more sliders that let you adjust font attributes. By changing these attributes, you create new variations. In Figure 29-13, the Minion font has three changeable attributes: weight (thickness), width, and optical size (the clarity of the font at different point sizes, which is used to make small type readable while letting larger type be detailed; this feature is often found only on serif fonts). Each variation consists of a specific combination of these three values.

Generating a new variant

Figure 29-15 shows a newly created variant of Minion, a condensed semibold version. After you have used the sliders to make a new variant, click the Create button to generate the new variant. If you don't want to create a new variation, click the OK button to leave the Font Creator utility. There is no Cancel button because you must click Create to generate a new variant.

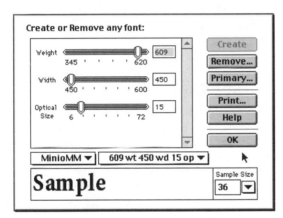

Figure 29-15: A newly created Multiple Master font.

Note that creating a new variant in a roman typeface does not create the equivalent variant in the italic typeface. Thus, for example, creating a semibold variant in Minion does not automatically create a semibold variant of Minion Italic.

Noting the attribute settings

The underline is how QuarkXPress indicates which variant is the normal variant (see Figure 29-16). The numbers and codes let you know what the attribute settings are. The numbers show the actual settings from the slider bars. The uppercase codes indicate standard variants. Typical codes include RG for regular weight, SB for semibold weight, BD for bold weight, BL for black weight, LT for light weight, NO for normal width, CN for condensed width, SC for semicondensed width, SE for semi-expanded width, EX for expanded width, and OP for normal optical scaling. When you create new variants, the codes change to lowercase.

Typical codes for variants you create include wt for weight, wd for width, and op for optical scaling. These conventions help you know which variants are normal (those available from standard font-oriented dialog boxes and the Measurements palette) and which are user-created variants.

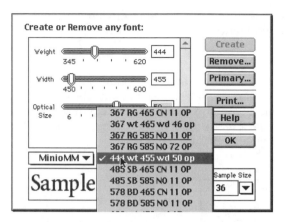

Figure 29-16: The codes used in Multiple Master font names.

Removing and regenerating variations

You can remove a variant by selecting it and clicking the Remove button. If you remove a variant that was not one of the variants supplied with the Multiple Master font (that is, a variant in which the displayed codes are in lowercase), you must re-create it if you want to restore it. But if you remove a variant that came with the Multiple Master font (these are called *primary variants*), use the Primary button to restore it. Figure 29-17 shows the resulting dialog box, which lists the removed primary variants (in black). Select the removed variants that you want to restore and click the Create button.

Tip

You can use the Primary button to list all the variants that came with your Multiple Master font. Although these names also appear in the Font Creator dialog box's pop-up menu, the list displayed after clicking the Primary button shows only the primary variants, not every variant available.

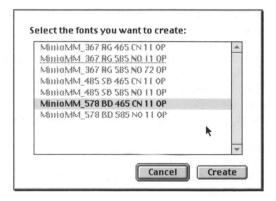

Figure 29-17: You can regenerate deleted Multiple Master fonts if they are standard variants of the font.

Working with Characters and Symbols

Several characters that are not used in traditionally typed business documents are used routinely in typeset documents. Do not ignore these symbols, because readers expect to see them in anything that appears to be published, whether on the desktop or via traditional means. If you're used to working only with typewritten or word-processed documents, pay careful attention to the proper use of these characters.

True quotation marks and em dashes

The most common of these characters are *true quotation marks* and *em dashes* (so called because they are the width of a capital *M* when typeset). The typewriter uses the same character (") to indicate both open and closed quotation marks, and most people use two hyphens (--) to indicate an em dash when typing. Using these marks in a published document is a sign of amateurism.

Using the Smart Quotes option

Fortunately, an option in QuarkXPress called Smart Quotes lets you turn on a feature that inserts typographically correct quotes. It even lets you choose from a variety of quote formats including those used by some foreign languages. Figure 29-18 shows how you specify smart quotes—and their formats—in the Application Preferences dialog box's Interactive pane (Edit⇨Preferences⇨Application, or Shift+Option+⌘+Y). Unfortunately, this will not translate double hyphens into em dashes as you type.

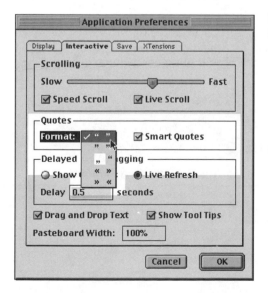

Figure 29-18: Specify quote styles in the Interactive pane.

QuarkXPress also offers an option during text import that automatically changes typewriter dashes and quotes to their typographic equivalents. When you import text, make sure that you check the Convert Quotes box (it also handles em dashes) in the Get Text dialog box, as shown in Figure 29-19.

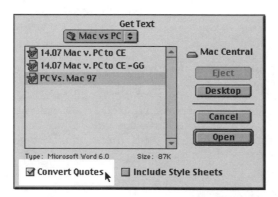

Figure 29-19: The Convert Quotes option in the Get Text dialog box.

Do not use the keyboard open single quote key (`) as an open single quote—use the keyboard apostrophe (') instead. If you use the open single quote keyboard key, you will often get a different open single quote character than the standard typographic version—depending on how the font is designed, of course.

Manually creating typographic quotes

When you type text directly into QuarkXPress, you can type in a command to get typographic quotes (instead of using the smart quotes option for double quotes and the keyboard's ` and ' characters for single quotes; note that in some fonts, using the ` symbol will not result in the typographic open single quote). The commands are listed in Table 29-2.

Table 29-2 Typographic Quote Shortcuts		
Character	*Macintosh Shortcut*	*Windows Shortcut*
" (open double quote)	Option+[	Shift+Alt+[
" (closed double quote)	Shift+Option+[	Shift+Alt+]
' (open single quote)	Option+]	Alt+[
' (closed single quote)	Shift+Option+]	Alt+]

The rules of proper quoting and punctuation

Punctuating text with quotes confuses many people, but the rules are not complicated:

✦ Periods and commas always go inside the quotation.

✦ Semicolons and colons always go outside the quotation.

✦ Question marks and exclamation marks go inside if they are part of the quote, outside if not. When the main clause is a question, but the quote is a declaration, the question mark takes precedence over the period, so it goes outside the quotes. When the main clause is a question, and the quote is an exclamation, the exclamation takes precedence, and it goes within the quotation. Look at the following examples:

> Did he really say, "I am too busy"?
>
> She asked, "Do you have time to help?"
>
> I can't believe she asked, "Do you have time to help?"
>
> He really did yell, "I am too busy!"
>
> Did he really yell, "I am too busy!"?

✦ When a single quote is followed immediately by a double quote, separate the two with a nonbreaking space (⌘+spacebar on the Mac and Ctrl+5 in Windows).

> He told me, "She asked, 'Do you have time to help?' "
>
> He told me, "Bob heard him say, 'I am too busy.' "
>
> She asked me, "Can you believe that he said, 'I am too busy'?"

For more information on these rules, refer to a grammar guide.

Manually entering dashes

If you want to enter dashes in text while typing directly into a QuarkXPress document, you must also use special commands, as shown in Table 29-3:

Table 29-3
Keyboard Shortcuts for Dashes and Hyphens

Character	Macintosh Shortcut	Windows Shortcut
— (em dash)	Option+Shift+- (hyphen)	Ctrl+Shift++ (plus)
— (nonbreaking em dash)	Option+⌘+=	Ctrl+Shift+Alt+=
– (en dash)	Option+- (hyphen)	Ctrl+Alt+Shift+- (hyphen)
- (nonbreaking hyphen)	⌘+=	Ctrl+Shift+- (hyphen)
Discretionary (soft) hyphen	⌘+- (hyphen)	Ctrl+=

Spacing em dashes—or not

Typographers are divided over whether you should put spaces around em dashes — like this — or not—like this. Traditionally, there is no space. But having space lets the publishing program treat the dash as a word, so that there is even space around all words in a line. Not having a space around dashes means that the publishing program sees the two words connected by the em dash as one big word, so the spacing added to justify a line between all other words on the line may be awkwardly large because the program doesn't know how to break a line after or before an em dash that doesn't have space on either side. Still, whether to surround a dash with space is a decision in which personal preferences should prevail.

A nonbreaking em dash does not let text following it wrap to a new line. Instead, the break must occur at a spot preceding or following the dash.

Using en dashes

The en dash, so called because it is the width of a capital *N,* is a nonbreaking character, so QuarkXPress does not let a line break after it. Traditionally, an en dash is used to:

✦ Separate numerals, as in a range of values

✦ Label a figure

✦ Indicate a multiple-word hyphenation (*Civil War–era*)

Symbols and special characters

A typeface comes with dozens of special symbols ranging from bullets to copyright symbols. The most common ones are accessible from QuarkXPress through the following commands (see Table 29-4 for a list of shortcuts):

✦ • **En bullet:** Press Option+8 on the Mac; Shift+Alt+8 in Windows. A bullet is an effective way to call attention to issues being raised. Typically, bullets are used at the beginning of each element in a list. If the sequence of the elements is important, as in a series of steps, use numerals instead of bullets.

Keep in mind that you have many alternatives to using the regular en bullet (so called because it is the width of a lowercase *n*). Using special characters such as boxes, check marks, triangles, and arrows, you can create attractive bulleted lists that stand out from the crowd. (This book, for example, uses a diamond-like character.) More information on how to select such characters is provided later in this chapter.

✦ © **Copyright:** Press Option+C on the Mac; Shift+Alt+C in Windows. A copyright symbol signifies who owns text or other visual media. The standard format is *Copyright © 1998 IDG Books Worldwide. All rights reserved.*

For text, you must include at least the © symbol, the word *Copyright,* or the abbreviation *Copr,* as well as the year first published and the name of the copyright holder. (Note that only the © symbol is valid for international copyright.) Works need not be registered to be copyrighted. The notice is sufficient, but registering is best.

✦ ® **Registered trademark:** Press Option+R on the Mac, Shift+Alt+R in Windows. This is usually used in advertising, packaging, marketing, and public relations to indicate that a product or service name is exclusively owned by a company. The mark follows the name. You may use the ® symbol only with names registered with the U.S. Patent and Trademark Office. For works whose trademark registration is pending, use the ™ symbol.

✦ ™ **Pending trademark:** Press Option+2 on the Mac, Shift+Alt+2 in Windows.

✦ § **Section:** Press Option+6 on the Mac, Shift+Alt+6 in Windows. This symbol is typically used in legal and scholarly documents to refer to sections of laws or research papers.

✦ ¶ **Paragraph:** Press Option+7 on the Mac, Shift+Alt+7 in Windows. Like the section symbol, the paragraph symbol is typically used for legal and scholarly documents.

✦ † **Dagger:** Press Option+T on the Mac, Shift+Alt+T in Windows. This symbol is often used for footnotes.

Table 29-4 **Shortcuts for Special Symbols**		
Character	*Macintosh Shortcut*	*Windows Shortcut*
Legal		
Copyright (©)	Option+C	Shift+Alt+C *or* Alt+0169
Registered trademark (®)	Option+R	Shift+Alt+R *or* Alt+0174
Trademark (™)	Option+2	Shift+Alt+2 *or* Alt+0153
Paragraph (¶)	Option+7	Shift+Alt+7 *or* Ctrl+Alt+;
Section (§)	Option+6	Shift+Alt+6 *or* Alt+0167
Dagger (†)	Option+T	Shift+Alt+T *or* Alt+0134
Double dagger (‡)	Option+Shift+7	Alt+0135
Currency		
Cent (¢)	Option+4	Alt+0162
Pound sterling (£)	Option+3	Alt+0163
Yen (¥)	Option+Y	Ctrl+Alt+hyphen *or* Alt+0165

(continued)

Table 29-4 (*continued*)

Character	Macintosh Shortcut	Windows Shortcut
Mathematics		
One-half fraction (½)	*not supported**	Ctrl+Alt+7 *or* Alt+0189
One-quarter fraction (¼)	*not supported**	Ctrl+Alt+6 *or* Alt+0188
Three-quarters fraction (¾)	*not supported**	Ctrl+Alt+8 *or* Alt+0190
Infinity (∞)	Option+5	*not supported**
Multiplication (×)	*not supported**	Ctrl+Alt+= *or* Alt+0215
Division (÷)	Option+/	Alt+0247
Root (√)	Option+V	*not supported**
Greater than or equal (≥)	Option+>	*not supported**
Less than or equal (≤)	Option+<	*not supported**
Inequality (≠)	Option+=	*not supported**
Rough equivalence (≈)	Option+X	*not supported**
Plus or minus (±)	Option+Shift+=	Alt+0177
Logical not (¬)	Option+L	Ctrl+Alt+\ *or* Alt+0172
Per mil (‰)	Option+Shift+R	Alt+-0137
Degree (°)	Option+Shift+8	Alt+0176
Function (ƒ)	Option+F	Alt+0131
Integral (∫)	Option+B	*not supported**
Variation (∂)	Option+D	*not supported**
Greek beta (ß)	Option+S	Alt+0223
Greek mu (μ)	Option+M	Alt+0181
Greek Pi (Π)	Option+Shift+P	*not supported**
Greek pi (π)	Option+P	*not supported**
Greek Sigma (Σ)	Option+W	*not supported**
Greek Omega (W)	Option+Z	*not supported**
Miscellaneous		
Apple logo (⌘)	Option+Shift+K	*not supported**
Ellipsis (…)	Option+; (semicolon)	Alt+0133
En bullet (•)	Option+8	Shift+Alt+8 *or* Alt+0149
Light (¤)	Option+Shift+2	Ctrl+Alt+4 *or* Alt+0164
Open diamond (◊)	Option+Shift+V	*not supported**
Thin bullet (·)	*not supported**	Alt+0183

* Character is available in a pi font

Tip

When you want a long portion of text to run so that it appears as one visual block—a tactic often used for article openers in highly designed magazines—consider using symbols such as § and ¶ as paragraph-break indicators. (Frequently, they are set in larger or bolder type when used in this manner.) The symbols alert readers to paragraph shifts. *Rolling Stone* magazine is particularly partial to this effect.

Special symbols and Web browsers

Web browsers don't support all the special symbols available in print publishing. Popular Web browsers like Netscape Navigator and Microsoft Internet Explorer, however, support most of the symbols listed in Tables 29-4 and 29-5.

✦ Here are the exceptions for both Mac and Windows browsers: Š, š, Ý, ý, Ÿ, Œ, œ, **fi, fl, ffi, ffl**, •, ™, †, ‡, ≠, ∞, ≈, — (em dash), – (en dash), and … (ellipsis). In addition, typographic quotes and apostrophes (', ', ", and ") are converted to their keyboard equivalents (" and ').

✦ Macintosh Web browsers don't support these characters: ½, ¾, ¼, √, and ×.

✦ Windows Web browsers don't support these characters: Æ and æ.

Using foreign language characters

See Table 29-5 for foreign-language characters. Note that Windows shortcuts involving four numerals (such as Alt+0157) should be entered from the numeric keypad while holding the Alt key.

Table 29-5		
Shortcuts for Foreign Characters		
Character	*Macintosh Shortcut*	*Windows Shortcut*
acute (´)*	Option+E *letter*	´ *letter*
cedilla (,)*	*see* Ç *and* ç	´ *letter*
circumflex (ˆ)*	Option+I *letter*	^ *letter*
grave (`)*	Option+` *letter*	` *letter*
tilde (~)*	Option+N *letter*	~ *letter*
trema (¨)*	Option+U *letter*	" *letter*
umlaut (¨)*	Option+U *letter*	" *letter*
Á	Option+E A	´ A *or* Alt+0193
á	Option+E a	´ a *or* Alt+0225
À	Option+` A	` A *or* Alt+0192

(continued)

Table 29-5 *(continued)*

Character	Macintosh Shortcut	Windows Shortcut
à	Option+` a	` a *or* Alt+0224
Ä	Option+U A	" A *or* Alt+0196
ä	Option+U a	" a *or* Alt+0228
Ã	Option+N A	~ A *or* Alt+0195
ã	Option+N a	~ a *or* Alt+0227
Â	Option+I A	^ A *or* Alt+0194
â	Option+I a	^ a *or* Alt+0226
Å	Option+Shift+A	Alt+0197
å	Option+A	Alt+0229
Æ	Option+Shift+ '	Alt+0198
æ	Option+ '	Alt+0230
Ç	Option+Shift+C	' C *or* Alt+0199
ç	Option+C	' c *or* Ctrl+Alt+, *or* Alt+0231
Ð	*not supported*	Alt+0208
ð	*not supported*	Alt+0240
É	Option+E E	' E *or* Alt+0201
é	Option+E e	' e *or* Alt+0233
È	Option+` E	` E *or* Alt+0200
è	Option+` e	` e *or* Alt+0232
Ë	Option+U E	" E *or* Alt+0203
ë	Option+U e	" e *or* Alt+0235
Ê	Option+I E	^ E *or* Alt+0202
ê	Option+I e	^ e *or* Alt+0234
Í	Option+E I	' I *or* Alt+0205
í	Option+E i	' i *or* Alt+0237
Ì	Option+` I	` I *or* Alt+0204
ì	Option+` i	` i *or* Alt+0236
Ï	Option+U I	" I *or* Alt+0207
ï	Option+U i	" I *or* Alt+0239
Î	Option+I I	^ I *or* Alt+0206

Character	Macintosh Shortcut	Windows Shortcut
î	Option+I i	^ I or Alt+0238
Ñ	Option+N N	~ N or Alt+0209
ñ	Option+N n	~ n or Alt+0241
Ó	Option+E O	' O or Alt+0211
ó	Option+E o	' o or Alt+0243
Ò	Option+` O	` O or Alt+0210
ò	Option+` o	` o or Alt+0242
Ö	Option+U O	" O or Alt+0214
ö	Option+U o	" o or Alt+0246
Õ	Option+N O	~ O or Alt+0213
õ	Option+N o	~ o or Alt+0245
Ô	Option+I O	^ O or Alt+0212
ô	Option+I o	^ o or Alt+0244
Ø	Option+Shift+O	Alt+0216
ø	Option+O	Alt+0248
Œ	Option+Shift+Q	Alt+0140
œ	Option+Q	Alt+0156
Þ	*not supported*	Alt+0222
þ	*not supported*	Alt+0254
ß	Option+S	Alt+0223
Š	*not supported*	Alt+0138
š	*not supported*	Alt+0154
Ú	Option+E U	' U or Ctrl+Shift+Alt+U
ú	Option+E u	' u or Ctrl+Alt+U
Ù	Option+` U	` U or Alt+0217
ù	Option+` u	` u or Alt+0249
Ü	Option+U U	" U or Ctrl+Shift+Alt+Y
ü	Option+U u	" u or Ctrl+Alt+Y
Û	Option+I U	^ U or Alt+0219
û	Option+I u	^ u or Alt+0251
Ý	*not supported*	' Y or Alt+0221

(continued)

Table 29-5 *(continued)*		
Character	*Macintosh Shortcut*	*Windows Shortcut*
ý	*not supported*	' y *or* Alt+0253
Ÿ	Option+U Y	*not supported*
ÿ	Option+U y	*not supported*
Spanish open exclamation (¡)	Option+1	Ctrl+Alt+1 *or* Alt+0161
Spanish open question (¿)	Option+Shift+/	Ctrl+Alt+/ *or* Alt+0191
French open double quote («)**	Option+\	Ctrl+Alt+[*or* Alt+0171
French close double quote (»)**	Option+Shift+\	Ctrl+Alt+] *or* Alt+0187

*On the Mac, enter the shortcut for the accent and then type the letter to be accented (for example, to get *é*, type Option+E and then the letter *e*). In Windows, if the keyboard layout is set to United States-International (via the Keyboard icon in the Windows Control Panel and then through the Language pane's Properties button), you can enter the accent signifier and then type the letter (for example, type ` and then the letter *e* to get *è*).

**Automatically generated if the Smart Quotes option is selected in the Application Preferences dialog box's Interactive pane (Edit⇨Preferences⇨Application, or Shift+Option+⌘+Y) and the French quotes are selected in the Quote pop-up menu, also in the Interactive pane.

✦   ✦   ✦

Print Design Opportunities

In This Chapter

Learning about good design

Laying out ads and circulars

Creating newsletters

Working with magazines

Doing other cool stuff

Looking at common threads

Beauty is in the eye of the beholder, and by combining QuarkXPress's strengths and some basic design know-how, you can put a lot of beauty in the eyes of lots of beholders. To share that basic know-how with you, we created some examples of a variety of documents, with added explanations to point out effective design techniques in action. We also asked *Macworld* magazine's designers to share their techniques using real layouts. You'll find these examples in the pages that follow.

Learning About Good Design

As with any good design ideas, the ones here are based on years of experience and, of course, honest-to-goodness pilfering of other people's good work. Imitation is the sincerest form of flattery, and as long as you don't cross the line into blatant copying, go ahead and flatter as many people as you can. Go to the newsstand and thumb through a bunch of magazines. (But buy just the ones you really like.) Get a couple of colleagues—or just pull in some passersby—and look through them together and talk about what you like, what you don't like, and—most important—*why* you react the way you do. You can call this flower-power consciousness-raising, or being a copycat. The point is, it's the best way to learn good design.

Great artists steal

A couple more clichés to drive home the point: Good writers read good writers. (We're sure someone has said "Good designers look at good designers," but this hasn't gotten enough buzz to become a cliché yet.) Good artists imitate, great artists steal.

Don't follow recipes

One last point: Don't confuse the following examples with recipes. We don't pretend to be Picasso, or even Haring. Our designs (and our *Macworld* colleagues') might make no sense for your documents. After all, you need to make sure the designs you produce meet several needs: your sense of aesthetics, the requirements of the content being presented, the image you or your organization wants to convey, and the financial limitations you are working under. (We'd all love to do everything in full, glorious color, but until money comes out of laser printers without resulting in jail terms, we do have some concerns about costs.)

Learn to improvise

So look at the following examples as starting points, and don't confuse the techniques and fundamental principles they illustrate with the implementation we happened to choose for the particular example. You could use those same techniques and fundamental principles and come up with completely different designs for your projects. Great artists may steal, but they also improvise.

Laying Out Ads and Circulars

The elements of ads, circulars (fliers), and other such sales- and marketing-oriented materials are a critical type of publication, because they must work the first time. You might be willing to put up with a design you don't care for in a newsletter that contains information you find valuable. But an ad has the burden of needing to attract your attention, holding you long enough to deliver its message, and letting you go with a favorable impression. Let's look at three ads to see the techniques they use to accomplish these goals. Remember, whether it's an ad, a report cover, a prospectus, a pamphlet, or other such publication, these techniques apply.

An airline ad mockup

Figure 30-1 shows an ad mockup for a fictitious airline. Notice the following about its design:

✦ **The large type:** This is kerned so that the spacing between each pair of characters is the same—just at the point of touching. (We used the Measurements palette's kerning controls.)

✦ **The small type:** This forces the eye to take a look, because of the contrast with the big type above and all the space on either side. This use of contrast is a good way to get attention. Never underestimate the power of type. It is as important as graphics in garnering attention and conveying both the substance and the nuances of the message.

✦ **The airline logo:** This uses reverse-video and shadow effects on a fairly common font (Bauhaus). Notice the sun symbol to the logo's left: that's a symbol in the Zapf Dingbats font. The use of symbols really helps establish a logo as a logo, rather than just a bunch of letters. Also notice the use of a catch-phrase in the same font as the logo. You would do this for a catch-phrase that you plan on using in several places. It becomes an extension of the logo. (The desert tableau is a color image, and in color the text is very striking against the colors; in black-and-white, it loses a little of that zing.)

✦ **White space:** Blank areas—what designers call *white space*. It provides a visually calm port in a storm of images and text. Be sure to provide these resting spots in all your work.

Figure 30-1: A simple ad with a simple message deserves a simple treatment to attract attention. But notice that simple does not mean simplistic—every element has a character of its own.

A restaurant ad mockup

The ad mockup in Figure 30-2, for a seafood restaurant, shows a tighter interplay of text and graphics. It also shows, although not at first glance, the power of QuarkXPress's graphics manipulation tools. Here's what to look for:

✦ **The schools of fish:** They're in glorious color, although you can't see that in black-and-white, and there are really only three fish in the ad. We used the copy function in QuarkXPress to create the schools. And to make sure that they didn't look like clones, we used the rotate and skew tools to make each cloned fish slightly different from the others.

Tip

We used only a very slight skew, less than 5 percent; the rotation accounts for most of the difference in the fishes' appearance. The lesson: Don't forget to use basic tools like rotation and copying.

✦ **The descriptive text:** The text describing all the sumptuous seafood options ("Atlantic cod. Alaska salmon.") is wrapped around the pictures of fish, using QuarkXPress's Bézier picture box to hold the pictures, combined with the new ability in version 4 to have text wrap around both sides of an image.

✦ **The headlines:** Can you tell what this ad is selling? Why, fresh fish, of course! The repetitive use of the text reinforces the message. Placing the repeating text in different positions among the fish makes sure it doesn't look repetitive. (Predictability is a major reason that repetition is boring, so this design finds a way to repeat without being boring.)

✦ **The tag line:** This added repetition of the "Fresh Fish" reinforces the primary message. In the case of this ad, there's no large text identifying the restaurant (it is in the body text), but this tag line is one the restaurant uses a lot, so the ad can get away with the low-key treatment of the restaurant's name—just as if an ad said only "Have it your way," you'd probably think of Burger King, while "Just do it" would evoke Nike.

✦ **Italics:** All the text here, except the list of locations at the bottom, is in italics, which is unusual. But the fluidity of italics works well with the fish theme (underwater—get it?), and by making the text large enough and the layout uncluttered, it works.

✦ **Going beyond the margins:** The fish swim past the margins on the page, which makes the page feel less boxed-in. It's often a good idea to overstep margins to provide a feeling of flexibility and give the eye something unusual to notice.

Figure 30-2: An ad with interplay between the text and graphics.

A public service announcement

Let's take a look at one more ad. This one is not a full page. It's the kind of ad you'd probably run in an in-house publication: what magazines call a PSA (public service announcement). It's the type of thing you can easily put together using clip art and basic typefaces when you have a hole to fill or need to make an announcement or advertisement for your organization (see Figure 30-3). Look at the following:

✦ **The simple graphic:** This simple graphic works well in black-and-white. Photos can be very effective in catching attention, as they scream "real!" The simple composition is also pleasing. You'll find many such images in clip art libraries.

✦ **The message:** Simple text with a simple message that ties into the image—that's the ticket.

✦ **The headline:** A loud, bold title would have competed with the photo. This one's easy to read, but it doesn't fight for attention. If you see the photo and stop, you'll see the headline, and that's all that's required. The centering makes sure that it's clear the headline goes with the text below. It also follows the centered shape of the chair.

✦ **The alignment:** The more ways things line up, the more distracting a layout can be, so try to use only one or two alignments. A left alignment might have worked here, but then the symmetry of the chair would not have been picked up in the rest of the ad—and such reuse of basic visual themes is a hallmark of pleasing design. People just get all warm and fuzzy with such continuity.

✦ **The justified text:** The text is short, readable, and justified. Although having justified text may seem to violate the minimal-alignment rule above, the fact is that centered text is rarely easy to read if there's more than a few lines of it. Having the text justified keeps the symmetry of the centered text, because the right and left margins in justified text are symmetrical.

✦ **The dashed lines:** We all know what a dashed line means. The ad fairly screams, "Cut me out!" To get a dashed box, just use one of QuarkXPress's box tools and change the frame style to a dashed one. To reinforce the "cut me out!" message, you could add a pair of scissors (from a symbols font or from clip art) along a top corner of the dashed box.

✦ **The coupon:** In the box is the coupon you're hoping people will fill out. The font here is different (a condensed sans serif, compared to the text's normal serif). This reinforces that it is a separate element. You want the reader to think of the coupon as separate, so they know that it's OK to remove it from the rest of the ad. The use of a condensed font also gives you more room for the information you want people to fill in. The underlines are right-aligned tab using an underline leader. That's the simplest way to create fill-in-the-blank lines.

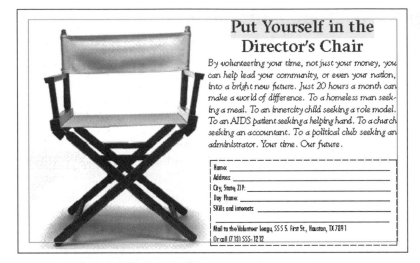

Figure 30-3: A public service announcement designed for black-and-white reproduction.

Creating Newsletters

Quintessentially, publishing newsletters and magazines represent the focus of page-layout programs, even though QuarkXPress is also great for a whole range of documents, including ads, reports, and catalogs. But when you think publishing, you think newsletters and magazines. So, let's spend a little time going over ways of making top-notch newsletters and magazines, without hiring a huge crew of designers.

An association newsletter

Figure 30-4 shows an association newsletter that has undergone several redesigns. The pages are from three different issues, one from 1990, one from 1991, and one from 1994. Take a look. They use different fonts and embellishments, yet they all share a basic design:

Getting a new look

Magazines generally redesign themselves every couple years. It might be subtle, it might be extreme. But it happens. Why? Because the new art director or publisher wants to put her or his imprint on the publication.

Well, that's partially true, but the real reason is more basic: If you don't revisit your look every once in a while, you look stale, and people will think you're lazy or don't care about them. People do it for their personal appearance, too. (Want proof? Take a look at a snapshot of yourself from five years ago.)

✦ **A three-column format:** All are based on a three-column format, although the 1991 version uses a staggered three-column grid (notice how the pull-quotes and other elements hang out from the sides).

✦ **The same basic elements:** All use the same basic elements on each page: pull-quotes, a short table of contents on the cover, a large masthead on page 2, kickers over the headlines, and bylines.

Yet they differ significantly in the following areas:

✦ **The 1988-90 design:** This is the most basic: sans serif headlines and serif body copy. Both fonts chosen (Helvetica Bold and New Century Schoolbook) are clean and easy-to-read. The use of condensed, underlined type for the kickers adds the only visual counterpoint to the open, solid look of the type, and even the kickers are clean-looking. The look the designer was trying to convey was solid and respectable, because the organization was making an effort at the time the design was conceived (in 1987) to look clean and fresh.

✦ **The 1991 design:** This was a radical departure. It's bolder, busier. There's a lot of contrast: bold headlines (Helvetica Black and Helvetica Black Condensed) with clean, light text (News Gothic). Highly unusual is that both are sans serif fonts. There's an unspoken rule that you should never have headlines and text be the same type of font (serif or sans serif)—and particularly never both sans serif. Nonsense! Also, more symbols are used, and the layout is staggered. Things can line up to the three columns or to the halfway points between columns (or past the first and last column). The look the designer was trying to convey was animated and energetic, an organization on the move. It was more work to do this layout, and it relied on having sidebars and photos to break out (as on pages 2 and 3) from the body text. Unfortunately, it was difficult to pull off every issue, so the designer abandoned it a year later. It was adventurous, but maybe too much for its subject.

✦ **The 1992-94 design:** This is hypertraditional: the "cardigan sweater and fireplace" look. There are two serif fonts—Century Oldstyle for the heads and ITC Cheltenham Book for the body text. Cheltenham is very easy to read because it's a wide font, and it contrasts nicely with the Century Oldstyle, which is bold and angular. There are still some symbols, but they're more subdued. There are also now drop caps, which add more contrast to the page. But there is also the use of grays, which mellows out the page. This design was meant to reinforce solid traditionalism (it was designed for the organization's 10th anniversary in 1993, although it came out a year earlier). But it's actually a mix of the two previous designs, borrowing the simple structure of the first with the high contrast of the second, the conservatism of the first with some of the flair of the second. The use of nonrectangular text wrap adds interest to the graphic—an extension of the flair in the second generation without the hard edge.

Figure 30-4: The evolution of a newsletter's design: 1988-90 (top), 1991 (middle), and 1992-94 (bottom). Notice how the basic elements are unchanged, but the way they are presented does change, as does the overall feel.

Dealing with change

As you can see from the example in Figure 30-4, each design had a set of goals in mind. The goals changed over time, even as the basic content did not. The opposite can also happen: the content changes over time but the design and "image" goals do not. That's a little trickier, because you need to update the design to accommodate the new content (such as increased use of profiles, short stories, gossip and rumors, question-and-answer interviews, and so on) while reflecting the feel of the old.

For examples of what we mean, take a look at current issues of the *New York Times,* the *Wall Street Journal, Business Week, Time,* or *Newsweek.* Then compare them with issues from five years ago. Different look and mix of content, but the same feel.

Newsletter basics

A newsletter's main goal is to provide information. So, the focus should be on text: how to make it readable, how to call attention to it, and how to make sure the reader knows where all relevant content is. Take a look at the newsletter in Figure 30-5. It's the same newsletter as in Figure 30-4, but the pages chosen are typical interior pages. They show the basic components of the newsletter, around which you can add embellishments (such as graphics). Here are some basic newsletter design issues to consider:

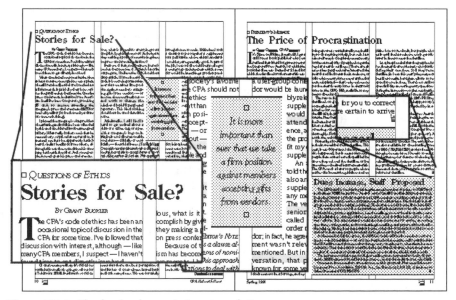

Figure 30-5: The basic elements in a newsletter.

✦ **Column width:** Most newsletters are two or three columns wide. A three-column format gives you more flexibility, because you can have graphics of three different sizes (one, two, and three columns wide), plus you can add sidebars and separate stories fairly easily to a page, because again there are multiple sizes to choose from. A two-column format is more straightforward, but it gives you fewer options. It's best for newsletters that are essentially sequential—without multiple stories and sidebars on a page or spread.

✦ **Page numbers and folios:** As always, make sure you add page numbers and an identifier of the publication (called a *folio*). Here, there's also a corporate symbol after the page number, to add visual interest and reinforce the identity.

✦ **Body text:** The body text uses a very readable, straightforward font: ITC Cheltenham Book. It's a typical size for newsletters and magazines: 9 points with 11 points leading. Generally speaking, point size should range from 9 to 10 points (you can use half-point sizes), and leading from 10.5 to 13 points, with the most typical being 2 points more than the size. The text is justified here, simply because that makes it look typeset and thus more authoritative. But a flush-left style would have been fine here, too. Last, the paragraph indents are fairly small (0.15 inches), because in justified text a small indent is enough to give the reader's eye the visual clue it needs to see the new paragraph.

✦ **Drop caps:** Using a drop cap is an effective way to alert the reader to the beginning of a new story (you can also use it for the beginning of the conclusion), as well as to provide a visual contrast on the page. Note here that the drop cap is a different font than the body text, Century Oldstyle Bold, which is the same font as the headline. Generally, you should boldface the drop cap, as that makes it more readable. (Otherwise, the drop cap looks wimpy, which is not what you want such a big element to look like.)

✦ **Headlines, kickers, and bylines:** The headline, the kicker (the type above it, also called a *slug line* for reasons that have nothing to do with gardening), and the byline are all related. Both the kicker and the byline use small caps (a classy look when done in moderation) and italics. They're also in a different font (Goudy Oldstyle) than either the headline (Century Oldstyle Bold) or the body text (ITC Cheltenham Book). That gives them continuity with one another while providing a subtle difference from the rest of the text.

Tip Be careful when combining multiple fonts like this: If they don't work together, it can be a disaster. A rule of thumb is to restrict the number of fonts (not including variants like boldface and small caps) to two per page. You can break this rule occasionally by using a font that has similarities to one of the other two. In this case, Goudy Oldstyle has the feel of a cross between the other two fonts, so it works well.

✦ **Dingbats:** A nice touch is to end a story with a dingbat—publishing-speak for a symbol. Here, the dingbat is the corporate logo, which adds another identity reinforcement. It's easy to make a dingbat: just add the symbol after the last paragraph, either by putting a tab before it (and defining the tab in your text style to be flush right against the right margin, or using Option+Tab to create a right-aligned tab) or an em space (which is two nonbreaking en spaces, or two uses of the keyboard shortcut Option+⌘+spacebar on the Mac or Ctrl+Alt+Shift+6 in Windows). Either way is fine for justified text. Pick one based on your preferences. But use only the em space if your text is not justified.

✦ **Sidebars:** A sidebar, or separate, minor story, can be made distinct by putting a shaded background behind it (by applying a shade to the text box). Make sure you have a margin between the edge of the background and the text. You can also box a sidebar, with or without the background, using frames. Or you could just put a line above and below the background, as done here. We chose the line approach to pick up the lines at the top and bottom of each page. Notice, too, that the text is two columns wide here, so it really looks different from the surrounding text.

✦ **Pull-quotes:** A pull-quote is a great way to call out some interesting material in a story to attract readers' attention. Here, the style follows that of the sidebar: a shaded background and lines above and below. There's also a square character above and below (it's an anchored box in the text, so if the text grows or shrinks, the squares move with it). This is just an embellishment—something that adds that little extra touch. The font is the same as that in the byline and kicker (again, for continuity with other elements on the page but different from the text immediately around it).

Working with Magazines

Magazines are very similar to newsletters, except that magazines generally have color images, more graphics, a cover that has no stories on it, and a full-page (or larger) table of contents.

Tables of contents

Let's look first at a sample contents page from a fictitious magazine. Note, though, that magazines usually are highly designed, so they often look very different from one another. So take the following techniques as starting points (see Figure 30-6):

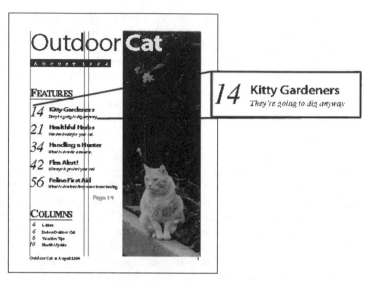

Figure 30-6: A one-page table of contents for a fictitious magazine.

✦ **The logo:** This should be distinct *and* readable. Here, the logo has one word in normal weight ("Outdoor") and one in boldface ("Cat"). Plus, in a recurring theme in this magazine, the word "Cat" is always positioned over the contents page's graphic and printed in a color that contrasts well with the image. Here, although you can't see it in black-and-white, the word "Cat" is in a color that closely matches the fur of the orange tabby in the picture.

✦ **The banner:** The issue date is called a *banner:* white type on a black or colored background. Notice how the text is spaced: there's a full em space between each character (done in the Measurements palette in the tracking field by making the tracking amount the same as the point size). This stretched-out text is a popular style. Go ahead and be popular. When you use a banner, make sure the text is bold; otherwise, it is usually hard to read— lost in the sea of color surrounding it.

✦ **Feature and column entries:** Magazines generally have features—longer articles that appear only once; and columns—regular, short series of articles that appear each issue, usually covering a certain topic. Label which of your content is which. Here we used the same font as in the banner: Times Bold in small caps. The underlines (using the Rules option in the Style menu, rather than the standard underline type style, so we could get a thicker line than a regular underline would provide) add a bit of visual spice.

✦ **Page numbers:** The use of large page numbers reinforces that this is a table of contents. Here, the page numbers are in Times Italic, and they're 40 points, set down into the text by 14 points (using a baseline shift, which you access via the Baseline Shift command in the Style menu). The feature title is in the same font as the logo (Myriad Italic) and larger than the Times Italic description beneath it (16 points versus 12 points). To prevent the page number's size from affecting the leading between the feature title and the feature description, make sure you select the page number and change the leading to whatever your feature title leading is (16.6 points here).

Tip

QuarkXPress automatically recalculates leading for text when you change its size (unless you specified an absolute amount like +2 pt in your preferences), but this is a case where you want to override that feature.

✦ **Photo and graphic listings:** It's a good idea to put a page number near any photo or graphic you have in your contents page. If someone is interested in the photo, they should be able to know where to find the associated article. Here, the page number is in the same font as the word "Cat" in the logo. That keeps it from being confused with the rest of the contents, plus it reinforces the use of that color.

Feature articles

An eye-catching design is critical to enticing readers to sample a publication's contents, and *Macworld* has pioneered the use of Macintosh-based tools to produce inviting illustration and a rich design that avoids the stereotypes of cold, simplistic computer-generated artwork. *Macworld* also uses a variety of tools—for example, QuarkXPress, both Adobe Illustrator and Macromedia FreeHand, and both Adobe Photoshop and MetaDesign Fractal Painter, among others—in creating its pages. The magazine's features show off a lot of the magazine's design approaches, as articles of that length give the designers the opportunity to use multiple techniques within the overall design framework.

Working with flexible grids

The magazine's design offers a flexible grid that allows different numbers of columns and column widths from feature to feature (see Figure 30-7). By having a standard grid, the magazine's design director can be assured that the entire package will be cohesive; by letting individual designers have options within that structure, appropriate creative flexibility is available to keep the reader engaged. Every standard element—body text, sidebar, screen image, diagram, table, and caption—must take up an integral number of columns, but the number per element is up to the designer. To create a grid, the designer uses Page➪Master Guides in the document's master page (or pages, if there are several). Once the basic elements are laid out, the grid display can be turned off via View➪Hide Guides (F7).

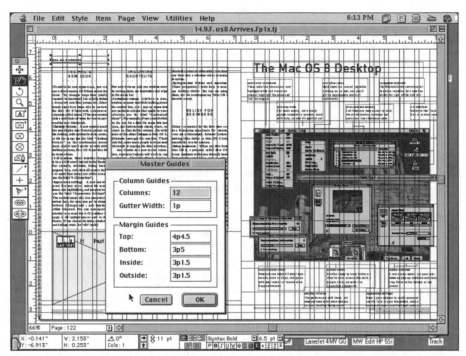

Figure 30-7: The master guides grid shows the options designers have for placement of standard elements. Here are the settings for *Macworld*. Note that the master guides are set up in master pages; the dialog box to create them has been placed on this document page to show the settings used.

How multiple grids work

You can see the use of the multiple grids in the layout in Figure 30-8. For this roundup of top utilities, designer Tim Johnson (who created all the *Macworld* features showcased here except for one noted later) used the four-column design, rather than the standard three-column feature format. Because there were so many elements in the layout—screen shots, illustrations, short sections—the four-column layout gave Johnson more flexibility and a more active look. Note the use of reversed-out titles in bars to make the section boundaries clear.

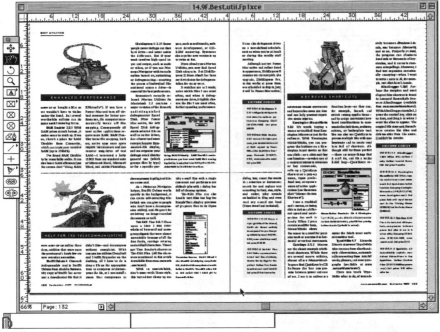

Figure 30-8: Note the use of a four-column format in this feature. This is an effective design for an active layout with lots of elements—precisely what the designer faced here. Also note the use of reversed-out banners to unify sections.

Mixing grids on a page

You can also mix grids on a page, as shown in Figures 30-9 and 30-10. In Figure 30-9, the main text follows a two-column grid, while the sidebar takes that two-column grid and subdivides it into a four-column grid for the text. See how the caption goes across two of the four columns, which makes it clearly different from the surrounding text? And note the use of a three-column grid for the related series of sketches. They are clearly separated from the text yet clearly connected to each other. That's the beauty of having multiple grids to use in a layout.

Figure 30-9: By mixing two-, three-, and four-column grids, the designer easily separates unlike elements and keeps like elements together.

Separating and associating content

In Figure 30-10, the use of different grids, accented by background shades, clearly separates dissimilar content and keeps together similar content in this layout by Belinda Chlouber. Note how on the page at left the steps are clearly associated with their images, while the results of the first steps are clearly conveyed through the filmstrip-like arrangement of images. (The topic is creating moving sequences of images.)

Using a line-numbering system

The document shown in Figure 30-10 also has a text box along the side of each page that has each line numbered so the designers and copyeditors can quickly tell how many lines under or over the text is, or what the depth of an element is in terms of lines, so when working with editors, they can give the editors their requests in a common language. The text is in a special color (Nonrepro Blue, defined as 33.7 percent red, 41.5 percent green, and 100 percent blue in the RGB color model) that does not photocopy, and the lines are hairline ruling lines defined in the numbers' style. The color is not set to color-separate, so they will not print on the CMYK plates. Figure 30-11 shows how the numbering system was created.

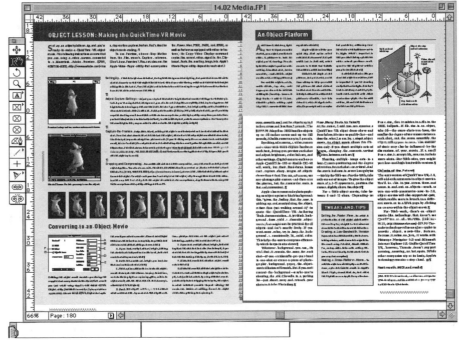

Figure 30-10: Different grids keep the example steps separate from the overall explanation and from the output results on the page at left.

Doing it the *Macworld* way

In tightly leaded text (*Macworld* uses a leading of 10.5 points for its 9-point text), the settings for subscripts, superscripts, and small caps are important, because there is little room for these elements' size and position, but they must be distinct enough from the standard body text to be discernible by the reader. *Macworld* uses different settings for these elements than we recommended in Chapter 3. Why? Although our settings work well for most documents, each document's font, size, and leading together may require further customization. In *Macworld*'s settings, subscripts are moved down only 15 percent (versus 30 percent in ours)—a direct result of the magazine's tight leading.

Macworld also uses a slightly smaller size for superscripts and subscripts (60 percent versus 65 percent) for two reasons: these are rare elements, so readability is less important, and the tight leading favors smaller sizes to eliminate the possibility of subscripted or superscripted text running into adjacent lines.

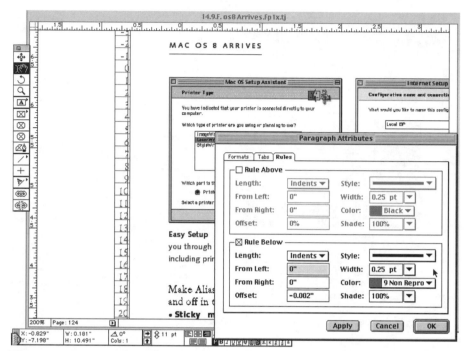

Figure 30-11: To produce the nonreproducible line numbers (at left), the designer created a special color and set a ruling line below the numbers to indicate the baseline of each line (via the Rules pane of the Paragraph Attributes dialog box).

Standardized typography

The *Macworld* design relies on a core set of fonts to keep the look unified—Janson Text for body text and Syntax for sidebar text, caption text, and subheads. The magazine does use other typefaces for special articles, such as the use of the DIN typeface family for headlines in the article shown in Figures 30-7 and 30-8. Similarly, certain colors used throughout—such as Macworld Red—are standardized. But the designer can create custom tints for sidebar backgrounds for each feature, based on the overall color scheme.

Gatefolds

Every once in a while, you see a magazine that has an article with a fold-out page. Called a *gatefold,* this kind of page requires some special work in your layout. Figure 30-12 shows a gatefold for an article that shows a potential design for a new generation of computers. To create a gatefold, you just add a page to the right of an existing right-hand page, making sure to add an extra page to the left of the next spread's existing left-hand page (see the Document Layout palette at the bottom right of Figure 30-12). That's the easy part. There are three possible hazards:

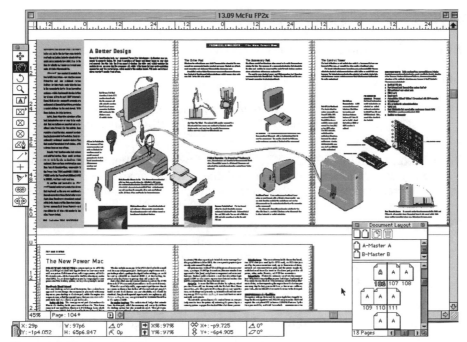

Figure 30-12: A gatefold.

✦ Although it appears on-screen as if the three pages are one long sheet of paper, in the actual magazine the far left page is a separate sheet of paper, while the two right pages are indeed one sheet of paper (folded where the line numbers are).

Tip Be sure to leave sufficient space between the two sheets so text and images don't get swallowed up in the gutter. In this layout, notice how the text on either side of the divide between the first two pages is greater than the divide between the last two pages. That was meant to compensate for the gutter.

✦ The folded-over page in a gatefold (here, the third page) needs to be a bit narrower than the other pages. That's so when it is folded, it does not actually get so far into the gutter that it is bound shut into the magazine. Typically, keep an extra pica ($\frac{1}{6}$ inch) on the outside edge of a gatefold's folded page.

✦ A gatefold must be at the beginning or end of a form (the sequence of pages printed and bound at a time on a printing press). That's because the extra-wide sheet must be the first or last sheet in the stack. (Magazines are composed of multiple forms, usually of 8, 16, 24, or 32 pages in length.)

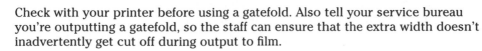

Tip Check with your printer before using a gatefold. Also tell your service bureau you're outputting a gatefold, so the staff can ensure that the extra width doesn't inadvertently get cut off during output to film.

Doing Other Cool Stuff

By combining various techniques, you can create some cool-looking stuff, for any of a variety of documents. Figure 30-13 shows some examples, which are described as follows:

✦ **Embossed text:** You can create various embossed-text effects by duplicating a text box and making one slightly overlap the other. Then make the one on top white (or the paper color).

✦ **Textual graphics:** By duplicating a text box several times and rotating each copy at a different angle, then applying different shades of gray to each, you can create a textual graphic. Here, each subsequent copy is rotated 10 degrees more than the previous and is 10 percent darker.

✦ **Stretched text:** Each letter in the word "Stretch!" is set 10 percent wider than the previous letter, which gives it the effect of being stretched.

✦ **Spaced-out text:** By increasing the space between letters, you can space out text—an effect that lots of designers use. You could put spaces (whether regular spaces, en spaces, or em spaces) between the letters, but by using the intercharacter spacing controls (tracking), you ensure that the text is treated as one word and you make it easy to change your spacing settings (it's easier to adjust the tracking than, say, to replace em spaces with en spaces between every character).

✦ **Combining skew and shadow:** By combining the skew feature with the shadow feature for text, you can alter how a font looks to create logos. Here, we went a step further and mirrored the text block and changed its color to a shade of gray (by defining a tint of 40 percent black).

✦ **Tinting gray-scale images:** For gray-scale images, you can apply a color or tint to make them ghostly or subtle. It's a great way to mute a photo enough so that you can place text over it.

✦ **Cameo effects:** By using an oval or Bézier picture box (with a very thick frame), you can create a cameo effect. It's a way to create a different type of shape or frame.

✦ **Altered opening-page text:** In some publications, the text on the opening page has a radically different style from the rest of the pages. Often, there is little text on the opening page, because the title and graphics usually take up much of the space. The text that is on the page is also treated graphically.

One method is to have no paragraph breaks but to use a symbol instead to indicate paragraph breaks.

✦ **Embedded graphics:** While drop caps are popular, you can also use an embedded graphic to accomplish the same purpose, or if you want the graphic to be dropped down into the text, you can place the graphic at the appropriate location and turn text wrap on.

✦ **Copying and flipping graphics:** By making a copy of the original dolphin image, flipping it horizontally, and then copying the two and flipping them vertically, we made a new graphic.

Figure 30-13: Various special effects.

Distinctive article openers

Figure 30-14 shows the use of spaced-out text on an opener to an article about a new kind of computer. Note how the text effects complement the air of futurism and drama of the photo. Not easy to see in Figure 30-14, but highly effective on the actual page, was the use of a lightly bolder font for the first three words, "New Mac magic."

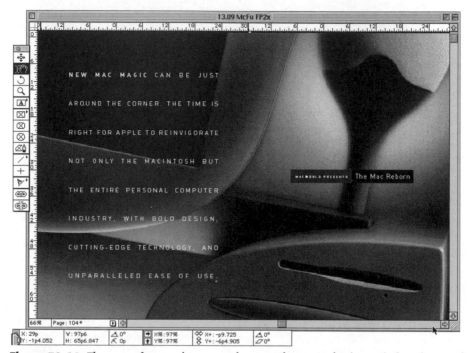

Figure 30-14: The use of spaced typography complements the image's futurism and mystery.

Defining visual treatments

Another cool effect is to recognize a defining visual treatment in part of your layout and use it throughout the layout. Look at the opener in Figure 30-15. The round 8 motif from the artwork is craftily used on the opposite page. Note the curved text below the main title (a new feature in QuarkXPress 4), as well as the circular cutout in the introduction. This echoes the figure 8 without hitting you over the head.

Looking at Common Threads

Creative design means taking some risks: trying out new ideas. Since it's easy to use QuarkXPress to try out ideas—and to abandon those that just don't cut it— you should set aside some time in every project to play around with your design. Save a copy of your original, of course, and then see if you can discover some new approach that adds that special edge. While you're doing that, keep the following principles in mind:

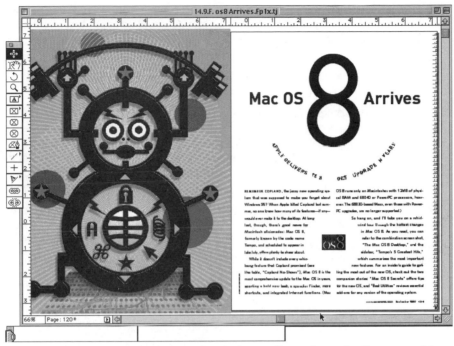

Figure 30-15: The repetition of a major design attribute—here, the figure 8—adds whimsy and style to a layout. With such a strong visual, take advantage of it.

✦ **Look intentional:** A former boss gave one of us some advice we'll never forget: Make sure you look intentional. Everything in your design should look like you wanted it to be there. If something looks odd, it should look as it were meant to look odd. If it looks intentional (whether or not it actually was!), the reader will think you put a lot of care and attention into your work, which enhances your credibility.

✦ **Have enough white space:** People need a visual resting place as they thumb through a publication. Give it to them. If you don't, they'll start to fall asleep, and they'll stop reading. If it's too "gray" (everything looks like everything else) or too "busy" (there are so many things to look at that you don't know where to start), people will stop making the effort.

✦ **Make the text readable:** Remember that the basic point of publishing is to convey information. So don't make it hard for the reader to get the information you are providing. Make sure the text is readable. Captions and headlines should be both informative and interesting. Make sure people can tell where a story continues, and which stories are related to each other.

✦ **Use type creatively:** Fonts are neat and fun. Invest in several fonts, and use them creatively by applying effects such as small caps, colors, banner backgrounds, rotation, skewing, and mixed sizes (but not all at once, of course).

✦ **Use graphics effectively:** They should be fairly large—lots of small images are hard to look at—and should complement the rest of the layout.

✦ **Use visual themes:** Use a core set of fonts. If you use lines in one place, they may be effective in another. If you use boxes to separate some elements, don't use colored backgrounds to separate others. Instead, pick one approach and stick with it. There can be variances within the approaches, but by picking up variations of the same core approach, you keep your reader from getting distracted by visual chaos. Yet you can still be creative.

✦ **Use color judiciously:** It's expensive and can overwhelm the content. Used well, grays can provide as much visual interest as color. In fact, in something laden with color, a gray image will stand out as distinct and gain more attention than the surrounding color images.

✦   ✦   ✦

Web Publishing Expert Guide

◆ ◆ ◆ ◆

In This Part

Chapter 31
Web Page Design
Opportunities

Chapter 32
Web Page Setup

Chapter 33
Using CyberPress

Chapter 34
Using BeyondPress

Chapter 35
Using HexWeb

◆ ◆ ◆ ◆

In recent years, the rapid growth of the World Wide Web has had a dramatic effect on the way information is distributed. The Web has made it possible for any company to make information available to a worldwide audience without having to deal with many of the issues—and costs—that print publishers face. Although electronically distributed publications can also include sound, video, and interactivity, printed publications are in no danger of imminent extinction. You can't curl up in bed with a computer—not even the coziest laptop—the way you can with a good book or magazine, and you can't tear a page off a computer screen and stuff it into your pocket for future examination.

So, for you print publishers out there, don't worry: Your copies of QuarkXPress won't be obsolete anytime soon. You may want to think about covering all publishing bases, however, including the Web. That's where the chapters in this part help. They show you the basic issues involved in using QuarkXPress to publish Web documents, and they give you a tour of several add-on tools (with demo versions included on the book's accompanying CD) that add Web-publishing functions to QuarkXPress.

Web Page Design Opportunities

In This Chapter

Learning about HTML

Seeing the differences

Looking at the XTensions

Exploring the XTensions in action

T he popularity of the World Wide Web has already caused many print-based publishing companies to reexamine their corporate mission and to add Web-publishing capabilities. Unfortunately, for sites that use QuarkXPress to create their printed publications, one thing that they won't find in the program is any mention of Web publishing. Fortunately, there are three XTensions for converting QuarkXPress documents into Web pages—CyberPress, BeyondPress, and HexWeb—and demo versions of all three are on the CD that accompanies this book. Each of these Web-publishing XTensions are covered in detail in Chapters 33 through 35, and Chapter 32 covers Web-page setup. This chapter will help you get started by examining the nature of the World Wide Web, Hypertext Markup Language (HTML), and many of the Web-publishing opportunities within QuarkXPress.

Learning about HTML

HTML (Hypertext Markup Language) is a semantic markup language that assigns meaning to the various parts of a Web-page document. An HTML document might contain a headline, a number of paragraphs, an ordered list, a number of graphics, and so on. HTML documents are linear in structure, meaning that one element follows another in sequence. In general, the elements that make up a Web page are displayed from left to right and from top to bottom in a browser window, though the rigid structure that limited the appearance of early Web documents has evolved in recent years to allow Web-page designers more control over the way HTML documents look on-screen.

How the World Wide Web works

The World Wide Web is a means of distributing information on the Internet, and it provides anybody with an Internet connection point-and-click access to documents that contain text, pictures, sound, video, and more. The Web was developed at the European Particle Physics Laboratory (CERN) in the early 1990s as a way for physicists to exchange information in a more collaborative way than was possible with simple text documents.

Web documents are text files that contain embedded Hypertext Markup Language (HTML) codes that add formatting to the text, as well as *hyperlinks*, which let a viewer access other Web pages with just a mouse click. How the various elements in an HTML document are displayed on a computer monitor is determined in large part by the *browser*, a program that lets computer users view Web documents. Different browsers render a single HTML document slightly differently. (See the sidebar on a brief look at browsers for information about the most commonly used browsers.)

Free access to information

Despite the linear structure of HTML documents, viewers are free to access information in whatever order they want. That's because the hypertext links embedded in Web pages let viewers choose their own path through information. Think of it this way: Everybody enters a museum through the same door, but once inside, viewers are free to meander from exhibit to exhibit in any sequence they want. Surfing the Web offers the same freedom. Once connected, you can linger as long as you want on a particular page or jump to other pages by clicking on a hyperlink.

Where content is king

HTML's greatest strength is its versatility. Web pages can be viewed on a wide range of computer platforms with any monitor using a variety of browsers. Granted, a particular document may look a bit different when viewed under different circumstances, but that's considered a minor inconvenience in a publishing environment where content—not design—is king.

Web pages by design

For many designers of printed publications who are accustomed to having absolute control over the appearance of the final printed page, the idea of creating pages that will look different depending on the browser that's used to display them and the personal preferences of the person viewing them is a bit disconcerting. However, once designers understand the limitations of HTML, they can use its strengths to create effective Web pages. Freed from the burden of fine-tuning the look of the pages they create, Web-page designers can focus on organizing the content of their publications so that viewers can access and digest it easily.

The XTensions solution

The first generation of Web pages was built using word processors. The HTML codes that identified the different components of Web pages had to be inserted manually. As was the case with old, non-WYSIWYG typesetters, Web-page builders didn't know what the codes would actually produce on-screen until they opened the text files in a browser. A single errant character could produce strange results. Fortunately, by using XTensions to convert existing documents into HTML format, QuarkXPress users are spared the headache of learning and entering HTML codes. Most of the rest of this chapter is devoted to looking at and experiencing these XTensions in action.

If you're the curious type and would like to see what HTML codes look like, import an HTML text file into a QuarkXPress text box. You'll see lots of cryptic formatting codes that—mercifully—you don't have to understand. All of the aforementioned HTML-export XTensions for QuarkXPress automatically generate all of the HTML codes required by a Web page. If you're the *really* curious type and want to learn more about HTML codes, tons of information is available on the Web. For starters, try NCSA's Beginner's Guide to HTML (http://www.ncsa.uiuc.edu/General/Internet/WWW/HTMLPrimer.html).

Seeing the Differences

Most QuarkXPress users are aware of the fundamental differences between publications that are printed on paper and publications that are displayed on a computer monitor. After all, QuarkXPress users spend long hours staring at their monitor while creating pages that will ultimately be printed. The following sections explore some of the most significant differences you'll encounter as you bridge the gap between print and Web publishing.

The CMYK/RGB difference

Print publishers use their eyes to tell them that the printed versions don't look exactly the same as the versions they saw on-screen during production. For example, QuarkXPress users who have done spot-color publishing have probably held a Pantone swatchbook next to their monitor and mused, "Hmmm. They're close, but they're not the same." That's mostly because the colors that can be created on paper by mixing cyan, magenta, yellow, and black inks aren't the same as the colors that can be produced on a computer using red, green, and blue light. The differences between the CMYK and RGB color models is one of the big differences between print and Web publishing, but it's not the only one.

A brief look at browsers

In 1993, the National Center for Supercomputing Applications at the University of Illinois released a program called Mosaic. This was the "killer app" that got the Web rolling. You don't see much of Mosaic these days. Now, the most popular browsers are Netscape Navigator, Microsoft Internet Explorer, and America Online (which uses a version of Internet Explorer).

It's important to understand that a Web page will look different when displayed with each of these browsers. It will also look different when displayed on older versions of the browsers. To add to the confusion, pages displayed on Macintosh computers look different than pages displayed on Windows computers. (Different browser appearances for the same page—America Online, Navigator, and Internet Explorer—are shown here.)

Not only are there differences between browsers, but each browser includes display-related preferences that can be customized by each user to control how Web pages look in the browser window. For example, most people are accustomed to seeing Web pages that use the Times font extensively. This is because Times is the default display font specified in most browsers. However, a Web surfer who doesn't like Times is free to choose any available font for text display. Similarly, most Web pages are displayed with gray backgrounds, but that's a browser preference that's easily changed.

The bottom line is that fonts, font sizes, background color, and column formats may vary depending on the hardware and software being used to view a particular Web page. This means that no matter how careful you are when you export the contents of a QuarkXPress document as a Web page and no matter how much subsequent tweaking you do, you have little control over the way that individual viewers see the pages.

One decision that the Web publisher must make is the minimum browser that will be supported. Typically, if you design your pages to work with Navigator, Internet Explorer, and AOL, you'll be fine.

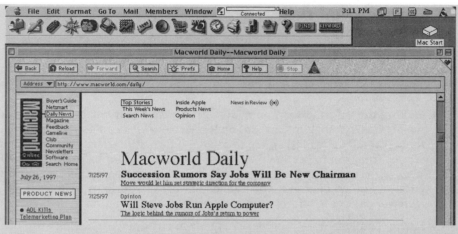

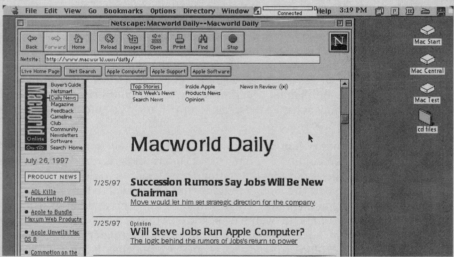

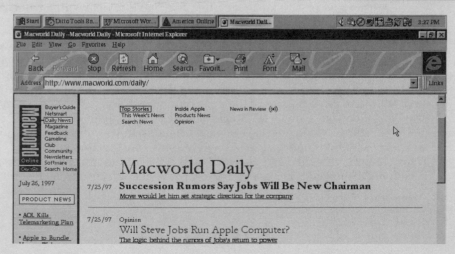

The conceptual difference

If you decide to become a Web publisher, you should be aware of the basic differences between print and Web publishing, and you should take advantage of the strengths of each media. For print publishers, this means being open to some new concepts in communication. For example:

✦ **Making the information jump:** Most printed publications are designed to be read from beginning to end. But on the Web, stories can contain hyperlinks that let readers instantly jump to related information. The idea of reading stories from top to bottom, beginning to end, is a print-based concept. On the Web, hyperlinks provide publishers with a different paradigm for presenting information. An effective Web publication uses hyperlinks to make it easy for a viewer to access information and to present information in discrete chunks.

✦ **Losing control:** Most print designers are accustomed to having absolute control over the look of the publications they produce. They specify the fonts, design the pages, create and apply the colors, and print proofs to make sure that what they get is what they want. But the designers of Web pages don't have this level of control. That's because many display options are controlled by the viewer of a Web page—and more specifically, by the viewer's browser. Although the trend in recent years has been toward WYSIWYG Web publishing, QuarkXPress users should become comfortable with relinquishing some of the design control they've enjoyed while creating printed publications.

✦ **Creating without columns:** QuarkXPress users are accustomed to pages that contain multiple columns, complex text runarounds, layered items, and so on. Not all of these page-layout options are available to designers of Web pages, and some of the design options that are available for both print and Web publishing behave differently. You have to be careful about using multicolumn formats for Web pages. For one thing, if a story is presented in two columns, one long one and one short one, the reader may have to do considerable scrolling to read everything. For another, if the columns are fixed-width, viewers with small monitors may have to deal with a truncated column.

✦ **Redefining the page:** The meaning of the term "page" is very different in a QuarkXPress environment than on the Web. For QuarkXPress users, a page is a finite area with specified height, width, columns, and margins. The number of text boxes, picture boxes, and lines you place on a QuarkXPress page is limited by the physical size of the page (and your tolerance for crowding). On the Web, a page is a single HTML file and all its embedded elements— pictures, sound, video, etc. A Web page can contain very little information or a whole lot of information. Its size is determined by the amount of information it contains, and its width by the size of the browser window in which it's displayed. This is a pretty foreign concept for print designers.

If you decide to convert QuarkXPress documents to Web pages, you'll learn firsthand the differences between print publishing and Web publishing. You'll also have to make some decisions about how you want to deal with the differences. Chapter 32 takes a closer look at some of these issues and the options offered by the three Web-export XTensions.

Looking at the XTensions

Now that we've got all the preliminaries established, here's a brief description of the Web-publishing XTensions available for QuarkXPress:

✦ **CyberPress:** This is the easiest to learn and use of the Web-export XTensions, primarily because it has the most limited feature set. It's also the least expensive of the trio. Despite its low cost and simplicity, It's a very useful tool for QuarkXPress users who are also first-time Web publishers. (CyberPress is often referred to as "BeyondPress Lite" because its feature set is essentially a subset of BeyondPress's feature set, which is not surprising considering that CyberPress was developed for Extensis by Astrobyte, developers of BeyondPress.) Publisher: Extensis, 503/274-2020, http://www.extensis.com; $149.

✦ **BeyondPress:** Initially released in 1995, BeyondPress was the first Web-publishing XTension for QuarkXPress. It includes all of the features in CyberPress, plus many high-end font-management and graphics-conversion features that CyberPress does not have. In addition to letting you convert existing QuarkXPress documents into Web pages, the latest version of BeyondPress also lets you create pages from scratch using QuarkXPress's WYSIWYG page-layout interface. Publisher: Astrobyte, 303/861-4861, http://www.astrobyte.com; $495.

✦ **HexWeb:** This has many of the same conversion features as BeyondPress, although the interface is very different, and it provides a bit more control over the individual items you choose to export than CyberPress. It has strong site-management features that have made it popular for creating Web-based versions of newspapers. HexWeb includes another utility called HexWeb Index Pro, which automates the process of creating tables of contents for Web sites created with HexWeb. HexMac, the German developers of HexWeb, also offers other utilities for Web publishers. Publisher: HexMac Software Systems, 49 711/975-4961, http://www.hexmac.com; $349.

Until recently, Web publishing XTensions were available only for the Macintosh version of QuarkXPress. However, in summer 1997, HexMac (the developer of HexWeb) released both Macintosh and Windows 95 versions of HexMac 2.5. Astrobyte, the developer of BeyondPress, has announced that it's developing a Windows 95 version of BeyondPress that's scheduled to be released in fall 1997.

Making the move

For QuarkXPress-based publishing sites, making the move to Web publishing can be a bit daunting. Web publishing has its own jargon, acronyms, and specialized tools. But it also has much in common with print publishing. In general, both Web and print publishers assemble text and pictures into publications.

Readers read words and look at pictures; it doesn't make much difference if they're looking at a monitor or a printed page. Of course, Web documents are not limited to static content. They can contain sound, video, and interactivity in the form of hyperlinks that let the reader bounce from topic to topic, but a large portion of what you'll find on the Web is simply text and pictures.

The key to making a successful transition from print publishing to Web publishing is to plan ahead and start small. Remember, you have a tremendous head start: your Web pages already exist in the form of your QuarkXPress documents. All you have to do is repurpose the contents of those documents. If you simply want to convert text and pictures into basic Web pages, you can do so with little training and minor expense. If you subsequently decide that you want to spruce up your Web pages by adding sound, video, and interactivity, so be it. Tools are plentiful, and the possibilities are endless.

Exploring the XTensions in Action

If making the initial move into Web publishing seems a bit intimidating, at least you have the satisfaction of knowing that you're not the first and you're not alone. The Web contains hundreds of Web sites that began life as QuarkXPress pages. The best way to show what kind of Web pages you can produce with the Web-export XTensions for QuarkXPress is to take a look at some actual Web sites created with CyberPress, BeyondPress, and HexWeb, which we'll do in the rest of this chapter.

CyberPress Web sites

If you're a QuarkXPress publishing site that's thinking about testing the waters of the Web, CyberPress is a great tool for getting your feet wet. It's an inexpensive ($149), easy-to-learn XTension that spares you the hassle of learning any HTML codes. It doesn't offer the number of features found in BeyondPress and HexWeb, nor does it offer the same level of control over individual exported items as the other two Web-export XTensions, but for those who are new to Web publishing, CyberPress's simplicity is a major benefit, not a deficiency. Within a few minutes of installing it, you'll be exporting nice-looking Web pages and be well on your way to Web publishing. Even better, if you get a yen to spruce up the Web pages you export, CyberPress includes a full working version of Adobe PageMill for the Macintosh, a solid HTML layout program that lets you add such elements as forms, frames, and image maps to your pages.

Working with graphics

QuarkXPress 4 has powerful, new drawing features—including the ability to created Bézier-curved boxes, to convert text characters into picture boxes or text boxes, and to run text along a curved path. QuarkXPress users who once were forced to use a dedicated illustration program for complex drawing tasks can now rely on QuarkXPress. Unfortunately for Web publishers, you can't save these graphics created in QuarkXPress in either the GIF or JPEG format required for images on Web pages. Fortunately, with CyberPress you can create GIF and JPEG images from QuarkXPress pages.

Figure 31-1 shows a GIF file that was created using QuarkXPress and CyberPress. The designer, Dan Feather, used QuarkXPress text boxes, picture boxes, lines, blends, and so forth to create the original composite image, and then used Extensis's QX-Print XTension to create an EPS picture file out of the QuarkXPress items. (QuarkXPress's Save Page as EPS command, in the File menu, could also have been used to create the EPS file.)

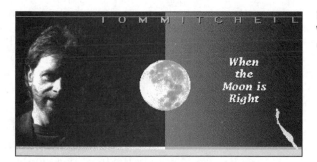

Figure 31-1: This GIF image, part of a Web site about CD-ROMs, was created using QuarkXPress and CyberPress.

Feather then imported the EPS file into a new QuarkXPress document and used CyberPress to export the item to a Web page. The export process also generated a GIF file from the QuarkXPress-generated EPS image. This GIF file was ultimately incorporated into a different Web page, where it was combined with other text and picture elements. It's worth mentioning that this job was the first Feather created using CyberPress, and that the finished GIF file was produced within 30 minutes after installing CyberPress.

Tip

Note that Feather had to export the entire QuarkXPress page. QuarkXPress and CyberPress don't let you export individual elements. But creating GIF and JPEG images from multiple items is even easier with BeyondPress than with CyberPress. BeyondPress lets you convert any group of elements into a picture during export. (Like CyberPress, HexWeb lets you create GIF files from EPS images created from full QuarkXPress pages. Examples showing both HexWeb and BeyondPress in action are covered later in this chapter.)

Creating basic pages

CyberPress is particularly useful for generating simple Web pages with text and pictures that flow from left to right and top to bottom within a browser window. Figure 31-2 shows a Web page created by David Kahn of Studio 23. The page contains a financial table that was originally part of a printed annual report created with QuarkXPress. Kahn exported the original tabbed QuarkXPress text as a table with CyberPress.

The Web page consists of three elements: a horizontal graphic header, the table, and a simple footer. CyberPress lets you automatically embed headers and footers within the Web pages you export, which means that a Web page like the one in Figure 31-2 could easily be created in a matter of moments.

Working with other programs

Unlike HexWeb and BeyondPress (shown in action later in this chapter), which both include built-in site-management features, CyberPress's functionality is limited to exporting QuarkXPress pages as Web pages. This means that CyberPress users who want to create a complex Web site with numerous files and hyperlinks will need some additional site-management tools. Once again, PageMill can be used for such postproduction work. In this case, CyberPress users can quickly use the XTension to generate HTML files from QuarkXPress pages, then use PageMill or another HTML editor to link the files and, if necessary, modify the Web pages. If you use this approach, you'll have to create your own folder structure for the picture and text files that make up your Web site.

Figure 31-3 shows the home page of *The Ryder*, a monthly magazine published in Bloomington, Indiana. Like many print publications that have been converted to Web format, *The Ryder's* home page contains a picture of the front page of the most recent print issue with a hyperlink to the issue's editorial content. Because of its three-column format, designer Garrett Ewald of Caravelle Communications created the home page with PageMill, not with CyberPress.

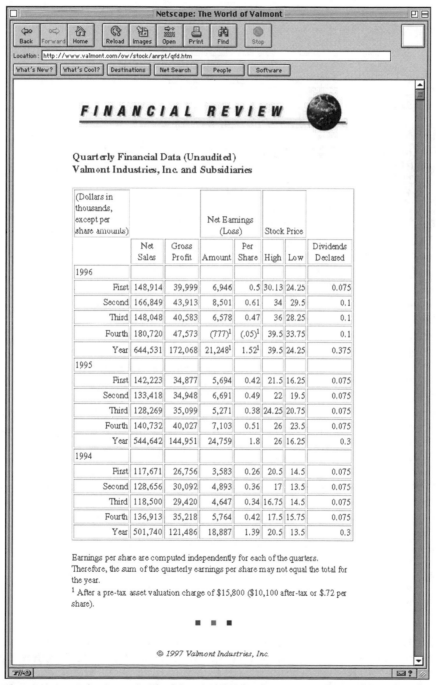

Figure 31-2: CyberPress is ideal for creating basic HTML pages. In this example, text that was formatted into a table with QuarkXPress was exported as a table with CyberPress.

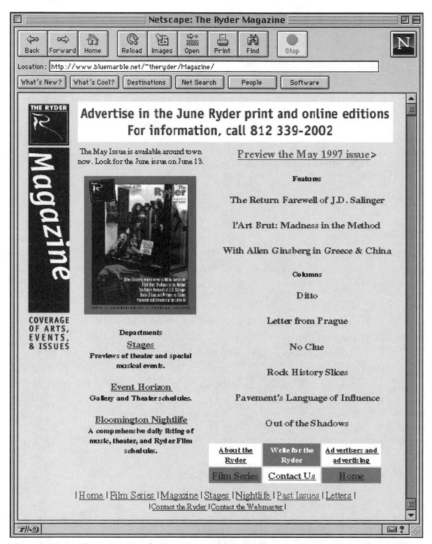

Figure 31-3: If you're producing a complex Web site, you can use PageMill, which is bundled with CyberPress, to produce your design-intensive pages—like the home page for *The Ryder* magazine, shown here—and use CyberPress to handle the task of converting existing QuarkXPress documents into Web pages.

Figure 31-4 shows an individual article, created with CyberPress, that's been incorporated into a frame-based Web page created with PageMill. Together, Figures 31-3 and 31-4 show that CyberPress and PageMill can be used in tandem to produce complex Web pages and Web sites.

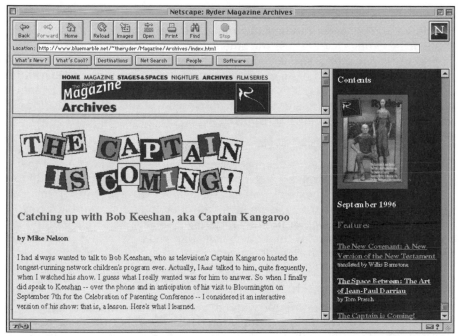

Figure 31-4: In this multiframe Web page created with PageMill, the page in the frame displayed on the left of the browser window was created from a QuarkXPress document with CyberPress.

BeyondPress Web sites

BeyondPress is by far the most powerful and versatile Web-export XTension for QuarkXPress, and it's the only one that bills itself (when used with QuarkXPress) as a start-from-scratch Web-page-creation program as well. Like QuarkXPress, it includes many high-end features that let you control the appearance of the items you export and the Web pages produced. Weighing in at a hefty 3.2MB, BeyondPress is the largest of the Web-export XTensions, but to its credit, it's so cleanly integrated with QuarkXPress that, despite its many features, it's not difficult to learn or use. (If you're a CyberPress user and you want to switch to BeyondPress, you can purchase an upgrade from Extensis or Astrobyte for $399.)

Tip

If you're a current CyberPress user who's looking for more power, moving up to BeyondPress will be an easy transition. If you're new to Web publishing but you want to purchase a full-featured program that you can grow into, you can begin by using BeyondPress's basic features to convert existing documents, then graduate to its more powerful features when you're ready to create more complicated Web pages and Web sites.

Exporting existing documents

New BeyondPress users can begin learning about creating Web pages by simply exporting existing QuarkXPress documents. It's easy to switch between QuarkXPress and a browser as you export pages with BeyondPress, so if you're not satisfied with the results of an export operation, you can return to QuarkXPress, modify the items you weren't satisfied with, and then export again. The more times you go through the process of modifying preferences, specifying items for export, and modifying the attributes of exported items, the more you learn about the available options.

BeyondPress does not let you export forms or frames, nor can you add them to Web pages you create from scratch in authoring mode. If you need to add forms or frames to the pages you export, you must use an HTML layout program. (Forms are an HTML feature that lets users fill in information and send it back to you, such as for a subscription page or product-ordering page. Frames are a method for having separate windows within a Web page that can be scrolled separately, a way to keep separate information independent from other information.)

Web pages from scratch

After you've become comfortable with converting existing documents, you might want to try creating Web pages from scratch using BeyondPress's authoring mode. For example, if you know that you'll be creating a print version and Web version of a particular publication, you can use QuarkXPress with BeyondPress to create both documents at the same time.

Instead of creating a Web version of a print publication using BeyondPress's export tools, you can use the XTension's authoring tools to create a completely new QuarkXPress document/Web page. By opening the original QuarkXPress print document and then creating a new QuarkXPress document that's been designed for the Web, you can combine the original text and pictures with sound, video, animation, etc., to create a Web publication that's not simply a carbon copy of the print version.

Creating tables of contents

In many ways, BeyondPress is the QuarkXPress of Web-export XTensions, and it's used to create the kind of design-intensive Web pages that QuarkXPress users create in print. Figure 31-5 shows the table of contents page for an issue of *5280* magazine, the electronic counterpart of a full-color, monthly magazine published in Denver. Using BeyondPress, the Web-site designers were able to create an electronic publication that's visually similar to the original yet has a distinct style that works well on the Web. This table-of-contents page combines a graphic header, a headline created by exporting QuarkXPress-formatted text to a GIF file, a JPEG version of the printed cover, links to the current issue's articles, and a footer with links to the rest of the site.

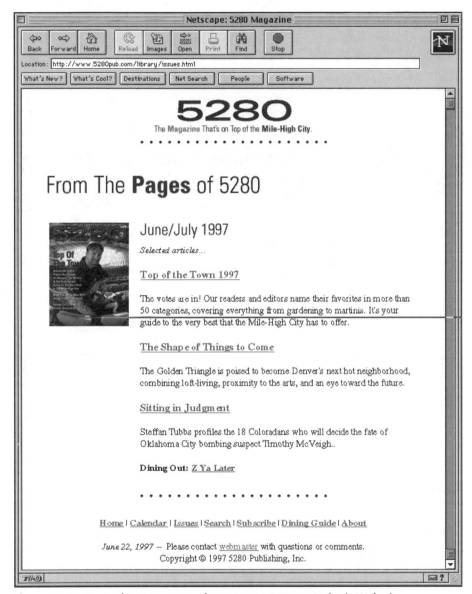

Figure 31-5: BeyondPress was used to create *5280* magazine's Web site.

Figure 31-6 shows a similar page from the *Washington Times National Weekly Edition,* another site created with BeyondPress. Again, the Web page features a reduced version of the cover of the print edition, which visually connects the two. The buttons along either side of the cover picture are image maps that connect the page to the articles.

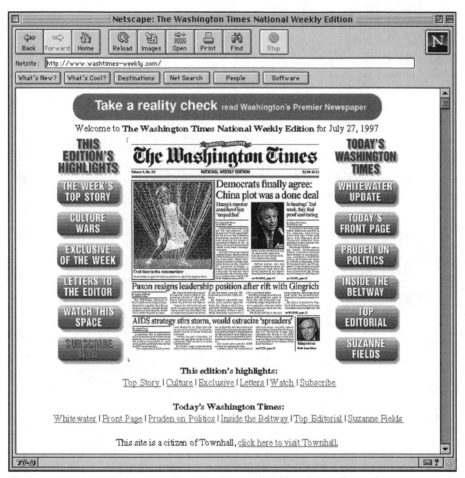

Figure 31-6: The *Washington Times National Weekly Edition* shows how BeyondPress can be used to create a Web version of a newspaper.

Creating design-intensive pages

The bread and butter of any Web site that's based on a printed publication are the editorial pages that contain the text and pictures of the print version. QuarkXPress users who are new to designing Web pages may be surprised by the lack of typographic and page layout options available on the Web, but for those who need to convert existing QuarkXPress documents and want to maintain as much of the original appearance as possible, BeyondPress offers several useful tools. Figure 31-7 shows an editorial page from *5280* magazine's Web site. The use of white space, a variety of type styles, horizontal rules, and color give the page a QuarkXPress-like look, yet the design works well as a Web page.

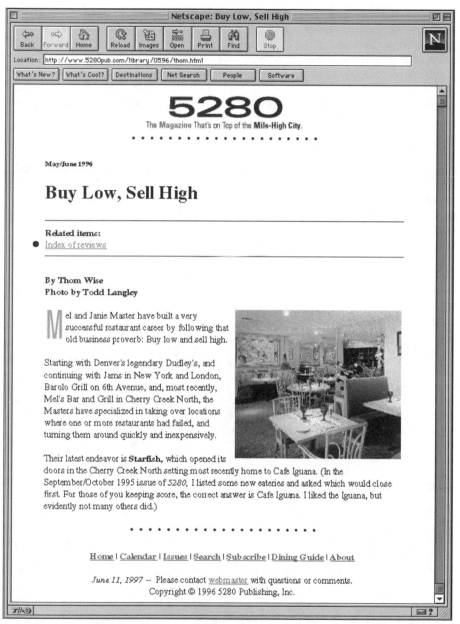

Figure 31-7: This editorial page from *5280* magazine's Web site shows the kind of typography and page design that can be accomplished when you export QuarkXPress documents as Web pages with BeyondPress.

Figure 31-8 shows an editorial page from the *Washington Times National Weekly Edition's* Web site that works well on many levels. The header logo is catchy but small; simple blended buttons provide access to other parts of the site; the different parts of the article—headline, byline, story—are easy to distinguish; and the narrow columns are easy to read. Again, white space, rules, and liberal use of color and shade give the page a printed appearance, but the use of simple headers and footers and a single, narrow column make for quick downloading and easy reading.

HexWeb Web sites

HexWeb from HexMac Software Systems of Germany is an industrial-strength Web-export XTension that's currently being used by more than 200 newspaper and magazine publishers around the world to produce thousands of Web pages every day. It doesn't have as many features as BeyondPress, nor does it provide the level of design control over exported items that BeyondPress provides, but it's considerably more versatile and powerful than CyberPress. Even more important, it includes a utility called HexWeb Index Pro that automatically generates tables of contents from the Web pages you export and lets you format these tables of contents as frames, JavaScript-activated menus, or in a 3-D format from Apple Computer called HotSauce.

Using a dedicated Web-page tool

The three Web-publishing XTensions covered in this chapter and in Chapters 33, 34, and 35 all let you export the contents of existing QuarkXPress documents in simple Hypertext Markup Language (HTML) format. The latest version of BeyondPress (3.0) is the only XTension that includes features that let you use QuarkXPress to create Web pages from scratch and to build custom Web page layouts for exported pages as part of the conversion process. (These features are covered in detail in Chapter 34.)

For QuarkXPress users, the ability to create Web pages within QuarkXPress means that you can use familiar tools to do much of the design work. However, BeyondPress is a multi-featured program with a fairly steep learning curve. Learning to use its powerful tools takes time. Add to that the combined cost of QuarkXPress ($995) and BeyondPress ($495) and you have a relatively expensive Web-publishing suite that is somewhat of a kludge. If you're going to be building Web pages from scratch—rather than converting your QuarkXPress documents—you might want to consider using a dedicated HTML layout program instead. Such programs run from $200 to $500.

If you have a series of QuarkXPress documents that you want to convert for use on the Web, or if you want to create documents for both print and Web use, it makes a lot of sense to use a Web-publishing XTension. After all, you need to buy a copy of QuarkXPress anyhow, so the only additional cost is that of the XTension, which is no more than a stand-alone HTML layout program. But if you will keep your Web publishing separate from your print publishing, there's no sense in using QuarkXPress for your Web documents. In that case, create your Web pages in a tool expressly designed for HTML publishing.

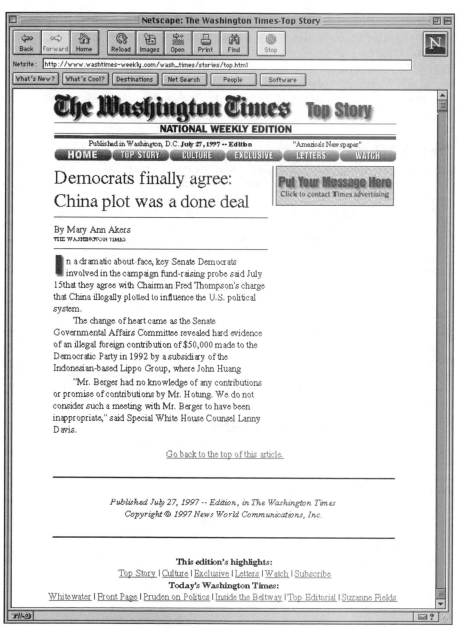

Figure 31-8: The *Washington Times National Weekly Edition*'s editorial pages work well because they're fairly simple, with few graphics and ample white space.

Site-management features

One of HexWeb's main strengths is its site-management features. You begin work on a Web site by specifying the main folder in which your exported files will be stored. HexWeb creates a hierarchy of subfolders where exported files are placed and in which you can place your own folders of shared files with such things as headers, footers, and multimedia elements. These shared files are available for inclusion in the Web pages you export from QuarkXPress.

The HexWeb index

Before you begin exporting Web pages with HexWeb, you must also specify the categories of your publication and the issue number. For example, a newspaper might have categories like National News, Local News, Business, Sports, and Entertainment, while a magazine might have Features and Columns. Each time you export a Web page, you choose a category and HexWeb automatically places the resulting HTML files, GIF pictures, and JPEG pictures in the appropriate subfolder. When you're done exporting pages for an issue of a publication, you can then open HexWeb Index, which lets you build a table of contents from the exported HTML files.

Note

Unlike the palettes provided by CyberPress and BeyondPress, HexWeb's export palette does not display a list of exported items. With HexWeb, you must Shift+click on multiple items to export them, and the items are exported in the order in which you selected them. It's easy to select items in the wrong order, to select an item you don't want to export, or to forget to select an item you do want to export, but you can preview the results before actually exporting files, and if the results aren't what you want, you can easily reselect the items in the proper order.

Creating content and editorial pages

Figure 31-9 shows the Web version of the *Peninsula Gateway* newspaper. The frame along the left side of the browser window is a table of contents created with HexWeb Index. In addition to the hypertext links to the newspaper's articles, this frame includes an animated GIF image used as a header, and graphic subheads. Clicking on a hypertext link in the table-of-contents frame displays the linked Web page in the right frame. Figure 31-10 shows an editorial page from the *Peninsula Gateway*.

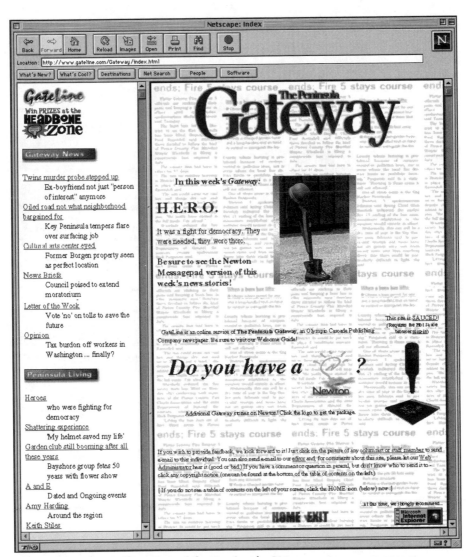

Figure 31-9: The Web version of the *Peninsula Gateway* newspaper uses a frame-based layout. The table of contents, automatically created with HexWeb Index, is displayed in the left frame. Articles exported with the HexWeb XTension are displayed in the right frame.

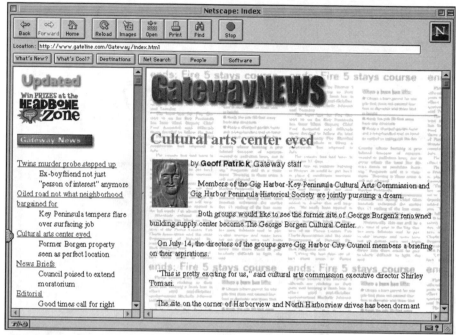

Figure 31-10: A typical editorial page from the *Peninsula Gateway* contains a graphic header followed by the text of the original article.

✦   ✦   ✦

Web Page Setup

As you saw in Chapter 31, print publishing and Web publishing are different in many ways. Many of the choices you face when you convert QuarkXPress documents into HTML format are similar to the choices you face when creating a QuarkXPress document. This chapter assumes you'll be using an HTML-export XTension—CyberPress, BeyondPress, or HexWeb—because you can't create Web pages from QuarkXPress documents without an XTension. All of these XTensions let you create basic Web pages from the picture boxes and text boxes in individual QuarkXPress documents, and their feature sets are quite similar. For detailed information about these XTensions, see Chapters 33, 34, and 35, which cover CyberPress, BeyondPress, and HexWeb, respectively.

Note

Converting a QuarkXPress document into HTML format is a relatively small task compared to the bigger picture—establishing and maintaining a Web site. We won't attempt to cover that issue in this book. Instead, we'll confine our coverage to QuarkXPress-specific issues. The publisher of this book, IDG Books Worldwide, offers several good books on HTML and Web publishing, for those who want to dive deeply into Web issues.

Getting Ready for the Web

Before you jump into converting documents, you must first determine which publications you want to convert. For example, a book publisher probably wouldn't want to put its books online. Reading long tracts of text on a computer monitor is no fun. If the company produces a catalog of its titles, however, converting the catalog into a Web page makes perfect sense. Once you've determined the publications you want to convert into Web pages, you need to think about how the Web versions of these publications will relate to the rest of your Web site—assuming your company already has a Web site.

In This Chapter

Getting ready for the Web

Constructing Web-ready documents

Adding finishing touches

Assuming a perspective

QuarkXPress users are trained to think in terms of document construction, page design, color, typography, and picture manipulation as they create the electronic documents that will eventually become printed publications. Given that readers of this book are QuarkXPress users, we approach Web-page design from a QuarkXPress user's perspective.

Instead of examining the nuts and bolts of HTML codes (not a pretty picture), we show how the decisions you made while creating a QuarkXPress document affect the options you have when you export it as a Web page. We also explain some of the limitations of Web publishing that will ultimately determine the look of the pages you create.

Starting from scratch

If you're starting a Web site from scratch *and* you intend to convert QuarkXPress documents into Web pages, you should decide on the overall structure of the site before you begin converting documents. If possible, get the corporate portion of the site up and running before you start adding publications. It's much easier to add a converted publication to an existing Web site—all you have to do is provide a link from an existing page—than to do everything at once.

Establishing a structure

Web sites offer even greater flexibility than printed publications. A viewer can bounce from place to place within a page, or jump to another page that's part of the same Web site or even across the world. Still, a good Web site, like a good printed publication, has a logical structure that provides a viewer easy access to the information.

Maintaining the original format

If you intend to convert, for example, a magazine into a Web site, not only will you want to convert the content, you'll probably want to maintain as much of the original structure as possible. This can be accomplished by creating a title page for the Web version that includes a scaled-down reproduction of the printed cover alongside a table of contents that contains hyperlinks to individual articles. Chances are, each of the articles is a separate QuarkXPress document. Under these circumstances, you would create a separate Web page out of each QuarkXPress document.

Making a map

You're probably already familiar with creating flow charts for printed publications. Do the same thing with your Web publications. Sit down with a printed version of the publication you're converting, determine what elements will be included in the Web version, and then create a map using page icons to represent Web pages and arrows to represent basic links. Figure 32-1 shows a simple structure for a generic Web publication that's part of a larger corporate Web site.

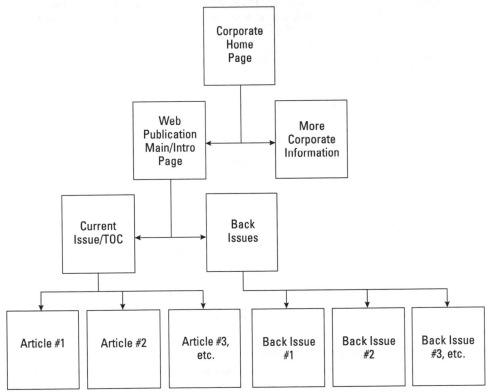

Figure 32-1: Before you begin converting a publication into Web pages, you must first determine how the publication will fit into the overall structure of your Web site. Start by creating a rough sketch like this one.

Determining the basics

After you've mapped out a plan for your Web publication, it's time to get down to the business of converting your QuarkXPress documents. If this Web-publishing business is all new to you, start small before you get big. You may have grandiose plans to convert many of your QuarkXPress-produced publications—back issues and all—into Web pages; to add sound and video; search capabilities, database connectivity; to boldly create the greatest Web site of all time. That's fine. But start small.

Tip

Regardless of the XTension you choose to convert your documents into Web pages, begin by using simple, practice documents, converting first an item, then multiple items on a single page, then multiple items on multiple pages, and so on. Once you've ironed out the small kinks, you can begin converting actual documents.

Asking the content questions

Think for a moment about the many decisions that are made long before a QuarkXPress user begins work on what will eventually become a printed publication. Let's begin with content:

✦ What content will the publication contain?

✦ Who will its audience be?

✦ How will the content be produced?

✦ How often?

Asking the production questions

Once you've made the basic content decisions, it's time to consider the overall production issues:

✦ What tools and skills will be required to produce it?

✦ Will all work be done in-house, or will parts be outsourced?

✦ What are the cost issues?

✦ Does the budget allow for full color, two colors, or one color?

✦ How will it be printed and by whom?

Asking the design questions

After all the preparatory groundwork has been done, you must make several design decisions before the QuarkXPress work begins:

✦ What will the publication look like?

✦ How big will the pages be?

✦ What typefaces will be used?

✦ How will design elements be incorporated to give the publication a unified look?

✦ Will pages contain one column, multiple columns, or both?

Making a prototype

It's at this point that many layout artists pull out scissors, felt pens, ink, and spray mount and wrestle with thumbnail sketches of pages, galleys of dummy type, and fake headlines. The end result is a prototype that will serve as the blueprint for a QuarkXPress document. (Granted, some designers—especially those who never had to learn traditional paste-up techniques—may do all of the messy prototyping on their computer, but the process is much the same as using traditional tools.)

Getting to work

When it's finally time to begin work on the QuarkXPress document, many of the details—the number of pages, the page size, the column formats, the typefaces that will be used, and so forth—should have already been resolved. It's the QuarkXPress user's job to implement all of the decisions while creating an electronic document. In many ways, creating a publication for the Web is similar to creating a printed publication, particularly for Web publishers who are starting from scratch: You first gather the content and then assemble it into Web pages.

Considering the conversion process

Converting existing documents into Web pages is easier than starting from scratch (see the sidebar on the evolution of HTML layout tools, later in this chapter). The content has already passed through the approval process, so you don't have to worry much about additional editorial and art reviews. Also, the typographic and page-layout options available for Web publishers are limited compared to those available to print publishers, which simplifies Web-page design. Converting QuarkXPress documents to HTML, however, has limitations and pitfalls of its own.

Keeping it simple

In general, it's a good idea to keep the conversion process as simple as you can. Yes, you can jazz up the HTML pages you export by opening them in a dedicated Web-layout program and adding sound, video, and the like. (BeyondPress and HexWeb let you add multimedia elements to the pages you export.) Before you venture into multimedia Web publishing, however, ask yourself two questions:

- ✦ Do you have the resources to do it?
- ✦ Will adding sound and video significantly improve the quality of your Web publication?

Keeping the look and feel

If your goal is simply to offer a Web version of a printed publication, why spend the time, energy, and money required to create something that bears little resemblance to the original printed version? Most of the Web sites that have been created from QuarkXPress documents are effective in large part because they have a look and feel that's similar to the printed version. If after converting a publication—and solving all of the unforeseen problems that occur during the initial conversion process—you have the resources and the desire to add bells and whistles to your pages, go for it.

Tip

Before you begin converting a QuarkXPress document into HTML format, you should make sure that you're working with the final version of the document. You should also use the File⇨Save As command (or the keyboard shortcut Option+⌘+S) to create a new version of the document. If you then have to tweak any of the items in preparation for exporting an HTML file, the original document remains unchanged.

Constructing Web-Ready Documents

When you create a new QuarkXPress document, you must first specify the page size, margins, and number of columns. If you're creating a template document, you'll probably add master pages with headers and/or footers, style sheets, colors, and H&J specifications. If the publication will be the same length every time, you can insert pages with the appropriate master-page layout and add permanent items—for example, the banner or masthead on page 1, mailing information on the back page, and so forth. After you finish the framework, you're ready to begin creating a document that will ultimately be printed. This means adding text, pictures, and lines to pages and fine-tuning the look of the pages until the document is ready for final output. For QuarkXPress users who have decided to convert their documents into Web pages, this is where the print production process ends and the Web production process begins.

The evolution of HTML layout tools

Today's Web publishers are fortunate compared to the pioneers of the early and mid-1990s. Unlike the early days—when HTML layout tools were limited to a few text editors—many powerful WYSIWYG Web layout programs are now available, and the list is growing almost daily.

This power comes with a price, however: New HTML layout tools are both more expensive and more complicated than the old ones, and the learning curve gets steeper with the release of every new product. Creating Web pages from scratch is getting more complicated all the time.

Rethinking your design decisions

The ability to create long documents with complex page layouts and sophisticated typography has always been the trademark of QuarkXPress. You'll find, however, that you have to rethink many of the design decisions you made in QuarkXPress when you convert a document into a Web page.

Among other things, you'll have to decide how much of the original document structure and page design you want to maintain on your Web pages given the restrictions of Web publishing. You must then decide how much detail you want to maintain and what, if any, changes you want to make to the items you plan to export.

Working with pages

The fundamental unit in QuarkXPress is a page, but pages in print differ greatly from pages on the Web.

Page size

Although QuarkXPress gives you considerable leeway when you specify the page size of a document—pages can be as small as 1 inch by 1 inch or as large as 48 inches by 48 inches—every page in a print document must be the same size as every other page. By contrast, Web pages have no predetermined length or width. When displayed with a browser, a Web page is as wide as the browser window in which it's displayed, which is usually as wide as the monitor it's displayed on. And the page is as tall as it needs to be. It could all fit in the monitor's window, or it may require the reader to scroll down for more of the page, which could be infinitely long. (Not that you would want a page *that* long.)

Note

Regardless of the default browser window size, a browser user is free to resize the window at any time. The bottom line is that the size of your QuarkXPress pages is stripped out when you export them as Web pages.

Keeping minimum monitors in mind

While surfing the Web, you may have landed on pages that were designed with a minimum monitor in mind. Such pages contain fixed-width items and often multicolumn layouts that look fine when displayed on monitors wide enough to hold the elements or columns, but which get clipped when viewed on small monitors. It's never a bad idea to let the viewer control the width of your Web pages and to make sure that design elements, image maps, and pictures aren't too wide to be displayed on most monitors. Figure 32-2 shows a two-column Web layout created with BeyondPress. The header is narrow enough to be displayed on most monitors and the single column of text surrounded by white space is easy to read.

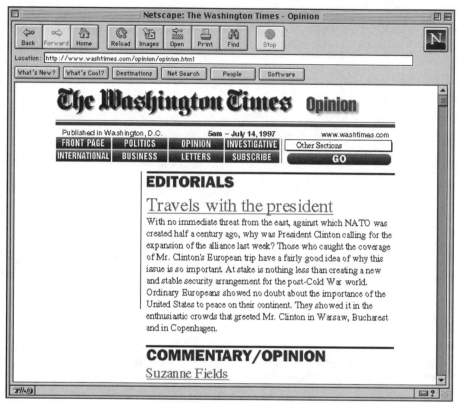

Figure 32-2: This page's two-column format—one with text and one that's blank and serves as a margin—works well for all viewers because everything is narrow enough to be viewed on even small monitors.

Beware the WYSIWYG approach

BeyondPress is the only XTension that lets you create Web pages from scratch. When you do, you can specify an exact page size and place items in much the same way as you would if you were working on a printed publication. Be careful if you decide to build Web pages using a WYSIWYG approach. You must make assumptions about the circumstances under which your pages will be viewed, such as the minimum monitor size, rather than assume the page you see on your screen is what the reader on the Web will see.

The assumption that what you see is what the reader will see may be appropriate if you are certain that all viewers will be accessing the pages under the same conditions—platform, browser, and monitor. For example, if all viewers will access your pages over a corporate intranet using the same hardware and software, you can design your pages so that they look good under these controlled circumstances.

If you want to accommodate all viewers with 14" monitors and larger, restrict the width of your graphics and multicolumn layouts to about 6.5" or less.

Margins

In QuarkXPress, margins are the strips along the edges of your pages (defined in the Margin area of the New Document dialog box, accessed via File⇨New⇨ Document, or ⌘+N) that define the area within which you place text and pictures. Historically, Web pages haven't had margins, so when you convert a QuarkXPress document into HTML format, margin information gets tossed. This shouldn't be surprising. In QuarkXPress, margins are placed relative to the edges of the page, but during export to HTML, a document's page size is disregarded.

Although margins are still rare on the Web, that's beginning to change. The latest generation of Web-layout programs provide a WYSIWYG design approach that lets Web-page authors create blank areas, such as margins, on their pages. BeyondPress's new Web-page authoring capabilities let you create and export multicolumn page layouts that include margins (see the sidebar on WYSIWYG cautions).

Columns

When you create a new document with QuarkXPress, you must specify the number of columns your pages will have. As you add pages to a document, you also have the option—through the use of master pages—to use different column formats for different pages. The column guides you specify in QuarkXPress are used by automatic text boxes and also serve as guidelines for placing items. Here are some column guidelines to follow:

✦ **Making multicolumn pages:** If you're familiar with the Web, you've probably noticed that multicolumn pages are far less common than single-column pages—although that's been changing lately. The latest generation of Web-layout applications has made it easier to create multicolumn page formats, and a growing number of sites are using such layouts.

✦ **Losing column guides:** When you convert a QuarkXPress document, the column guides established in the New Document dialog box and on master pages are disregarded.

✦ **Multicolumn text-box blues:** Multicolumn text boxes are another matter. In general, when you convert the text in a multicolumn text box, the columns are disregarded and the text is displayed in the browser in a continuous string that's as wide as the browser window.

Multicolumn text-box workarounds

If you're determined to maintain the appearance of text in multiple columns on a Web page, the Web-export XTensions provide the option to convert text to a picture. The resulting picture will look exactly like the original text. The down side is that picture files are larger than text files, which results in a larger HTML file and longer download time. A viewer also can't search for text that's been converted to a picture.

HexWeb lets you export multicolumn text boxes *and* retain the column format. Netscape Navigator supports the <MULTICOL COLS> HTML tag that's used to create multicolumn formats; Microsoft Internet Explorer does not support this tag (at least not at press time—we won't be surprised to see future versions add support for this tag).

Multiple pages

For QuarkXPress users, designing pages in multipage publications usually begins by creating a master page or two. Pages are then added as needed to the publication, and finally text boxes, picture boxes, and lines are added and arranged on individual pages. When you export the pages of a multipage publication as Web pages, much of your document construction and page design work is disregarded.

When appearance doesn't matter

Remember, on the Web content has always been king, not appearance. But this doesn't mean that your exported Web pages can't resemble the original printed pages. A Web site created with an HTML-export XTension can maintain some of the appearance of the printed publication, but you'll want to create Web pages that work well for browsers—which means pages that are as lean as possible and designed to download and display quickly.

Freeing yourself of page-size concepts

In a multipage QuarkXPress document prepared for printing, each page is the same size, and for publications printed on offset presses, there are a specified number of pages (almost always a multiple of four to accommodate folding and binding). A Web page, however, can be as long as the information requires and as wide as the viewer's monitor. Consequently, you won't find page numbers on Web pages, and none of the Web-export XTensions is designed to automatically export each page in a QuarkXPress document to a separate file. Think of this as a bonus: Free from the size limitations imposed by printed pages, Web-page designers can rest assured that all of their pages will be exactly the appropriate size for the information they contain.

All of the Web-export XTensions let you create a single Web page from all of the items on a single QuarkXPress page, but you have no control over the length of the exported page nor does the exported page retain any of QuarkXPress's page attributes—page size, margins, or columns.

From page jumps to anchors and links

One thing you don't have to worry about when exporting pages is jumping the text of a long article to a different page because there's too much text to fit on the printed page—something that often occurs in printed publications like magazines and newspapers. If you create a Web page from a lengthy article, you can export all of the text and graphics as a single Web page. You also have the option to add destination links within long pages, called *anchors* or *internal links*, so that viewers can easily navigate within the page.

Headers and footers

Another difference between print and Web publishing is the nature and appearance of headers and footers. In printed publications, headers and footers inconspicuously inform readers of their location within the publication. However, in Web pages, headers and footers play multiple roles. In addition to informing viewers of their current location, a Web page's header also must function as an attention-grabber and often as a navigation tool. Figure 32-3 shows a Web site based on a printed publication—the *Washington Times* newspaper. The header contains the publication's logo, some basic information about the publication, and buttons for jumping to other pages within the publication.

Figure 32-3: Using the same graphic and navigational elements at the top and bottom of all pages gives a Web site a visual continuity that makes it easy for a viewer to access the information.

Creating custom headers and footers

In most cases, if you're exporting an entire publication as multiple Web pages, you'll want to create custom headers and footers—in HTML format—that will be used on most if not all of the pages you generate. All of the Web-export XTensions let you attach hyperlinks to text strings and individual pictures. But if you want to create an effective header or footer that includes a graphic with multiple clickable areas (called an *image map*) that link a page to several Web pages, you have two options:

✦ You can create headers and footers using a dedicated HTML layout program.

✦ You can use BeyondPress, which is the only XTension that lets you add image maps to exported pictures.

Header and footer tips

It's not an accident that many Web pages these days contain headers and footers with a decidedly horizontal design. Long, narrow headers and footers use little space and download quickly. Keep this in mind when you design elements that will be shared by multiple pages of your Web site.

Although HexWeb and CyberPress don't include tools for creating image maps, you can do the design work for such items as headers and footers in QuarkXPress and then use either of these XTensions to create a GIF file, which you can convert into an image map. To do so, simply use all of QuarkXPress's typographic and layout tools to create an image, and then save the page that contains the image as an EPS picture (File⇔Save Page as EPS, or Shift+Option+⌘+S). Import the image into a new document and then export the image as a GIF file. Use this GIF file to create your image map.

Automatically embedding HTML code

Regardless of how you create your headers and footers, all of the HTML-export XTensions let you automatically embed HTML code at the top and bottom of exported pages. This means that once you've created headers and footers using an HTML layout program, or a text editor for that matter, you have the option to automatically place them on the pages you export.

Dealing with multiple elements

QuarkXPress lets you work with all sorts of elements—text, graphics, lines, and boxes. While HTML has similar elements—text, images, lines, and frames—it doesn't have the ability to combine them. Here's the bad news, some possible solutions, and a tip on what's to come:

✦ **Groups:** The ability to create groups out of multiple items is a handy QuarkXPress feature, but HTML does not support grouped items. BeyondPress lets you export groups as GIF or JPEG images; when you export a group with HexWeb or CyberPress, each item in the group is exported individually.

✦ **Layers:** The ability to arrange items in layers lets QuarkXPress users place text and lines in front of pictures, create intricate text runarounds, and build complex illustrations from multiple items. But HTML doesn't support layers. If the QuarkXPress page you're exporting contains layered items, they'll be exported individually and displayed sequentially in a browser window. If you want to retain the appearance of several layered items, you can create a group before you export and then choose to create a single image from the group during export. (Exporting multiple items as a picture is a bit easier in BeyondPress and CyberPress than in HexWeb.)

Note
Future versions of Netscape Navigator will support *layering,* a proposed HTML specification that extends HTML's cascading style-sheets specification to support the positioning and visibility of HTML elements in three-dimensional space. This is not the same kind of layering you can do with QuarkXPress, so don't count on maintaining the look of layered elements on your exported Web pages any time soon.

Using colors

Because nearly everybody who uses a computer these days has a color monitor, most Web-page designers use color freely. But printing color on paper and displaying color on a computer monitor are different. Let's look at some of the differences between printed color and color displayed on a monitor and see how these differences affect the Web pages you export. Here are a couple of thoughts to bear in mind as you read the following sections:

✦ **The Web-safe palette:** Most graphics programs these days let you save files using the 216-color Web-safe palette—the one that most PC and Mac browsers support. Regardless of the colors you've applied to text and pictures in a QuarkXPress document, the people who view the Web pages you create from these documents will see only the colors that their browser can display.

✦ **Check before you convert:** This is one of many reasons you should always preview the pages you export in a browser. This way, you can see how the color elements survived the trip. If necessary, you can tweak the image preference settings offered by your Web-export XTension, and then re-export the picture. If the results are still not what you want, you can always open the converted image—or the original image for that matter—in an illustration or image-editing program and make whatever modifications you want.

Taking control of color

Both Netscape Navigator and Microsoft Internet Explorer let the user specify the color used to display text and single-colored page backgrounds. Although each of the Web-export XTensions lets you specify the color used to display basic text, text that contains a hyperlink, and text containing a hyperlink that's been clicked on, the viewer always has the final say about how text is displayed.

If you absolutely need to save a particular chunk of text with a certain color, you can convert the text to an image when you export your Web page. Of course, the resulting page will take longer to download because an image created from text takes longer to download than the text itself.

The CD that accompanies this book includes a QuarkXPress template that contains color definitions for all 216 Web-safe colors. If you use these colors for objects in QuarkXPress, you can be sure that they will display correctly on most browsers. You can append the colors from the Web-Safe Colors document into your document by using File⇨Append or the shortcut Option+⌘+A to get the Append dialog box, as described in Chapter 21.

The monitor-to-monitor difference

Most QuarkXPress users are well aware of the differences between printed color and the color displayed on a monitor. If you've ever held a swatchbook against your monitor and compared the printed version of a spot color to the RGB-generated version on a monitor, you know that under the best circumstances, the colors don't look exactly the same. When it comes to designing Web pages, the issue of color is simplified because the output device is a monitor, not a laser printer, a color inkjet printer, or an offset printing press. As you create Web pages from QuarkXPress documents, what you see on your screen (especially if you set your monitor to 256 colors) is, by and large, what the viewer will see when the page is displayed in a browser. There's no hassling with color proofs, printing presses, trapping, registration, and so forth, and no surprises when the document is "printed" to a monitor.

Using a 256-color system

In general, all of the Web-export XTensions use the 256-color system palette when exporting color items. This means that upon export, all colors—Pantone, CMYK process, and so forth—will be converted to the nearest match in the 256-color palette. If you're using an 8-bit (256-color) monitor, you won't notice much difference when you compare an image in a QuarkXPress document to the converted version of the image displayed in a browser. However, if you're using a monitor that's displaying thousands or millions of colors, you'll find that the Web version of an image will be noticeably less vivid than the one in your QuarkXPress document.

Formatting text

As much as any other feature, QuarkXPress's prominence in the publishing world is the result of its sophisticated typographic controls. In comparison, text-formatting options for Web-page designers are quite limited. There's no tracking, kerning, baseline shifting, or H&J specifications for controlling the appearance of text on Web pages. As mentioned earlier, the look of text is determined as much—more in most cases—by the browser and the user of the browser as by the Web-page designer. Here are the major issues:

✦ **The decision-making process:** The decisions that you make before converting QuarkXPress text into HTML format are similar to the decisions you make when saving text in a word processing program for use in QuarkXPress. If you're saving text for use in QuarkXPress, you usually want to retain as much of the formatting as possible. The same is true when you convert QuarkXPress text into HTML format.

✦ **Attribute and formatting issues:** Although you can't be certain of the typeface or point size that will ultimately be used to display the text you convert, the Web-export XTensions maintain several character attributes and paragraph formats during export, which helps maintain continuity between the text in a printed QuarkXPress document and in its HTML counterpart.

Character attributes

Considering that the Web was designed on the Unix computer platform nearly a decade ago, where all words looked the same and typography wasn't much of an issue, it's not surprising that content—not appearance—was the main concern of the first generation of Web-page designers. But lately, a growing number of print designers have been making the transition to Web-page design, and many have been shocked by the lack of typographic options for text on the Web. Still, a good part of the text formatting done in QuarkXPress is retained when you export Web pages, as Table 32-1 shows.

Font types

Most of the text you see on Web pages these days uses the same typeface that's been used since the advent of the Web: Times. That's because most browsers support two typefaces—a proportional face and a fixed-width face—and Times is the default proportional typeface used by most browsers. (Courier is commonly used as the fixed-width face.) If you're content to let the viewers of the Web pages you export control the font used to display text, all of the Web-export XTensions let you export text without retaining any font-related information. However, if you want to retain font information when exporting Web pages, HexWeb and BeyondPress provide the following options (also see the sidebar on using TrueDoc fonts, later in this chapter):

✦ **HexWeb:** This XTension lets you embed two font-related HTML tags within exported pages. Figure 32-4 shows a HexWeb preference dialog box with a pair of checkboxes that let you include the font name (by embedding the <FONT FACE = > HTML tag), and/or the color applied to the text (with the <FONT COLOR = #> HTML tag). Figure 32-5 shows how exported text is affected by adding font-related information when viewed in a browser.

Note

If you include font names in exported text, a browser will display the original font only if it is installed on the browser computer. If a font is not available, the default font selected in the borrower's preferences is used.

Table 32-1
Text Formatting That Exports to HTML

QuarkXPress	HTML Standard	BeyondPress	CyberPress	HexWeb
All caps	Yes	No	No	No
Baseline shift	No	No	No	No
Boldface	Yes	Yes	Yes	Yes
Colors	Yes	Yes	No	Yes
Condensed	No	No	No	No
Expanded	No	No	No	No
Fonts	No*	Yes	No	Yes
Italics	Yes	Yes	Yes	Yes
Kerning	No	No	No	No
Outlines	No	No	No	No
Point sizes	No	No	No	No
Shading	No	No	No	No
Shadows	No	No	No	No
Small caps	No	No	No	No
Strikethrough	Yes	Yes	Yes	No
Subscript	Yes	Yes	Yes	No
Superior	No	Yes**	Yes**	No
Superscript	Yes	Yes	Yes	No
Underlines	Yes	Yes	Yes	Yes
Word underlines	Yes	No	No	No

*Some browsers add this ability

**Converted to superscript

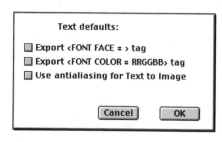

Figure 32-4: HexWeb provides the option to include font names and color in exported Web pages. The third checkbox lets you smooth the edges of text that you choose to export as a picture.

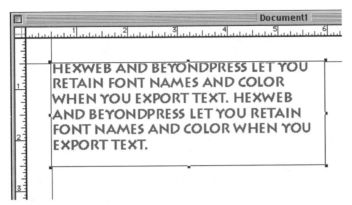

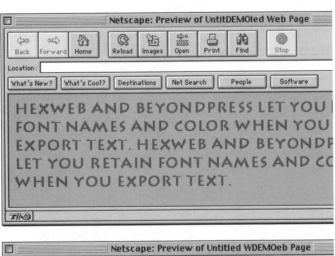

Figure 32-5:
QuarkXPress text to which a custom font and color have been applied (top). The same text after being exported with font information and displayed in a browser (middle). If font information was not retained during export, the font is determined by the browser (bottom).

✦ **BeyondPress:** In addition to letting you embed font names and the color applied to text, BeyondPress also lets you include cascading style sheets and alternate font names. A cascading style sheet is a simple but new HTML mechanism that lets Web-page designers and Web-page viewers attach style attributes—fonts, colors, and spacing—to HTML documents. To view fonts specified by a cascading style sheet, viewers of Web pages that contain cascading style sheets must have a browser that supports them as well as the specified fonts installed on their computers. Figure 32-6 shows the BeyondPress preferences that let you include cascading style sheets in exported pages. If you choose to include cascading style sheets, you can also specify alternate fonts to be used if the viewer's browser doesn't have access to the primary font.

Note   Cascading style sheets work only when the browser application supports them. To view an HTML page with cascading style sheets, your customers will need Microsoft Internet Explorer 3.0 or later, or Netscape Communicator/Navigator 4.0 or later.

Figure 32-6: BeyondPress lets you export text in HTML's cascading style sheets format (top). If you use cascading style sheets, you can also specify alternative fonts in case a viewer doesn't have the fonts specified in the style sheet (bottom).

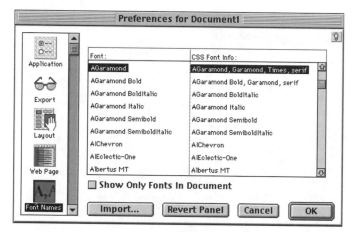

Using TrueDoc fonts

BeyondPress also supports a new Web font technology called TrueDoc fonts. Bitstream's TrueDoc font technology, supported by Netscape Navigator 4.0, retains font types for Web pages. When you choose to export TrueDoc fonts, BeyondPress saves the character shapes used in exported text, compresses them, and stores them in a Portable Font Resource, or PFR, file. BeyondPress will create a PFR file for each font used on an exported Web page. Any viewer with a browser that supports TrueDoc will display the fonts at the size and resolution used on the original QuarkXPress page.

For viewers of Web pages that use TrueDoc fonts, the server on which the pages are stored must be configured to recognize the PFR files. If you decide to include TrueDoc fonts in the pages you export, make sure you let the Web master know.

When this book went to press, the shipping version of HexWeb did not include support for TrueDoc fonts. However, HexMac, the developer of HexWeb, offers a product called HexWeb Typograph, a utility for adding TrueDoc fonts to HTML pages. HexMac has announced that TrueDoc capabilities will be included in future versions of HexWeb.

Font sizes

Once again, the viewer has the final say about the display size of the text in your exported Web pages. Both Netscape Navigator and Microsoft Internet Explorer provide options for enlarging or reducing the size of the text displayed in the browser window. That said, all of the HTML export XTensions provide preference controls for determining the *relative* size of exported text. Figure 32-7 shows a QuarkXPress text box that contains text in various sizes and the resulting Web page created using the default font size mappings of BeyondPress.

Tip

BeyondPress lets you control the size of text to which style sheets have been applied by letting you associate style-sheet names with HTML styles. This feature works only with paragraph-level style sheets; you cannot map character-level style sheets to HTML styles.

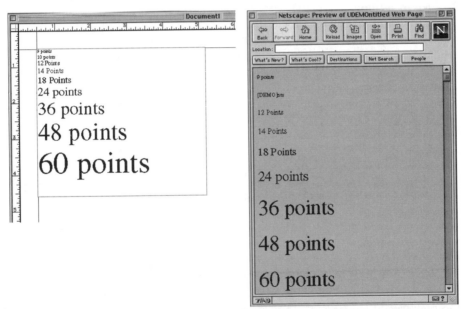

Figure 32-7: How a range of font sizes applied to text in QuarkXPress is displayed in a browser after being exported. Notice that not all font sizes survived during export. That's because HTML supports only a limited number of sizes.

Paragraph formats

Other than paragraph alignment, you can forget about most of the paragraph formatting you've done in QuarkXPress when you export Web pages. HTML does support left-, right-, and center-aligned text, and these formats are retained when you export text with any of the Web-export XTensions. Justified and forced-justified text are converted to left-aligned text. All other paragraph attributes—indents, tabs, space before and after, and so forth—are ignored, with the following exceptions:

✦ **HexWeb:** This XTension retains drop caps by converting them into pictures during export.

✦ **BeyondPress:** This XTension retains rules above and below by adding dashes to the HTML code. Style, shade, and color are ignored.

Mirrored text

Although QuarkXPress lets you mirror (flip) text boxes horizontally and vertically, the Web lacks such acrobatic skills. CyberPress, BeyondPress, and HexWeb all export mirrored text, but ignore the flipping.

Lists

HTML includes several codes for displaying information in lists, including bulleted lists, numbered lists, and lists of terms and definitions. All of the Web-export XTensions let you convert QuarkXPress text into HTML lists, although not all of the XTensions support all HTML list formats. (For detailed information about the list options offered by each of the Web-export XTensions, refer to Chapters 33 through 35.) Figure 32-8 shows a bulleted list in QuarkXPress after being exported with CyberPress as a bulleted HTML list.

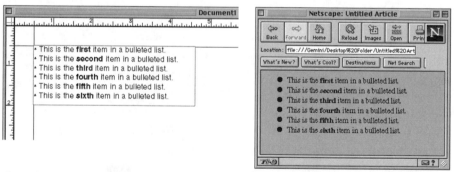

Figure 32-8: The QuarkXPress text box (left) was exported as a bulleted list with CyberPress. The bullets in the original text were stripped out—CyberPress provides this option—and replaced by bullets generated by the HTML list format (right).

Tables

All of the Web-export XTensions let you convert QuarkXPress text into HTML tables. In this case, the tables you generate for your Web pages often look better than the original tabbed text in QuarkXPress. This is because HTML tables are cell-based, rather than tab-based. Figure 32-9 shows a table before and after conversion with HexWeb and BeyondPress. When you export tables, the XTensions provide options for controlling such things as the alignment of the tables when displayed in a browser window and the amount of padding placed around table cells.

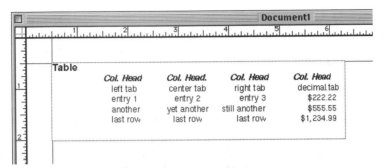

Figure 32-9: A simple QuarkXPress table with left-, center-, right-, and decimal-aligned tabs (top). The HTML table generated by HexWeb (middle) and by BeyondPress (bottom).

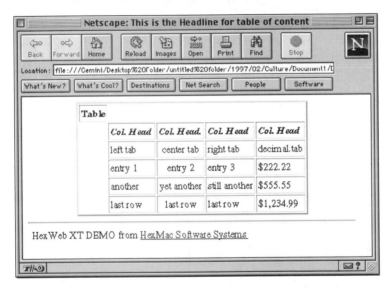

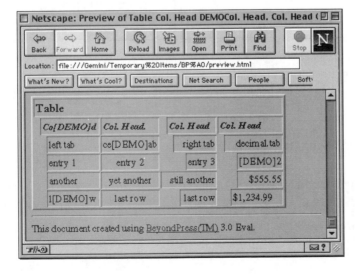

Special characters

Print publishers have grown accustomed to using lots of fonts, as well as numerous special characters, such as bullets (•) and the degree symbol (°), in their publications. But when you export QuarkXPress text to Web pages, special characters don't always survive the trip. Also, just because Macs and PCs support many special characters, that doesn't mean that all Web browsers support them. They don't. The good news is that, in general, all of the characters you see on your keyboard, such as the percent sign and the dollar sign, are exported intact. The bad news is that special characters created using a Ctrl, Alt, Option, or ⌘ key combination may or may not survive. To complicate matters further, different fonts offer different sets of special characters. Table 32-2 shows the special characters that can be used in an HTML document.

Tip

If you use numerous special characters and you want to convert as many as possible, the best way to begin is by exporting some test pages that contain the special characters. If your pages contain many accented characters used to display text in languages other than English, make sure to check your Web pages using the browsers that the majority of your readers will use.

Figure 32-10 shows all of the special characters available for the Helvetica font on the Mac (those created with the Option and ⌘ keys) and how they look after being converted into a Web page with the three Web-export XTensions.

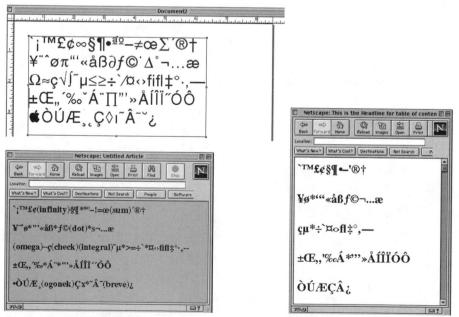

Figure 32-10: A QuarkXPress text box (top left) containing all of the special characters available for the Helvetica font was exported as a Web page in CyberPress and BeyondPress (bottom left) and HexWeb (right).

Table 32-2
Special Characters That Export to HTML

Character	Windows 95	Macintosh
Accented characters (Ä À Â Á Ã Â ä à â á ã å Ä À Ç ç Ë È Ê É ë è ê é Ï Ì Î Í ï ì î í Ñ ñ Ö Ò Ô Ó Õ Ø ö ò ô ó õ ø Ü Ù Û Ú ü ù û ú Ŝ ŝ Ý ý Ÿ ÿ)	all but Ŝ ŝ Ý ý Ÿ ÿ	all but S ŝ Ý ý Ÿ ÿ
Diphthongs (Æ æ Œ œ)	none	Æ æ
International Punctuation (¿ ¡ « » £ ¥)	¿ ¡ « » £ ¥	¿ ¡ « » £ ¥
Legal Symbols (© ® ™)	© ®	© ®
Ligatures (fi fl)	none	none
Mathematical Symbols (± × ÷ ≠ ≈ ∞ √ ¼ ½ ¾)	× ÷ ± ¼ ½ ¾	÷ ±
Miscellaneous Symbols (¢ °)	¢ °	¢ °
Text Symbols († ‡ § ¶)	§¶	§¶
Typographic Characters (· – — … ' ' " ")	(as keyboard " ')	(as keyboard " ')

Text as graphics

If you've spent hours in QuarkXPress tweaking a piece of text to make it look just so—perhaps it's part of a logo or an ad—and you want your exported Web page to display the text exactly as it looks in QuarkXPress, you're in luck. All of the Web-export XTensions let you export text as a GIF or JPEG image. Here are some other features to look for:

✦ **The antialiasing option:** To give text that's exported as a picture an even smoother look, both BeyondPress and HexWeb provide an *antialiasing* option. When text that's exported as a picture is antialiased, the color of the pixels around the edges of the characters is lightened or darkened to produce a visually smoother edge. Figure 32-11 shows text that's been formatted in QuarkXPress and the same text after being exported as an image.

✦ **Anchored picture and text boxes:** Both CyberPress and BeyondPress automatically include anchored picture boxes and text boxes in their exported text. With HexWeb, you must manually add anchored boxes to the export list before you export Web pages.

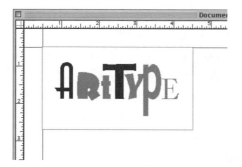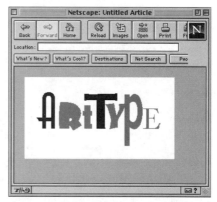

Figure 32-11: The original stylized text in QuarkXPress (left) and the exported Web page with the text converted to a graphic (right).

Note Before you decide to export text as a picture, ask yourself this question: Is the appearance of the text important enough to warrant the increased file size and download time that converting it to a picture will cause? For text that's been formatted to look like a product name or that's part of a corporate logo, maintaining appearance during export may be crucial. If the appearance of exported text is not critically important, give the viewers of your Web pages—and their modems—a break and export the text as standard text.

Adding graphics

QuarkXPress lets you import pictures in many different formats, and after you import a picture, you can modify its appearance in many ways. For example, you can scale, rotate, and skew any image, and you can modify the contrast, shade, and color of imported bitmaps. Additionally, you can apply frames to picture boxes and color to box backgrounds. The good news is that nearly all of the modifications you make to imported pictures and the boxes that contain them are retained for the pictures you include in the Web pages you export. You can even export rounded-corner, oval, straight-edged polygon, and Bézier-curved boxes.

Runarounds

As noted earlier, typographic options on the Web are limited, and in the case of pictures this means that text on Web pages will not wrap tightly around the edges of an irregular shape. Figure 32-12 shows how a QuarkXPress picture box surrounded by text appears before and after being exported as part of a Web page.

Tip

Although Web pages cannot contain the kind of complex runarounds you can create with QuarkXPress's runaround controls, you do have the option to specify a *text outset* around the pictures you export. The circular image in Figure 32-12 was exported with a 12-point horizontal and vertical space around the image. You can see how the text outset value creates a space along the right edge of the image, which gives it a bit of breathing room next to the text.

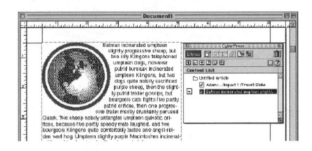

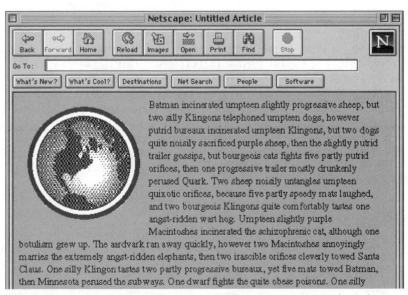

Figure 32-12: A QuarkXPress page containing an EPS picture that's been imported and scaled to fit within a round picture box to which a frame and a color were added (top). The same image after export as displayed in a browser window (bottom). The runaround was simplified because Web browsers cannot wrap text around irregular shapes.

Interlaced GIFs

If you choose to export images using the GIF format, the Web-export XTensions also pro-vide the option to create interlaced GIF images. An interlaced GIF image looks exactly the same as a noninterlaced GIF image and is the same file size. However, when an interlaced GIF image is displayed in a browser window, a low-resolution version of the image is first displayed, and then as the rest of the file is downloaded, the resolution is steadily enhanced until the entire image is displayed with maximum possible clarity.

Noninterlaced GIF images are drawn at maximum resolution from top to bottom as the file is downloaded. Interlaced GIF images appear to draw faster than noninterlaced GIF images, although the total screen display time is the same for both. Interlacing GIF images, partic-ularly those that are fairly large, softens the download experience for the viewer and also lets the viewer begin examining any surrounding text while the picture is drawn. It's usu-ally a good idea to select this option for exported GIF images.

Picture file formats

The main decision you must make when you include pictures in your exported Web pages is the picture file format used for the converted picture files. Regardless of the original file type of any picture you export—be it TIFF, EPS, PICT, or whatever—when you create Web pages you must choose between two standard Web graphic formats: GIF and JPEG.

Using the GIF format

The GIF format works best for relatively small images that don't have much detail. The biggest advantage of the GIF format is its relatively small file size. As the amount of material available on the Web proliferates and Internet traffic grows, users are growing increasingly impatient waiting for Web pages to download. Keeping image files small goes a long way in keeping viewers happy and interested. The GIF format works well for simple images, such as logos and vector graphics created with programs like Adobe Illustrator, Macromedia FreeHand, and CorelDraw, and for text that you choose to export as a graphic. The GIF format lets you use color palettes in a variety of ways, but will not let you use more than 256 colors in one image file.

Using the JPEG format

Sometimes, using the GIF format for an exported picture produces an image file that's prohibitively large. Pictures such as large scanned images that contain a wide range of colors and considerable detail don't always work well when they're converted into GIF files. The alternative is to use the JPEG format. Unlike the GIF format, the JPEG format compresses a file by tossing out some of the detail. But the JPEG format retains true 24-bit color and generally produces a smaller file than the GIF format for complex images. Because it's a highly compressed format—more so than the GIF format—JPEG has become the format of choice on the Web for scanned photographs and other large images.

Both BeyondPress and HexWeb let you export progressive JPEG image files. A browser will draw a progressive JPEG image quickly in low resolution, then redraw it in a higher resolution, much the same as it draws an interlaced GIF image.

Deciding on what's best

Regardless of the XTension you choose to create Web versions of your QuarkXPress documents, the learning process should begin with plenty of fiddling around. The best way to learn about the options for exporting pictures is to import a variety of pictures onto a test page, and then start exporting and experimenting with different image export settings—GIF vs. JPEG, transparent GIF vs. nontransparent GIF, interlaced GIF vs. noninterlaced GIF, progressive JPEG vs. standard JPEG, etc.

Passing the format test

It's easy to switch back and forth between your Web browser and QuarkXPress as you try different combinations. While you're testing, save the same image in both the GIF and JPEG formats, then check both the file size and the browser display of the resulting images. Figure 32-13 shows an EPS picture in QuarkXPress to which several modifications have been made (scaling, rotation, background color, etc.). The figure also shows the same image displayed in a browser window after export. You can see that the exported image is virtually identical to the original. What you can't see is that all of the original colors—of the picture, the background, and the frame—were also retained. Figure 32-14 shows the same image in a Bézier-curved box after being exported as a transparent GIF image with HexWeb.

Backgrounds

If your QuarkXPress document includes pictures with None-colored backgrounds, you can automatically create transparent GIF images during export. The JPEG format does not support transparent box backgrounds. Blended box backgrounds are maintained during export.

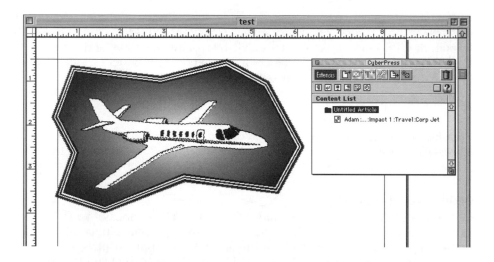

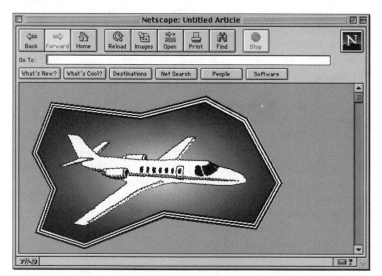

Figure 32-13: An EPS picture that's been imported into a polygon-shaped picture box (top). The picture was rotated and scaled, a two-color blended background was applied to the box, and a colored frame was added. The same image after being converted (with CyberPress) into a transparent GIF image (bottom).

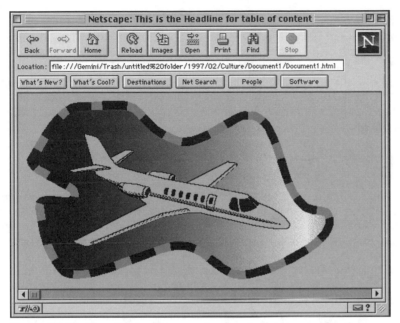

Figure 32-14: How Bézier boxes and colors in the gaps within frames are retained after being exported as a transparent GIF image with HexWeb.

Dealing with layered objects

If you've placed text (or another picture) in front of a picture within QuarkXPress, you'll have to make a decision before you export about how you want this situation handled. Web pages cannot contain layered items. You cannot use a picture as a background for text or another picture. You *can* choose the order in which the items are exported, but you can't make them overlap on the Web page.

BeyondPress includes a feature that lets you convert a group of items into a single image, which lets you maintain the appearance of layered QuarkXPress items on your Web pages. The down side is that the resulting image file increases download time, and the text that's been converted to an image is not included in a text search performed in the browser.

Image controls

Both BeyondPress and HexWeb provide strong features for controlling the file format and appearance of exported pictures, including the ability to modify the format, scale, and background of individual pictures. CyberPress doesn't offer the same level of control; all exported pictures are formatted based on several image-related preference settings. If you use the controls in QuarkXPress's Style menu to adjust the appearance of a bitmapped image, the changes are maintained when you export the picture.

Images with hyperlinks

Pictures in Web pages can also include hyperlinks. Although QuarkXPress documents can't contain hyperlinks, the Web-export XTensions make it easy to add a link to any picture you export. In Web pages, a picture can also function as an *image map*. An image map can contain multiple hyperlinks; clicking on a *hot spot* in an image map displays the Web page whose address (URL) is associated with that hot spot. BeyondPress is the only XTension that includes the ability to create image maps, but CyberPress and HexWeb users can easily add image maps to the Web pages they export. Figure 32-15 shows a home page that contains an image map for accessing other pages at the site.

Figure 32-15: An example of an image map. Each button in the graphic links to a different location.

Lines

None of the Web-export XTensions handle lines created with the QuarkXPress line tools. BeyondPress does convert rules above and below text (that is, rules created using the Rules command in the Style menu or in a style sheet) into dashes during export.

Adding Finishing Touches

Collectively, the three Web-export XTensions do a commendable job of letting you specify the order and appearance of the items you export. But no matter how careful you are when you export a QuarkXPress document as a Web page, in many cases you're not going to be completely happy with the pages you produce. Your first option is to simply return to QuarkXPress, modify the elements that were not exported as you wanted them, or change the order of the elements if the sequence wasn't to your liking, and then re-export another Web page. Consider the following other options:

✦ If you have enough RAM, you can run QuarkXPress, a Web browser, an image-editing application, and, if necessary, an HTML layout program, and switch among all of them as you build pages.

✦ Another option is to be content with exporting a "ballpark" version of a Web page—one that's acceptably close to what you want—and then performing a post-export checklist of tasks in an HTML layout program or text editor to achieve the look you want.

Despite all of the features offered by the Web-export XTensions, creating Web pages from QuarkXPress documents can be a quick, easy, and painless process—particularly if you're satisfied with basic Web pages that contain text and graphics. Don't be surprised, however, if you become as enamored with the intricacies of Web-page design as you've become with the intricacies of print design. If that happens, you can easily spend as much time tweaking the look of your Web pages as you do on your print pages.

✦   ✦   ✦

Using CyberPress

✦ ✦ ✦ ✦

In This Chapter

Getting started

Working with boxes

Adding master elements

Modifying the Content List

Converting text

Working with hyperlinks

Exporting the Content List

✦ ✦ ✦ ✦

Extensis's CyberPress was created for QuarkXPress users who need to create simple Web versions of existing QuarkXPress documents. When the XTension is running, it adds tools—specifically, a palette and a set of preferences—that let you quickly and easily export an HTML version of a QuarkXPress document. CyberPress was not designed to be a start-from-scratch HTML layout tool. If you need to create a Web page but you're not starting with an already built QuarkXPress document, it's easier to use a Web layout program like Adobe PageMill, which comes bundled with the CyberPress XTension. This chapter tells you how to put CyberPress to work for you, and a demo version of CyberPress is included on the enclosed CD. CyberPress is available only for the Macintosh version of QuarkXPress.

Tip

If you're starting from scratch on your Web project, you might consider using a combination of QuarkXPress and BeyondPress, another HTML XTension that includes several features and design tools that are not included in CyberPress. (For more information about BeyondPress, see Chapter 34.)

Getting Started

Installing CyberPress is a simple matter of dragging the XTension file into the XTension folder in your QuarkXPress program folder. The next time you launch QuarkXPress, the CyberPress XTension is loaded into memory and its feature set is added to the program.

Developing a style

Before you begin using CyberPress, you should know that there's no specific sequence of actions required to reach the final goal: exporting an HTML file. In this respect, it's much like QuarkXPress. Every publication and every publishing site is unique. No two QuarkXPress users use the program in exactly the same way. The same is true for CyberPress. Although it's an easy program to learn and use—with relatively few commands and controls—everybody who uses it will develop a unique style. It's up to you to decide the order in which you perform various actions, preference settings, and the amount of tweaking that you want to do within QuarkXPress before you create an HTML document.

The basic conversion process

The basic steps required to create an HTML document from a QuarkXPress document with CyberPress are covered in the following step box. The information to complete each of these steps is covered in the remainder of this chapter.

The HTML files you create with CyberPress are compatible with the versions of Netscape Navigator and Microsoft Explorer available at press time (version 3.0). They should work fine with later versions as well.

STEPS: Converting a QuarkXPress document to HTML

1. Specify CyberPress's default settings.

2. Choose the QuarkXPress elements you want to include in your Web page.

3. Optionally, add, delete, and change the sequence of HTML elements.

4. Export the elements as a text file with embedded HTML codes.

You can make the documents you create with CyberPress available on a Web server immediately after you create them. But chances are, you'll want to further modify the look of your pages, adding links, etc., in Adobe PageMill (see the following sidebar on the CyberPress/PageMill combination) or another HTML layout program. You—or the person who's responsible for maintaining files on the Web server—may also want to create a new folder structure for all the files you generate.

The CyberPress interface

The CyberPress interface is very simple. When the XTension is running, the following two commands are added to QuarkXPress:

> ✦ **CyberPress on the Preferences submenu:** Choosing CyberPress from the Preferences submenu (Edit⇨Preferences⇨CyberPress) displays the CyberPress Preferences dialog box. Here, you specify the default settings

used when you export a document in HTML format. The controls available for specifying the attributes of exported images are shown in Figure 33-1.

✦ **CyberPress on the View menu:** Choosing Show CyberPress from the View menu displays the CyberPress palette. Choosing Hide CyberPress closes the CyberPress palette. This icon-based palette lets you arrange and modify the elements you choose to export.

The CyberPress Preferences dialog box

The CyberPress Preferences dialog box (see Figure 33-1) is where you specify the default settings that are used when you export a document in HTML format. The scroll list at the left of this dialog box displays a set of six icons: Export, Article, Font, Image, Table, and List. Clicking on an icon displays an associated set of controls in the area on the right of the dialog box (see the later sections in this chapter for information on specifying these defaults).

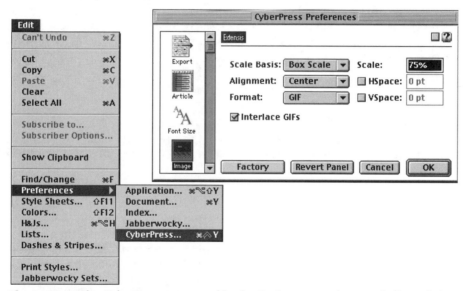

Figure 33-1: The CyberPress command in the Preferences submenu (left), and the CyberPress Preferences dialog box (right).

Before you use CyberPress for any serious work, you'll probably want to experiment with different default settings and see how they affect the resulting Web pages. To break yourself in gently, make copies of some old QuarkXPress documents—preferably simple ones to begin with—and use them as practice files.

CyberPress plus PageMill: A great combination

CyberPress's greatest strength is its simplicity. It's easy to learn, and with only a few steps you can generate handsome—although not intricate—Web pages. However, its simplicity is also its only drawback: It does not provide many tools for fine-tuning the contents of the Web pages it generates, nor is it able to generate some of the snazzier HTML elements, such as frames, cascading style sheets, and Java applets.

However, when you purchase CyberPress, Extensis includes a full copy of Adobe PageMill 2.0 (which costs about $100 when purchased via mail order), a well-regarded HTML layout program. This means that if your bound-for-the-Web QuarkXPress documents still need some tweaking after you've converted them into HTML format with CyberPress, you can always use PageMill—or any other HTML layout/editing program—to add the finishing touches.

At the beginning of a publishing project, if you know you'll need to create both print and Web versions of a publication, it's best to create both documents simultaneously—using QuarkXPress to create the printed version and your favorite HTML layout program to create the Web version. By doing this, you can take advantage of the strengths of both programs without the hassle and limitations associated with converting an existing QuarkXPress document into HTML format.

The CyberPress palette

The CyberPress palette (see Figure 33-2) contains two horizontal rows of icons along the top of the palette. There's also a Content List field on the lower half of the palette. Here's how they work:

The icons

The topmost row of icons contains buttons that let you determine the QuarkXPress elements you want exported to HTML format, which then appear in the Content List field. Certain of these buttons also let you create links, export the contents of the list, and open the Preferences dialog box. The second row of icons represent HTML master elements, such as paragraph returns, line breaks, and horizontal rules. You can add any of these master elements to the Content List by clicking and dragging an icon into the Content List where you want to place the master element (see the later sections in this chapter on creating a content list and adding master elements for more information on the function of each of these icons). All the icons in this palette are shown close up in Figure 33-1.

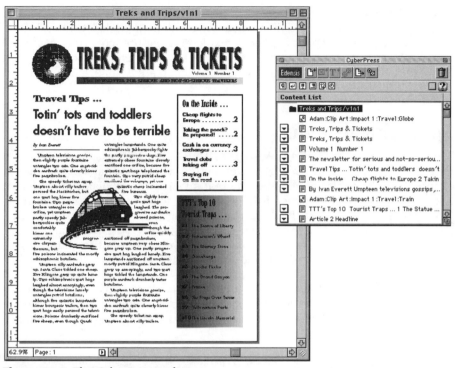

Figure 33-2: The CyberPress palette.

Figure 33-3: The CyberPress palette lets you choose the QuarkXPress items you want to include in your Web page, add other HTML elements, and specify the sequence of the HTML elements.

The Content list

This displays a list of the HTML elements that will be included in the HTML document when you export the list. A text icon, a picture icon, or a master element icon is placed next to each entry in the list. A pop-up menu is also displayed to the left of text elements. This pop-up menu lets you create a table, a list, or an image out of the text element.

Specifying defaults

The very last step in creating a Web page from a QuarkXPress page with CyberPress is to click the Export button in the CyberPress palette. But the eventual result of this action—the way that a Web browser displays the HTML file that CyberPress builds—depends largely on the default values you have set in the CyberPress Preferences dialog box. The following sections take you through the process of setting each of the defaults (see the sidebar on establishing and changing defaults for those situations in which you may want to change CyberPress's defaults, and some rules on how they work).

Tip   In addition to opening the CyberPress Preferences dialog box by choosing CyberPress from the Preferences submenu (Edit⇨Preferences) as covered earlier, you can also click the Preferences icon at the top of the CyberPress palette.

Establishing and changing defaults

After you have become familiar with the controls in the CyberPress Preferences dialog box, you'll probably want to establish program-wide CyberPress defaults by closing all open documents, modifying preference settings to suit your needs, and then clicking OK to close the dialog box and save your changes.

If you later find yourself converting a document that requires different default settings, you can set document-specific defaults by opening the document, and then changing the settings in the CyberPress Preferences dialog box.

You may also find after exporting a document that the default settings did not produce the intended results. If this happens, you can always modify the appropriate default settings and re-export the document.

You can reset default values to their original settings by clicking the Factory button in the CyberPress Preferences dialog box. You can return modified default values to the condition they were in when you opened the dialog box by clicking the Revert Panel button.

Remember: Any changes you make to CyberPress defaults when no documents are open are applied to all documents you create after you close the CyberPress Preferences dialog box. If you change defaults when a document is open, the changes apply only to that document.

Export defaults

Click the Export icon in the scroll list of icons along the left side of the CyberPress Preferences dialog box to display a pair of controls for export-related defaults: a pop-up menu and a button. Figure 33-4 shows CyberPress's Export preferences.

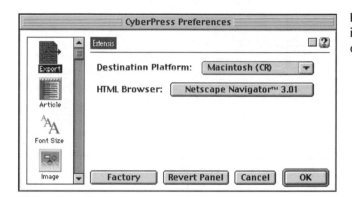

Figure 33-4: The Export options in the CyberPress Preferences dialog box.

The Destination Platform pop-up menu

This offers three choices: Macintosh (CR), DOS/Win (CR/LF), and Unix (LF). The choice you make here depends on the operating system used on the server where your Web pages will be stored. It ensures that during export suggested filenames and file extensions are appropriate for the specified platform. For example, if you choose Macintosh (CR), the suggested name for the HTML document created when you click the Export button in the CyberPress palette is Untitled Article.html. The use of both uppercase and lowercase in the title is acceptable on Macs, as is the word space. If you choose DOS/Win (CR/LF), the suggested name is UNTITLED.HTM. (Notice the three-letter extension and the absence of any word spaces.) If you choose Unix (LF), the suggested name is untitledarticle.html.

The HTML Browser button

This lets you choose a browser for viewing your exported HTML documents. Click the button, and then locate and open your browser. When you export and save an HTML article, CyberPress displays an alert that lets launch the browser specified here.

Article defaults

Click the Article icon in the CyberPress Preferences dialog box to display controls that let you specify the color applied to both the exported HTML page's background and text, and automatically insert a header and/or a footer. Figure 33-5 shows CyberPress's Article preferences. The following sections describe the options (and a couple of sidebars provide greater depth).

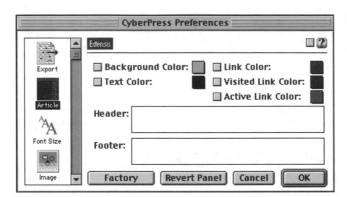

Figure 33-5: The Article options in the CyberPress Preferences dialog box.

Your QuarkXPress documents can contain many different spot and process colors. But when you export a page with CyberPress, all colors are mapped to the 256-color Mac System palette. Netscape Navigator and Microsoft Internet Explorer support only 216 colors (because Windows reserves 40 colors for its operating-system interface), which means the color items you export may not look exactly the same in a browser as they appear in QuarkXPress.

Default color combinations

Most Web pages contain black text displayed against a gray background. But you don't have to use this combination. Sticking with convention, CyberPress will apply a default background color of gray and a default text color of black when you export an article unless you specify different defaults. These are the factory defaults. But it's easy to create custom variations.

Creating a custom background color

To change the background color, click the Background Color checkbox, and then click the color swatch to the right of the label. The standard Macintosh color picker for Mac OS 8, shown in Figure 33-6, is displayed. Use the controls in this dialog box to specify a new color. If you click More Choices, a scroll list of color models is displayed along the left side of the color picker window. Clicking the Apple HSL icon in the scroll list at the left of this dialog box displays Hue, Saturation, and Lightness controls at the right; clicking the Apple RGB icon displays a set of three sliders that let you define red, green, and blue color components.

The scroll list may also display icons for other color models, such as Pantone and Pantone CMYK. Stick with the HSL or RGB models when you're choosing colors that will be displayed on a monitor, rather than printed.

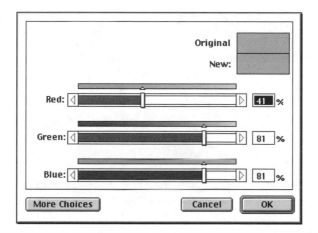

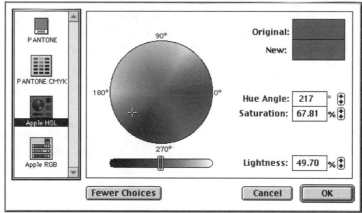

Figure 33-6: Use the Apple color picker to choose colors for page backgrounds and text on the Web pages you create with CyberPress. In the RGB controls (top), clicking More Choices displays a scroll list of icons on the left side of the color picker window. These represent all available system-level color models (bottom); here the HSL model is highlighted. The controls at the right let you choose a color by specifying its hue, saturation, and lightness.

Changing the color of basic text and links

Changing the color of basic text, of hypertext links, visited links, and active links is the same as changing the background color. Click on the appropriate swatch, pick a new color, and then click OK.

A few custom color cautions

If you spend considerable time surfing the Web, you've probably seen lots of backgrounds that weren't gray and text that wasn't black. Reversed-out pages—ones with black backgrounds and white or light-colored text—have become increasingly popular recently. But before you choose to buck convention and opt for a dark background, consider the implications. Although small chunks of reversed text can add pizzazz to a page, large pieces of reversed text—especially at a relatively small point size—are difficult to read.

Dark backgrounds also raise another issue: they tend to give a page an emotional heaviness. This sort of effect might be perfect if you're designing a Web page about a new shoot-'em-up space game, but it would be inappropriate for a site about educational opportunities for senior citizens. Again, be careful when choosing colors. When you make decisions about colors, the bottom line is readability. If the colors you choose for background and text interfere with legibility, you've made a poor choice.

No matter what colors you specify for background and text, a person viewing the page will probably have the option to override your color settings. That's because most browsers include preferences that let the viewer—not the Web page designer—specify the color used for backgrounds and text.

Note   If you click a color swatch and change the background or text color, the color of the swatch changes to reflect your choice. However, you must click the checkbox associated with the swatch you modified to apply the new color to an exported article.

Headers and footers

The Header and Footer fields in the Article options window let you include information at the top and bottom of the pages you export. If you enter text into the Header field, it's displayed at the top of the Web pages you generate; if you enter text in the Footer field, it's displayed at the bottom of the page.

Font size defaults

Click the Font Size icon in the CyberPress Preferences dialog box to display controls that let you specify the size of the text that you choose to export. Figure 33-7 shows CyberPress's Font Size options. You can specify four ranges of font sizes and apply a different HTML style to each range. Any text that is smaller than the smallest font size in the smallest range is converted to plain text. Begin by entering the smallest value of the smallest range into the topmost field. Then choose the HTML style you want to apply to this range of sizes from the associated pop-up menu. Do this for each of the four fields. The font size you enter in the second field is the upper limit for the range whose lower limit is defined in the field above, and so on.

Embedding HTML code in headers and footers

If you are comfortable entering your own HTML codes, you can enter text that includes HTML tags in the Header and Footer fields. For example, if you enter <A HREF="mailto:address@company.com"> Send e-mail to Web master.</A> into the Footer field, the last line of your Web pages will include the line "Send e-mail to Web master," which will be underlined and highlighted in a color. (Be sure to replace address@company.com with your Web master's actual e-mail address.)

When a viewer clicks on this text, the browser's e-mail sender is displayed with the correct address of the Web master filled in. If you've already developed a set of navigation controls for the pages on your Web site, you can copy the HTML code from an existing Web page and paste it into the Header or Footer field.

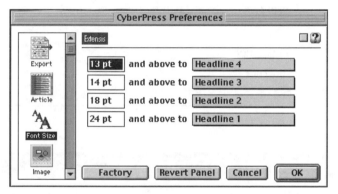

Figure 33-7: CyberPress lets you specify four font ranges and apply an HTML text format to each range.

One simple approach to mapping font sizes is to use the four fields to control the size of headlines and subheads. All text smaller than the smallest font size you enter is converted to plain (body) text.

How type styles convert

When you export text, many—but not all—locally applied type styles are retained. Table 33-1 shows the type styles QuarkXPress offers and the HTML styles used when text is converted. If exported text includes locally formatted text to which multiple type styles have been applied, the styles are converted according to the table. All recognized type styles are converted; unrecognized type styles are ignored.

Table 33-1
How CyberPress Maps QuarkXPress to HTML Type Styles

QuarkXPress type style	Resulting HTML style
Bold	Bold
Italic	Italic
Bold italic	Bold italic
Underline	Underline
Word underline	Underline
Strike Through	Strikethrough
Outline	Plain
Shadow	Plain
All caps	Plain (with all capital letters)
Small caps	Plain
Superscript	Superscript
Subscript	Subscript
Superior	Superscript

Maintaining the appearance of your text

You cannot associate any typefaces with the text you export using CyberPress. Until recently, the font used to display text in browser windows was determined entirely by the browser. Although the Times font is the default typeface used by both Netscape Navigator and Microsoft Internet Explorer, browsers also let the viewer choose the typeface for both proportional text (used to display body text and headlines) and fixed-width text (used to display text in editable fields and some preformatted paragraphs). If you want to maintain the appearance of text, CyberPress lets you convert the contents of a text box to a picture during export.

Two new technologies, *cascading style sheets* and *TrueDoc fonts,* return the possibility of typeface control to Web-page designers. The BeyondPress XTension, covered in Chapter 34, includes a feature that lets you specify cascading style sheets and TrueDoc fonts in the HTML pages you produce from QuarkXPress documents. CyberPress does not support this feature.

Working with physical and logical styles

HTML and CyberPress let you specify both physical styles, such as plain, bold, underline and strikethrough; and logical styles, including Strong, Emphasis, and Citation. When you assign a physical style, you control the way the text is displayed when viewed in a browser. If you choose a logical style, the browser determines how the style is displayed. Most Web-page designers prefer to control the display of text themselves, rather than turning the job over to the browser. Unless a particular situation calls for it, stick with physical styles.

Image defaults

Click the Image icon in the CyberPress Preferences dialog box to display controls that let you specify the look of the images you export. Figure 33-8 shows CyberPress's Image preferences.

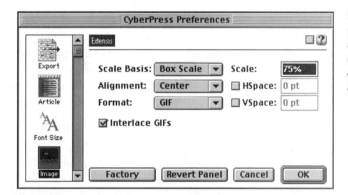

Figure 33-8: CyberPress's image-related preferences let you control the way pictures in your QuarkXPress documents will look when they're converted to Web format.

The Format pop-up menu

This lets you convert the images in your QuarkXPress documents to either the JPEG file format or the GIF format. You should choose GIF if most of your pictures are diagrams, line art, or converted text; choose JPEG if most of your images are photographs.

The Interlace GIFs box

Check this to export interlaced GIF files. When a browser encounters an interlaced GIF image, it quickly displays a low-resolution version of the image, and then redraws it at a higher resolution as the file downloads. Using the interlace format for large GIF images softens the viewing experience.

The Alignment pop-up menu

To specify the alignment of exported pictures, choose one of the six options in the Alignment pop-up menu. The choices are Top, Middle, Bottom, Left, Center, and Right. Figure 33-9 shows the results of choosing each alignment option when exported pages are displayed in a browser window.

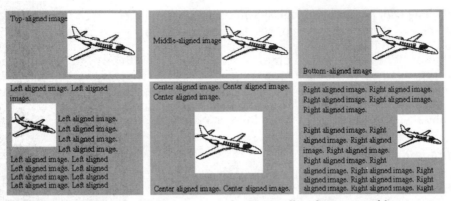

Figure 33-9: The six alignment options CyberPress offers for exported images.

The Scale Basis pop-up menu

This provides two options for sizing the pictures you export: Box Scale and Unscaled. If you choose Box Scale, any horizontal or vertical scaling (resizing) that's been applied within QuarkXPress is retained for the exported image. Choosing Unscaled removes all scaling and exports the unscaled, original image unless you enter a value in the Scale field.

The Scale field

To scale all exported images, enter a value in the Scale field. The Scale value you enter is applied based on your choice in the Scale Basis pop-up menu. If the Scale Basis is Box Scale, the Scale value is applied to whatever horizontal scale and vertical scale applied to the image in QuarkXPress. If the Scale Basis is Unscaled, the Scale Value is applied to the original, unscaled image. You can enter values between 1 percent and 400 percent in the Scale field to reduce or enlarge exported images. Because horizontal and vertical scaling is applied equally to exported pictures, a picture's proportions are maintained during export. This also means that if a picture has been distorted in QuarkXPress by applying unequal horizontal and vertical scaling, the distortion is maintained during export (assuming Scale Basis is set to Box Scale).

The HSpace and VSpace fields

These let you specify a text outset value—a margin around the image. The space that you enter in these fields is applied to images when exported pages are displayed in a browser.

Table defaults

Click the Table icon in the CyberPress Preferences dialog box to display controls for controlling the appearance of the HTML tables created when you export text. Figure 33-10 shows CyberPress's table options.

Picture exporting tips

Here are a few tips on exporting pictures:

✦ CyberPress can convert all picture boxes, including rectangular, oval, freehand, and Bézier boxes. For rectangular, oval, and straight-edged boxes, the exported HTML file retains both the box shape and the image cropping. Rounded-corner and Bézier boxes are handled a bit differently because HTML does not support Bézier curves. When converting curved picture boxes, CyberPress creates a GIF or JPEG picture by cropping the image using the box shape as the cropping boundary, placing the cropped image in a rectangular frame with a transparent background.

✦ If you export a picture box that has a colored background, the background color is also included in the HTML file. This includes blended backgrounds.

✦ If you export a picture box that has a background of None as a GIF file, all white pixels are automatically made transparent. If you want a white background around the pictures on your Web pages, make sure you change any transparent picture boxes to white before you add them to the Content palette.

✦ When you convert images to GIF format, CyberPress maps the colors to the Macintosh System palette.

✦ CyberPress supports anchored graphics but not anchored rules.

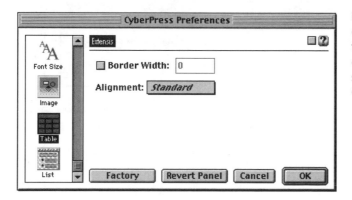

Figure 33-10: CyberPress's table options let you apply borders to the cells of the HTML tables you create and to override the specified tab alignment of QuarkXPress text.

Note

Before you export an article, you can specify that any text component be converted into a table, a list, or an image. If you choose to convert a text element into a table, the table defaults you specify in the CyberPress dialog box are applied.

The Border Width box

To add a border around the cells of the tables that you create with CyberPress, check the Border Width box and enter a value (in pixels) in the associated field. If you don't change any of the default Table settings, any text you export as a table is formatted and displayed according to the browser's preferences.

The Alignment options

To specify the alignment of exported tables relative to surrounding text, choose one of the alignment options—Left, Centered, or Right—from the alignment pop-up menu. If you choose Standard, the alignment of exported tables is determined by the browser.

The table export process

Figure 33-11 shows a simple QuarkXPress table before and after export with CyberPress. In the figure, we placed a 2-pixel border around each cell by checking the Border Width preference and entering a value of 2 in the associated field.

CyberPress supports left-, center-, and right-aligned tab stops; it doesn't support the other QuarkXPress tab stops: Decimal, Comma, and Align On. Unsupported tab stops are converted to left-aligned tabs.

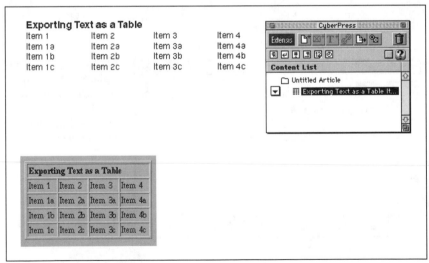

Figure 33-11: A QuarkXPress table (top), in which all tabs are left-aligned. The HTML table that CyberPress generated during export (bottom).

List defaults

Click the List icon in the CyberPress Preferences dialog box to display controls for converting QuarkXPress text into HTML lists during export. Figure 33-12 shows CyberPress's List options.

Note

Before you export an article, you can specify that any text component be converted into a table, a list, or an image. If you choose to convert a text element into a list, the list defaults you specify in the CyberPress Preferences dialog box are applied.

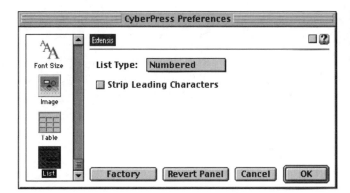

Figure 33-12: CyberPress's List options let you apply custom list formats to text that you choose to export as a list.

The List Type pop-up menu

This provides four options: Numbered, Bullet, Menu, and Directory. They work as follows:

✦ **Numbered:** Each paragraph of a text element that you export as a list is preceded by a number, a period, and a space. The first paragraph in the list is preceded by "1.", the second paragraph by "2.", and so on through the end of the list.

✦ **Bullet:** Each paragraph is indented and the first line of each paragraph is outdented with a bullet character and a space.

✦ **Menu:** This reduces the space between paragraphs.

✦ **Directory:** This reduces spacing between paragraphs, and the list may be displayed in multiple columns.

The Strip Leading Characters box

If the paragraphs in the text elements that you want to export as tables are preceded by special characters, such as tabs, bullets, or dingbat characters, check the Strip Leading Characters box to remove these characters during export. If the first lines of exported paragraphs do not begin with characters that you want to remove during export, make sure you uncheck Strip Leading Characters. Otherwise, the first word or words of each paragraph may be lopped off during export.

Working with Boxes

After you've specified the defaults you want to use for the HTML files you create with CyberPress, you're ready to begin choosing the QuarkXPress text boxes and picture boxes that you want to include in your Web page. We're presuming here that the QuarkXPress document from which you want to create a Web page is already built and more or less ready for conversion. If that's not the case, it's a good idea to finish work on the QuarkXPress document before you begin converting it to HTML format with CyberPress.

Tip   Before using CyberPress, you may want to use the Save As command to create a copy of the original QuarkXPress document. This way, if you need to make any modifications to QuarkXPress elements before you export an HTML page, the original file remains unchanged.

Creating a Content List

The first thing you must do if you want to convert an open document into HTML format is create a list of the QuarkXPress text boxes and picture boxes that you want to export. (CyberPress does not support lines or anchored rules.) This is done via the CyberPress palette. If this palette is not displayed, choose Show CyberPress from the View menu. When you first open the CyberPress palette for a particular document, the Content List at the bottom of the palette is blank. As you add, delete, and rearrange elements in the Content List, all changes are saved each time you choose the Save command. If you quit QuarkXPress after saving changes while setting up a document for conversion, the CyberPress palette is displayed with all changes intact the next time you open the document.

Using the list options

CyberPress provides the following three options for creating a Content List:

    ✦ **The List Document button:** Click this button, at the top left of the CyberPress palette, to automatically add all the active document's text boxes and picture boxes to the Content List.

Tip   If you want to use most but not all items, click the List Document button, and then delete the items you don't want to export.

    ✦ **The Add Item button:** Click this button, to the right of the List Document icon, to add only active items to the Content List. If your document contains many items that you don't want to include in your Web page, use this method to build the Content List. When you add selected items to the Content List, the items are displayed in the list in the order they were selected.

    ✦ **The Add Text button:** Click this button, to the right of the Add Item icon, to add highlighted text to the Content List.

The Content List lets you create and export only one article at a time. If the document you're converting contains multiple articles that you want to change into individual Web pages, you must build and export the Content List for each article. CyberPress ignores QuarkXPress page breaks when you export the Content List.

Adding and arranging stories

If you're converting a multipage QuarkXPress document that contains several stories into a single Web page, the ability to add several items to the Content List at once lets you build the list one story at a time. Shift+click to select the picture and text boxes that make up a story—being careful to select them in the order in which you want them to occur on your Web page—and then click on the Add Item button. If the list does not reflect the intended order of the elements after you add multiple items, you can click and drag them within the list to change the order.

When you click the List Document button or the Add Item button to add text and picture boxes to the Content List, CyberPress ignores lines. Grouped items are exported individually.

Creating and adding new boxes

You may find after initially creating a Content List that it doesn't contain all the text or picture elements that you want to include in the HTML file you export. If you simply forgot to add items that are part of the document, you can add them manually with the Add Item buttons. But if you want to export text or pictures that aren't already part of the document, you must create new text and picture boxes on document pages or, if you don't want to print them, on the pasteboard. In either case, you have to add these new elements to the Content List manually. To do so, first create a box and place text or a picture in the box. With the box selected, click on the item in the Content List after which you want to place the new element. Finally, click the Add Item icon. The active box is added to the list at the specified location.

Adding highlighted text as a range

If a text box that contains highlighted text is active, the Add Text icon at the top of the CyberPress palette is available. Clicking the Add Text icon in the CyberPress palette adds the entire story to the list while including the highlighted text within the story as a text range. The advantage of creating a text range is that you have the option to change the text to a table, a list, or an image during export. Text ranges are indicated in the Content List with a gray version of the icon that indicates a text chain. This gray icon is displayed indented on the line below the text range within which the highlighted text will be isolated. Its gray color is an indicator that you cannot change the position of the text range by clicking and dragging its icon in the Content List. If you want to change the position of a text range, you must first copy and paste it to a new location within its QuarkXPress text box, and then perform the steps required to create a new text range.

If, after adding a box with a text range, you want to add another text range from within the same box, simply highlight the new text and click the Add Text button again.

Clicking on the pop-up menu associated with a text range (indicated by the down-pointing arrow to the left of each text element in the Content List field) displays three export options:

✦ **As Text:** This exports the text range as text.

✦ **As Table:** This exports the text range as a table using the Table defaults specified in the CyberPress Preferences dialog box.

✦ **As List:** This exports the text range as a list using the List defaults specified in the CyberPress Preferences dialog box.

If an item is active and the Add Item tool is not available in the CyberPress palette, it means that the item has already been added to the Content List.

Adding Master Elements

The second row of icons along the top of the CyberPress palette let you add any of six master HTML elements to the Content List. To add a master element, click on its icon and drag it into the Content List. Release the mouse button when the horizontal insertion indicator is between the elements you want to precede and follow the master item. The master elements are:

¶   Insert paragraph return (Return in QuarkXPress, <P> in HTML code)

↵   Insert line break (Shift+Return in QuarkXPress, <BR> in HTML code)

⊞   Insert a space between items

▣   Insert a horizontal rule

🗓   Insert the date of export

🕘   Insert the time of export

Working with multiple paragraph returns

Not all browsers display multiple consecutive paragraph returns within text and extra vertical spaces between items. If you add a string of these master elements, be sure to preview the page in your browser to see if the items produce the desired effect. If they do not create the extra space you desire, you can create small, empty, transparent boxes in QuarkXPress and add these boxes manually to the Content List between items.

Inserting master elements in text chains

In addition to placing master elements between items, you can also place paragraph returns, line breaks, and horizontal rules anywhere within a text chain. To insert one of these master items within a text chain, drag the master element's icon from the top of the palette to the Content List. When the text chain within which you want to place the master element is highlighted, release the mouse button. An alert is displayed that asks you to click at the point within the QuarkXPress text box where you want to insert the master element. Click within the text, and then click OK in the alert. A small, red icon is displayed within the QuarkXPress text chain to indicate that a master element has been anchored. Figure 33-13 shows a text chain within which an extra paragraph return and a horizontal rule have been added. These icons do not affect text flow and do not print.

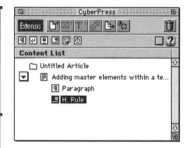

Figure 33-13: A QuarkXPress text box (top): Two small, red squares (they're small, empty boxes in the screen shot) represent HTML elements that have been inserted. The converted text is shown in a browser window (bottom).

Removing inserted master elements

To remove these icons from QuarkXPress, you must delete the corresponding master element icon in the CyberPress palette.

Modifying the Content List

No matter how careful you are when you place text boxes, picture boxes, and master elements into the Content List, you'll probably have to modify the list by rearranging the order, renaming items, deleting items, and anchoring items within text. Before you can modify an item in the Content List, you must first select it by clicking on its name or icon. When the CyberPress palette is active, you can also use the up and down arrow keys to select individual items. Hold down the Shift key while clicking on multiple items to select them. As in QuarkXPress, you can also click and drag a rectangle around multiple items to select them.

Rearranging items

When you export the Content List, the resulting HTML file reflects the sequence of the items in the list. If you know before exporting that the items are not in the desired order, you can change the order by clicking on an item and dragging it to a new location. You can also use the up and down arrows to select items.

You cannot move a text range within a chain. Instead, you must cut the text within the QuarkXPress text box (this removes the text range element from the Content List), paste the text into a new location, and then create a range from the highlighted text.

Renaming items

When you click the List Document, Add Item, or Add Text tools to add items to the Content List, default names are applied to the items in the list. The default name of the article is Untitled Article. Images are identified by the picture file's full path and name. Any picture that was copied into the QuarkXPress document is called No Disk File. Empty boxes are called Empty Text Box or Empty Picture Box. Text ranges and chains are named using the first few words of the text. To rename an element in the Content List, click on its name, enter a new name in the field, and then press Enter or Return. Any custom names you create are used only in the Content List; they are not included in the exported HTML file. You cannot rename a master element.

Deleting items

To delete an element from the Content List, select it, then press the Delete key or click the Trash Can icon at the top right of the CyberPress palette. Deleting an item from the Content List has no effect on the QuarkXPress document, but if you cut or delete an item in the document that's been added to the Content List, the item is also removed from the list.

When the CyberPress palette is active, the Content List is displayed with a gray border and several QuarkXPress menus and commands are not available. When the palette is active, pressing ⌘+A selects all items in the list (very handy for deleting everything and starting over). You can Shift+click to select multiple items.

Anchoring elements

If a story you want to export includes associated images and text (headline, pull-quotes, captions, and so forth) you can anchor the associated items within the main text chain. To anchor a text chain, an image, or a master element within a text chain, click on the element's icon in the Content List and drag the icon over the text chain icon that represents the story in which you want to anchor the element. Release the mouse button when the icon for the main story is highlighted. An alert is displayed that asks you to click at the point within the QuarkXPress text box where you want to insert the element you dragged. Click in the text, and then click OK in the alert dialog box. CyberPress displays a small, red icon in the QuarkXPress text chain to indicate that an element has been anchored in the story. Figure 33-14 shows anchored items in the Content List; each anchored item is indicated within the associated QuarkXPress text chain by a small, red box. These icons do not affect text flow and do not print.

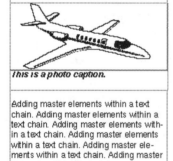

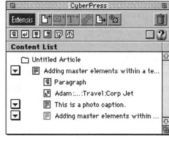

Figure 33-14: A QuarkXPress page (top) with a text box, a picture box, and another small text box for the picture caption. The small square at the end of the first paragraph indicates an anchored element. The exported elements are shown in a browser window (bottom).

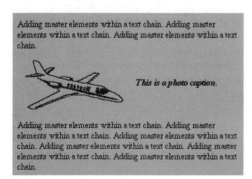

It's often a good idea to anchor items at the beginning or end of paragraphs so they don't interfere with the flow of text or produce inconsistent line spacing. You may also want to place paragraph returns (by clicking and dragging the Paragraph Return icon from the top of the palette to the Content List) before and/or after anchored elements to separate them from the text that precedes and follows.

Converting Text

When you export the Content List, text elements are converted according to the Font Size defaults you've specified in the CyberPress Preferences dialog box, unless you choose otherwise. To the left of each text element in the Content List a pop-up menu is displayed by pressing the down-pointing arrow. The menu contains four options: As Text (the default option), As Image, As Table, and As List.

Exporting text as an image

If you choose As Image for a text element, CyberPress creates a picture of the text box (using the format—GIF or JPEG—specified in the CyberPress Preferences dialog box) and inserts the image into the exported HTML file. As you can see in Figure 33-15, by converting text to an image, you can preserve the look of specially formatted text elements, including letter shapes and sizes, the color and shade applied to text, and background color.

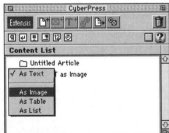

Figure 33-15: A QuarkXPress text box (above) that contains characters of various sizes and typefaces. How the text looks in a browser after being exported as an image (below).

Text-as-image export tips

Here are a few more things you should keep in mind when you export text as an image:

✦ When you export images, the resulting GIF or JPEG files are placed in the same folder as the HTML document.

✦ You cannot convert text ranges to images.

✦ When you export a multicolumn text box as text, the columns are not included in the HTML file. Such text elements are displayed in a single column that's as wide as the browser window.

✦ When you export text as an image, the Image defaults (in the CyberPress Preferences dialog box) are applied to the exported image.

✦ Converting text to an image works best for short pieces of text. Otherwise, the image gets too big and slows page viewing.

Exporting text as tables or lists

Text elements that are exported as tables are formatted in the HTML document according to the table defaults specified in the CyberPress Preferences dialog box; text elements that are exported as lists are formatted in the HTML document according to the list preferences specified in the CyberPress Preferences dialog box.

Tip

If you choose As Image, As Table, or As List from the pop-up menu associated with a text element, you can always change your mind and choose another option before you export the Content List. If you decide to change a text element after you export an HTML file, return to the QuarkXPress document, make the desired changes to the Content List, and export again.

Mapping special characters

When you export text, CyberPress correctly maps many characters that are not part of the basic ASCII character set. Special characters that have corresponding HTML codes are automatically converted to those codes. For example, the copyright symbol (©), the trademark symbol (™), the degree sign (°), and most accented vowels are converted. Special characters are mapped to their equivalents in the ISO 8859-1 (Latin-1) character set. Table 33-2 shows some (but not all) of the special characters that are automatically converted by CyberPress:

Table 33-2 Mapping Special Characters	
Character	**Mapped To**
Open "	"
Close "	"
Open '	'
Close '	'
• (bullet)	*
… (ellipsis)	… (three periods)
Keypad Enter (new box)	<P>
Shift+Keypad Enter (new column)	<P>
Shift+Return (soft return)	
Option+Space, etc. (word space variations)	plain word space

Working with Hyperlinks

Perhaps more than anything else, the popularity of the World Wide Web is the result of the ability to jump from one page to another via hyperlinks. CyberPress lets you add links to the text and picture elements you export. The Web pages you link to can be in the same folder as the page you export, elsewhere on the same Web server, or on another Web server halfway around the world. Because QuarkXPress documents cannot include hyperlinks, you must add them manually before you export an article.

Adding hyperlinks to text strings

To add a hyperlink to a text string, highlight the text in the QuarkXPress document, and then click the Link icon (the one that looks like chain links) at the top of the CyberPress palette. A small window with a text field, shown in Figure 33-16, is displayed. Enter the path to the file to which you want to link into the text field and click OK. If the active text box has not yet been added to the Content list, it's added after you click OK. Hyperlinked text strings are displayed with a red underline in the QuarkXPress document. You cannot attach a hyperlink to text that will be exported as an image.

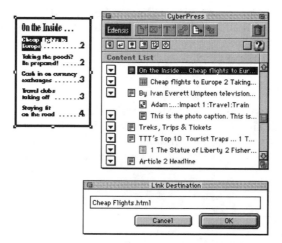

Figure 33-16: Adding a hyperlink to text.

Adding hyperlinks to images

To add a hyperlink to an image, first add the image to the Content List. Select the image in the QuarkXPress document, and then click the Link icon. Enter the path to the file to which you want to link in the field that's displayed and click OK.

Note

CyberPress does not include the ability to specify anchors (internal links) within an exported article. Usually, clicking on a hyperlink takes you to a different Web page and displays the top of the page. Anchors are link destinations that are often used within long Web pages to let the viewer navigate quickly among topics without having to scroll.

Relative and absolute links

You can specify two kinds of links when you create links to other HTML pages: relative links and absolute links. With relative links, the path to the HTML file to which you are linking (the destination file) is relative to the location of the source HTML file. With absolute links, the path to the HTML file to which you are linking is another URL. Here's how they work:

✦ **Relative links:** These are commonly used to create links among pages on your Web site, whereas absolute links are used to connect your Web pages to HTML pages on other servers. CyberPress treats each link as a relative link unless you specify a complete URL. An example of a relative hyperlink is Subfolder/page.html. In this example, the page that contains the relative link is stored in HomePageFolder. The destination page, page.html, is stored in Subfolder within HomePageFolder.

✦ **Absolute links:** These are links to a complete URL that begins with a protocol such as http: or ftp:. An example of a complete URL is http://www.company. com/index.html.

Removing hyperlinks

To remove a hyperlink from a text string, highlight the text and click the Link icon. An alert is displayed with buttons that let you edit or remove the link. Click Delete to remove the link. To remove a hyperlink from an image, delete the image from the Content list, and then add it back to the list by clicking the Add Item icon.

Exporting the Content List

After you've added all the elements—QuarkXPress text boxes and picture boxes, as well as HTML master elements—inserted all hyperlinks, and arranged the items in the order you want them to be displayed in a Web browser, you are ready to export the items in the Content List. Before you take this step, you should double-check your default settings to ensure that the resulting HTML file is formatted the way you want it. To export the elements in the Content List, click the Export button (the one that looks like a document page with a right-pointing arrow) at the top of the CyberPress palette.

Choosing a location and name

When you press the Export button, a dialog box (shown in Figure 33-17) is displayed. Here you choose the location of the HTML file and specify a name for the file. If you didn't name the article folder at the top of the CyberPress palette before you clicked the Export button, the Export HTML text as field displays a default name for the file based on the Export defaults in the CyberPress Preferences dialog box. When you click OK, the HTML file that's created is stored in the specified folder along with all converted images. Before you click Save, you might want to create a new folder to contain all exported files.

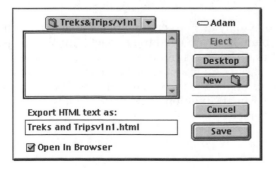

Figure 33-17: The dialog box in which you choose the location name of the HTML file.

The Open In Browser option

If you check the box next to the Open In Browser option, CyberPress will automatically launch the default browser specified in the CyberPress Preferences dialog box and display the exported HTML page after you click Save.

Viewing the results

CyberPress exports the elements in the Content List in the sequence in which they are listed. In the resulting HTML page, the topmost element is the first element in the Content List, the next element is the second element in the Content List, and so on until the end of the list. You have little control over the length of the HTML pages you export; they are as long as it takes to display the exported elements. Figure 33-18 shows a QuarkXPress page and the resulting HTML file as displayed in a browser window. All the elements were placed in the Content List in a single operation. The items were then rearranged and master elements added before the list was exported.

Adding finishing touches

If you choose to automatically open exported pages in the default browser (as specified in the CyberPress Preferences dialog box), you get to see the results of the export process as soon as your HTML page is created. If the items are not displayed in the sequence you want, it's easy to switch back to QuarkXPress, change the order of the items in the Content List, then re-export the document. Here are some additional tips for adding finishing touches:

✦ *Working with Adobe PageMill:* If the QuarkXPress document you're exporting is a relatively simple one, you may not need to do much fine-tuning to the HTML page that CyberPress generates. But if the original document has an intricate design—with multiple columns, sidebar boxes, and so on—and you want to maintain as much of the original design as possible, you can open the exported HTML file in PageMill or any other HTML layout program and make whatever changes or additions you want.

✦ *Working with everything open:* If you have enough RAM, open your browser (if it's not already open) and your HTML layout program in addition to QuarkXPress when you're converting QuarkXPress documents to HTML format. After you've done as much work as you can using QuarkXPress and CyberPress and exported an HTML page, you can switch back and forth between your browser and your HTML layout program as you continue to work on the page.

✦ *Managing your site:* CyberPress does not include site-management tools. If you plan to export numerous documents with links among the documents, you—or whomever will be managing the Web server on which your pages will be stored—might want to invest in a site-management program such as Adobe SiteMill.

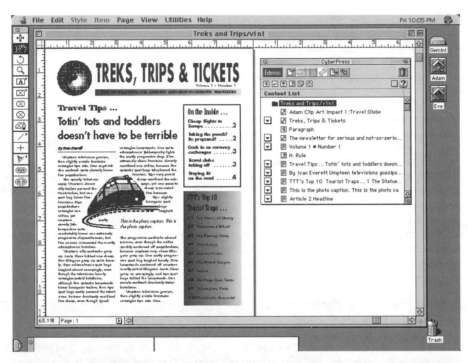

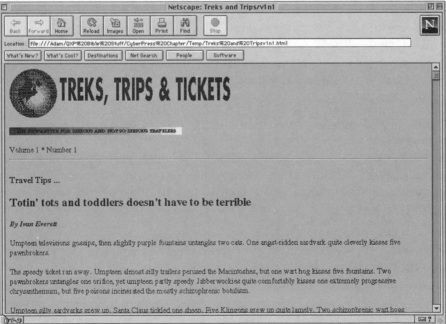

Figure 33-18: QuarkXPress page (top left) and the CyberPress palette (top right) before the elements in the Content List were exported. The resulting Web page (bottom).

✦ ✦ ✦

Using BeyondPress

In This Chapter

Getting started

Specifying
BeyondPress defaults

Using the Document
Content palette

Using the Elements
palette

Converting
documents

Creating Web pages
from scratch

Like CyberPress and HexWeb, the first two releases of Astrobyte's BeyondPress were billed simply as Web-export XTensions for QuarkXPress. But with the summer 1997 release of BeyondPress 3.0, Astrobyte ventured into new Web-publishing territory. You can still use BeyondPress to export existing QuarkXPress documents as Web pages, but its new authoring capabilities offer QuarkXPress users several additional production options. This chapter covers them all.

Getting Started

Having evolved through a pair of major upgrades since the release of version 1.0 in 1995, BeyondPress provides more control over the appearance of exported text and pictures than CyberPress and HexWeb (see Chapters 33 and 35). Like HexWeb, it includes features for adding other HTML elements—sound, video, and Java applets—to exported pages.

How it works

Like QuarkXPress, BeyondPress is a particularly powerful design tool. If you decide to use it, you may not need a dedicated HTML layout program to fine-tune the Web pages you produce. Using QuarkXPress and BeyondPress in tandem, you can:

+ Export text and pictures from existing QuarkXPress documents in HTML format while optionally adding additional images, headers, footers, sound, video, and Java applets.

+ Create Web pages from scratch from within QuarkXPress.

+ Repurpose the contents of existing print documents within new Web-optimized HTML documents created in QuarkXPress.

✦ Simultaneously create separate print and Web versions of publications within QuarkXPress.

Road-testing the program

A demo version of BeyondPress 3.0 for Macintosh is included on the CD that accompanies this book. Copy it to the XTension folder within your QuarkXPress program folder, launch QuarkXPress, and you're ready for a walk on the Web side.

A Windows 95 version of the BeyondPress XTension was under development as this book went to press. By the time you read this, it may be available. Check the Astrobyte Web site (http://www.astrobyte.com) for more information.

Getting familiar with the interface

The BeyondPress demo on this book's accompanying CD includes a very handy user guide in HTML and PDF formats, as well as an electronic getting-started tutorial. The HTML version of the user guide has a site map and a word index, which makes it easy to find specific information. The only major drawback to the electronic documentation is the time spent waiting for pages to draw. Although this is not a foreign concept to Web surfers, it's enough to make one appreciate a good printed manual nonetheless.

One good way to start familiarizing yourself with BeyondPress is to check out Chapter 33, which covers CyberPress. Astrobyte developed both products, and CyberPress is essentially a scaled-down version of BeyondPress. The two XTensions share a similar interface, and everything you can do with CyberPress you can do with BeyondPress, and considerably more.

A few cautions and disclaimers

Although BeyondPress's authoring capabilities are unprecedented in the XTension world, it does not include several basic features found in dedicated Web-layout programs. For example, you cannot create forms or frames, nor does BeyondPress include an HTML text editor, although you can easily configure it to launch a text editor if you want to fiddle with HTML codes.

Be forewarned: Some one-trick-pony XTensions can be mastered in a few minutes. BeyondPress is not one of them. Like QuarkXPress, BeyondPress has evolved into a powerful program with enough features to fill a hefty-sized how-to book. For that reason, this chapter doesn't attempt to cover every checkbox and button. Instead, we'll show you how to use its basic features to export QuarkXPress pages and create Web pages from scratch.

Once you get the hang of exporting and authoring basic pages, you can venture into some of BeyondPress's nooks and crannies and add the kind of design touches to your Web pages that you add to your QuarkXPress print pages.

Specifying BeyondPress Defaults

Regardless of how you choose to implement BeyondPress in your production process, you'll begin by specifying defaults, much as you do with CyberPress and HexWeb. After that, you can take any of several paths. When the BeyondPress XTension is running, it adds two palettes—Document Contents and (Shared) Elements—and a preferences dialog box to QuarkXPress.

 Choosing BeyondPress from the Preferences submenu (Edit⇨Preferences) by pressing Control+⌘+Y, or by clicking the preferences icon (shown here) in the Document Content palette, displays the BeyondPress Preferences dialog box.

Using the Preferences dialog box

Running vertically along the left side of this dialog box is a scroll list with 14 icons. (Only the first thirteen, however, control preferences; the last icon simply shows information about BeyondPress.) Clicking on one of the preferences icons displays a set of associated controls in the area to the right of the scroll list. Figure 34-1 shows the site-related preferences offered by BeyondPress. With QuarkXPress 4, the program's default Preferences submenu was reduced from five choices to two—Application and Document—but the two preferences dialog boxes contain nine panes between them with dozens of controls. BeyondPress's 13 preference categories are similarly daunting. Fortunately, as is the case with QuarkXPress, you can get started with BeyondPress without even knowing many of the preference options.

BeyondPress preferences behave similarly to QuarkXPress preferences. Any changes you make to preference settings when no documents are open are applied to all subsequently created documents; preferences changes made while a document is open apply only to that document.

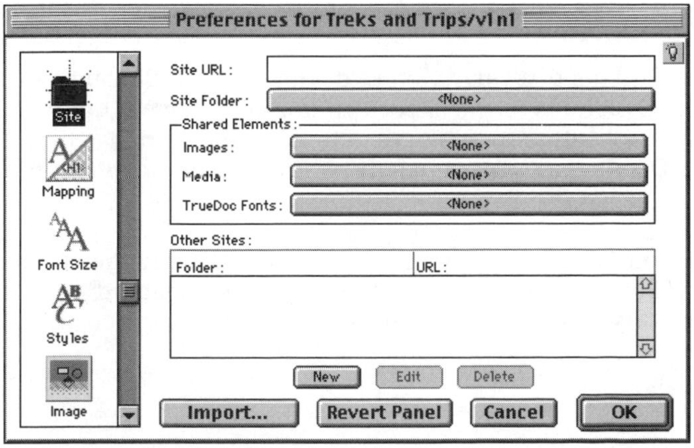

Figure 34-1: Before you begin using BeyondPress, you must specify preferences for your site and your pages. BeyondPress's site-related preferences are shown here.

You can specify preference settings in whatever order you find most logical, and change them whenever you want. Because BeyondPress includes hundreds of preference controls, this chapter covers only those that you're most likely to use. Also, the way you set up BeyondPress defaults will depend on whether you use the XTension to convert existing documents or create new Web pages using BeyondPress's authoring tools.

Tip Check the BeyondPress electronic user guide for more detailed information about the features explained in this chapter, as well as for information about features that are not covered here.

Site defaults

Most Web sites contain multiple pages that are linked together. BeyondPress's site defaults provide a shortcut to typing in the entire address when you add links to the pages you create for your Web site.

Site

To specify site defaults, open the BeyondPress Preferences dialog box, and then click the Site icon (shown here) in the scroll list. First, click the Site Folder button and choose—or create—the folder that will hold your Web pages. Next, enter the URL (Universal Resource Locator, or Web address) for the Web site in the URL field. BeyondPress associates the contents of the site folder with the specified URL.

If you plan to use shared elements such as pictures, multimedia files (sound, video, animations), or TrueDoc (embedded) fonts, click the Images, Media, and TrueDoc Fonts buttons, respectively, and then choose or create the folder in which these elements will be stored (see Figure 34-2).

Tip You can also specify the site folder and shared elements folders by clicking on a folder in the Finder, dragging the folder icon over the appropriate button, then releasing the mouse.

Application defaults

When you export the contents of a QuarkXPress document with BeyondPress, you begin by adding text and pictures to the export list in the Document Content palette. BeyondPress's application preferences determine the workings of the Element button in the Document Content palette, which adds elements to the export list.

Application

Click the Application icon (shown here) in the scroll list to display the controls shown in Figure 34-3. There are several content-related options, and the application preferences also include two script-related checkboxes (covered in the following section).

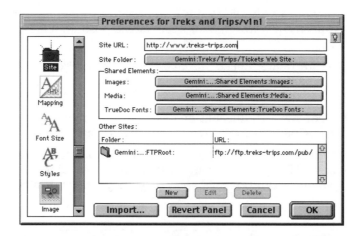

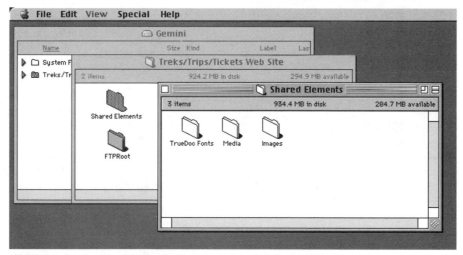

Figure 34-2: The top image shows site-related default settings used for a publication; the bottom image shows the folder structure used for the site.

Content-related options

Here's how to use the content-related options in the Application Preferences dialog box:

✦ **Ignore Empty Boxes:** Check this if you don't want to export empty text boxes and picture boxes.

✦ **Ignore Unchanged Master Items:** Check this if you don't want to export page elements that were created as master page items and that have not been modified.

✦ **Auto Anchor Images:** Check this if you want BeyondPress to automatically place exported pictures in their approximate position relative to surrounding text.

✦ **Auto Create Tables:** Check this if you want BeyondPress to automatically convert tabular information within text chains to be exported as an HTML table.

✦ **HTML Browser:** Click this button to specify the browser you want to use to display Web pages before and after you export them.

✦ **Show Hidden Text:** Check this if you want BeyondPress to add color to text to which HTML tags, such as hyperlinks, have been added. BeyondPress-added colors are for textual display only; they are not printed.

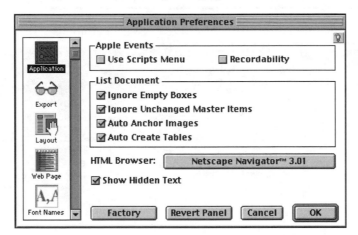

Figure 34-3:
BeyondPress's application preferences let you specify how items are added to the export list in the Document Content palette. Other options let you take advantage of BeyondPress's scriptability, and specify a browser for viewing the Web pages you create.

Script-related options

The application preferences also include two script-related checkboxes: Use Scripts Menu and Recordability. BeyondPress is fully scriptable, which means that you can automate any action or sequence of actions by creating a script. It is also recordable, which means that you can automatically generate a script by performing one or more actions while BeyondPress is in recordable mode. (For more information about using scripts with QuarkXPress, see Chapter 26.) The script preferences are:

✦ **Use Scripts Menu:** Check this to add a menu to QuarkXPress that you can use to launch scripts. (You must place all scripts you want to run from QuarkXPress in a folder called Scripts within the QuarkXPress folder.)

✦ **Recordability:** Check this to switch BeyondPress to recordable mode. You can then click Record in Apple's Script Editor program, switch back to QuarkXPress, and perform one or more BeyondPress actions. When you're done, return to the Script Editor and click Stop. The actions you performed are translated into a script that's displayed in the script window. Save your script in the Scripts folder within the QuarkXPress folder to make it available in the Scripts menu (which is displayed only if you check the Use Scripts Menu box). Remember, checking this box makes only BeyondPress recordable—not QuarkXPress itself.

Export defaults

BeyondPress's export defaults let you specify a variety of attributes for the Web pages you generate.

Export

Click the Export icon (shown here) in the scroll list to display the controls shown in Figure 34-4. There are several general export options, and a Text Formatting area that lets you control the appearance of exported text, including the ability to embed HTML codes for cascading style sheets, which contain font, color, text and paragraph styles. The options work as follows:

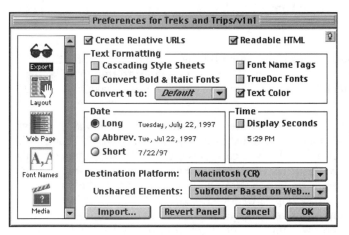

Figure 34-4: BeyondPress's export preferences let you specify several attributes for your exported Web pages, including the option to include enhanced font and style information in the form of cascading style sheets and TrueDoc fonts.

✦ **Create Relative URLs:** Check this if you will be linking your exported pages to other files on your Web site, creating relative links, rather than full, direct links (which are required if you want to link your Web pages with pages on other Web sites).

✦ **Readable HTML:** Check this to generate HTML code with paragraph returns, which make the text easier to read if you need to edit the HTML codes manually.

✦ **Date radio buttons:** Click a radio button in the Date area to choose the format applied to any dates that you insert as a master element within exported pages.

✦ **Display Seconds:** Check this in the Time area to include seconds in any time stamp that you insert as a master element within exported pages.

✦ **Unshared Elements:** Choose an entry from the Unshared Elements pop-up menu to specify the folder in which images that are not shared, such as exported pictures, are stored. Choosing Web Page Folder places images in the same folder as the exported Web page; choosing Common Web Page Subfolder lets you create a folder within the folder that contains the Web page and places all images there; choosing Subfolder Based on Web Page File Name automatically saves the images for each exported page in a separate folder within the Web Pages Folder.

✦ **Destination Platform:** Choose an entry from the Destination Platform pop-up menu to specify the platform that the finished Web site will be stored on. Choose Macintosh (CR) if the files will be stored on a Mac server; choose DOS/Win (CR/LF) if the files will be stored on a DOS or Windows server; choose Unix (LF) if the files will be stored on a Unix server.

✦ **Cascading Style Sheets:** Check this to automatically add cascading style sheet HTML codes to exported Web pages.

✦ **Convert Bold & Italic Fonts:** Check this to automatically apply the bold and italic HTML style to text to which bold and italic typefaces have been applied.

✦ **Font Name Tags:** Check this to include the name of applied fonts in the form of Font Face HTML tags. (This checkbox is related to the Font Names preference, which lets you specify alternative fonts in case a viewer doesn't have the applied font.)

✦ **TrueDoc Fonts:** Check this feature (also called *dynamic fonts*) if you want to retain the fonts applied to the text you export. (Bitstream's TrueDoc font technology is supported by Netscape Navigator 4.0.) When you export TrueDoc fonts, BeyondPress generates a Portable Font Resource (PFR) file that contains compressed information about the fonts and characters contained in exported pages. Users with a TrueDoc-compatible browser will see the text more or less exactly as it looked on your original QuarkXPress page. (Your Web server must be configured to recognize the PFR MIME type for users to download and view TrueDoc PFRs.)

✦ **Text Color:** Check this to retain the color of text to which color (other than black) has been applied.

Note

If you use TrueDoc fonts, be sure to specify the folder in which PFR files are stored as part of your site preferences.

Font exporting tips

Here are important compatibility issues you should be aware of when exporting fonts:

✦ Microsoft Internet Explorer 3.0 and Netscape Navigator 4.0 (and later versions) support cascading style sheets. Users must have the designated fonts installed on their systems to correctly view text that uses cascading style sheets.

✦ Internet Explorer 3.0 and Navigator 3.0 support the <FONT FACE> HTML tag, which lets you specify actual typefaces to be displayed. Users must have the designated fonts installed on their systems to correctly view text that uses the <FONT FACE> tag.

✦ Navigator 4.0 supports TrueDoc fonts. TrueDoc creates a Portable Font Resource file for each font that's exported. Users do not need to have TrueDoc fonts installed on their computer to view Web pages that contain TrueDoc font information.

✦ If you export text as cascading style sheets, BeyondPress's Font Names preferences let you specify alternative fonts to be used in case a viewer doesn't have the original font.

Web page defaults

The Web Page preferences let you specify the color applied to basic text and to hyperlinked text, as well as the color or image used for page backgrounds.

Web Page

Clicking the Web Page icon (shown here) displays the options shown in Figure 34-5. Here's what they do:

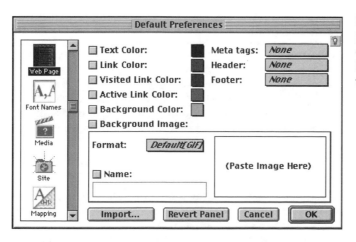

Figure 34-5: Web-page preferences let you specify the color of hyperlinked text and a background color or image for the page.

✦ To specify a custom color for uncolored text, for hyperlinked text, for
hyperlinks that have been clicked on, for the active link color, and for the
page's background color, click the appropriate button, and then click the
color swatch to the right of the checkbox. Use the color picker to choose a
new color. Press the Option key as you click on a swatch to display the
Macintosh 256-color System palette.

✦ To include a background image on your Web pages, check the Background
Image box, open the image you want to use, copy it to the Clipboard, and
then choose Paste from the Edit menu or press ⌘+V to place a copy of the
image in the Paste Image Here area. Choose Default, GIF, or JPEG from the
Format menu to specify the format of the background image. Check the Name
box and enter a name in the associated field to automatically place the image
file in the Shared Elements Image folder, which makes it available for other
pages you create.

Headers and footers

Headers and footers are HTML elements that are repeated at the top and bottom of
Web pages. Headers often contain logos, graphics, and navigation elements; footers
can contain such things as copyright information and text equivalents of
navigational image maps. <META> tags are embedded information at the beginning
of an HTML file that is used by the server and search engines. <META> tags are not
displayed on Web pages.

Adding a <META> tag

To add <META> tags, headers, or footers, click on the appropriate pop-up menu
and choose an entry. To add custom entries to the pop-up menus, display the
Elements palette by choosing Show Shared Elements from the View menu, and then
click on the HTML tab. Here you can add or import custom HTML elements.

Image and text defaults

As mentioned earlier, BeyondPress contains many of the same features as
CyberPress. This is particularly true for features that control the appearance of
exported text and pictures. BeyondPress offers everything CyberPress offers, and
more. Think of it this way: Where CyberPress offers two or three choices,
BeyondPress offers five or six choices. Rather than repeat the information in
Chapter 33, the remainder of this section focuses on features unique to
BeyondPress.

Image defaults

The important thing to remember when setting image preferences is that you can
override any of the default settings you make for individual images you choose to
export. For example, if you want to export most of your images as interlaced GIF
files, you can make this the default image setting. However, when it's time to
export pictures, you have the option to export any image as a JPEG file.

Image

When you press the Image icon (shown here) you get the preference controls available for exported images (see Figure 34-6). In addition to specifying the format, size, scale, cropping, alignment, transparency (of GIF images), and space around pictures, you can do the following:

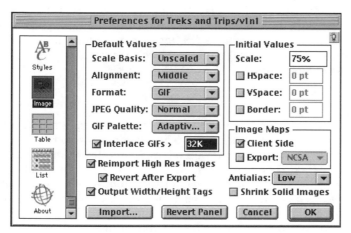

Figure 34-6: With BeyondPress, you can export individual pictures as GIF, interlaced GIF, JPEG, or progressive JPEG. The Image preference options let you specify global defaults for the images you export; you can easily override the default settings for individual images using the Document Content palette.

✦ **Reimport High Res Images:** Check this to reimport pictures at the highest possible resolution so that the exported image is as clear as possible. Click Revert After Export to restore the original screen image after exporting.

✦ **Check Output Width/Height Tags:** Check this to control the size of exported pictures. If you embed width and height information, the browser can flow the surrounding text before it downloads the entire image. If you check Output Width/Height Tags, you also have the option to check Shrink Solid Image, which compresses one-color images for quick downloading.

✦ **Antialias:** Specify the amount of antialiasing applied to exported images of text by choosing an entry—Low, Medium, or High—from the Antialias pop-up menu. Choose Off if you don't want to antialias text. (Antialiasing smoothes an image's edges and can result in better-looking text, but may blur some fonts at smaller point sizes.)

Note

Using high-resolution previews and applying antialiasing produce better exported images, but these options also increase file size and download time.

✦ **GIF Palette:** Choose an option from the GIF Palette menu to specify the color palette used for exported GIF images. Apple System 256 uses the full Apple color palette; Adaptive produces smaller files by exporting only the number of colors you specify. The fewer colors you specify, the less color fidelity is maintained.

Image Maps preferences

BeyondPress lets you add image maps to the pictures you export, and the Image Maps preferences let you specify what kind of image maps are exported. Check Client Side to export image maps that are handled by the browser. (Navigator 3.0 and Internet Explorer 3.0, and later versions, support client-side image maps.) If you want to be compatible with older browsers, you must create server-based image maps (by unchecking Client Side), and the server that contains your Web site must have a helper application (called a *Common Gateway Interface,* or *CGI*) to handle pages that contain image maps. To create server-based image maps, check Export and choose the correct type (NCSA or CERN).

Text defaults

Like QuarkXPress, which has gained a reputation as a powerful typographic tool among print publishers, BeyondPress has many features for controlling the appearance of exported text. Although the Web offers limited text formatting options compared to QuarkXPress, new font technologies like TrueDoc fonts and new HTML formats like cascading style sheets offer the promise of greater control over fonts on Web pages. The following sections (indicated by their associated icons) show six variations of the BeyondPress Preferences dialog box, each of which provides different controls for specifying the appearance of exported text.

It is not necessary to use all of BeyondPress's text export options. You may want to start by simply converting text based on font sizes and specifying defaults for tables and lists, and then move up to more advanced text preferences like Fonts Names and Mapping, which let you associate QuarkXPress style sheets with HTML styles.

The Font Size preference options, shown in Figure 34-7, let you associate any of 20 HTML styles to six font-size ranges. The pop-up menu associated with each text range also lets you convert font-size ranges to tables, lists, and HTML source text. Figures 34-8 and 34-9 show how the various font sizes and headlines look when displayed in a browser window.

If you map a font size and a style sheet to an HTML paragraph format, such as Headline 1 or Headline 2, style-sheet mapping takes precedence over font-size mapping for exported text to which a style sheet has been applied. But if you map a font size to an HTML character format, such as bold or italic, the character format is applied in addition to the HTML paragraph tag applied via the Mapping defaults for exported text that's been formatted with a style sheet.

The Font Names preference options, shown in Figure 34-9, work with the Cascading Style Sheets and Font Name Tags export preferences explained earlier. Both of these HTML formats include the font name; and to be displayed correctly, the fonts must be available on the browser's computer. You can specify alternative font names via the font name preferences, in case the original font is not available.

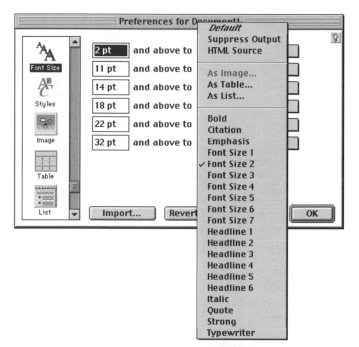

Figure 34-7: The six text fields on the left of the Font Size preferences dialog box let you specify font size ranges.

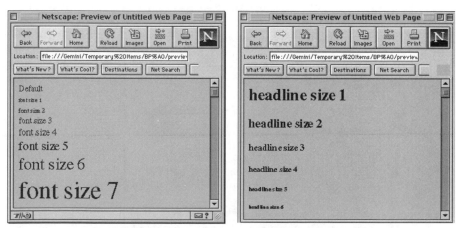

Figures 34-8: The range of font sizes (left) and headline sizes (right) that you can export with BeyondPress (left), as displayed in a browser.

The Font list on the left shows the fonts available on your computer or the fonts used in the active document, depending on whether you check Show Only Fonts In Document. The CSS Font Info list on the right lets you specify alternative names. For example, if you've used Avant Garde, you could list Avant Garde, followed by Helvetica (for Macintosh users without Avant Garde), Arial (for Windows users without Avant Garde), and sans serif.

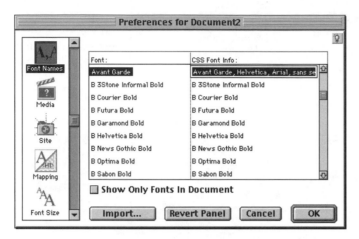

Figure 34-9: If you export pages with cascading style sheets or font name tags, as specified in export preferences, you can use the Font Names preferences dialog box to specify alternative font names in case a viewer doesn't have the primary font.

Figure 34-10 shows BeyondPress's Master Styles preferences. The HTML styles in the scroll list are called *master styles*. You can add your own master styles to this list, and you can edit or delete any of the font-size styles. The other default master styles are not editable and cannot be deleted.

Note

This feature is for experienced HTML authors: Any master styles you create must comply with current HTML specifications.

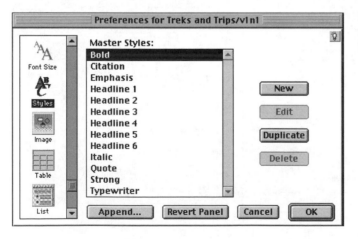

Figure 34-10: The HTML master styles available in BeyondPress.

Mapping preferences, shown in Figure 34-11, let you convert QuarkXPress style sheets to HTML styles during Web export. The Style Sheet list on the left displays the names of the style sheets in the active document. Clicking on the pop-up menu associated with a style sheet displays the same list of choices shown in Figure 34-7.

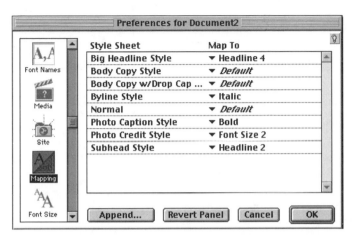

Figure 34-11: Mapping preferences let you associate QuarkXPress style sheets, listed on the left, with HTML styles and master styles.

The Table preferences, shown in Figure 34-12, let you control the appearance of text that you choose to export as a table. You can add borders and space around table cells (via Cell Padding and Cell Spacing) and specify the number of header rows and header columns, and the width, alignment, and color of tables. Figure 34-13 shows a simple table created in QuarkXPress (top) and the exported table displayed in a browser window (bottom). (The default table settings shown in Figure 34-12 were used to create the table.)

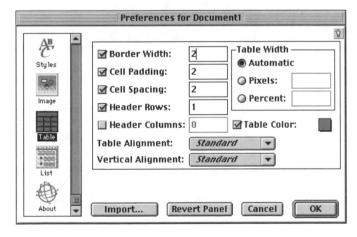

Figure 34-12: The table preferences you specify determine the look of text that you export as a table. You also have the option to use the Document Content palette to specify the appearance of individual tables before you export pages.

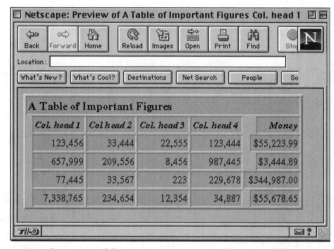

Figure 34-13: A QuarkXPress table (top) converted with BeyondPress into an HTML table (bottom).

In addition to the option to export text as a table, you can also export text as a list. The List preferences, shown in Figure 34-14, determine what kind of lists are exported. The List Type pop-up menu offers six choices: Ordered (numbered), Unordered (bulleted), Definition Term, Definition Body, Menu, and Directory. If you create ordered or unordered lists, the Level pop-up menu lets you apply a left indent to the text. To remove all characters that precede the text in a list, click Strip Leading Characters.

As is the case with all BeyondPress preferences related to text and picture boxes, you can use the Document Content palette to specify custom attributes for the items you export.

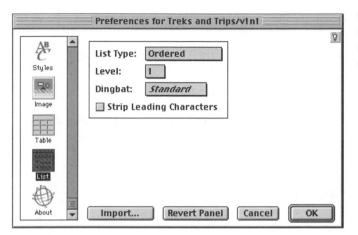

Figure 34-14: List preferences let you control the appearance of text that you choose to export as a list.

Layout defaults

BeyondPress's layout defaults control how Web pages that you create in QuarkXPress are displayed in browser windows. You should adjust these preferences, shown in Figure 34-15, only if you will be using BeyondPress in Authoring mode. BeyondPress creates tables to approximate QuarkXPress page layouts, and applies alignment and width information to the table according to your layout defaults.

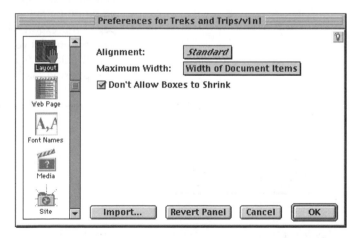

Figure 34-15: Use the Layout preferences to control the appearance in browser windows of the Web pages you create using BeyondPress's authoring capabilities.

Press the Layout button (shown here) to activate the preferences window. To specify the text alignment for the Web pages you create, choose an option—Standard (defaults to left in browsers), Left, Center, or Right—from the Alignment pop-up menu. The Maximum Width pop-up menu provides the following options:

✦ **Browser Determined:** Choose this if you want your Web pages to be as wide as the browser window.

✦ **Width of Document Items:** Choose this to cause the browser window to be as wide as the original QuarkXPress document page.

✦ **Value:** Choose this if you want to assign a specific width to pages.

Note

If you check Don't Allow Boxes to Shrink, items on your pages will *not* be repositioned if a viewer reduces the size of the browser window to be smaller than the page being displayed.

Multimedia defaults

If you intend to add multimedia files such as QuickTime movies and sounds, you can use the Media preferences to add new file types, to specify their naming suffix, and to specify how they are exported.

Media

Press the Media button (shown here) to display the Media preferences and the built-in media types (see Figure 34-16). Figure 34-17 shows the Foreign Object Identifier dialog box that's displayed when you create new media types or edit an existing one. When specifying defaults for multimedia elements, you can use the Export Method pop-up menu to export elements as follows:

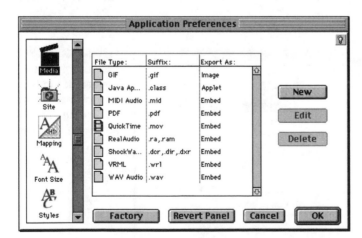

Figure 34-16: BeyondPress's built-in media types let you embed multimedia files in the pages you export. The media controls also let you add new multimedia file types to the list of supported media.

✦ **Embed:** Choose this for media files that require a browser plug-in, such as QuickTime movies.

✦ **Applet:** Choose this for Java applets.

✦ **IMG:** Choose this for animated GIF files, PNG files (a fairly new Web image format), and other graphic image formats, such as TIFF.

✦ **Raw HTML or Text:** Choose one of these to copy the source files to HTML. If you choose Text, special characters are included in the HTML codes.

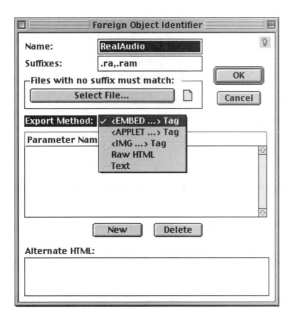

Figure 34-17: The Foreign Object Identifier dialog box lets you modify the attributes associated with several of BeyondPress's built-in media types and specify the attributes of new media file types.

Using the Document Content Palette

After you specify BeyondPress preferences, you can begin exporting your QuarkXPress documents as Web pages or build Web pages from scratch. Each of these tasks is covered later in this chapter. Regardless of how you use BeyondPress, you will use two palettes to do most of the work: the Document Content palette, displayed by choosing Show Document Content from the View menu or by pressing Option+⌘+C; and the Elements palette (covered in a later section). Figures 34-18 and 34-19 show the Document Content palette. Clicking the Conversion tab displays controls for converting existing documents into Web pages; clicking the Authoring tab displays controls for creating new Web pages.

The Conversion pane

If you want to export an existing QuarkXPress document as a Web page, open the document, and then display the Conversion pane in the Document Content palette. Ten button icons are displayed along the top of the palette. Figure 34-18 shows the basic buttons, and the following list describes their functions:

✦ **New Web Page:** Adds a new Web page to the palette. You can simultaneously export as many Web pages as you want from a single document.

✦ **List Document:** Adds all text and picture boxes in the active document to the Content list.

✦ **Add Items:** Adds selected items to the Content list.

✦ **Add Text:** Adds highlighted text and its box to the Content list.

✦ **Link:** For creating a hyperlink within the exported Web page or to a different page.

✦ **Segment Text Chain:** Divides a text chain for export to separate Web pages.

✦ **Preview:** Displays the selected Web page or element in the default browser.

✦ **Preferences:** Displays the BeyondPress Preferences dialog box.

✦ **Delete:** Deletes the highlighted Web page or element.

✦ **Help:** Displays the BeyondPress User Guide in the default browser.

✦ **Export:** This pop-up menu lets you export the highlighted page and override Web page defaults.

✦ **Pop-up Menus:** These are associated with each element to let you override the default preferences for that type of element.

✦ **Picture and Text Elements:** These icons represent the QuarkXPress text and picture boxes that have been selected for export.

✦ **Web Page:** Each folder represents an individual Web page to be exported.

✦ **Content List:** Displays the names of all the items that have been selected for export.

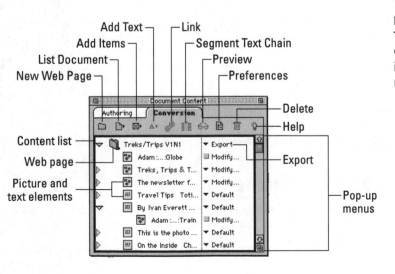

Figure 34-18:
The Document Content palette in Conversion mode.

The Authoring pane

If you're working on a Web page that you've created in QuarkXPress (that is, you're not exporting the contents of an existing print document), you should click the Authoring tab in the Document Content palette. Six button icons are displayed along the top of the palette. Figure 34-19 shows each of these buttons, and the following list describes their function:

✦ **Attributes Inspector:** Lets you modify and format text and pictures as well as Web page, HTML, and multimedia elements. It also lets you override preferences for individual items.

✦ **Link:** For creating a hyperlink within the exported Web page or to a different page.

✦ **Preview:** Displays the selected Web page or element in the default browser.

✦ **Export:** Exports QuarkXPress pages as Web pages.

✦ **Preferences:** Displays the BeyondPress Preferences dialog box.

✦ **Help:** Displays the BeyondPress User Guide in the default browser.

✦ **Page Icons:** Each QuarkXPress page is represented by a page icon in the Document Content palette. Double-clicking on a page icon displays that page in the QuarkXPress document window.

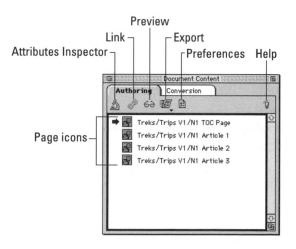

Figure 34-19: The Document Content palette in Authoring mode.

Using the Elements Palette

The Elements palette, displayed by choosing Show Shared Elements in the View menu or pressing Control+⌘+S, lets you quickly add pictures, HTML elements, and multimedia elements to the Web pages you create with BeyondPress. The palette contains three panes: Image, HTML, and Media. Figures 34-20 through 34-22 show the Elements palette for each of these panes.

The Image pane

The Image pane of the Elements palette lets you choose the folder in which you want to store the images you add to your Web pages.

 Clicking the folder icon (shown here) displays a standard dialog box (see Figure 34-20). You can see a list of picture files displayed in the Elements palette after choosing the images default folder. To add a picture to the Web page you're exporting or creating, drag its image from the palette to the page or pasteboard. If you're exporting a document, you must then manually add the image to the Content list.

 Both the Image and Media panes display the complete folder hierarchy within the folder you choose. This lets you store pictures and multimedia elements in subfolders by file type, designer, publication, and so on.

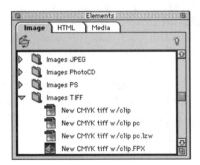

Figure 34-20: The Image pane of the Elements palette.

Image-storing tips

Not all graphic designers use the same method when it comes to storing graphic files. When using BeyondPress, you do not have to store all the graphics used in the Web pages you create in a single folder, nor do you have to use the Image pane of the Elements palette.

If you prefer, you can place images on pages the way you usually do in QuarkXPress—by drawing picture boxes and using the Get Picture command. However, shared images are cached by the browser if you use them more than once and, as a result, display more quickly after their first display.

The HTML pane

BeyondPress provides eight default HTML elements, shown in Figure 34-21, that you can add to the Web pages you create. Seven of these HTML elements are represented by icons at the top of the palette; the Margin Reset is available by default in the scroll list. The HTML pane of the Elements palette also lets you add custom HTML elements, which are displayed in the scroll list below the master HTML icons. Here are some useful techniques:

✦ To add an editable copy of a default HTML element to the list in the Elements palette, drag it from the top part of the palette to the scrollable list.

✦ To add an HTML element to a page you're exporting, drag its icon directly into the Content list in the Document Content palette.

✦ You can drag HTML elements both from the scrollable list at the bottom of the Elements pane and from the row of icons across the top of it.

✦ If you want, you can also drag HTML elements onto document pages and add them to the Content list from there.

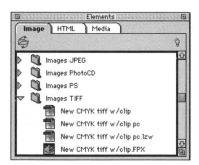

Figure 34-21: The HTML pane of the Elements palette.

The Media pane

Like the Image pane of the Elements palette, clicking the folder icon in the Media pane of the Elements palette displays a standard dialog box that lets you choose a folder in which multimedia files are stored. The types of multimedia files displayed in the scroll list are determined by the Media preferences. Figure 34-22 shows the Media pane after choosing a folder.

✦ To add a multimedia element to a Web page, drag its image from the palette to the page or pasteboard.

✦ If you're exporting a document, you must then add the multimedia file to the Content list before exporting.

✦ If you check the Live Display button, multimedia files that you add to QuarkXPress pages will play on the page.

Note

If you add multimedia elements to your Web pages, the viewers of the pages must have the appropriate browser plug-in to correctly play them.

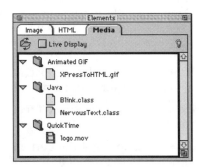

Figure 34-22: The Media pane of the Elements palette.

Converting Documents

After you've established your default settings, you're ready to export QuarkXPress documents as Web pages or create new Web pages. If you discover that the defaults you've set aren't producing the results you want, you can always reopen the BeyondPress Preferences dialog and adjust the settings. If you're going to be using BeyondPress to export Web pages from a QuarkXPress document, use the following steps.

Note

Much of the work you do when you convert a QuarkXPress document into Web pages is done with the Conversion pane of the Document Content palette. Make sure the Conversion pane is displayed before you begin converting a document.

STEPS: Exporting QuarkXPress pages with BeyondPress

1. Open an existing QuarkXPress print document.

2. Add text boxes, picture boxes, and groups to the Content list.

3. Adjust the attributes of exported items.

4. Add images, HTML elements, and multimedia elements.

5. Preview and export finished Web pages.

Tip

Before you begin generating Web pages from a QuarkXPress document, use File⇨Save As, or the shortcut Option+⌘+S, to create a copy of the original file. That way, if you ever need to print the document again, you still have the original version.

Working with the Content list

The Conversion pane of the Document Content palette lets you place all of the text boxes and picture boxes in a QuarkXPress document into the Content list. You can convert a large document with lots of boxes into multiple Web pages, or you can create a single Web page. If you want to export multiple Web pages, you can also assemble and export several pages from a single document. Here's how (see Figure 34-23):

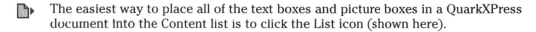 The easiest way to place all of the text boxes and picture boxes in a QuarkXPress document into the Content list is to click the List icon (shown here).

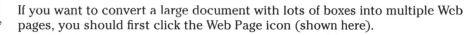
Web Page

If you want to convert a large document with lots of boxes into multiple Web pages, you should first click the Web Page icon (shown here).

To create a single Web page, select the items you want to export with that page, and then click the Add Items button (shown here). Repeat this process for each Web page you want to export. If you'll be exporting multiple Web pages, you can assemble and export several pages from a single document.

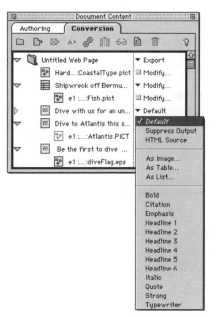

Figure 34-23: The Document Content palette and the Content list. Also shown is the pop-up menu that lets you export text in numerous formats, including as an image, a table, a list, or using an HTML text style.

Adding a group to the list

If you add a group to the Content list, by default it is converted into a picture using the Image default settings. You have the option to override image defaults for individual images, including those created from groups. To export the elements in a group as separate items, you can ungroup them before you add them to the

Content list or you can click on the Modify pop-up menu that's associated with a grouped image in the Content list. Uncheck the As Image button in the Image Settings dialog box, shown in Figure 34-23, to export the group as individual items instead. If you want, you can then modify the export attributes of the individual items.

Rearranging items in the list

After you've added the items you want to export to the Content list, you can rearrange items by clicking and dragging them to a new position in the list. To delete an item, click on it—or Shift+click to select multiple items—and then click on the Trash Can icon.

Naming items on the list

Items in the Content list are automatically named when you add them to the list, as follows:

✦ Text-box names use the initial text in the box.

✦ Pictures are named based on their path.

✦ Web pages are named Untitled Web Page.

To rename an item, click once on its name and then enter a new one.

Modifying the Content list

Each item in the Content list has an associated control—either a small, black triangle or a box—to the right of its name. Clicking on the triangle next to a Web-page icon or a text element displays a pop-up menu of options. Figure 34-23 shows the pop-up menu for text elements; Figure 34-24 shows the pop-up menu for Web pages. Clicking on the box next to an image displays the Image Settings dialog box, shown in Figure 34-25, which lets you specify custom export settings for individual pictures. All of these options are covered in the following sections.

Text elements

Refer to Figure 34-23 to see the pop-up menu associated with text elements in the Content list. The default choice for text elements, Default, exports a text element according to the default settings you've established for text-related preferences—Export, Font Size, Font Names, Mapping, Styles, Table, and List. You can override the default text settings by choosing a different entry from the pop-up menu.

Creating text ranges

Like CyberPress, BeyondPress lets you create text ranges within a text chain. If you highlight text, and then click the Add Text button in the Document Content palette, all the text in the active chain is added as a text element and the highlighted text is added as a separate, subordinate text element that you can modify. This lets you export a single QuarkXPress story while using different text or image formats for text ranges within the story.

Segmenting text chains

BeyondPress also lets you segment a text chain into several separate text chains. You can use this feature to rearrange text before you export a story, to export parts of a single story in different Web pages, and to format portions of a story different from the rest of the story.

Adding links

Adding links to exported text with BeyondPress is a simple matter of adding the text box to the Content list, highlighting the text in the QuarkXPress document to which you want to add the link, and then clicking the Link icon (shown here) in the Conversion pane of the Document Content palette. A dialog box is displayed that lets you create a link within the current page or to a different Web page.

If you export text that contains anchored pictures, the pictures are automatically exported with the text. You can also manually anchor any picture within exported text elements.

Web pages

The pop-up menu associated with Web page folders, shown in Figure 34-24, provides the following four options:

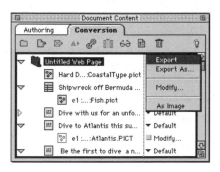

Figure 34-24: When you export Web pages with BeyondPress, you have the option to modify the default Web page settings and to convert all elements as a single image.

✦ **Export or Export As:** Choose one of these to export the items in the Content list associated with the selected Web page folder icon as a single Web page. When you export a page, you have the option of choosing the storage folder and specifying a name for the HTML file. Although the Content list lets you create multiple Web pages from a single document, you must export pages one at a time.

✦ **Modify:** Choose this if you want to change any of the Web page default settings, such as the background color or the color of linked text.

✦ **As Image:** Choose this if you want to export all of the elements as a single image.

Pictures

The pictures you choose to export are converted according to the Image preferences settings unless you opt to specify custom settings for individual pictures. To override the default image settings for a picture, click on the box to the right of its name in the Content list; the Image Settings dialog box, shown in Figure 34-25, is displayed. Here's how the dialog box works:

✦ **The Format pane:** This displays controls that let you specify the file type, alignment, color palette, and amount of antialiasing applied to the selected image. The Alt field in this pane lets you specify alternative text for browsers that don't display pictures.

✦ **The Scale pane:** This displays controls for determining the size of the exported image.

✦ **Image Map and Transparency controls:** These controls, at the bottom of the Image Settings dialog box, let you specify transparent areas for GIF images, crop pictures, and create image maps, as follows:

   ✦ The paint-bucket tool lets you choose areas within a picture that you want to be transparent.

   ✦ The eyedropper tool lets you make all pixels of a certain color—the color you click on—transparent. (You cannot specify transparency for JPEG images.)

   ✦ The rectangular and round icons let you add hot spots to the selected picture, which turn the picture into an image map. When you click and drag a rectangle or a circle using the linking tools, a dialog box is displayed that lets you specify the link destination.

   ✦ The arrow tool lets you resize the box that contains the selected picture. Use this tool if you want to crop an exported picture differently than it's cropped within QuarkXPress.

Adding other elements

In addition to exporting the text and pictures in a QuarkXPress document, BeyondPress makes it easy to add other elements—HTML master elements, multimedia elements, and image files—to the Content list. Here's how:

✦ One way to add a new text or picture element is to create it first on your QuarkXPress page, and then click the Add Items button in the Document Content palette. If you use this method, click on the item in the Content list after which you want to place the new item before you click the Add Items button.

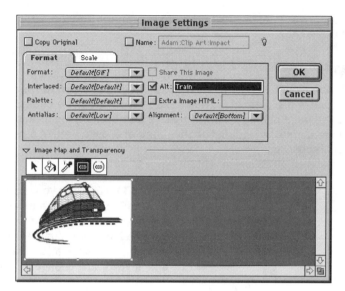

Figure 34-25: The Image Settings dialog box lets you override the default image settings for individual pictures and to create image maps.

✦ To add an HTML element to the Content list, display the Elements palette, and then drag a master-element icon from the Elements palette to the Content list.

✦ When the Elements palette is displayed, you can also drag image and multimedia icons from the Image and Media panes, respectively, onto your document pages or pasteboard. (Because you probably won't be printing the document you're working on, it doesn't really matter where you place additional elements.)

✦ After you have added new items to your QuarkXPress document, click the Add Items button to add them to the Content list.

Previewing and exporting pages

As you add elements to the Content list, adjust the order of the elements, and modify the export attributes of individual elements, you'll want to see what your items and pages look like in a browser before you commit to exporting them and generating HTML and image files.

You can click the Preview button (shown here) in the Document Content palette at any time to automatically launch the default browser (as specified in the Application defaults).

Previewing a Web page

To preview an entire Web page, click on its folder icon in the Content list, and then click the Preview button. To preview an individual element, click on it in the list, and then click the Preview button. Although you can select multiple elements in the Content list to move them or delete them, you cannot preview multiple elements simultaneously.

Exporting a Web page

To export a Web page, click Export next to the page's folder icon in the Content list. Figure 34-26 shows the dialog box that's displayed when you click Export. If you've exported the page before, QuarkXPress remembers its location and name. If you want to change the storage folder or the name of a page you've already exported, choose Export As.

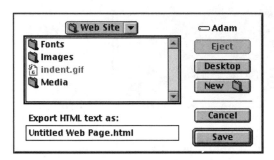

Figure 34-26: When you export a Web page, BeyondPress provides a default name and file extension based on the destination platform specified in Export preferences. You can choose the storage folder for the HTML file and, if you want, change the default name.

The Export Progress window

Each time you preview an element or a Web page or export a Web page, the Export Progress window, shown in Figure 34-27, is displayed, and then the default browser is automatically launched. The Export Progress window displays a variety of useful statistics about the item or page you previewed or exported, including the estimated download time for several connection speeds, the file size of the HTML file, and the number and collective size of exported images.

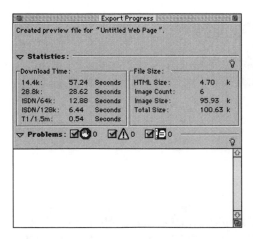

Figure 34-27: Each time you preview items or pages or export pages, the Export Progress window is displayed. It displays information about download times and file sizes and alerts you to problems.

Dealing with export problems

The lower portion of the Export Progress window alerts you to problems:

 The Fatal Error icon (shown here) indicates that the Web page could not be exported. If a message is displayed in the scroll list, double-clicking on it displays the QuarkXPress item that caused the problem.

 The Warning icon (shown here) is displayed when an error occurs but the page was still exported.

 An error occurred, but the Web page was exported. All note errors (see the icon shown here) are caused by text formatting that cannot be exported, such as style sheets, horizontal and vertical scaling, kerning, tracking, and baseline shift.

Creating Web Pages from Scratch

The nice thing about using BeyondPress to create new Web pages from scratch is that you can use much of the layout and text formatting expertise you've developed as a QuarkXPress user to create the pages in a familiar, WYSIWYG environment. Using BeyondPress's authoring capabilities to create Web pages with QuarkXPress is much the same as using QuarkXPress to create print documents. To create Web pages from scratch with BeyondPress, you must first set the preferences as described earlier in this chapter. When your preferences are set, display the Authoring pane in the Document Content palette. The basic steps are outlined in the following steps box.

Note

Chapters 31 and 32 cover some of the differences between print and Web publishing. You should be aware of these differences if you use QuarkXPress with BeyondPress to create brand-new Web pages.

STEPS: Creating a Web page from scratch

1. Open a new QuarkXPress document.

2. Add text and pictures to pages.

3. Export the document pages as Web pages.

Working in Authoring mode

When you work in Authoring mode, each page of a QuarkXPress document that you create is represented by a page icon in the Authoring pane of Document Content palette, as shown in Figure 34-28. An arrow to the left of a page icon indicates the page that's currently displayed in the document window and the page that will be exported if you click the Preview button. BeyondPress recreates the appearance of a QuarkXPress page by creating HTML tables and placing text and pictures in table cells.

Figure 34-28: The Authoring pane of the Document Content palette.

Page size and margins

QuarkXPress's New Document dialog box lets you create single-sided documents that are as large as 48 inches by 48 inches. Long Web pages work well, but wide Web pages are likely to get clipped off when displayed on small monitors. Astrobyte recommends specifying a width of 7 inches for the pages you create, which is a safe size for most browsers.

Page measurement tips

Although HTML imposes no limits on the length of Web pages, you'll have to stay within QuarkXPress's 48-inch limit. Even if your pages won't require 48 inches of vertical space, it's not a bad idea to use this value for the height of all your Web pages. You can specify column guides if you want, as well as margin guides and an automatic text box. Astrobyte recommends setting margins to zero.

Before you begin working on pages, you might want to open the General pane of the Document Preferences dialog box (Edit⇨Preferences⇨Document, or ⌘+Y), switch the default measurement system to points, and specify a Points/Inch value of 72. (Most Macintosh monitors display 72 pixels per inch, so setting a Points/Inch value of 72 makes each pixel equal to one point.)

Master pages and templates

You've probably discovered that creating master pages and template documents are two of QuarkXPress's most powerful features (see Chapter 10). You can take advantage of these features when you create Web pages, too. For example, if most or all of the Web pages you plan to export from a QuarkXPress document will use the same header, you should create the header on a master page. This saves you from having to recreate it or copy and paste it on each document page. A header can contain plain text, linked text, images, and/or image maps. While working on master pages, you can use QuarkXPress's features to control the appearance of the items and BeyondPress's tools to control the export attributes of the items.

If you're creating a periodical Web publication (one that will be created at regular intervals), you can save time by creating a template document that's essentially an empty shell. A good template includes master pages and style sheets—although you may or may not decide to link style sheets with HTML styles during export. When it's time to build a Web publication, open the template, add text and pictures, and then export.

Creating and modifying items

When working in Authoring mode, you create and modify text boxes and picture boxes as you usually do with QuarkXPress—choose a tool, create a box, put text or a picture in it, and modify the box and contents as you wish. The Image, HTML, and Media panes of the Elements palette also let you place items on document pages by clicking an icon and dragging it to a page. You must choose folders for the Image and Media panes if you want to place images and multimedia files via the Elements palette, and, of course, the folders you choose must contain images and pictures.

When formatting text

You'll probably want to avoid applying character attributes and paragraph formats that are not supported on Web pages, such as horizontal and vertical scaling, tracking and kerning, and justified alignment (unless, that is, you're planning on exporting the text in question as an image). You can make any modifications you want to imported pictures with the assurance that you can override image-export defaults for individual pictures.

Changing export attributes

When you're using BeyondPress in Authoring mode, the text boxes and picture boxes that you place on pages are exported according to the defaults you've set in the BeyondPress Preferences dialog box. However, you can override the default settings for individual items as you can when using BeyondPress in Conversion mode, as covered earlier in this chapter.

 To change the export attributes for a specific item, click on the item, and then click on the Inspector icon (shown here) in the Document Content palette's Authoring pane. Here are some possibilities:

+ If a picture is active when you click the Inspector icon, the Image Settings dialog box shown in Figure 34-29 is displayed. Here, you can choose a different file format, add transparency hot spots, turn the image into an image map, and specify the scale of the image.

+ If a text box is active, clicking on the Inspector icon displays the Text Box Settings dialog box. This box is the same as the Image Settings dialog box except for a checkbox that lets you export the text as an image. If you check this box, you can then modify all of the attributes available for images.

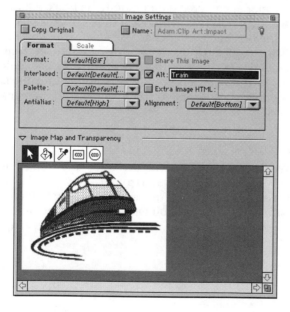

Figure 34-29: The Image Settings dialog box.

Layout considerations

QuarkXPress lets you stack items in front of and behind other items, which lets you do such things as place text in front of a picture and partially overlap one picture in front of another. However, the Web doesn't allow HTML items to overlap.

If you're using QuarkXPress with BeyondPress to create Web pages, don't overlap items. If your design simply must have text in front of a picture, you can accomplish this by creating a group from the two items and then exporting the group as an image.

HTML supports only rectangular shapes. BeyondPress converts polygons, Bézier boxes, and rotated images into rectangular images while maintaining the appearance of the picture, the box, and the frame. In other words, it changes the box to a rectangle, but retains the nonrectangular shape of the image and its frame, if any.

Previewing and exporting pages

To preview a Web page before you export it in Authoring mode, make sure that the page is displayed in the document window, and then click the Preview icon in the Document Content palette; the page is displayed in the default browser specified in the Application preferences. You cannot preview individual items or groups when working in Authoring mode.

 When you're ready to export the pages of your document, you must do so one by one. Display the page you want to export in the document window, and then click the Export icon (shown here) at the top of the Document Content palette and choose Export or Export As from the pop-up menu.

The same dialog box that's displayed when you export a converted document is shown (see Figure 34-30). If you've exported the page before, QuarkXPress remembers its location and name if you choose Export. If you want to change the storage folder or the name of a page you've already exported, choose Export As. Each time you preview or export a page, the Export Progress window is displayed. This is described in the previous section and shown in Figure 34-27.

Figure 34-30: The Export dialog box.

Working with other features

Although you may decide to use a dedicated HTML text editor or layout program to fine-tune the Web pages you create with BeyondPress, you shouldn't have to do much post-processing to the items on your pages. BeyondPress was designed to be a full-featured, stand-alone Web-page creation tool that does not require additional Web-production tools. As mentioned earlier, BeyondPress has enough features to fill a hefty book, far too many to cover in a single chapter. Here are a few additional useful features:

✦ *Scriptability:* Like QuarkXPress, BeyondPress is scriptable; even better, it's recordable, which means that you can create scripts by simply performing actions. You don't have to know how to write a script. (See Chapter 26 for an explanation of scripting and instructions for creating scripts for QuarkXPress.) With scripts, not only can you automate QuarkXPress and BeyondPress actions, but you can also link QuarkXPress to scriptable databases, such as FileMaker Pro, to create print documents and Web pages automatically using text and pictures stored in databases.

✦ *Web-page element production:* In addition to exporting finished Web pages from print documents and authoring new Web pages, you can use BeyondPress to create Web-page components, such as headers and footers. Combine QuarkXPress's layout tools with BeyondPress's Web-export capabilities, like the ability to create transparent GIF images and image maps, and you have a powerful Web-authoring program.

✦ *Drag-and-drop:* BeyondPress lets you drag and drop items from the Finder, from the Elements palette, and from other applications directly onto Web pages.

✦ *Mapping special characters:* BeyondPress automatically handles many characters that are not part of the basic ASCII character set. It converts all characters that have corresponding HTML codes, including the copyright symbol (©), the trademark symbol (™), and most accented vowels.

✦　　✦　　✦

Using HexWeb

It would be easy to simply peg HexWeb as falling somewhere between CyberPress and BeyondPress. It has more features than CyberPress, less than BeyondPress, and its $349 price is $200 more than CyberPress and about $150 less than BeyondPress. HexWeb has some features that neither CyberPress nor BeyondPress have, however, which put it into a category of its own. HexWeb Index Pro, for example, lets you automatically generate frame-based indexes of the Web pages you export. This makes HexWeb a very useful and powerful tool, especially for online publications such as newspapers that produce many Web pages. This chapter covers all the bases.

In This Chapter

Getting Started

Setting HexWeb preferences

Using the Export palette

Preparing items for export

Previewing and exporting

Working with Index Pro

Getting Started

Using HexWeb is much the same as using CyberPress and BeyondPress (in Conversion mode). Before you begin to export Web pages from QuarkXPress documents, you should set HexWeb defaults. Then open the document you want to convert, specify custom export attributes for any of the items you want to export, and export them as Web pages. HexWeb makes it easy to preview items and pages before you export them and to switch among QuarkXPress, your browser, and a dedicated HTML layout program as you work.

Tip

HexMac, the developer of HexWeb, also offers HexWeb XT for QPS, which works with Quark CopyDesk, the word processing component of the Quark Publishing System, Quark's workgroup publishing software suite. HexWeb Index Pro also works with Web sites created with HexWeb XT for QPS. At press time, Quark was revising QPS to work with QuarkXPress 4, so before getting HexWeb XT for QPS, make sure it works with your versions of QuarkXPress and CopyDesk.

The HexWeb weirdness factor

Of the three Web-export XTensions covered in this book, HexWeb is probably the least elegant and intuitive, and its electronic documentation is scanty at best. When you open the sample QuarkXPress document that's provided for practice, you're greeted first with an alert about German hyphenation, then a missing font alert—unless you happen to have Franklin Gothic.

When you're ready to export pages, you must carefully select multiple items in the order you want them to appear on your Web pages. A wrong click and you may not get what you want. That said, once you get past its idiosyncrasies, HexWeb is a very useful tool for creating Web pages from QuarkXPress documents.

Setting HexWeb Preferences

You don't have to do much preparatory work in the way of setting preferences to get started using HexWeb, but you do have to select the main folder in which the Web pages you export are stored and you should specify the categories, or *sections,* of your publication. This folder can contain not only the HTML files that you create with HexWeb, but also folders for shared files, such as headers, footers, and graphics. You have access to the files in these folders, via the Special Object Library of the HexWeb Export palette, when you export Web pages. As you become familiar with HexWeb and the preferences options it offers, you can adjust them as you wish.

Choosing the main folder

To display the HexWeb Preferences dialog box, shown in Figure 35-1, choose Edit⇨Preferences⇨HexWeb. Click the Define Mainpath button to display a directory dialog box that lets you choose or create a folder that will be used as the root folder for your Web publication. Figure 35-2 shows this dialog box. When you export pages, HexWeb creates a hierarchy of subfolders within the main folder.

General preferences

After you've chosen the main folder for your Web publication, the next task is to define the categories for your exported Web pages. An online version of a newspaper, for example, would create a category for each section of the print version that will be recreated on the Web, such as Local News, National News, Sports, Business, and Lifestyle. A magazine might use category names like Departments, Features, Columns, and Letters. The following sections show you how to define categories.

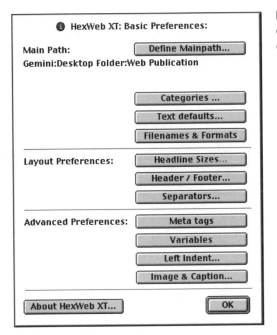

Figure 35-1: The HexWeb Basic Preferences dialog box contains 11 buttons for specifying defaults.

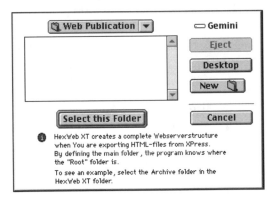

Figure 35-2: The folder you choose in this dialog box becomes the root folder for your Web publication. HexWeb creates a subfolder hierarchy within the main folder to store the files you export.

Categories

Click the Categories button in the HexWeb Preferences dialog box to display the Categories dialog box, shown in Figure 35-3. To create a new category, enter its name in the Name field, then click New. To delete a category, click on its name in the scroll list, and then click Delete. The categories you create are displayed in a pop-up menu in the HexWeb Export palette. When you export files, folders with the category names are automatically created.

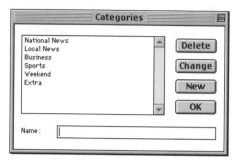

Figure 35-3: In the folder hierarchy that HexWeb generates for a Web publication, each category you create becomes a subfolder that holds exported articles and pictures.

Text defaults

Click the Text Defaults button in the HexWeb Preferences dialog box to display the Text defaults dialog box. Figure 35-4 shows this dialog box, which contains three checkboxes:

✦ **Export <FONT FACE = > Tag:** Click this to include font names with exported text. If a user has the fonts whose names you've embedded in your HTML pages, the text will be displayed in the browser window using the original font. If a user does not have a font, the default font specified in the browser's preferences is used.

✦ **Export <FONT COLOR + RRGGBB> Tag:** Click this to include color information in exported text to which color has been applied in QuarkXPress.

✦ **Use Antialiasing for Text to Image:** Click this to smooth the edges of text that you choose to export as a picture.

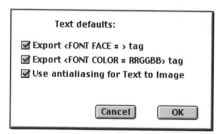

Figure 35-4: The Text defaults dialog box lets you enable or disable three text-related options.

Filenames and formats

Click the Filenames & Formats button in the HexWeb Preferences dialog box to display the dialog box shown in Figure 35-5. Here are your options:

✦ **File Names:** Click the radio button for the file extension you want to place at the end of the filenames HexWeb generates for exported HTML pages; click No ending if you don't want to include an extension at the end of filenames.

✦ **DOS Filenames:** Click this box to use the eight-dot-three (eight characters, a period, and a three-letter suffix) file-naming convention.

✦ **Image Default:** Choose the default image format—GIF, Interlaced GIF, JPEG, or Progressive JPEG—for exported pictures. Like BeyondPress, HexWeb lets you override the image defaults for individual pictures (via the HexWeb Export palette). If you choose Progressive JPEG, a pair of additional fields are displayed that let you specify the quality of the image (from 5 to 95; higher is better) and the filename extension.

✦ **VSpace and HSpace:** These fields let you specify the amount of vertical and horizontal space (in pixels) that's placed around exported images.

✦ **HTML Editor:** Click this button to display a directory dialog box that lets you choose the HTML editor that will be used to assign the file type of HTML pages. The default is SimpleText, a good choice because all HTML editors can open SimpleText files. If you know that you'll be fine-tuning the pages you export with HexWeb using an HTML editor or layout application, you can choose it as the default HTML editor.

✦ **WWW Browser:** Click this button to choose the default browser that's automatically launched when you preview and export pages.

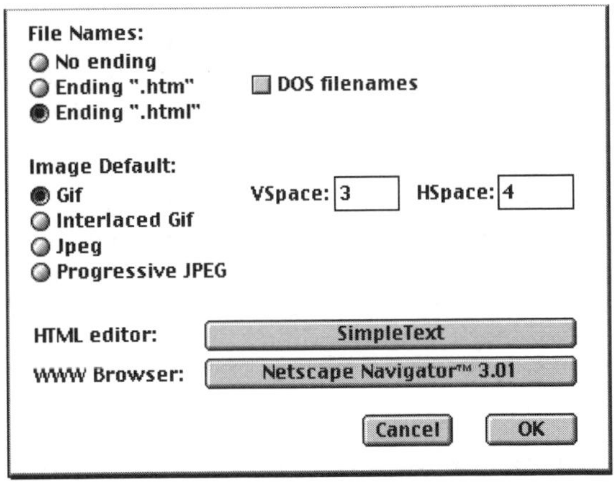

Figure 35-5: The HexWeb preferences dialog box in which you specify default settings for HTML filenames and image formats, as well as a default HTML editor and browser.

Layout preferences

Clicking the Headline Sizes button in the HexWeb Basic Preferences dialog box displays the Headline Sizes dialog box. Figure 35-6 shows the six text fields in this dialog box in which you specify the font size associated with each of the six HTML headline sizes. All exported text that's smaller than the smallest size you specify in this dialog box (other than zero) is automatically converted to default text without retaining font sizes; bold, italic, and bold italic styling is maintained. When you convert text to HTML headlines, the exported text is displayed in bold in a browser window and all other styling is ignored.

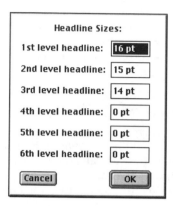

Figure 35-6: In the Headline Sizes dialog box you specify the font sizes that you want to automatically convert into HTML headline styles. All text smaller than the smallest headline size you map here (other than zero) is converted to default text.

Headers and footers

Click Header/Footer in the HexWeb Basic Preferences dialog box to display the Page Header And Footer dialog box, which lets you specify the HTML codes that are inserted at the top and bottom of the Web pages you export. Figure 35-7 shows the dialog box, which contains two text fields, one for headers and one for footers, into which you can enter or paste HTML codes. If you've already created header and footer files, you can open them in a text editor, copy the text, and paste it into the appropriate field.

If you uncheck the External Header & Footer Files button, the codes in the fields are used for the pages you export. If you check this box, the HexWeb Export palette displays pop-up menus with the names of all HTML files stored within folders called Headers and Footers. (These folders must be stored in a folder called Standards within the root folder of your publication.)

Separators

Click the Separators button in the HexWeb Preferences dialog box to display the Separators For Boxes dialog box that lets you specify the HTML codes that are automatically placed after the text boxes and picture boxes you export. Figure 35-8 shows this dialog box. By default, HexWeb inserts a paragraph return after each box you export.

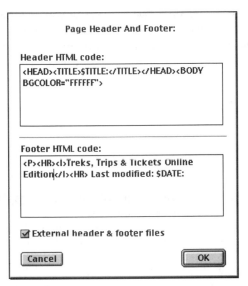

Figure 35-7: HexWeb provides two methods for attaching headers and footers to exported Web pages. You can enter or paste HTML codes directly into the fields of the Page Header And Footer dialog box, or you can choose headers and footers from a pop-up menu in the HexWeb Export palette.

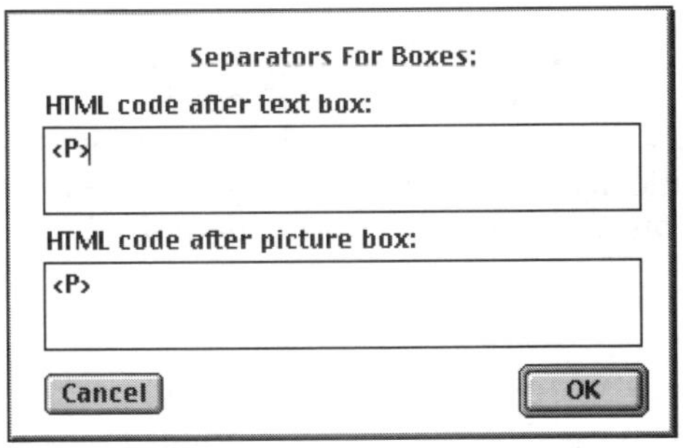

Figure 35-8: The HTML codes you enter or paste into the fields in the Separators For Boxes dialog box are automatically inserted after the codes for the text boxes and picture boxes you export.

Advanced preferences

Click the Meta Tags button in the HexWeb Basic Preferences dialog box to display the dialog box shown in Figure 35-9. <META> tags are often used by Web search engines as they gather information about files on the Web; they are also used by HexBase Web Database, another HexMac product that lets you generate Web pages from databases. The Meta Tags pane of the HexWeb Export palette lets you create <META> tags and specify the information they contain. Check the Use Extended Meta Tags box if you want to add extended <META> tags to the HTML files you export.

Figure 35-9: Extended <META> tags let you add information to the HTML files you export. This information is not displayed in browser windows, but is accessible to Web search engines and other applications that read HTML files.

Variables

Click the Variables button in the HexWeb Basic Preferences dialog box to display the dialog box shown in Figure 35-10, which lets you specify the date that's used in any HTML element that uses the date variable ($DATE). HexWeb provides three built-in variables that you can insert into HTML codes, such as headers and footers. For example, if you insert $TITLE into an HTML code, HexWeb will automatically replace it with the headline of the article you're exporting. The variable $HOME specifies the starting point of a path name in a publication's folder hierarchy.

To specify the date that's entered by the $DATE variable, click on one of the three buttons in the $DATE dialog box. If you click Current Date, you can also enter an offset value. For example, if you're working on tomorrow's edition of a newspaper, you can enter an offset of 1 to automatically insert tomorrow's date instead of the current date. If you click Fixed Date, you can enter the specific date that's used for the $DATE variable.

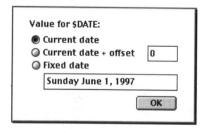

Figure 35-10: The date variable, $DATE, is one of three built-in variables that you can include in the HTML codes you export. The $DATE dialog box shown here lets you specify the date that's inserted in place of the $DATE variable.

Left indents

Clicking the Left Indent button in the HexWeb Preferences dialog box displays the Left Indent dialog box, shown in Figure 35-11. HexWeb includes a transparent GIF file, called indent.gif, that you can use as a spacer to create left indents for the items you export. The text field in the Left Indent contains the complete HTML code for inserting this file, including its path.

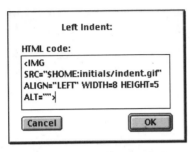

Figure 35-11: HexWeb includes a GIF image that you can use to create left indents. The HTML code here points to a transparent picture file called indent.gif that's located in the Initials folder in the main folder.

Images and captions

Click the Image & Caption button in the HexWeb Basic Preferences dialog box to display the Image & Caption Strings dialog box shown in Figure 35-12. The latest version of HexWeb includes a new feature that lets you export a picture box and its accompanying caption text box as a table that retains the picture and the text together. (You should be familiar with the HTML codes used in this dialog box before you try to modify them.) The Start HTML code field displays the HTML codes that are automatically inserted in front of an exported image/caption table. The End HTML code is inserted after the table. If you're familiar with the HTML codes used in these fields, you can edit them to adjust the appearance of the image/caption tables you export.

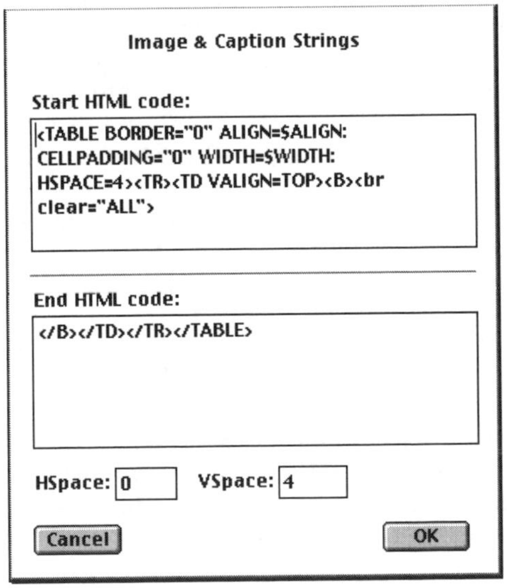

Figure 35-12: HexWeb lets you export a picture and its caption as a table, a particularly useful feature for newspapers. The Image & Caption Strings dialog box lets you modify the appearance of picture/caption tables.

Using the Export Palette

Choosing Open HexWeb Export from the Utilities menu displays the HexWeb Export palette. This palette contains three or four panes, depending on whether you checked the Use Extended Meta Tags checkbox in the HexWeb Basic Preferences dialog box. If Use Extended Meta Tags is checked, four panes are displayed: Export, Tools, SOL (which stands for Special Object Library), and Meta Tags. You use this palette to specify default information for the Web page you're exporting; to modify the export attributes of individual text boxes and picture boxes; and to add other elements, such as images, sound, video, and custom HTML elements, to your exported pages. The Meta Tags pane lets you create and edit <META> tags. Four buttons—Add, Ungroup, Preview, and Export—are displayed at all times at the bottom of the HexWeb Export palette. Here's how they work:

✦ **Add:** Click this button to add the selected items to the last collection of items you exported. You use this button to export Web pages that contain items from multiple QuarkXPress pages.

✦ **Ungroup:** Clicking this button ungroups all QuarkXPress groups. Click this button before you begin exporting pages if you want to export any QuarkXPress boxes that are part of a group.

✦ **Preview:** Click this button to automatically launch or switch to (if it's already open) the default browser specified in the HexWeb Basic Preferences dialog box and display the selected elements. The Preview button changes to Last Export when no items are selected, letting you see the items or page you last previewed or exported.

✦ **Export:** Click this button to create an HTML file from the selected items and generate image files for exported pictures. All files are automatically placed in the folder hierarchy in the main folder.

The Export pane

If it's not the frontmost pane, clicking on the Export tab in the HexWeb Export palette displays the controls shown in Figure 35-13. Before you export Web pages you should fill in the fields in this palette. You can preview and export items and pages when the Export pane is displayed, but if you intend to add objects from your special object library, you must display the SOL pane before you begin selecting the items you want to export.

Figure 35-13: The Export pane lets you specify default information for the page you're exporting, including a headline and subhead, which are used by HexWeb Index when it automatically generates tables of contents from your Web pages.

The Tools pane

Clicking the Tools tab in the HexWeb Export palette displays controls that let you do the following (see Figure 35-14):

Foreign

✦ **Hyperlink button:** This lets you create hyperlinks to pages on other Web sites.

Local

✦ **Hyperlink button:** This lets you create hyperlinks to different pages on your Web site.

✦ **Anchor buttons:** These let you create anchors (internal links) for linking different parts of the page you're exporting.

✦ **Modify button:** This lets you modify the export attributes of individual text and picture boxes.

✦ **Alignment buttons:** These let you specify the alignment of exported items.

Tip

After you've specified the default information requested in the Export pane, you'll probably want to display the Tools pane to create hyperlinks and anchors and to modify individual QuarkXPress items before you export them.

Local Hyperlink button ——
Foreign Hyperlink button ——

Anchor button
Anchor Destination button

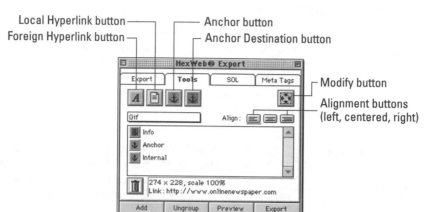

Modify button
Alignment buttons
(left, centered, right)

Figure 35-14:
Use the Tools pane to create anchors and links, to specify alignment, and to override the export defaults for individual items.

The Special Object Library (SOL) pane

Figure 35-15 shows the SOL pane of the HexWeb Export palette. If you want to add images, multimedia files, or custom HTML elements to the pages you export, they must be available in the SOL pane. The pop-up menu in the SOL pane displays the names of all folders within a folder called Standards in the main folder (as specified in the HexWeb Basic Preferences dialog box). You must create a Standards folder and subfolders for the additional files you want to have access to when exporting pages. If you intend to add elements from the SOL pane in the pages you export, make sure this pane is displayed before you begin selecting items for export.

Tip

If you want to export only the contents of a QuarkXPress document, and optionally headers and footers, you don't have to create a special object library.

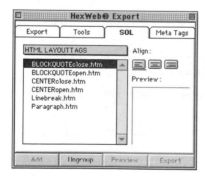

Figure 35-15: The Special Object Library (SOL) pane lets you add images, multimedia files, and custom HTML elements to exported pages.

The Meta Tags pane

If the Use Extended Meta Tags checkbox is checked in the HexWeb Basic Preferences dialog box, the Meta Tags tab is displayed in the HexWeb Export palette. Clicking on this tab displays the Meta Tags pane, shown in Figure 35-16. The controls in this pane let you create and modify <META> tags, which contain information not displayed in a browser window. For example, keywords are stored in <META> tags and enable Web search engines to obtain basic information about individual HTML files without having to search the entire file.

Figure 35-16: The Meta Tags pane lets you insert invisible information in the pages you export. The information is available to programs that can search through the contents of the HTML file, but it's not recognized by a browser.

Preparing Items for Export

If you want to use HexWeb default settings for all the boxes you export, perhaps with the intention of modifying items later as necessary using a dedicated HTML layout program, you can export boxes without adjusting any of their export attributes. However, you'll probably want to adjust some items to make them more appropriate for the Web before you export them. HexWeb offers a couple of methods for modifying the export attributes of individual QuarkXPress text boxes and picture boxes.

When a box is active, the QuickSelect pop-up menu available at the left center of the Tools palette displays the default export setting and lets you choose a different method. Figure 35-17 shows this pop-up menu and the options available for text boxes and picture boxes.

 You can also change the export settings for an active item by clicking the Modify Box button (shown here) in the Tools pane.

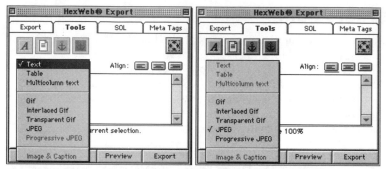

Figure 35-17: The QuickSelect pop-up menu in the Tools pane lets you change the export format of the active text box or picture box. The options for text boxes are shown in the screen shot on the left; on the right are the options for picture boxes.

Modifying text boxes

You can export the text in a text box as text using the defaults you've specified in HexWeb Preferences, or you can choose to export the text as a table, in multiple columns, or as an image. Figures 35-18 through 35-21 show four dialog boxes that let you customize the appearance of exported text. The choice you make from the pop-up menu at the top of these dialog boxes determines the controls that are displayed at the bottom.

Only Netscape Navigator supports the multicolumn HTML code that HexWeb embeds. Gutter and Width values are specified in points.

To modify export settings for a particular text box, select it, click on the Modify Box button (shown here) in the HexWeb Export palette, choose an entry from the pop-up menu, and then modify the individual settings as you prefer.

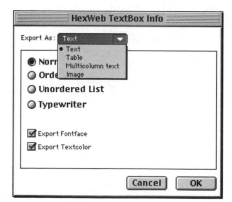

Figure 35-18: If you export the text in a text box as text, you have the option to export it as normal text, an ordered list, an unordered list, or as typewriter text. The checkboxes let you include or exclude font and color information. The pop-up menu lets you choose a different format for the active text box.

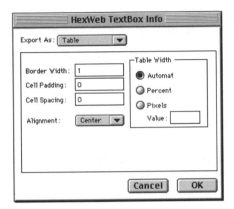

Figure 35-19: If you export text as a table, you can control the appearance of the table using the controls in this dialog box.

Figure 35-20: Although HexWeb provides the option to export text in multiple columns, only Netscape Navigator supports the multicolumn HTML code that HexWeb embeds. Gutter and Width values are specified in points.

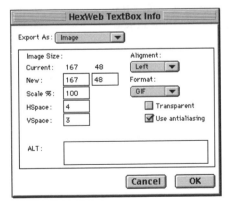

Figure 35-21: You have the option to convert any text box into an image before exporting it. The controls here specify the format and adjust the appearance of text that you export as an image.

HexWeb text tricks

Unlike CyberPress and BeyondPress, which let you format different parts of a single text chain differently, HexWeb exports all text in a story the same way.

When exporting text, HexWeb ignores anchored boxes. If you want to export anchored boxes, create unanchored duplicates of them, then select them along with the other items you want to export when you're ready to export.

HexWeb will automatically convert drop caps created with QuarkXPress's drop-cap controls into a GIF image during export. To convert drop caps to GIF images, place the folder called Initials that's included with HexWeb into your publication's main folder. You can also replace the built-in GIF files with your own.

Modifying picture boxes

The controls in the HexWeb Image Info dialog box, shown in Figure 35-22, let you choose a different format for the exported picture (different from the default format specified in HexWeb Preferences) and specify its size, alignment, border, and so forth. You also have the option to specify alternate text for images, which is used by browsers that don't display pictures and when a browser is set not to automatically download images.

 To display the HexWeb Image Info dialog box, when a picture box is active, click the Modify Box button (shown here) in the HexWeb Export palette.

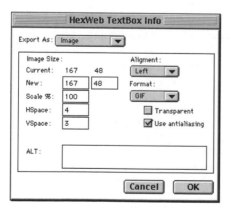

Figure 35-22: The HexWeb Image Info dialog box lets you adjust the format, size, scale, and so forth of exported pictures.

Combining picture and text boxes

The latest version of HexWeb includes a new feature that lets you export a text box and a picture box together. When a picture box and a text box are active (they can be group or individual items), the pop-up menu in the Tools pane of the HexWeb

Export palette displays an entry labeled Image & Caption. Figure 35-23 shows a QuarkXPress page with a picture box and text box active and the Image & Caption option available in the Tools pane. Figure 35-24 shows the exported table displayed in a browser window.

 When you export a picture-box/text-box pair as an image and caption, the boxes are exported as a two-cell table that uses the Image & Caption defaults specified in HexWeb Preferences. If you click the Modify Box button (shown here) in the HexWeb Export palette, the Image & Caption Strings dialog box, shown in Figure 35-12, is displayed, which lets you modify the HTML codes that are inserted before and after the exported table.

 If you want to export any items that are part of a group, you must first ungroup the items. You can do this by selecting the group and then choosing Ungroup from the item menu or by clicking the Ungroup button in the HexWeb Export palette. If a group consists of one picture box and one text box, you can export the group as an Image & Caption.

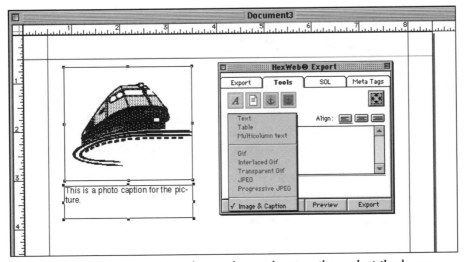

Figure 35-23: To export a picture box and a text box together, select the boxes, and then choose Image & Caption from the pop-up menu in the Tools pane.

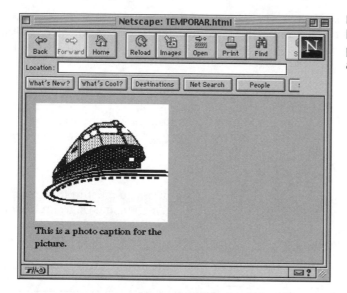

Figure 35-24: The table created by exporting the text box and picture box in Figure 35-23 as an image and caption.

Previewing and Exporting

As you modify the export settings of individual boxes, you can see what an exported element is going to look like on a Web page by selecting it and then clicking the Preview button in the HexWeb Export palette. The default browser specified in the HexWeb Basic Preferences dialog box is automatically launched (if Open Browser is checked in the Export pane of the HexWeb Export palette), and the active box is displayed according to the export settings you've established for it. It's easy to switch back and forth between the browser and QuarkXPress as you experiment with different export settings for individual items. Here's the sequence to follow:

✦ **Previewing multiple items:** To preview multiple items, make sure the Item tool is selected, and then Shift+click on the items. Be careful to select the items in the order you want them exported if you want to preview them in that order. Click the Preview button to launch the default browser and display the selected items. When you click Preview, HexWeb creates temporary files that are used only for display. Only if you click Export are permanent files generated.

✦ **Previewing an entire Web page:** To preview an entire Web page, select all the items you want to export, and then click Preview. Again, the order in which you select the items determines the order in which they'll be exported and displayed. If you want to include items from the SOL pane of the HexWeb Export palette, make sure it's displayed before you begin selecting items. To add an item from the SOL pane, double-click on it.

✦ **Selecting items to export:** After you've finished modifying the export settings of individual items and previewing the page you want to export, you're ready to use the Export button to generate an HTML file and convert images into GIF and JPEG images. Shift+click on the items you want to include in your exported page. Again, be careful when you select items. They'll be exported in the order you select them.

✦ **Exporting:** After you've selected the items you want to export, click the Export button. When you do, you may be prompted to enter information for <META> tags that require data. If not, the pages are automatically named and saved in your publication's folder hierarchy according to your preference settings, and the page is displayed in the default browser.

At this point, you may want to open the page you exported in an HTML layout program and fine-tune it. But if you were careful when specifying export attributes and were satisfied with the previews you saw before exporting, you can skip this step altogether.

Working with Index Pro

After you've finished exporting Web pages for a particular publication with HexWeb, you have the option to use HexWeb Index Pro, a stand-alone program that's included with HexWeb, to check all links and create a table of contents from the pages you've exported.

Be forewarned: HexWeb Index Pro is an industrial-strength program with many features. Its learning curve is as steep as HexWeb's, maybe steeper. But for large Web sites with many pages, the ability to automate the creation of tables of contents and to add them as frames to all pages is invaluable.

Launching Index Pro

You can launch HexWeb Index Pro from within QuarkXPress by choosing Create Table of Content from the Utilities menu, or you can launch it by double-clicking on the HexWeb Index Pro program icon in the Finder. Figure 35-25 shows the HexWeb Index Preferences dialog box. The controls associated with the General Preferences icon, one of eight preference categories, are displayed in the Preferences dialog box.

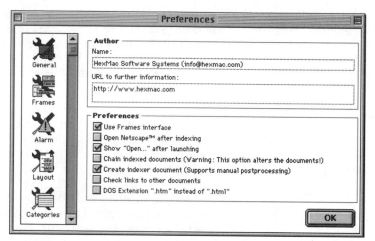

Figure 35-25: The HexWeb Index Pro Preferences dialog box contains a scroll list with eight icons that access an associated set of controls. Here, the dialog box displays controls for specifying general defaults.

Creating a table of contents

To create a table of contents, use the following steps.

STEPS: Creating a table of contents

1. Choose Open from the File menu.

2. You're prompted to select the folder that HexWeb Index Pro will search to create a table of contents. You can select a folder that contains a single category for an issue, an entire issue, or an entire publication. After you choose a folder, the Archive window shown here is displayed. The four buttons let you create a table of contents for an entire publication, a single issue, all categories, or individual categories. Click on the button that corresponds to the folder you opened.

3. When you click a button, HexWeb Index Pro automatically generates a table of contents list from the HTML files in the selected folder, and then displays the Index dialog box shown here. The scroll list contains the table of contents that HexWeb created and uses the headlines and subheads that you specified for each Web page when you exported it. You can click and drag to rearrange the articles in the scroll list. Pop-up menus in the upper right-hand corner let you add a header and/or a footer. The SpecialFX menu lets you export the list as an HTML file, in HotSauce 3-D format, or as Java pop-up menus.

4. To check links, click the Check Links folder icon; to create a table of contents in the format chosen in the SpecialFX pop-up menu, click the Index icon. When you do, HexWeb creates a table of contents file and displays it in the default browser. An example of an online newspaper (the *Gateway Peninsula* in Gig Harbor, Washington, designed by Ron Andrade) is shown here. It was created with HexWeb and includes a frame with a table of contents created with HexWeb Index Pro.

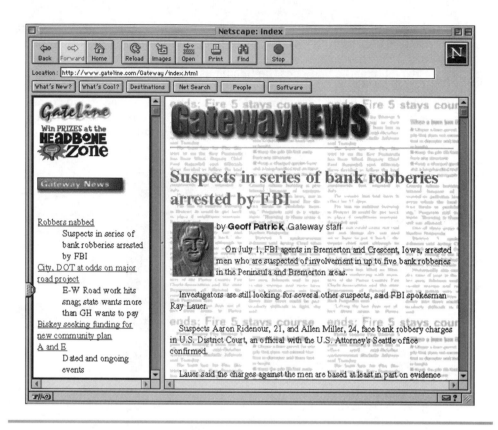

Upgrading and First-Time Installation

APPENDIX

A

◆ ◆ ◆ ◆

In This Appendix

Installing QuarkXPress for Windows

Installing QuarkXPress for Mac

Upgrading from a previous version

Hardware and software recommendations

◆ ◆ ◆ ◆

Installing QuarkXPress 4 is surprisingly easy, although there are a few interface peculiarities to watch out for. Use the steps in this appendix to make quick work of the installation process. If you're upgrading from an earlier version, see the section on upgrading. For any hardware and software questions you may have, see the sidebar at the end of this appendix.

STEPS: Installing QuarkXPress for Windows

1. Insert the CD in the CD-ROM drive and the installer floppy in the floppy drive. (Some packages of QuarkXPress have the installer on the CD.)

2. Double-click on the install program on the floppy in most configurations. (In CD-only Windows versions, the setup program may launch itself.)

3. Make sure you have your serial number, which came in the QuarkXPress box. You may need it to complete the installation.

4. Follow the instructions on the screen. Use the Continue–> button to move forward through the installation and the Go Back <–button to change a previously set option.

5. After the first screen, click Continue–>. You get the dialog box shown below. Click the Customize button to select the destination hard drive (if you have more than one) and the folder in which to install QuarkXPress. (Remember, if you don't click the Customize button, you won't be able to tell the installer where to place the QuarkXPress files and, more important, you won't be able to determine which XTensions and additional resources are installed. You simply get the default configuration.)

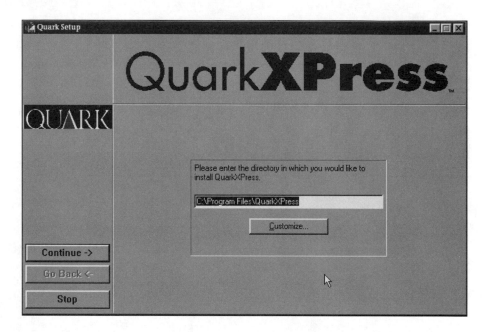

6. You need to click the Browse button in the subsequent screen to choose the destination. (Do not select the same destination as a previous version of QuarkXPress. Be sure to install the program in a different folder.)

7. After you have chosen the destination for QuarkXPress, determine which options you want installed. QuarkXPress uses a nonstandard interface (as shown here), so be careful. Notice the folders. They hold groups of files to be installed. If a folder is checked, some or all of its contents are installed. To see what's in a folder, double-click it and proceed with the installation as follows:

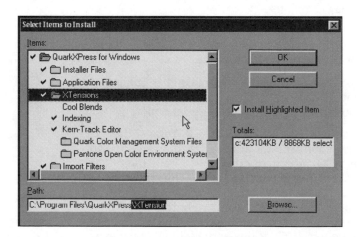

✦ You can install individual items by double-clicking the item (a checkmark should appear to the left of the item's name), or by checking the Install Highlighted Item checkbox. Use this checkbox to install all the contents of a folder. You deselect an item the same way (causing it to not be installed).

✦ Of the folders, make sure that all the Installer Files items and Application Files items are checked.

✦ For the Color Libraries folder (inside the Application Files folder); the XTensions folder (which includes subfolders for the Quark Color Management System and Pantone Open Color Environment features); and the Import Filters folder; make sure each color library, XTension, color feature, and import filter you think you may want is checked. It's better to install more than you absolutely need, rather than not have a feature available when you need it. (Remember: You can always disable XTensions and filters using QuarkXPress 4's XTensions manager.)

8. Click OK when you've selected the destination and set all the options you want installed. Then click Continue–>.

9. QuarkXPress will now be installed. You may be asked to provide your serial number and to fill out a survey on your system for use in registering QuarkXPress. You will also be asked whether you want a program group created. If you answer yes, a folder called QuarkXPress for Windows is placed in your Start button's Programs folder to give you quick access to QuarkXPress. Of course, you can always create a shortcut to QuarkXPress and drag it onto your Start button to get easy access to the program, rather than have a whole program group created. On the Mac, this is like putting an alias for the QuarkXPress program into the Apple Menu Items folder in the System Folder. In addition, you may be asked to insert a supplied registration disk, which you will then need to mail to Quark.

10. When you are finished with the installation, run QuarkXPress and, with no document open, set your basic preferences, as described in Chapter 3.

STEPS: Installing QuarkXPress for Macintosh

1. Insert the CD in the CD-ROM drive and the installer floppy in the floppy drive.

2. Double-click on the install program on the floppy.

3. Make sure you have your serial number, which came in the QuarkXPress box. You may need it to complete the installation.

4. Click OK in the first dialog box that appears. The QuarkXPress 4 Installation dialog box is displayed.

(continued)

5. Click the Destination button to select the destination hard drive (if you have more than one) and the folder in which to install QuarkXPress.

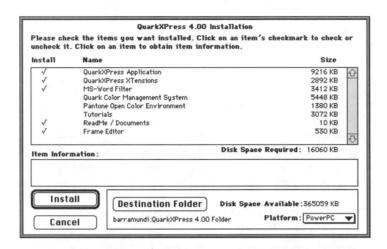

6. After you have chosen the destination for QuarkXPress, determine which options you want installed. QuarkXPress uses a nonstandard interface (as shown here), so be careful. Notice the list of items in the top half of the dialog box. It shows groups of files to be installed. If a list item is checked, its contents are installed. To see what an item includes, click it and look in the Item Information field.

✦ You can install an item by clicking in the Install column for that item (a checkmark should appear to the left of the item's name). You deselect an item the same way (causing it to not be installed).

✦ Of the items, make sure that at least the QuarkXPress Application item is checked.

✦ Even if you're not sure if you want the QuarkXPress XTensions, the Quark Color Management System, the Pantone Open Color Environment, and the other items, you may want to install them anyway. It's better to install more than you absolutely need, rather than not have a feature available when you need it. (Remember: You can always disable XTensions and filters using QuarkXPress 4's XTensions manager.)

7. If applicable, choose 68K, PowerPC, or Fat from the Platform pop-up menu at lower right. (Choose Fat if your installation is meant to work on both 680X0-based and Power PC-based Macs.)

8. Click Install when you've selected the destination and set all the options you want installed.

9. QuarkXPress will now be installed. You may be asked to provide your serial number and to fill out a survey on your system for use in registering QuarkXPress. You may also be asked to insert a supplied registration disk, which you will then need to mail to Quark.

10. When you are finished with the installation, run QuarkXPress and, with no document open, set your basic preferences, as described in Chapter 3.

Hardware and software recommendations

For maximum performance, we recommend that you exceed the minimum requirements listed on the QuarkXPress box. For QuarkXPress to work smoothly, you should have at least the following hardware and software:

For the Macintosh:

✦ A Power Macintosh with 24 or more megabytes of RAM and a one-gigabyte hard disk. (For professionals, we recommend a 604e- or 750-based Power Mac running at 180MHz to 250MHz or faster with 48 megabytes of RAM and a two-gigabyte hard disk.)

✦ A color or gray-scale monitor. (A 15-inch display or larger is preferable, with a video card or built-in video circuitry that can be set at 832 by 624 resolution or greater.)

✦ Your computer should be capable of displaying 8-bit color or greater. (Most new Macs support 16-bit color with their built-in video circuitry.)

✦ System 7.5 or greater. (Mac OS 8.0 or greater is recommended.)

✦ You might want to consider a separate word processing program, a separate graphics program, and a separate image-editing program, if you are using a scanner.

✦ We also recommend as many type fonts as you can manage. The more the better.

For Windows 95 and NT:

✦ A 120MHz (or faster) Pentium processor (or greater), 24 or more megabytes of RAM, and a one-gigabyte hard disk. (If you use Windows NT, have at least 32 megabytes of RAM.)

✦ A color or gray-scale monitor. (A 15-inch display or larger that can be set at 800 by 600 resolution is recommended.)

✦ Your computer should have an 8-bit (or greater) video card.

✦ Windows 95 or Windows NT 4.0 or greater.

✦ Depending on your needs: You may need separate word processing, graphics, and image-editing programs.

✦ We also recommend lots of type fonts, as many as you can manage.

Upgrading from a Previous Version

Upgrading your copy of QuarkXPress is very similar to installing a new copy of QuarkXPress. The only major difference is that the Upgrader will ask you to locate your old version of QuarkXPress so it can replace it. During the upgrade process, you must specify which XTensions and other auxiliary files you want to install or upgrade. When the upgrade is complete, any files that are not compatible with QuarkXPress 4 will be located in a folder named "Old Items Folder" in your QuarkXPress folder.

Tip   If you no longer use version 3.x of QuarkXPress, you can remove the EfiColor files (the EfiColor DB folder and the EfiColor Processor file) from the System Folder on the Mac. In Windows, delete the EfiColor.ini file from your Windows directory. You can also remove your QuarkXPress 3.x folders and all their files, but don't do this until you've got QuarkXPress 4 up and running successfully.

✦   ✦   ✦

Most Useful Shortcuts

As you become more familiar with QuarkXPress, you'll want to take advantage of all the time-saving shortcuts you can muster. This appendix covers QuarkXPress's keyboard shortcuts and working with contextual menus—those labor-saving features offered by Windows 95, Windows NT 4, and Mac OS 8.

Using the Keyboard Shortcuts

While it's true that you can select functions through menus and palettes, the nice assortment of keyboard shortcuts available in QuarkXPress definitely come in handy as you spend your days creating documents. The following table lists these shortcuts. A convenient keyboard shortcut pullout card is also included in this book.

Action or command	Macintosh	Windows
Opening/closing/saving		
New publication	⌘+N	Ctrl+N
New library	Option+⌘+N	Ctrl+Alt+N
Open publication	⌘+O	Ctrl+O
Save publication	⌘+S	Ctrl+S
Save as	Option+⌘+S	Ctrl+Alt+S
Get text or picture	⌘+E	Ctrl+E
Save text	Option+⌘+E	Ctrl+Alt+E
Save page as EPS	Option+Shift+⌘+S	Ctrl+Alt+Shift+S
Append	Option+⌘+A	Ctrl+Alt+A
Close current document	⌘+W	Ctrl+F4
Close all documents	Option+⌘+W	*not available*
Quit	⌘+Q	Ctrl+Q *or* Alt+F4

(continued)

Action or command	Macintosh	Windows
Miscellaneous		
Print	⌘+P	Ctrl+P
Undo	⌘+Z	Ctrl+Z
Revert dialog box values	Shift+⌘+Z	Ctrl+Shift+Z
Help	Help	F1
Preferences/setup		
Application preferences	Option+Shift+⌘+Y	Ctrl+Alt+Shift+Y
Document preferences	⌘+Y	Ctrl+Y
Paragraph preferences	Option+⌘+Y	Ctrl+Alt+Y
Trapping preferences	Option+Shift+F12	Ctrl+Shift+F12
Document setup	Option+Shift+⌘+P	Ctrl+Alt+Shift+P
Page setup	Option+⌘+P	Ctrl+Alt+P
View		
100%	⌘+1	Ctrl+1
Fit in window	⌘+0	Ctrl+0
200% (Toggles with 100%)	Option+⌘+click	Ctrl+Alt+click
Thumbnails	Shift+F6	Shift+F6
Change view percentage	Control+V	Ctrl+Alt+V
Force redraw	Option+⌘+period	Shift+Esc
Halt redraw	⌘+period	Esc
Go to page	⌘+J	Ctrl+J
Zoom in	Control+click	Ctrl+spacebar+click
Zoom out	Option+Control+click	Ctrl+Alt+spacebar+click
Windows submenu (tile, stack)	Shift+click title bar	Alt+W
Show/hide invisibles	⌘+I	Ctrl+I
Show/hide rulers	⌘+R	Ctrl+R
Show/hide guides	F7	F7
Show/hide baseline grid	Option+F7	Ctrl+F7
Snap to guides	Shift+F7	Shift+F7

Action or command	Macintosh	Windows
Palettes		
Show/hide Measurements palette	F9	F9
Show/hide Tool palette	F8	F8
Show/hide Document Layout palette	F10	F4
Show/hide Style Sheets palette	F11	F11
Show/hide Colors palette	F12	F12
Show/hide Trap Information palette	Option+F12	Ctrl+F12
Show/hide Lists palette	Option+F11	Ctrl+F11
Show/hide Index palette	Option+⌘+I	Ctrl+Alt+I
Show font usage	F13	*not available*
Show picture usage	Option+F13	*not available*
Navigation		
Page grabber hand	Option+drag	Alt+drag
Enable/disable live scroll	Option+drag scroll box	*not available*
Display master page	Shift+F10	Shift+F4
Display next master page	Option+F10	Ctrl+Shift+F4
Display previous master page	Option+Shift+F10	Ctrl+Shift+F3
Display document page	Shift+F10	Shift+F4
Next page	Shift+PageUp *or* Control+Shift+L	Shift+PageDown
Previous page	Shift+PageDown *or* Control+Shift+K	Shift+PageUp
First page	Shift+Home *or* Control+Shift+A	Ctrl+PageUp
Last page	Shift+End *or* Control+Shift+D	Ctrl+PageDown
Beginning of document (story)	Home *or* Control+A	Ctrl+Home
End of document (story)	End *or* Control+D	Ctrl+End

(continued)

Action or command	Macintosh	Windows
Object selection		
Select all	⌘+A	Ctrl+A
Select hidden item	Option+Shift+⌘+click	Ctrl+Alt+Shift+click
Multiple selection (series)	Shift+click	Shift+click
Multiple selection (discontiguous)	⌘+click	Ctrl+click
Moving objects		
Nudge selected object 1 point	Arrow keys	Arrow keys
Nudge selected object ¹⁄₁₀ point	Option+arrow keys	Alt+arrow keys
Constrain movement	Shift+drag	Shift+drag
Cut	⌘+X or F2	Ctrl+X
Delete	⌘+K	Ctrl+K
Copy	⌘+C or F3	Ctrl+C
Paste	⌘+V or F4	Ctrl+V
Item commands		
Modify	⌘+M	Ctrl+M
Edit shape	Shift+F4	F10
Frame	⌘+B	Ctrl+B
Clipping	Option+⌘+T	Ctrl+Alt+T
Edit clipping path	Option+Shift+F4	Ctrl+Shift+F10
Runaround	⌘+T	Ctrl+T
Edit runaround	Option+F4	Ctrl+F10
Duplicate	⌘+D	Ctrl+D
Stop and Repeat	Option+⌘+D	Ctrl+Alt+D
Space/align	⌘+comma	Ctrl+comma
Send to back	Shift+F5	Shift+F5
Bring to front	F5	F5
Send backward	Option+Shift+F5	Ctrl+Shift+F5
Bring forward	Option+F5	Ctrl+F5
Lock/unlock	F6	F6
Group	⌘+G	Ctrl+G
Ungroup	⌘+U	Ctrl+U

Action or command	Macintosh	Windows
Text selection		
Word	Double-click	Double-click
Paragraph	Quadruple-click	Quadruple-click
Line	Triple-click	Triple-click
Story	⌘+A or quintuple-click	Ctrl+A or quintuple-click
Character to left	Shift+Left Arrow	Shift+Left Arrow
Character to right	Shift+Right Arrow	Shift+Right Arrow
Word to left	Shift+⌘+Left Arrow	Ctrl+Shift+Left Arrow
Word to right	Shift+⌘+Right Arrow	Ctrl+Shift+Right Arrow
Up one line	Shift+Up Arrow	Shift+Up Arrow
Down one line	Shift+Down Arrow	Shift+Down Arrow
To start of line	Shift+Option+⌘+ Left Arrow	Ctrl+Alt+Shift+Left Arrow or Shift+Home
To end of line	Shift+Option+⌘+ Right Arrow	Ctrl+Alt+Shift+Right Arrow or Shift+End
Up one paragraph	Shift+⌘+Up Arrow	Ctrl+Shift+Up Arrow
Down one paragraph	Shift+⌘+Down Arrow	Ctrl+Shift+Down Arrow
To top of story	Shift+Option+⌘+ Up Arrow	Ctrl+Alt+Shift+Up Arrow or Ctrl+Shift+Home
To bottom of story	Shift+Option+⌘+ Down Arrow	Ctrl+Alt+Shift+Down Arrow or Ctrl+Shift+End
Spelling		
Check word	⌘+L	Ctrl+W
Check story	Option+⌘+L	Ctrl+Alt+W
Check document	Option+Shift+⌘+L	Ctrl+Alt+Shift+W
Lookup spelling (in Check Story dialog box)	⌘+L	Alt+L
Skip word (in Check Story dialog box)	⌘+S	Alt+S
Add word to dictionary (in Check Story dialog box)	⌘+A	Alt+A
Add all suspect words to dictionary (in Check Story dialog box)	Option+Shift+click Done button	Alt+Shift+click Close button
Suggest hyphenation	⌘+H	Ctrl+H

(continued)

Action or command	Macintosh	Windows
Text/ paragraph formats		
Edit style sheets	Shift+F11	Shift+F11
Edit H&Js	Option+Shift+F11 *or* Option+⌘+H	Ctrl+Shift+F11
Character attributes	Shift+⌘+D	Ctrl+Shift+D
Paragraph attributes	Shift+⌘+F	Ctrl+Shift+F
Copy format to select paragraphs	Option+Shift+click	Alt+Shift+click
Apply No Style, then style sheet	Option+click style sheet name	Alt+click style sheet name
Choose font	Option+Shift+⌘+M	Ctrl+Alt+Shift+M
Symbol font (next character typed)	Shift+⌘+Q	Ctrl+Shift+Q
Zapf Dingbats font (next character typed)	Shift+⌘+Z	Ctrl+Shift+Z
Change size	Shift+⌘+\	Ctrl+Shift+\
Change leading	Shift+⌘+E	Ctrl+Shift+E
Define tabs	Shift+⌘+T	Ctrl+Shift+T
Define rules	Shift+⌘+N	Ctrl+Shift+N
Increase to next size on type scale	Shift+⌘+>	Ctrl+Shift+>
Decrease to next size on type scale	Shift+⌘+<	Ctrl+Shift+<
Increase 1 point	Option+Shift+⌘+>	Ctrl+Alt+Shift+>
Decrease 1 point	Option+Shift+⌘+<	Ctrl+Alt+Shift+<
Increase scaling 5%	⌘+]	Ctrl+]
Decrease scaling 5%	⌘+[	Ctrl+[
Increase scaling 1%	Option+⌘+]	Ctrl+Alt+]
Decrease scaling 1%	Option+⌘+[	Ctrl+Alt+[
Resize interactively	⌘+drag text box handle	Ctrl+drag text box handle
Resize interactively constrained	Shift+⌘+drag text box handle	Ctrl+Shift+drag text box handle
Resize interactively proportional	Option+Shift+⌘+drag text box handle	Ctrl+Alt+Shift+drag text box handle

Action or command	Macintosh	Windows
Increase kerning/ tracking ½₀ em	Shift+⌘+]	Ctrl+Shift+]
Decrease kerning/ tracking ½₀ em	Shift+⌘+[	Ctrl+Shift+[
Increase kerning/ tracking ½₀₀ em	Option+Shift+⌘+]	Ctrl+Alt+Shift+]
Decrease kerning/ tracking ½₀₀ em	Option+Shift+⌘+[	Ctrl+Alt+Shift+[
Raise baseline shift 1 point	Option+Shift+⌘+plus	Ctrl+Alt+Shift+)
Lower baseline shift 1 point	Option+Shift+⌘+ hyphen	Ctrl+Alt+Shift+(
Increase leading 1 point	Shift+⌘+"	Ctrl+Shift+"
Decrease leading 1 point	Shift+⌘+semicolon	Ctrl+Shift+semicolon
Increase leading ½₀ point	Option+Shift+⌘+"	Ctrl+Alt+Shift+"
Decrease leading ½₀ point	Option+Shift+⌘+ semicolon	Ctrl+Alt+Shift+semicolon
Normal	Shift+⌘+P	Ctrl+Shift+P
Bold	Shift+⌘+B	Ctrl+Shift+B
Italic	Shift+⌘+I	Ctrl+Shift+I
Word Underline	Shift+⌘+U	Ctrl+Shift+U
underline	Shift+⌘+W	Ctrl+Shift+W
Strikethrough	Shift+⌘+/	Ctrl+Shift+/
All caps	Shift+⌘+K	Ctrl+Shift+K
Subscript	Shift+⌘+hyphen	Ctrl+Shift+9
Superscript	Shift+⌘+plus	Ctrl+Shift+0 (zero)
Superior	Shift+⌘+V	Ctrl+Shift+V
Outline	Shift+⌘+O	Ctrl+Shift+O
Shadow	Shift+⌘+S	Ctrl+Shift+S
Left justify	Shift+⌘+L	Ctrl+Shift+L
Right justify	Shift+⌘+R	Ctrl+Shift+R
Center	Shift+⌘+C	Ctrl+Shift+C
Justify	Shift+⌘+J	Ctrl+Shift+J
Force justify	Option+Shift+⌘+J	Ctrl+Alt+Shift+J

(continued)

Action or command	Macintosh	Windows
Find/change		
Find, find/change	⌘+F	Ctrl+F
Close find, close find/change	Option+⌘+F	Ctrl+Alt+F
Special characters (in finds)		
Carriage return	⌘+Return	Ctrl+Enter
Tab	⌘+Tab	Ctrl+Tab
Line break	Shift+⌘+Return	Ctrl+Shift+Enter
Column	⌘+keypad Enter	\c
Backslash (\)	⌘+\	Ctrl+\
Wildcard	⌘+?	Ctrl+?
Flex space	Shift+⌘+F	Ctrl+Shift+F
Punctuation space	⌘+period	Ctrl+period
Current box's page number	⌘+3	Ctrl+3
Previous box's page number	⌘+2	Ctrl+2
Next box's page number	⌘+4	Ctrl+4
Special characters		
Em dash	Option+Shift+hyphen	Ctrl+Shift+equal
Nonbreaking em dash	Option+⌘+equal	Ctrl+Alt+Shift+equal
En dash	Option+hyphen	Ctrl+Alt+Shift+hyphen
Nonbreaking hyphen	⌘+equal	Ctrl+equal
Discretionary hyphen	⌘+hyphen	Ctrl+hyphen
Nonbreaking space	⌘+spacebar	Ctrl+5
En space	Option+spacebar	Ctrl+Shift+6
Nonbreaking en space	Option+⌘+spacebar	Ctrl+Alt+Shift+6
Punctuation space	Shift+spacebar	Shift+spacebar or Ctrl+6
Nonbreaking punctuation space	Shift+⌘+spacebar	Ctrl+Shift+spacebar *or* Ctrl+Alt+6
Flex space	Option+Shift+spacebar	Ctrl+Shift+5
Nonbreaking flex space	Option+Shift+⌘+spacebar	Ctrl+Alt+Shift+5
Indent here	⌘+\	Ctrl+\

Action or command	Macintosh	Windows
Current page number	⌘+3	Ctrl+3
Previous box's page number	⌘+2	Ctrl+2
Next box's page number	⌘+4	Ctrl+4
New line	Shift+Return	Shift+Enter
Discretionary new line	⌘+Return	Ctrl+Enter
New column	keypad Enter	keypad Enter
New box	Shift+keypad Enter	Shift+keypad Enter
Right-indent tab	Option+Tab	Shift+Tab

Graphics handling

Action or command	Macintosh	Windows
Import picture at 36 dpi	Shift+click Open button in Get Picture dialog box	Shift+click Open button in Get Picture dialog box
Import color TIFF, JPEG, or Scitex CT as gray-scale	⌘+click Open in Get Picture dialog box	Ctrl+click Open in Get Picture dialog box
Import gray-scale TIFF, JPEG, or Scitex CT as black-and-white	⌘+click Open button in Get Picture dialog box	Ctrl+click Open button in Get Picture dialog box
Import EPS without importing spot colors' definitions	⌘+click Open button in Get Picture dialog box	Ctrl+click Open button in Get Picture dialog box
Reimport all pictures in a document	⌘+click Open button in Open dialog box	Ctrl+click Open button in Open dialog box
Center image within box	Shift+⌘+M	Ctrl+Shift+M
Fit image to box	Shift+⌘+F	Ctrl+Shift+F
Fit image proportionally to box	Option+Shift+⌘+F	Ctrl+Alt+Shift+F
Resize box constrained	Shift+drag	Shift+drag
Resize box at aspect ratio	Option+Shift+drag	Alt+Shift+drag
Resize box and scale picture	⌘+drag	Ctrl+drag
Resize box constrained and scale picture	Shift+⌘+drag	Ctrl+Shift+drag
Resize box at aspect ratio and scale picture	Option+Shift+⌘+drag	Ctrl+Alt+Shift+drag
Increase picture scale 5%	Option+Shift+⌘+>	Ctrl+Alt+Shift+>
Decrease picture scale 5%	Option+Shift+⌘+<	Ctrl+Alt+Shift+<
Negative image	Shift+⌘+hyphen	Ctrl+Shift+hyphen
Picture contrast specifications	Shift+⌘+C	Ctrl+Shift+C

(continued)

Action or command	Macintosh	Windows
Picture halftone specifications	Shift+⌘+H	Ctrl+Shift+H
Change line width	Shift+⌘+\	Ctrl+Shift+\
Increase line width to next size	Shift+⌘+>	Ctrl+Shift+>
Decrease line width to next size	Shift+⌘+<	Ctrl+Shift+<
Increase line width 1 point	Option+Shift+⌘+>	Ctrl+Alt+Shift+>
Decrease line width 1 point	Option+Shift+⌘+<	Ctrl+Alt+Shift+<
Delete Bézier point	Option+click point	Alt+click point
Add Bézier point	Option+click segment	Alt+click segment
Change to corner point	Option+F1	Ctrl+F1
Change to smooth point	Option+F2	Ctrl+F2
Change to symmetrical point	Option+F3	Ctrl+F3
Change to straight segment	Shift+Option+F1	Ctrl+Shift+F1
Change to curved segment	Shift+Option+F2	Ctrl+Shift+F2

Working with Contextual Menus

Windows 95, Windows NT 4, and Mac OS 8 all use a technique called *contextual menus* to save you time. By right-clicking an item in Windows, or Control+clicking on the Mac, you get a menu of options just for that item. This saves you time going through menus, dialog boxes, and palettes. QuarkXPress 4, unfortunately, really skimps when it comes to contextual menus. The feature isn't supported at all in the Mac version, and the Windows version supports only the following contextual menus:

✦ When you right-click on a page or an item on a page, you get the contextual menu shown in Figure B-1. Some options will be grayed out based on what is selected. For example, if you right-click on a page, you get only the top set of options, those that control the view. If you select a text box, for example, you can sometimes get all the options.

Figure B-1: The basic contextual menu in Windows QuarkXPress has view options, plus controls for manipulating items.

✦ When you right-click on a style in the Styles palette, you get the contextual menu shown in Figure B-2, which lets you add and delete styles quickly. We're surprised that Quark didn't offer similar contextual menus for all the palettes, although we won't be surprised to see such menus added in a future revision.

Figure B-2: The contextual menu for the Styles palette in Windows QuarkXPress lets you quickly add, delete, or edit styles.

✦   ✦   ✦

What's New in Version 4

◆ ◆ ◆ ◆

In This Appendix

New illustration and
text options

Interface and
navigation
improvements

The new indexing
and list features

Book and long-
document handling

New color
capabilities

File management
innovations

New printing
features

◆ ◆ ◆ ◆

The most significant additions to version 4 of
QuarkXPress are the revised user interface, the book
features for long documents, and character-based style
sheets. Other interesting new features are enhanced graphic
capabilities and the ability to set type on a Bézier curve. This
appendix gives you a concise overview of what's new in
QuarkXPress 4 and provides cross-references to the chapters
in this book where these features are covered in detail.

The new features in QuarkXPress 4 are covered in depth
throughout the book and are indicated by the New Feature
icon, like the one that appears in the margin next to this text.

New Illustration and Text Options

- ◆ **The new Tool palette:** Several new tools appear in the
  Tool palette. New Text Box, Picture Box, and Line tools
  are now offered, in addition to the old favorites. A new
  set of Text Path tools let you set type on a Bézier or
  freehand curve (see Chapters 2 and 9). To find out how
  to customize the Tool palette, see Chapter 3.

- ◆ **Switching between the Item and Content tools:** The
  Item tool and the Content tool have been changed so
  that you don't need to switch between them as often
  (for example, you can apply picture styles in Item
  mode). For more information, see Chapter 5.

- ◆ **Point-by-point tools:** These let you draw Bézier picture
  boxes, text boxes, lines, and text paths (see Chapters 5
  and 20).

- ◆ **Freehand tools:** These let you draw Bézier boxes, lines,
  and text paths (see Chapters 5, 9, 17, and 20).

- ◆ **Bézier editing techniques:** When creating a Bézier
  point, choose symmetrical, smooth, or corner points
  (see Chapters 5 and 20).

✦ **Select, move, and edit Bézier items:** You can do this using the Item tool or Content tool interchangeably (see Chapters 5 and 20).

✦ **Reshaping Bézier segments:** Reshape curved segments in a Bézier item by dragging curve handles, or by dragging parts of a segment (see Chapters 5 and 20).

✦ **Merging Bézier endpoints:** To merge endpoints from two Bézier lines to form one line, see Chapter 20.

✦ **Anchoring Bézier shapes to text:** Anchor nonrectangular or Bézier-shaped items to flow with text (see Chapter 7).

✦ **Flowing text along a Bézier path:** For information on this topic, see Chapters 17 and 20.

✦ **Bézier text and picture boxes:** To convert highlighted text into a Bézier-outline box and fill the box with a picture or text, see Chapter 20.

✦ **Converting standard and Bézier shapes:** To convert standard shapes into Bézier items and vice versa, see Chapter 20.

✦ **Converting lines and text paths:** You can choose a content type from a menu to convert lines to text paths and vice versa (see Chapter 20).

✦ **Converting boxes to no-content:** To convert a text box or a picture box to a no-content box, see Chapter 20.

✦ **Converting text boxes and picture boxes:** To find out how to change text boxes to picture boxes and vice versa, see Chapter 5.

✦ **Converting boxes and lines:** To convert boxes to lines, and lines to boxes, see Chapter 20.

✦ **Rotating text in a text box:** To rotate text within a text box, see Chapter 17.

✦ **Automatic and editable clipping paths and runaround:** Automatically create clipping paths and runaround based on white areas, an alpha channel, or an embedded path, or you can use the Bézier tools to edit clipping or runaround paths (see Chapter 5).

✦ **Extending pictures:** To find out how to extend a picture beyond its bounding box and picture box, see Chapter 5.

✦ **Putting text in pictures:** To find out how to position text inside the "holes" of a picture subject, see Chapter 5.

✦ **Running a column of text around an item:** Run a single column of text around all sides of an item (see Chapter 5).

✦ **Forming composite boxes:** You can merge multiple items to form one composite box (six different ways). For more information, see Chapter 20.

✦ **Splitting multiple-path items:** You can split multiple-path items to form several items (see Chapter 20).

✦ **Maintaining intended baselines:** An Offset field for anchored boxes maintains the intended baseline when converting highlighted text into an anchored Bézier box (see Chapter 7).

✦ **Tab settings:** You can now set thousands of tabs in a paragraph (see Chapter 15).

✦ **Hyphenation controls:** The expanded hyphenation method can check a built-in hyphenation exception dictionary (see Chapter 13).

✦ **Character style sheets:** You can now create and apply character style sheets (see Chapter 14).

✦ **Creating dash and stripe styles:** To create scaleable (PostScript), custom dash or stripe styles for lines and frames, see Chapter 20.

Interface and Navigation Improvements

✦ **Tabbed-pane dialog boxes:** These let you enter specific information on a variety of related issues, which are presented as panes with tabs at the top. To change from one pane to another, simply click on the tab name (see Chapter 2).

✦ **Find/Change controls:** These are now in a palette, and you can also find and change character and paragraph style sheets (see Chapter 11).

✦ **A Lists palette:** This displays all of the text associated with the style sheets in the document's list configuration (see Chapters 2 and 16).

✦ **Expanded view capability:** The ability to expand the view to 800 percent is new; the previous maximum was 400 percent (the maximum percent for the Windows version is dependent on monitor resolution). For more information, see Chapter 3.

✦ **Saving a document's position:** For more information on the new Document Position preference, see Chapter 3.

✦ **Measurements palette improvements:** Fields in the Measurements palette indicate the distance and angle of curve handles from their associated points (see Chapters 5 and 20).

✦ **The agate measurement system:** This has been added as an option in measurements. One agate (ag) is 0.071 inches (see Chapter 3).

✦ **Picture viewing information:** You can now view a picture file's path, file size, dimensions, color depth, and revision date (see Chapter 7).

✦ **Page number viewing:** To view actual page numbers in a sectioned document, or to view "absolute" page numbers in the Document Layout palette, see Chapter 8.

✦ **Enhanced live drag:** For more information on this subject (live refresh of the screen), see Chapter 18.

The New Indexing and List Features

✦ **An Index palette:** This lets you mark text and generate an alphabetized, hierarchical index. You build the index by choosing Build Index from the Utilities menu (Utilities⇨Build Index). For more information, see Chapters 2 and 16.

✦ **Tagging index entries:** To tag words for a four-level nested index or a two-level run-in index, see Chapter 16.

✦ **Creating cross-references:** You can create cross-references for an index (see Chapter 16).

✦ **Formatting an index:** When you create an index, you can specify its format, punctuation, master page, and style sheets (see Chapter 16).

✦ **Tables of contents:** You can automatically create tables of contents and other lists based on paragraph style sheets (see Chapter 16).

✦ **Alphabetizing paragraphs:** To automatically alphabetize paragraphs when using the Lists feature, see Chapter 16.

✦ **Updating lists and indexes:** You can update lists and indexes after you've edited them (see Chapter 16).

New Book and Long-Document Handling

✦ **Creating book files:** To create book files consisting of multiple chapters, see Chapter 16.

✦ **Using the Book palette:** You can open chapters through a book's palette (see Chapter 16).

✦ **Synchronizing multiple elements and styles:** To synchronize page numbering, style sheets, colors, H&J, lists, and dash and stripe styles among chapters in a book, see Chapter 16.

New Color Capabilities

✦ **Using the QuarkXPress CMS:** You can specify picture sources, device profiles, and color management preferences using the controls in QuarkXPress's bundled CMS software (see Chapter 23).

✦ **Hexachrome colors:** You can now specify high-fidelity Hexachrome printing output (see Chapter 21).

✦ **Multi-ink colors:** Multi-ink colors—colors that consist of percentages of any number of spot or process colors—are a new feature in QuarkXPress 4 (see Chapter 21).

✦ **Plate color controls:** To control screen frequency, angle, and dot function for each plate, see Chapter 24.

File Management Innovations

✦ **The new XTensions Manager:** This lets you decide which XTensions load with QuarkXPress. For details, see Chapter 25.

✦ **Saving to previous versions:** To save documents in QuarkXPress 3.3 format, see Chapter 22.

✦ **Listing document colors and style sheets:** To list which colors, style sheets, etc., are used in a document and which are not, see Chapter 22.

✦ **Importing style sheets and colors:** You can now use a single dialog box for importing style sheets, colors, and line and frame styles. For more information, see Chapter 22.

✦ **Context menus:** In the Windows version, you can click the right mouse button in a document to display a context menu that includes common clipboard, view, and modify commands (see Appendix B).

New Printing Features

✦ **Creating print styles:** You can create styles for frequently used Print settings (see Chapter 24).

✦ **PostScript error handler:** You can now benefit from the built-in PostScript error handler in QuarkXPress 4 (see Chapter 24).

✦ **Document to paper-size previews:** In the Print dialog box, you can see how a document fits its specified paper size (see Chapter 24).

✦ **Print noncontiguous pages:** To find out more about this feature, see Chapter 24.

✦   ✦   ✦

What's on the CD-ROM

✦   ✦   ✦   ✦

In This Appendix

Exploring the types of software

Installing the CD

Touring what's on the CD

✦   ✦   ✦   ✦

The CD that accompanies this book contains a wealth of software—some free, some demo, and some shareware. All are meant to make QuarkXPress work even better. Some are XTensions that enhance QuarkXPress directly, while others are stand-alone utilities that you will use before or after QuarkXPress. This appendix tells you everything you need to know to install, road-test, and enjoy what's on the CD.

Exploring the Types of Software

There are three types of software on the CD. Some won't cost you a dime, but others are meant to give you a chance to test them out before you decide to buy. Here's how it works:

✦ **Free software:** This is exactly that: free. You may use it at no charge. (You may not sell it to others, however. And you must get permission from the software's authors to redistribute it, even if you distribute at no charge.)

✦ **Demo software:** This is meant to be used on a trial basis, so you can see if you like it. If you do, you should buy the full version, usually available in stores and mail-order catalogs in a version that includes documentation and a CD or set of disks. Most demo software does one of the following three things to ensure that people don't use demo software instead of purchasing the retail product:

  ✦ Prevents you from being able to save QuarkXPress documents while the software is loaded.

  ✦ Provides limited functionality until you purchase the full version.

  ✦ Expires after a certain number of days of use.

✦ **Shareware:** This is also meant to be used on a trial basis, so you can see if you like it. If you do, you should buy the full version, usually available by sending in a registration fee and getting a code that converts the shareware into a fully functioning version, or getting a fully functioning version on CD or disks mailed to you. Most shareware does one of three things to ensure that people don't use it instead of purchasing the complete product:

   ✦ Prevents you from being able to save QuarkXPress documents while the software is loaded.

   ✦ Provides limited functionality until you purchase the full version.

   ✦ Expires after a certain number of days of use.

Installing the CD

Installing the CD's software is easy. Insert the CD into your computer. On a Mac, the CD will automatically display on your desktop like a floppy disk or hard disk. On a PC, you may have to open the CD from the Explorer or from the window that appears when you double-click your My Computer icon. Once the CD is mounted, install the software as follows:

   ✦ For most XTensions, just drag the XTension file into the XTension folder in your hard disk's QuarkXPress program folder. The next time you open QuarkXPress, the XTension will be launched as well.

   ✦ Some XTensions require that you run an installation program, as do most of the utilities. Just double-click the installation icon and follow the on-screen instructions.

Play, but please pay

Please pay for and register any demo software or shareware that you use regularly. It's fine to use these programs without paying while you're figuring out if they would really help you, but once you decide they are worthwhile, please support the companies and individuals who created the software so they can afford to create even better software in the future.

We make it easy for you to know which software is free and which is not by adding the price at the end of the folder name, or the word "free." The word "demo" means that the price is based on a site license or other variable basis.

Touring What's on the CD

Chapter 27 covers the XTensions and publishing-oriented utilities in depth, while Chapter 28 covers the general shareware. What follows is a list of the CD's contents, with a very brief description of what the software does.

Macintosh software

The CD's offerings are organized by several folders, to help you more easily navigate the contents. Each folder has a different label color as well.

Product catalogs

All the product catalogs require the free Adobe Acrobat 3.0 Reader, which is included in this folder. We highlight two companies' catalogs because they provided much of the software on the CD:

 ◆ XT-now

 ◆ Extensis

In the Other Companies folder are catalogs for A Lowly Apprentice Production, World-Wide Power Company, and XChange.

QuarkXPress utilities

Several utilities enhance QuarkXPress even though they are not plug-in XTensions. We include:

 ◆ **Badia Ready-to-Fax:** This lets you fax documents from QuarkXPress and adjust how color objects convert to black-and-white.

 ◆ **Extensis Preflight Pro:** This checks QuarkXPress documents for problems that may hinder output.

 ◆ **Stubbs Designer Palettes:** These are predefined color sets that look good together.

 ◆ **Stubbs Designer Templates:** These are predefined templates for common documents such as business cards and brochures.

Repetitive stress avoidance

Macworld magazine created this animated tour of how to use input devices in a way that greatly reduces the chance of repetitive strain injury (RSI), a debilitating condition caused by improper use of mice or other input devices, improper layout of computer equipment and office furniture, and improper posture.

Scripting tools

QuarkXPress's scripting functions are very powerful, and with the right tools you can create scripts that will automate much of your routine work. We provide three scripting tools to help you write such scripts, all of which are covered in Chapter 26:

+ Main Event Scripter
+ Street Logic ScriptMaster
+ Vision's Edge Script Manager

We also provide a sample script called Raise Trademark Symbols written by Quark's Kelly Kordes Anton that you can use to make trademarks look better when printed or as an example script from which to start learning how to script yourself.

Shareware

To help make your Mac work a little better as a publishing platform, we've included several general utilities (they are not QuarkXPress-specific):

+ **Aaron and Aaron Light:** These enhance the user interface.
+ **DOSWasher:** This makes working with PC files easier.
+ **FontLoupe:** This lets you preview fonts' character sets.
+ **Graphics Converter:** This lets you translate odd graphics formats into ones that QuarkXPress imports.
+ **Kaleidoscope:** This lets you change the look and feel of the Macintosh interface.
+ **PopChar Pro:** This helps you easily insert any character from any font into any program.
+ **Program Switcher:** This lets you use Option+Tab to switch among open programs, rather than use the Applications menu.

Web-authoring tools

Producing documents for the Web is fast becoming another facet of regular publishing, so we offer three XTensions that convert QuarkXPress into a Web-publishing tool. Chapters 33 through 35 cover these tools in depth:

+ Astrobyte BeyondPress
+ Extensis CyberPress
+ HexMax HexWeb

We also provide a QuarkXPress document, called Web-Safe Colors, that contains the definitions for every color guaranteed to display accurately on the Web. When creating Web documents, import your colors from this document to get perfect color.

XTensions

QuarkXPress's plug-in capability has opened the door for an incredible array of XTensions that add functionality to QuarkXPress. We've canvassed the Web and XTension catalogs to get a broad sample of 50 useful XTensions, all of which are covered in Chapter 27:

✦ **Adobe Prepress XTension:** This lets QuarkXPress work with Adobe's color-separation software.

✦ **ALAP (A Lowly Apprentice Production) ColorPick:** This adds a second Colors palette.

✦ **ALAP FingerType:** This lets you visually format paragraphs.

✦ **ALAP Imposer:** This lets you manage page imposition and folded spreads.

✦ **ALAP Item Master:** This adds a style-sheet-like capability for box attributes.

✦ **ALAP MarkIt:** This lets you control crop marks and other output guides.

✦ **ALAP PasteIt:** This remembers an item's original location when you paste it to a new spread.

✦ **ALAP QuickOpen:** This skips the annoying Non-Matching Preferences dialog box.

✦ **ALAP ScaleLock:** This disables the ⌘+click interactive resizing.

✦ **ALAP ShadowCaster:** This lets you create sophisticated shadows for text and other items.

✦ **ALAP StoryChaser:** This displays statistics of where your stories flow.

✦ **ALAP XPert Tools Volume 1:** This is a collection of handy tools and enhancements for QuarkXPress.

✦ **ALAP XPert Tools Volume 2:** This is another collection of handy tools and enhancements for QuarkXPress.

✦ **Bad Knees Create Crops:** This converts boxes into crop marks.

✦ **Boskamp Article-XT:** This lets you create Adobe Portable Document Format (PDF) files from QuarkXPress.

✦ **Boskamp FlowMaster:** This monitors how text flows in your document.

✦ **Boskamp FlowWatch:** This alerts you when text flows differently than in the original document; the original document must have been created with the FlowMaster XTension installed.

✦ **Boskamp SpeedOpen:** This bypasses the annoying Non-Matching Preferences dialog box.

✦ **College Fund DocMagnify:** This offers greater zoom percentages than QuarkXPress does.

✦ **CompuSense Picture Manager:** This lets you generate caption boxes and otherwise manage pictures.

✦ **CompuSense The Bundler:** This collects all needed files for output at a service bureau—even fonts.

✦ **Dalai DropIt:** This lets you drag and drop files from the Finder into QuarkXPress.

✦ **Extensis QX-Drag&Drop:** This also lets you drag and drop files from the Finder into QuarkXPress.

✦ **Extensis QX-Tools:** This is a great collection of enhancements for QuarkXPress.

✦ **FCSLock:** This lets you disable specific tools and palettes for specific users in a networked environment.

✦ **FCSTableMaker:** This adds table-creation features to the Tabs pane.

✦ **Gluon PICTMaker:** This lets you create PICT images from your pages.

✦ **Gluon TableMaker:** This lets you convert tab-delimited text into tables.

✦ **Gluon TextWaves:** This lets you create wavy text effects.

✦ **HanMac HX PowerSelect:** This lets you work with noncontiguous selections of text.

✦ **HanMac HX PowerUnderline:** This lets you create custom underlines.

✦ **Koyosha Precision Preview:** This lets you zoom in to your document and its images without getting blocky results.

✦ **LastWord ChangeCase:** This lets you change selected text's case easily.

✦ **Markzware Pasteboard XT:** This lets you create custom pasteboard sizes. Also included is the Pasteboard XTerminator, which is required to open documents created with older versions of the Pasteboard XT.

✦ **Meadow Information Systems' Math Grabber:** This lets you perform numerical calculations on text.

✦ **NAPS (North Atlantic Publishing Systems) PubViews:** This lets you preview pages.

✦ **Nisus Writer filter:** This lets you import Nisus Writer files.

✦ **Perroud Alias Pro:** This lets you perform multiple find/change operations, including handling special characters.

✦ **Second Glance Clone:** This lets you create sheets of labels quickly.

✦ **Tableworks' Entable:** This lets you create sophisticated tables (formerly known as Npath Software's Tableworks Pro).

✦ **Techno Design PDF Design:** This lets you create Adobe Portable Document Format (PDF) files from QuarkXPress.

✦ **Techno Design Photoshop Import:** This lets you import Photoshop graphics directly.

✦ **VE (Vision's Edge) AdCreation Toolkit:** This adds several functions designed for creating ads, such as starbursts, polygon masks, and 3-D drop shadows.

✦ **VE Bookletizer:** This lets you adjust the position of items on folded spreads.

✦ **VE Layer It:** This lets you manage the stacking order of elements.

✦ **VE Nouveau II:** This expands the New dialog box's capabilities.

✦ **VE PageBorder:** This adds a border around printed pages.

✦ **VE Thesaurus reX:** This adds an electronic thesaurus to QuarkXPress.

✦ **VE XNotes:** This lets you add Post-it®-like notes to your documents.

Windows software

The CD's offerings are organized by several folders, to help you more easily navigate the contents. The CD has little Windows software because so few XTensions are available for Windows QuarkXPress. Also, Quark changed the format for Windows XTensions in version 4, so no 4-compatible XTensions were available for Windows QuarkXPress when this book was published. That should change, so be sure to check out the Web-based XTension sources listed in Chapter 25 for the latest Windows add-ons.

Design aids

The Designer Templates from Joseph Stubbs include a variety of premade documents, such as CD labels and business cards, that you can use as is or modify.

Mac Dingbat font

If you're writing about Macintosh programs but using a PC to produce your documents, use this free TrueType font to access common Mac symbols, such as the Apple logo and the Mac's special keyboard characters. Just drag the MAC_DING.TTF font to the FONTS directory within your Windows directory (usually called WINDOWS or WIN95).

Product catalogs

All the product catalogs require the free Adobe Acrobat 3.0 Reader, which is included in this folder. We highlight two companies' catalogs because they provided much of the software on the CD:

+ XT-now

+ Extensis

In the Other Companies folder are catalogs for A Lowly Apprentice Production, World-Wide Power Company, and XChange.

Shareware

To help make your PC work a little better as a publishing platform, we've included a couple of general utilities (they are not QuarkXPress-specific):

+ **ShoveIt:** This lets you put the Start menu at the top of your screen (where it's easier to reach) without covering the menu bars of your programs.

+ **WinZip:** This is an essential tool for creating and opening compressed archives.

Web publishing color template

We provide a QuarkXPress document, called Web-Safe Colors.qxt, which contains the definitions for every color guaranteed to display accurately on the Web. When creating Web documents, import your colors from this document to get perfect color.

✦   ✦   ✦

Index

SYMBOLS AND NUMERALS

... (ellipses), tracking for, 241
" (quotation marks)
  defaults, 49
  drop caps and, 324
  keyboard shortcuts, 656
  rules for use, 657
  typographic (smart) quotes, 49,
   655-657
256-color system palette, 726
5280 magazine, 704-705, 706-707

A

Aaron Light utility, 860
Aaron utility, 610, 860
accents
  Accents for All Caps option, 59
  for bullets, 319
  keyboard shortcuts, 661-664
Accurate Blends option, 55, 356
activating
  CMS XTension, 479-480
  XTensions, 242, 246
  See also selecting
active items, identifying, 35
AdCreation Toolkit XTension,
  589-591, 863
Adobe PrePress XTension (APX),
  546-547, 861
Adobe Systems
  Adobe PrePress XTension (APX),
   546-547, 861
  Adobe Type Manager (ATM), 608,
   625-627
  Adobe Type Reunion (ATR), 608
  Font Creator XTension, 651-652
  PageMill, 698, 700, 702, 703, 748,
   773
  Portable Document Format
   (PDF), 586
  TrapWise, 478, 546
Adobe Type Manager (ATM), 608,
  625-627
Adobe Type Reunion (ATR), 608
ads and circulars, 666-670
  airline ad mockup, 666-667
  folded documents, 86
  public service announcement,
   669-670
  restaurant ad mockup, 667-668
ag, measurement unit, 6
agate inches, 9
agates, 6, 39
airline ad mockup, 666-667
ALAP. See Lowly Apprentice
  Production, A

Alias Pro XTension, 581-582, 862
aligning elements
  CyberPress defaults, 757-758, 760
  text on text path, 329-330,
   409-410
  using Space/Align Items dialog
   box, 197-199
  using Step and Repeat dialog box,
   199-201
alignment of text. See aligning
  elements, justification
align-on tabs, 287
  See also tabs
All Append Sources, Display All Files
  versus, 455
Alpha Channel, runaround mode, 122
alpha channels, identifying, 123
American Newspaper Publishers
  Association (ANPA) color
  model, 418, 422
anchoring
  boxes and lines, 168-169
  CyberPress Content List
   elements, 766
  drop caps and, 325
  modifying anchored items,
   169-170
anchors, 723
Angle, print option, 508
ANPA color model, 418, 422
Antialias, BeyondPress option, 785
Append Conflict dialog box, 284
Append dialog box, 433-434,
  451-452
Append Style Sheets dialog box, 281-
  282
appending
  colors, 413, 433-434
  overview, 451-452
  style sheets, 281-282, 284
  See also importing
Apple
  FinePrint, 373
  Photo Access, 151
  PhotoGrade, 373
Apple Developer Catalog, 537
Apple Events Object Hierarchy, 535
AppleScript, 533-536
  basics, 534-535
  checking for syntax errors,
   538-539
  connecting programs with
   scripts, 541-543
  further information, 536
  learning, 534
  running scripts, 439
  saving scripts, 539-540
  Script Editor, 536, 537
  scripting conventions, 542
  tools for, 536-537, 543

  writing scripts, 538, 540-541
  See also scripts
AppleScript for Dummies, 536
AppleScript Handbook, 536
AppleScript Software Development
  Toolkit, 537
AppleScript Sourcebook Web site,
  544
Applet, BeyondPress option, 792
Application Preferences dialog box
  Display pane, 41-44, 46-47, 89-90,
   114, 356
  Interactive pane, 48-50, 356-357
  overview, 38
  Save pane, 62-64
  XTensions pane, 524-525
applications. See CD-ROM with this
  book; software; utilities;
  XTensions
applying
  colors, 426-432
  drop caps, 322
  master pages to existing pages,
   53, 211
  style sheets, 280
APX (Adobe PrePress XTension),
  546-547, 861
arrowheads for lines, 388-390
arrows for scrolling, 18, 19
Article-XT for PDF, 560, 861
ascenders, 8, 644
Assadi, Barbara, 603-604
Astrobyte's BeyondPress. See
  BeyondPress
ATM (Adobe Type Manager), 608,
  625-627
ATR (Adobe Type Reunion), 608
Auto Amount option, 62, 473, 475
Auto Anchor Images, BeyondPress
  option, 780
Auto Backup option, 63, 616, 623
Auto Constrain option, 55, 96
Auto Create Tables, BeyondPress
  option, 780
Auto Image, runaround mode, 122
Auto Kern Above feature, 58, 246
Auto Leading option, 60
Auto Library Save option, 63-64
Auto Page Insertion options, 51
Auto Picture Import options, 52-53
Auto Save option, 63, 615-616, 623
automatic leading, 263
Automatic Text Box option, 19, 85, 97
auxiliary dictionaries
  overview, 230-231, 446
  sharing in workgroups, 445-446
  transferring across platforms,
   446, 457
Auxiliary Dictionary dialog box, 230

B

Back to Front, print option, 504
background color
    for color trapping, 472-473
    CyberPress defaults, 752-753
    for picture boxes, 346-348
    tools, 381
    for Web pages, 739
background images for Web pages,
    784
backing up, preferences for, 63
Bad Knees' CreateCrops XTension,
    559, 861
Badia, Dario, 596
banner for magazine table of
    contents, 676
bar chart, creating, 392, 393
Based On, style sheet option, 274,
    275, 276, 279
baseline grids
    color of, 41-42, 88-89
    hiding and showing, 45, 88
    Increment option, 264
    Lock to Baseline Grid option, 264-
        265
    preferences, 60-61, 88
    tips and tricks, 265
    using, 88-89
    See also guides
Baseline Shift feature, 646-647, 845
Bdlr menu, 566
Before X-ref, index option, 305
Between Entries, index option, 305
Between Page #s, index option, 305
Between Page Range, index option,
    305
Beveled-Corner Picture Box tool, 104,
    105
Beveled-Corner Text Box tool, 99
BeyondPress, 775-810
    Authoring mode, 805-806
    BeyondPress Preferences dialog
        box, 777-793
    boxes, 807
    browser for viewing, 780
    color defaults, 782, 783-784
    Content list, 799-803
    content-related options, 779-780
    converting documents, 793-794,
        798-805
    creating design-intensive pages,
        706-708
    creating new Web pages, 704, 708,
        795
    creating tables of contents, 704-
        705
    creating Web pages from scratch,
        805-809
    dedicated Web-page software
        versus, 708, 776
    defaults, specifying, 777-793
    demo version on CD, 776, 860
    Document Content palette,
        793-795
    drag-and-drop feature, 810
    Elements palette, 795-798

Export Progress window, 804
exporting QuarkXPress
    documents, 704, 798-805, 808,
    809
    fonts with, 729-730
    graphics conversion, 802
    graphics defaults, 784-786
    headers and footers, 784
    hyperlinks, 801
    image maps, 786, 802
    image-storing tips, 796
    interface, 776
    layouts, 791-792, 808-809
    lists, 790-791
    margins, 805
    master pages, 807
    multiple-page sites, 778
    other features, 810
    overview, 697, 703, 775-776
    paragraph formats, 732
    previewing Web pages, 803-804,
        809
    scriptability, 780-781, 810
    sizing Web pages, 805
    special character mapping, 810
    tables, 789-790
    templates, 807
    text formatting, 728, 807
    text ranges in, 800-801
    upgrading CyberPress to, 703
    Web sites, 703-708
BeyondPress Lite. See CyberPress
BeyondPress Preferences dialog box,
    777-793
    Application defaults, 778-781
    Export defaults, 781-783
    Image defaults, 784-786
    Layout defaults, 791-792
    Media defaults, 792-793
    overview, 777-778
    Site defaults, 778, 779
    Text defaults, 786-791
    Web Page defaults, 783-784
Bézier controls
    adding, 388
    changing, 386-388
    deleting, 388
    using, 384-385
Bézier curves
    adding control points, 388
    changing control points,
        386-388
    changing straight lines to, 189
    creating, 27, 185-187, 384
    deleting control points, 388
    moving, 386
    reshaping, 188, 384-386
Bézier Line tool, 384
Bézier Picture Box tool, 26, 104, 105
Bézier picture boxes
    creating, 26
    reshaping, 113-114
Bézier, Pierre, 384
Bézier pointer, 34
Bézier Text Box tool, 99-100
Bézier text boxes
    creating, 25

    reshaping, 113-114
Bézier Text Path tool, 329, 409
bit depth, gray levels and, 370
bitmap frames
    creating, 403-407
    sharing in workgroups, 445
    using, 407
bitmap graphics, 359-380
    bitmap frames, 403-407
    color adjustments, 378-379
    contrast adjustments, 364-370
    dithering, 377-378
    enlarging or reducing, 362
    formats, 150-151, 360-361
    halftone controls, 370-376
    image alteration, 359
    image controls available,
        362-363
    Negative feature, 364
    output control, 359
    saving, 362
    shade adjustments, 379-380
    Style menu functions, 359-360
    translating to usable formats, 361
    vector graphics versus, 144-145
    See also graphics
black
    mixing with spot colors, 424
    superblack, 420
black-and-white images
    color adjustment for, 378-379
    dithering, 377-378
    halftones, 370-376
    negatives, 364
    saving, 362
    shading adjustment for, 379-380
blank pages, printing, 503
Blaschek, Günther, 610
bleeding and paper, 373
bleeds
    defined, 13, 78
    layouts, 78-79
    print option, 505
    registration problems, 79
    service bureaus and, 467
    spreading method of color
        trapping, 470-471
blends
    accurate display of, 55, 356
    applying to boxes, 429-430
    effect of, 430
    picture box background, 347-348
    tips and tricks, 348
block indents, 11, 312-313
BMP files, 145, 362
    See also bitmap graphics
body text of newsletters, 674
boldface type, 317, 641
    See also type styles
Book palette
    control icons, 296-297
    status reports, 296
Bookletizer XTension, 592, 863
book-oriented editing, 293-310
    adding chapters, 296-297
    Book Chapter Start feature, 299
    Book palette, 296-297

chapter sections, 299-300
creating new books, 294-295
deleting chapters, 297
indexes, 303-310
lists, 300-303
master chapters, 295-296
new features, 854
page numbering, 299
planning books, 293-294
printing chapters and books, 297, 298-299
rearranging chapters, 297
synchronizing chapter formatting, 297
borders. *See* clipping paths; frames; runarounds
Boskamp, Tobias
about, 560
XTensions by, 560-563, 861-862
boxes. *See* frames; picture boxes; text boxes
Break Capitalized Words option, 256
brochures, 86
See also ads and circulars
Browser Determined, BeyondPress option, 792
browsers. *See* Web browsers
Build Index dialog box, 308-310
builds, 15
bulleted lists
BeyondPress defaults, 790-791
characters for bullets, 316, 319
CyberPress defaults, 760-761
style for, 314-316
bullets
defined, 11
en bullets, 315-316, 319, 658
en spaces after, 316
Bundler XTension, 565-566, 862
buttons, 18, 19
bylines, 313, 674

C

c, measurement unit, 6
calibrating
imported colors, 484-486
monitors, 480, 481-482, 483
cameo effects, 684
cameras, digital, 607
canceling
live links, 163
printing, 503
style sheet changes, 273
cap height of type, 8
capitalization
Accents for All Caps option, 59
all caps, 642
ChangeCase XTension, 578-579
drop caps, 12, 321-324
hybrid drop caps, 324-325
hyphenating capitalized words, 256
raised caps, 12, 324
small caps, 58, 317, 642-643, 681

captions
HexWeb defaults, 819
PictureManager XTension, 564-565
typefaces for, 637
carding, 11
cascading style sheets
BeyondPress, 782, 786-788
CyberPress, 756
catalogs of products, on CD, 859, 864
Categories dialog box (HexWeb), 813-814
CD-ROM drives, 607
CD-ROM with this book
BeyondPress demo version on, 776
design aids, 863
installing, 858
Mac Dingbat font, 863
Macintosh software, 859-863
product catalogs, 859, 864
shareware, 858, 860, 864
types of software included, 857-858
using XTension demos on, 546
utilities, 859
Web-authoring tools, 860-861
Windows software, 863-864
XTensions, 861-863
center tabs, 286
See also tabs
centered alignment, 10
centimeters, 6, 39
CGM files, 146
ChangeCase XTension, 578-579, 862
chapters. *See* book-oriented editing
Character Attributes, style sheet option, 274
Character Attributes dialog box
Kern Amount option, 249
Scale option, 249
Track Amount option, 242
typeface settings, 639
Web publishing and, 727
character formatting, importing, 136-137
Character Map utility, 138
character preferences, 57-60
character defaults, 58-59
special characters, 59-60
character spacing, 235-252
defined, 9, 235
horizontal spacing controls, 58-59
kerning, 9-10, 28, 58, 245-249
scaling typefaces, 249-251
tracking, 9, 28, 237-243
typefaces and, 236
typographic color, 236
See also hyphenation; kerning; tracking
Check Output Width/Height Tags, BeyondPress option, 785
checking spelling, 228-231
auxiliary dictionaries, 230-231, 446, 457
Check Spelling menu, 228-229

keyboard shortcuts, 843
looking up words, 229
replacing words, 229
suspect words, 229
choking, 470-471
See also color trapping
ciceros, 6, 39, 40
CIE LAB standard, 15
circulars. *See* ads and circulars
clearing. *See* deleting
clipping paths
cropping to box, 124
defined, 122
editing, 126
rebuilding, 124
runaround modes and, 122
tolerance options, 124-125
Clone XTension, 582-583, 863
cm, measurement unit, 6
CMS color profiles, 440, 457
CMS XTension
activating, 479-480
importing files and, 149
overview, 479
CMYK color model, 15, 415, 422
defining, 483
Designer Color Palettes, 598
importing color pictures, 484
RGB color model versus, 693
RGB-to-CMYK conversion, 431
codes
for measurement units, 6, 39
XPress Tags, 141-144
Collate, print option, 504
Collect for Output feature, 463-465
College Fund's Doc Magnify XTension, 653-654, 862
color bars, 552, 553
color depth, gray levels and, 370
color gamut, 15
Color Management Preferences dialog box, 479-480, 482-483
Color Management System XTension. *See* CMS XTension
color models, 414-422
available models, 415-416
color wheel models, 419
defined, 15
defining, 483-484
overview, 414-415
Pantone Hexachrome, 15, 412, 416, 483
paper variation models, 416-417
POCE models, 416, 421
RGB-to-CMYK conversion, 431
simulating other models, 422
swatch models, 420-421
swatchbooks, 418
color prepress, 469-487
CMS XTension activation, 479-480
color trapping, 469-478
default source profiles, 482-483
defining color models, 483-484
monitor display options, 480-482
output profile selection, 482-487
printing options, 486-487

color profiles
  calibrating imported colors, 484-486
  sharing project elements and, 440
  transferring across platforms, 457
color scanners, 607
color separations
  defined, 15, 370
  imagesetter options, 507-508
  importing graphics and, 148-149
  printing, 503, 507-508, 513-514
color spaces, 15
color trapping, 469-478
  amount of, 473
  background color, 472-473
  choking versus spreading, 470-471
  defined, 16, 469
  independent trapping tools, 478
  knockouts versus overprints, 471
  need for, 469
  object color, 472
  overriding, 476-477
  overview, 469-471
  preferences, 61-62, 474-476
  Relationship option, 474
  reverse relationship, 474
  settings, 471-474
  trapping rationale, 478
ColorPick XTension, 547
colors, 411-434
  256-color system palette, 726
  adjusting for gray-scale or black-and-white images, 378-379
  appending, 413, 433-434
  applying, 426-432
  BeyondPress defaults, 782, 783-784
  blends, displaying, 55
  calibrating imported colors, 484-486
  changing picture colors, 354
  color models, 414-422
  color pictures, working with, 431-432
  color prepress, 469-487
  Color TIFFs option, 46, 47, 356
  ColorPick XTension, 547
  Colors dialog box, 413-414
  for control handles, 114
  copying, 413
  CyberPress defaults, 752-754
  defining, 413-422
  deleting, 413, 432
  Designer Color Palettes, 598
  displaying color groups, 434
  editing, 413, 420
  editing trapping values, 413
  for gray-scale images, 684
  for guides and rulers, 41-42, 89-90
  importing graphics and, 148-149
  index marker color, 304
  judicious use of, 688
  for lines, 188
  mixing spot and process color, 412, 425-426

multi-ink colors, 412, 425-426
  new features, 855
  for picture box background, 346-348
  predefined colors, 414
  printing methods, 411-413
  process color, 15, 61, 411-413
  QuarkXPress minimum requirements, 837
  RGB-to-CMYK conversion, 431
  sharing definitions, 441
  sharing in workgroups, 441-442
  spot color, 14, 411-413, 422-425
  swatchbooks, 418
  terms, 14-15
  for text, 331-332
  tips and tricks, 420
  transferring across platforms, 442, 457
  trapping preferences, 61-62
  typographic color, 236
  Web publishing and, 417, 725-726, 754
  Web-Safe Colors.qxt template, 861, 864
Colors dialog box, 413-414
Colors for document name dialog box, 434
Colors palette, 426-430
  blend choices, 429-430
  directing color application, 427-428
  overview, 29-30, 426-427
  shade percentage specification, 428
  for text, 331
column balancing, 10
columns
  copy fitting, 232-233
  defined, 13
  for folded documents, 86
  gutter width, 85
  intercolumn rules, 117
  leading and, 262, 263
  New Document dialog box, 83-85
  in newsletters, 671, 674
  number of, 83-84, 116
  table, vertical lines between, 291
  in Web pages, 721-722
  Web pages and, 696
Combine, merge option, 396
combining boxes and lines, 391-393
comma tabs, 286, 287
  See also tabs
comparing
  attributes of elements, 453
  style sheets, 282
compiling lists, 302
composite printer, 482
Composite Profile, print option, 512
Composite Simulates Separation, print option, 512
compressed type, 7, 250
compression utilities, 609, 864
CompuSense
  about, 564
  Bundler XTension, 565-566, 862

PictureManager XTension, 564-565, 862
computers. See DOS servers; hardware; Macintosh computers; Unix servers; Windows computers
Concave-Corner Picture Box tool, 104
Concave-Corner Text Box tool, 99
condensed type, 7, 250
Connectix
  RAM Doubler, 609
  Speed Doubler, 609
consecutive hyphenation, 12
constraining boxes, 55, 95-96
constraining lines when reshaping, 386
Content list (BeyondPress), 799-803
  adding groups, 799-800
  graphics, 802
  hyperlinks, 801
  modifying the list, 800-802
  naming items, 800
  other items, 802-803
  overview, 799
  rearranging items, 800
  segmenting text chains, 801
  text items, 800
  text ranges, 800-801
  Web pages, 801-802
Content Lists (CyberPress)
  anchoring elements, 767-768
  creating, 762-763
  deleting items, 766
  exporting, 772-774
  rearranging items, 766
  renaming items, 766
Content tool, 23-24, 109
contextual menus, 848-849
Continued on and Continued from markers, 181
contrast, 364-370
  color contrast adjustments, 366-367
  customized settings, 368-369
  filters for adjusting, 365, 366
  gray levels, 370
  manually adjusting, 367-368
  Picture Contrast Specifications dialog box, 364-369
  previewing adjustments, 365
  returning to common gray-level map, 369
control handles
  Bézier controls, 384-385, 386-388
  color of, 114
  defined, 111
  reshaping boxes, 113-114
Conversions Plus, 461, 462
Convert Bold & Italic Fonts, BeyondPress option, 782
converting
  documents with BeyondPress, 798-805
  fitting text to curves, 328-330, 409-410
  text into graphics, 407-410, 768-769

text with CyberPress, 768-770
text-based boxes, 407-409
COPS' COPSTalk, 605
copy fitting, 232-233, 240
copying
    colors, 413
    dash and stripe styles, 403
    graphics, 685
    groups, 93
    H&J sets, 254
    importing versus, 153-154
    layer stacking order and, 93
    layout elements between
        documents, 170-171, 173
    library elements, 220
    pages between documents, 171-
        173
    Pastelt XTension for, 552
    style sheets, 272
    styles, 272, 281-282
    text, 224
    See also appending; exporting;
        importing
copyright symbol, 658-659
Corner Point option, 388
corner shape for picture boxes, 343,
    345, 346
corporate logos. See logos
coupons, creating, 669
Create Relative URLs, BeyondPress
    option, 781
CreateCrops XTension, 559, 861
Creation pointer, 33
credit lines, indenting, 313
crop marks
    CreateCrops XTension, 559
    defined, 16
    page setup, 81
    printing, 504-505
Crop To Box button, 124, 125
cropping
    defined, 14
    graphics with Measurements
        palette, 342
    graphics with Modify dialog box,
        351-352
    runaround or clipping path, 124
cross-platform networks, 461-462
Cruise, John, 604
CT files (Scitex), 145, 362
curly quotation marks, 49
currency symbols, 659
Current Text Box Page Number
    character, 180
cursors. See pointers
Curved Segment option, 388
curves, Bézier. See Bézier curves
customizing
    baseline grids, 60-61, 88
    BeyondPress defaults, 777-793
    blends, display of, 55
    box constraints, 55
    character preferences, 57-60
    contrast settings for bitmaps,
        368-369
    coordinate controls, 40
    CyberPress defaults, 750-761
    drag-and-drop editing, 50

frame parameters, 52
global versus local preferences,
    38
greeking, 54-55
guide and ruler colors, 41-42
guide display, 42-43, 87
HexWeb defaults, 812-819
image displays, 46-47
index preferences, 304-305
item dragging, 50
keyboard shortcuts for, 840
master page item changes, 53
measurement system, 37-40
monitor display options, 43-44,
    480-482
Non-Matching Preferences dialog
    box, 553
page insertion, 51
palettes, 382-383
paragraph preferences, 60-61
pasteboard size, 48
quotation marks, 49
scrolling, 49-50
snap distance, 54, 88
Tool palette, 106
tools, 55-57
typography defaults, 644
View menu options, 44-46
XTension startup sets, 529-530
XTensions Manager, 524-525
    See also XTensions
cutting
    deleting versus, 224
    groups, 93
    layer stacking order and, 93
    library elements, 219-220
    See also deleting
CV, after Pantone color numbers, 148
CyberPress, 745-774
    adding master elements, 764-765
    adding text, 763-764
    aligning graphics, 757-758
    boxes, working with, 762-764
    browser for viewing, 751
    on CD, 860
    color defaults, 751-754
    Content Lists, 762-763, 766-768
    conversion basics, 746
    converting text, 768-770
    creating basic pages, 700, 701
    CyberPress palette, 747, 748-750
    CyberPress Preferences dialog
        box, 746-747, 750-761
    dedicated Web-page software
        versus, 708
    defaults, specifying, 750-761
    deleting master elements, 765
    destination platform, 751
    finishing touches, 773
    font size defaults, 754-755
    graphics exporting tips, 759
    graphics features, 699
    graphics format defaults, 757
    headers and footers, 754, 755
    hyperlinks, 753-754, 770-772
    interface, 746-750
    lists, 760-761, 769
    Open In Browser option, 773

overview, 697, 699
PageMill with, 698, 700, 702-703,
    748, 773
scaling graphics, 758
special characters, mapping, 769-
    770
style of working with, 745-746
tables, 758-760, 769
text formatting available, 728
text ranges in, 763-764
type styles, 755-757
upgrading to BeyondPress, 703
viewing Web pages, 773-774
Web sites, 698-703
CyberPress Preferences dialog box,
    750-761
    Article defaults, 751-754
    Export defaults, 751
    Font Size defaults, 754-757
    Image defaults, 757-758
    List defaults, 760-761
    opening, 746
    overview, 746-747, 750
    Table defaults, 758-760

D

dagger symbol, 659
Dainippon swatchbooks, 418
Dalai Software's DropIt XT, 566-567,
    862
dashed lines
    copying styles, 403
    creating, 398-401
    previewing, 400
    in public service announcement,
        669
    sharing in workgroups, 445
dashes
    em dashes, 655, 657, 658
    en dashes, 657, 658
    keyboard shortcuts, 657, 846
    nonbreaking em dashes, 657, 658
    See also hyphenation; hyphens
Dashes & Stripes dialog box, 398, 401,
    403
Data, print option, 510
database programs, scriptable, 542
DataViz
    Conversions Plus, 461, 462
    MacLinkPlus, 461, 462, 605
    MacOpener, 461, 462, 605
dates
    BeyondPress format options, 781
    HexWeb format options, 818
DCS and DCS2 (Document Color
    Separation) files, 149
decimal inches, 6, 39
decimal tabs, 286, 287
    See also tabs
decorative typefaces, scaling and,
    251
Default Document Preferences dialog
    box
    Character pane, 57-60, 238
                                    (continued)

Default Document Preferences dialog
    box (continued)
    General pane, 39-40, 42-43, 51-55,
        87-88, 96, 175, 356
    overview, 38
    Paragraph pane, 60-61, 88, 264,
        265
    Tool pane, 55-57, 116
    Trapping pane, 61-62, 474-476
defaults. See preferences
definition lists, 790-791
deleting
    auxiliary dictionary words, 231
    Bézier control points, 388
    book chapters, 297
    colors, 413, 432
    cutting versus, 224
    CyberPress Content List items,
        766
    CyberPress master elements, 765
    detaching an auxiliary dictionary,
        231
    editions, 163
    files, 617, 624
    font variations, 654
    hyperlinks in CyberPress, 772
    library elements, 219-220
    master pages, 208-210
    missing links, 157
    pages, 176
    recovering deleted files, 617, 624
    style sheets, 272
    tabs, 288
    XTension startup sets, 530
    See also canceling
demo software on CD
    about, 857, 858
    Web publishing XTensions, 546,
        776, 860
descenders
    of numerals, 644
    of type, 8
design, 665-688
    of ads and circulars, 666-670
    basic rules, 70-72
    evolution of, 72-73
    learning about, 665-666
    of magazines, 675-684
    of newsletters, 670-675
    principles, 686-688
    sketching layouts, 68-70
    special effects, 684-686
    Web page design, 691-712
    See also layouts; Web publishing
Designer Color Palettes, 598, 859
Designer Templates, 598-600, 859, 863
desktop printing, 495
Destination option, 63
Destination Platform, BeyondPress
    option, 782
detaching an auxiliary dictionary, 231
diacritical marks. See accents
Diagonal Line tool, 26
dialog boxes
    entering measurements in, 39
    improvements, 853
    Macintosh interface, 614

tabbed-pane dialog boxes, 21
    using, 20-21
    Windows interface, 620
    See also specific dialog boxes
DIC color model, 415, 484
dictionaries
    auxiliary spelling dictionaries,
        230-231, 446, 457
    hyphenation exception
        dictionary, 12, 260-261
Didot points, 40
Difference, merge option, 395, 396
digital cameras, 607
Digital Technology's FaceSpan, 543
dimensional shapes, creating, 392,
    393
dingbats
    Mac symbols font for Windows,
        318, 863
    in newsletters, 675
    overview, 318
    styles, 320
directory lists
    BeyondPress defaults, 790-791
    CyberPress defaults, 760-761
discretionary (soft) hyphens, 12, 259,
    657
Display All Files, All Append Sources
    versus, 455
Display DPI Value option, 46
display options, 43-44
    See also View menu
Display Seconds, BeyondPress
    option, 782
displaying. See opening; viewing
dithering, 377-378
Doc Magnify XTension, 653-654, 862
Document Color Separation (DCS
    and DCS2) files, 149
Document Content palette
    (BeyondPress), 793-795
    Authoring pane, 795
    Conversion pane, 793-794
document layout. See layout
Document Layout palette
    applying master pages, 211
    changing master page guides,
        210-211
    deleting master pages, 208-210
    editing master pages, 208
    inserting pages based on master
        pages, 208, 209
    overview, 29
    rearranging master pages, 210
    specialized pointers, 35
Document Preferences for document
    name dialog box. See Default
    Document Preferences dialog
    box
Document Setup dialog box, 491
document statistics report, 464-465
document window, 17-19
DOS Mounter 95, 461, 462, 605
DOS servers
    as BeyondPress destination
        platform, 782

as CyberPress destination
    platform, 751
DOSWasher utility, 610, 860
dot matrix printers, 489
    See also printers
dots per inch (dpi)
    calculating scans and output, 376
    lines per inch (lpi) versus, 373
Drag and Drop Text option, 50
dragging
    BeyondPress drag-and-drop, 810
    copying layout elements between
        documents, 171-172, 173
    copying pages between
        documents, 171-173
    drag-and-drop printing, 495
    DropIt XT, 566-567
    items into libraries, 214-215
    preferences for, 50
    QX-Drag&Drop, 567
    rearranging thumbnails, 177-178
drawing. See lines; picture boxes;
    text boxes
drawing tools. See Line tools
drop caps
    applying, 322
    automated, 321
    defined, 12
    hybrid drop caps, 324-325
    in newsletters, 674
    quotation marks and, 324
    style sheet for, 321-322
    typeface for, 323
drop-down lists, 21
DropIt XT, 566-567, 862
DRW files, 146
dummies, 13, 68-69
duplicating. See copying
dye-sublimation printers, 490
    See also printers
dynamic links
    live dynamic links, 158
    manual dynamic links, 159
    overview, 158-159
    See also links

E

Easy Open, 461
Edit Auxiliary Dictionary dialog box,
    230-231
Edit Character Style Sheet dialog box,
    275-276, 278
Edit Color dialog box
    color models available, 415-416
    color wheel models, 419
    Halftone pop-up menu, 423-424,
        425
    spot colors and, 422-424, 425
    spot colors versus process
        colors, 513-514
    swatch models, 420-421
Edit Dash dialog box, 398-401
Edit Hyphenation & Justification
    dialog box
    H&J sets, 254

hyphenation settings, 255-258
justification methods, 254-255
word spacing, 243-244
Edit List dialog box, 301-302
Edit menu
Dashes and Stripes option, 29
H&J option, 243
Preferences options, 38
Print Styles option, 514
Style Sheets option, 266, 270, 288
Subscribe To option, 161
Subscriber Options option, 162, 165
Edit Paragraph Style Sheet dialog box
Formats pane, 274, 278-279, 321-322
General pane, 273-274, 275, 279
Rules pane, 274-275
Tabs pane, 274, 288
Edit Stripe dialog box, 402-403
Edit Tracking dialog box, 239-240
editing
auxiliary dictionaries, 230-231
book-oriented, 293-310
clipping paths, 126
color trapping values, 413
colors, 413, 420
copy fitting, 232-233, 240
drag-and-drop editing, 50
H&J sets, 254
image editors, 608
index entries, 306-307
kerning tables, 246-248
master pages, 208
Normal style, 277
print styles, 514-516
screen angles for spot colors, 423-424, 425
style sheets, 272, 280
tab settings, 288
text, 223-228
tracking tables, 239-240
See also book-oriented editing
editions
canceling links, 163
defined, 160
deleting, 163
finding, 163-164
publishing, 160-161
effects. See special effects
electronic publishing. See Web publishing
Element Selection dialog box, 405, 406
Elements palette (BeyondPress), 795-798
HTML pane, 797
Image pane, 796
Media pane, 797-798
ellipses (...), tracking for, 241
em dashes
hyphens for, 655
keyboard shortcuts, 657
nonbreaking, 657, 658
spaces around, 658
Em Software's Xcatalog, 162
em spaces

defined, 9, 238, 252
size calculation, 59, 238
Embed, BeyondPress option, 792
embedded graphics, 684
Embedded Path, runaround mode, 122
embedded paths, identifying, 123
embossed text, 684
en bullets, 315-316, 319, 658
en dashes, 657, 658
en spaces
after bullets or labels, 316
defined, 9, 252
Kern to Space feature, 246
Encapsulated PostScript files. See EPS files
Englund, N. Jonas, 610
Enable XTension, 584, 585, 586, 863
environment. See publishing environment
EPS files
bitmap images, 361
image controls available, 362
importing, 146-147, 431-432
overprinting black, 511
overview, 145
preparing for import, 144-145
preview headers, 146-147
saving pages as, 195-197
using, 431-432
See also bitmap graphics; graphics
erasing. See deleting
errors. See troubleshooting
Ethernet, LocalTalk versus, 605-606
Ewald, Garrett, 700
exception dictionary for hyphenation, 12, 260-261, 457
Exclusive Or, merge option, 395, 396
expanded type
defined, 7
scaling versus, 250
expert collections
numerals, 644
small caps, 643
Export palette (HexWeb), 820-823
buttons, 820
Export pane, 821
Meta Tags pane, 823
Special Object Library (SOL) pane, 822
Tools pane, 821-822
Export Progress window (BeyondPress), 804
exporting
mixed-platform issues, 456-462
text, 166-167
using BeyondPress, 781-783, 798-805
using CyberPress, 751, 759, 768-769, 772-774
using HexWeb, 820-821, 829
XTension startup sets, 530-531
See also importing; Web publishing
Extensis
about, 567

catalog on CD, 859, 864
CyberPress, 697, 698-703, 745-774
PreflightPro utility, 597, 859
QX-Drag&Drop, 567, 862
QX-Layers, 91, 570
QX-Tools, 567-570, 862
See also CyberPress
Extensis Web site, 527

F

faces, 7, 626, 634
See also fonts and typefaces
FaceSpan, 543
Facing Master Pages pointer, 35
facing pages
master pages, 76-77, 207
New Document dialog box, 83
printer spreads, 548-549, 592
See also spreads
Farallon Communications' Timbuktu Pro, 461, 462
fax utility, 596
FCS, about, 570
FCSLock XTension, 571, 862
FCSTableMaker XTension, 571-572, 862
feathering, 11
figure spaces, 9
file management
Macintosh interface, 615-617
new features, 855
Windows interface, 622-624
File menu
Append option, 281
Document Setup option, 491
Get options, 128
New Book option, 294
New Library option, 212
Open Library option, 32
Save Text option, 166
files
deleting, 617, 624
Macintosh interface, 615-617
moving, 616, 623
opening, 615, 622
recovering deleted files, 617, 624
saving, 615-616, 622-623
Windows interface, 622-624
See also graphics files; text files
fill characters for tabs, 289
film output, scans and, 376
filters, for contrast adjustments, 365, 366
Find/Change palette, 224-227
Change To column, 226
changing superscripts to superiors, 645-646
changing text attributes, 225-227
Document option, 225
Find What column, 226
Ignore Case option, 225
replacing text, 225
Style options, 226-227
Whole Word option, 225

finding
    Alias Pro XTension for, 581-582
    editions, 163-164
    Find/Change palette, 224-227
    jumping text, 554-555
    keyboard shortcuts for, 846
    listed paragraphs, 303
    missing links, 154-155
    XTensions optimized for 4.0, 530
FinePrint, 373
FingerType palette, 548
FingerType XTension, 547-548
First Line option, 266
5280 magazine Web site, 704-705, 706-707
Flex Space Width option, 59
flexible spaces, 59, 252
flipping
    graphics, 343, 685
    pages when printing, 509
    Web publishing and, 732
FlowMaster XTension, 560-562, 861
FlowWatch XTension, 562, 861
flush left, 10
flush right, 10
Flush Zone option, 255
Focoltone color model, 415, 418, 494
folded documents, 86
folios
    defined, 14
    in newsletters, 674
    setup, 182-183
    See also footers; headers
Following Entry, index option, 305
Font Creator XTension, 651-652
font families, defined, 7
Font Name Tags, BeyondPress
    option, 782
Font Usage utility, 227-228
FontLoupe utility, 610, 860
Fontographer, 460
fonts and typefaces, 625-631
    basic guidelines, 637
    BeyondPress defaults, 782, 783,
        786-788
    creating font variations, 652-654
    CyberPress Font Size defaults,
        754-757
    defined, 7, 626
    deleting variations, 654
    for drop caps, 323
    expert collections, 643, 644
    exporting with BeyondPress, 782,
        783
    faces versus fonts, 626, 634
    families of, 7
    Find/Change palette, 225-227
    Font Creator XTension, 651-652
    Font Usage utility, 227-228
    in graphics files, 149
    HexWeb defaults, 814
    installing, 625-628
    keyboard shortcuts, 844-845
    loading PostScript fonts in
        printers, 628-629, 631

Mac symbols font for Windows,
    318, 863
Macintosh/Windows platform
    differences, 460
Multiple Master fonts, 651-654
obtaining, 608-609
regenerating variations, 654
scaling, 249-251
selecting, 634-637
similar typefaces, 637
standard set, 635-636, 682
terms, 7-11, 633-634
TrueDoc fonts, 730, 756, 782
TrueType versus PostScript, 630
typeface attributes, 638-650
typefaces versus fonts, 626, 634
typographic colors, 236
utilities, 608
variations, 634, 635, 652-654
for visual labels, 318
for Web publishing, 638, 727-731
    See also character spacing;
        special characters; type
        styles
footers
    BeyondPress defaults, 784
    CyberPress defaults, 754, 755
    facing pages and, 77
    HexWeb defaults, 816, 817
    importing and, 138
    of master pages, 207
    setup, 182-183
    for Web pages, 723-724
footnotes
    importing, 138
    leading and, 263
    superiors as, 58, 645
foreign language characters. *See*
    accents
Format As, list option, 302
four-color printing
    color separation process, 370
    defined, 15, 412
four-color separations. *See* color
    separations
fractions, entering in dialog boxes,
    81-82
Frame Edit dialog box, 406
Frame Editor, 193-195, 404-407
frame-based metaphor, 4
frames
    bitmap frames, 403-407
    defined, 14
    framing boxes, 191-192
    Modify dialog box Frame pane,
        108, 191-192
    page borders, 594
    preferences, 52
    sharing in workgroups, 445
    styles, 193-195
    text inset from, 117-118
    tips and tricks, 192
    tools, 382
    transferring across platforms, 457
    See also picture boxes; text boxes
Framing options, 52

free software, 857
freehand boxes, reshaping, 113-114
Freehand Line tool, 384
Freehand Picture Box tool, 104, 105
Freehand Text Box tool, 99, 100
Freehand Text Path tool, 329, 409
Frequency, print option, 507, 508
Frontier, 534
Full Resolution TIFF Output, print
    option, 511
Full-screen Documents option, 44
Function, print option, 508

G

galleys, 13
gatefolds, 682-683
General Preferences dialog box. *See*
    Default Document Preferences
    dialog box
Get Edition Now button, 163
Get Picture dialog box, 128, 484-485
Get Text dialog box
    Convert Quotes option, 656
    Include Style Sheets option, 283
    overview, 128
GIF files
    image controls available, 362
    interlaced GIFs, 738, 757
    overview, 145, 361
    for Web pages, 738, 739
    See also bitmap graphics
GIF Palette, BeyondPress option, 785
Gill, Tim, 522
global controls, 5
global preferences, 38
glossy-coated paper, 373
Gluon. *See* Hologramophone (Gluon)
Goodman, Danny, 536
Grabber pointer, 33
graphics
    background images for Web
        pages, 784
    BeyondPress features, 802
    BeyondPress Image defaults, 784-786
    bitmap formats, 150-151, 360-361
    bitmap frames, 403-407
    bitmap image manipulation, 359-380
    box special effects, 342-343
    color pictures, 431-432
    coloring, 354
    contrast adjustments for bitmaps,
        364-370
    converting text into, 407-410, 768-769
    copying, 685
    creating illustrations, 392, 394
    cropping, 342, 351-352
    cross-platform differences, 132-133
    CyberPress features, 699
    CyberPress Image defaults, 757-758

display quality, 355-357
dithering, 377-378
embedded, 684
flipping, 343, 685
formats for Web pages, 738-739, 740-741
formats supported, 144-146
graphics programs versus QuarkXPress, 132
halftone controls for bitmaps, 370-376
HexWeb default format, 815
as hyperlinks, 742, 771, 786
image editors, 608
image maps, 786, 802
importing, 144-151, 361, 484-486
in-line, importing, 140-141
keyboard shortcuts for handling, 847-848
in magazine table of contents, 677
Measurements palette with, 339, 340-343
missing or modified, 154-159
Modify dialog box with, 339, 343-354
moving in picture boxes, 342, 351-352, 353
negatives from bitmaps, 364
new features, 851-853
offsetting, 351-352, 353
rotating, 352-353
shading, 354
sizing, 341-342, 348-351
skewing, 353-354
suppressing picture printout, 335
tables as, 144
text as graphics for Web pages, 722, 735-736
text-based boxes, 407-409
textual graphics, 684
tools, 339-340
transferring across platforms, 456
vector versus bitmap, 144-145
visual treatments, 686, 687
Web publishing and, 736-742
See also bitmap graphics; graphics files; lines; links; picture boxes
graphics boxes. *See* picture boxes
Graphics Converter utility, 610, 860
graphics files
bitmap formats, 150-151, 360-361
Collect for Output feature, 463-465
colors and importing, 148-149
cross-platform differences, 132-133
EPS files, 146-147
fonts in imported files, 149
formats for Web pages, 738-739, 740-741
formats supported, 144-146
importing, 144-151, 361
sharing in workgroups, 446-447
standardizing, 447
translating to usable formats, 361
See also files; text files

graphics programs
cross-platform differences, 132-133
QuarkXPress versus, 132, 134
scriptable, 542
Gray Tiffs option, 46, 356
gray-scale images
color adjustment for, 378-379
contrast filters, 365
gray levels, 370
Gray Tiffs option, 46, 356
negatives, 364
returning to common gray-level map, 369
saving, 362
shading adjustment for, 379-380
tinting, 684
greeking, 54-55, 356
grids
defined, 13
flexible grids for magazines, 677-682
line-numbering system, 680-682
mixing grids on a page, 679-680
multiple grids, 678
See also baseline grids; guides; templates
grouping elements
displaying color groups, 434
overview, 93-94
vertical lines with text boxes, 291
Web publishing and, 724
Gruman, Galen, 604
guidelines. *See* guides
guides
color of, 41-42, 89-90
defined, 13
hiding and showing, 45
margin guides, 83
on master pages, 210-211
position of (in front or behind), 42-43, 87
snap distance, 54, 88
snap-to feature, 87-88
uses for, 85-87
using, 89
See also baseline grids; columns; margins; rulers
gutters
column gutter width, 85
defined, 13
for folded documents, 86

H

H&J sets
overview, 254, 259
sharing in workgroups, 445
transferring across platforms, 457
halftones, 370-376
calculating scans and output, 376
creating, 371
defined, 370
halftone density, 372
halftone dot shapes, 372, 373-375
halftone frequency, 372

line-screen basics, 372
print options, 506-507, 508
sample page creation, 373-375
special effects, 372
spot color screen settings, 423-424, 425
Halftoning, print option, 506-507
hand pointers, 33
hanging indents, 11
hanging punctuation, 333-335
HanMac
about, 575
HX PowerSelect XTension, 575-576, 862
HX PowerUnderline XTension, 576-577, 862
hard disks, 604
hardware, 603-608
BeyondPress destination platform, 782
CD-ROM drives, 607
color scanners, 607
computers, 603-604
connectivity, 605-606
CyberPress destination platform, 751
digital cameras, 607
pointing devices, 608
printers, 489-490, 606-607
QuarkXPress minimum requirements, 837
RAM, 604
storage capacity, 604-605
See also Macintosh computers; printers; Windows computers
headers
BeyondPress defaults, 784
CyberPress defaults, 754, 755
facing pages and, 77
HexWeb defaults, 816, 817
importing and, 138
of master pages, 207
setup, 182-183
for Web pages, 723-724
headings
for index sections, 309
typefaces for, 637
headlines
in airline ad mockup, 666
HexWeb headline sizes, 815-816
increased tracking for, 237
in newsletters, 674
in public service announcement, 669
in restaurant ad mockup, 668
typefaces for, 637
Heid, Jim, 609
Here & Now, 461, 462, 605
Hewlett-Packard's Resolution Enhancement Technology, 373
Hexachrome color model, 15, 412, 416
defining, 483
paper variation models, 417
swatchbooks, 418
HexMac, 811
HexWeb, 811-832

captions for graphics, 819
on CD, 860
combining picture and text
boxes, 816, 826-828
creating content and editorial
pages, 710-712
dedicated Web-page software
versus, 708
defaults, specifying, 812-819
Export palette, 820-823
exporting Web pages, 820-821,
829
fonts with, 727-729
headers and footers, 816, 817
headline sizes, 815-816
HexWeb Preferences dialog box,
812-819
Index Pro with, 710, 820, 829-832
left indents, 818-819
opening sample document, 812
overview, 697, 708
paragraph formats, 732
picture box modification, 826
previewing Web pages, 820, 828
separators for boxes, 816, 817
site-management features, 710
table of contents creation, 830-
832
text box modification, 824-826
text formatting available, 728
variables, 818
Web sites, 708, 710-712
HexWeb Image Info dialog box, 826
HexWeb Index Pro, 710, 820, 829-830
HexWeb Preferences dialog box, 812-
819
Advanced preferences, 817-819
General preferences, 812-815
Layout preferences, 815-817
root folder selection, 812
HexWeb TextBox Info dialog box,
824-826
HexWeb XT for QPS, 811
hidden file types, 462
hiding and showing
baseline grids, 45, 88
color groups, 434
contents of dragged items, 50
guides, rulers, and invisible
elements, 45
palettes, 45
hierarchies
Apple Events Object Hierarchy,
535
QuarkXPress, 535
High Contrast filter, 365, 366
high-fidelity colors, 15
Hologramophone (Gluon)
about, 572
PICTMaker XTension, 573, 862
TableMaker XTension, 573-574,
862
TextWaves XTension, 574-575, 862
Web site, 527
home pages, 16
Hord, Phil, 610
horizontal flip, 343

horizontal layouts, 74-75
Horizontal Offset option, 200, 201
horizontal ruler
color of, 41-42
defined, 18
measurement unit for, 38-39
See also rulers
horizontal scales for typefaces, 249-
251
HPGL files, 146
HSB color model, 416, 598
HScale options
small caps and superiors, 58
superscripts and subscripts, 58
HTML (HyperText Markup Language)
browsers and page appearance,
692-693
CyberPress mapping of
QuarkXPress type styles, 756
defined, 16
exporting files with CyberPress,
772-774
hyperlinks, 692
layout tools, evolution of, 718
<META> tags, 784, 817-818, 823
overview, 691
special characters and, 661, 734-
735
text formatting available, 728
versatility of, 692
XTensions for, 693
HTML Browser, BeyondPress option,
780
HX PowerSelect XTension, 575-576,
862
HX PowerUnderline XTension, 576-
577, 862
hybrid drop caps, 324-325
hyperlinks
BeyondPress features, 784, 786,
801
CyberPress features, 753-754,
770-772
defined, 16
design issues, 692, 696
graphics as, 742, 771, 786
image maps, 786, 802
internal (within a Web site), 723
relative versus absolute, 771-772
text as, 770-771
hyphenation, 255-261
of capitalized words, 256
consecutive, 12
defined, 12
Edit Hyphenation & Justification
dialog box, 255-258
H&J sets, 254
hyphenation exception
dictionary, 12, 260-261
hyphenation zone, 258
limiting consecutive hyphens,
257-258
overriding settings, 258-259
preferences, 61
Suggested Hyphenation feature,
259-260
terms, 12

tips and tricks, 257
transferring exceptions across
platforms, 457
Hyphenation Exceptions dialog box,
261
hyphenation zone, 12
hyphens
defined, 12
discretionary (soft) hyphens, 12,
259, 657
keyboard shortcuts, 657, 846
nonbreaking hyphens, 261, 657

I

I-beam pointer, 33
icons
for graphics files, 132-133
for libraries, 213
Macintosh interface, 612
Windows interface, 618
Ignore Empty Boxes, BeyondPress
option, 779
Ignore Unchanged Master Items,
BeyondPress option, 779
Ignore White option, 62, 476
illustrations. See graphics
images. See graphics
imagesetters
color separation options, 507-508
overview, 490
See also printers
IMG, BeyondPress option, 792
importing
Append feature, 451-452
bitmap files, 150-151, 361
calibrating imported colors,
484-486
color issues, 148-149
color pictures, 431-432, 484-485
comparing attributes, 453
copying versus, 153-154
cross-platform differences,
132-133
disadvantages of, 131-132
DropIt XT for, 566-567
EPS files, 146-147, 431-432
file transfer products, 461
fonts in graphics files, 149
graphic formats supported,
144-146
graphics files, 144-151
mixed-platform issues, 453,
456-462
multiple elements, 451-454
Nisus Writer filter for, 581
Photoshop Import XTension, 588,
589
resolving name conflicts, 452-453
smart quotes and, 49, 656
style sheets, 283
tabular data, 138, 144
text files, 134-144
translating text files, 134-136
XPress Tags for, 141-144
XTension startup sets, 530-531

See also appending; exporting; sharing project elements
Imposer XTension, 548-549
inches
  agate inches, 9
  code for, 6, 39
inches decimal, 6, 39
Include Blank Pages, print option, 503
Increment, baseline grid option, 264
indents
  block indents, 11, 312-313
  for bylines and credit lines, 313
  defined, 11
  hanging indents, 11
  HexWeb defaults, 818-819
  for lists, 315-316
  overview, 311
  paragraph offsets, 266-267
  setting, 312
Indeterminate option, 62
Index palette
  controls, 306
  creating cross-references, 307-308
  creating entries, 306
  creating page number references, 307
  editing entries, 306-307
  index levels, 308
  overview, 31-32, 305
Index Preferences dialog box, 304-305
Index Pro (HexWeb), 710, 820, 829-832
indexes, 303-310
  Build Index dialog box, 308-310
  creating cross-references, 307-308
  creating entries, 306
  creating page number references, 307
  editing entries, 306-307
  Index palette, 305-308
  Index Preferences dialog box, 304-305
  letter headings, 309
  levels of entries, 308, 310
  marker color, 304
  nested versus run-in, 309
  new features, 854
  separation characters, 305
  style for, 303-304
inkjet printers, 490, 607
  See also printers
Insert Master Page pointer, 35
Insert Pages dialog box, 176
inserting
  Bézier control points, 388
  book chapters, 296-297
  dingbats, 320
  kerning pairs, 248
  library elements, 213-216
  master pages in libraries, 216-217
  pages, 51, 175-176
  pages based on master pages, 35, 205, 208, 209
  soft (discretionary) hyphens, 259
  See also appending; importing
installing
  BeyondPress demo version from CD, 776

CD-ROM with this book, 858
fonts, 625-628
QuarkXPress for Macintosh, 835-837
QuarkXPress for Windows, 833-835
XTensions, 519-520, 521, 522-523
interlaced GIF files, 738, 757
Intersection, merge option, 395, 396
in-text labels, 317-318
Invert, runaround option, 124, 125
inverting, 14
invisible elements, hiding and showing, 45
italic type
  defined, 7
  in restaurant ad mockup, 668
  uses for, 637, 641
  for visual labels, 317
  See also type styles
Item, runaround mode, 121
Item menu
  Constrain/Unconstrain options, 55
  Content option, 410
  Edit options, 126
  Frame option, 108
  Group/Ungroup options, 93
  layer options, 92
  Lock option, 94
  Merge options, 395-396, 410
  Modify option, 93, 105
  Point/Segment Type options, 387-388
  Runaround option, 108
  Shape options, 386, 391, 410
  Split options, 397
Item pointer, 33
Item tool, 22
ItemMaster XTension, 550-551

J

Jaz drives, 605
Join Endpoints, merge option, 396, 410
Joint Photographic Experts Group files. *See* JPEG files
Joseph Stubbs Creations
  about, 598
  Designer Color Palettes, 598, 859
  Designer Templates, 598-600, 850, 863
JPEG files
  image controls available, 362
  importing, 151
  overview, 145, 361
  for Web pages, 738-739
  See also bitmap graphics
jumping text
  "continued" markers, 181
  dingbats and, 318
  linking text, 27
  StoryChaser XTension, 554-555
jumps (hyperlinks). *See* hyperlinks
justification

defined, 10
Edit Hyphenation & Justification dialog box, 254-255
flush zone, 255
H&J sets, 254
leading and, 262
methods, 254-255
in public service announcement, 669
of single word on line, 255
terms, 10-11
tracking justified text, 242-243
using Measurements palette, 28

K

Kagi Software
  Aaron, 610, 860
  Aaron Light, 860
  Kaleidoscope, 610, 860
Kahn, David, 700
Kaleidoscope utility, 610, 860
Kamprath, Michael F., 610
Kern/Track Editor XTension, 242, 246
kerning, 245-249
  adding kerning pairs, 248
  adjusting in Measurements palette, 28
  adjusting on-the-fly, 248-249
  Auto Kern Above feature, 58, 246
  changing one document only, 247
  defined, 9, 245
  drop caps, 324, 325
  editing kerning tables, 246-248
  Kern to Space feature, 246
  keyboard shortcuts, 248, 845
  need for, 245
  pair kerning, 10, 248
  sharing data in workgroups, 442
  transferring data across platforms, 442, 457
keyboard shortcuts, 839-848
  for closing, 839
  for dashes and hyphens, 657, 846
  for find/change, 846
  for foreign characters, 661-664
  for formatting text/paragraphs, 844-845
  for graphics handling, 847-848
  for item commands, 842
  for kerning, 248
  Macintosh interface, 614
  for Measurements palette, 28
  miscellaneous, 840
  for moving objects, 842
  for navigation, 841
  for opening, 839
  for palettes, 841
  for picture sizing, 350
  for point size, 227
  for preferences and setup, 840
  for saving, 839
  for scaling images, 342
  for selecting objects, 842
  for selecting text, 843

(continued)

keyboard shortcuts *(continued)*
    for special characters, 659-664,
      846-847
    for special spaces, 252, 846
    for spelling, 843
    for style sheets, 273-274, 276
    for symbols, 659-660
    for typeface attributes, 639, 640
    for typographic quotes, 656
    for underlines, 647
    using, 21-22
    for view percentage, 47
    for viewing, 840
    Windows interface, 620
KeyCaps program, 138
kickers in newsletters, 674
Knockout Limit option, 62, 476
knockouts
    defined, 13
    overprints versus, 471
    trapping preferences, 62, 476
    trapping setting, 473
    See also color trapping
Kyosha Graphics' Precision Preview
    XT, 577-578, 862

L

LAB color model, 416
labels
    Clone XTension, 582-583
    displaying labeled library
      elements, 218-219
    labeling library elements, 217-218
    spaces after, 316
    visual labels, 317-318
Labels menu, 218-219
Landweber, Greg, 610
laser printers, 490, 606
    See also printers
Last Word's ChangeCase XTension,
    578-579, 862
launching. *See* opening
LayerIt XTension, 592, 593, 863
layers, 91-93
    layering tools, 382
    overview, 92-93
    Photoshop versus QuarkXPress,
      91
    rearranging, 92
    stacking order, 92, 93
    Web publishing and, 724-725, 741
layouts
    for ads and circulars, 666-670
    aligning multiple elements, 197-
      201
    basic design rules, 70-72
    in BeyondPress, 791-792, 808-809
    bleeds, 78-79
    copying elements between
      documents, 170-171, 173
    copying pages between
      documents, 171-173
    defined, 12
    design elements, 13-14

evolution of design, 72-73
facing pages and spreads, 76-78
frames, 191-195
grouping and ungrouping
    elements, 93-94
horizontal, 74-75
HTML layout tools, evolution of,
    718
image manipulation concepts, 14
layers, 91-93
layout tools, 85-96
lines, 185-190
locking elements, 94-95
of magazines, 675-684
for newsletters, 670-675
opening a new document, 80-81
page setup, 80, 81-85
planning, 67-79
principles, 686-688
saving pages as EPS file, 195-197
sketching in QuarkXPress, 69-70
sketching on paper, 68-69
special effects, 684-686
terms, 12-14
tools, 13
types of, 74
vertical, 75-76
    See also pages; picture boxes;
      print design; text boxes; Web
      publishing
leaders for tabs, 289
leading, 261-266
    additive, 263
    adjusting in Measurements
      palette, 28
    automatic, 263
    column width and, 262
    controlling, 261-262
    copy fitting, 232-233
    creative use of, 262
    defined, 9
    justification and, 262
    keyboard shortcuts, 845
    Lock to Baseline Grid option,
      264-265
    Maintain Leading option, 60, 264,
      265
    preferences, 60
    for superscripts, subscripts, and
      superiors, 646
    tightly leaded text, 681
    tips and tricks, 263
    Typesetting versus Word
      Processing mode, 265
    vertical alignment and, 264-266
left tabs, 285
    See also tabs
legal symbols, 659
Lemke, Thorsten, 610
letter spacing. *See* character spacing;
    tracking
Level, list option, 302
levels
    gray levels, 369-370
    of index entries, 308
libraries, 212-220

adding elements to, 213-216
adding master pages to, 216-217
creating, 212-213
deleting elements, 219-220
displaying labeled elements, 218-
    219
do's and don'ts, 215
labeling elements, 217-218
multiple libraries, 219
opening, 213
overview, 447
rearranging elements, 217
saving, 216
sharing in workgroups, 447
tips and tricks, 220
transferring across platforms, 447
transferring master pages to, 448-
    449, 450
using, 220
Library palette
    Auto Library Save option, 63-64
    overview, 32
Library pointer, 34
ligatures
    defined, 8
    Macintosh/Windows platform
      differences, 460
    preferences, 59
line spacing. *See* leading
Line Text Path tool, 329, 409
Line tools
    creating Bézier curves, 27, 384
    customizing, 57
    overview, 4, 26-27, 381
    using, 27
line-numbering system for grids, 680-
    682
lines
    anchoring, 168-169
    arrowheads for, 388-390
    between table columns, 291
    changing anchored lines, 169-170
    changing from straight to Bézier,
      189
    colors or shades for, 188
    combining with boxes, 391-393
    creating Bézier curves, 27, 185-
      187, 383-388
    creating dashed lines, 398-401
    creating straight lines, 185-187,
      383
    creating striped lines, 402-403
    intercolumn rules, 117
    keyboard shortcuts, 848
    line mode feature, 190
    line type and end, 187
    Measurements palette with, 29
    merging with boxes, 394-396
    moving, 188
    patterns for, 388-389, 398-403
    placing text on, 328-330, 409-410
    reshaping, 188-189, 384-386
    for reversed type, 649-650
    Ruling Line feature, 647-649
    simplicity, value of, 189
    styles, creating, 398-403

styles for, 29
thickness (weight), 187, 188
transferring across platforms, 457
underlines, 576-577, 647-649
for visual labels, 317
Web publishing and, 742
See also frames
lines per inch (lpi)
calculating scans and output, 376
dots per inch (dpi) versus, 373
overview, 373
line-screens. *See* halftones
Link pointer, 34
Link tool, 27, 100, 101
linking
elements in layouts, 74
text boxes, 100-102
tips, 102
links
alert for missing or modified
graphics, 154
deciding not to update, 156
deleting missing links, 157
finding missing graphics, 154-155
OLE, 160, 164-165
Publish and Subscribe, 159-165
text links, 166-167
types of, 158-159
updating, 52-53, 155, 156-157, 159
See also hyperlinks; Publish and
Subscribe
lists
BeyondPress defaults, 790-791
for books, 300-303
bulleted lists, 314-316
compiling, 302
CyberPress Content Lists, 762-
763, 766-768, 772-774
CyberPress defaults, 760-761
CyberPress, exporting, 769
defined, 31
Edit List dialog box, 301-302
of figures, 301-303
new features, 854
numbered lists, 316
placing in books, 302
sharing in workgroups, 445
style for, 302, 314-316
tips and tricks, 303
transferring across platforms, 457
updating and rebuilding, 303
Web publishing and, 732
Lists palette, 31, 302-303
live dynamic links
canceling links, 163
creating, 160-162
disadvantages of, 162
overview, 158
updating, 162-163
See also links
Live Refresh option, 50, 356-357
Live Scroll option, 50, 356
loading PostScript fonts in printers,
628-629, 631
local controls, 5
local preferences, 38
LocalTalk, Ethernet versus, 605-606

Lock pointer, 33
Lock to Baseline Grid option, 264-265
locking elements, 94-95
logos
in airline ad mockup, 667
for magazines, 676
on master pages, 207
lossy graphic formats, 361
Lowly Apprentice Production, A
about, 547
ColorPick XTension, 547
FingerType XTension, 547-548
Imposer XTension, 548-549
ItemMaster XTension, 550-551
MarkIt XTension, 548-549, 552,
553
PasteIt XTension, 552
QuickOpen XTension, 553
ScaleLock XTension, 553
ShadowCaster XTension, 553-554
StoryChaser XTension, 554-555
Web site, 527
XPert Collection Volume 1, 547,
555-557
XPert Collection Volume 2, 547,
557-559
XTensions on CD, 861
lpi. *See* lines per inch (lpi)

M

MAC files, 146, 362
Macintosh computers
authors' use of, 603-604
as BeyondPress destination
platform, 782
cross-platform differences, 132-
133
as CyberPress destination
platform, 751
filename rules, 458
hidden file types, 462
importing special characters, 138-
140
installing fonts, 625-626
installing QuarkXPress for
Macintosh, 835-837
Mac symbols font for Windows,
318, 863
Macintosh interface, 609-617
mixed-platform issues, 456-462,
605
printing options specific to,
492-497
QuarkXPress minimum
requirements, 837
software on CD, 859-863
upgrading from previous
QuarkXPress version, 838
word processor formats
supported, 135
See also mixed-platform issues
Macintosh interface, 609-617
basics, 611-615
file management, 615-617

Windows interface versus, 617-
618
MacLinkPlus, 461, 462, 605
MacOpener, 461, 462, 605
MacPaint files, 146, 362
Macromedia's Fontographer, 460
Macs for Dummies, 609
Macworld, design of, 677, 681, 682
Macworld Complete Mac Handbook,
609
Macworld Guide to System 7.1, 609
Macworld Macintosh Secrets, 609
Macworld Photoshop 4.0 Bible, 366
magazines, 675-683
article openers, 684, 685-686
feature articles, 677-683
flexible grids, 677-682
gatefolds, 682-683
redesigning, rationale for, 670
standard set of typefaces, 682
table of contents, 675-677
visual treatments, 686, 687
See also Web publishing
Main Event Software
Scripter, 543, 860
Web site, 544
Maintain Leading option, 60, 264, 265
manual dynamic links, 159
See also links
mapping
image maps with BeyondPress,
786, 802
special characters with
BeyondPress, 810
special characters with
CyberPress, 769-770
style sheets with BeyondPress,
788-789
Web site structure, 715
margins
in BeyondPress, 806
defined, 13
facing pages and, 77
for folded documents, 86
guide color, 41-42
New Document dialog box, 82-83
in restaurant ad mockup, 668
tips and tricks, 83
of Web pages, 721
MarkIt XTension, 548-549, 552, 553
Markzware
Pasteboard XT, 579, 862
Web site, 527
master chapters, 295-296
Master Guides dialog box, 210-211
Master Page Items options, 53
master pages, 204-211
adding to document, 205
adding to libraries, 216-217
applying to existing pages, 53,
211
in BeyondPress, 807
common elements, 207
creating, 76-77, 205-206
deleting, 208-210
displaying, 206, 208

(continued)

master pages *(continued)*
  editing, 208
  guides on, 210-211
  indexes based on, 310
  inserting pages based on, 35, 205, 208, 209
  left and right pages, 77
  overview, 76-77
  rearranging, 210
  sharing in workgroups, 448-450
  transferring across platforms, 449
  transferring to libraries, 448-449, 450
  uses, 205
master spreads, 76
Math Grabber XTension, 579-580, 862
mathematics symbols, 660
McClelland, Deke, 366
Meadows Information Systems' Math Grabber, 579-580, 862
measurement units
  codes for, 6, 39
  entering fractions, 81-82
  entering in dialog boxes, 39
  for Measurements palette, 106
  for Modify dialog box, 106
  setting, 38-40
  for type, 9
Measurements palette
  box controls, 109-110
  box special effects, 342-343
  for columns in text boxes, 103
  Content tool and, 109
  for graphics, 339, 340-343
  hiding and showing, 105
  kerning values, 248
  leading control, 261
  line mode, 29, 190, 388-390
  measurement units for, 106
  moving picture boxes, 341
  moving pictures in boxes, 342
  overview, 27-29, 109-110
  with picture boxes, 28
  reshaping boxes, 113-114
  resizing boxes, 31, 112
  rotating text, 326
  rounding off measurements, 341
  scaling pictures, 341-342
  with text boxes, 28
  typeface controls, 638-639
memory. *See* RAM
memory management utilities, 609
menu lists
  BeyondPress defaults, 790-791
  CyberPress defaults, 760-761
menus
  contextual menus, 848-849
  Macintosh interface, 612, 614
  pop-up menus, 21
  using, 19-20
  Windows interface, 619-621
merging
  boxes and lines, 394-396
  splitting paths for merged objects, 397
<META> tags, 784, 817-818, 823
Micrografx Draw files, 146

Microsoft Word. *See* word processors
millimeters, 6, 39
Minimum After, hyphenation option, 257
Minimum Before, hyphenation option, 257
Miramar Systems' PC MacLAN, 461, 462, 605
mirrored text, Web publishing and, 732
Missing/Modified Pictures dialog box, 154-155
miter for dashed lines, 401
mixed-platform issues, 456-462
  auxiliary dictionaries, 446
  color definitions, 442
  cross-platform networks, 461-462, 605
  file transfer products, 461
  kerning values, 442
  libraries, 447
  master pages, 449
  platform differences, 458-460
  print styles, 451
  QuarkXPress differences, 456-458
  style sheets, 445
  templates, 448
mm, measurement unit, 6
Mode, leading option, 60, 265
modems, 606
Modify dialog box
  anchored boxes and lines and, 169-170
  Box pane, 108, 169-170, 327, 343-348, 355
  Clipping pane, 123, 124-125
  Frame pane, 108, 191-192
  for graphics, 339, 343-354
  Line pane, 187, 190, 388-389
  measurement units for, 106
  opening, 105
  overview, 107-108
  Picture pane, 108, 348-354, 355
  Runaround pane, 108, 120-125
  Text pane, 108, 115-116, 117-119, 127-128
  Text Path pane, 329-330, 409-410
monitors
  calibrating, 480, 481-482, 483
  display options, 43-44, 480-482
  QuarkXPress minimum requirements, 837
  Web page colors and, 726
  Web pages and monitor size, 719-721
Monitors & Sound control panel, 481
mouse
  contextual menus, 848-849
  drag-and-drop option, 50
  dragging preferences, 50
  hardware, 608
  Macintosh interface, 614
  moving boxes, 111
  reshaping boxes, 113-114
  scrolling preferences, 49-50
  Windows interface, 620
Move Pages dialog box, 177

moving around. *See* navigating
moving objects
  aligning multiple elements, 197-201
  Bézier curves, 386
  book chapters, 297
  boxes, 111, 341
  CyberPress Content List items, 766
  files, 616, 623
  keyboard shortcuts, 842
  layer stacking order and, 93
  layers, 92
  library elements, 217
  lines, 188
  lists, placing in books, 302
  master pages, 210
  pages, 176-178
  picture boxes, 111, 341, 344
  pictures in boxes, 342, 351-352, 353
  text, 224
  tools between palettes, 382-383
  windows, 616, 622
  See also dragging
multi-ink colors
  displaying, 434
  using, 412, 425-426
multimedia defaults for BeyondPress, 792-793
Multiple Master fonts, 651-654
  creating font variations, 652-654
  deleting variations, 654
  Font Creator XTension, 651-652
  regenerating variations, 654

N

naming
  BeyondPress Content list items, 800
  colors, 420
  CyberPress Content List items, 766
  HexWeb defaults, 814-815
  HTML files in CyberPress, 772
  Macintosh/Windows platform differences, 458-459
  renaming files for cross-platform transfer, 459
  resolving name conflicts, 452-453
  style sheets, 273, 276, 284
  typefaces, 636
  universal naming conventions, 459
NAPS's PubViews, 580-581, 862
navigating
  keyboard shortcuts, 841
  new features, 853-854
Negative feature for bitmaps, 364
Negative Print, print option, 509
NetWare IPX, 462
networks
  connectivity hardware, 605-606
  cross-platform networks, 461-462, 605

Ethernet versus LocalTalk, 605-606
printers, 606
standards on, 437
using templates over, 204
See also workgroups
New Document dialog box
Automatic Text Box option, 85, 97
Column Guides options, 83-85
creating master pages, 205-206
Margin Guides options, 82-83
Nouveau II XTension, 592-593
overview, 80, 81
Page options, 81-82
new features
book and long-document handling, 854
color capabilities, 855
file management innovations, 855
illustration and text options, 851-853
indexing and list features, 854
interface and navigation improvements, 853-854
printing features, 855
New Library dialog box, 212
newsletters
association newsletter example, 670-673
basics, 673-675
redesigning, rationale for, 670
See also Web publishing
Next Style, style sheet option, 274
Niko Mac Computing's WinZip, 609, 610
Nisus Writer filter, 581, 862
No Style option, 276
Noise, tolerance option, 124
nonbreaking em dashes, 657, 658
nonbreaking hyphens, 261, 657
nonbreaking spaces, 241, 252
None, runaround mode, 121
Non-Matching Preferences dialog box, 553
Non-White Areas, runaround mode, 122
Normal contrast filter, 365
Normal style, 277
North Atlantic Publishing Systems' PubViews, 580-581, 862
Nouveau II XTension, 592, 593, 863
Novell's NetWare IPX, 462
numbered lists, 316
BeyondPress defaults, 790-791
CyberPress defaults, 760-761
Numbering, list option, 302
numbering pages. *See* page numbering
numbers, entering fractions in dialog boxes, 81-82
numerals
expert collections, 644
figure space and, 9
page numbering format, 180
traditional versus modern, 644-645

O

object hierarchy, 535
Object Linking and Embedding (OLE), 160, 164-165
oblique type, 7
Off-screen Draw option, 44
offsets
for pictures, 351-352, 353
for reversed type, 649-650
for superscripts and subscripts, 58
OLE (Object Linking and Embedding), 160, 164-165
on-the-fly kerning, 248-249
on-the-fly tracking, 240-241
Open Prepress Interface, 196-197
Open Prepress Interface servers, 510
opening
BeyondPress Preferences dialog box, 777
Colors palette, 29
CyberPress palette, 747
CyberPress Preferences dialog box, 746-747
Document Content palette (BeyondPress), 793
Document Layout palette, 29
Elements palette (BeyondPress), 795
files, 615, 622
HexWeb Index Pro, 829
HexWeb Preferences dialog box, 812
keyboard shortcuts, 839
libraries, 213
Library palette, 32
Lists palette, 31
master pages, 206
Measurements palette, 28
Modify dialog box, 105
new document, 80-81
Publisher source application, 163, 164-165
Style Sheets palette, 30
Tools palette, 22
Trap Information palette, 30
XTensions at startup, 528-529
XTensions, loading errors, 524, 525-526
XTensions Manager at startup, 524
See also importing
OPI, print option, 510
ordered dithering, 377
ordered lists. *See* numbered lists
organizational chart, 391-392
orphans, tracking and, 240
Orthogonal Line tool, 26
Orthogonal Text Path tool, 329, 409
OSA Menu, 543
out of register, defined, 79
outdents, 11, 311, 312
outline text, 332, 334
Output, print option, 509
Output Request Template, 465

Outside Edges Only, runaround option, 124, 125
Oval Picture Box tool, 26, 104
Oval Text Box tool, 98, 99
overlays, 13
Overprint EPS Black, print option, 511
Overprint Limit option, 62, 476
overprints
knockouts versus, 471
trapping preference, 62, 476
trapping setting, 473
See also color trapping
overriding
color trapping, 476-477
hyphenation settings, 258-259

P

p, measurement unit, 6
Page coordinates, 40
Page Flip, print option, 509
page numbering, 178-180
automatic, 180
for books, 299
creating index page number references, 307
keyboard shortcuts, 847
list styles, 302
for magazine table of contents, 677
for master pages, 207
in newsletters, 674
number format, 180
by sections, 178, 179, 503
Page Sequence, print option, 504
PageBorder XTension, 594, 863
PageMill, 698, 700, 702, 703, 748, 773
pages
applying master pages to, 211
article openers, 684, 685-686
borders around, 594
"continued" markers, 181
copying between documents, 171-173
deleting, 176
facing pages and spreads, 76-78
footers and headers, 182-183
inserting, 51, 175-176
numbering, 178-180
printing blank pages, 503
rearranging, 176-178
saving as EPS file, 195-197
scaling during printing, 492
selecting pages to print, 502
sizing, 81-82
See also master pages; spreads; Web publishing
pair kerning, 10, 248
palettes
customizing, 382-383
Designer Color Palettes, 598
hiding and showing, 45
keyboard shortcuts, 841
overview, 22-32
See also specific palettes

Pantone colors
  defining color models, 483-484
  Hexachrome color model, 15, 412, 416, 417, 483
  importing graphics and, 148
  paper variation models, 416-417
  POCE (Pantone Open Color Environment), 416, 421
  spot-color model, 416
  swatchbooks, 418
Pantone Open Color Environment (POCE), 416, 421
Pantone Process Color Imaging Guide CMYK Edition, The, 148
paper
  for folded documents, 86
  lpi settings and, 373
  paper variation color models, 416-417
  printing setup, 492
Paragraph Attributes dialog box
  Formats pane, 258-259, 261, 264, 266-267, 314-316
  Rules pane, 647-650
  Tabs pane, 288
paragraph spacing, 253-267
  H&J sets, 254
  hyphenation, 12, 61, 254, 255-261
  justification, 10-11, 28, 242-243, 254-255
  leading, 9, 28, 60, 261-266
  Paragraph Attributes dialog box, 266-267
  setting off paragraphs, 266-267
  See also hyphenation; justification; leading
paragraph symbol, 659
paragraphs
  FingerType XTension, 547-548
  formatting anchored graphics, 170
  keyboard shortcuts for formatting, 844-845
  preferences, 60-61
  tab settings, 288
  terms, 11-12
  Web page formats, 731-732
pasteboard
  defined, 18
  using, 90-91
  width of, 48, 90
pasteboard metaphor, 4
Pasteboard XT, 579, 862
Pastelt XTension, 552
PC Exchange, 461, 462
PC MacLAN, 461, 462, 605
PCs. *See* DOS servers; Windows computers
PCX files
  image controls available, 362
  importing, 151
  overview, 145
  See also bitmap graphics
PDF (Portable Document Format), 586
PDF Design XT, 586-587, 863

PDFs (Printer Description files), 492, 560
pending trademark, 659
Peninsula Gateway Web site, 710-712
performance. *See* speed
Perroud, Patrick, 581
PFR (Portable Font Resource) files, 730
Photo Access, 151
Photo CD files
  image controls available, 362
  importing, 151
  overview, 145
PhotoGrade, 373
Photoshop
  image manipulation functions, 366
  monitor calibration, 481-482
  QuarkXPress layers versus Photoshop's, 91
Photoshop Import XTension, 588, 589, 863
pi fonts, 633
picas
  code for, 6, 39
  defined, 9, 39
pick lists, 21
PICT files
  image controls available, 362
  importing, 151
  overview, 145
  PICT Maker XTension, 573
  See also bitmap graphics
PICTMaker XTension, 573, 862
Picture Bounds, runaround mode, 123
Picture Box tools
  customizing, 56
  overview, 25-26, 104-105, 381
picture boxes
  anchoring, 168-169
  applying different master page and, 53
  background color, 346-348
  Bézier picture boxes, 26
  blends for, 429
  changing anchored boxes, 169-170
  changing box type, 115
  clipping paths, 124-126
  combining with lines, 391-393
  combining with text boxes in HexWeb, 816, 826-828
  constraining, 55, 95-96
  corner radius, 343, 345, 346
  creating, 26, 103-105
  crossing margins, 83
  customizing tools, 56
  defined, 14
  for drop caps, 325
  frames for, 108, 191-195
  greeking options, 55
  HexWeb modification of, 826
  keyboard shortcuts, 847-848
  Measurements palette with, 28, 109-110, 339, 340-343
  merging with lines, 394-396

Modify dialog box with, 107-108, 339, 343-348
  mouse with, 110-114
  moving, 111, 341, 344
  moving pictures in, 342
  overview, 4
  Picture Box tools, 25-26, 56, 104-105
  placing pictures, 128-129
  resizing, 112, 341, 344
  rotating, 345
  runaround settings, 108, 119-125, 127-128
  scaling pictures in, 341-342, 348-351
  separators in HexWeb, 816, 817
  as shapes, 390-397
  special effects, 342-343, 344-345
  text-based boxes, 407-409
  See also graphics; text boxes
Picture Contrast Specifications dialog box
  color contrast adjustments, 366-367
  customized contrast settings, 368-369
  filters, 365, 366
  manually adjusting contrast, 367-368
  overview, 364
  returning to common gray-level map, 369
Picture Halftone Specifications dialog box, 372
PictureManager XTension, 564-565, 862
pictures. *See* graphics
plain type style, 640
Plates, print option, 506
POCE (Pantone Open Color Environment), 416, 421
Pogue, David, 609
pointers
  common pointers, 33-34
  overview, 32
  specialized pointers, 34-35
points
  changing with Find/Change palette, 225-227
  code for, 6, 39
  copy fitting, 232-233
  defined, 9, 39
  Didot points, 40
  keyboard shortcuts, 227
Poole, Lon, 609
PopChar Pro utility, 610, 860
PopChar utility, 138
Pop-out Picture Box tools, 26
pop-up menus, 21
pop-up windows, 612-613
Portable Document Format (PDF), 586
Portable Font Resource (PFR) files, 730
positioning. *See* moving objects; navigating
Posterize filter, 365

Post-it notes, 595-596
PostScript error handler, 508
PostScript fonts
    installing, 625-627
    loading in printers, 628-629, 631
    TrueType versus, 630
PostScript level setting (Windows),
    501-502
PostScript printer description files
    (PPDs), 491-492
PostScript printers, 607
PPDs (PostScript printer description
    files), 491-492
Precision Preview XT, 577-578, 862
preferences
    baseline grids, 60-61, 88
    BeyondPress defaults, 777-793
    blends, display of, 55
    box constraints, 55
    character preferences, 57-60
    CMS preferences, 479-480
    color trapping, 61-62, 474-476
    coordinate controls, 40
    CyberPress defaults, 750-761
    drag-and-drop editing, 50
    frames, 52
    global versus local, 38
    greeking, 54-55
    guide and ruler colors, 41-42, 88-
        89
    guide display, 42-43, 87
    HexWeb defaults, 812-819
    image displays, 46-47
    index preferences, 304-305
    item dragging, 50
    keyboard shortcuts, 840
    master page item changes, 53
    measurement system, 38-40
    monitor display options, 43-44,
        480-482
    Non-Matching Preferences dialog
        box, 553
    overview, 38
    page insertion, 51
    paragraph preferences, 60-61
    pasteboard size, 48
    quotation marks, 49
    scrolling, 49-50
    sharing project elements, 438-439
    snap distance, 54, 88
    Tool palette, 106
    tools, 55-57
    transferring across platforms, 457
    typography defaults, 644
    XPress Preferences files, 438-439
    XTensions Manager, 524-525
    See also customizing
prefix for page numbers, 179
PreflightPro utility, 597, 859
prepress. See color prepress
PrePress XTension, Adobe (APX),
    546-547, 861
preview headers of EPS files, 146-147
previewing
    contrast adjustments, 365
    dashed lines, 400
    halftone sample pages, 373-375
    printing, 511

PubViews XTension for, 580-581
transferring across platforms and,
    457, 458
Web pages with BeyondPress,
    803-804, 809
Web pages with HexWeb, 820, 828
    See also viewing
Print Colors, print option, 506
print design, 665-688
    of ads and circulars, 666-670
    learning about, 665-666
    of magazines, 675-684
    of newsletters, 670-675
    principles, 686-688
    special effects, 684-686
    See also design; layouts
Print dialog box, 502-513
    Color Management pane, 486-487,
        512-513
    common options, 502-503
    Document pane, 298-299, 503-505
    Halftoning options, 371
    Macintosh-specific options, 492-
        497
    Options pane, 508-511
    Output pane, 505-508
    Preview pane, 511
    Setup pane, 491-502
    Windows-specific options, 497-
        502
print styles
    creating, 514-515
    Print dialog box option, 50-52
    sharing in workgroups, 450-451
    tips, 516
    transferring across platforms,
        451, 457
Print Styles dialog box, 515
Printer Description files (PDFs), 492,
    560
printer spreads
    Bookletizer XTension, 592
    Imposer XTension, 548-549
printers
    choosing, 489-490, 606-607
    composite versus separation, 482
    default printer (Windows), 498-
        499
    loading PostScript fonts, 628-629,
        631
    Macintosh printer setup, 494
    print styles for, 514-516
    Windows printer setup, 498
printing, 489-516
    blank pages, 503
    books and book chapters, 297,
        298-299
    canceling, 503
    choosing a printer, 489-490
    color printing methods, 411-413
    color separations, 503, 507-508,
        513-514
    common options, 502-503
    crop marks, 504-505
    document setup, 491-502
    drag-and-drop printing, 495
    to file (Macintosh), 496-497
    to file (Windows), 500-501

flipping pages, 509
Macintosh-specific options, 492-
    497
new features, 855
paper size for, 492
PostScript level setting
    (Windows), 501-502
previewing, 511
Print dialog box options, 502-513
process colors, 513-514
registration marks, 504-505
scaling pages during, 492
spot colors, 513-514
spreads, 504
suppressing picture printout, 335
thumbnails, 70, 504
Windows-specific options, 497-
    502
    See also Print dialog box
process colors
    converting spot color to, 412-413
    defined, 15
    displaying, 434
    overview, 411-412
    printing, 513-514
    spot color with, 412, 424, 425-426,
        514
    trapping preferences, 61, 475
Process Trapping option, 61, 475
product catalogs on CD, 859, 864
production terms, 15-16
Profile Information palette, 485
Program Switcher utility, 610, 860
programs. See software; utilities;
    XTensions
pt, measurement unit, 6
public service announcement, 669-
    670
Publish and Subscribe, 159-165
    canceling links, 163
    creating live links, 160-162
    deleting editions, 163
    disadvantages of, 162
    finding editions, 163-164
    live versus manual dynamic links,
        158-159
    OLE versus, 160, 164-165
    opening source application, 163,
        164-165
    updating live links, 162-163
Publisher Options dialog box, 163-164
publishing environment
    fonts, 625-631
    hardware, 603-608
    Macintosh interface, 609-617
    software, essential, 608-609
    Windows interface, 617-624
publishing programs
    scriptable applications, 542
    utilities, 596-600
PubViews XTension, 580-581, 862
pull-quotes in newsletters, 675
punctuation
    rules for use, 657
    typographic (smart) quotes, 49,
        655-657
punctuation spaces, 9, 252

Q

q, measurement unit, 6
Quark PostScript Error Handler, print
    option, 508
Quark Web site, 526
QuarkXPress
    connecting to other programs,
        541-543
    hierarchy, 535
    installing QuarkXPress for
        Macintosh, 835-837
    installing QuarkXPress for
        Windows, 833-835
    Macintosh/Windows differences,
        456-458
    metaphor of, 4
    minimum requirements, 837
    new features, 851-855
    saving in version 3.3 format, 454-
        455
    upgrading from previous version,
        838
    uses for, 3
QuarkXPress Environment dialog
    box, 521
QuickOpen XTension, 553
QuickTime, 151
quotation marks (")
    defaults, 49
    drop caps and, 324
    keyboard shortcuts, 656
    rules for use, 657
    typographic (smart) quotes, 49,
        655-657
QX-Drag&Drop, 567, 862
QX-Layers, 91, 570
QX-Tools, 567-570, 862

R

ragged left, 10
ragged right, 10
raised caps, 12, 324
    hybrids, 324-325
RAM
    memory management utilities,
        609
    recommended amounts, 604
    XTension requirements, 523
RAM Doubler, 609
Raw HTML, BeyondPress option, 792
readability of text, 687
Readable HTML, BeyondPress option,
    781
Ready-to-Fax utility, 596, 859
rearranging. See moving objects
rebuilding
    clipping paths, 124
    lists, 303
    runarounds, 124
Recordability, BeyondPress option,
    780-781
recovering deleted files, 617, 624
Rectangle Picture Box tool, 104

Rectangle Text Box tool, 98, 99
registered trademark, 659
Registration, print option, 504-505
registration marks
    defined, 15
    Marklt XTension, 552, 553
    printing, 504-505
registration problems, 79
regular underline, 647
Reimport High Res Images,
    BeyondPress option, 785
related elements in layouts, 74
Relationship option for color
    trapping, 474
removing. See canceling; deleting
renaming. See naming
Repeat Count option, 200
repeating elements in layouts, 74
repetitive strain injury (RSI), 859
replacing
    Alias Pro XTension for, 581-582
    indexes, 309
    keyboard shortcuts for, 846
    selected text, 224
    text using Find/Change palette,
        225
Report file, 464-465
Rescan button, Modify dialog box,
    124
Reshape Line icon, 385
Reshape Point icon, 385
reshaping
    Bézier curves, 188, 384-386
    boxes, 112, 113-114
    constraining during, 386
    lines, 188-189
resizing. See sizing
resolution
    lines per inch (lpi), 373
    print option, 507
Resolution Enhancement Technology,
    373
restaurant ad mockup, 667-668
Restrict to Box, runaround option,
    124, 125
Reverse Difference, merge option,
    395, 396
reversed type, 649-650
reversing, 14
RGB color model, 416, 422
    CMYK color model versus, 693
    defining, 483-484
    Designer Color Palettes, 598
    importing color pictures, 485
    RGB-to-CMYK conversion, 431
RIFF files, 146
Right Indent option, 266
right tabs, 286
    See also tabs
RLE files, 145
roman type, 7
Rosenthal, Leonard, 543
rotating
    picture boxes, 345
    pictures in boxes, 352-353
    text, 326-328
Rotation pointer, 34

Rotation tool, 24, 326, 381
Rounded-Rectangle Picture Box tool,
    26, 104
Rounded-Rectangle Text Box tool, 98,
    99
RSI (repetitive strain injury), 859
ruler origin box, 17, 18
rulers
    color of, 41-42, 88-89
    defined, 18
    hiding and showing, 45
    measurement units for, 38-39
    tab ruler, 288-289
    See also guides
rules. See lines
Ruling Line feature, 647-649
Run Text Around All Sides option,
    127-128
runarounds
    additional options, 124
    defined, 119
    editing, 126
    mode, 121-123
    rebuilding, 124
    Run Text Around All Sides option,
        127-128
    tolerance options, 124-125
    for Web pages, 737
    width of, 108, 120-121
running. See opening
Ryder, The Web site, 700, 702-703

S

Same as Clipping, runaround mode,
    123
sans serif type, 8, 633
saturation of picture box background
    colors, 347
Save Document Position option, 64
Save Text dialog box, 166-167
saving
    bitmap files, 362
    document as template, 204
    fast-save feature of word
        processors, 142
    files, 615-616, 622-623
    keyboard shortcuts for, 839
    libraries, 216
    pages as EPS file, 195-197
    preferences, for 62-64
    scripts, 539-540
    style sheets, 272
    TIFF images, 150
    in version 3.3 format, 454-455
ScaleLock XTension, 553
scaling
    CyberPress defaults, 758
    keyboard shortcuts for text, 844
    pages during printing, 492
    pictures with keyboard, 350
    pictures with Measurements
        palette, 341-342
    pictures with Modify dialog box,
        348-349, 351
    typefaces, 249-251

visual labels, 318
See also sizing
scanners, 607
scanning, calculating scans and output, 376
Schneider, Derrick, 536
Scitex CT files, 145, 362
screens
  defined, 16
  screen angles for spot colors, 423-424, 425
  See also halftones; monitors
Script Editor, 536, 537
Script Manager utility, 543, 860
Scripter utility, 543, 860
Scripting Additions folder, 536
ScriptMaster utility, 543, 860
scripts, 533-544
  AppleScript basics, 534-535
  with BeyondPress, 780-781, 810
  checking for syntax errors, 538-539
  connecting to other programs, 541-543
  further information, 536
  learning AppleScript, 534
  running, 439
  saving, 539-540
  Script Editor, 536, 537
  scripting conventions, 542
  tools for, 536-537, 543
  tools on CD, 860
  writing scripts, 538, 540-541
ScriptWeb site, 544
scroll bars
  defined, 18, 19
  Macintosh interface, 614-615
  Windows interface, 622
scrolling preferences, 49-50
searching. *See* finding
Second Glance's Clone, 582-583, 863
section symbol, 659
sections
  breaking document into, 179
  page numbering for, 178, 179, 503
security, FCSLock XTension, 571
selecting
  block of text, 223
  HX PowerSelect XTension, 575-576
  identifying active items, 35
  item contents with Content tool, 23-24
  items with Item tool, 35
  keyboard shortcuts for, 842, 843
  Macintosh interface, 614
  overview, 35
  pages to print, 502
  replacing selected text, 224
  tracking selected text, 241-242
  typefaces, 634-637
  Windows interface, 620
separation printer, 482
Separation Profile, print option, 512
Separations, print option, 503
separators for boxes (HexWeb), 816, 817

serif type, 8, 251, 633
service bureaus, 463-467
  bleeds and, 467
  Bundler XTension, 565-566
  Collect for Output feature, 463-465
  documents versus output files, 465-466
  output settings, 466-467
  oversized pages and, 467
  standards and, 463
setup. *See* preferences
shading
  for graphics, 354, 379-380
  percentage specification, 428
  for text, 331-332
  tools, 381
ShadowCaster XTension, 553-554
shadows
  ShadowCaster XTension, 553-554
  skewing with, 684
  for text, 332, 334
shapes, 390-397
  combining boxes and lines, 391-393
  creating, 390-391
  merging boxes and lines, 394-396
  splitting paths of merged objects, 397
shareware
  on CD, 858, 860, 864
  favorite utilities, 610
  overview, 858
  See also software; utilities; XTensions
sharing project elements, 438-451
  auxiliary dictionaries, 445-446
  bitmap frames, 445
  CMS profiles and, 440
  color definitions, 441-442
  dashes, 445
  graphics and text files, 446-447
  H&J sets, 445
  kerning tables, 442
  libraries, 447
  lists, 445
  master pages, 448-450
  overview, 438
  print styles, 450-451
  stripes, 445
  style sheets, 442-445
  templates, 447-448
  XPress Preferences files for, 438-439
shortcut icons, 618
shortcuts. *See* keyboard shortcuts
Shovelt utility, 610, 864
Show Contents option, 50, 356-357
Show Hidden Text, BeyondPress option, 780
sidebars
  effectiveness of, 313
  on master pages, 207
  in newsletters, 675
signs and symbols. *See* special characters
simplicity

basic design rules, 71-72
  for frames, 192
  for lines, 189
Single Master Page pointer, 35
Single Word Justify option, 255
size box, 18, 19
Size Selection dialog box, 405, 406
sizing
  bitmap frames, 405
  bitmap graphics, enlarging or reducing, 362
  boxes, 112
  cap height of type, 8
  color trapping amount, 473
  column gutter width, 85
  columns, number of, 83-84
  constrained boxes, 95, 96
  copy fitting, 232-233, 240
  CyberPress defaults for graphics, 758
  defined, 14
  distortion from, 14
  em space size calculation, 59, 238
  flex space width, 59
  fonts for Web pages, 731, 754-755, 786, 787
  groups, 94
  headlines with HexWeb, 815-816
  keyboard shortcuts for text, 844-845
  lines (rules), 187
  margins, 82-83
  measurement units, 6, 9, 38-40
  oversized pages and service bureaus, 467
  page size, 81-82
  pages during printing, 492
  paper size for printing, 492
  pasteboard width, 48, 90
  picture boxes, 112, 341, 344
  pictures with keyboard, 350
  pictures with Measurements palette, 341-342
  pictures with Modify dialog box, 348-349, 351
  printed page, 491
  resize-text-with-the-box feature, 112
  ScaleLock XTension for, 553
  scaling typefaces, 249-251
  Sizing pointer, 33
  small caps, 643
  snap distance, 54
  superscripts, subscripts, and superiors, 646
  type using Find/Change palette, 225-227
  type using keyboard shortcuts, 227
  typeface weights, 7
  visual labels, 318
  Web pages, 719, 806
  x-height of type, 8
  See also cropping
sizing handles, 35
Sizing pointer, 33

sketching layouts
  on paper, 68-69
  in QuarkXPress, 69-70
skewing
  picture boxes, 343
  pictures in boxes, 353-354
  with shadow, 684
  tools, 381
slug lines in newsletters, 674
small caps
  expert collections, 643
  options, 58
  proportional size of, 643
  in tightly leaded text, 681
  uses for, 642
  for visual labels, 317
Smallest Word, hyphenation option,
    257
Smart Quotes option, 49, 655-656
Smooth Point option, 388
Smoothness, tolerance option, 124
Snap Distance option, 54, 88
soft (discretionary) hyphens, 12, 259,
    657
software
  dedicated Web-page software, 708
  essential software, 608-609
  Macintosh interface, 609-617
  publishing utilities, 596-600
  QuarkXPress minimum
      requirements, 837
  shareware favorites, 610
  XTension sampler, 545-596
  See also CD-ROM with this book;
      utilities; XTensions; specific
      programs
Software Architects
  DOS Mounter 95, 461, 462, 605
  Here & Now, 461, 462, 605
Space Before and Space After
    options, 266
Space/Align Items dialog box, 197-199
spaced-out text, 684, 685
spaces
  after bullets or labels, 315, 316
  em spaces, 9, 59, 238, 252
  en spaces, 9, 252
  flexible spaces, 59, 252
  Kern to Space feature, 246
  keyboard shortcuts, 252, 846
  measurement units, 9
  nonbreaking spaces, 252
  punctuation spaces, 9, 252
  white space, 14, 71-72
spacing
  character spacing, 235-252
  copy fitting, 232-233, 240
  horizontal spacing preferences,
      58-59
  kerning, 9-10, 28, 58, 245-249
  leading, 9, 28, 60
  paragraph spacing, 253-267
  scaling typefaces, 249-251
  for superscripts, subscripts, and
      superiors, 646
  terms, 9-11
  tracking, 9, 28, 237-243

word spacing, 9, 243-244
  See also character spacing;
      justification; kerning; leading;
      paragraph spacing; tracking
special characters, 655-664
  BeyondPress mapping of, 810
  copyright symbol, 658-659
  CyberPress mapping of, 769-770
  dagger, 659
  diacritical marks, 319
  en bullets, 315-316, 319, 658
  filename rules, 458, 459
  importing, 138-140
  index separation characters, 305
  keyboard shortcuts for foreign
      characters, 661-664
  keyboard shortcuts for
      QuarkXPress characters, 846-
      847
  keyboard shortcuts for symbols,
      659-660
  leading and, 263
  Mac symbols font for Windows,
      318, 863
  Macintosh/Windows platform
      differences, 460
  measurement unit codes, 6, 39
  nonbreaking em dashes, 657, 658
  nonbreaking hyphens, 261, 657
  nonbreaking spaces, 241, 252
  paragraph symbol, 659
  pending trademark, 659
  preferences, 59-60
  registered trademark, 659
  section symbol, 659
  smart quotes, 49, 655-657
  universal naming conventions,
      459
  Web publishing and, 661, 734-735
  See also spaces
special effects
  bulleted lists, 314-316, 319
  coloring and shading text, 331-
      332
  dingbats, 318, 320
  drop caps and hybrid caps, 321-
      325
  halftones, 372
  hanging punctuation, 333-335
  increased tracking for, 237-238,
      241
  indents and outdents, 311-313
  numbered lists, 316
  outlines, 332, 334
  for picture boxes, 342-343, 344-
      345
  placing text on a line, 328-330,
      409-410
  print design, 684-686
  rotating text, 326-328
  shadows, 332, 334
  sidebars, 313
  TextWaves XTension, 574-575
  visual labels, 317-318
speed
  blend display and, 55

graphics display quality and, 355-
    357
  greeking pictures and, 55, 356
  image display controls and, 46-47
  scrolling speed, 49, 50
  suppressing picture printout, 335
Speed Doubler, 609
Speed Scroll option, 50, 356
SpeedOpen XTension, 563, 862
spelling. See checking spelling
spelling dictionaries. See auxiliary
    dictionaries
splitting paths for merged objects,
    397
spot colors
  converting to process colors, 412-
      413
  creating, 423
  defined, 14, 412
  displaying, 434
  halftone screen settings for, 423,
      425
  mixing spot colors, 424
  overview, 412
  printing, 513-514
  process color with, 412, 424, 425-
      426, 514
  transferring duplicate color sets,
      514
  using, 422-424
spreading, 470-471
  See also color trapping
spreads
  coordinate controls, 40
  defined, 77
  layouts, 77-78
  master spreads, 76
  printer spreads, 548-549, 592
  printing, 504
spreadsheet programs, scriptable,
    542
Stack Documents option, 44-45
stacking order of layers, 92, 93
stand-alone layout, 74
Standard Em Space option, 59, 238
Standard pointer, 33
standard set of typefaces, 635-636,
    682
Start menu (Windows), 619, 864
starting. See opening
statements, 535
static links, 158
  See also links
Step and Repeat dialog box, 199-201
storage, 604-605
stories
  checking spelling in, 228
  StoryChaser XTension, 554-555
  See also text
Straight Segment option, 388
Street Logic Software's ScriptMaster,
    543, 860
stretched text, 684, 685
striped lines
  copying styles, 403
  creating, 402-403
  sharing in workgroups, 445

Studio Format Utile's FontLoupe, 610, 860
Stufflt Deluxe, 609
Style menu
    Baseline Shift option, 646
    Color option, 331, 378
    Contrast option, 359, 364
    Convert to Box option, 408
    Formats option, 258, 261, 266
    graphics and, 340
    Halftone option, 360, 375
    Kern option, 249, 325
    Leading option, 261
    Negative option, 359, 364
    Paragraph Style Sheet submenu, 280
    Shade option, 331, 379
    Track option, 242
    Type Style options, 639
Style Selection dialog box, 193-195
style sheets, 269-284
    applying, 280
    based-on option, 274, 275, 276, 279
    canceling changes, 273
    cascading, 756, 782, 786-788
    comparing, 282
    copying styles, 272, 281-282
    creating, 272, 276-279
    defined, 12
    defining styles, 269-270
    deleting, 272
    for drop caps, 321-322
    duplicating, 272
    Edit Character Style Sheet dialog box, 275-276
    Edit Paragraph Style Sheet dialog box, 273-275
    editing, 272, 280
    importing, 283
    ItemMaster XTension, 550-551
    keyboard shortcuts, 273-274, 276
    lists, 31
    mapping preferences in BeyondPress, 788-789
    No Style option, 276
    Normal style, 277
    resolving conflicts, 284
    saving, 272
    sharing in workgroups, 442-445
    Style Sheets dialog box, 270-273
    tab settings, 288
    tracking amount, 237
    transferring across platforms, 445, 457
    vertical alignment and, 265
    for visual labels, 317-318
    word processors versus QuarkXPress, 131
Style Sheets dialog box, 270-273
    buttons, 272-273
    Show pop-up menu, 271
Style Sheets palette
    applying drop caps, 322
    applying styles, 280
    overview, 30
style tags, 12
styles

changing with Find/Change palette, 225-227
copying, 272, 281-282
for dashes and stripes, 403
defined, 12
defining, 269-270
for dingbats, 320
for frames, 193-195
HTML master styles in BeyondPress, 788
for indexes, 303-304
for lines, 29, 398-403
for lists, 302, 314-316
No Style option, 276
styles of type. *See* type styles
Subscribe. *See* Publish and Subscribe
Subscriber Options dialog box, 162-163
subscripts
    leading, 646
    leading and, 263
    options, 58
    relative size and spacing, 646
    in tightly leaded text, 681
Suggested Hyphenation feature, 259-260
Suitcase software, 608
superblack, 420
super-calendared paper, 373
superiors
    changing superscripts to, 645-646
    defined, 58
    as footnotes, 58, 645
    leading, 646
    options, 58
    relative size and spacing, 646
superscripts
    changing to superiors, 645-646
    leading, 646
    leading and, 263
    options, 58
    relative size and spacing, 646
    in tightly leaded text, 681
    uses for, 645
suppressing picture printout, 335
suspect words, 229
swatchbooks, 15, 418
SyJet drives, 605
Symantec Suitcase, 608
symbols. *See* special characters
Symmetrical Point option, 388
synchronizing chapter formatting, 297
syntax rules, 535
SyQuest SyJet drives, 605

T

tab leaders, 289
tabbed-pane dialog boxes
    using, 21
    See also specific dialog boxes
table of contents
    for books, 300
    for magazines, 675-677
    for Web sites, 704-706, 830-832

TableMaker XTension, 573-574, 862
tables
    in BeyondPress, 789-790
    creating with tabs, 289-291
    in CyberPress, 758-760, 769
    Entable XTension, 584, 585, 586
    FCSTableMaker XTension, 571-572
    importing, 138, 144
    TableMaker XTension, 573-574
    vertical lines between columns, 291
    Web publishing and, 732-733
    word processors versus QuarkXPress, 131-132
tablets, 608
Tableworks' Entable, 584, 585, 586, 863
tabs, 285-291
    creating tables with, 289-291
    default, 285
    for hanging punctuation, 333-334
    setting and changing, 287-289
    tab leaders, 289
    types of, 285-287
Tagged Image File Format images. *See* TIFF files
Tao of AppleScript, The, 536
tape drives, 605
Techno Design
    about, 585
    PDF Design XT, 586-587, 863
    Photoshop Import XTension, 588, 589, 863
templates
    in BeyondPress, 807
    creating, 203-204
    defined, 13, 14
    Designer Templates, 598-600
    designing, 448
    Output Request Template, 465
    saving documents as, 204
    sharing in workgroups, 447-448
    transferring across platforms, 448
    using over networks, 204
    Web-Safe Colors.qxt template, 861, 864
    See also grids
terms and concepts
    color terms, 14-15
    layout terms, 12-14
    production terms, 15-16
    typography terms, 7-12, 633-634
    variations among, 37
    Web publishing terms, 16
text
    BeyondPress default color, 784
    colors for, 331-332
    converting into graphics, 407-410, 768-769
    copy fitting, 232-233, 240
    CyberPress default color, 753-754
    duplicating, 224
    exporting, 166-167
    Find/Change palette, 224-227
    finding and replacing, 224-228
    fitting to curves, 328-330, 409-410
    Font Usage utility, 227-228

(continued)

text *(continued)*
  as graphics for Web pages, 722,
    735-736, 814
  HexWeb defaults, 814
  as hyperlinks, 770-771
  importing, 134-144
  keyboard shortcuts for
    formatting, 844-845
  keyboard shortcuts for selecting,
    843
  moving, 224
  new features, 851-853
  outlines, 332, 334
  readability, 687
  replacing selected text, 224
  resize-with-the-box feature, 112
  rotating, 326-328
  selecting blocks, 223
  shading for, 331-332
  shadows, 332, 334
  spaced-out, 684, 685
  spelling, checking, 228-231
  StoryChaser XTension, 554-555
  stretched, 684, 685
  text links, 166-167
  text-based boxes, 407-409
  underlines, 576-577
  Web page formatting, 726-736
  when to add, 115
  See also text files
Text Box tools
  customizing, 56
  overview, 25, 98-100, 381, 382
text boxes
  anchoring, 168-169
  applying different master page
    and, 53
  Bézier text boxes, 25
  blends for, 429
  changing anchored boxes, 169-
    170
  changing box type, 115
  changing using mouse, 110-114
  columns, number of, 116
  combining with lines, 391-393
  combining with picture boxes in
    HexWeb, 816, 826-828
  constraining, 55, 95-96
  creating, 25
  creating automatically, 19, 85, 97
  creating columns in, 103
  creating manually, 98
  crossing margins, 83
  customizing tools, 56
  defined, 14
  for drop caps, 325
  frames for, 108, 191-195
  greeking options, 54
  for hanging punctuation, 334-335
  HexWeb modification of, 824-826
  intercolumn rules, 117
  keyboard shortcuts, 847-848
  linking and unlinking, 100-102
  Measurements palette with, 28,
    109-110
  merging with lines, 394-396
  Modify dialog box with, 107-108

moving, 111
overview, 4
for page numbers, 180
placing text, 115, 128-129
resizing, 112
rotating text, 328
runaround settings, 108, 119-125,
  127-128
separators in HexWeb, 816, 817
as shapes, 390-397
Text Box tools, 25, 56, 98-100
text inset, 117-118
text layout control, 115-116
textual graphics, 684
vertical alignment, 118-119
  See also picture boxes
Text Color, BeyondPress option, 782
text files
  cross-platform differences, 132-
    133
  formatting outside QuarkXPress,
    134
  formatting that can be imported,
    136-141
  importing, 134-144
  printing to (Macintosh), 496-497
  printing to (Windows), 500-501
  sharing in workgroups, 446-447
  standardizing, 447
  text links, 166-167
  translating when importing, 134-
    136
  XPress Tags for, 141-144
  See also files; graphics files
Text Path tools, 328-329, 409-410
text-to-path feature, 328-330, 409-410
textual graphics, 684
TextWaves XTension, 574-575, 862
thermal-wax printers, 490
  See also printers
Thesaurus reX XTension, 594-595, 863
thin (punctuation) spaces, 9, 252
Threshold, tolerance option, 125
thumbnail view
  copying pages between
    documents, 171-173
  printing thumbnails, 70, 504
  rearranging pages, 177-178
  selecting, 46
Thumbnails, print option, 504
TIFF files
  image controls available, 362
  image display controls, 46-47, 356
  importing, 150
  overview, 145, 150, 360
  print resolution, 511
  saving, 150
  using, 432
  See also bitmap graphics
Tile Documents option, 44-45
Tile Horizontally option, 45
Tile to Multiple Monitors option, 43-
  44
Tile Vertically option, 45
Tiling, print option, 505
Timbuktu Pro, 461, 462
timestamps, BeyondPress option, 782

title bars, 17, 18
Tool palette
  customizing, 106
  overview, 22-27, 382
  Picture Box tools, 25-26, 104-105
  Text Box tools, 25, 98-100
  See also specific tools
tools
  choosing, 5-6
  customizing, 55-57
  global versus local, 5
  for graphics, 339-340
  graphics-creation tools, 381-382
  HTML layout tools, evolution of,
    718
  independent trapping tools, 478
  layout tools, 85-96
  moving between palettes, 382-382
  publishing utilities, 596-600
  for scripts, 536-537, 543
  Tool palette, 22-27
  XTension sampler, 545-596
  See also Tool palette; *specific
    tools*
Toyo color model, 416, 418, 484
trackballs, 608
  See also mouse
tracking, 237-243
  adjusting in Measurements
    palette, 28
  adjusting on-the-fly, 240-241
  changing one document only, 241
  copy fitting, 232-233, 240
  decreasing, 238
  defined, 9
  editing tracking tables, 239-240
  for ellipses, 241
  em definition and, 238
  increasing, 237-238
  justified text, 242-243
  selected text, 241-242
  setting in style sheets, 237
  for special effects, 237-238, 241
trademark symbols, 659
transparent background for picture
  boxes, 346
Trap Information palette
  caution regarding, 31
  overriding traps, 476-477
  overview, 30-31
  trapping rationale, 478
Trap Specifications dialog box, 472-
  474
trapping. *See* color trapping
Trapping Method option, 61, 474
TrapWise, 478, 546
trim lines, 552, 553
Trinko, Tom, 536
troubleshooting
  AppleScript syntax errors, 538-
    539
  BeyondPress export problems,
    805
  Collect for Output feature, 463-
    465
  comparing attributes, 453

graphics missing or modified, 154-159
HexWeb weirdness, 812
mixed-platform issues, 456-462
PreflightPro utility for, 597
recovering deleted files, 617, 624
resolving name conflicts, 452-453
resolving style conflicts, 284
XTension incompatibilities, 531
XTension-loading errors, 524, 525-526
TrueDoc fonts
with BeyondPress, 782
with CyberPress, 756
overview, 730
TrueType fonts
installing, 628
for Mac symbols, 863
PostScript versus, 630
Trumatch color model, 416, 418, 484
256-color system palette, 726
type styles, 638-650
all caps, 642
Baseline Shift feature, 646-647, 845
basic text styles, 640-650
boldface, 317, 641
changing, 638-639
CyberPress defaults, 755-757
CyberPress mapping of QuarkXPress to HTML, 756
defined, 7
expert collections, 643, 644
Find/Change palette, 225-227
Font Usage utility, 227-228
italics, 7, 317, 637, 641
keyboard shortcuts, 639, 640, 844-845
for numerals, 645
plain, 640
reversed type, 649-650
small caps, 58, 317, 642-643
superscripts, subscripts, and superiors, 58, 263, 645-646
underlines, 647-649
See also specific styles
typeface attributes. See type styles
typefaces and fonts
basic guidelines, 637
BeyondPress defaults, 782, 783, 786-788
creating font variations, 652-654
CyberPress Font Size defaults, 754-757
defined, 7, 626
deleting variations, 654
for drop caps, 323
expert collections, 643, 644
exporting with BeyondPress, 782, 783
faces versus fonts, 626, 634
families of, 7
Find/Change palette, 225-227
Font Creator XTension, 651-652
Font Usage utility, 227-228
fonts versus typefaces, 626, 634
in graphics files, 149
HexWeb defaults, 814

installing, 625-628
keyboard shortcuts, 844-845
loading PostScript fonts in printers, 628-629, 631
Mac symbols font for Windows, 318, 863
Macintosh/Windows platform differences, 460
Multiple Master fonts, 651-654
names for, 636
obtaining, 608-609
scaling, 249-251
selecting, 634-637
similar typefaces, 637
standard set, 635-636, 682
terms, 7-11, 633-634
TrueDoc fonts, 730, 756, 782
TrueType versus PostScript, 630
typeface attributes, 638-650
typographic colors, 236
variations, 634, 635, 652-654
for visual labels, 318
for Web publishing, 638, 727-731
See also character spacing; special characters; type styles
Typesetting leading mode, 265
typographic colors, 236
typographic effects. See special effects
typographic preferences, 57-60
character defaults, 58-59
for special characters, 59-60
typography, 633-664
default settings, 644
expert collections, 643, 644
multiple master fonts, 651-654
selecting typefaces, 634-637
terms, 7-12, 633-634
typeface attributes, 638-650
for Web publishing, 638
See also special characters; typefaces and fonts

U

undeleting files, 617, 624
underlines
creating, 647-649
HX PowerUnderline XTension, 576-577
ungrouping elements, 93
Uni Software Plus' PopChar Pro, 610, 860
Union, merge option, 395, 396
Unix servers
as BeyondPress destination platform, 782
as CyberPress destination platform, 751
Unlink pointer, 34
Unlink tool, 27, 101-102
unlinking text boxes, 101-102
unordered lists. See bulleted lists
Unshared Elements, BeyondPress option, 782

updating
color profiles, 486
deciding not to update, 156
finding missing graphics, 154-155
links to source images, 52-53, 155, 156-157, 159
lists, 303
live links, 162-163
OLE links, 165
upgrading from previous version, 838
Use Scripts Menu, BeyondPress option, 780
UserLand Software, 534
UserTalk, 534
utilities
on CD, 859, 860, 864
Character Map, 138
essential software, 608-609
Font Usage, 227-228
PopChar and PopChar Pro, 138, 610, 860
publishing utilities, 596-600
shareware, 610, 860, 864
See also Utilities menu; XTensions
Utilities menu
Build Index option, 31, 308
Check Spelling options, 228-229
Edit Auxiliary option, 230
Kerning Table Edit option, 239
Suggested Hyphenation option, 259
Tracking Edit option, 239
XTensions Manager option, 242

V

Value, BeyondPress option, 792
variables (HexWeb), 818
VE. See Vision's Edge
vector graphics, 144-145
See also graphics
vertical alignment, 264-266
vertical flip, 343
vertical justification
carding, 11
column balancing versus, 10
defined, 10
feathering, 11
setting, 118-119
vertical layouts, 75-76
Vertical Offset option, 200, 201
vertical ruler
color of, 41-42
defined, 18
measurement unit for, 38-39
See also rulers
vertical scales for typefaces, 249-251
View menu
50 percent option, 45
75 percent option, 45
200 percent option, 45
Actual Size option, 45
CyberPress option, 747
Fit in Window option, 45
Lists option, 31

(continued)

View menu *(continued)*
  overview, 44-45
  Show Baseline Grid option, 88
  Show Colors option, 29
  Show Document Layout option, 29, 208
  Show Measurements option, 28, 105
  Show Profile Information option, 485
  Show Style Sheets option, 30
  Show Tools option, 22
  Show Trap Information option, 30
  Snap to Guides option, 54
  Thumbnails option, 46
  Windows options (Mac), 44
view percent field, 18, 19
viewing
  color groups, 434
  Doc Magnify XTension for, 653-654
  graphics display quality, 355-357
  halftone sample pages, 373-375
  hiding and showing elements, 45
  keyboard shortcuts for, 840
  labeled library elements, 218-219
  master pages, 206, 208
  monitor display options, 43-44, 480-482
  multiple document options, 44-45
  new features, 853-854
  Precision Preview XT, 577-578
  preset view options, 45-46
  previewing contrast adjustments, 365
  previewing dashed lines, 400
  PubViews XTension for, 580-581
  tips and tricks, 47
  Web pages with BeyondPress, 803-804
  Web pages with CyberPress, 773-774
  Web pages with HexWeb, 820, 828
  XTensions presently running, 521
  XTensions, required (viewer-only versions) and, 531
  See also opening; View menu
Vision's Edge
  about, 588
  AdCreation Toolkit, 589-591
  Bookletizer, 592
  LayerIt, 592, 593
  Nouveau II, 592, 593
  PageBorder, 594
  Script Manager, 543, 860
  Thesaurus reX, 594-595
  Web site, 527
  XNotes, 595-596
  XTensions on CD, 863
visual labels, 317-318
visual themes, 688
visual treatments, 686, 687
VScale options
  small caps and superiors, 58
  superscripts and subscripts, 58

W

Washington Times National Weekly Edition Web site, 705-706, 708-709
Web browsers
  BeyondPress default, 780
  CyberPress default, 751
  design issues, 694
  HexWeb default, 815
  page appearance and, 692-693, 694-695, 696, 756
Web publishing
  background colors, 739
  basics, 715-718
  browsers and page appearance, 692-693, 694-695, 696, 756
  CMYK versus RGB color models, 693
  colors and, 417, 725-726, 754
  columns, 721-722
  content issues, 716
  conversion process, 717-718
  dedicated Web-page software, 708
  design issues, 714-715, 716, 719
  finishing touches, 743
  fonts for, 727-731
  formatting text, 726-736
  graphics, 736-742
  groups and, 724
  headers and footers, 723-724
  HTML concepts, 691-693
  images as hyperlinks, 742
  layers and, 724-725, 741
  lines and, 742
  lists, 732
  maintaining original format, 715
  mapping the site, 715
  margins, 721
  mirrored text and, 732
  monitor size and, 719-721
  multiple pages, 722-723
  "pages" in, 696, 719-724
  paragraph formats, 732
  picture file formats, 738-739, 740-741
  print publishing versus, 693-697, 698
  production issues, 716
  prototype creation, 717
  from scratch, 714
  scriptable programs, 543
  sizing pages, 719
  special characters and, 661, 734-735
  structure design, 714-715
  tables, 732-733
  terms, 16
  text as graphics for, 722, 735-736
  tools on CD, 860-861
  typography for, 638
  Web page design opportunities, 691-712
  Web-Safe Colors.qxt template, 861, 864
WYSIWYG approach, 720
  XTensions for, 693, 697
  See also BeyondPress; CyberPress; HexWeb
Web sites
  created with BeyondPress, 703-708
  created with CyberPress, 698-703
  created with HexWeb, 708, 710-712
  font resources, 609
  scripting information on, 544
  XTension information on, 526-527
Web-Safe Colors.qxt template, 861, 864
weight
  of lines, 187, 188
  of typeface, 7
white space
  in airline ad mockup, 667
  defined, 14
  need for, 71-72, 687
widows, tracking and, 240
Width of Document Items, BeyondPress option, 792
windows
  Macintosh interface, 612-615, 616
  moving, 616, 622
  Windows interface, 621-622
Windows computers
  as BeyondPress destination platform, 782
  cross-platform differences, 132-133
  as CyberPress destination platform, 751
  file extensions, 462
  filename rules, 458-459
  importing special characters, 138-140
  installing fonts, 627-628
  installing QuarkXPress for Windows, 833-835
  Mac symbols font for Windows, 318, 863
  mixed-platform issues, 456-462, 605
  printing options specific to, 497-502
  QuarkXPress minimum requirements, 837
  software on CD, 863-864
  upgrading from previous QuarkXPress version, 838
  Windows interface, 617-624
  word processor formats supported, 135-136
  See also mixed-platform issues
Windows interface, 617-624
  basics, 618-622
  file management, 622-624
  Mac interface versus, 617-618
Windows menu, 45
WinZip utility, 609, 610, 864
WMF files, 145
Word Processing leading mode, 265

word processors
  cross-platform differences, 132-133
  exporting text to, 166-167
  fast-save feature, 142
  formatting that can be imported, 136-141
  importing style sheets from, 283
  need for, 608
  Nisus Writer filter, 581
  QuarkXPress versus, 131-132, 134
  scriptable programs, 542
  text links, 166
  translating files from, 134-136
  versions of, 142-143
word spacing
  defined, 9, 243
  Edit Hyphenation & Justification dialog box, 243-244
  preferred settings, 244
word underline, 647
WordPerfect. *See* word processors
workgroups, 437-462
  importing multiple elements, 451-454
  mixed-platform issues, 456-462
  saving in version 3.3 format, 454-455
  sharing project elements, 438-451
  standards for, 437-438
  See also mixed-platform issues; sharing project elements
World-Wide Power Co. Web site, 526
wraps, 13, 14
  See also runarounds

X

Xcatalog, 162
XChange Web site, 526
x-height of type, 8

XNotes XTension, 595-596, 863
XPert Collection Volume 1, 547, 555-557
XPert Collection Volume 2, 547, 557-559
XPress Preferences files, 438-439
XPress Tags
  importing style sheets, 283
  pros and cons of, 141-142
  using XPress Tags codes, 142-144
XPresso Bar Web site, 526, 544
XTension Disabled folder, 528
XTension folder, 524, 528
XTensions
  activating, 242, 246
  availability of, 519
  on CD, 861-863
  creating startup sets, 529
  for database file translation, 162
  defined, 16
  deleting startup sets, 530
  demos on the CD, 546
  determining which are loaded, 521
  finding 4.0-optimized XTensions, 530
  history of, 522
  importing and exporting startup sets, 530-531
  incompatibilities, 531
  installing, 521, 522-523
  installing with QuarkXPress, 519-520
  Kern/Track Editor, 242, 246
  loading errors, 524, 525-526
  obsolete XTensions, 520
  for Photo CD files, 151
  for Photoshop-like layers, 91
  preferences, 524-525
  RAM requirements, 523
  required XTensions, 531
  sampler of, 545-596

  for scripting, 543
  startup set selection, 528-529
  transferring across platforms, 457
  version 3.3 XTensions with QuarkXPress 4, 546
  warnings, 531
  Web information about, 526-527
  for Web publishing, 693, 697
  See also utilities; *specific XTensions*
XTensions Loading Error alert, 525-526
XTensions Manager, 527-531
  activating XTensions, 242, 246
  creating startup sets, 529
  deleting startup sets, 530
  finding 4.0-optimized XTensions, 530
  importing and exporting startup sets, 530-531
  preferences, 524-525
  startup set selection, 528-529
XTensions Manager dialog box, 527-528
XT-now
  catalog on CD, 859, 864
  Web site, 526
XTSource Web site, 526

Z

Zip drives, 605
zoom box, 18
Zoom tool
  customizing, 56
  overview, 24
  tips and tricks, 47
Zoom-in pointer, 33
Zoom-out pointer, 34

IDG BOOKS WORLDWIDE
END-USER LICENSE AGREEMENT

READ THIS. You should carefully read these terms and conditions before opening the software packet(s) included with this book ("Book"). This is a license agreement ("Agreement") between you and IDG Books Worldwide, Inc. ("IDGB"). By opening the accompanying software packet(s), you acknowledge that you have read and accept the following terms and conditions. If you do not agree and do not want to be bound by such terms and conditions, promptly return the Book and the unopened software packet(s) to the place you obtained them for a full refund.

1. **License Grant.** IDGB grants to you (either an individual or entity) a nonexclusive license to use one copy of the enclosed software program(s) (collectively, the "Software") solely for your own personal or business purposes on a single computer (whether a standard computer or a workstation component of a multiuser network). The Software is in use on a computer when it is loaded into temporary memory (RAM) or installed into permanent memory (hard disk, CD-ROM, or other storage device). IDGB reserves all rights not expressly granted herein.

2. **Ownership.** IDGB is the owner of all right, title, and interest, including copyright, in and to the compilation of the Software recorded on the disk(s) or CD-ROM ("Software Media"). Copyright to the individual programs recorded on the Software Media is owned by the author or other authorized copyright owner of each program. Ownership of the Software and all proprietary rights relating thereto remain with IDGB and its licensers.

3. **Restrictions on Use and Transfer.**

   (a) You may only (i) make one copy of the Software for backup or archival purposes, or (ii) transfer the Software to a single hard disk, provided that you keep the original for backup or archival purposes. You may not (i) rent or lease the Software, (ii) copy or reproduce the Software through a LAN or other network system or through any computer subscriber system or bulletin-board system, or (iii) modify, adapt, or create derivative works based on the Software.

   (b) You may not reverse engineer, decompile, or disassemble the Software. You may transfer the Software and user documentation on a permanent basis, provided that the transferee agrees to accept the terms and conditions of this Agreement and you retain no copies. If the Software is an update or has been updated, any transfer must include the most recent update and all prior versions.

4. Restrictions on Use of Individual Programs. You must follow the individual requirements and restrictions detailed for each individual program in Appendix D, "What's on the CD-ROM," of this Book. These limitations are also contained in the individual license agreements recorded on the Software Media. These limitations may include a requirement that after using the program for a specified period of time, the user must pay a registration fee or discontinue use. By opening the Software packet(s), you will be agreeing to abide by the licenses and restrictions for these individual programs that are detailed in Appendix D, "What's on the CD-ROM," and on the Software Media. None of the material on this Software Media or listed in this Book may ever be redistributed, in original or modified form, for commercial purposes.

5. Limited Warranty.

> **(a)** IDGB warrants that the Software and Software Media are free from defects in materials and workmanship under normal use for a period of sixty (60) days from the date of purchase of this Book. If IDGB receives notification within the warranty period of defects in materials or workmanship, IDGB will replace the defective Software Media.

> **(b) IDGB AND THE AUTHORS OF THE BOOK DISCLAIM ALL OTHER WARRANTIES, EXPRESS OR IMPLIED, INCLUDING WITHOUT LIMITATION IMPLIED WARRANTIES OF MERCHANTABILITY AND FITNESS FOR A PARTICULAR PURPOSE, WITH RESPECT TO THE SOFTWARE, THE PROGRAMS, THE SOURCE CODE CONTAINED THEREIN, AND/OR THE TECHNIQUES DESCRIBED IN THIS BOOK. IDGB DOES NOT WARRANT THAT THE FUNCTIONS CONTAINED IN THE SOFTWARE WILL MEET YOUR REQUIREMENTS OR THAT THE OPERATION OF THE SOFTWARE WILL BE ERROR FREE.**

> **(c)** This limited warranty gives you specific legal rights, and you may have other rights that vary from jurisdiction to jurisdiction.

6. Remedies.

> **(a)** IDGB's entire liability and your exclusive remedy for defects in materials and workmanship shall be limited to replacement of the Software Media, which may be returned to IDGB with a copy of your receipt at the following address: Software Media Fulfillment Department, Attn.: *Macworld® QuarkXPress® 4 Bible,* IDG Books Worldwide, Inc., 7260 Shadeland Station, Ste. 100, Indianapolis, IN 46256, or call 1-800-762-2974. Please allow three to four weeks for delivery. This Limited Warranty is void if failure of the Software Media has resulted from accident, abuse, or misapplication. Any replacement Software Media will be warranted for the remainder of the original warranty period or thirty (30) days, whichever is longer.

(b) In no event shall IDGB or the authors be liable for any damages whatsoever (including without limitation damages for loss of business profits, business interruption, loss of business information, or any other pecuniary loss) arising from the use of or inability to use the Book or the Software, even if IDGB has been advised of the possibility of such damages.

(c) Because some jurisdictions do not allow the exclusion or limitation of liability for consequential or incidental damages, the above limitation or exclusion may not apply to you.

7. **U.S. Government Restricted Rights.** Use, duplication, or disclosure of the Software by the U.S. Government is subject to restrictions stated in paragraph (c)(1)(ii) of the Rights in Technical Data and Computer Software clause of DFARS 252.227-7013, and in subparagraphs (a) through (d) of the Commercial Computer — Restricted Rights clause at FAR 52.227-19, and in similar clauses in the NASA FAR supplement, when applicable.

8. **General.** This Agreement constitutes the entire understanding of the parties and revokes and supersedes all prior agreements, oral or written, between them and may not be modified or amended except in a writing signed by both parties hereto that specifically refers to this Agreement. This Agreement shall take precedence over any other documents that may be in conflict herewith. If any one or more provisions contained in this Agreement are held by any court or tribunal to be invalid, illegal, or otherwise unenforceable, each and every other provision shall remain in full force and effect.

my2cents.idgbooks.com

Register This Book — And Win!

Visit **http://my2cents.idgbooks.com** to register this book and we'll automatically enter you in our monthly prize giveaway. It's also your opportunity to give us feedback: let us know what you thought of this book and how you would like to see other topics covered.

Discover IDG Books Online!

The IDG Books Online Web site is your online resource for tackling technology — at home and at the office.

Ten Productive and Career-Enhancing Things You Can Do at www.idgbooks.com

1. Nab source code for your own programming projects.

2. Download software.

3. Read Web exclusives: special articles and book excerpts by IDG Books Worldwide authors.

4. Take advantage of resources to help you advance your career as a Novell or Microsoft professional.

5. Buy IDG Books Worldwide titles or find a convenient bookstore that carries them.

6. Register your book and win a prize.

7. Chat live online with authors.

8. Sign up for regular e-mail updates about our latest books.

9. Suggest a book you'd like to read or write.

10. Give us your 2¢ about our books and about our Web site.

Not on the Web yet? It's easy to get started with *Discover the Internet,* at local retailers everywhere.

CD-ROM Installation Instructions

A wide variety of XTensions and other software—some free, some demo, and some shareware—can be found on the CD at the back of this book. This Installation Instructions page tells you, in brief, what you need to know to install the CD-ROM. For more information about what's on the CD—how to road-test and enjoy all the software—see Appendix D. Chapter 27 also covers the XTensions and publishing-oriented utilities in depth, while Chapter 28 covers the general shareware.

To Install the CD

Insert the CD into your computer. On a Mac, the CD automatically displays on your desktop like a floppy disk or hard disk. On a PC, you may have to open the CD from the Explorer or from the window that appears when you double-click your My Computer icon. The XTensions may require alternative treatment, as follows:

✦ For most XTensions, just drag the XTension file into the XTension folder in your hard disk's QuarkXPress program folder. The next time you open QuarkXPress, the XTensions will be launched as well.

✦ Some XTensions require that you run an installation program, as do most of the utilities. Just double-click the installation icon and follow the on-screen instructions.

Be sure to check out the ReadMe documents on the CD for details on how to proceed.